ArchiLab

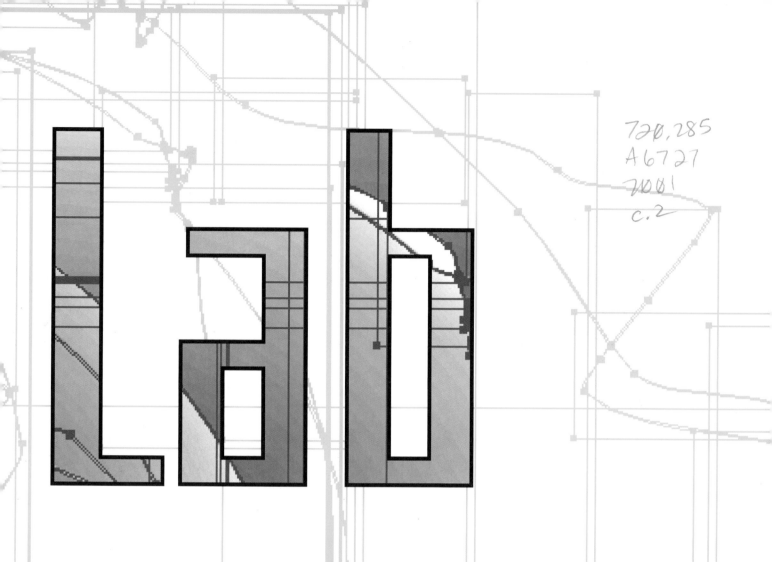

Lab

Radical Experiments in Global Architecture

Edited by Frédéric Migayrou and Marie-Ange Brayer

With over 2300 illustrations

 **Thames & Hudson**

+Contents

Essays

This book is published in conjunction with the ArchiLab conferences and exhibitions, which took place in 1999 and 2000 in Orléans, France. It was sponsored by the city of Orléans and organized by Frédéric Migayrou and Marie-Ange Brayer.

ArchiLab © 2001 the city of Orléans
Architects' texts and images © 2001 the architects
Essays © 2001 the authors

First published in paperback in the United States of America in 2001 by Thames & Hudson Inc., 500 Fifth Avenue, New York, New York 10110

Library of Congress Catalog Card Number: on file
ISBN 0-500-28312-5

Designed by Laurent Pinon

Printed and bound in England by Butler & Tanner, Frome

The Archilab International Architectural Conference in Orléans is a showcase for the most innovative architectural research programmes. The conference is the brainchild of the city of Orléans, in partnership with the Centre Region, and enjoys the back of the Ministry of Culture and Communications and the cooperation of the Centre Regional Contemporary Art Fund (FRAC). In 1999 and 2000 young architects from around the world showed their projects in Orléans, where they also participated in an unprecedented forum of discussions and meetings, focusing on the challenges facing architecture today. The conference, which is attended by a broad public, is now an indispensable point of reference for architectural and cultural circles.

I am keen to express my warmest thanks to Thames & Hudson for publishing, at the dawn of the third millennium, the English version of the catalogues produced for the occasion.

There can be no doubt that this volume will help increase the international feedback about this event, with its enthusiastic emphasis on creativity and pluralism.

At a time when there is a growing need to rethink cities and to devise new forms of urban living, ArchiLab encourages people to discover architectural works through experimental proposals and designs by particularly innovative teams. So we hereby cordially invite you to visit this and all future ArchiLab conferences in Orléans.

Jean-Pierre Sueur
Mayor of Orléans

Architects

✛ Generic Architectures

| FRÉDÉRIC MIGAYROU |

Does architecture still have a cultural, political and social function? Is it still that art of arrangement, which raises an issue to do with origins, in the classical tradition--the issue of a beginning, of a proximity that still reverberates in the concept of inhabiting, in the social fascination with house and home, inclusion and territorial belonging? Architects who are coming to the fore, within a new international coherence that is thoroughly transcultural and hybrid, are at the same time combining specific factors coming from here, there and everywhere, are energetically asserting a practical determination to be effectual. What then do these architects have in common, architects whose research seems formally quite distinct, and whose tools, languages and practical contexts are disparate?

Where lies the reality of architecture? Is this reality still that of a reflective work to do with the means, language and uses of a discipline, which, well ahead of the techniques of the image, managed to mingle procedures and know-how, in order to bring building to a state of effectiveness moulded by these contradictions and permeated by political, economic and social definitions? The idea of an overall industrialization of procedures, of a calculated dispossession of architects' decision-making capacities by a corporate culture with all its sights set on standardization, profit and endless market expansion will end up by doing away with the architect's acknowledged area of qualification and expertise. Architecture that is built, day in and day out, involving millions of square metres is an architect-less architecture, where industry endlessly renews the selfsame formulae in an ironical denial of the architect's very craft. So all that remains is a few isolated atolls, those monuments and representative facilities granted to a handful of creative people finally isolated from the mainland where major decisions are made about developments and facilities. Where sweeping urban developments, major civil engineering projects and structural facilities are concerned, the political world has learnt to bow to the corporate world, controlled by a few lobbies, which by way of their subsidiaries renew, on a worldwide scale, a standardized network of highrise office blocks, communications thoroughfares, airports and shopping malls, thus constructing a distressing landscape typified by unprecedented standardization. It has taken just a few years for the merry-go-round to be joined by the last bastions of the East and Asia, now confronted by the absurd contradiction between the flattening effects of globalization and endless nationalistic fallback on specific features, be they regional, religious or ethnic. What is architecture's place where the claims of a neo-regionalist, vernacular, heritage-oriented discipline are the precise counterpoint of a far-reaching dispossession produced by the global economy, communications and the excessive planning of territorial management? Those very territories which seem to be becoming the eulogists of a traditionalist and identity-based discourse bolstering the means of production and development, also underscore territorial destructuring and the rejection of specific geographical and cultural factors.

How is a person to be an architect where the profession has seen its area of activity shrink to next to nothing? How is the architect's area of expertise to be enhanced where technical knowledge has spawned so many interventions and skills, eluding the very logic of the project or denying that architectural creation has any specific character? The timing of the project, situational analysis, preliminary study, programme drafting, design, engineering study, choice of materials and cost study are all bound by a policy of optimization, which at any given moment comes up with prefabricated solutions sold like any other service by engineering and design departments. The architect is caught in a lethal trap, where this permanent reification of the practice has stereotyped solutions, and where this agreed delegation of qualifications and skills pigeonholes him in a role that he has, in the final analysis, always rejected: architect-cum-designer — losing the real sense of a free form of expression, which pales against the seriousness of those builders who, where architecture is concerned, are interested solely in functionality and profitability.

Nowadays, architecture is obliged to deal with this problem of sovereignty, identity and legitimacy. It must win back its area of activity. It must redefine the conditions in which it stays close to the real, and become interventionist in every area involved by the industrial production of the building, from which it has been bit by bit excluded. The very conditions formulating this issue of identity define both the challenge and the deadlocks in which the cultural, social and political positioning of architecture is entangled. All our mainly Western conceptions of architecture, and the way it has become a discipline and an area of learning and knowledge, have been adapted to an identity-related conception where the principle of foundation had to be defined at some remove from the real, at some remove from the complexity of the world conceived as an intolerable tower of Babel. As a sin of empiricism or dogmatism, the issue of the ark, of foundation and of a beginning seems to be inextricably bound up with any attempt to define architecture – an origin that must be wrenched from the loam of the real to establish an architectural legitimacy, normalcy, prescriptiveness and truth. Architecture has always been modern, by relentlessly renewing its relationship with the classical foundation, by shifting the order or Alberti-inspired harmony towards an independent foundation, rooted, first and foremost, in the abstraction of measurement, then becoming thoroughly organized around a rational foundation striving to become a system. Architecture has been modern ever since it gave way to the architectonic, to that desire to unify knowledge under one idea: mastery of space and time defined by Kantian schematics, independence of a foundation of idealism that has ultimately never been challenged. This self-foundation on the part of architecture, its foray into the order of reasons, has thus always exercised architects by renewing a normativeness, the principles of sound architecture, and shifting the rules of foundation to criteria and standards endeavouring to inspect and step aboard the real. Space, time, body, functions, practices, social arena, city, machine – modern architecture has attempted to redefine the proper use of reality. Clean body, purified spaces, light and functionality are all the flipside of a universalist discourse, which still owes everything to the ideology of the Enlightenment. Architecture has always been postmodern by failing to perpetuate this basic grammar, by highlighting its finest achievements in failure, drift, falsification, in the hijacking of the codes and standards it had provided itself with.

Be it modern or postmodern, it is indeed architecture that has updated this cultural contradiction, which nowadays seems to sum up the deadlock of our aesthetic domains, taking all the various disciplines together, trying to define the depletion of a conception of knowledge. Jean-François Lyotard said it quite emphatically: postmodernism is not the historical state of an after-modernism but merely the realization of modernism in other forms. The contrast with Jürgen Habermas is quite explicit, and refuses that renewal of history that ill conceals the desire to perpetuate a materialistic ratio-

nality. When Jean-François Lyotard writes that 'the principle of a universal meta-language is replaced with that of the plurality of formal and axiomatic systems capable of arguing denotative statements',[1] he not only sets out what he calls the great narratives and their normative, prescriptive capacity and their desire for truth, but he also seeks to understand how a normative, prescriptive system is based on the effectiveness, sound performance and interconnectedness of knowledge. So how are we to understand this modern/neo-modern contradiction which would renew historical rationality, or the fragmentary reality of a divided foundation, in altered forms? By borrowing directly from the vocabulary of architecture a notion of the postmodern that will thrive, Lyotard ushers in the idea of a simultaneity of times, of historical moments in the absence of any rational and defined orientation of history. Architecture becomes the metaphor for a switch in the status of knowledge, the learning of the Enlightenment 'ceasing to be, in itself, its own end', to leave room for a general commercialization of information. It is the whole emancipatory value of learning and history-the value of *Bildung* – which thus seems to topple, taking with it the hopes of a person such as Jürgen Habermas, who is still Kantian, and who attempts to get social theory across as the ultimate rational model.[2]

Quests for a local foundation, for a more human relationship with architecture, will assume the multifaceted forms that seem to be making an echo-like comeback today. Architecture which is at the forefront must have negotiated all forms of regression in trying to renew, more or less adroitly, the idea of the particular or proper versus a dispossession undertaken by the mercantile society. The parts of *La Dialectique de la Raison* denouncing a culture where art, and thus architecture, reduced to the standing of goods, have lost their 'mediatory function',[3] still attempt to renew the model of an emancipatory reason. We are familiar with the critical fortunes of this logic of dispossession for people like Guy Debord, Jean Baudrillard and even Paul Virilio, turning Kantian teleology into an apocalyptic vision, a subordination to the simulatory realm of ends. Architectural theory has thus seized upon this latest renewal of a normative anchor point with the *tendenza*, in which E.N. Rogers and Aldo Rossi attempt to perpetuate the latest forms of a historicist rationality by trying to save a few transcendental models based on social practice, and the sedimentation of the historical city. These latest renewals of the modern which, under the leadership of Vittorio Gregotti, seem to have frozen European architecture, shore up this impossible quest for a lost legitimacy.

Conversely, how are we to interpret this global fascination with contemporary French philosophy, where it would seem impossible to write any university essay or critical tract without sprinkling quotations from Jacques Derrida,

Gilles Deleuze and Michel Foucault throughout it? What a paradox to see what was set up like some vast critical undertaking of identity-related forms of discourse turning back into an unfathomable lack of understanding, into an authoritative discourse eager to renew an ultimate dimension of the modern, new spaces, new technologies, new hermeneutics. The notion of 'difference', initially conceived as a shift of issues of foundation, turns into a claim to do with identity. The episode of deconstruction offers a clear response to this impossibility of constructing a discourse of foundation for the architecture to come, and this impossibility of maintaining the illusion of a disciplinary truth. This has formed the bulk of the research carried out by Bernard Tschumi, Peter Eisenman and Daniel Libeskind, endeavouring to devise a primary disposition of the architectural identity while at the same time permanently shifting the gestures of foundation. The fact that Derridian deconstruction, which was the ultimate form of a system of hermeneutics, should raise questions about the processes of creating meaning did not, however, directly permit its application in the objective, architectural space. The fact that deconstruction has become a formalism is obvious to one and all, and perhaps this has to do with the ultimate renewal of a Kantian form of intuition hidden behind the spatial metaphors that hamper the designation of a legal anchor point. Mark Wigley, incidentally, sidestepped the issue. The disparate prestigious gathering of famous architects that made up the exhibition 'Deconstructivist Architecture' at the New York MoMA simply attested to the formal inability of the architectural object to reinstate the unity of its meaning.[4] The visual passion brought on by this presentation of the chaotic as a negative form seemed to be borne along by the illusory belief in a new modernity. French philosophy itself, still permeated by phenomenology, has incidentally been nurtured by a boundless register of spatial metaphors broadly taken up by architectural criticism.[5] The current fortunes of these topological metaphors respond to this difficulty in challenging discourses of foundation, often in a misinterpretation about their use.

How are we to reorganize an understanding of the singularity of form, of the spatial continuum, without resorting to the actual structure of a Kantian aesthetics which, from Ernst Cassirer to Erwin Panofsky, has espoused Kantian schematics as a unilateral matrix for constituting space? From Emil Kaufman to Joseph Rykwert, the circle that muddles the modern reason of Enlightenment architecture with the rationalism of modern functionalism has described narrow limits that, be it modern or post-modern, fixed architects in an endless confrontation over the truth of architecture. If Manfredo Tafuri and Kenneth Frampton have stressed this loss of identity in architecture, they have nevertheless failed to construct any new legal domain, and the lost reference to modernism remains the negative model of a new relativism, looking for its standards in an architectural syntax rendered independent, semantic and historicist for one, and tectonic for the other. Conversely, having different thoughts about normativeness in the absence of universalist models is to introduce 'a plural, micrological rationality, turned towards registering the singular, the complex, and the different'.[6] Architecture can no longer carry this universal discourse on emancipation, renewed for the most part by a Le Corbusier relentlessly decreeing the laws of a sound architectural code. Neo, post, super, hyper, the reference to the modern movement once more organizes the critical positions as a permanent reference, never declared to any legal definition of architecture – the definition that consists in undoing an order, hierarchies, an ongoing relationship with primary principles and with an origin and an exclusive foundation. Architecture must dodge this temptation 'of an essentialist and absolute foundation of its legitimacy'.[7]

Rem Koolhaas's impact, rematerializing the critical field of architecture by giving himself a 'concrete universal', as philosophy puts it, in other words, the context of globalization as the horizon of a practical universality, made it possible to render the placement of a practical and immediate normativeness effective. Conceiving architecture in the context of globalization, where lifestyles become unilateral under the effects of a total exploitation of the territory, the distribution of functional zones between suburban dwellings, industrial estates, shopping malls, natural parks and wasteland awaiting attention, is tantamount to accepting this de facto state of the physical complexity of architecture and city planning as a material that must be worked with. The 'terrifying beauty of the twentieth century', which makes the landscape, as is, an inexhaustible resource of invention, enabled Koolhaas to sketch out a method where he offers himself, as the physical domain, an actual phenomenality of the real, authorizing every manner of assimilation, cross-fertilization and hybridization, in a never-ending ode to complexity. Against the simplistic typologies of a real rendered commonplace, he imposes an immediate reading of the noise of the city, of mixtures of light, matter, functions, for which he offers to draw up new genealogies, by seeking 'for each bastard a genealogical tree'.[8] These quests for origins over, Koolhaas invites us to think of the generic city on a global scale, a model of universality for one and all, a repetitive city with no history. The city is freed of concentric forms of logic, of the centre; it drifts towards the outskirts; it accepts all simultaneous presences; it concentrates at one and the same time the hyperlocal and the hyperglobal; it is multicultural and multiracial. Involved here is neither empiricism seeking models in the reality of the post-industrial world, nor relativism bent on establishing the conventional values of an average world, for what Koolhaas is after is authentically ground-breaking: it clearly describes the outlines of the architectural domain, a domain with no withdrawal, an area of skill whose normativeness must spring from use and praxis. As if to say: 'What's left, once the identity is laid bare? The generic?'[9]

By updating such a radical shift of the most basic structures of modern rationalism, Rem Koolhaas seems to have reasserted all the architect's abilities in terms of intervention. A good many critical texts and writings do in fact lay claim to this new modernism, this hypermodernism, which, oddly enough, is keen to embrace the real as an area of application. This certainly has to do with the ambiguous culture of the image enjoyed by the architect, editing work, sequences, that seem to renew an idea of the plan, of the still-schematic frame. Upcoming architects mix the consequences of a collapse of the age-old rational status of architecture and this pragmatic necessity, which shatters the schematic value of space and time. It is the architect's whole craft, his procedures and his know-how, that need reviewing. The project – the *Entwurf*, to borrow the Kantian term – can no longer be kept at a remove and capsizes distance, the precondition of architectural conception. The programme can no longer abide by this preliminary definition; it no longer responds to the Kantian *monogramma*, which had a bearing on the definition of the whole and its division into parts. The line of thought about the diagram nowadays in progress enhances the permanent interactivity of the conception, a simultaneity of the process; 'the place of the diagram corresponds to an operational, intersubjective field, which is put together over a given period of time, where meanings are formed and deformed in an interactive way'. Form itself is no longer that receptacle of intuition, it loses its unity, it is constituted in movement and in a permanent interrelation. 'More than an entity formed just by its inner definition, topological surfaces and forms are arranged in interaction with the field which forms them.'[10] Architects are in the process of weaving the framework of a new horizon of objectives, and they are doing this, without references, by openly sidestepping all forms of logic of the modern sphere.

This is why it would be illusory to proffer any manifesto, or try immediately to give an overall coherence to the whole of the research front that is being established. So this essay merely aims to stake out the narrow path of an outlet for age-old issues, which had frozen the architectural debate and slowly evicted the architect from its own area of skill. The architecture that is now happening is plural, pluralist, multifaceted; it intermingles discourses, practices and techniques. It is efficient and embraces the industrial world like an inexhaustible register of materials and procedures, from which it is necessary to draw in order to regenerate our relationships with the limitless urban sphere that looms ahead. Usages do not necessarily correspond to uses and it is all the forms of hierarchization presupposed by the profession that are upset. Architecture is laid bare, it denies its positivist emphasis, it remains tempted by withdrawal, a minimalist aspiration, or minimum architecture. With cheap materials and the optimization of expertise, it provides immediate, local, clearly defined answers and rejects style and generalization of praxis. As separation and distribution, the old economy of an abstract space is adversely affected by a whole register of constituent connections, where space is only presented in a local way. As interpenetration of interior and exterior, proliferation of ramps and folds, assertion of a tectonic that links or detaches zones of coherence, architecture seeks mutating forms, a morphogenesis that prompts new spatial motifs, an exchange between processes of dissipation and other processes of aggregation. The digital tool is not the instrument of abstraction, of a final transcendence of the design; it simply increases the range of an exploration of dimensional changes as well as perceptual and visual changes. Nothing must be frozen as principles, everything remains within a convention expressed by words that seem to halt what is common, shared by everyone, fluidity, hybridization, complexity, morphogenesis. ArchiLab stands at the threshold of these exchanges at a moment when it is architecture itself that is becoming generic, regaining a fully-fledged capacity for indication and intervention, at the precise instance when the architect is becoming a distinct figure, proposing solutions that no other professional body can henceforth snatch from him. ❖

1. Jean-François Lyotard, *La Condition Postmoderne* (Minuit, 1979), p.72.
2. Jürgen Habermas, *Knowledge and Human Interest*, 1968 (London: Heinemann, 1978).
3. Max Horkheimer, Theodor W. Adorno, *La Dialectique de la Raison*, 1944 (Gallimard, 1974), p.169.
4. Philip Johnson, Mark Wigley, *Deconstructivist Architecture* (MoMA, New York, 1988), p.19. 'Such an analysis brings together highly conceptual architects with pragmatists. They join together in the production of disquieting objects which interrogate pure form, in a way that exposes the repressed condition of architecture'.
5. Frédéric Migayrou, 'Une figure sans traits, la pensée sans façon', *Exposé*, n. 2 (Editions HYX, 1995), p.206.
6. Francis Guibal, 'Penser le temps du risque' in *Témoigner du différend, Autour de Jean François Lyotard*, *Osiris*, 1989, p.13.
7. Hans van Dijk, *Architecture and Legitimacy* (NAI Publishers, 1995), p.15.
8. Rem Koolhaas, 'The Terryfing Beauty of the Twentieth Century' in *S,M,L, XL* (The Monacelli Press/010 Publishers, 1995), p.208.
9. Ben van Berkel and Caroline Bos, 'Diagrams, interactive instruments in operation' in *ANY*, n. 23, 1998, p.19.
10. Greg Lynn, *Animate Form* (Princeton Architectural Press, 1998). p.32.

✛ Graphs
The Sloughing of the Paradigm

| MARIE-ANGE BRAYER |

'The glimmering parergon!'
HERMAN MELVILLE

Architecture, nowadays, is a body that has sloughed off all its layers. It would seem that paradigm, model and reference have shifted towards other metonymic arenas. If architecture is a map, it is an imploded map, between the local and the global. If architecture is a text, it is a hypertext altered by its many different writers, readers and places. If architecture is a body, it is a body streaked with flows.

Sifting through the extremely varied research of the thirty architects taking part in this first *ArchiLab*, one inevitably enters the feisty field of a claimed merger between theory and praxis – a vehement thrust decompartmentalizing once-exogenous disciplines. Today, an architects' agency incorporates designers, philosophers, artists, art critics, geographers and musicologists (Atelier Seraji/Nexus Atelier; UN Studio/Van Berkel & Bos). It explores the cognitive sciences and the media (Neil M. Denari; Peter Zellner) and modal territorial dimensions (Roche, DSV & Sie. P, FOA, Njiric + Njiric, MVRDV). The way it works has become ellipsoidal. Likewise, the instruments have been modified and diversified. But, running counter to a deterministic approach to new technologies which have affected new spatial concepts, it might be suggested that none of this is new, that we have never been so close to the projective geometry of Desargues (circa 1640), that, back in his day, Piranesi's 'Carceri', activating the heterotopy of the architectural place, and advocating the semantic void of objects in their discontinuous assembly ('Campo Marzio') plunged the architectonic object, in its unity, into crisis, as was demonstrated by Manfredo Tafuri. And from Konstantin Melnikov's Pavilion erected in Paris in 1925, we journey towards the open systems of Coop Himmelblau and the tributes of Pauhof. From the early nineneenth century modular aggregates of J.N.L. Durand to Le Ricolais's radiolarian structures in the 1950s, from the folded sheet metal of Yona Friedman's late 1950s 'spatial towns' to Greg Lynn's 'blobs', from the 1960 cells of Häusermann and Chanéac to Oosterhuis's single-celled bodies, and from the sloping planes of 'Architecture-Principe' (Parent/Virilio) in the mid-1960s to the NOX's interactive H_2O eXPO pavilion – what history is to be reactivated?

The critical interpretation of contemporary 'movements' has often tended to fall back on easy pleonasm: modernity is modern, deconstruction deconstructs in its proclaimed discontinuity, and today people would tell us that architecture is on the move, it has become fluid, while taking us back to archaic dualities, for example, that of liquid and solid, real and virtual. It could actually be argued that volume has given way, today, to envelopes, unchangingness to contingency, fixedness to motion, articulation to assembly. It is also possible to factor in semantic recurrences: topology, fold, node, fretwork, sheath, mutation, affect, hybridization, indeterminacy, distortion, transformation, flexibility, discontinuity, instability, transitory, cognitive, evolutive, interactive, organic, haptic, texture, morphogenesis, liquid, digital, biological, network, connection, immersion, flux, fluids, fluctuations … but this, surely, only ushers in a hollow rhetoric. 'Why still talk about the real and the virtual, the material and the immaterial? Here, these categories are not in opposition or in some metaphysical disagreement, but more in an electroliquid aggregation, enforcing each other, as in a two-part adhesive; constantly exposing its metastability to induce animation,' observes Lars Spuybroek of NOX ('Motor Geometry').

Today, Leibniz, Spinoza and Husserl all act as references, and it would appear that topology has shed Euclid's shell. The Spinozan plane of immanence, which, along with Bergson, has been such an inspiration to Gilles Deleuze for his 'Mille Plateaux', might open up for us the extensive field of architecture. Similarly, a new 'eidetic' reduction of architecture might transform it into a cognitive gene, leading to the new opticality of a paradigmless architectonic object: not an occlusive figure, but a generative proposition of evolutive space-time.

Leibniz's *Ars Combinatoria* (1666) developed a theory of complexity, a universe 'founded on exchanges of identity', which would certainly mark Greg Lynn's fluid and connective forms. These new techniques of fluctuation come across like intensive and reactive fields. Steeped in vitalist philosophies (Leibniz, Bergson, Whitehead, Deleuze), Lynn develops the 'blob' notion, a topological monad whose ever-changing form manages to merge the continuity of the global in the heterogeneity of the local. This body is always growing and self-adjusting like an ecosystem. New paradigms are emerging: relation, connection, combination, fusion, inflection. Unlike deconstructivism, and 'an architecture of contradictions, superpositions and accidental collisions', Greg Lynn's folding systems are capable of 'engendering unpredicted connections with contextual, cultural, programmatic, structural and economic contingencies by vicissitude' (Greg Lynn, 'The Folded, the Pliant and the Supple'). With its differential intensities, the ground of the

Yokohama International Port Terminal, currently being built by FOA (Foreign Office Architects, Alejandro Zaera-Polo, Farshid Moussavi), is a folded surface enabling shifts between different states that are at once dynamic and static. FOA is examining the conflict between global systems and local singularities. In order to 'sidestep mimetic, symbolic and typological mediation', they have used a three-dimensional topography: 'having recourse to folds as structural devices redirects the forces of gravitational verticality towards the oblique and helps us to get rid of traces of gravity in space' (A. Zaera-Polo). The separation between envelope and structure is here done away with in favour of the 'materiality of a continuum, of a continuous and differentiated space', which denies all external paradigm.

Running counter to the current denial of Euclidean geometries, which possibly veils a comeback of traditional spatial metaphor, Bernard Cache (Objectile) shows us that these geometries nevertheless encompass topology and that there is no contradiction, but rather a bifurcation, between Euclid and, for example, Frédéric Klein's theory of transformation. 'Because topological structures are often represented with somehow indefinite curved surfaces, one could think that topology brings free curved shapes to architecture, but this is a misunderstanding ... One should not think of Euclidean geometry as cubes opposed to the free interlacing of topology.' But this does not mean that the Euclidean space is the sole form of spatial intuition, as Kant suggested, but that 'multidimensionality is not the exclusive privilege of topology, there also exist Euclidean hyperspaces as well as projective hyperspaces' ('Plea for Euclid'). So topology has not ushered in the continuity of transformation.

So what exactly is this upheaval in the epistemic field, leading us from the Lucretian 'clinamen', from René Thom's catastrophe theory, to a new dystopic field of the 'hyper', sequential in the form of 'bits' of information, data-saturated networks, in the quest for non-transcendence and stereo-complexity? Behind this mixedness, the hybridization of these new paradigms, is there not a hidden new formalism of the surface on which one surfs as a techno-nomad? Yet Neil Denari's 'gyroscopic horizons', stripped of any physical anchorage, and Neil Spiller's DNA- and cell-inspired structures seem to involve a fissure of the paradigm, a twisting of referencing, for other similarities which are no longer alienated from the metaphysical order of meaning, but draw their vitality from the dynamics of the connections, from the 'link' that joins the heterogeneous factions of the real.

Nor is this link the exclusively deterministic link of the new technologies. It is also what pushes Tom Kovac towards the organic forms of English sculptors such as Moore and Hepworth, eluding the categories of cast or sculpted form; what leads Dominique Lyon towards Merce Cunningham and Sophie Calle, and dECOi towards William Forsythe. The field of reference is no longer the real, but mathematics and computer calculus for Objectile and Nox, and the iconic complexity of the media for Neil Denari, or, alternatively, the disruption of accident and chaos in the seismographic drawings of Reiser + Umemoto.

The object, either isolated or set in its context, is replaced by a new sequence which draws us into changing phenomenological spaces. This, the continuum achieved by Van Berkel in his Möbius House, built in the Netherlands, where the space-time loop in the form of a Möbius strip makes interior and exterior reversible; or CJ Lim's 'Guest House', which exists only through the temporal nature of the moment: the architecture – a prosthetic body – mutates on the basis of climatic variations and the movements of the occupants who bring life to it. The house is a fleeting, dismembered body, at times open, at times closed in on itself, at times moving, like a caterpillar, at times suspended in a catatonic state. In it, a wall may turn into a floor, and the house may be buried in the ground or hoisted upward like a ship's prow. The 'Guest House' project almost becomes the allegory of this mutating time. This fleeting, dismembered body is in quest of a time of congruity and simultaneity – the time of Moholy Nagy and Delaunay, by way of the body broken down into movements by someone such as the physician Etienne-Jules Marey. This new 'plane of immanence', which encourages us to summon up the stuff of Spinoza and its attributes, its modal saliences which develop new communities, has twisted the subject into the object. The process under way is a generative one – from Oosterhuis's ecosystems to Greg Lynn's 'folds'. The status of the object has itself become ambiguous. It is the state of 'smectic' (layered) indeterminacy for dECOi, hovering between liquid and solid. The whole representational logic is turned inside out. The primary object has dissolved in the process. The paradigm bifurcates towards referents that are vectorialized, suspended, compressed, dissolved and involuted. Mark Goulthorpe (dECOi), again, talks to us about the 'trauma of reference': 'The world may have become visual to an extent never before imagined, for the logics of representation, and the opticality they presuppose, have liquefied – become chemical.' Linearity has given way to flows and biological rhythms. The recurrence of morphing (a sequential dissolve of images), used by Nox from the 1980s on, which we find today with Roche, DSV & Sie. P, clearly embraces these extrusions in time which is at once suspended and compressed. In the same breath, these extensive strategies lend a structural role to ornament (dECOi, Objectile), henceforth presented as a 'node' weaving the surface into the volume and the line into the depth, while at the same time intentionally doing away with the hierarchic order of the architectonic components, now turned back into paratactical mesh.

The essentialist categories of form have likewise been replaced, in present-day research, by the diagram in its graph form – neither figure nor background, neither abstract nor concrete, the diagram can no longer be this Kantian scheme, between image and concept, like the hyphen of a two-part thought. This diagram is, for example, the genetic graph of Oosterhuis's Freshwater Pavilion, which comes over in speed, in the accelerated sloughing of temporal processes. This element of differentiation is an expanded writing of space, a cognitive phrase of the process, which destructures representational forms of logic. The diagram thus crosses a new culture of flows and multiplicities, where solid bodies have disappeared in favour of the cinematic textures of video, morphing and virtuality.

It recurs in the inscrutability of the notion of object in dECOi or, alternatively, in the procedural engineering of Ben van Berkel, architect of the Erasmus Bridge in Rotterdam. Van Berkel designs his projects 'through diagrams which are conceptual techniques of virtual organization before they become material technologies of concrete assemblage' ('Forms of Expression: The Proto-Functional Potential of Diagrams in Architectural Design'). For Ben van Berkel, 'the condensation of meaning in a diagram makes it a unique instrument today. The diagram conveys an essence which is unspoken, and unconnected with any ideal or ideology; it is haphazard, intuitive, subjective, and not associated with any linear logic; all this is physical, structural, probably even technical. The diagram offers a stable moment in the design process which is more and more a fluctuation involving computers, sketches, discussions, programmatic analyses and models, in no particular order. The abstraction of the diagram is well removed from any modernist or purist ideal. Rather, it is the plurality of meanings and the generative nature of the diagram which lend it its specific value.' Scaleless, non-linguistic, a summary of typology and genealogy, the diagram is the connective tool of tools that eludes all representation and ushers in deterritorialization.

'The new architectural body, which encompasses diversity, conflict and change within itself, attests to qualities peculiar to our age,

including the transformability and virtually boundless absorption of information,' declares Ben van Berkel, in an apology for an 'active science,' inherited from Nietzsche, 'capable of interpreting real activities and relations between forces.' Architecture as 'exact transformation' (Dominique Lyon), architecture as 'transformational strategy' (Ben van Berkel) is nowadays overlaid with a host of identities that exist simultaneously. Architecture has got rid of its great mimetic body to explore the currents, forces, actions, information and intensity in a world marked by the plasticity of social, economic and political distribution. How are we 'to recreate a cohesive identity from multiplicities?' (Van Berkel) 'Today looking has come to mean calculating rather than depicting external appearance. As architects we used to be obsessed with the cube and the sphere; now we have become obsessed with a cloud or a flock, with a traffic jam, with the behaviour of a dog, with the substance and the surface of water... We have stopped modelling form from the outside and generate it from the inside instead' (Lars Spuybroek, 'The Motorization of Reality').

'This whole new world is within our reach', Xenakis declared in the 1950s. His 'Metastasis' – 'inflections of curved surfaces, amplifications, reductions, twists' – involved an architectonic space, with undulating acoustic ranges, a space of the 'glimmering parergon' (Melville), where the incorporation of many and varied data no longer has any stable referent. A time when possible identities emerge and flow together, a 'metastasic' architecture, with a synthetic field of activity that has turned the architect into 'possibly the last general practitioner in a world of specialists' (Bart Lootsma), embracing a plurality of areas of reflection and action which radically exceed the domain traditionally earmarked for architecture. The architect has become a cartographer, a geneticist of the visible, a surveyor of mixed territories and a narrator of moving topologies. But this does not involve forms of technological 'hypnerotomachy'. Quite to the contrary, the complexity of the experiments currently being developed by these architects has already managed to find a form. Its perceptible achievement goes hand in hand with the vigorous enthusiasm of their research. ◆

Offshore Architecture: Accelerated Reconfigurations of a Praxis

| CHRISTIAN GIRARD |

Close this book and open it again in six months, or a year, or two years, or ten. Or even later when perhaps no printed books will ever be published. The advantage of this postponing will be that all the works shown in this compendium will no longer be topical. For an architect's work, nothing is worse that being subjected to the realm of the ephemeral, even if, these days, it is crucial to be able to work in cahoots with it. Meanwhile, all the project illustrations in this publication and plenty more produced by architects from the four corners of the global village will circulate faster and faster. Once the paper medium – this book, this essay – has cooled, it will perhaps tolerate an analytical, aloof eye. In a year's time, some of the architects brought together here will already be well removed from what they are proposing today or, conversely, they will be in the throes of actually carrying through their projects. Others will have broadened their research and their urban and architectural experiments. They will also have built architectures and their laboratories will have gone on working out programmes of relevance to the city. At times, their approaches will have become very common by dint of duplications, or else they will have remained solitary in their singularity. Whatever, the sum of experience compiled and summarized here will have pursued the vital undertaking of rewriting and overhauling the urban architectural discipline.

It would have been so comfortable just to let oneself be 'globalized' on the spot, locally, as close as possible to our cultural customs, as close as possible to our own front door, in our own neighbourhood and our own city. On-the-spot globalization and armchair internationalization have turned into almost commonplace ways of being. Now architecture, too, is undergoing this development, where the main rule of play is instant cross-border trade. Something as symbolically loaded as human blood was already the target of globalization/internationalization in the 1980s.[1] With it, it was not just immaterial money movements and digital imagery which circulated, but human substances. If 'organless bodies' – in the strict sense of the term – can be negotiated, put up for grabs and exported from continent to continent, it is even more straightforward to broadcast projects involving territorial spaces and developments. Architecture is also put in a stance of generalized exchange in real time, beyond charted lands. Globalization goes hand in hand with architecture's new capacity to escape from its own disciplinary boundaries..

An architecture of complexity has been developed of late. I call it 'offshore architecture', because it lies beyond the borderlines between disciplines, and it tacks outside the territorial waters of known learning. The very word 'architecture' starts to hamper any understanding of the new potential role of practitioners, who are more in touch with the latest developments in information technologies than with the history of their discipline. They respond to a programme, which is all the more quintessential than any programme to do with giving shape to the built space, and consists in defining new possibilities of tangible inclusion in an ever-changing real.

Félix Guattari made distinctions between 'Euclidean spaces' (where no ambiguity is allowed), 'projective spaces' (where the imaginary gets the better of reality) and 'labyrinthine topological spaces' (where pride of place goes to affects and emotions, based on a geometry of body wrapping). In so doing, he strikingly anticipated the changes occurring in architecture.[2] At issue is not so much a formal diversity and a fragmentation of aesthetics, but a challenge to the accepted concepts of programme, use and context, which govern this praxis. By virtue of their attention to situations and their spatial incorporation – those new 'collective enunciative arrangements' ['agencements collectifs d'énonciation'] which Guattari talked about, meaning often imperceptible changes to social configurations – projects may sometimes give rise to cultural patterns and models of the relationship between, on the one hand, individuals and social groups, and, on the other, the world.

At the same time, a lushness never seen before in architecture is at work, as it is everywhere else. Plenty of projects produced by computer graphics have polished, smoothed surfaces, almost edible moiré effects, supple wrappings, sensual coatings and precise metal or plastic skins. An effect of visual/physical fission appears, associating the optical and the tactile. An extension of the architectural space is aimed at by most architects concerned with this disciplinary upheaval. On the French scene, one pointer to the development under way was given in March 2000 by the projects submitted to the international competition at the Quai Branly Museum. An immeasurable gap opened up here between proposals frozen within a common conception of the architectural object (Ando, Foster, Piano, Portzamparc and Berger, not forgetting the winner, Nouvel) and those candidly exploring approaches freed from both narrow contextualism and any reference to typologies (mainly the projects of two firms: Eisenman, Jakob & MacFarlane). Shackled by its incestuous bond with the profession, architectural journalism thus saw here merely a question of style, although a more far-reaching change was probably at work.

Indeed, whether the cutting edge of international architecture can be exhibited, is not self-evident. What might have been an undisputed novelty twelve months ago sinks into oblivion at the speed of light – oblivion or the repetitiousness of advertising. Screen architecture, plant-rich architecture, cyber-spatial rendering, 'land-artized' architecture, and so on, bore us no sooner than they are promoted.

The spectre of speed brandished by Paul Virilio really does have its effects, and the absolute reign of Jean Baudrillard's simulation is forever being scrutinized. Construction sites, alone, seem to be still withstanding the squeeze of time – but for how much longer? The faster you erect a skyscraper the better. The real and matter have their requirements, including the material to which too many architects have naïvely thought they were attributing properties of immateriality – glass, that 'blue jeans of contemporary architecture', to quote one of the architects in this volume, responsible for a short scathing analysis of transparency.[3]

Safe from any drift into the illusion of form and matter, the critical architect who drastically reinterprets functions and uses, reinvents programmes and steps beyond methods of sectoral activity in territories. Such an architect does contribute to the emergence of the events that make up the contemporary city. ✦

1. Rabinow, Paul, *French DNA: Trouble in Purgatory* (Chicago, The University of Chicago Press, 1999). This describes the mechanism by which the voluntary blood-giving became embroiled in international monetary systems.
2. Guattari, Felix, *Cartographies schizo-analytiques* (Paris, Editions Galilée, 1989), p. 298
3. 'Le verre et la violence' in Ricciotti, Rudy, *Pièces à conviction*, Paris (Sens & Tonka, 1998), pp. 74-81.

✛ Building Terminal

| Ole Bouman |

Many people think that the new media are pushing architecture into the role of helpless victim. It can only stand by and watch how millions of people are spending more and more of their valuable time in digital surroundings; they no longer need architecture as the backdrop to the important moments of their lives. On top of this, the role of permanent carrier of cultural meaning has lapsed. The mother of the arts is becoming a marginal phenomenon. Others take a more optimistic view of things. As far as they are concerned, the only interesting architecture is computer-generated architecture. In this essay I will explore the fertile area between these two extremes.

The key question for the coming years is whether architecture will succeed in developing other strategies besides the rationalization of existing practice. What other options are there apart from cost-cutting and streamlining? Equally important is the question of whether potential new strategies will in fact constitute genuine alternatives within the practice of building. Will creative innovation at the conceptual level really get a look-in? In any event, for this to happen designers must not merely take note of the new technology but also seek out its creative potential. Rather than automatically adjusting to current practice, they should adjust current practice where necessary to the new ideas. In this way architecture is able to conquer a new field of activity in a digital era. It can produce environments we have as yet barely encountered. It can create experiences we have never had before. It can also organize itself in a way that challenges professional certitudes and makes the existing role play look hopelessly old-fashioned.

Before going into the nature of the new environments and experiences, we must first pause to consider the artistic mentality necessary for their creation. In order to be able to intervene actively in the development of the new media an architect must be adequately mentally equipped. A key element of this question of mentality is the relationship with technology itself. In architecture, as in other areas, it is possible to distinguish three broad attitudes to the new media. The first is the negative attitude where people stubbornly stick to the old familiar way of working and simply ignore the cultural significance of the new media. At the very best, since the computer has become indispensable for drawing, they will employ someone to take care of this side of the business. The whiz-kid as alibi for not making any substantive changes. The architecture continues to look the same as ever.

The second attitude is that of an unabashed surrender to the hype in which the new media are lauded with quasi-religious fervour as architecture's saviours. The design identity of these architects is synonymous with their use of the computer. In the final analysis, they are asked only by virtue of their reputation as a computer apostle, a preacher of the digital gospel. However versatile their designs, it is above all their use of the computer that attracts attention. For those who adopt this attitude it is then only a small step to restrict themselves voluntarily to this stance. Eventually, they can talk of nothing else. At which point a true community of faith is born.

Finally there is the pragmatic attitude in which the two domains are seen side by side, as two parallel worlds. Such pragmatists have no difficulty accepting the existence of virtual reality, of digital networks, and they are also prepared to use the computer for the design of architecture. At the same time, however, they stick to the production of a physical, analogue world, appropriate to the functions we have always known and adapted to the physical movements we have always made. Even if the entire office is computerized, the benefits of the new technology are barely if at all conceptualized and as such taken into account in the designs. Media remain what they are: means. Nothing more.

There is, however, a fourth attitude possible. Something that has so far received much less attention is the possibility of allowing the physical and virtual domains to merge, of integrating them. By refusing to let oneself be reduced to either a worn-out dinosaur or a stressed-out cybernaut, a whole range of innovative possibilities capable of injecting architecture with enormous vitality comes into view. It is a matter of crossing the analogue and digital worlds, of hybrid environments that can no longer be classified as one thing or the other. The behaviour of such worlds is similarly hybrid, consisting partly of biological and physical reactions, partly of cybernetic acts appropriate to a cyborgian existence. The environmental quality of such a hybrid world can never again be reduced to the typical architectural parameters that have stood us in good stead for centuries. All previous architectural definitions, from Vitruvius to Peter Eisenman, run up against their limits here. Beauty and functionality and solidity, tectonic and cladding, programme and meaning, all these old concepts acquire a new connotation. The task is to chart the architectural potential of a digital world, not in spite of, not instead of, not even alongside, but in the physical world. This I will do by exploring the concept of architecture conceived as terminal. As such it's still a building, an object. But it is also a computer, an interface. As a nodal point in a wider communication network.

What if architecture were to become no more than a prop for a display or projection screen? If the separation between its two main functions, shelter and symbol, were to become definitive and the sheltering function were to divest itself of any iconographic ambition and withdraw behind the exterior? What would remain of architecture as we know it if spatial expression were to become a mere adjunct and all designing capacity and visual intelligence were to be put into directing the surface? Would architecture survive if the entire tectonic tradition of construction and making connections were to vanish as a source of design inspiration in favour of the visual story on façades and interior walls? What does the future hold for architecture when any of its buildings can be animated and transformed by projections and electronic displays? What is left of architecture if our architectural 'sign' language is no longer etched in stone?

In the past, architecture also needed sunlight in order to be seen. As soon as darkness fell it lost its shape and substance. Meaning vanished, cloaked in shadows. Even when it became fashionable to spotlight monumental buildings, it was above all the building as volume, as object, that was emphasized. Out of the nocturnal gloom there suddenly rises up a majestic object, a representative of the realm of things, that must try to last until dawn. Until the invention of neon light. Nearly everyone has memories of the flashing lights of Times Square, Shinjuko, Piccadilly Circus or Place Pigalle. These places provided the defining images of the metropolis at night. Simple light-switching circuits strung along the upper edge of urban elevations created a deliriously metropolitan atmosphere that owed virtually nothing to the materiality of the architecture. The absolute acme of such urban animation (partly because of countless famous film scenes) is The Strip at Las Vegas. The ultimate funfair. But neon signs are only part of its story nowadays. Entire virtual edifices are contrived by means of lighting effects. Gigantic Jumbotron and Napcom displays dominate the scene. The best the visual display industry has to offer is on show here. And it is growing all the time. Ever larger LCD and magma screens. Ever finer resolution, ever sharper pictures. And although a surface of around 2 x 3 metres quickly runs into millions of dollars in production and management costs, the price of hardware looks set to fall. Façades and walls could be brought to life by designers and provided with a new, dynamic iconography. Now that a good deal of public life is conducted indoors, in shopping malls or car parks, the game can continue by day. No longer must the use of light in architecture wait for nightfall.

At first glance, it would seem that these developments need not really affect architecture. They could remain an addition, a revitalization. But of course there is something far more fundamental going on here. It concerns a new role for architecture in a pervasive visual culture where the mass media have less and less need of the enclosure of the box (TV, cinema). The audio-visual media continue to find new outlets in the city. For the static nature of the architecture, bound up as it is with

concepts like foundations, durability, inertia and tradition, this has serious implications. Mobilization, which has long had society in its grip, is now impinging upon the material environment. When stationary objects are visually animated they lose their objectness, their fixity. However sturdy their construction may still be, they appear to be moving. It looks as if we have here the next step in the rich history of parallax manipulation. Where the baroque played the game of convex and concave and investigated the trompe l'œil, where neo-classicism discovered the mirror, where nineteenth-century engineering heroized the free-standing structure, where modernism turned the free façade and the free ground plan into ideology, we are now on the threshold of a new development in the psychological game of spatial design. For this new spatial effect the physical space is no longer strictly necessary, although duplication has its attractions. The great leap consists of uncoupling spatial perception and architectural structure. Now that really is 'lite' architecture. In addition to striving after ever lighter structures, transparent and translucent walls and gravity-defying, curvilinear forms, architecture can now, via film, become truly immaterial. Contours fade, forms become fluid. The relationship between human beings and architecture is no longer polar or dialectical, but 'immersive'. You can quite literally be swallowed up in it...

Who will be the first architect to win the Oscar or Golden Palm for best director?

I offer you the following scenario. Suppose that architects were to incorporate video walls and projections in their initial sketch designs. Suppose that in their negotiations with the client, investment by the likes of Fuji, Coca-Cola or Lucky Strike, by Sharp, Zeiss Ikon or Polaroid, by Silicon Graphics or Alias WaveFront, could be calculated in their budgets from the start. It might then be possible to use the image-carriers thus procured for non-commercial, experience-heightening effects. Apart from one-dimensional messages from the multinationals, urban façade displays could at given moments become total theatre, with the architect as director, as creative brain. This is the urbanism of the future. In addition to the advertisements, conscious and unconscious sensations are evoked. A mixture of film loops and abstract images affords artistically profound experiences. The consciousness industry, to resurrect that old concept, will help energize the public domain. And as if that were not enough, we are also continuing to develop interactive paint, contorted façade surfaces and curved windows, to use sandblasted or LCD-programmed glass, with zinc and aluminium cladding. One can imagine a whole range of architectural interventions aimed at intensifying this projection game. And who will invent the double-curved display screen? Frank Gehry's Bilbao fantasia will be child's play in comparison with the building that really (re) acts as a terminal. ❖

✦ World Trade

| Mark Robbins |

It's 4 a.m. inside a darkened 1940s dance hall in New York. Strobe lights, fog machines and deafening sound heighten the disorientation of the dancers in the kinesthetic drive of music and ecstasy. Thousands of bodies in sync get lost with other dancers on the floor, reflected on walls of full-length mirrors. The crowd is in constant flux, a huge amoebic mass, containing visible strands, clusters and single cells. Like a school of fish it is diffuse in formation, figural at one moment, dispersed at another. Groups hang together watching, a spectacle for others. Like a religious experience, the evening offers the warm seduction of a glimpse beyond one's own body, the possibility of fusing with a group, a virtual experience.

Restructuring boundaries is part of the kick and promise of the virtual technology, spatially and politically, that offers universal and unconditional access. It opens a range of possibilities for the presentation of gender, physique and even voice. There is an ease in simulating that 'you are there'. The telephone first allowed this bodiless transportation; the dream of interactive TV is now played out by the web and c-u c-me technologies. VR with strap-on prosthetic viewing devices gives a physical sense of presence. In very short order the net has evolved in our lives, from e-mail to direct time-based interaction. Chat lines with delayed text were amplified with the addition of audio and video. Like spectators under glass, the net offers perfect hygienic engagement, projected wholly and passionately on the fragmentary evidence on a screen. Giddy at the first simple contact, the users of technology now get a greater sense of reality that approaches the proximate senses, the last set of senses left out. In the increased capacity to sever ties with the actual, elaborate invention is employed to make a virtual connection complete.

While already separated as individuals through mechanical advances into self-sustaining units (the car, the air-conditioned home), Americans cluster in discrete suburbs. Event shopping and theme parks prosper, allowing for highly ritualized ways of being together through commerce. The mall and Cineplex act as a convincing stage double for the commune. At the same time, the culture has been thoroughly connected through radio and TV waves, and increasingly wired with cables. A common source for information and goods establishes community in spatial exile through the web. Home shopping with call-ins helps resurrect a sense of community with the pervasive structure of evangelism. (Twelve thousand sold, fifty people on line', redemption and inclusion through a 'sale' or 'love donation'.) In testimonials for food dryers or healing waters, an onstage chorus echoes the enthusiasm of the pitch: they've tried it and it's changed their lives.

The net promises an antidote to our own geographic limits, offering access to a multinational bazaar. With a credit card, access code and a PC, all the things once associated with the metropolis are available from home: entertainment, companionship, contact without disclosure. The world at our port. Like other myths of progress, the changes will not be total or provide universal access. The net is neither inherently liberating nor demonic, and truly global access remains problematic in the delivery. There is an analogy between the hopes for modernism, the expectations for a global culture and the flow of information on the web. The totality of master planning gives way to the infil, the particular. It's always a hybrid condition, closer to *Bladerunner* than Utopia.

The corollary to our current fascination with the possibilities of the virtual is the preoccupation with the 'real'. Advertising breathlessly asserts its desirability, building a youthful market. At the supermarket, seemingly handwritten labels on a product line note, 'real food for people'. (One assumes the elided 'real' as a qualifier for people). Beyond Coke's 'real thing', 'in the back of your mind, what you're hoping to find', it's probably not a soda. Vogueing, the intense simulation of identity, takes the consumer imperatives of fashion and beauty and represents them with a vengeance. Coded in hyperbolic performances, voguers assume desired identities from pop diva to Brooks Brothers executive drag. The prized 'realness' marks the degree of success in passing. The apotheosis of the consumer's dream of stardom is played back with cutting irony.

Architecture, like the physical body, in fact is limited, fixed in place. Attempts by designers at achieving a mutable space, through moveable or transparent walls, a fascination of early modernists, continue. The explorations present catalogues of possible configurations or a graphic fluidity of form. The insertion of video or choreographed lighting offers a sense of speed and movement in a building, but it's basically a leaden proposition, fixed in space. The building can simulate MTV with rapidly alternating sound and light, but more powerfully orchestrate the congregation of bodies in space. It offers the tactile possibilities of direct interaction.

If the building, however, is no longer the dominant purveyor of meaning, its attempts to capture a broader narrative within culture are significant. Buildings continue to hold a place in our consciousness, though often finding purchase through style and décor, in the theatricality and simulation of Williamsburg or Graceland (the 'Old South' under a high-tech roof, the trees bound with metal mesh to assure their lollipop shape). Disney's Celebration serves up a past we desire as it did the World of Tomorrow. That architecture supports a set of fixed notions of what a community looks like and about who inhabits it. In less saturated versions across the country the vocabulary finds imitations in home and product design, a national style.

American developers have recognized the popularity for gathering and being seen, and labour to set the stage in appealing ways. Configured at the periphery as new 'town centres' or with less bucolic images for urban settings, malls are offered as safe but engaging public space. Marketed with saturated colours and programmed with activities, like a Ritalin-deprived kid, they are always running. Using the techniques of film – Eisenstein translated through music videos – they are bright, full of stimuli. The space competes with newer faster technologies, with analogues of the graphic spin of .coms.

Umberto Eco and others have plumbed the hyperreal turf of Disneyworld and adventure parks for a sense of our national culture. This is not news. In the recent blossoming of themed events and entertainment shopping, however, there is an aggressive blurring between authentic public experience and its simulation: Universal Walk in L.A. and the representations of New York, Venice and now Paris as Las Vegas casinos. They offer distance without the trouble of travel, the exoticism without the risk.

Metreon recently opened in San Francisco at Yerba Buena as part of a public-private partnership on a long-vacant urban renewal site downtown. It is a good example of an agora for commerce, with its great fragmented interior vaults, a palace to give the net a run for its money, offering tactile participation in this 'retail baroque'. As physical engagement and cultural narrative, it compares well with the formal and propagandistic effects of eighteenth-century pilgrimage churches and residences. Here too the edges are blurred, the viewer swept into the atmospheric event, the perspectival experience of heaven and hell, paradise in mirrored, panelled interiors. Typical of this new generation, the interior is spatially complex, themed with futuristic references reminiscent of Flash Gordon and an industrial deco. Distinct zones between the retail are erased with vistas that cut through shopping areas, from computer stores to coffee shops to a video-game parlour in some intergalactic style. (Sony did the interiors). The movement of people plays against the hyperanimated surfaces. At the top level of the escalator ascent is the multiplex. This is the final darkened repose in stadium seating, with

instructions on how to behave in a public theatre, before the rumbling show in Dolby sound.

In the mall we enter the realm of the spectator in an audience with objects and each other. It is a space in-between, as in the apprehension of art described by critic Rosalind Krauss as 'virtual'. Grappling famously with Clement Greenberg, she wrote in the late 1980s about abstract art 'rendering substance entirely optical... incorporeal, weightless', rooted, she continues, in the 'pulverization of the edge, the setting up of the illusion that one cannot secure the experience of distinct objects because one cannot locate the contours. The viewer floating in front of the work as pure optical ray... a dematerialization into the virtual.' She proposes this as a pure desiring subject 'constructed by pop' and the 'world of media and the solicitation of advertising'. It's a description and a technique that apply to virtual media and to the tactile field. It is evident in the blurring of the baroque and high modern space – one through hyperbolic pattern, the other through transparency – a layering of glassy and reflective surfaces, oscillating between inside and out.

The use of visual simulation as a marketing device is not particularly new, traced by Douglas Rushkoff in his book *Coercion to Frank Baum*, who in the 1890s began testing blends of colour, light, glass and mirrors, to stimulate positive responses to certain products. In 1902 Theodore Dreiser identified the use of mannequins as having the ability to create 'an atmosphere of reality that aroused enthusiasm'. Rushkoff describes the creation of controlled spaces, using props, light, sound and smell. The casino , the mall, the stadium spectacle are all environments carefully orchestrated to disorient or reorient the viewer to make a specific pitch effective. 'The exclusion of all real world sensory stimuli meant that patrons were dependent on manufactured cues for their behavior. Eliminating all external stimuli prevented any random... reactions.' While virtual modes become more sophisticated in providing an approximation of tactile environments into which we can lose ourselves, so does environmental or atmospheric design. We are disoriented but the use of familiar visual and aural cues, even, for example, the scent of baking cinnamon rolls exhausted to the interior, helps us feel comfortable, at home.

Rushkoff introduces the term 'techno-real' used by a group of authors to restrategize the commercial control of the net, 'to reclaim the Internet as public space rather than one dominated by market forces', fusing tech and real. Tech becomes a means to an authentic, real end, rather than a substitute. In reverse, Intel offers, 'can't do it in life do it on the web'.

The theatrics of the newer commercial architecture make most of the decisions for the audience, selecting theme, sequence, activity and behaviour, as if going to a movie that you can be in. In describing this increasingly sophisticated genre, journalist Susan Doublilet writes of the complex production in the terms of a movie, with a narrative and a script. A host of designers, from industrial to graphic design, interior, lighting, architecture, assemble a believable storyline for the retail experience.

Artist and writer Amy Rankin wrote in 1987 about the ways that the 'unruly real' is banished from our public life through what she terms the symbolic 'mapped over the imaginary'. The pointed use of simulation has become a popular, subversive strategy in art practices, one that challenges the passive digestion of our own image. The critical distance toward representation used famously by artists like Warhol, or later Hans Haacke or Fred Wilson, destabilizes assumptions and stereotypes. The image, Rankin continues, 'produces pleasure precisely where it fixes meaning least', the complexity and ambiguity that 'bear a faint stain of the real'. Artists leave questions in place, with quotations repositioned, leaving things open for interpretation by active viewers. Complexity, though, is generally not what the consumer wants and commerce instead trades on easy black and white equations between product and effect. Ads smooth out difference and offer a seamless depiction of how we live what we desire. The pitch is direct and offers happiness and membership in an imagined community, however remote.

The bulk of media is generated for profit and the realities offered are those that most readily sell. Like most forms of advertising or narrative representations, they exclude non-conforming types . As in post–Hays Code movies and later on TV, the representations of us are controlled, the way we speak, dress, decorate. The movies not only trained us in an easy reception of conventions for the medium, the way film images generate meaning, but also of a dominant set of social ones. Chorus girls from Lima, Ohio, trained by diction coaches spoke an odd Anglo patois, prostitutes became 'hostesses', closed doors signified sex, women were pale, men rugged. Archetypes of wealth and poverty were reinforced.

Corporations have always understood that multiple buyers exist, the trick was to appeal to them without losing the mass market. Advertisers precisely identify different groups in the search of new markets that offer significant enough niches. Target stores open up the idealization of the American family to Latino and African-Americans, showing sunny outings worthy of Martha Stewart. IKEA courts the gay market, showing a mix of couples that could be partners or friends. In an odd way the ads offer the promise of democratic access that legislation and good intentions often fail to deliver. Personal and the particular responses are a hedge against the homogenizing force of the market. They are generated by larger ideas and riskier, richer propositions, about programme, use and form, which must be allowed to exist. Not all will succeed or even appeal, but the aspiration of designers and artists is necessary for a public realm in which the difficult exchange of ideas can occur.

In *Transfiguration of the Commonplace*, philosopher Arthur Danto presents a case for the relation between art and mere real things, which goes back to the earliest discussions of art, imitation and reality. He loosely quotes Plato asking, 'Who would choose the appearance of a thing over the thing itself; who would settle for a picture of someone he could have, as it were, in the flesh?' The virtual and the tactile do jockey for our attention. Who could not be impressed with the continued force of the imagination in the face of the void: a power to reproduce and invent? Both have the potential for freedom and co-option, making other possibilities or only an international market share. ✦

✦ Two Stories for the Avant-garde

| Michael Speaks |

I have always found charming the late English architecture critic Colin Rowe's story about modern architecture's trip across the Atlantic Ocean; how its physique flesh and its morale word, or its form and ideology, became separated; how ideology either remained in Europe or dropped off somewhere in the cold waters of the Atlantic; how form arrived on American shores to become the style of corporate America; and how, as a result of American postwar military and cultural supremacy, this formalist architecture became the 'international' style sold to the rest of the world as truly modern.

Rowe's little story is equally applicable to 'theory', that set of mostly French, German and Italian philosophical tracts that arrived in the United States in the late 1970s through departments of comparative literature and were disseminated to the rest of American academe as a wonderful new mode of contemporary thought. Theory, like modern architecture, was detached from its Continental origins and replanted in the U.S., where it took on a lighter, more occasional existence. This was enabled by the decoupling of philosophy and other traditional disciplinary fields, such as anthropology, from their real material – from field analysis in the case of anthropology – by way of semiotic methodologies which purported to offer a more scientific, universal understanding obtained by analyzing the structures of social organization. Language became pre-eminent, as was suggested even about our psyche in Jacques Lacan's assertion that the unconscious was structured in the most radical way like a language. Linguistics broke down disciplinary boundaries to such an extent that one could become a specialist in 'theory' without disciplinary or material affiliation of any kind.

Theory was portable – it could be attached to almost any field of study, film, literature, anthropology, art history, even architecture. Portable also because by definition theory was translated into American English and could slip the surly bonds of national identity or specialist claims – everyone was reading theory in their second language, even American academics, many of whom had developed French theory expository styles and modes of analysis that appeared foreign to their colleagues. Theory carried all the punch of philosophy without the windy German preambles and recondite French qualifications, without, that is, years of study, political affiliation or deep knowledge. Theory was a weapon of the young, the post-1968 generation wearied by the morality and slowness of their elders who seemed so untheoretical, whether they embraced or rejected theory. Theory was fast philosophy and it made its way through various sectors of U.S. academe in the 1970s and 1980s and arrived to architecture, late, as Mark Wigley has so famously and so frequently pointed out. And when it did, it was inevitable that theory and the formalist modern architecture described by Rowe would cross paths.

Driven by an attempt to reconnect form and ideology, Rowe's storyline gives us a way to understand more clearly the contemporary avant-garde's ambitions to re-establish the social mission of modern architecture, and to do so in a formal vocabulary that is recognizably modern. Nowhere has this been more evident than in journals such as Oppositions, Assemblage and ANY, and exhibitions such as 'Deconstructivist Architecture' (1988) at MoMA or the 'Autonomy and Ideology Symposium' also at MoMA (1996). In all of these endeavours, but especially in the 'Deconstructivist Architecture' exhibition, theory (deconstruction) was attached to experimental form in an attempt to create a critical, resistant, avant-garde architecture with left-leaning sympathies. But some time in the mid- to late 1990s the avant-garde desire to reconnect form and ideology diminished as form began to melt into blobs and fields of data while ideology loosened up and became reconfigured as identity branding and lifestyle. As pop science, new computer technologies and branding became more pressing issues in architecture, the 'critical' position ostensibly enabled by theory began to loose its hold on the avant-garde. Resolutely critical and resistant to an emergent commercial reality driven by the forces of globalization; weighed down by its historical attachment to philosophy; and unable to recognize itself as a new mode of commodified thought, theory has not been free or quick enough to deal with the blur of e-commerce and open systems. Ultimately, theory and the avant-garde project it enabled have proven inadequate to the vicissitudes of the contemporary world. And so today we stand at the end of a historical period of experimentation dominated by Rowe's little story. But it is passing and another story has already begun to take its place.

Rarely told but no less influential on the direction and ambition of contemporary architecture, it is a story whose trip across the Atlantic in fact moves in the opposite direction of Rowe's story – from America to Europe – and is motivated not by ideology and form but by pragmatic lessons learned from Manhattan. That story has to do with the discovery of an American architecture different from the formalist one Rowe narrates, and is told by Rem Koolhaas in his famous book Delirious New York. Koolhaas makes several discoveries in his research on New York, which serve to trigger the emergence of an experimental practice of architecture that has moved beyond the narrow ambitions of the avant-garde. Though many of the arguments for a new species of BIG architecture would not emerge until some years after the publication of Delirious New York, Koolhaas focused in that book on an architecture less concerned with form and ideology than with the shaping forces, logics and technologies of the metropolitan condition; an architecture of quantity not quality, where density and scale provide opportunities that outstrip the enfeebled art of architecture; and on an architecture that exploits opportunities presented under conditions of constraint. All of this was brought together in Koolhaas's 'Retroactive Manifesto for Manhattan', in which he argues for an architecture that needed no manifesto, no ideology or set of avant-garde ideas in order to be implemented; such an architecture, he argued, had already occurred in America, without genius, without authority and, more importantly, it had accumulated more than enough evidence to be convincing.

Of course the discoveries made in *Delirious New York* became a framework for the work of Koolhaas's Office of Metropolitan Architecture (OMA) during the following years in Europe, but it also triggered the emergence of a new practice of architecture in the Netherlands. In an exhibition entitled 'BIG SOFT ORANGE', which went on tour in the U.S., I argued that this new practice was one of the first responses to the emergent conditions of globalization, identified in the exhibition title. The 'Big' focused on the requirement to deal with quantity expressed in the Dutch Vinex requirement to build more than a million new dwellings over the next twenty years; the 'soft' signalled the emergence of a new approach evident in a renewed emphasis on the analysis and manipulation of material and immaterial processes, logics and codes and in the growing importance of scenario planning, profiling, as well as other temporal steering mechanisms. The third, related feature of this new approach I identified as an avowed post-avant-garde attitude accompanied by an acceptance of the market as the pre-eminent reality of contemporary architectural and urban practice. My argument was that many of these young Dutch offices preferred to deal pragmatically though aggressively with the ORANGE reality of commercialism and artificialization, those two very 'Dutch' historical concerns which with globalization are rapidly becoming the concern of huge patches of the globe. Unlike early-twentieth-century avant-gardes that wanted to clear away what was already there in order to establish a new social order, and unlike the theory avant-gardes of the 1980s which sought to resist what they found already there, many young Dutch offices, I argued, focus very precisely on what is 'just there', on the constraints and limitations of a global market which they see not as an evil to be resisted but as a new condition of possibility.

Though I focused on this emergent Dutch architecture, it is today clear that many new practices and forms of architecture are arising to meet the challenge posed by globalization and many of them deal in one way or another with the three conditions catalogued in the 'BIG SOFT ORANGE' show. Though these practices are singular and unique, many have begun to conform to an experimental managerial approach attempting to deal with the reality of a world dominated by Kevin Kelly's 'New Rules for the New Economy': 1) embrace the swarm; 2) increasing returns come with increasing connections; 3) focus on plentitude not scarcity; 4) follow the free; 5) feed the web first; 6) let go at the top; 7) from places to spaces; 8) no harmony, all flux; 9) develop soft relationships of all kinds; 10) focus on opportunities before efficiencies.[1] Indeed, around the world today, and especially in North America and Europe, there has emerged a new romance with business and corporate culture. Much of this attention has been focused on a new breed of managers and entrepreneurs who are now showcased in business lifestyle magazines such as *Business 2.0*, *Fast Company* and *Red Herring*. Bolstered by the overwhelming success of the IT industries and fuelled by virulent and aggressive strains of venture capital that have sprung up in northern California, these new managers have emerged as heroes in the struggle to tame and make sense of the complex world that has been thrown up by the forces of globalization.

Though witnessed primarily in the fast-paced world of global corporations, these managerial avant-gardists (and surely this is not the proper name for a class of doers who have altogether outstripped the ambitions of any historical avant-garde) are showing up with greater frequency in the world of high design, architecture and urban planning. Indeed, it is this managerial approach, and not an interest in the work of Gilles Deleuze, post-Euclidean geometries, diagrams or data, that unites the work of the freshest architectural practices around the world today, including for example those such as Greg Lynn Form, Reiser and Umemoto, Cortex, UN Studio, MVRDV, FOA, O.C.E.A.N., and others here at ArchiLab. A great deal of attention is now being paid to this new approach, especially in schools of architecture; one of the most aggressive is the AA's new Design Research Laboratory, the DRL, run by Patrik Schumacher, Brett Steele and Tom Verebes. The real import of this work – its managerial ambitions – has been obscured, however, because the primary focus has been on the more palatable, quasi-academic problem of 'research'. *Daidalos*, in fact, devoted an entire recent issue to this topic, which featured the work of many of the offices just mentioned, and championed Rem Koolhaas and the OMA as pioneers and innovators in this new research-based practice. In a yet unpublished essay entitled 'Junk Space' Koolhaas admits as much when he suggests that his work at the Harvard's Graduate School of Design allows him intellectual latitude denied by the normative practice of architecture. The real ambitions and intent of this managerial approach become clear, however, only when we look closer at how research is understood in relation to corporate culture, and the multiplicitous ways in which globalization is transforming the practice of architecture. DRL co-head, Patrik Schumacher, writes: 'Why research? The business of architecture is not excepted from the challenge of competitive innovation. The accelerating economic restructuring is affecting the organization of architectural production as much as every other sphere of production ... In a time of momentous restructuring, questions concerning design product and process can only be addressed within an academic framework that understands architecture as a research-based business rather than a medium of artistic expression.'[2]

The assertion is very bald, very clear: architecture should no longer recoil from the degraded world of business and corporate thinking; on the contrary, it should aggressively seek to transform itself into a research-based business. Though not recognized as adherents of such a research-based business approach to architecture, I think it is fair to say that this managerial approach provides the intellectual infrastructure necessary for the fleet-footed generation of architects and urbanists who have emerged to meet the challenges presented by globalization: namely, the challenge presented by quantity and commercialization to develop softer design strategies flexible enough to deal with the challenges of the market. The tools of these new managerialists are no longer those of the traditional architect or planner but those of the scenario planner and animation specialist. Animation softwares such as those used by Greg Lynn or Datascapes employed by MVRDV are means of testing architecture's ability to interact with and transform hidden or embedded shaping forces.

Consistent with Koolhaas's story, Kelly, in 'New Rules for the New Economy' argues that in the near future three features will distinguish the new economy: it will be global, it will favour intangible, soft things over tangible, hard things, and it will be networked. Consistent with this, contemporary design practices favour time, interactivity and innovation while space, originality and the search for the new have fallen away as concerns altogether. Perhaps the most significant change in contemporary concerns the category of 'the new', for which Jeffrey Kipnis argued so strongly in the *AD: Folding in Architecture* episode in the mid-1990s. Kipnis, along with Sanford Kwinter, who never tires of offering and then retracting manifestos, and even to some extent Koolhaas himself, often find themselves playing parts in Rowe's little narrative. Even though initiated by Koolhaas, the second story has taken off and in many ways has moved beyond Koolhaas's own flirtations with the market in his analyses of Jerde, Portman and shopping. One often gets the impression that Koolhaas is slumming, getting a taste of the degraded world of commerce so as to distinguish his avant-gardism from the old-fashioned, theory-dominated avant-garde of the 1980s and 1990s. The real point is that the avant-garde interest in the new has today been eclipsed by a demand for innovation. The new requires manifestoes of the kind that Kipnis offered in his five points for a new architecture in *AD: Folding* and that Kwinter has so desperately tried to articulate for the last four years. Even Koolhaas's break with the Rowe narrative is enabled by a 'retroactive manifesto'. Unlike the modernist, avant-garde obsession with the new, innovators do not first create ideas or ideologies (designs or plans) and then implement them in the real world (final design). Ideas and things, the materialism that is so often invoked by the last and most hysterical of the theory avant-garde, should themselves become part of a constantly transforming design in which design is never understood as a static object but is always a

dynamic movement. This kind of design approach is perhaps best seen today in the emerging world of rapid-prototyping where the search for 'new' prototypes that solve specific problems has been replaced by prototypes that are focused on binding together teams that innovate. It is a world that follows closely on management innovator Peter Drucker's insistence on exploiting opportunities rather than solving problems. Harvard Business School Professor Michael Schrage argues along the same lines in his recently published book, *Serious Play: How the Best Companies Simulate to Innovate*. Quickly and continuously converting new product ideas into crude mock-ups and working models turns traditional perceptions of the innovation cycle inside out: instead of using the innovation process to come up with finished prototypes, the prototypes themselves drive the innovation process. This is the status of design animations or datascape; they are not final products but innovative designs that lead to more innovation. This was the status of a design created by MAXWAN and Crimson for a 30,000-house extension for the city of Utrecht. In a recent essay entitled 'Orgwars' Crimson principal Wouter Vanstiphout recounted the ambitions of this soft plan: 'Leidsche Rijn is an urbanism of negotiation, and proud of it. The negotiations were not done to get the design realized; the design was made to negotiate with, to get the city built.'

As one story ends and another begins confusion will be the only constant. Witness Sanford Kwinter's hysterical 'FFE: Trahison des Clercs', published in a recent issue of *ANY* magazine. In this bi-monthly column, Kwinter attacks MVRDV and 'BIG SOFT ORANGE' as B-versions, second-rate rip-offs of what he calls the 'greater sovereignty' of Rem Koolhaas and the OMA. Treason, sovereignty, religion? However out of touch with contemporary reality, Kwinter identifies correctly the genius of these new managerialists when he says that they are 'Disencumbered of all social or physiological intensity – that is, of anything with the historical, existential thickness of ideals, dreams, or "transvaluing values"'. Blissfully free from the historical mission to create the future, the designers he attacks are able to intervene in the contemporary. The difference between Kwinter's assessment of them and my own is that what he sees as negative or evil, I see as affirmative and opportunistic. Caught between two stories, Kwinter, like many of us, is struggling to find a new part to play. ✦

1. Kevin Kelly, *New Rules for the New Economy: 10 Radical Strategies for a Connected World* (New York, Penguin, 1999).
2. Patrik Schumacher in *Daidalos*, n. 69/70 (Berlin, 1998–99).

✤ Architecture in the Second Modernity

| Bart Lootsma |

The city is no longer, if we may believe Rem Koolhaas.[1] Of course, this is a paradox, when we realize that in the last decade of the twentieth century we have finally reached the point when over half of the world's six billion people live in towns and cities[2]. Urbanity has become the dominant, generic condition in which people live. This is paralleled in the same decade by drastic changes in society. The full impact of globalization and individualization is becoming visible, no longer only in the larger cities and metropolises, but, under the influence of international media networks and a sharp increase in individual mobility, literally everywhere. The impact, which is based on new technologies, is so enormous that we can speak about a Second Modernity. The city is no longer synonymous with the spatial manifestation of one community with a clear – preferably hierarchical – structure. This also means that one can no longer draw conclusions about the structure of a society based on the physical, morphological structure of a city we used to do. The city is no longer simply the enumeration of more of the same things, it is the enumeration of many different things. Architecture and urbanism always dealt with how these things relate to each other. But what happens to architecture and urbanism when they are polarized into the small, intimate scale of the highly individual and the huge, abstract scale of the global? Or is that maybe not the issue and is there a different way in which this new society manifests itself in architecture?

Individualization

If I still use the word 'city' here, it is just because better or more specific words do not yet exist. I would like to use it here in the broadest sense of 'urbanized area'. A number of smaller and larger communities find space side by side and in continually changing combinations in this sprawling, practically unbounded field. These communities are no longer defined here by their consistent spatial proximity within a limited territory. Increasingly, communities are formed by active conscious choice and by proximity measured in time spans. This goes beyond the half-baked and vague hints of something that is often referred to as the 'multicultural society', which, however well intentioned, invariably connotes the 'invasion' of aliens from outside. The real multicultural society develops just as well from within. In a text on the history of the Maaskantflat in Rotterdam, one of the highlights of modern postwar reconstruction of the city, Adriaan

Geuze has shown enormous differences in the homogeneity and sense of community between the original inhabitants and those who have moved into apartments that became vacant in recent years. Here he is speaking not of people from different countries but of mainly young people with a more individualistic way of life.[3] Sociologists such as Ulrich Beck, Anthony Giddens and Scott Lasch view individualization as an unavoidable and necessary intermediate phase on the way to a new form of society.[4] While in classical society there were direct connections between class, family, sexual role patterns, the division of labour between men and women, marriage and architectural typologies, today many more people have the opportunity to replace the standard biography with one they have chosen themselves – a 'do-it-yourself biography', as Roland Hitzler has called it, or, as Giddens puts it, a 'reflexive biography'. According to Ulrich Beck, individualization means 'first the disembedding and second, the re-embedding of industrial society's ways of life by new ones, in which the individuals must produce, stage and cobble together their biographies themselves'.[5] The reflexive element consists not so much in an active reflection, but in the confrontation with others. Of course, these confrontations happen more often and play a more and more crucial role when society is becoming more and more congested at the same time. All of this turns our conception of culture in the broadest sense of the word on its head, particularly when it is a matter of those aspects of culture that take effect in public space and owe their legitimacy to the public sphere, such as architecture and the visual arts. Traditionally, architecture mediates between the individual desires of a person commissioning a work and the public interest. Public art traditionally produces symbols in which society as a whole is supposed to be able to recognize itself. Even if this represented a highly individual expression by the maker, it was always legitimized by the special position of the artist in society. Architecture and art are always legitimized on the basis of a – constantly changing – discourse about 'Art' and 'Architecture', which would be imposed from 'High Culture'. But today, everyone can receive twenty or thirty television stations at home, and there are at least as many subcultures. Each of these cultures seeks its own programme or creates its own mix out of various programmes. And each of these cultures listens to its own mix of music and dresses in its own combination of articles of clothing, which, individually or together, tell a story about the wearer's position in society. The same holds true for the cars people buy – often specially equipped with significant accessories – as well as their interiors, gardens and homes. People know what they want and make their own choices – even if these choices have been prepared by the industry. But the industry has to be given credit as well for having learned to 'listen' to their clients more and more. They have developed marketing and production strategies that allow them to make more and more individual products. Roemer van Toorn has characterized this new society as the 'Society of the And' in contrast to the 'Society of the Either/Or'. 'Thinking in terms of good and evil no longer legitimates our civilizing process. Either/or categories such as East/West and left/right have dissipated. The end of the Cold War has precipitated a crisis of victory in the West, which is why the question of a social sense of possibilities now has to be posed in a completely new way. Previously, the dominant criteria were differentiation, specialization, transparency and predictability; now we speak of the quality of simultaneity, of a multicultural society, of uncertainty, alienation, chaos, theories, networks, hubs and nodal points, interaction, hybrid ambivalence, paradoxes, schizophrenia, liquid space, cyborgs and so on'.[6] The Society of the And is a great rhizome, defined by endless libidinous couplings, endless incidents produced by technological means. But what does all this mean for architecture? How are we to judge the architectural quality of a project or a building, when we know that it is just the result of strictly individual preferences, desires, demands or necessities? What will the public interest be in this new situation? How can we formulate it and how will this change urban design and planning, for example? Will the theme park be the definitive model for urban design?

Terence Riley, the curator of 'Un-private House' exhibition that took place at the Museum of Modern Art in New York in 1999, gave a preview of the exhibition beforehand in a lecture at the Berlage Institute in Amsterdam.[7] It is intriguing to see that the houses he selected are all designed for specific people, who live their life in a particular way. They work at home, for example, they may have a homosexual relationship or be single, they may be handicapped, as in the case of the owner of the villa in Bordeaux by OMA. The houses are all tailor-made for the clients. On the other hand, even though some of the selected houses are quite radical in their design, somehow they all fit in the traditional scheme of what 'good' architecture is supposed to be. We know the architects from publications or because they teach at Ivy League universities. And even though these houses all experiment with new typologies, the style is still more or less homogeneous. Let's call it simply 'modern' here for the sake of argument, even if we could have more refined arguments about it – something we would normally immediately indulge in. Taste, in this case the individual taste of a curator of an important museum, still seems to play a crucial role in the selection process and that becomes more and more problematic if we take individualization really seriously. Terence Riley is very conscious of this problem. He started the lecture with a presentation of his own work as an architect, which more or less set the stage for the second part of the lecture: it would have been strange if the were too far away from what he is doing himself as an architect. And later on during the lecture he referred to this problem in a different way, quoting a remark by Peter Eisenman about Frank Gehry's Guggenheim Museum in Bilbao: is it simply great architecture or is it a theme park or both? Is Architecture with a big A as we have always known it becoming a theme park in itself, just one category among the many other categories that exist? Has it become just another niche in the market? The answer seems to be yes, and some would even argue that this has always been the case. But hasn't architecture, at least in Europe, always played a more important and broader public role than that? And shouldn't we somehow try to maintain that role, even if it is in a different way?

Market Democracy

'The West is confronted by questions that challenge the fundamental premises of its own social and political system. The key question we are now confronting is whether the historical symbiosis between capitalism and democracy that characterized the West can be generalized on a global scale without exhausting its physical, cultural and social foundations,' writes the sociologist Ulrich Beck.[8] Beck himself sees opportunities in this phase of the modernization process – which he calls 'reflexive modernization' – for achieving a totally new society, one that offers individuals a bigger role on numerous levels but also one in which individuals form a new image of the mass of which they are part and the consequences this has – for example, for the environment. 'This concept does not imply (as the adjective "reflective" might suggest) reflection, but (first) self-confrontation'.[9] Beck is interested in a new form of politics – what he calls 'sub-politics' – in which society takes shape from the bottom up. 'The instrument of power' in sub-politics is congestion (in the direct and the figurative sense) as the modernized form of the involuntary strike. The phrase that Munich motorists can read at a typical congestion location – 'You are not in a jam, you are the jam' – clarifies this parallel between strike and congestion'.[10] When Terence Riley presents twelve individual houses for wealthy clients with large pieces of land he can still avoid this problem. But that is a pity, because it is exactly here, in this moment of congestion and the collision of individual interests, that we might find the big new challenge for architecture. It is the point or the line where different interests meet and possibly clash. Because individuals do not just mind their own business: the high level of education has made them assertive. What could a new image of collectivity then be? New legislation, reflecting the dual goals of an open market and minimal government interference, is characterized both by deregulation and by the effects of consultation procedures and the possibility for individuals to lodge appeals against a whole range of initiatives taken by government or private parties. Government and industry together reach agreements about production norms but special-interest groups can also organize themselves and in turn negotiate on norms and rules with both government and industry. Apart from legislation, the 'empirical laws' that investors develop on the basis of economic analyses and prognoses also have a considerable effect on the direction in which society is steered. All these parties, in an effort to appear as 'objective' and as strong as possible, use 'scientific' research in their argumentation. At the same time the various parties dispute one another's methods and findings. The only thing they have in common is that all these studies are presented in the form of numbers, statistics and charts. Even when instinctive or emotional arguments play a role in the decision-making process, they can nearly always be quantified – for example, because they are carried by a collective. This is the case, for instance, with referendums, opinion polls and market research. With a touch of cynicism one might dub this situation a market democracy. Quantities are the new language of this international form of government. The computer is not only the tool used to manipulate quantities; it also, as a means of communication, serves to enforce this language as the new individual standard. The new market democracy has consequences for everybody, but especially for architects and urbanists. The field in which they must work is becoming more and more complex, chaotic and unstable. The process that leads to an architectural or urban design and its eventual realization involves a great many parties. Some of these, such as the client or his representatives, the local council, the urban planner, the various technical advisers, the contractors and subcontractors, may sit around the same negotiating table with the architects. Other parties operate in the background and pop up at the most unexpected moments in the hope of catching the architect red-handed. These may be local residents or future employees of the client, public utilities, journalists, local politicians or any other directly or indirectly involved figure whatsoever. In addition, architecture itself entails countless rules, norms, empirical laws and jurisprudence. These too have an enormous impact on architecture, even greater perhaps than the individual architect or urban designer. Many architects and urban designers find it very difficult to play along with the new market democracy. In the 1980s many of them cherished the proud idea that they should resist these developments and that the only way of saving architecture was to regard it as an autonomous discipline. Their research was directed at the historical definition of the discipline and at its language. For these architects, the new rules and norms governing architecture and urbanism were merely obstacles to the achievement of their ideals. They were restrictions imposed from outside. In fact it was thought that the new situation would admit only a limited number of building typologies and that the creative role of the architect would be confined to that of some kind of aesthetic adviser. This impending homogenization was parried in the official architectural debate with an incredibly rapid succession of styles and themes. In recent large urban design projects, this has lead to rather bizarre patchworks lacking in continuity. With market influences strengthened, architecture has increasingly come to be regarded as a consumer item rather than as the delimiter of public space. People want their own highly individual home, one that not only houses them but also expresses their identity. This has led to a situation in which, as MVRDV put it, 'Everything can be made, every object is imaginable and nothing seems weird or extravagant any more'.[11] On one hand, this offers the architects who cherish an autonomous position the opportunity for a kind of 'branding' of their work, resulting in a kind of over-emphasizing of their individual attitude and language in lectures, publications and exhibitions. On the other, it becomes clear that this is only a temporary solution. To get a grip on larger developments it will be necessary to deal with all the influences from outside the discipline again and to abandon the idea that the architect has an autonomous position.

Synthetic regionalization

The idea that globalizing tendencies would lead to an increasingly homogeneous built environment is one that we even find being mooted by Rem Koolhaas, although in 'Generic City' he does wonder what the positive aspects of this trend might be.[12] Yet in recent years more and more architects have also been arguing quite the reverse – like Alejandro Zaera-Polo, for instance, who claims that globalization actually leads to 'the enhancement of diversification and heterogeneity by increasing our awareness of differences, the particularities of a location and its specificities'. According to Zaera: 'We witness an artificial regionalization, an artificially enhanced nature, where the local flavour becomes synthetic'.[13] This landscape of multiple differences is experienced at most because of the radically increased (auto) mobility. This produces a *dérive* the Situationists couldn't have dreamt of. More and more, this *dérive* is taken into account in the urban design process. Willem Jan Neutelings has come up with the concept of the 'Patchwork Metropolis', based on an urban study for the area between The Hague and Rotterdam in 1989–90, but clearly indebted to 'The Naked City', the psychogeographical map of Paris by Asger Jorn and Guy Debord. Each 'patch' has a specific programme and a specific physical structure, according to Neutelings. 'In this diversified surface the fragments belong to a complex, non-physical order subject to a changing equilibrium of political, economical, historical and cultural forces. From these fragments the inhabitants of this carpet form their own personal city... It is chaos, or rather order of a greater complexity, one that makes possible a rich diversity of intense experiences and thus can be considered of great quality.'[14] In a similar way, according to Adriaan Geuze, the new city is 'a well-aired metropolis of villages, urban centres, suburbs, industrial areas, docks, airfields, woods, lakes, beaches, reserves and the monocultures of hi-tech farming'.[15] 'The urbanite is constantly changing guise and environment, taking his leisure on the Maasvlakte [The Rotterdam Harbour, which is used for all kinds of modern and motorized sports] and in the Alps, hanging around in dark alleys, tearing through the landscape, sleeping and working at different places, while his family and friends don't live in the same street.'[16]

Datascapes

MVRDV, too, is unconvinced by the notion of a situation that is converging on homogeneity, believing instead that it is possible to identify 'gravity fields' in the apparent chaos of developments, hidden logicalities that eventually ensure that whole areas acquire their own special characteristics. 'These gravities reveal themselves when sublimated beneath certain assumed maximised circumstances or within certain maximized constraints'.[17] And they give a whole series of examples: 'Because of tax differences the borders between Belgium and the Netherlands are occupied with vast numbers of villas generating a linear town along the frontier'. 'Market demands have precipitated a "slick" of houses-with-a-small-garden in Holland.' 'Political constraints in Hong Kong cause "heaps" of dwellings around its boundaries.' 'In their wish for a nineteenth-century lookalike town, Berlin puts its new buildings into tight envelopes. This pushes the majority of the vast programmes underground, turning the streets into elements in the middle of vast programmes'. 'Monumental regulations in Amsterdam limit the demand of modern programmes, causing 'mountains' of programme invisible from the street behind medieval façades'. 'Accessibility demands cause almost enclosed types of infrastructure and thus a series of linear towns through the Ruhrgebiet.' 'In order to avoid the high-rise rules, in Paris-La Défense massive programs appear as Ziggurats with 18 metre-high accesible 'steps' so that all the offices can be entered by the maximum length of the fire-ladders'.[18] In fact the entire built environment is governed by such force fields. Apart from the fact that they create differences in the landscape, they hold the key to understanding how society manifests itself in contemporary architecture. Because there are usually several of these force-fields operating at the same time and none is truly dominant, it is difficult to detect the impact of individual forces. Which is why MVRDV came up with the concept of datascapes. Datascapes are visual representations of all the quantifiable forces that may influence the work of the architect or even steer or regulate it. These influences could be planning and building regulations, technical constraints, natural conditions such as sun and wind, but they could just as well be legislation, for example on minimum working conditions, or political pressure from interest groups both inside and outside the commissioning organization. Each datascape deals with only one or two of these influences and reveals their impact on the design process by showing their most extreme effects. Hence, a site normally contains more than one datascape. Over the last two years, MVRDV have developed a whole catalogue of datascapes in collaboration with students from the AA in London and the Berlage Institute in Amsterdam.[19] Together they demonstrate a new image of what collectivity could be in the Second Modernity. Datascapes are in fact visualizations of what the sociologist Anthony Giddens calls 'expert systems' and 'abstract systems': bureaucratic systems in which faith in the system is based on the presumed expertise in a specific field.[20] The status of a person in one system says nothing about his or her status in another system. But that is not all: the information produced by the different expert systems is also open to dispute. Contemporary society is governed by a multiplicity of such 'abstract systems' and they have replaced the traditional systems that were based on authority. What makes the datascapes so fascinating is that in many cases they actually generate schemes that apparently approach something that may be called an architectural project. As such, they certainly have an aesthetic appeal of their own. Also, the method and the results are sometimes very similar to actual designs, for example, some of those by Greg Lynn, who is also interested in formal reactions to forces from outside his projects. But datascapes are not architectural projects, even though they are, just like architectural projects, at the same time both abstract and real. They are more like updated versions of what architects used to refer to as the site or the plot. Whereas in the case of Greg Lynn the input is chosen by the architect in order to produce a specific spatial effect, the datascapes are given, so that every architect has to work with them whether he or she wants to or not. 'What makes datascapes wholly unlike the "normal" architectural project today is their deliberate denial of the endless negotiation between competing forces, regulations, planning criteria familiar as the planning procedure by which all space is administered today: in the sense that Tafuri has written, a complex managerial task that largely characterizes the profession of architecture and defines its principal forms of labour'.[21] The visualization of the often contradictory datascapes that play a role in a project, marks the start of a process of negotiation involving all the participants. This process may finally lead to the project itself or at least help to show what is possible should the architect opt for other starting points. The superimposition of the various datascapes relevant to the location, which often have totally contradictory consequences, gives rise to a complex spatial envelope that reflects not just the restrictions but also the possibilities and outer limits of the design. The datascapes show how complex and unstable the contemporary urban landscape has become. As Detlef Martins puts it: 'It is here at the limits of the possible that architecture must take a stand, at the point where the reasonable becomes unreasonable, the normal abnormal and vice versa'.[22] ✤

1. Rem Koolhaas, 'Generic City' in Rem Koolhaas, *S, M, L, XL* (Rotterdam/New York, 1995).
2. David Clark, *Urban World/Global City* (London/New York, 1996).
3. Adriaan Geuze, Onze Flat in *Over Rotterdam* (Rotterdam, 1994).
4. Ulrich Beck, Anthony Giddens, Scott Lash, *Reflexive Modernization, Politics, Tradition and Aesthetics in the Modern Social Order* (Cambridge, 1994).
5. Ulrich Beck, *The reinvention of Politics*, see note 4.
6. Roemer van Toorn, 'The Society of The And, Constructing Progressive Reflexivity in The And', unpublished manuscript, 1998.
7. Terence Riley, conference at Berlage Institute, Amsterdam, March 1999.
8. See note 5.
9. Idem.
10. Idem.
11. MVRDV, 'Datascape, The Final Extravaganza', *Daidalos*, n. 69/70 (December 1998–January 1999). See note 1.
12. Alejandro Zaera Polo, 'Order out of Chaos, The Material Organization of Advanced Capitalism' in *Architectural Design*, Profile No. 108 (London, 1994).
13. Willem Jan Neutelings, 'Patchwork Metropolis' in *Willem Jan Neutelings, Architect* (Rotterdam, 1991).
14. Adriaan Geuze, 'Accelerating Darwin' in Gerrit Smienk (ed.), *Nederlandse Landschapsarchitectuur, tussen traditie en experiment* (Amsterdam, 1993).
16. Adriaan Geuze, 'Wliderness' in Anne-Mie Devolder (ed.), *Del Alexanderpolder, waarde stad verder gaat* (Bussum, 1993).
17. See note 11.
18. Idem.
19. MVRDV, *Datascapes* (Rotterdam 1999).
20. Anthony Giddens, 'Living in a Post-Traditional Society'; see note 4.
21. Brett Steele, 'Data Escape', conference at Architectural Association, London, July 1997, unpublished manuscript
22. Detlef Martins, memo to Winy Maas, Toronto, June 1997.

Operative Lands

| Manuel Gausa |

Land-Links

'Tenerife: Group of Tourists around a Swimming Pool', 1994. Andreas Gursky's image conveys to perfection the 'informal' character so peculiar to today's landscape(s): the 'informality' peculiar to leisure and recreation (associated with contemporary freedom, flexibility and mobility) but also the 'informality' present in most processes to do with land use, lying at the root of the way our present-day cities are growing. These processes refer to basic movements of aggregation and distancing, the variable appropriation of available free areas, and separation; specific densification and dilation. Processes that are accumulative, unstable, opportunistic, open. Movements – patterns of behaviour – produced within evolving, dynamic systems, which tend to encourage self-organization, interaction and, in many instances, its own distortion based on the ongoing transformation of immediately 'prior' situations. Forever-changing systems, complex and non-linear, frequently defined as 'chaotic'.

Nowadays, we are apparently puzzled and disarmed in the face of what Ian McHugh has called 'the spectre of unbridled growth in the contemporary city'. A relatively recent scenario, which has replaced the old idea of centrality, continuous spread, linear coherence and development with complex, polynuclear, matrical, heterogeneous and incoherent structures, open to non-linear developments. Our task, as architects and town planners, is nevertheless to define new organizational machinery, new arrangements capable of dealing with this apparent lack of order, which in fact comes manifests itself as a new form of a more ambiguous order that cannot be composed. Designing open systems capable of making their way into reality and giving it new momentum. At once blunt and supple. Intrusive and yet collusive. Meant to upset the initial data but without turning them down. Flexible systems – dispositions rather than compositions – that are changeable and tactical. Reactive. Like beautiful contemporary prostheses – independent (artificial) and contingent (specific). Neither classical nostalgic evocations nor modern mechanical prototypes, but reactive instruments – arrangements – capable of being abstract (global) and singular (local), all the same time. Capable of replying at once 'artificially, tactically and flexibly' in order to give momentum back to a body – a reality – that no longer wants to be regenerated, but rather restructured.

In this context, the landscape appears like a real operative factor: supple, versatile, capable of being instrumentalized and 'decoded'.

Ironing the landscape

Not just as a provocative action, therefore, but as a tactical idea: ironing, repairing, but also revising and redefining. In a belligerent and truly open

interpretation, the landscape or countryside today can be the authentic 'building' of the new city. The structuring element of a possible large-scale, new order – more flexible and level-headed – and not the possible residue of the former planning. An open order, capable of introducing itself and handling the casual and uncontrolled developments of present-day urban structures, and producing more versatile connective systems 'resonating' with the actual metropolitan dynamics being released today. Dynamics that would witness the yielding of the old boundaries of what had been defined for centuries as a 'city' to the new scales of this 'urban-territorial' space, where presences and absences, pre-existences and latencies all co-exist: consolidated nuclei and vague margins, bastard kinds of growth and ground stripped of its natural aspect. A reality defined by the accumulation of apparently unconnected fragments proclaiming the new hybrid condition of the territory, gradually colonized and forever unfinished. The infrastructures of communications and transport come across as the most obvious signs of this complicated territorial system. A basic, referential grid, made of 'fibrous' networks, which irrigate the territory and organize the appearance of discontinuous developments, occupied archipelagoes between which are produced interstices, residual terrains, fringe areas and large chunks of neglect working in a 'negative' way. Open voids that can be recycled, likely to involve a more unusual instrumentation of the land, in a flexible and expressive way.

Like an ink blot over the territory, the crystalline form of the primitive city tends gradually to break up into a heterogeneous spread of blotches and voids: a patchwork of interwoven realities, of places and between-places, of conflicts (tensions) and 'beauties' (attractions) precisely encouraged by this potential for mobility, interchange and displacement, which, in less time, makes it possible 'not only to go further but, above all, to reach a greater number of places'. What is involved here is an uneven progressive dynamic that encourages the development of interactive structures emerging from the combination of different situations of 'planning', 'self-organization', 'prudent approach'. These are combinatory structures, which, in spite of the apparent impression of disorder and arbitrariness that they convey, possess – like certain self-generated forms which exist in nature – inner 'codes' adjusted to formatory rules referring here to elementary movements of agglomeration and distancing aimed at giving rise, over time, to multifaceted and discontinuous complex procedures. So the city is no longer a single 'place', or a single defined 'form'; it is not even a single evolving state – an alternative model – but rather an accumulation of many different but simultaneous phenomena, states and experiences: a polynuclear and 'many-layered', gradually diversified system, produced by discontinuous, stratified and non-fixed realities, which eliminate natural aspects, pervert and continually alter the actual elementary diagrams of development producing them. Over and above the ancient metropolis (the linear development of an organism – the urban one – in a precise geographical framework or place), the contemporary 'metapolis' (to borrow François Asher's term) appears like a defined, staccato, vibratory system, more than through representations and relations; a system of articulatory networks and layers of information that can be overlaid with vague, moveable and variable outlines. A polyhedral scenario that can no longer be represented on the basis of unambiguous and literal representations, but from partial, selected aspects that can be rendered instrumental, issuing from a reality which simultaneously refers to several areas of coordinates. This is the essence of the contemporary city: being a multiple structure, at once analogous and different. A structure in effect made up of similar movements on an overall scale but also made up of collisions, encounters and specific intersections, which end up by producing singular, plural and variable combinations. An abstract, diagrammatic system that is distorted in every instance, in each particular case, in order to be 'contextual' and different. This gives a multiple overview of identical and different 'cities' which, in their turn, are complexes of several 'cities within cities'. This, too, is the essence of the contemporary metapolis, being a 'hyper-place', a 'place of places'. A rich abstract – total – a kaleidoscope of offers, situations and contingent – local – opportunities.

The harmonious music of a complete and balanced city thus gives way to the evidence of a complex, arhythmic music with, at times, possible melodic fragments, but on the whole with a syncopated and atonal arhythmia made up of points and counterpoints which might help to assimilate the contemporary urban space to a permanently incomplete body that is changeable in time. The interesting thing about trying to understand the inner processes that take place in these progressively fragmented and heterogeneous realities that are our large cities of today, comes from an activist intent: that of designing new mechanisms of restructuration – over and above traditional planning (or the interference of luck and chance) – capable of effectively articulating, on a large scale, the future developments of these organisms that are in constant entropic evolution. Far removed from old temptations to do with the compositional mastery of the form that has hallmarked the disciplines of urban matters, we need rather to come up with battle plans, well-intentioned tactics, at the same time open to the unforeseen. Technicians, agents, administrations and communities should be capable of encouraging reflections in this direction. It is important, today, to explore new arrangements – at once incisive and flexible – capable of tackling the actual casual and infrastructural dimension of city

and territory. Scientific study of 'dynamic systems' leads to an analysis of similar – chaotic – complex processes typified by a high degree of indeterminism, instability, incoherence, infiniteness, in other words, informality. These are systems which may refer uniquely to simulations of possibilities (arrangements): their trajectories actually show a host of possible protocols open to surprising and spontaneous dynamics. But they may also show recurrent movements – 'strange attractors' – that make it possible to deduce a certain idea of order associated with the appearance of an internal 'genetic code'. These more or less complicated diagrams usually outline rhizomatic, fractal structures characterized by: matrical self-organization, entanglement, sequentiality and discontinuity, infinite evolution, absence of scale, organic rather than mechanical development and, above all, the importance of void/solid seriation.

There thus emerges the power of the space 'in reverse' or 'negative', as it were, not like a remnant – a residual reserve – 'between things', but like a 'structuring gearing'. And the landscape thus appears, in the context of our present-day urban structures, like a 'sub-system' that is as important as the urban system – an infrastructure in turn – capable, within possible tactical seriations, of organizing the appearance of events, by balancing the force of the different forms of volumetry with the value of surfaces; by alternating dense opaque spaces and vast horizons, obtaining productive zones and relational spaces. By retrieving the value of the sky, the dimension of the ground, the presence of textures, different vegetation, and patches of colour. In other words, work with openings, fade-outs and re-cuts, rather than with the constructional geometry of the building.

In this context, the new city can no longer go on being interpreted as the classical concentric and radial movement – one-off, continuous, regular and deterministic – around a centre, but as a multiple and non-linear structure of movements, events and relational spaces combined in strategic networks designed to encourage exchange, interrelation and mixedness, as well as a greater 'freedom of election'. One future target is to reconvert these 'spider's webs' – absurd and anti-functional – which currently run alongside most of our territories in effective new linkages, articulating tactical sequences of components: historical nuclei, modern developments, new focal sub-centres, halo-like growths and spaces to be recycled, flexible colonization zones, natural areas and new 'operative landscapes', thus forming this rich kaleidoscope of 'realities' represented by the contemporary city. It is no longer a matter of contrasting 'natural area' and 'urban area', but of getting them to co-exist in structuring systems. A rhythmic sequence on the territory would be configured in this way, with retractions and dilations, with extensions and re-cuts, complying with a basic mixed scheme, open to possible developments, but always referring to the tactical arrangement of the linking elements: land-links, connective areas capable of providing sequential developments – both locally and globally – in which, as in entwined virtual fingers, links of places and of places between places, of voids and solids, would be produced on differing scales, the way they are in the actual fractal systems. 'Relational' areas and spaces associated with leisure, rest and recreation, with thematic play or mixed activity and with all those other complementary uses, each time more important in the new society that is drawing closer. Perhaps the technological breakthrough in the field of telecommunications has ended up by eroding the traditional link between 'place' and 'activity', but it has also encouraged a new dimension of leisure, which includes nature understood as a relational event. This broadening of the concept of leisure and its arena of action in turn encourages the transformation of large free zones into new 'landscapes for distension': 'pauses' in territorial developments and 'pauses' in our own productive activities. This 'at once functional and sustainable colonization' of the landscape should nevertheless be broached with new models of intervention in which the old 'component' vocation – the old and frenzied imposition of building 'forms' – would ultimately be replaced with new, less conventional relations, emerging from an effective and ambiguous relationship with the environment made up of 'gentle caresses and trenchant decisions'. The age-old dichotomy of town planning between 'areas that can be planned' and 'areas that cannot be planned' might give way to simple strategies of colonization and occupation of the landscape, differing according to the specific calling of the place. Strategies that might replace stable land use (linked with property and ownership) by another type of models, based on a possible 'reversible occupation', capable of accommodating temporal, not to say 'precarious' uses: this, particularly, would involve a possible 'ephemeral colonization' of the landscape – linked up to light construction systems, calling for the tactical forecasting of certain soft 'colonization areas', with low density and low impact (in temporal conditions of use), preferably associated with the recycling of disused land in need of requalification (quarries, former farmland, residual marginal areas). In any event, if the contemporary city was typified until not so very long ago by the materialization of a constructed, more or less homogeneous fabric, in which the formal desire for a specific culture had been forged, today the new plural and polyhedral temporal dimension of the contemporary city proclaims the end of any wish for continuity and coherence – and predominance – be it semantic or cultural, and the appearance of a

new type of organization, hybrid, flexible and varied, based on heterogeneity and syncope. In other words, this possible 'yin-yang', 'positive-negative', 'void-solid' seriation, which is well outlined on every scale, would encourage diversity, contrast and identify different episodes – places – as a result of the role attributed to the cadences of incision and articulation and to 'silences', to voids, like gears that provide sequences and links between developments, while giving rise to an authentic dynamic of social membership. It is a question here of considerations making reference to the 'figure-ground' dichotomy so ably described by Douglas R. Hofstadter in his book *Gödel, Esher, Bach*: by drawing a figure (or a positive space) within a frame, its complementary form is also drawn: this is the 'ground' or 'negative space'. In most drawings, the figure-ground relationship plays a lesser role; the figure is much more interesting than the ground. But on some occasions, for all this, the ground gives rise to an interaction. It is thus possible to establish a distinction between two types of spatial use: the 'cursive', where the ground appears as a by-product of the act of drawing, and the 'recursive', where the ground may be seen in its own right as a figure with a similar entity.

If, in the traditional city, compact, coherent and monocentric growth gave rise to the predominance of solid over ground, we have already mentioned how, in the fractal multicity, though with an apparently more chaotic development, it may conversely be easier to design 'recursive', dovetailed structures capable of interlocking and interconnecting as if in virtual fields of pixels, areas of development – presences – and operative reserve areas – absences.

Lands in Lands
Let us imagine the 'land in land' concept – 'operational landscape' over 'Amphitryon landscape'. In the same way as the city has dispersed the boundaries that separate it from old extramural territories, the architectural project may dissolve its outlines into new 'functional geographies'. Topography rather than volumetry. An 'architecture of the void' may then be imagined, in tune with the qualities of a 'landscape-cum-open space', that is, in sum, realized by virtue of its own 'vacant' qualities like a 'field' of forces, open, permeated by broad vanishing lines, where, in a muted way, the surfaces, horizons and meetings between earth and sky come across quite distinctly. This therefore involves an architecture of dovetailed surfaces; 'areas on other areas', 'presences-absences' envisaged on the basis of the, albeit paradoxical, combination between 'densification and disappearance'. If we imagine the surfaces of the territory like the stone floors of certain living rooms (dotted with coloured rugs sowing various patterns and designs), we can then also imagine shifts in the landscape, possible 'architectures' conceived, in their turn, like virtual rugs or carpets – thick, dense areas on free and receptive ground. So it is no longer a matter of 'dividing up spaces' and 'partitioning' them, any more than it is a matter of 'brandishing uses'.

Rather, it is a matter of organizing activities in a preferably fluid, free space, with some 'concave' service surfaces – rugs/carpets (like accumulators in reverse) revealing a concern with the colonization of the landscape by devices of infiltration and distancing, not linked with any strict geometric arborescent masses (preferably with deciduous leaves), by the incorporation – above all in partitions or divisions – of light materials that alter over long periods (copper, wood)... And, in most cases, the relationship between architecture and time. The transformation of the living. The importance of the evolutive. Many of the references mentioned here have no place in handbooks of 'disciplinary' architecture, but do have a place in the research carried out in other experiments. This transversality, in which contributions from Arte Povera and Land Art (from Mario Merz to Christo, from Richard Long to Joseph Beuys) intersect with intuitions about the theory of landscape design and the new geography, anthropology and biology, and so on, is included in the critique of the star work-object that has stamped much of the 1980s and 1990s. Experimenting with form but also having confidence in a benevolent invention of alternative and imaginative formulae capable of encouraging this new 'natural contract' in which the complicitous appearance of an architecture in syntony with the landscape (rather than integrated in this landscape) would precisely involve its ability to incorporate surprising technical and visual solutions that are unusual, enriching and never paralyzed or intimidated by the presence of nature, but on the contrary stimulated by the possibility of incorporating it, reinforcing it and reformulating it: of enriching it more than preserving it... New Landscape Architectures, in other words, to meet the new demands of a society troubled by the geological frenzy of the city. ❖

layouts, but with freer and more deliberate configurations. Devices capable of 'inserting', 'densifying' and 'preserving' at the same time... A fashioned void in which the project is no longer already carried out on the basis of the priority configuration of the mass constructed vertically – architecture as 'edification' – but on the basis of the restructuring of the horizontal surfaces: dunes, hills, bowls, trenches, folds, like topomorphic manifestations of a possible artificial geography that is not far removed – in its spatial imagery – from natural geography... Like faces flattened up against a window, old cut-out prismatic containers against the sky thus give way to new magmatic forms squashed on the ground; forms 'lying in wait', in which – in a fecund paradox – the roof of a building is at the same time its own floor. So it is no longer a question of creating 'volumes beneath light' but 'ambiguous landscapes beneath the sky'. Hybridized enclaves capable of generating their own energy. Fields inside other fields. Lands in lands.

In Landarch
The power of work with the idea of landscape has to do precisely with its capacity to take on new dimensions, to bestride new boundaries, to blur the silhouettes and redraw the familiar outlines of what was hitherto understood by the term 'architecture'. This possibility has clearly assisted the transition from a generation obsessed by the relationship between architecture and city (city as a stable stage, outcome of edification) to another generation that is more sensitive to a new contract with nature (epic nature, it goes without saying, hybrid and wild, rather than tamed and bucolic). Shifts within which architecture is formed together with the landscape, and the landscape becomes architecturalized. A mischievous, strange transgression, which is rich by being mongrel, made up of new ecological/environmental aromas, but also of decidedly contemporary strategies, with a determination unabashedly to transform things and their images, at a clearly casual pace, or one that is phonily ingenuous and sometimes even too insolently elementary (by the acceptance of direct systems of manipulation: modelling, camouflage, graphic actions, packaging, analogy games, metaphors and fables, and as many other devices again, all serving to prompt new references in the imagination). Land and arch, never an abrupt graft, but a possible interlock, a hybrid contract between two hitherto alien categories... Constructions which artificially incorporate movements – or moments – of nature, at times architecturalizing the landscape (by modelling, cutting out, folding), by proposing new topological forms, at times 'landscaping' (by packaging, wrapping, covering) an architecture in an ambiguous state of synergy with the strange nature surrounding it. A nature obtained by the intrusion of plants – organic or synthetic – by the insertion of

✦ Architecture in Limbo

| Aaron Betsky |

Any architecture today must answer the question: how can we be at home in, make sense of and find our way through a landscape that changes in computer and communication technologies and the massive redevelopment of physical, social and cultural space they occasion continually make unrecognizable to us? It is no longer enough (if it ever was) to make elegant compositions in façade or plan, to make things that are sensible or sensuous or to make forms that make sculptural sense. We must do all of these things, but we must do them in such a way that they work in a situation dominated by mobile phones, the Internet, urban sprawl and global culture. Making single buildings is not enough when all we see is signs and all we experience is the screen in front of our face.

I write this in Shanghai for a conference I will attend in a few weeks. Outside, new skyscrapers fade off in all directions into the polluted haze that is punctured only by the sharp colours of advertising for brands we know everywhere. Inside, air-conditioning and the cushioning blandishments of not-quite-natural materials pad the cell. In front of me, the screen presents the face of invisible technology that courses all around me, all the way back to my home in San Francisco. Plugged in and removed from the street, I could be anywhere. I am in limbo.

Such an experience of floating in the haze of sameness, slick surfaces, spaces defined by codes, familiar signage and a materiality that always everywhere recedes is not just reserved for those traveling along the lanes of business. We all wait endlessly for our train, in traffic, in fast-food restaurants. We work in our offices, factories and institutions housed in the same boxes of absence. We live in always changing surroundings defined by economy and codes as much as by our own sense of ourselves and surrounded by a web of social relations whose contours are indefinable and uncertain. The massive dislocations caused by the globalization of our economy give this world a violent undercurrent that to many millions is a distinct reality.

It is not, in other words, just a question of the boredom of the haves. For those who have not, or have very little, the glare of fluorescents, the blare of advertising, the disappearance of any sense of horizon, the imprisonment by closed forms and the lack of variety are inexpressibly worse. The very logic of global capitalism is evident not in the abstractions of statistics, but in the experience of everyday life. We may try to alleviate such conditions by designing better housing or giving offices windows that open, but in the end such blandishments are already subject to the iron laws of economics that provide the commissions.

What I would suggest is that architecture in such a world must first – as always – respond to the context in which we construct its artefacts. It must make what Michael Bell has called 'slow space': mirrors to the limbo effect that suspend us wilfully and clearly within the web of modernization in such a way that, encased and removed from it, we can understand it. Certainly the clarity of materials, the abstraction of form and the deformation of shape that are mainstays of modernist architecture can help achieve such an effect, though they run the danger of so far removing the building that it becomes a monument to values and sensibilities rather than an active antidote to modernization.

It is when such tactics lead to a sense of the unhomely (*unheimlich*) that architecture becomes more effective. The 'come-back effect' of the familiar, which is somehow now strange because of changes in use, scale or form can deepen a sense of the unreality of the world we make for ourselves. Such work has the effect of being enigmatic. It continually awakens our wonder, awe and fear in such a way that we cannot consume the object, space or image. Making the strange part of our everyday lives, such work reminds us of the strangeness of that existence.

Further, an architecture that would mirror our suspended landscape would itself be uncertain in its relation to that datum that we think mediates between others, the physical landscape and ourselves. Architecture must be an unfolding of the landscape, rather than the placing of an object upon it. Against the tyranny of the orthogonal or the smoothness of the buildings shaped by codes and conventions, it poses the elongated, the cantilevered, the provisional and the continuous. An architecture without beginning or end in section or plan can accommodate and respond to modernization.

Such an architecture would be a collage of forms gathered together from the world around it rather than the invention of something new. For reasons that are only too obvious, we must recycle and reuse. In order to make forms that all those who are not architects do not see as merely alien, we must make out of the culture around us, rather than against it. The rich stew of images that rises every day around the globe waits for us to mine it for our constructions. We must build in such a way that our buildings continue the weave of our environment, rather than stand out from it. We must understand our statements as restatements. Finally, we may have to accept the fact that architecture is not building. Rather, what we think of as the articulation of form built in such a way as to reflect critically the site on which it appears – whether that is a social, economic or physical one – might find its place within the realms of art or in the unreal world of the electrosphere. Architecture has an effective place in the organization of information in such a way that it does not just communicate, but becomes something in which we can be at home. At the same time, architecture can be a form of unbuilding that reveals the world to us. Many architects and those who practise architecture are engaged in experiments towards the making of such slow space. As I sit in the cocoon this writing has created for me, I await the astonishment of such space with eager anticipation. ✦

Architects

(SPAIN)

Actar Arquitectura

| Manuel Gausa (*1959) | Oleguer Gelpi (*1964) | Ignasi Pérez Arnal (*1965) |
| Florence Raveau (*1965) | Marc Aureli Santos (*1960) |

Antitypes Architecture has been used for a long time to design objects. These days, it must be concerned with relationships. It must project not unambiguous forms (compositions) but plural 'contracts' between places and events (arrangements). These arrangements suggest both combinations and distributions in space, as well as flexible forms of logic. Their effectiveness lies in the sound design of their operating system: the specific logic of relationship and internal combination; articulation and infrastructure; the mechanism of exchange and 'glocal' relationship (between individual interests – local – and combined objectives – global). This hybrid and at times 'anti-natural' contract, which can bring together in one and the same project differing formation codes, in fact refers to the actual division between the parties to the project and the contemporary city: twinned crystals, cuttings, grafts and pairings are all recent anti-compositional illustrations that convey undisciplined, impure and indeterminate orders and 'eccentric' forms (uncentred but also extreme and cursory, almost spontaneous) in continuity with the particular interpretation of a space, that of the present-day Metapolis, which can only be effectively represented by the changeable, opportunistic and unprejudiced overlay of different and differentiated layers and networks (as is the case with scanner readings and GPS maps). In a way, these contracts are 'antitypes', associated with scenarios once and for all devoid of any formal typification; antitypes in which, as in the contemporary world, different layers of movements, actions and activities overlap, no longer in the form of harmonic and coherent bodies, but of simultaneous landscapes in which 'commensal' structures, forms and identities co-exist. This is how we like to see Actar: like a strange antitype; a singular project issuing from the desire to bring together personalities, callings and fields of activity that are apparently diverse, but in fact linked: architectonic project and publishing project; creation and distribution; forward-looking action and critical eye. Dichotomies akin to others traditionally associated with the definition of the contemporary city and space (man-made/natural, urban/territorial, public/private, style/content, solid/void); dichotomies which have suddenly blurred the strict limits and given way to new and operative binomials or pairs. Mixed realities brought about by associations, transversalities and unexpected connections: links. It is precisely this desire for linkage that explains and orders Actar's hybrid identity and activity, oriented towards the interpretation and treatment of a complex space, subject to new technical and phenomenological conditions – keys to a specific environment and new scales of processes occurring therein; keys to the cultural phenomena of a thoroughly metropolitan (global) scenario, but one also attuned to the interests of the particular, the singular and the individual (local); keys leading to other types of arrangements based on direct forms of disinhibited logic, rather than to orthodox prefigurations, to the revaluation of situations rather than to their design, and to the creation of strategies (capable of encompassing complexity) rather than to the formulation of constructions. ✧

MANUEL GAUSA

✚ M'House Building

NANTES, FRANCE, 1997–2000

This project is presented like a 'menu' of interchangeable modules. These modules, which form a 0.90 x 4.50–meter grid on the ground, with a height of 2.80 meters, result from a fixed structural section, carefully studied so as to permit their lateral and vertical assembly, and the subsequent incorporation of floor, façade and partition units made of different materials, and with diverse textures and colours. They can be combined by juxtaposition and superposition, and offer a limitless number of configurations based on the variation of a limited number of standard spaces and flexible technical elements (accumulators, fitted walls, vertical circulation systems). The shape of this 'à la carte' building is not based solely on the choice of colour and the outside silkscreening but also on the particular and custom-built design of the standard. The theme of the 'catalogue house' is based here on a relationship between industry and design, conceived to encourage cheap, quick and simple systems, and technical solutions that are both precise and open. This construction, which can always be reversed, draws up an implicitly time-related 'contract' with the landscape. ✚

ISBN 84-605-1841-8

9 788460 518418

✚ Barcelona Land Grid
BARCELONA, SPAIN, 1996-99

This work of territorial investigation was presented as part of the exhibition: '1856-1999: Barcelona Contemporania' held at the Contemporary Cultural Centre in Barcelona in 1995. Its aim was to draw up an active and functional mapping of the metropolitan – and even metapolitan – area of Barcelona, a reading of the poly-nuclear reality in which it is inscribed today. Based on the idea of a flexible mesh, it reveals the presence of an infrastructural and landscape-oriented grid, closely bound up with the geography and articulating the territory. Once identified, this 'land grid', which is at once description and project, may, according to Actar, become the medium of a strategy of urban and territorial restructuring taking into account the complexity of the specific situations, processes and conditions of the contemporary metropolis: movements, relations and interconnections, but also differential relations between city and nature, between colonized spaces and preserved spaces, between global and local. ✚

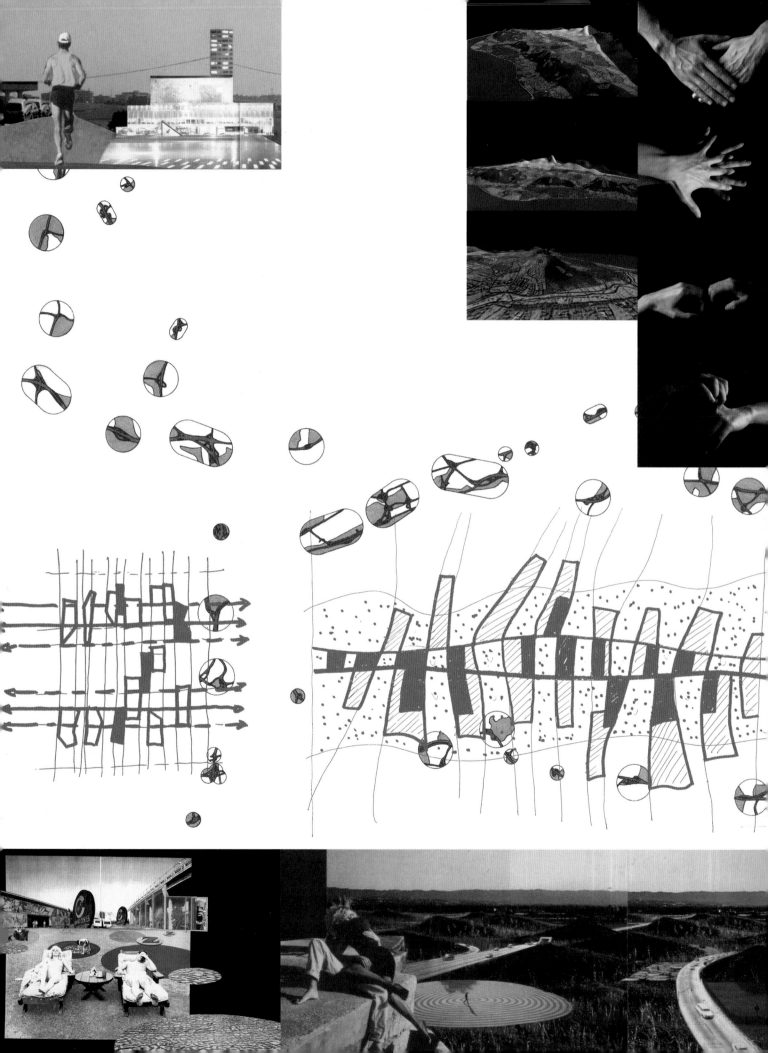

✚ Seventy Dwellings at Mont Hacho

CEUTA, SPAIN, 1998

This housing project, clinging to the sides of Mount Hacho, forming a natural amphitheatre looking over the Mediterranean, was designed as part of Europan 1999, where it was a finalist. Through an experimental transposition of literary narrative in architecture, Actar decided to 'recount' a host of particular stories in one and the same coherent grid: a landscape of terraces, surfaces, colours, textures and even many different viewpoints. Each unit is designed on the basis of a square 4 x 4-metre module – corresponding to the optimization of industrial prefabrication criteria – and a semi-fitted 'service wall'. This latter, containing bathtubs, basins, toilets, cupboards, kitchen modules, work surfaces and even stairways, works like a backbone along which there may be all the distributive and typological variations. This arrangement should permit a flexible and programmed adaptation to the individual backgrounds of the residents. ✚

✚ Picasso Square

ONTORNÉS DE VALLÈS, BARCELONA, SPAIN
1998–2000

The challenge of this project is to turn a large residual and irregular empty space, in the middle of Montornés de Vallès, into a public place, a truly 'relational' space. Here, rather than proposing a unitary and comprehensive design, Actar's intent is to develop an open system, capable of conveying diversity: not only organizing a space but also revealing its potential status as a 'place of places'. The project is presented as the blending of a lengthwise system of 'typological' strips – a street, a square, a passage, a grove of trees, a path – and a crosswise system of functional grids – an esplanade for collective activities, a playground, a pond and its shoreline, clearings and depressions for more individual pastimes. This interference is emphasized by an almost calligraphic intervention on the ground, i.e. by differentiated treatments of its colours, textures and materials, going with gradations between the busyness of the urban space and the inner quality of the grove of trees.

✚

passeig romàntic

avinguda central

carrer perimetral

bosc

plaça

ESQUEMA DE BANDES

cràters/racons

cultura

platja

jocs

esplanada

ESQUEMA DE ZONES

✚ Actar Arquitectura

Manuel Gausa (1959)
1986   Architectural Technical College of Barcelona

Oleguer Gelpi (1964)
1998   Architectural Technical College of Barcelona

Ignasi Pérez Arnal (1965)
1992   Architectural Technical College of Barcelona

Florence Raveau (1965)
1991   École d'Architecture de Paris la Défense

Marc Aureli Santos (1960)
1986   Architectural Technical College of Barcelona

1994   Creation of Actar at Barcelona

Principal buildings and projects
2000   M'House, five houses, Nantes, France (project)
2000–1999   Communal housing, Torrelles de Llobregat, Barcelona; Restaurant La Masia, Molins de Rei, Barcelona; Place Picasso, Montornés del Vallès, Barcelona (project)
1999   Individual house, Vallirana, Barcelona; Graz Maribor project, visiting consultant
1999–98   Ceuta housing, Europan Competition (special prize)

1998   Commission of 'Metapolis-01, 21 propositions for the new Barcelona'; 'Barcelona land grid'; Place Alfaro, Murcia (competition)
1996   Nodes proposal of preparks of perimetral activities, Collserola natural park, Barcelona
1994   Parc Bit, Mallorca (prizewinner)
1993   34 dwellings, Europan Competition, Madrid (mentioned)

Recent publications
1999   *In-Ex 01* Birkhaüser Verlag – In-Ex projects, Paris/Berlin; *Single housing* Actar/Birkhaüser Verlag, Barcelona/Berlin; *Punto de encuentro – Treffpunkt Zürich* exhibition catalogue of the Architektur Forum, Zurich; 'Wohnlandschaften' *Werk, Bauen+Wohnen* (1/2), Zurich; 'Housing: More for less' *Dau 7*, Barcelona; 'Territorio vibratil: reconocimiento en clave de accion' *Bau 14*, Madrid
1998   *Metápolis* 25 proposals for 21 teams, catalogue of the Festival de ideas para la futura multiciudad, Actar, Barcelona; 'Actar: Links' *Transversal* (no. 6) Barcelona
1997   *Housing: new alternatives, new systems*, Actar, Barcelona

Archi-Tectonics

| Winka Dubbeldam (*1960) |

TRANS-FORMAL ARCHITECTURES
GLOBULES, TEXTURES AND TRACES

G1 – GLOBULES
- Thing-shapes, or spatio-temporal individuations, corporeal occurrences with specific material qualities, almost smooth surfaces, and vaguely defined edges (*globule*: a tiny ball or globe, esp., a drop of liquid, *globoid*: shaped somewhat like a globe or ball).

T1 – TEXTURES
- A self-similar system where the micro resembles and informs the macro (*texture*: woven fabric, the arrangement of particles or constituent parts of any material).

T2 – TRACINGS
- Phoronomic shapes, formations developed out of tracings of gradual perfection, from which new constructions grow (*phoron*: a combining form meaning bearer, producer).

In the current fast-forwarded process of globalization, architecture is slowly sucked into the turbulent flux of changing urban conditions – conditions that are now no longer defined by local factors but by the increasing forces of global economies, immigration patterns and electronic communication infrastructures. This globalization of our living environment is creating external-internal stimuli, which calls for an intricate response mechanism to accommodate and integrate these cultural shifts. Science must be brought to bear on the realization of this complexity, with its multilayered systems demanding a new spatial order, to discover ways of bringing resolution/understanding to this global existence; architecture has the role of identifying this globality, extracting and transforming its many systems into a spatial construct. With information technology now linked so closely with the built environment, architects have become the translators of this information. For architecture, the study of science, like philosophy, mathematics or microphysics, will become of critical importance, causing the transformation from a mechanistic approach to an organismic, process-oriented approach. A shift in orientation has developed, which began in science with relativity theory, followed by quantum theory and systems theory. This organismic approach describes the notion that an organism is characterized by its immanent patterns of organization. This is similar to the notion of spirit also described by Leibniz as monads and by Hegel as '*Begriff*', or absolute ideas. These phenomena occur on all levels: in society, in behavioural processes, as well as in nature. The question which often comes up, Does this move?, is an expression of the mechanistic way of thinking that still persists. The organismic approach is process-oriented: it develops a space in the way a scientist works – it is based on research. The current global forces will define the behaviour of the system (urban textures) and finally distill the outcome (architectures) – not moving but moved – not a machine (Corbusier's machine for living) but a research resulting in a set of parameters that are traced, graphed and mapped to reflect the complex behaviour of urban forces, programmatic elasticity and the multiple layers of current modern architectures. ◆

WINKA DUBBELDAM

✛ Maashaven Towers
ROTTERDAM, THE NETHERLANDS, 2000

This project, which Winka Dubbeldam worked on within a
team of developers and engineers, involved revitalizing the
port district of Rotterdam. The economic changes taking place
in the port are actually translated into a shift of industrial
activities to the outskirts, thus permitting a potential inflow
of new functions. These benefit from the proximity of the city,
as well as from huge tracts of land beside the river Maas.
Here there is an immense grain silo on a disused wharf, which
had to be converted into offices and housing. As a noteworthy example of 1930s industrial architecture, part of the
building would be preserved to house offices. The grain storage area would be turned into a vast courtyard where sporting programmes would be held (tennis, track events, fitness
club). Housing units, constructed on the silo's concrete
foundation using a system of modular metal panels, would
close off the rear of this courtyard. On the
edge of the pier, three towers cantilevered
over the river would house duplex apartments. These three glass blades would
reflect the water and the city opposite. ✛

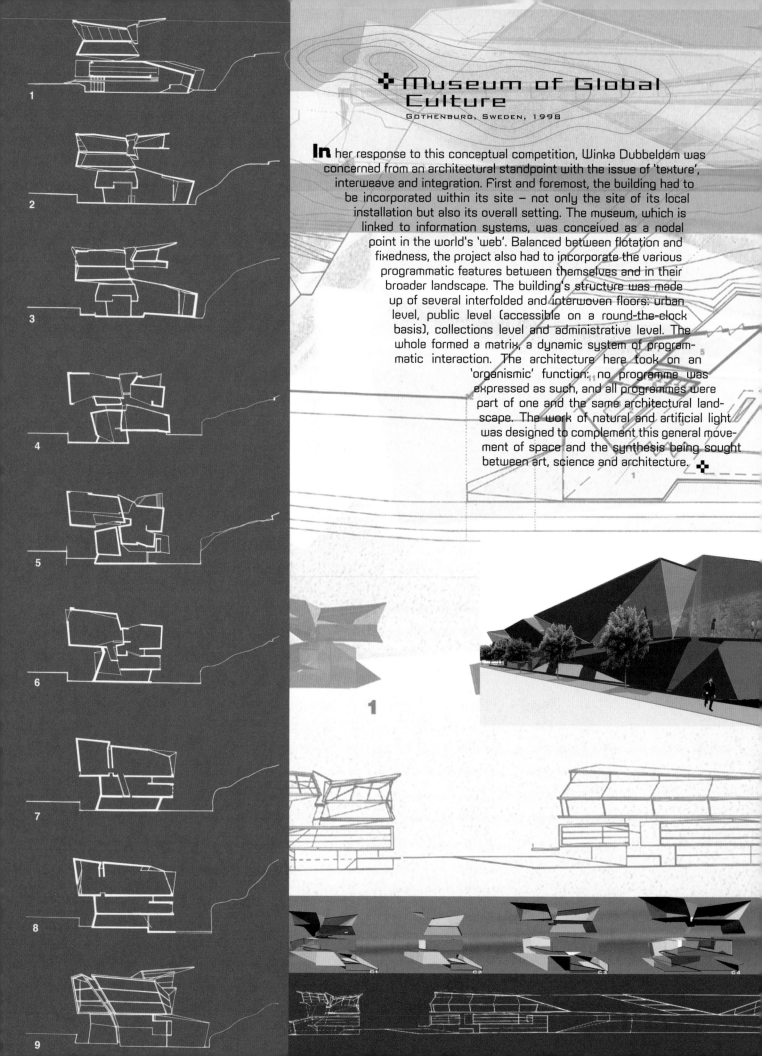

1
2
3
4
5
6
7
8
9

✤ Museum of Global Culture

GOTHENBURG, SWEDEN, 1998

In her response to this conceptual competition, Winka Dubbeldam was concerned from an architectural standpoint with the issue of 'texture', interweave and integration. First and foremost, the building had to be incorporated within its site – not only the site of its local installation but also its overall setting. The museum, which is linked to information systems, was conceived as a nodal point in the world's 'web'. Balanced between flotation and fixedness, the project also had to incorporate the various programmatic features between themselves and in their broader landscape. The building's structure was made up of several interfolded and interwoven floors: urban level, public level (accessible on a round-the-clock basis), collections level and administrative level. The whole formed a matrix, a dynamic system of programmatic interaction. The architecture here took on an 'organismic' function: no programme was expressed as such, and all programmes were part of one and the same architectural landscape. The work of natural and artificial light was designed to complement this general movement of space and the synthesis being sought between art, science and architecture. ✤

1

GROUND FLOOR P

GOTEBORG
SITE ANALYSIS

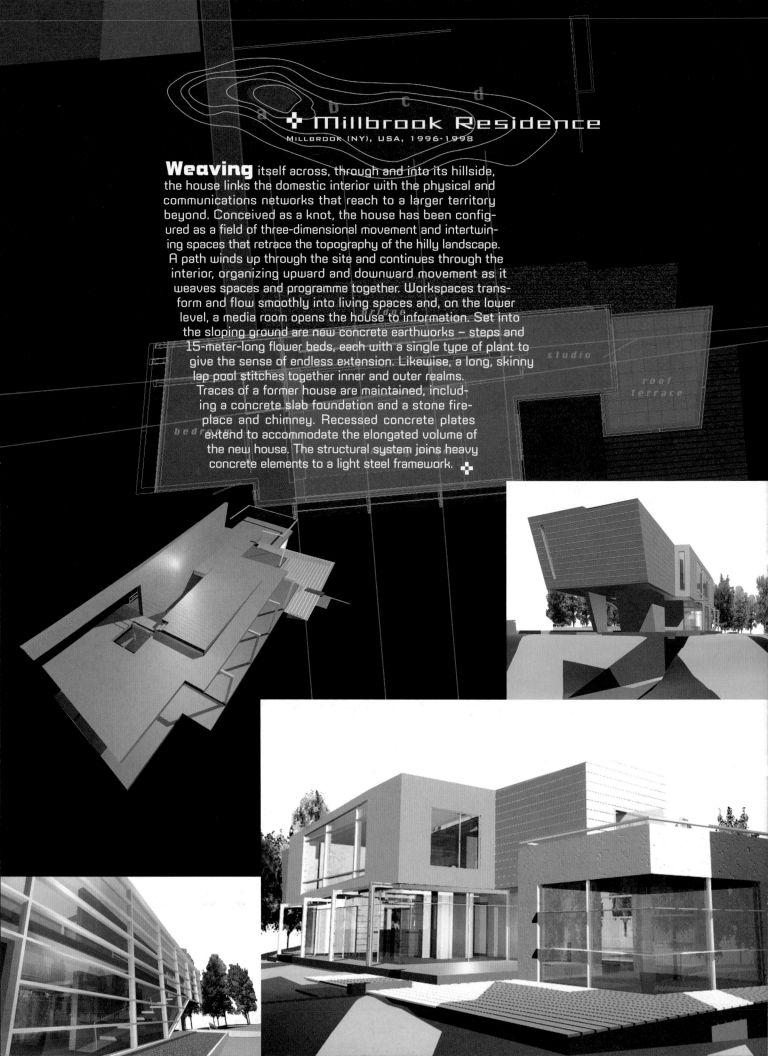

✛ Millbrook Residence

MILLBROOK (NY), USA, 1996-1998

Weaving itself across, through and into its hillside, the house links the domestic interior with the physical and communications networks that reach to a larger territory beyond. Conceived as a knot, the house has been configured as a field of three-dimensional movement and intertwining spaces that retrace the topography of the hilly landscape. A path winds up through the site and continues through the interior, organizing upward and downward movement as it weaves spaces and programme together. Workspaces transform and flow smoothly into living spaces and, on the lower level, a media room opens the house to information. Set into the sloping ground are new concrete earthworks – steps and 15-meter-long flower beds, each with a single type of plant to give the sense of endless extension. Likewise, a long, skinny lap pool stitches together inner and outer realms. Traces of a former house are maintained, including a concrete slab foundation and a stone fireplace and chimney. Recessed concrete plates extend to accommodate the elongated volume of the new house. The structural system joins heavy concrete elements to a light steel framework. ✛

Wooster Street Loft

NEW YORK, USA, 1998

FREE-STANDING BATHROOM

SUSPENDED KITCHEN

TERRACE

For this project, Winka Dubbeldam was asked to adapt the fifth floor of a converted SoHo loft building to residential space for an art collector. As the owner moves between London and New York, the Internet is his primary mode of communication, as an electronic link which connects these physically detached places. In the design for the loft, different zones are generated – public/private/guest areas, and the concept of 'connective cuts' is developed to produce continuity in separation. Planes are introduced as connective membranes, not only by means of translucency, but also by the slicing of these planes, separating them into suspended, floating and pivoting elements, conventional domestic elements are thus transformed. As a result, areas or fields of occupation have been formed, with fluid, continuous space flowing between them. Changes in the textures of the surfaces – walls, floors and windows further designate these areas as hard, soft and neutral zones. Doors and enclosures are replaced by shifts in volume, and transitions into different areas become 'hinge-points', while providing visual privacy. Overall, the continuity of these interlocking volumes creates a residence of overlapping intersections and interweaving space.

Greenwich Street Apartments
NEW YORK, USA, 2090

Located on the lower West End of Manhattan, a former six-storey warehouse will be renovated with an additional three-storey penthouse on top. Adjacent to the old brick-faced building, a new residential building of eleven storeys will be erected. The warehouse building will be completely gutted, enlarging the interior space for the introduction of an open loft plan. Large, treelike wood columns inside allow for the addition of the penthouse structure in glass and steel. The setback code of New York City is here taken as a design feature rather than a restriction; this 'sky exposure plane', as it is called, is introduced as a tilted glass plane, which separates the penthouses from the planar street façade. These two glass façades then inflect on each other, blurring their singularity and allowing for a folded spatial condition. The ground floor will be occupied by retail space and an art gallery, intended to foster a more active street and ease the transition from the former industrial area to an integrated residential neighbourhood. ✦

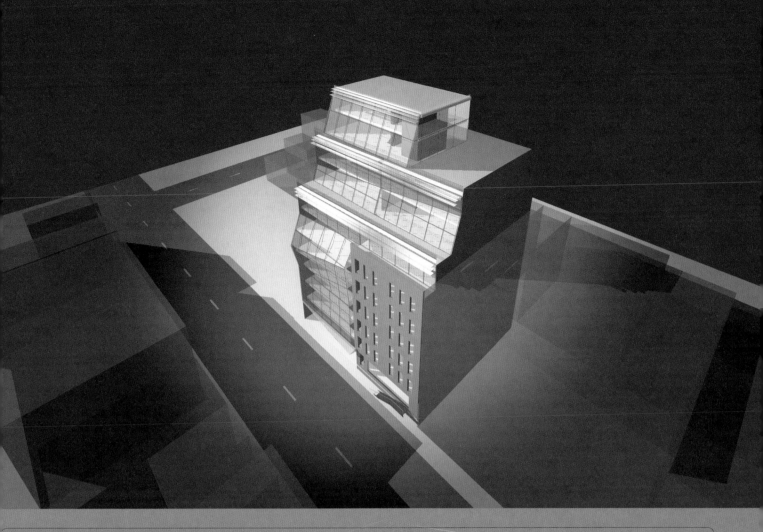

✛ Archi-Tectonics / Winka Dubbeldam

Winka Dubbeldam (1960)

1992   Master of Science in Advanced Architectural Design, Columbia University, New York

1990   Professional Degree in Architecture, Academy of Architecture, Rotterdam

1983   Professional Degree in Architectural Design, Academy of Art, Rotterdam

1994   Creation of Archi-Tectonics

Teaching

2000–1998 'Paperless' Design Studio, Columbia University, New York

2000–1994 'Paperless' Design Studio, University of Pennsylvania, Philadelphia

1997–95 Academy of Architecture, Rotterdam

Principal buildings and projects

2000   Maashaven Towers, Rotterdam (under construction); House in Aspen, USA (under construction); Urban design, Moscow (project); Warehouse 6+4 storeys, renovation (under construction); Duplex Store for a London Fashion Designer, Soho, NYC (under construction); Hair/Beauty Salon, NYC (realized); Townhouse in Hoboken, renovation (under construction); Redesign for an Architectural School, Rotterdam (under construction); Greenwich Street Apartments, New York (project)

1999   Duggal Max Digital Imaging Facility, New York (realized); *Gear Magazine* Office New York (realized)

1998   Wooster St Loft, New York (realized); Gothenburg Museum of World Culture (project)

1998–96 Millbrook House, New York (project)

1997   Wall Street Parallel Network Center, New York (competition)

1996   Governor's Island: Strategic (Re)occupations (competition), New York; Electronic Media Center, New York (project)

1995   Yokohama Ocean Liner Terminal (competition), Japan; Water Relief Urban Landscape, Dordrecht (project)

1994   Bio-Lab, Mojave Desert (competition); Cristine Gose Gallery, New York (realized)

Recent exhibitions

1999   'Archiprix' ARCAM, Amsterdam, 'The Un-private House' Museum of Modern Art, New York; FOE Gallery, Munich; T2 Art Gallery, New York; Parsons Gallery, New York

1998   'New York's Centennial of Greater NY Exhibition : 100 Ideas for the City that Could Be' Municipal Art Society, New York

Principal publications

1996   *Winka Dubbeldam Architect* 010 Publishers, Rotterdam

1995   *De Structuur van Water* Waabders, Netherlands, Waterwork

1994   'In Gesprek met Peter Eisenman' *Architect* (7/8)

1991   *Strategic Renewal of Moerwijk* 010 Publishers, Rotterdam

Selected bibliography

2000   *10x10* Phaidon Press, London

1999   *A+U* (no. 344); *Abitare* (May) *The Un-private House* Museum of Modern Art, New York; *Hybrid space: new forms in digital architecture* Peter Zellner, Thames & Hudson, London; *Lofts + apartments in New York* Edizioni l'Archivolto; 'Space travel in a loft' *New York Times* (23 Dec.)

1998   *Archimade* (March) 'Object 1998-1999'; *Interior Design* (April); 'Object 1998–1999'

1997   *Techno-Fiction* (vol. 1) : The 7th Bauhaus Kolloquium; *Elle* (April)

1996   *World Architecture* (Oct.); *Competitions* (autumn)

1995   *Space, Arts & Architecture and Environment* (Sept.); *Circuit* (Sept.)

Asymptote

| Lise-Anne Couture (*1959) | Hani Rashid (*1958) |

Asymptote opposes coincidence to siting, installation to foundation, in order to claim an emphatic right to build unencumbered by the traditional spatial order imposed by a foundation. 'Marinetti's locomotive has derailed', according to Hani Rashid in 'On Recent Non-Events'. The mobility and speed embraced by the Futurists have not, in the end, caused a radical change in how we conceive our relation to space. Only Lazlo Moholy-Nagy in 'Vision in Motion' possibly understood that the proliferation of optical instruments in the twentieth century has introduced such a fragmentation of the visible that a spatial inscription is no longer assumed a permanent referent. Asymptote proposes a reconfiguration of architecture through a radical mutation of its relation to space as an abstract referent, the one-dimensional space of geometry. Henceforth, architecture will organize material that is complex, perpetually over-determined, supported by permanent grafts and overlaps, deformed by use and enhanced by ever-changing symbolic interpretations. The architectural work is no longer relative only to its spatial inscription, the reified structure of an establishment that imposed a hierarchic ordering upon all political, economic and social parameters. Today architecture must organize itself into different configurations simultaneously, hybrid spatialities nourished by technology and media. As Hani Rashid and Lise-Anne Couture assert, architecture is entering an age of fluidity without the ontological anchor that geometrically defined space previously supplied; it must express and create new modalities, open up possible worlds. 'Amnesia' and 'anaemia' deny monumentality's static time, instead reclaiming presence, an infinite extension of the 'now', the desire to rediscover the principle of ambivalent memory that Jacques Derrida emphasized in 'Le puits et la pyramide'. Building should be autonomous; this would not liberate it from the traditional constraints of architecture, but these no longer determine form or function. Asymptote's claim to autonomy is its capacity to specify all elements – symbolic, technical and material – that could contribute to a project. 'Autonomy' is not the modernist term of idealism or abstraction denounced by social critics. Autonomy is the desire to think and to labour within the entire complex sphere of the real. The architectural work becomes an unfinished object, a permanent continuum of projects that have reached the limits of definition, that are limited both in their ability to define themselves and to be defined socially, through use. The definition of a project's unity is its pragmatism, its ability to reconstruct its universal meaning for each one of us. There is a silence of an idealized form, an architectural 'non-event', but an introduction to the eventual as something related to the event, the eventual that operates at the heart of the building, affirming an architecture in action, perpetually renewed. ✦

FRÉDÉRIC MIGAYROU

Los Angeles West Coast Gateway
(Steel Cloud), 1988
Collection Frac Centre

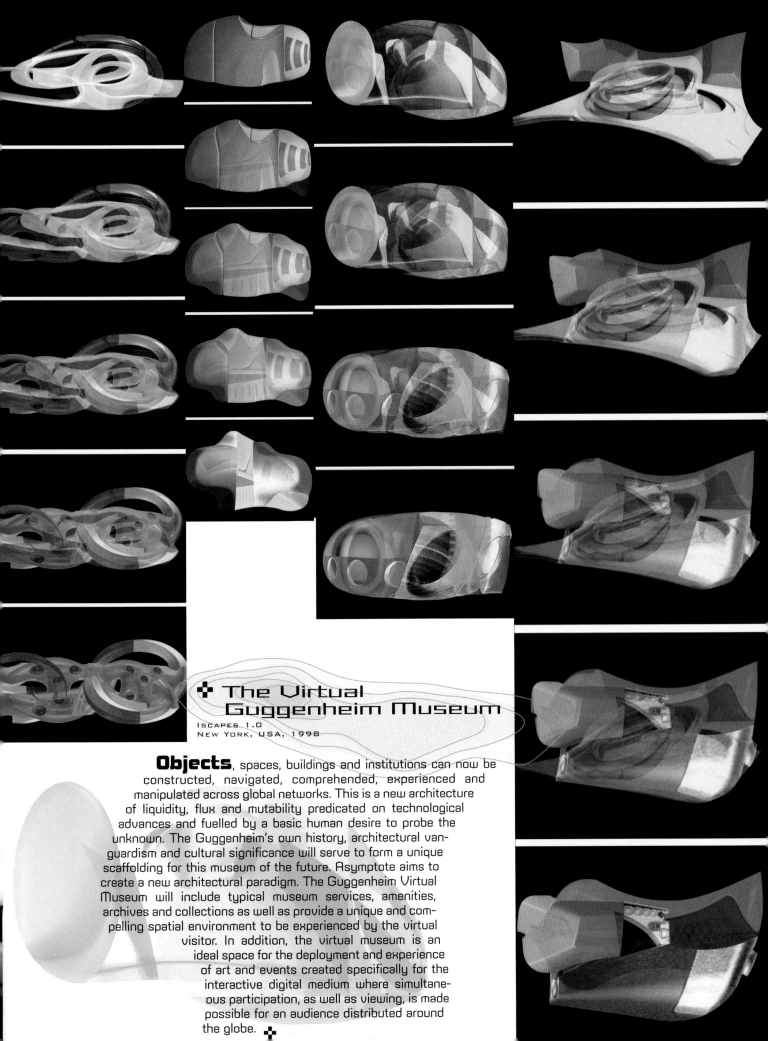

The Virtual Guggenheim Museum

ISCAPES 1.0
NEW YORK, USA, 1998

Objects, spaces, buildings and institutions can now be constructed, navigated, comprehended, experienced and manipulated across global networks. This is a new architecture of liquidity, flux and mutability predicated on technological advances and fuelled by a basic human desire to probe the unknown. The Guggenheim's own history, architectural vanguardism and cultural significance will serve to form a unique scaffolding for this museum of the future. Asymptote aims to create a new architectural paradigm. The Guggenheim Virtual Museum will include typical museum services, amenities, archives and collections as well as provide a unique and compelling spatial environment to be experienced by the virtual visitor. In addition, the virtual museum is an ideal space for the deployment and experience of art and events created specifically for the interactive digital medium where simultaneous participation, as well as viewing, is made possible for an audience distributed around the globe. ✛

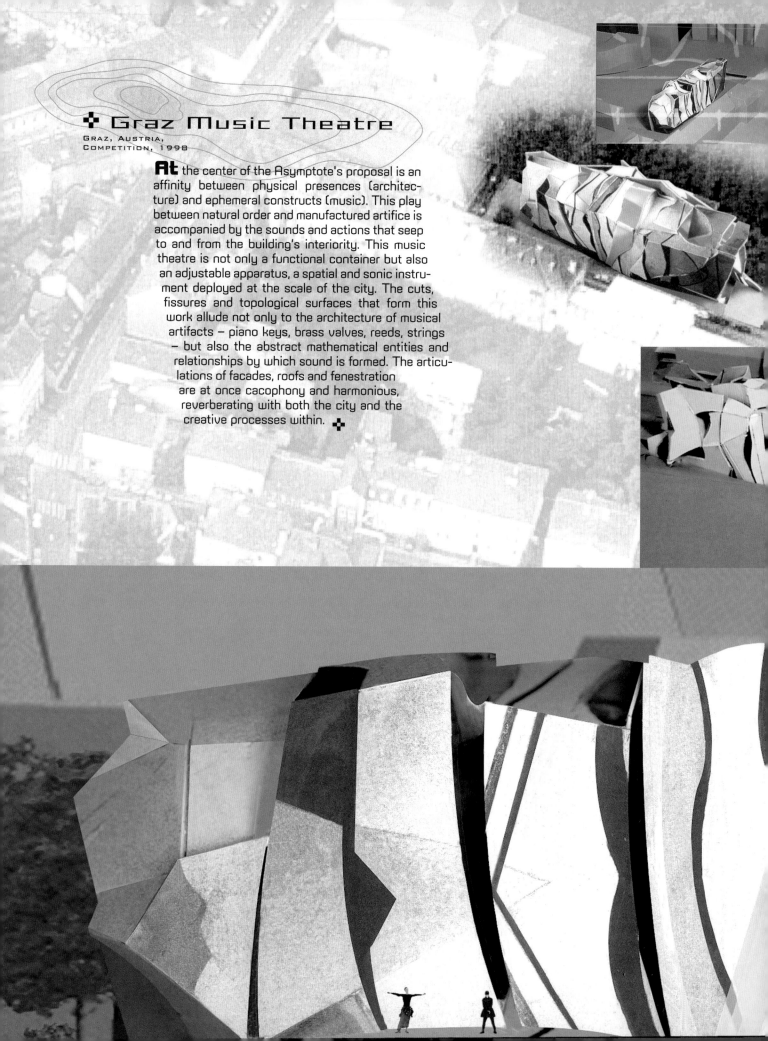

✦ Graz Music Theatre

GRAZ, AUSTRIA,
COMPETITION, 1998

At the center of the Asymptote's proposal is an affinity between physical presences (architecture) and ephemeral constructs (music). This play between natural order and manufactured artifice is accompanied by the sounds and actions that seep to and from the building's interiority. This music theatre is not only a functional container but also an adjustable apparatus, a spatial and sonic instrument deployed at the scale of the city. The cuts, fissures and topological surfaces that form this work allude not only to the architecture of musical artifacts – piano keys, brass valves, reeds, strings – but also the abstract mathematical entities and relationships by which sound is formed. The articulations of facades, roofs and fenestration are at once cacophony and harmonious, reverberating with both the city and the creative processes within. ✦

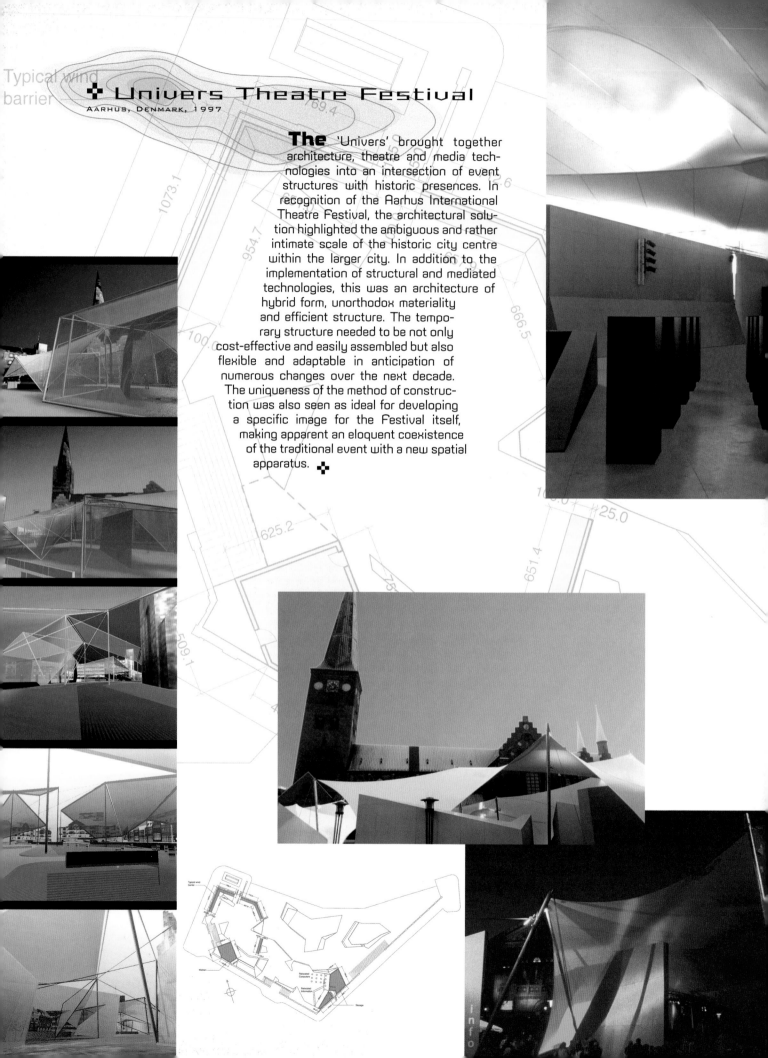

✦ Univers Theatre Festival
AARHUS, DENMARK, 1997

The 'Univers' brought together architecture, theatre and media technologies into an intersection of event structures with historic presences. In recognition of the Aarhus International Theatre Festival, the architectural solution highlighted the ambiguous and rather intimate scale of the historic city centre within the larger city. In addition to the implementation of structural and mediated technologies, this was an architecture of hybrid form, unorthodox materiality and efficient structure. The temporary structure needed to be not only cost-effective and easily assembled but also flexible and adaptable in anticipation of numerous changes over the next decade. The uniqueness of the method of construction was also seen as ideal for developing a specific image for the Festival itself, making apparent an eloquent coexistence of the traditional event with a new spatial apparatus. ✦

Information

863.0

340.9

68.0

76.8

Unibank

✦ Virtual NYSE

New York Stock Exchange
New York, USA, 1998

The 3DTFV is the first large-scale virtual-reality environment of its kind, incorporating the design and conceptualization skills of Asymptote as an architectural team. The 'data-scape' brings together information flows, data models and entities, and correlation models into a single seamless three-dimensional architectural environment. The virtual space is a real-time model displaying activity and events to users as a fully interactive navigable space with infinite possibilities of movement and viewing. The deployment of the 3DTFV alongside the actual trading floor in New York allows the operations personnel to gain a deeper and more precise understanding of the many variables and complexities that unfold during trading sessions. In addition to the model's functional requirements, special attention was paid to the overall quality of the virtual space, the control of form, light, texture and dynamics as well as methods of viewing and new means of navigation. ✦

✛ Asymptote

Lise-Anne Couture (1959)
1986 Master of Architecture, Yale University

Hani Rashid (1958)
1985 Master of Architecture, Cranbrook Academy of Art, Bloomfield Hills, Michigan
1987 Founded Asymptote Architecture in New York

Teaching
Lise-Anne Couture: 1999 – Parsons School of Design and Columbia University, New York; The University of Michigan, Ann Arbor; The Stadelschule, Frankfurt; Harvard University; The University of Montreal, Canada

Hani Rashid: 1999 – Graduate School of Architecture and Urban Planning, Columbia University, New York; Harvard University; The Stadelschule, Frankfurt; The Royal Danish Academy, Copenhagen; The Berlage Institute, Amsterdam; The Technical University, Vienna; Lund University, Sweden

Principal buildings and projects
1999 Virtual New York Stock Exchange – NYSE (under construction); Museum of Digital Art, Seoul, Korea (project); Multimedia Research and Edutainment Facility, Kyoto, Japan (project); The Guggenheim Virtual Museum (GVM), New York (project)
1998 Advanced Trading Floor Operations Center, New York Stock Exchange (realized)
1997 (Univers) Theater Festival, Aarhus, Denmark (realized)
1989 Los Angeles West Coast Gateway (Steel Cloud), (competition/prizewinner)

Recent exhibitions
Aedes Gallery, Berlin; The Kunsthalle, Vienna; The Museum of Modern Art, New York; Galérie Uzzan, Paris; Pavillon de l'Arsenal, Paris; Museum of Contemporary Art, Los Angeles; Centre Canadien d'Architecture, Montreal, Canada; Architecture Biennale at Venice

Publications (by Hani Rashid)
1994 *LAX: The L.A. Experiment AGIT(N)ATION Pseudo-Architecture*, SITES, Lumen Books

Selected bibliography
1998 *Architecture Design* 'Hypersurface Architecture' London; *Equal Partners*, exhibition catalogue, Smith College Museum of Art, Northampton, MA; The Virtual Dimension *The Difference-Scape* Princeton Architectural Press, NY
1997 *Architecture + Urbanism* 'Univers Theater' Tokyo, no. 323; *Architecture* 'Machine Dreams' Aaron Betsky, New York (June); *World Architecture* 'Designing the Unpredictable' Georgi Stanishev, London
1996 *Architecture for the Future* 'Asymptote Architecture' Pierre Terrail, Paris; *Paper Art 6 Catalog*, Dorethea Eimert, ed. Leopold-Hoesch-Museum; *Sites & Stations* 'LAXNYCYHM: Urban Triptych' Lusitania Press, New York; 'Die Schrift des Raumes' *Kunst Architecture Kunst* catalogue, Kunsthalle, Vienna/FRAC Centre
1995 *581 Architects in the World*; 'Asymptote Architecture: Rashid + Couture' Gallery Ma, Tokyo, Japan; *Arch +* 'Media City: Hani Rashid Studio' Berlin, September; *Instaurations de l'éventuel* Frédéric Migayrou, vol. 2, Orléans, France; *Architecture at the Interval Asymptote: Rashid + Couture* Rizzoli International; *40 Under 40* 'Brave New World' Beverly Russell, ed. Grand Rapids, Missouri; *Architecture + Urbanism* 'Asymptote' Tokyo, Japan (April); *Architectural Design* 'Film as Architecture as Film' Rashid and Couture, London
1993 *Assemblage 21* 'Analog Space to Digital Field: Asymptote Seven Projects' MIT Press, Cambridge, MA; *Theory & Experimentation Asymptote* Academy Editions, London

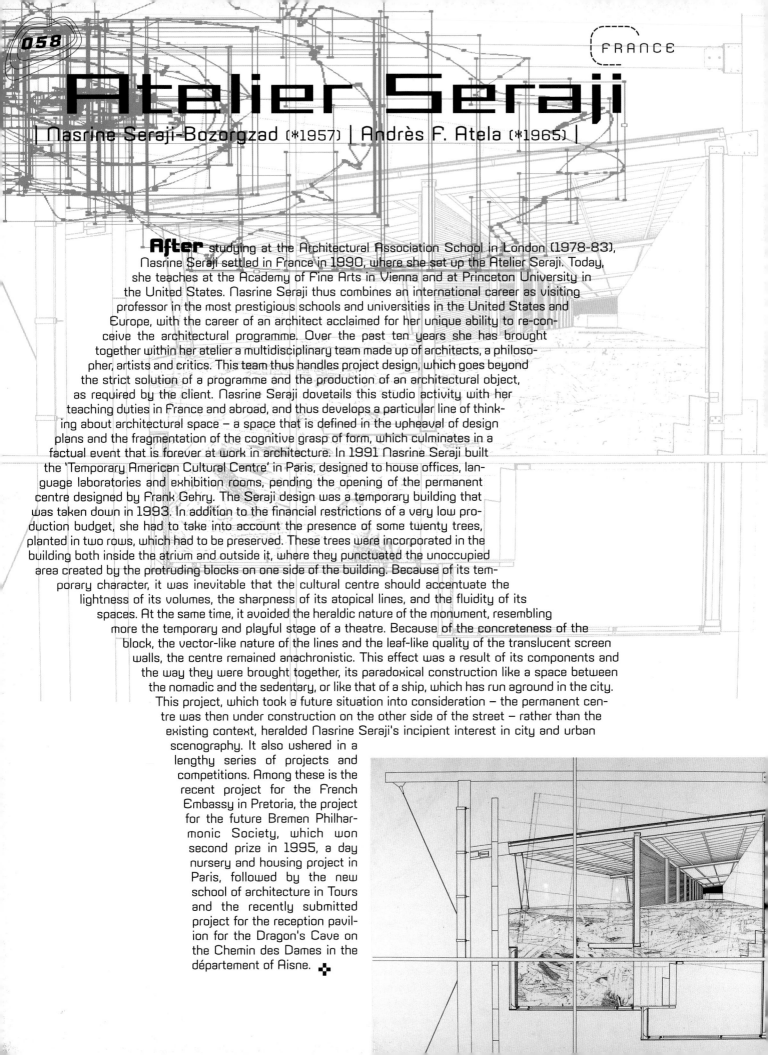

Atelier Seraji

| Nasrine Seraji-Bozorgzad (*1957) | Andrès F. Atela (*1965) |

After studying at the Architectural Association School in London (1978-83), Nasrine Seraji settled in France in 1990, where she set up the Atelier Seraji. Today, she teaches at the Academy of Fine Arts in Vienna and at Princeton University in the United States. Nasrine Seraji thus combines an international career as visiting professor in the most prestigious schools and universities in the United States and Europe, with the career of an architect acclaimed for her unique ability to re-conceive the architectural programme. Over the past ten years she has brought together within her atelier a multidisciplinary team made up of architects, a philosopher, artists and critics. This team thus handles project design, which goes beyond the strict solution of a programme and the production of an architectural object, as required by the client. Nasrine Seraji dovetails this studio activity with her teaching duties in France and abroad, and thus develops a particular line of thinking about architectural space – a space that is defined in the upheaval of design plans and the fragmentation of the cognitive grasp of form, which culminates in a factual event that is forever at work in architecture. In 1991 Nasrine Seraji built the 'Temporary American Cultural Centre' in Paris, designed to house offices, language laboratories and exhibition rooms, pending the opening of the permanent centre designed by Frank Gehry. The Seraji design was a temporary building that was taken down in 1993. In addition to the financial restrictions of a very low production budget, she had to take into account the presence of some twenty trees, planted in two rows, which had to be preserved. These trees were incorporated in the building both inside the atrium and outside it, where they punctuated the unoccupied area created by the protruding blocks on one side of the building. Because of its temporary character, it was inevitable that the cultural centre should accentuate the lightness of its volumes, the sharpness of its atopical lines, and the fluidity of its spaces. At the same time, it avoided the heraldic nature of the monument, resembling more the temporary and playful stage of a theatre. Because of the concreteness of the block, the vector-like nature of the lines and the leaf-like quality of the translucent screen walls, the centre remained anachronistic. This effect was a result of its components and the way they were brought together, its paradoxical construction like a space between the nomadic and the sedentary, or like that of a ship, which has run aground in the city. This project, which took a future situation into consideration – the permanent centre was then under construction on the other side of the street – rather than the existing context, heralded Nasrine Seraji's incipient interest in city and urban scenography. It also ushered in a lengthy series of projects and competitions. Among these is the recent project for the French Embassy in Pretoria, the project for the future Bremen Philharmonic Society, which won second prize in 1995, a day nursery and housing project in Paris, followed by the new school of architecture in Tours and the recently submitted project for the reception pavilion for the Dragon's Cave on the Chemin des Dames in the département of Aisne. ✦

INDIVIDUAL
MODULES.

3x4.
for
DIRECTORS.

FACADE.

ACCOUNTS
FIRST FL
WITH THE
PERSPEC

✦ American Cultural Centre
PARIS, FRANCE
1991

This temporary building, which was built pending
the construction of the centre's permanent premises,
designed by Frank Gehry, and subsequently taken
down in 1993, was located in a small triangular
square, between rue de Pommard and rue de Bercy in
Paris. Very simple blocks of reconstituted wood contained the offices, alternating with trees, included
within one side of the building and lining its other side.
The effect of this was to blur the distinctive identities
of building and trees. A block at the western end gave
the feeling that the building was about to start moving. A more continuous block to the south (made of
the same kind of wood) opened up a diagonal space
running the length of the building. It was accompanied by a translucent vertical plane and had a metal
structure. The roof, façade, uprights
and tie beams, with their optical directional character, produced a singular
movement, together with the blocks
(enclosed objects), with their almost
Kahn-like autonomy. A quasi-con-
structivist dynamic of openness and
enclosure was created, where only the
void between the objects became an
oriented fluid space. The building's
completeness gave the temporary centre the paradoxical guise of a permanent architecture. ✦

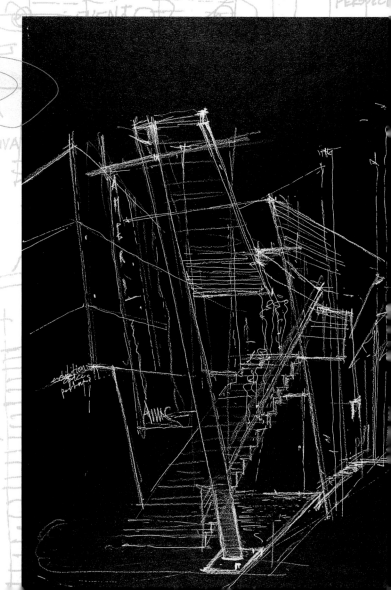

✚ School of Architecture

DEUX LIONS DISTRICT, TOURS, FRANCE
COMPETITION, 1997

The School of Architecture in Tours had to be built in the new Deux Lions district, like a landmark. The project is based on two axes: from east to west, the school organizes its three curricula of studies; from bottom to top, the different levels each embrace a programme theme with the help of different types of spaces and areas. In this way, the school's public and specific functions (exhibitions, lecture hall, café, reprographic shop, model workshop, student club premises) are concentrated on the ground floor around an atrium, the hub of movement. The first floor, for its part, houses the administrative premises, in a regular layout; the second floor houses the library, workshops and studios, here arranged in a dynamic plan; the third, the visual arts studios in an open-plan arrangement. The top floor, or 'eyrie', houses research premises. ✚

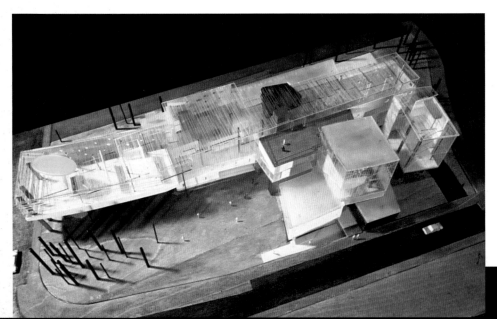

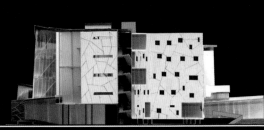

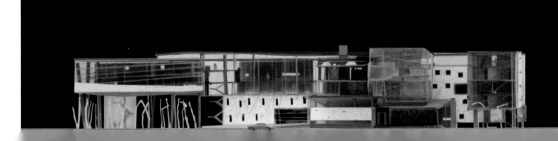

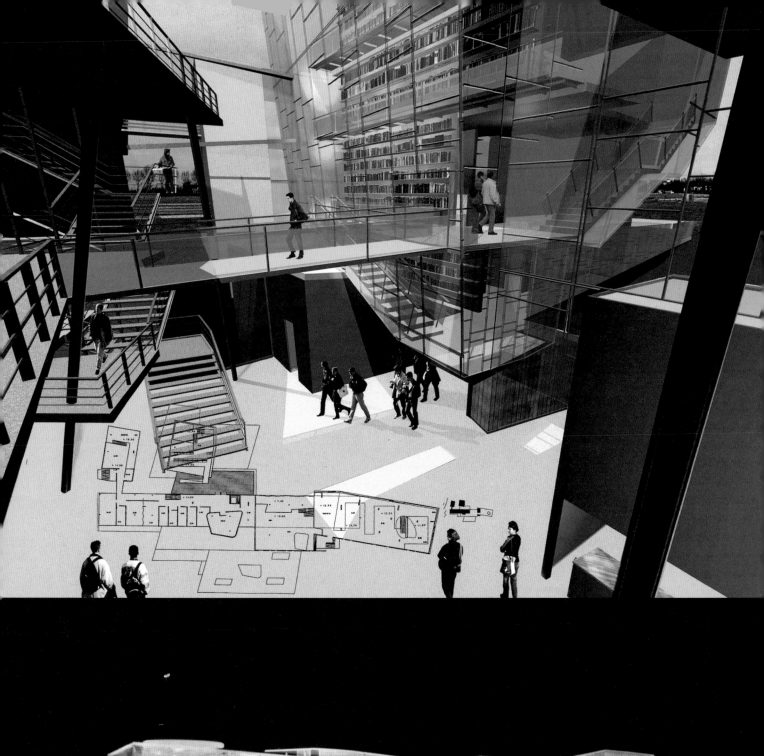

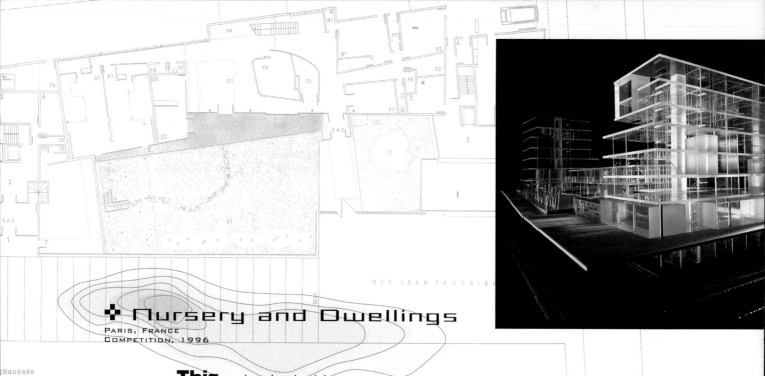

✦ Nursery and Dwellings

PARIS, FRANCE
COMPETITION, 1996

This project involved incorporating thirty-five housing units and
a sixty-place day nursery within the
same plot – a corner lot in a business
estate (ZAC) in the 13th arrondisse-
ment in Paris. The decision to expose
the outside areas of the nursery a to
the south meant turning these areas
towards the pedestrian street.
This also made it possible to
give the nursery breathing space
amid the density all round it. The two
tall wings, containing the housing
units, and the lower structure (the day
nursery) thus defined a garden-cum-
courtyard separated from the street
by a transparent wall. ✦

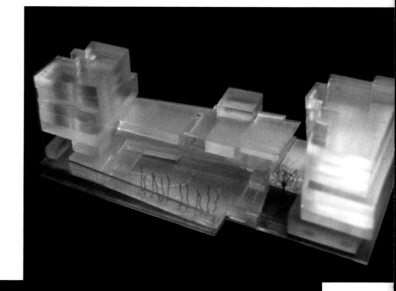

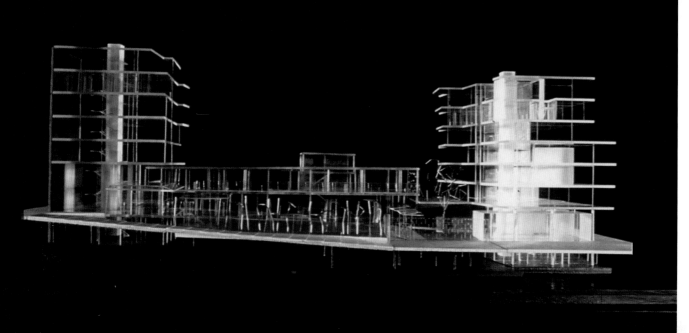

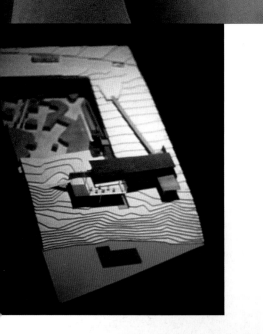

✚ Dragon's Cave

CHEMIN DES DAMES, AISNE
FRANCE.1998
(COMPETITION, 1996)

The Dragon's Cave is one of the most famous commemorative battle sites of the First World War. For months, its tunnels housed the troops opposing the enemy army. The project involves a reception pavilion where a visit to the underground museum begins, offering a threshold area between context and content, between the surrounding farmland and woodland, and the museum displays and exhibitions. This light pavilion is located below the access road, to minimize the impact of its mass for people arriving at the site. It is surmounted by a floating roof, a skewed surface which does not block the view over the environs. Ticket office, schools workshop, screening room and café are all linked together in a downward, theatrical sequence, leading to the entrance to the underground rooms. This pavilion was completed in 1998. ✚

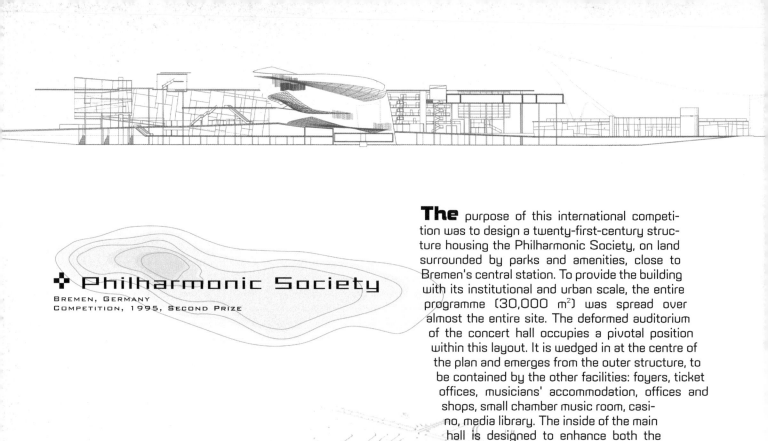

✚ Philharmonic Society

BREMEN, GERMANY
COMPETITION, 1995, SECOND PRIZE

The purpose of this international competition was to design a twenty-first-century structure housing the Philharmonic Society, on land surrounded by parks and amenities, close to Bremen's central station. To provide the building with its institutional and urban scale, the entire programme (30,000 m²) was spread over almost the entire site. The deformed auditorium of the concert hall occupies a pivotal position within this layout. It is wedged in at the centre of the plan and emerges from the outer structure, to be contained by the other facilities: foyers, ticket offices, musicians' accommodation, offices and shops, small chamber music room, casino, media library. The inside of the main hall is designed to enhance both the quality of individual listening and the collective celebration of music. ✚

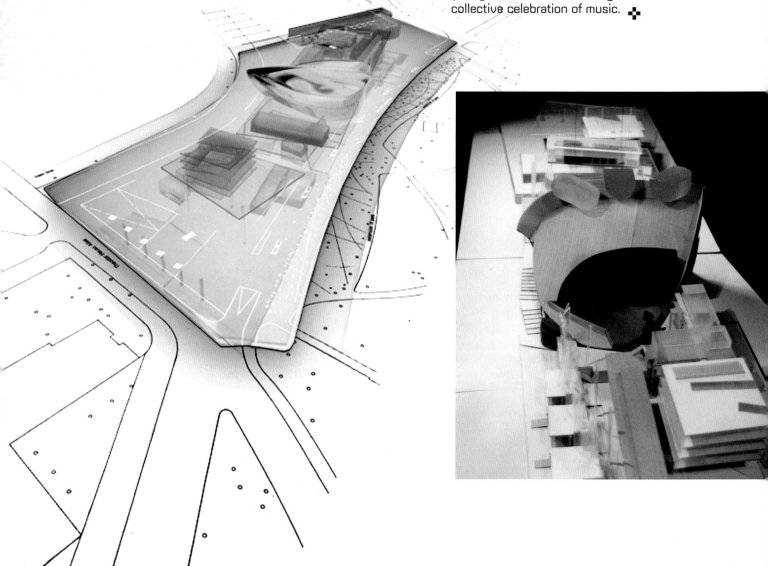

✤ Atelier Seraji

Nasrine Seraji-Bozorgzad (1957)
1983   Diploma from the Architectural Association, London

Andrés F. Atela (1965)
1994   Diploma from the Architectural Association, London; Atelier Seraji

1990   Founded Atelier Seraji in Paris

Teaching – Nasrine Seraji-Bozorgzad
1999–96   Vienna Fine Arts Academy, Austria: Professor and director of one of the two Architecture Master Schools; School of Architecture at Princeton University, USA: visiting professor

1998–93   School of Architecture of the Architectural Association, London: Dipl. Unit Master

1995   Special School of Architecture, Paris: visiting professor

1994   School of Architecture at Columbia University, New York: visiting professor School of Architecture at the University of Tulane, New Orleans, USA: visiting professor

1991–88   Foreign Studies Programme at the University of Toronto, Paris: visiting professor

Principal buildings and projects
1998   Reception pavilion at the Dragon's Cave, Chemin des Dames, Aisne (realized); Competition for the French Embassy at Pretoria (South Africa) Maison Confort EDF at Lyons (under construction)

1997   Competition for a school of architecture, Deux Lions district, Tours; Monument to the victims of the Holocaust, Berlin, competition with Jochen Gerz; Crèche and housing, rue Jean Fautrier, Paris 13e

1995   International competition for the New Philharmonia at Bremen: second place; Plan for the site of the gendarmerie barracks at Briey-en-Forêt (realized)

1994   Competition for the renovation of a block of fifty dwellings, Sarcelles. Submitted in 1997

1993   International competition for ideas for the new district of Spreebogen, Berlin

1991   Temporary American Centre, rue de Bercy, Paris: International competition submitted in 1991

Recent exhibitions
1998   Royal Institute of British Architects (RIBA) Architecture Centre, London

1997   Institut Français d'Architecture (IFA), Paris; Arc en Rêve Centre d'Architecture, Bordeaux; Librairie Minerva, Museum of Applied Arts (MAK), Vienna

1996   VIth Mostra Internazionale di Architettura (Biennale), Venice; AA, London

Recent conferences
1998   Faculty of Visual Arts and Design, Utrecht; The Berlage Institute, Amsterdam; Architectural Association, London; Zentralvereinigung der Architekten Österreichs, Vienna; Illinois Institute of Technology (IIT), Chicago

Principal publications
1998   'The architecture model' in *Triumph der Phantäsie: Barocke Modelle von Hildebrandt bis Mollinaro*, Michael Krapf, ed., Österreichische Galerie Belvedere, Vienna

1998   'Nexus-Atelier: Tools, Organization, Process' in *ANYhow*, Cynthia Davidson, ed., MIT Press, Cambridge, MA

1996   'Diversion' in *The Architect Reconstructing Her Practice*, Francesca Hughes, ed., MIT Press, Cambridge, MA

Selected bibliography
1998   *Architektur & Bau Forum* (Germany); *Casabella* (Italy)

1997   *Building Design* (UK); *Design Book Review* (USA); *l'Architecture d'aujourd'hui* (France); *Le Moniteur-AMC* (France); *RIBA Journal* (UK); *UME* (Australia)

1996   *AD: Architectural Design Profile* (UK); *Arch+* (Germany)

1995   *De Architect* (Netherlands); *Space* (Korea)

1993   *AA Files* (UK); *Assemblage* (USA); *Bauwelt* (Germany); *Progressive Architecture* (USA)

1992   *Abitare* (Italy)

1991   *Le Moniteur–AMC* (France)

Shigeru Ban

| Shigeru Ban (*1957) |

In my first work, the installation design of the Emilio Ambasz Exhibition, I designed screens of fabric to serve as partitions. The fabric was delivered in rolls with paper cylinder cores (paper tubes). I took many of the paper tubes back to my office. Later, when I was designing the installation for the Alvar Aalto Exhibition, it occurred to me to use the light brown paper tubes still in my office. I visited a paper tube factory. I discovered that the tubes made of recycled paper were inexpensive and could be made in almost any length, diameter and thickness. I wondered if they might be usable as structural material in architecture. In 1990 I began to design a multi-purpose hall (Odawara Pavilion East Gate). Professor Gengo Matsui kindly agreed to cooperate with me on the work of 'paper architecture'. There was no precedent anywhere in the world for the use of paper as a structural material and so we began with experiments on paper tubes as material. The paper-tube structure (PTS) used in the 'Paper House' was approved by the Ministry of Construction. One of my favourite buildings is the Farnsworth House by Mies van der Rohe. This was a revolutionary work that achieved complete continuity between inside and outside by means of a totally glazed exterior. However, there is no physical continuity as in traditional Japanese residential spaces, where various openable screens exist between inside and outside. The 'Curtain Wall House' was formed with an authentic exterior curtain wall. Other works are a response to the 'Universal Space' proposed by Mies, that is, the idea of a fluid space generated under a large continuous roof by means of furniture-like cores and partitions. Up to now I have used paper tubes as columns or framed trusses, but in 'Paper Domes' I designed a large frame with arches spanning 28 metres with a rise of 8 metres using paper tubes as a material under axial compressive force. The paper tube arches are now being designed for the Expo 2000 Hanover in Germany. In this century large numbers of low-cost housing became necessary. Today ethnic and regional conflicts are breaking out all over the world, creating many refugees. In addition, the worldwide problem of the homeless and frequent disasters are producing a significant minority. The way architects serve society, particularly minorities, may be an important factor in determining the character of this era. The UNHCR (Office of the United Nations High Commissioner for Refugees) commissioned me to develop a paper refugee shelter using paper tubes. After the 1995 Hanshin earthquake, I served as a volunteer and constructed together with sudents from all over the country 'Paper Church'/ community centre and 'Paper Loghouse'/ temporary shelter on the site of a destroyed church. Even in disaster areas, as an architect, I want to create beautiful buildings, to move people and to improve people's lives. If I did not feel that way, it would not be possible to create works of architecture and to make a contribution to society at the same time. ❖

SHIGERU BAN

Wall-less House
Karoizawa, Nagano, Japan 1997

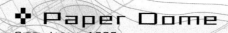

✦ Paper Dome

A large arched roof spanning 27.2 metres, 8 metres in height at the center and covering a space 22.8 meters wide, was created. Since paper tubes cannot be curved, the entire arch is divided into eighteen straight paper tubes 1.8 metres long, which are connected together by means of laminated wood joints. Horizontal rigidity is achieved by the use of structural plywood instead of bracing. Each panel of plywood is pierced by a circle which is as large as possible without compromising rigidity, in order to let natural light in through the corrugated polycarbonate panels. The ends of the paper tubes and joints are in full contact to transmit the loads for reducing the bending moment, but there are reinforcing steel tension members and braces provided as a precaution against sudden changes of load. ✦

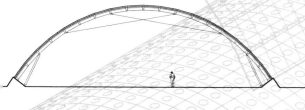

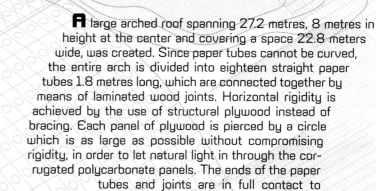

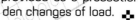

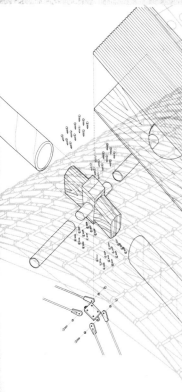

✦ Paper House
YAMANAKAKO, JAPAN
1995

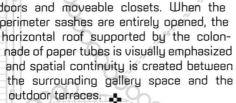

Lined up in an S-shape configuration on a square floor area 10 metres to a side, 110 'paper tubes' (2.7 metres high, 280 millimetres in diameter and 15 millimetres thick) define the living areas laid out inside and outside of the resulting composition of curved and straight planes. The project was the first in which paper tubes were authorized to be utilized as structural material in a permanent building. Ten of the paper tubes support the vertical load and the eighty interior paper tubes bear the lateral forces. The large circle surrounded by the eighty paper tubes forms an interior living area with a gallery around it. The living area in the large circle is represented as a universal space with no furnishings other than an isolated kitchen counter, sliding doors and moveable closets. When the perimeter sashes are entirely opened, the horizontal roof supported by the colonnade of paper tubes is visually emphasized and spatial continuity is created between the surrounding gallery space and the outdoor terraces. ✦

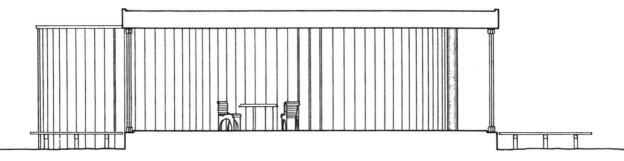

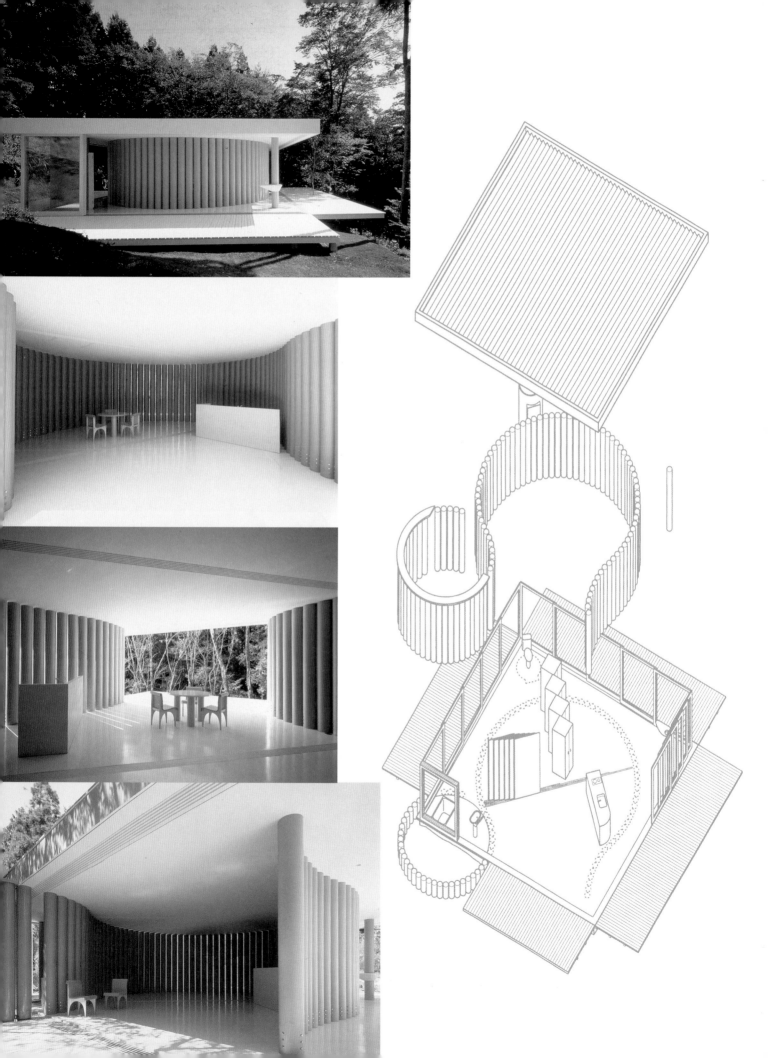

✦ Paper Loghouse

KOBE, JAPAN
1995

With this project, Shigeru Ban responded to an urgent issue: to provide decent temporary housing to the victims of the Kobe earthquake in 1995. The design criteria called for a cheap structure that could be built by anyone and quickly assembled. Ban's solution was to use a foundation of sand-filled beer cases, walls of paper tubes (diameter 108 millimetres, 4 millimetres thick), and the ceiling and roof of tent material. With this system there is no need to store anything and, as in Rwanda, it is possible to make the paper tubes on site. The floor area of 16 square metres is the same as that of the UNHCR basic shelter size for Africa. With the thermal properties of the paper tubes, these are being developed as prototypes suitable for many countries. At the Minamikomae Park in Kobe more than twenty units had been built. Not only did the loghouses compare favourably with other types of temporary housing in terms of cost and ease and speed of construction but they were easy to recycle after use and easy to store. ✦

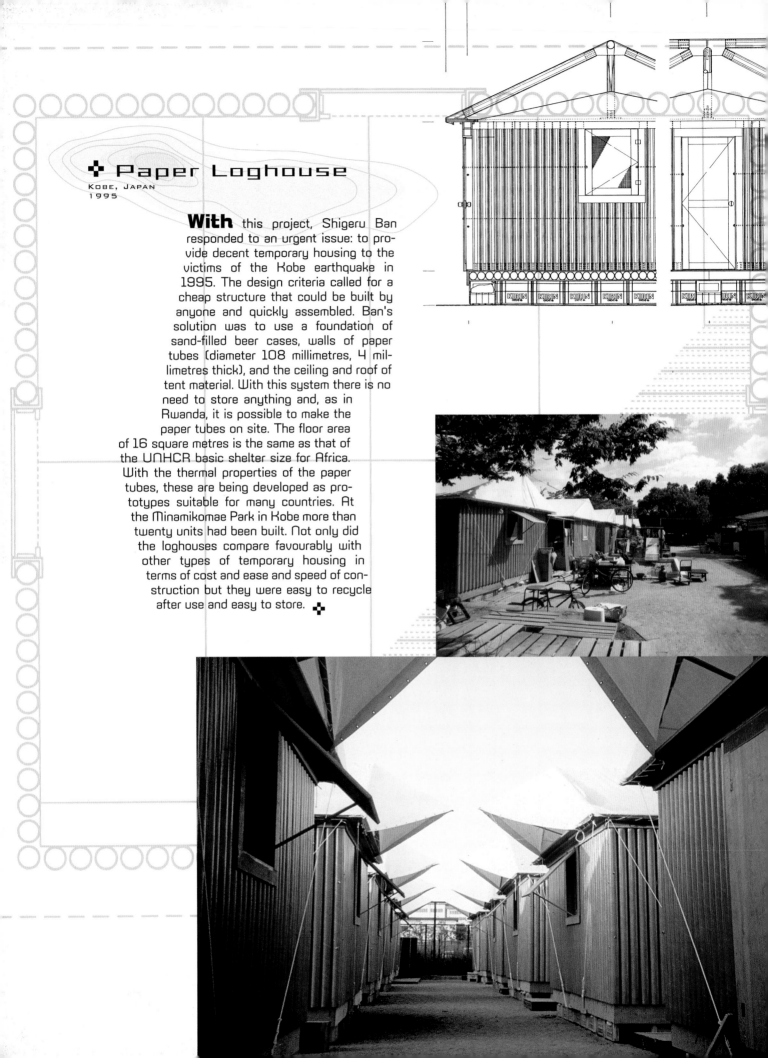

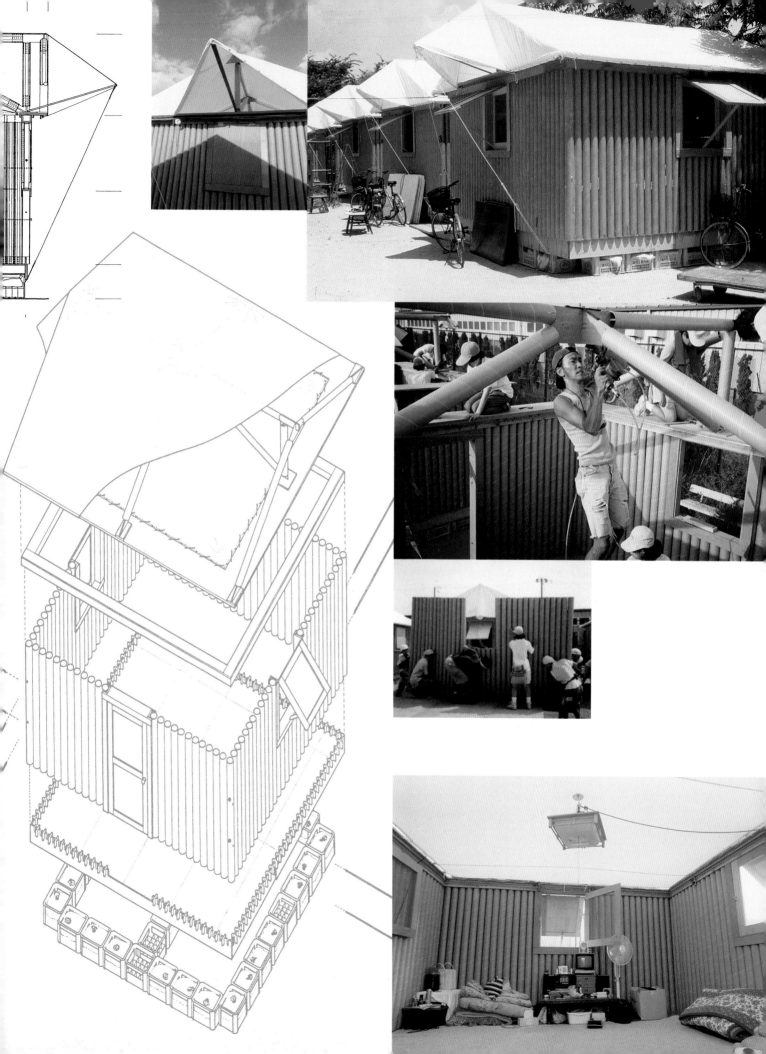

✤ Double-roof House

YAMANASHI, JAPAN
1993

This weekend villa was built on a sloping site overlooking Lake Yamanaka. The double-roof structure was created as a means of accommodating the snow load within a restricted budget without the need for a large structural framework. The upper roof structure is separated from the ceiling and folded steel plates of the minimum allowable dimension were used. The ceiling, not being suspended from the roof, is thereby freed from the deflection margin, and thus the ceiling becomes a roof with minimum live load. In addition, the upper roof provides shelter against direct sunshine in summer. Square-sectioned steel pipes that are normally used in temporary construction have been selected here as the material for the beams to support the corrugated-iron plated roof. Other structural elements below the roof are built of wood. The rooftop level above the bedroom-bathroom portion is a terrace, which provides a view toward Lake Yamanaka. ✤

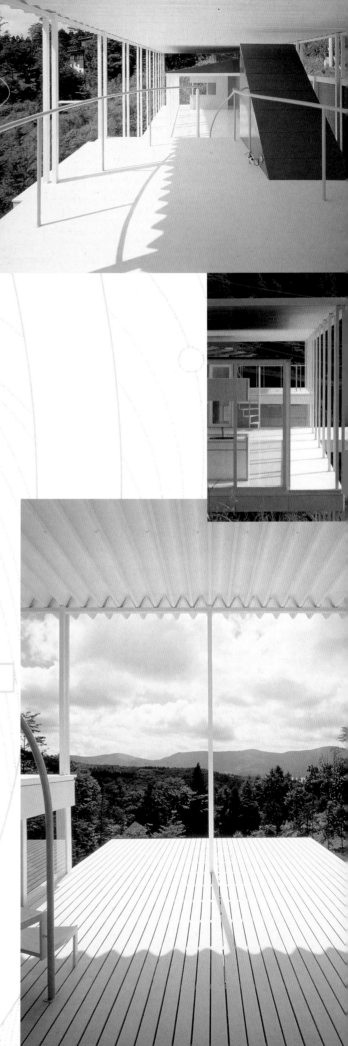

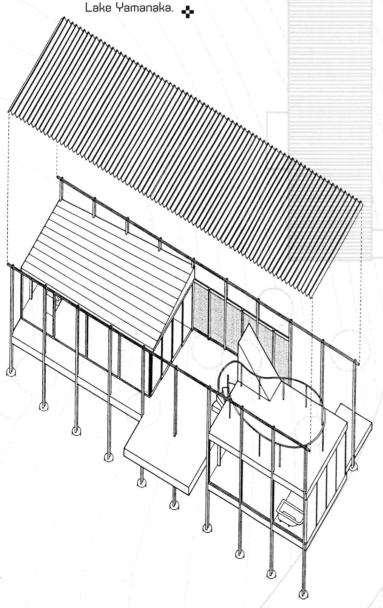

✤ Shigeru Ban

Shigeru BAN (1957)
1984 Bachelor of Architecture, Cooper Union
1982–80 Cooper Union School of Architecture, New York
1980-77 Southern California Institute of Architecture, Los Angeles
1985 Founded the practice at Tokyo, Japan
1995 Consultant to the High Commission for Refugees of the
      United Nations

Teaching
1996 Nihon University
1995 National University Yokohama
1995–93 Tama Art University

Principal buildings and projects
1998 Paper Dome, Gifu; Furniture House #3, Kanagawa; Ivy Structure
     House, Tokyo; Issey Miyake Collection Stage Set Design, Paris
1997 Wall-less House, Karuizawa, Nagano; JR Tazawako Station, Akita; 9
     Square Grid House, Kanagawa; Forest Hanegi, Tokyo; Paper Stage
     Design, Kabukiza Theatre, Tokyo, Paper Stage Design for Mannojo
     Nomura, Tokyo
1996 Furniture House #2, Fujisawa
1995 Paper Church – Paper Structure Tube #8 – Kobe, Hyogo; Paper
     Loghouse – Paper Structure Tube #7 – Kobe, Hyogo;
     Paper House – Paper Structure Tube #5 – Lake Yamanaka,
     Yamanashi; Curtain Wall House, Tokyo; Furniture House, Lake
     Yamanaka, Yamanashi
1994 House of a dentist, Tokyo; Paper Gallery, Tokyo
1993 Double-roofed House, Lake Yamanaka, Yamanashi; Factory at
     Hamura, Dengyosya, Tokyo; Station Gallery, Tokyo

Recent exhibitions
1998 Gallery GA, 'GA Japan League 98' – 'GA Houses Project 98'; JIA

Prize for the best young architect of the year
1997 Stool Exhibition 3, Living Design Center, Ozone; Gallery GA; 'GA
     Japan League 97'; Resurrection of Topos 3, Hillside Terrace Gallery
1996 Paper Church and Volunteers, Kenchikuka Club

Selected bibliography
2000 *Shigeru Ban* Emilio Ambasz, Shigeru Ban, Laurence King
     Publishing, London
1999 *Gallery MA Books 12*, 'Shigeru Ban, Projects in Process to
     Japanese Pavilion, Expo 2000 Hanover' Toto Shuppan;
     l'Architecture d'aujourd'hui (January) France; *GA Houses* no. 59,
     Japan; *AIT* (March) Germany
1998 *JA* no. 30; *Shinkenchiku-sha*, 'Paper Tube Architecture from Kobe
     to Rwanda' Chikuma Shobo Publishing Co. Ltd.; *Architectural
     Review* (Jan. and Nov.) UK; *Domus* (July/August) Italy; *Detail*
     (July/August) Germany; *AV 72* (July/August) Spain; *ID* (Feb.)
     USA; *Korean Architect* (Feb.) Korea
1997 *GG Portfolio*, Gustavo Gili; *Abitare* (March and August) Italy; *Form*
     (May) Sweden; *Arquitectura Viva* no. 52, Spain; *Monthly Design*
     (March) Korea
1996 *l'Architecture d'aujourd'hui* (Sept.); *Architectural Review* (Sept.)
     UK; *Detail* (August) Germany; *De Architect* (July/August),
     Netherlands; *l'Arca* (July/August) Italy; ARK (Feb./March) Finland;
     Architecture (Oct.) USA; *Ambiante* (Nov./Dec.) Germany; *Leonardo*
     (March) Germany
1995 *Architectural Review* (August) UK; *Living Architecture* no. 14,
     Denmark; *Bauwelt* (Nov.) Germany; *Architecture et Défi Ecologique*
     (Oct./Nov.) France
1994 *Abitare* (November and December) Italy; *l'Arca* (Dec.) Italy; *Interni*
     (Nov.) Italy
1993 *Metropolis* (Dec.) USA
1987 *Abitare* Annual 9, Italy

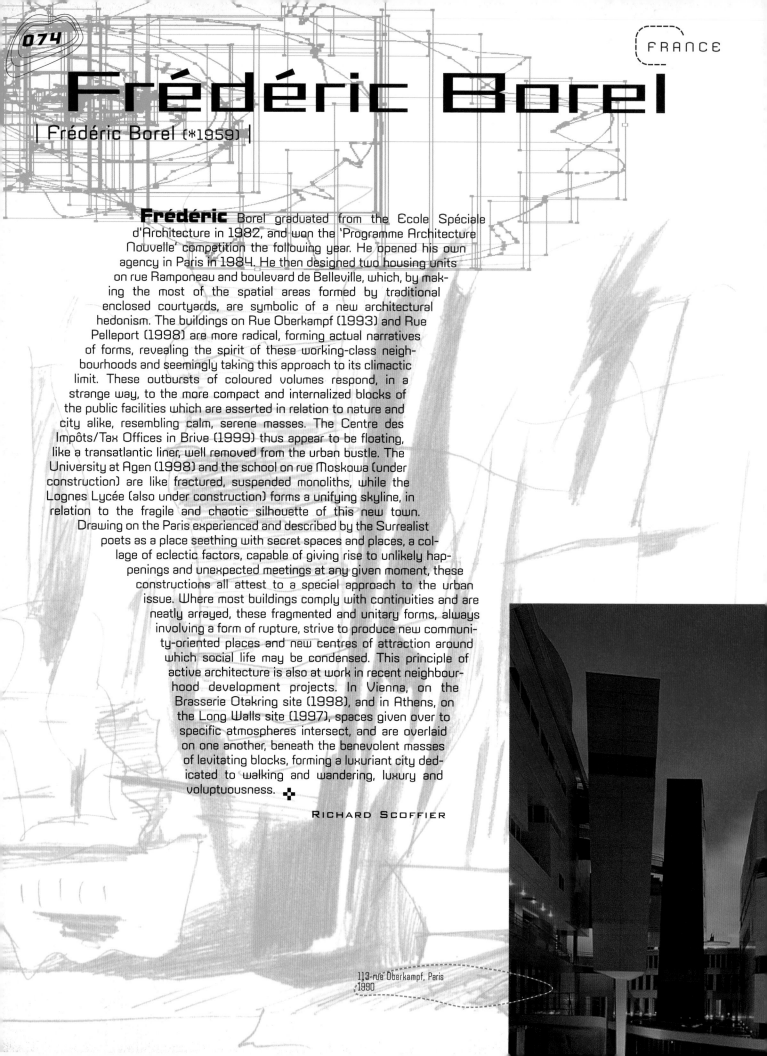

Frédéric Borel

| Frédéric Borel (*1959) |

Frédéric Borel graduated from the Ecole Spéciale d'Architecture in 1982, and won the 'Programme Architecture Nouvelle' competition the following year. He opened his own agency in Paris in 1984. He then designed two housing units on rue Ramponeau and boulevard de Belleville, which, by making the most of the spatial areas formed by traditional enclosed courtyards, are symbolic of a new architectural hedonism. The buildings on Rue Oberkampf (1993) and Rue Pelleport (1998) are more radical, forming actual narratives of forms, revealing the spirit of these working-class neighbourhoods and seemingly taking this approach to its climactic limit. These outbursts of coloured volumes respond, in a strange way, to the more compact and internalized blocks of the public facilities which are asserted in relation to nature and city alike, resembling calm, serene masses. The Centre des Impôts/Tax Offices in Brive (1999) thus appear to be floating, like a transatlantic liner, well removed from the urban bustle. The University at Agen (1998) and the school on rue Moskowa (under construction) are like fractured, suspended monoliths, while the Lognes Lycée (also under construction) forms a unifying skyline, in relation to the fragile and chaotic silhouette of this new town.

Drawing on the Paris experienced and described by the Surrealist poets as a place seething with secret spaces and places, a collage of eclectic factors, capable of giving rise to unlikely happenings and unexpected meetings at any given moment, these constructions all attest to a special approach to the urban issue. Where most buildings comply with continuities and are neatly arrayed, these fragmented and unitary forms, always involving a form of rupture, strive to produce new community-oriented places and new centres of attraction around which social life may be condensed. This principle of active architecture is also at work in recent neighbourhood development projects. In Vienna, on the Brasserie Otakring site (1998), and in Athens, on the Long Walls site (1997), spaces given over to specific atmospheres intersect, and are overlaid on one another, beneath the benevolent masses of levitating blocks, forming a luxuriant city dedicated to walking and wandering, luxury and voluptuousness. ✦

RICHARD SCOFFIER

113 rue Oberkampf, Paris
1990

131 rue Pelleport, Paris
1998

✦ PLI Residential Building

PARIS, FRANCE, 1998

Perched halfway up rue Pelleport, at the cross-roads of a cluster of adjacent streets, this small apartment building immediately surprises the onlooker with its formal and colourful busyness. This lavishness, which indicates a generosity that the approach to the building does not belie, reflects the keen attention that Borel has paid both to the organization of the housing units and to the setting in which this project stands—the heterogeneous context of a neighbourhood with lively topography and disparate constructions. The project brings together volumes and parts of coloured planes into a mass whose unusual outer cladding becomes a surface of exchanges with the features adjacent to the building: a seventeen-floor high-rise, scattered buildings of old Ménilmontant and those of rue Pelleport, all forming a homogeneous corridor. Frédéric Borel thus creates a unit and a mass that both match and contrast with the surroundings and are independent and binding: a building intentionally designed as a moment of incorporation and openness, like an urban event. ✦

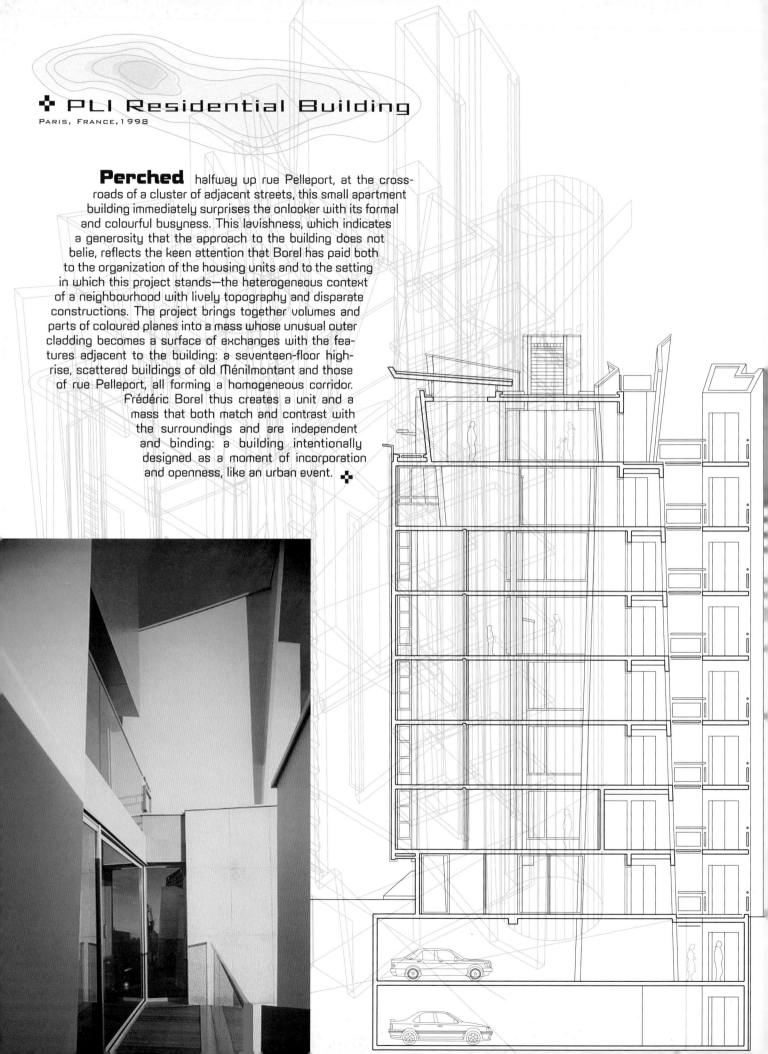

Science University at Agen

AGEN, FRANCE
FIRST PHASE: 1998; SECOND PHASE: IN PROGRESS

This is a simple construction, an elongated monolith, poised on a forest of V-shaped posts. But lurking behind this apparent simplicity is a certain persistent complexity. The outer structure of this block is covered with coloured fragments, which, by reducing the impact of the outlines, offset the might of the suspended mass. This design, painted in the bluish hues of distance, means that at certain times of day the building is totally absorbed by its site; at other times, on the contrary, by creating unlikely depths, it comes across like an event, imploding the monolithic mass in a host of slivers. The basic gesture thus remains as if suspended, favouring an atmosphere of osmosis with the site. The various parts of the programme create a sequence with a fluid succession of differentiated ambiences. The green space and the library, which seems to slide towards the backdrop, form a world removed from time, filled with levitating volumes, a garden of sciences put together like a 'garden of delights'. ✦

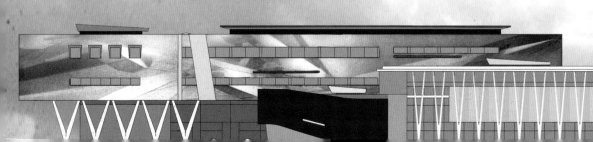

✦ Law Courts at Laval

LAVAL, FRANCE, COMPETITION, 1996

An enclosure of protective granite wraps three sides of a clearing whose slope extends into the depths of the project on the banks of the nearby river Mayenne. Under this gently sloping garden, folded and indented by a glass cylinder linking forecourt and the 'Salle des pas perdus', or main hall, various spaces are dynamically organized in relation to an axis of symmetry that runs through the composition. This establishes a balanced and tranquil whole, which is neither peremptory nor soothing, and thus coheres with the solemnity of the premises. Out of this garden, suspended between sky and earth, rise two blocks that contain courtrooms. Borel has created an an arrangement that condenses the history of judicial sites and the mythical tree of St Louis in contemporary glazed offices. Borel's project is neither a temple to justice inspiring fear and defiance, nor an administrative facility rendering the role of the legal institution commonplace. Rather, it strives to be part of the site and to represent a dignified and calming object, at once stable and open, cloaked in a certain strangeness while remaining familiar. ✦

✛ Valmy Day Nursery
PARIS, FRANCE, UNDER CONSTRUCTION

In the middle of a block filled with dense vegetation, the Récollets nursery clearly comes across as an accumulation of pure shapes. With its subtly expressed character and its simple volumes, this project contrasts with the elegant and refined city buildings, at once fragmented and articulate, usually built by Borel. It is as if, when faced with nature, it required experimenting with a more direct and more conceptual formal style. The structure consists of opaque blocks squeezed tightly against one another, as if levitating on glass crystals. With few means, the project seems to express of two pairs of contradictory ideas: attraction and expansion, heaviness and weightlessness. In the very movement with which the solid upper forms jostle about an extremely dense, invisible centre, the inner quality of the ground floor opens inexorably towards the outside, beyond its glazed partitions. This minor project, free of affectation and mannerism, and relentlessly informed by oxymoron — that rhetorical figure of speech that lends structure to many works by this architect — reconciles the opposites in a poetic ambiguity that is as deep as it is unfathomable.

✦ Frédéric Borel

Frédéric Borel (1959)
1982 Diploma from the Special School of Architecture, Paris
1983 Prizewinner in the competition 'Programme d'Architecture Nouvelle PAN XIII'
1985 Established the practice in Paris

Principal buildings and projects
2000 Ecole Maternelle de la rue Moskowa, Paris (under construction); Crèche Valmy, rue des Recollets, Paris (under construction)
1999 Théâtre à Ancenis (competition)
1998 Centre des Impôts, Brive (realized); 131, rue Pelleport, residential building, Paris (realized); University of Agen (realized); Ottakring District, Vienna, city planning (prizewinner in two phases of the competition)
1997 Long walls, Athens, city planning (project)
1996 Law courts at Laval (competition)
1990 113, rue Oberkampf, post office and housing, Paris (realized)
1986 100, Bd de Belleville, residential building, Paris (realized)

Principal publications
1997 'Parfaire la ville, même si parfois on la bouleverse' *Ville-Architecture* no. 3, Paris
1996 'Densité, réseaux, événements' *Mini PA* no. 15, Pavillon de l'Arsenal, Paris; 'Le Singulier, le volume, l'identité et l'altérité' *Bloc, le monolithe fracturé*, exhibition catalogue VIth Mostra Internazionale di Architettura at Venice, AFAA/HYX, Orléans
1992 *Le Dessin et l'architecte: Excursion dans les collections de l'Académie d'Architecture* Demi-Cercle/Pavillon de l'Arsenal
1990 'Architecture active' *Ouvertures*, exhibition catalogue, Arc-en-Rêve, Bordeaux
1984 'Romainville: Le déplacement comme élément constitutif de l'espace' *Pan XIII: Construire la banlieue*, Ministère de l'Urbanisme, Paris

Selected bibliography
2000–1989 Numerous French and international periodicals (*L'Oeil, GA, Architectural Review, Bauwelt, AMC, l'Architecture d'aujourd'hui,*
DBZ, Costruire, Architektur Aktuell (Vienna), *Architectural Design,* etc.)
1999 *GA Documents* no. 59
1998 *Re-Création: 21 architectures en France à l'aube du XXIème siècle* (1998/2000: travelling exhibition in Latin America) AFAA/Ministère de la Culture, France/Argentina; *Premises: Invested spaces in visual arts, architecture & design from France: 1958-1998* Guggenheim Museum, New York; *Paris côté cours: La ville derrière la ville* Pavillon de l'Arsenal, Picard, Paris
1997 *Paris des faubourgs: Formation transformation* Pavillon de l'Arsenal, Picard, Paris; 'Made in France 1947-1997' *Petit Journal de l'accrochage du musée*, Centre Georges Pompidou, Paris
1995 *Par exemple* catalogue of Ifa (travelling) exhibition, Interéseaux, France/Germany
1994 *Three French Architects* (O. Decq and B. Cornette, M. Kagan, F. Borel) catalogue of RIBA, London, exhibition, A3 Architecture Art Association, Paris; *Un Lieu, un architecte: 113, rue Oberkampf* Demi-Cercle, Paris; *GA Houses* no. 42, Japan
1990 *Le Jour se lève 100, Bd de Belleville*, Olivier Boissière, Demi-Cercle, Paris
1986 *Albums de la jeune architecture: Frédéric Borel* Ministère de l'Urbanisme, Paris

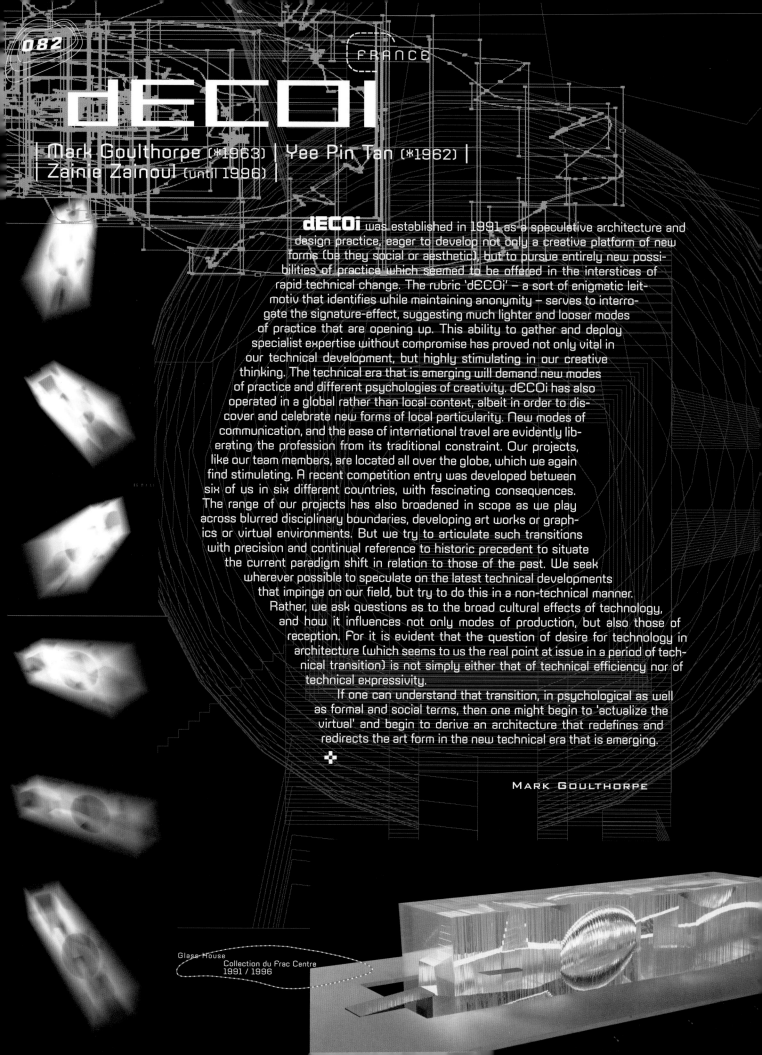

FRANCE

dECOi

| Mark Goulthorpe (*1963) | Yee Pin Tan (*1962) |
| Zainie Zainoul (until 1996) |

dECOi was established in 1991 as a speculative architecture and design practice, eager to develop not only a creative platform of new forms (be they social or aesthetic), but to pursue entirely new possibilities of practice which seemed to be offered in the interstices of rapid technical change. The rubric 'dECOi' – a sort of enigmatic leitmotiv that identifies while maintaining anonymity – serves to interrogate the signature-effect, suggesting much lighter and looser modes of practice that are opening up. This ability to gather and deploy specialist expertise without compromise has proved not only vital in our technical development, but highly stimulating in our creative thinking. The technical era that is emerging will demand new modes of practice and different psychologies of creativity. dECOi has also operated in a global rather than local context, albeit in order to discover and celebrate new forms of local particularity. New modes of communication, and the ease of international travel are evidently liberating the profession from its traditional constraint. Our projects, like our team members, are located all over the globe, which we again find stimulating. A recent competition entry was developed between six of us in six different countries, with fascinating consequences. The range of our projects has also broadened in scope as we play across blurred disciplinary boundaries, developing art works or graphics or virtual environments. But we try to articulate such transitions with precision and continual reference to historic precedent to situate the current paradigm shift in relation to those of the past. We seek wherever possible to speculate on the latest technical developments that impinge on our field, but try to do this in a non-technical manner. Rather, we ask questions as to the broad cultural effects of technology, and how it influences not only modes of production, but also those of reception. For it is evident that the question of desire for technology in architecture (which seems to us the real point at issue in a period of technical transition) is not simply either that of technical efficiency nor of technical expressivity.

If one can understand that transition, in psychological as well as formal and social terms, then one might begin to 'actualize the virtual' and begin to derive an architecture that redefines and redirects the art form in the new technical era that is emerging.

❖

MARK GOULTHORPE

Glass House
Collection du Frac Centre
1991 / 1996

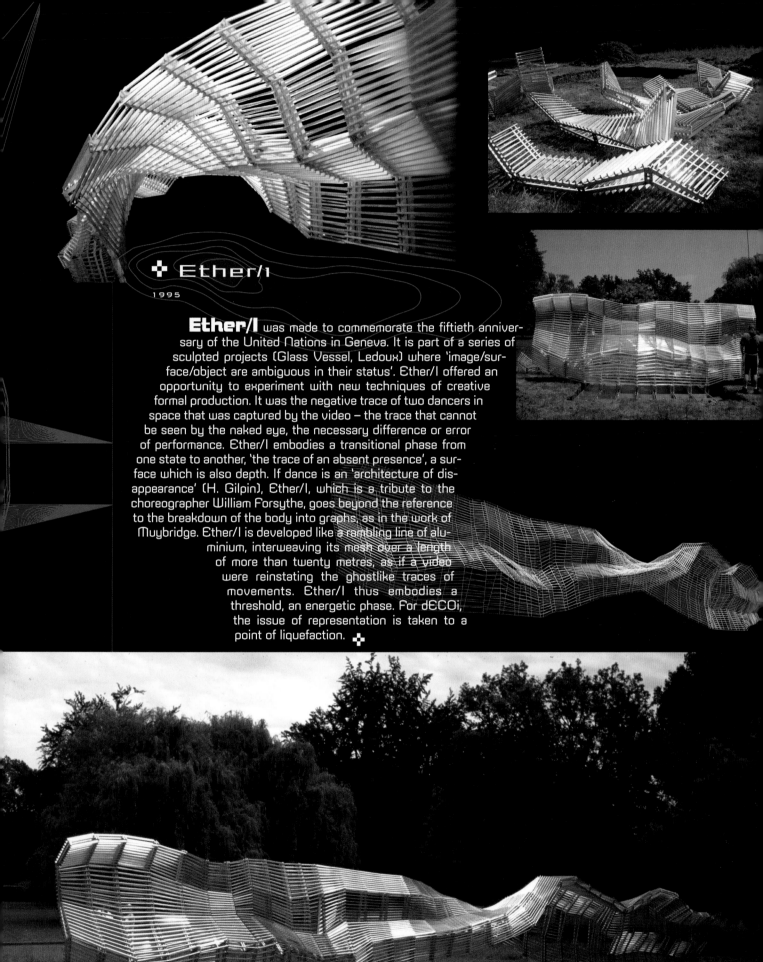

✛ Ether/1

1995

Ether/I was made to commemorate the fiftieth anniversary of the United Nations in Geneva. It is part of a series of sculpted projects (Glass Vessel, Ledoux) where 'image/surface/object are ambiguous in their status'. Ether/I offered an opportunity to experiment with new techniques of creative formal production. It was the negative trace of two dancers in space that was captured by the video — the trace that cannot be seen by the naked eye, the necessary difference or error of performance. Ether/I embodies a transitional phase from one state to another, 'the trace of an absent presence', a surface which is also depth. If dance is an 'architecture of disappearance' (H. Gilpin), Ether/I, which is a tribute to the choreographer William Forsythe, goes beyond the reference to the breakdown of the body into graphs, as in the work of Muybridge. Ether/I is developed like a rambling line of aluminium, interweaving its mesh over a length of more than twenty metres, as if a video were reinstating the ghostlike traces of movements. Ether/I thus embodies a threshold, an energetic phase. For dECOi, the issue of representation is taken to a point of liquefaction. ✛

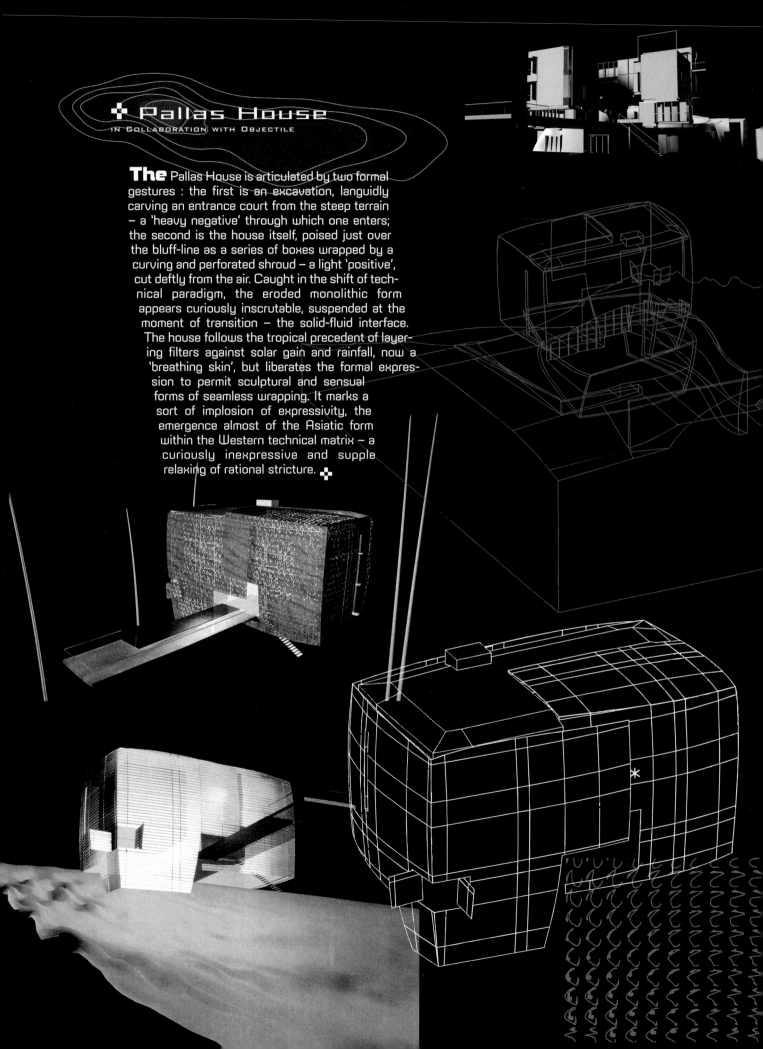

✦ Pallas House

IN COLLABORATION WITH OBJECTILE

The Pallas House is articulated by two formal gestures : the first is an excavation, languidly carving an entrance court from the steep terrain – a 'heavy negative' through which one enters; the second is the house itself, poised just over the bluff-line as a series of boxes wrapped by a curving and perforated shroud – a light 'positive', cut deftly from the air. Caught in the shift of technical paradigm, the eroded monolithic form appears curiously inscrutable, suspended at the moment of transition – the solid-fluid interface. The house follows the tropical precedent of layering filters against solar gain and rainfall, now a 'breathing skin', but liberates the formal expression to permit sculptural and sensual forms of seamless wrapping. It marks a sort of implosion of expressivity, the emergence almost of the Asiatic form within the Western technical matrix – a curiously inexpressive and supple relaxing of rational stricture. ✦

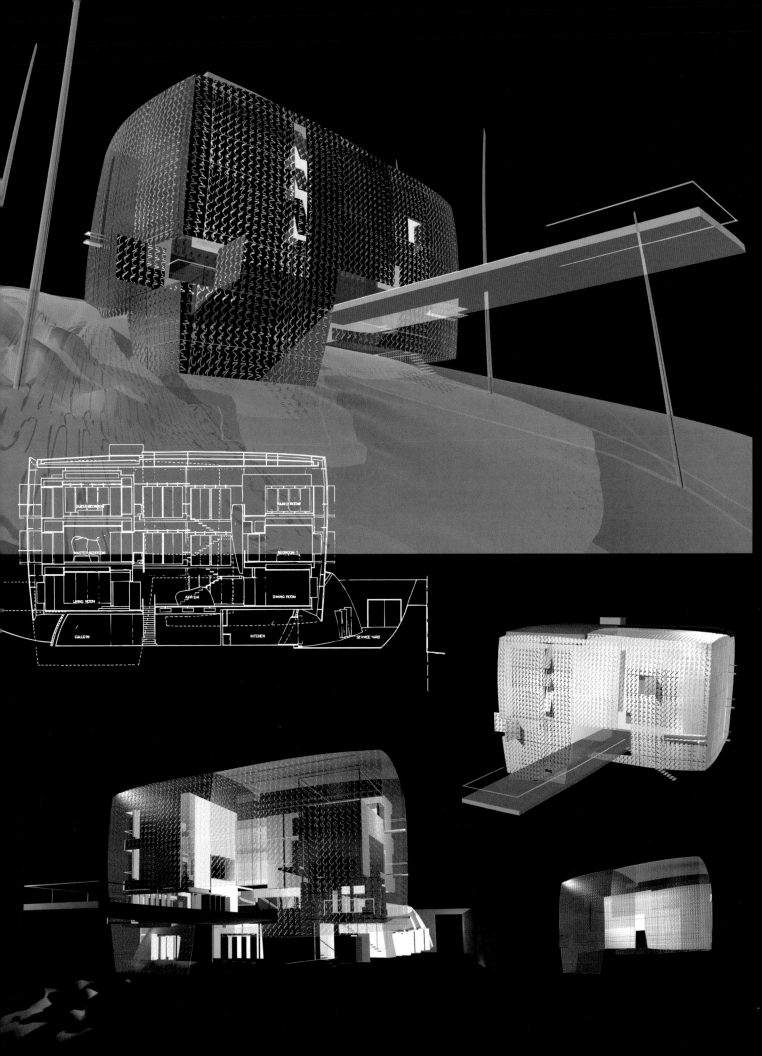

✦ ECO Taal
Ecological Centre
TAGAYTAY-TAAL, PHILIPPINES, 1997

ECO Taal was designed as the key element of a complex situated within the crater of the Taal volcano in the Philippines. This project is a response to what seemed to be the implicit challenge of this study: 'To develop a form that would disappear into the site, but which would remain clear in the mind – a kind of psychological involution'. Set on a steep, wooded slope, the project is like a carapace, a sort of swelling of the surface, giving the slope back its form, which is interrupted by the programme units (lecture and exhibition halls). Resembling an articulated coat of armour, the project is made up of disjointed leaves or slats which are distorted, slide and bend to the contour of the slope, offering a minimal presence in the site by being placed as close as possible to it, like a skin. Inside, the other side of the carapace is streaked with rays of changing light created by the disjointedness of the leaves. As a result, the vaults formed by these leaves are distorted, conveying the surprising experience of a curved space with an unexpected and changeable feel to it. ✦

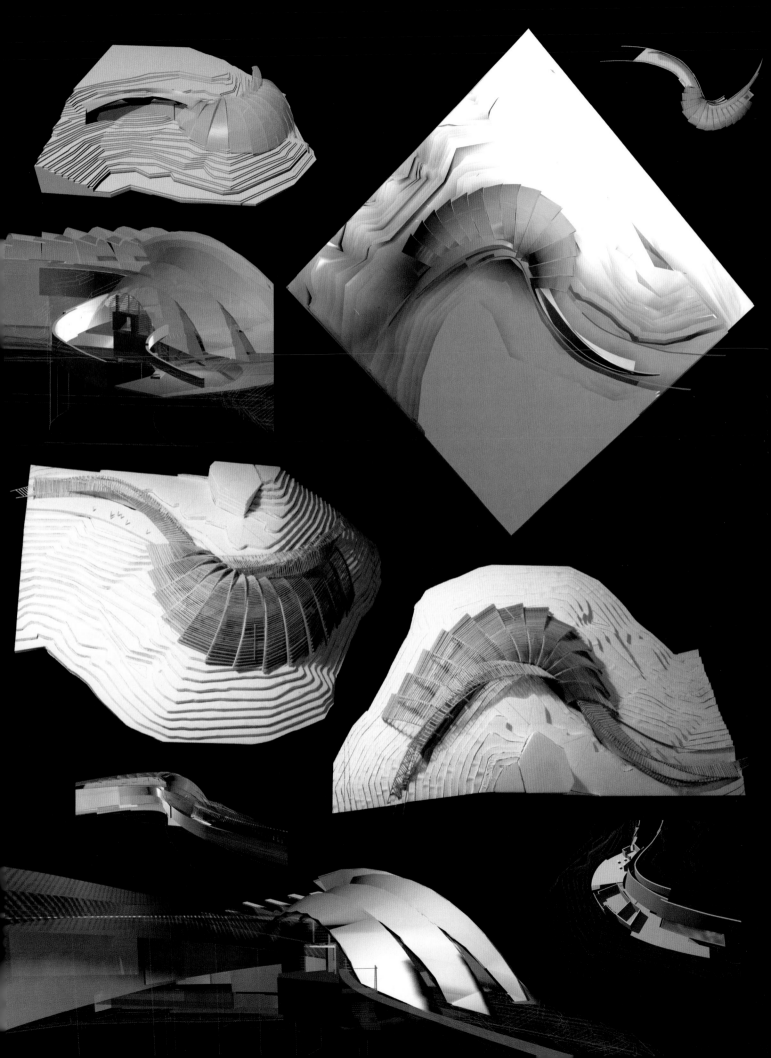

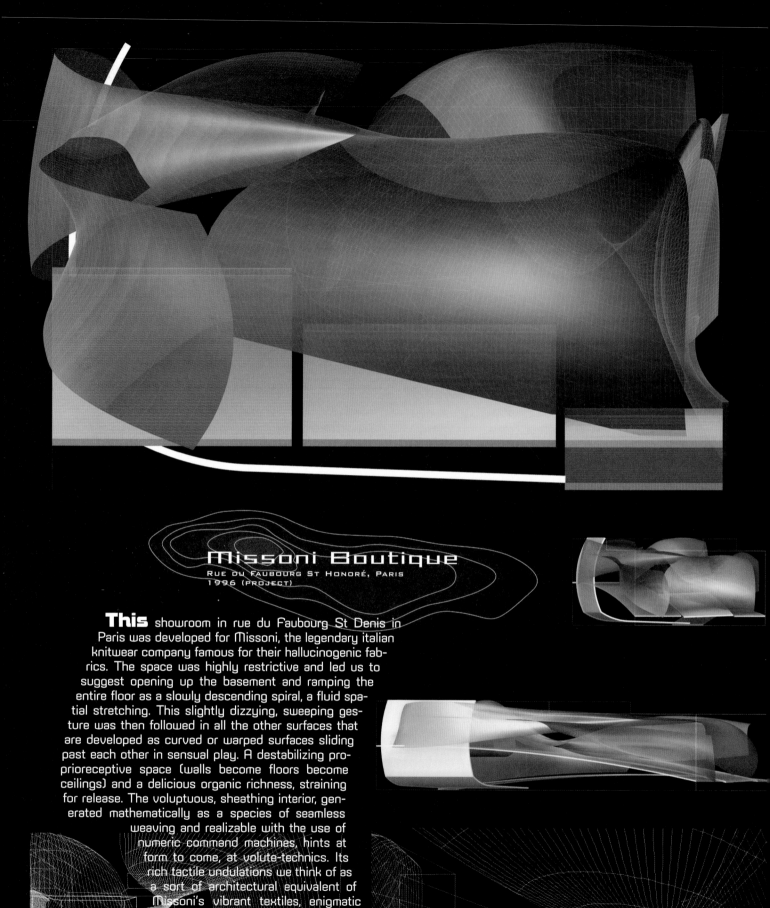

Missoni Boutique
RUE DU FAUBOURG ST HONORÉ, PARIS
1996 (PROJECT)

This showroom in rue du Faubourg St Denis in Paris was developed for Missoni, the legendary italian knitwear company famous for their hallucinogenic fabrics. The space was highly restrictive and led us to suggest opening up the basement and ramping the entire floor as a slowly descending spiral, a fluid spatial stretching. This slightly dizzying, sweeping gesture was then followed in all the other surfaces that are developed as curved or warped surfaces sliding past each other in sensual play. A destabilizing proprioceptive space (walls become floors become ceilings) and a delicious organic richness, straining for release. The voluptuous, sheathing interior, generated mathematically as a species of seamless weaving and realizable with the use of numeric command machines, hints at form to come, at volute-technics. Its rich tactile undulations we think of as a sort of architectural equivalent of Missoni's vibrant textiles, enigmatic and spontaneous combinations just glimpsed as traces in the gaps. ✦

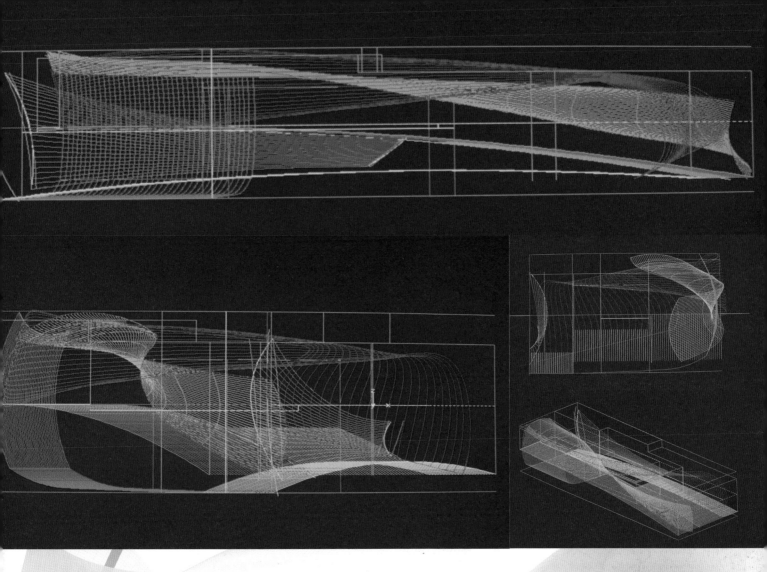

✦ dECOi

Mark Goulthorpe (1963)
1988   Diploma from the University of Liverpool (UK)

Yee Pin Tan (1962)

Zainie Zainoul (until 1996)
1991   Founded the practice at Paris; Royal Academy Award
1993   *Les Albums de la jeune architecture*, France
1996   Venice Biennale, French Pavilion, Italy; 'Architects on the Horizon', *AD Journal*, RIBA, London

Teaching
Mark Goulthorpe
1999–98 University of Kassel, Germany
1996–94 Architectural Association, London

Principal buildings and projects
1998   Luschwitz House, London (project); Gateshead Regional Music Centre, Gateshead, Tyneside (UK), and SwissRe Headquarters, Baltic Exchange Site, London (two technical and architectural studies for Sir Norman Foster); Hystera Protera, graphics
1997   Balai Taal Retreat, ECO Taal Ecology Centre, Tagaytay-Taal, Philippines (project); Yat Lye Showroom, Singapore (project)
1996   Pallas House, Kuala Lumpur, Malaysia (project); Missoni Showroom, Paris (project); Schlaff Apnia, set design for 'Sleepers Gut' by the Frankfurt Ballet; twenty holiday homes, Seremban, Malaysia (project)
1995   Nara/Toto World Architecture Triennale, Nara, Japan (grand prize); Museum of Korean Art, Los Angeles (competition); 'Ether/I' (sculpture)
1994   'Tour of Glasgow', Glasgow, UK (prizewinner)
1993   Law Courts, Reykjavik, Iceland (competition); 'Dans l'Ombre de Ledoux' (sculpture)
1992   Toto World Architecture Triennale, Nara, Japan (third prize); 'The most beautiful house in the world', Reggio Emilia, Italy (second Prize)
1991   Europan II: housing competition, Rhodes, Greece (first prize); Cultural Centre, Glasgow (special prize); 'Another glass house', Shinkenchiku-sha, Tokyo, Japan (first prize)

Recent exhibitions
1998   'Conference Any Time', Ankara, Turkey; 'TransArchitectures', Brussels, Berlin, New York, Tokyo; 'Smectic State', Melbourne, Australia
1995   Architectural Association, London
1994   '2020 Architecture Forum', Liverpool

Selected bibliography
1999   (in preparation): Exposé, 'La Maison, vol. 2', HYX; *Hybrid Space: New Forms in Digital Architecture*, Thames & Hudson, London; *Architectural Design*, 'The Contemporary House'
1998   *Pacific Edge: Contemporary Pacific-Rim Architecture* Thames & Hudson, London; *Paca Catalogue: Public Art Commissions Agency Ten-year Book*, PACA; *Monument* (June), Australia
1997   *ANY* (June), USA
1996   *A + U* (October), Japan; *Architectural Design* (August); *Bloc, le monolithe fracturé* catalogue of the Venice Biennale, HYX; *World Architecture* (May) UK; *Blue Print* (February), UK
1995   *Interstices*, New Zealand
1994   *Techniques & Architectures* (October), France; *A + U* (September), Germany
1993   *MODO* (October), Italy; *d'Architectures* (November), France; *Techniques & Architectures* (August), FranceZ

Décosterd & Rahm

| Jean-Gilles Décosterd (*1963) | Philippe Rahm (*1967) |

Like G.W.F. Hegel, we put architecture on the lowest rung of the world, in matter and gravity, below climatic variations and the passage of time, involved in physical, chemical, biological and electromagnetic relations with the environment and our body. An architecture of immanence, which accepts its material standing, its interdependence with external conditions as a modality. Our works are developing in this physical realm where architecture, at the outset, is nothing other than a Nietzschean struggle between a human desire for energetic growth and structural maintenance, on the one hand, and the external environment, which reduces, degrades and breaks up, on the other. We accommodate with interest these physical encounters, because in them we discover the fertility of ecological sequences, the variety of forms of causality, symbioses and biological predation, a tremendous expanding field with its own powerful behavioural patterns, capable of creating forms independently of the mind and semantic and visual tools. We are thus reassessing those factors of architecture represented by materials, structure, space and light, depending on their physical actions. We are examining and working on the physical, biological, electromagnetic and chemical impacts and exchanges between architecture, the environment and our organism. Matter is no longer restricted to a static and symbolic dimension, but involved in physical and chemical modifications with the exterior in the form of erosion, putrefaction and fermentation, and it takes on an alimentary value. Space is no longer empty, but defined like a certain amount of chemically constituted air, in which we are physiologically immersed by respiration and perspiration as much as materials are by oxidization. Likewise, light takes on an energetic dimension, through the thermal capacity of infrared rays, through chlorophyll photosynthesis, through the regulation of biological and hormonal rhythms. Our projects work like systems, identifying components, programming exchanges and making transformations possible. They proceed by way of emissions of information and energy expenditure, they recover and recycle, chemically altering the environment and electrically stimulating the human being. They are living entries into the physical world, a desire to understand the construction of forms and climates in accordance with the quantifiable reality of the concrete world. Our architecture is accepted as a living environment that goes beyond its sole status of aesthetic figure and political mediation. Our intent is to understand and work with real physiological mechanisms, very akin to present-day scientific and medical knowledge. These metabolic and ecological mechanisms might appear like a sort of fourth dimension of architecture, invisible and energetic, an architecture of particles making it possible to act in a tangible way in the world and produce real physical environments, open to life and to future developments. ✦

DÉCOSTERD & RAHM ASSOCIÉS

Suprachiasmatic nucleus

Optic chiasma

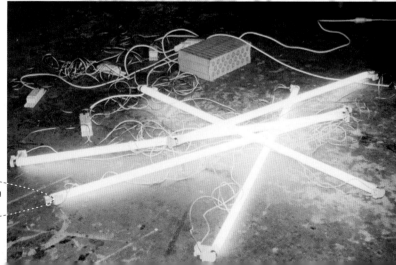

electromagetic field

1999

✛ Melatonin Room

2000

Melatonin Room is a physiological architecture that acts on the space itself by transforming its electromagnetic make-up. This room is defined as a space of hormonal stimulation. Two climates are produced, turn by turn. The first is defined by the emission of an electromagnetic radiation at 509 nm, at an intensity of 2000 lux, which eliminates the production of melatonin by the pineal gland. When secreted, this hormone provides information associated with tiredness and sleep. The space becomes a physically motivating place, which is also chemically stimulating. The second climate is a dissemination of ultraviolet rays, which, by contrast, stimulate the production of melatonin. Melatonin Room is a space without representation, which reduces to a maximum the medium between the emitter and the receptor, and acts on the chemical mechanisms of things between each other. It works on the new forms of communication created by the biotechnologies and by genetics, together with the analogical, the poetic, the aesthetic and the rhetorical. ✛

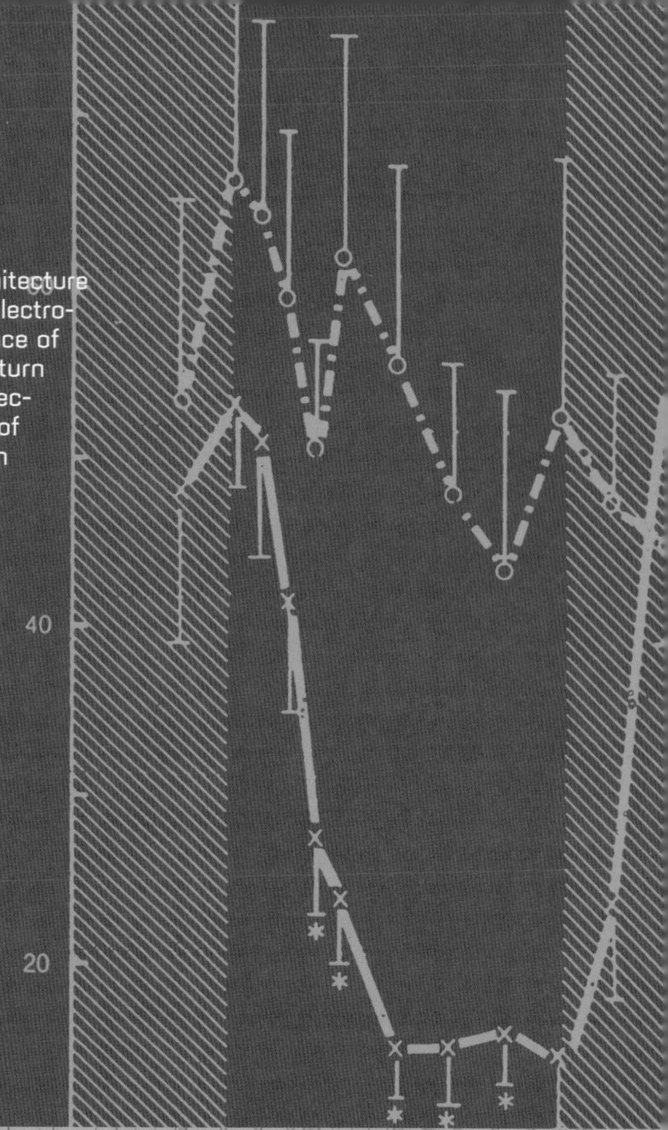

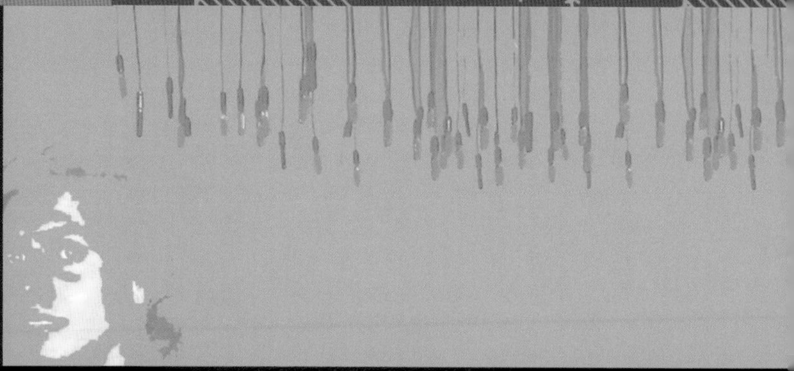

MELATONIN ROOM

MELATONIN ROOM

✦ Nomadic Dwellings

FOR ARTISTS ON THE COASTAL CONSERVATION AREAS OF
LANGUEDOC-ROUSSILLON, FRANCE, 1998
WITH GILLES CLÉMENT AND MICHEL AUBRY

Between the leather coat we wear and the piece of meat we eat, the habitat is made of cow hides, removed by knives, duly cleaned of flesh, immediately salted and folded, until they are laid over a self-tensioning kind of structure. The hairy side is innermost, forming an insulating climatic thickness between the grain of the leather and the flax of the interior finish. The flesh is outermost. The hides are constantly in a precarious state of equilibrium between what is liable to become putrid and what is not. Salt, against which people have battled on these seashores in their attempt to introduce farming, now becomes an ally in the maintenance of the inhabitable space in the form of temporary tanning. Revealed here, in an alimentary way, is the ceaseless energy exchange between man and his environment through architecture as parasitism and symbiosis. The habitat is placed on a field of Salicornia, like a link in the carbon cycle, accommodating the salty winds by frequently requiring an additional input of salt. As such, it remains a possible nutritive factor for wildlife and microorganisms, which pounce on it as soon as the inhabitant goes away. ✦

✚ Expo.01

DESIGN FOR THE ARTEPLAGE AT NEUCHÂTEL,
SWITZERLAND, 1998/1999
WITH MICHEL DESVIGNES AND YANN KERSALÉ

Décosterd & Rahm see the tension between Nature and Artifice as the gauge of the amount of energy expended to modify prior physical, chemical and biological conditions. Their architecture is set at this initial level of understanding of the world, ahead of cultural and symbolic forms. The Arteplage is organized around a luminous progression from the visible to the invisible. With a white light they impoverish the light spectrum by gradually getting rid of the shortest wavelengths until they come up to monochromatic purple light. They proceed into the invisible, as far as UVCs, and join up with infrared rays. In the invisible, an inner physiological relationship is set up between body and space, a medical relationship in which fermentation of vitamin D and an enzyme is stimulated, a dilatation of the blood vessels causing antigens to mobilize. Ultraviolet germicidal lights disinfect and purify the air. The space that was thought to be empty is presented as an invisible but physical environment, at once curative and harmful. ✚

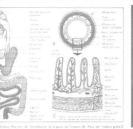
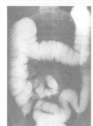
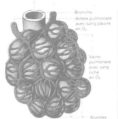

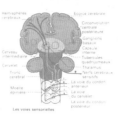
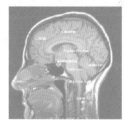

"DANS LA PEAU"
toucher

✤ Physiological Gardens

LA NEUVEVILLE, SWITZERLAND, 2000
COMPETITION WITH JÉRÔME JACQMIN

The gardens of Jean-Gilles Décosterd & Philippe Rahm deal with the senses, but with a knowledge of the chemical and medicinal interplays between the organism and the active substances of plants. They see the garden as a place where the body is plunged into the body of nature, to a point where the metabolism is altered and the chemistry of the organism is changed, giving rise to physiological interactions between plant and body, from the mouth to the stomach, from the skin to the blood, and from the nose to the brain. First garden: epidermis versus limbo, an itinerary among the softness of willow seeds to the Berce du Caucase involves ongoing phototoxic reactions. Second garden: from scents of roses that you inhale to Ambrosia and the risks of allergy it entails. Third garden: eat, with pleasure at first, sugar-sweet strawberries, then lose the flavour to belladonna, which causes tachycardia and urine retention. Fourth and last itinerary, which is almost psychic: between soothing plants such as verbena and giant hemlock, which causes cessation of breathing and asphyxia. ✤

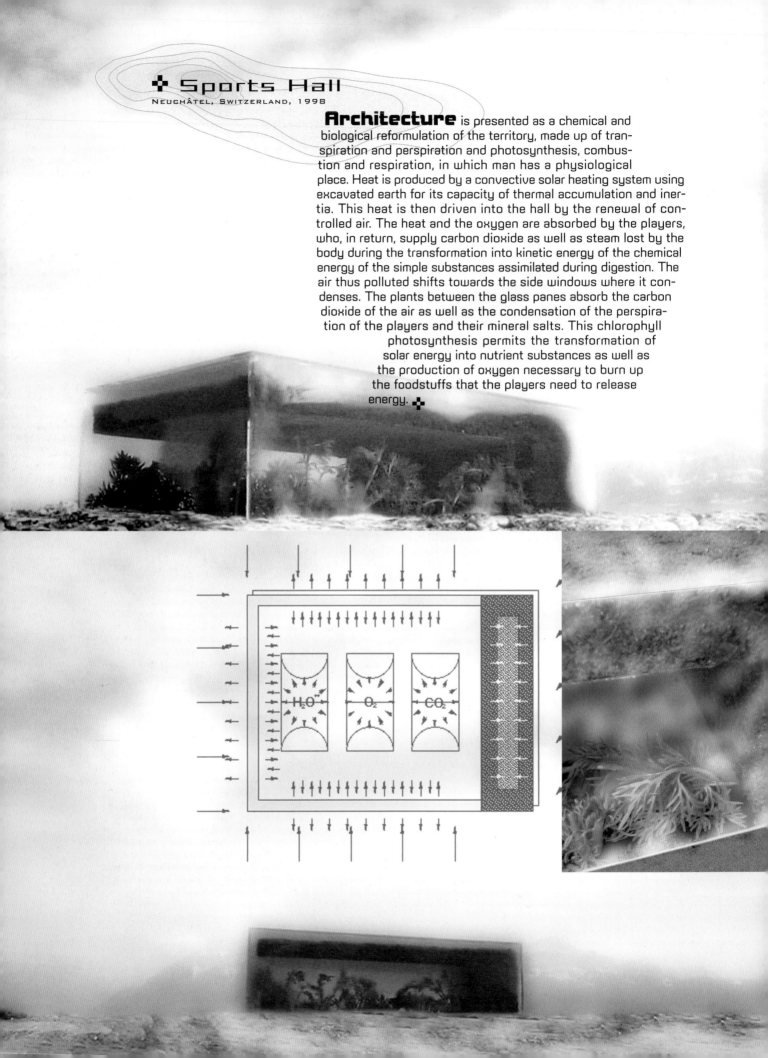

✦ Sports Hall
NEUCHÂTEL, SWITZERLAND, 1998

Architecture is presented as a chemical and biological reformulation of the territory, made up of transpiration and perspiration and photosynthesis, combustion and respiration, in which man has a physiological place. Heat is produced by a convective solar heating system using excavated earth for its capacity of thermal accumulation and inertia. This heat is then driven into the hall by the renewal of controlled air. The heat and the oxygen are absorbed by the players, who, in return, supply carbon dioxide as well as steam lost by the body during the transformation into kinetic energy of the chemical energy of the simple substances assimilated during digestion. The air thus polluted shifts towards the side windows where it condenses. The plants between the glass panes absorb the carbon dioxide of the air as well as the condensation of the perspiration of the players and their mineral salts. This chlorophyll photosynthesis permits the transformation of solar energy into nutrient substances as well as the production of oxygen necessary to burn up the foodstuffs that the players need to release energy. ✦

✦ Décosterd & Rahm, associés

Philippe Rahm (1967)
Jean-Gilles Décosterd (1963)
1993   Diplomas from the Ecole Polytechnique Fédérale de Lausanne

1993   Creation of Décosterd & Rahm, associés (Lausanne)

Principal buildings and projects
2000   A vaccination centre at Roundup, Lausanne jardins 2000 (completion summer 2000); Physiological Gardems, with Jérôme Jacqmin, Château de La Neuveville (second prize); 'Melatonin room' installation
1999   'The power of flowers', with Alternet Fabric, Lausanne Jardins 2000 (commercial competition); 'Dynamogénie' EPSIC Building, Lausanne (prizewinner first round); Expo '01, Arteplage de Neuchâtel, with Michel Desvignes, Yann Kersalé (selected project); 'Campement électromagnétique', installation, 'Open air' exhibition, galerie Chez Valentin, Paris
1998   Nomadic housing on the coastal conservation land, Sérignan, with Gilles Clément and Michel Aubry (project); 'Erodable money' festival Belluard Bollwerk International, Fribourg (realized); 'Heat' intervention for Neuchâtel archaeology museum at Neul (selected); 'Sport hall' Neuchâtel (project)
1997   Wild garden at Rôtillon, Lausanne Jardins 97 (realized); 'Cooked fields' rearrangement of the centre of Saint-Sulpice (prizewinner); 'Cadastral survey of cracks' Lausanne (special prize)
1996   VIP bar, Geneva-Arena (realized); House at Montreux transformation (realized); Shopping City-Disc, Lausanne (realized); Geological concrete, with Jean-Claude Deschamps, Uni-Dufour, Geneva (commercial competition); arrangement of a pedestrian zone, Bienne (project)
1995   'The lowest' Centre for Secondary Teaching, Morges, with Keller++Weber (mentioned); Nescafé bar, Geneva-Arena (realized); 'The natural contract' Place du Château-Lausanne for Mondada SA (mentioned); Concept for countryside and plantings at Cour-Lausanne, with W. W. Nossek (project)

1994   'The accursed child, a prefabricated garage, is that architecture?' Competition 'BTR/Prebéton' (prizewinner)
1993   'Some communal places', artistic intervention, Bellerives-Lausanne (first purchase)

Principal publications
1999   'The Chemical Lovers' *Parpaings*, Paris; *Elisabeth Creveseur* catalogue, Vidéos 1993-1999, MAC, Marseilles; 'Une architecture de l'immanence' *Inter* no. 72, Montréal
1998   'Les natures en ville' *Anthos* no. 1, rural review, Molondin; 'Soigner et construire, tel est le bâtir' *Quaderns* no. 220; 'Sous les pavés, l'herbe' *l'Architecture d'aujourd'hui* no. 317; 'Seconde genèse' exhibition catalogue of 'Mutations @morphes, R.DSV & Sie.P' FRAC Centre, Orléans
1997   'Les arbres devraient-ils avoir un statut juridique ?' *Quaderns* no. 217, Barcelona; 'La friche et la ville' *l'Architecture d'aujourd'hui* (Sept.); 'Gilles Clément, Traité succinct de l'art involontaire' *Art Press* no. 226
1996   'Sur le sol du monde sensible' *Art Press* no. 213; 'Roche DSV & Sie au Magasin, Grenoble' *l'Architecture d'aujourd'hui* (June)

Selected bibliography
2000   'Soleil Vert' *Parpaings* no. 12, Paris; 'Jardins 2000' *IAS* no. 05
1998   'Lausanne Jardins, une envie de ville heureuse' Péribole, Ecole Nationale Supérieure du Paysage de Versailles; *Inter* no. 69, Montréal
1997   *Architecture Suisse* no. 127, Lausanne; *Quaderns* nos 214 and 217, Barcelona; *Archimade* no. 55, Lausanne

Neil M. Denari Architects

| Neil Denari [*1957] |

During the last quarter century, forms of urbanization that emphasize the *terrain vague* of horizontal conditions have mirrored the decentralized structures of information industries. My home region, the Dallas Fort Worth area, is known as the Metroplex, a word invented to describe the phenomenon of the complex metropolitan environment. This region exemplifies how the technological landscapes of this time have come to embody the late-twentieth-century concept of what J.G. Ballard has called the unlimited possibility: desire × ingenuity = America. This is the cultural and physical landscape that forms the basis of my own developing identity. It is at once global in its implications and specific in its milieu. From 1983 to 1992 my work argued for relevance via an autobiographical positioning of ideas. Since 1992 my interest has shifted from the narrowly focused machine reference to the broad and open possibilities of cultural conditions not yet coded with an architectural symbol. I have recognized that a continuous series of cross sections must be cut through the global cultural structures that have come to dominate our contemporary lives so that the progress, ambivalence, possibilities and shifts recorded in these slices may inform my work. Indeed, if there is a self-consciousness to this work, it is based on movement, so that its plane of consistency is not secretly a box that limits. In cinema, even when Yasujiro Ozu's camera doesn't move (a technique we could call a limited box), the images multiply, an affect is generated. What is important is that the anomalies of movement become the essential point instead of being accidental or contingent. Since the early 1990s I have begun to understand how the popularity of technoscientific discourse and application has sponsored issues ranging from the crises of identity loss (due to homogenization) to the production of new and emergent cultural groups found in digital fields. It is impossible, therefore, for me to conceive of a relevant discourse in architecture that does not argue its presence through the pathways of culture. Here, culture has two forms. One is an apparition, like quicksand, a mirage or a blob, offering us an image that shifts, disappears or changes its shape instantly. Like a drunk walking in an earthquake, sometimes we do not notice the undulation of movement. The second form is a ferocious beast, consuming us at every turn. These twin phenomena of culture have come to mirror the logic of my work, which is built on the idea that the ambivalent fields of repetitive and processed spaces and the traditional desire to produce difference (the expressive *auteur*) exist together as a productive cultural condition. It acknowledges the forces (fatal, hegemonic or otherwise) that coordinate to both limit and open up the possible ways in which architecture can become simultaneously an extrapolator and a producer of culture. ✦

Tokyo International Forum (project)
Model, 1992
Free Centre Collection

Details Design Studio

NEW YORK, USA
1990-93

Originally commissioned in 1990 by a new division of Steelcase, this project is the result of five schemes developed over a three-year period. The company named Details asked for a 'wall' that would divide a large loft space in Soho downtown New York into two distinct spaces each of which would have a different but related function. One space is defined as clerical, the other as a design studio. The function of the wall, beyond its own properties of bisection, serves as a storage for books and prototypes, and one end houses a work table underneath the fiberglass skin. The project operates as an information cypher or vapour trail which passes through the space becoming reified in form within the room itself. The room, however, is considered to be insignificant and only serves to cut the information vapour that is wafting through the entire Euclidean matrix of Manhattan. The wall, therefore, is not site-driven and accommodates entry by merely making functional cuts into the white skin. ✛

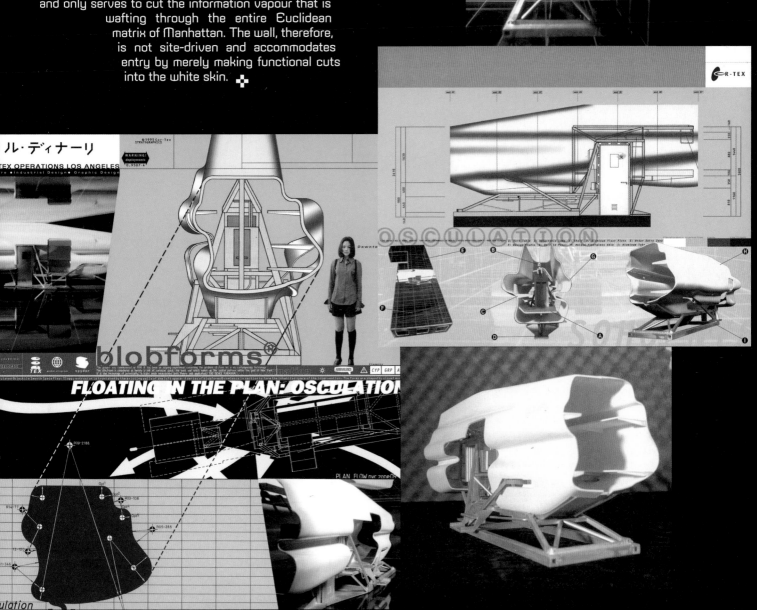

FLOATING IN THE PLAN: OSCULATION

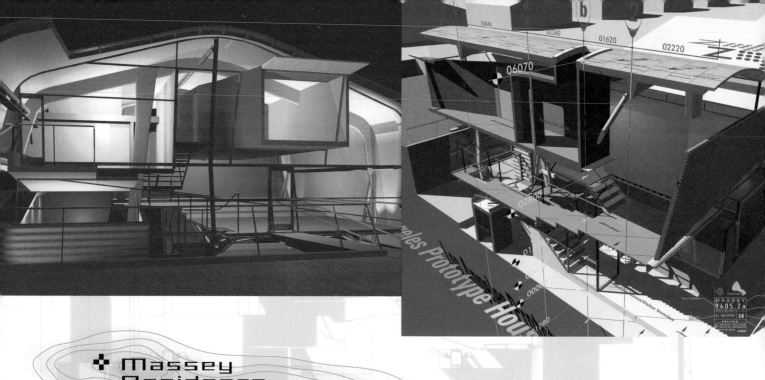

✦ Massey Residence
LOS ANGELES, USA
1995

This house is located on a typical sized L.A. site: 15 by 15 metres. It is the client's wish to explore the basic conditions of the North American suburban subdivision through a typical flat site and a typical programme of three bedrooms and two bathrooms. However, the house itself, though accommodating these ordinary factors, should be extraordinary. Like many smaller multi-unit apartment buildings in Los Angeles, this house has one level below ground and two above, thus disguising its size. The experience and concept of the house are about the section cut. The front and rear elevations show the roof skin and the basic extruded form of the overall volume. Inside, the circulation space revolves around a staircase, which connects seven different half-levels. This house sits as an ambivalent figure, committed to the preservation of site typology while internally engaging in an extreme criticism of architectural similitudes. ✦

main structural beams

intermediate glazing structure

MASSEY
9405 2a

X-RAY

△ geometry

CHLORINATED AIR

HALOGEN BUZZ

SEY RESIDENCE. @ (W) LOS ANGELES, CA. › © 1995 COR-TEX / NEIL M. DENARI, ARCHITECT
PUTER MODELING by.› ANDREW WAISLER / PROPELLERHEAD DESIGN

SLIPSTREA

04040

02340

01620

01220

Master Bedroom/Body Group

02800

01370

00630

00000

-01380

1995
R-TEX
RATOGRAPHICS

blobs, inc.

RROR VACUI PRODUCTIONS

-02600

∞
systems

✦ Kansai-Kan National Library

KANSAI, JAPAN
1996

In an era of the rise in digital communications systems, the scheme reasserts the power of architectural space. Given that the site allows distant views across it, a building of expressive potential was possible. Therefore, the temptations to make the building 'disappear' (underground) or become urbanized (as a wall to the street) were not explored. That the building would itself be a diagram of certain forms of contemporary knowledge was the only option as a reaction to an implicit privatization. The scheme breaks down into three parts, which function as both discrete and integrated elements. The entire stack programme is located within a concrete box on the southern edge of the site. As the site slopes up from north to south, the stack building is largely submerged into the ground. This building consists of two super-scaled world-sheets that interact to form continuous surfaces that themselves intersect with the matrix of floor plates and columnar systems of structure. ✦

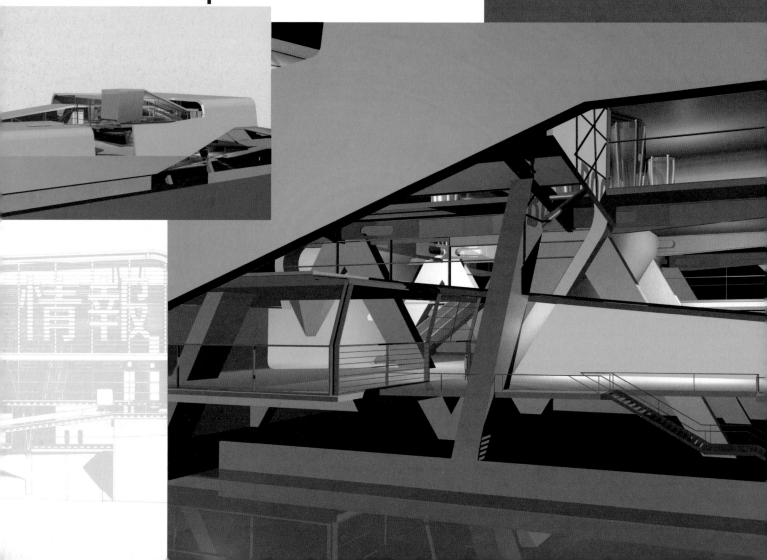

✚ Gallery MA

TOKYO, JAPAN
1996

Gallery MA in Tokyo is a space devoted to exhibiting architecture and related design. On the third level, an external quasi-Zen garden bounded by concrete walls cuts the floors above in half, creating an L-shaped building mass. A glass membrane divides the interior space from the garden and allows total visual invasion. The programme for the project was an experimental space. The design scheme for Gallery MA is developed from the Homolosine Interrupted map projection. The origin of the world map is a sheet on which to record territories. The Homolosine Projection depicts the world in a series of sheared ellipses; thus the green surface inside Gallery MA is an interrupted projection, as it deploys a flattened and empty global surface to form space. The surface bends and loops to form a three-dimensionally smooth yet complex geometry capable of merging with the graphically logoized world of visual codes and conventional signs. This is the 'world-sheet'. ✚

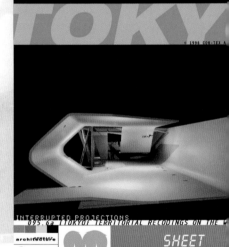

✦ Neil M Denari Architects

Neil M. Denari (1957)

1980 B.Arch., University of Houston
1982 Master if Architecture, Harvard University

1988 Studio Cor-Tex (called Neil M. Denari Architects since 1998) founded in Los Angeles

Teaching

1999–97 Dirige Southern California Inst. of Architecture (SCI-Arc) Los Angeles
1996–88 SCI-Arc, Los Angeles
1995 Columbia University, New York
1995–93 University of Texas, Arlington
1994 Bartlett School, University College of London
1992–90 Shibaura Institute of Technology, Tokyo

Principal buildings and projects

1996 Arlington (Texas) Museum of Art; 'Galerie MA', Tokyo; 'Kansaï-Kan of the National Diet Library' Japan (competition)
1995 Massey Residence (project); Sprawl Connectors LA (project); Orange County Exhibition Center (project)
1994 Yokohama International Port Terminal (competition)
1993 'Central Glass' – Museum of the 20th Century, Tokyo (competition)
1993–92 Tokyo Prototype House (project); Desert Center (project)
1993–90 Details Design Studio (project)
1992 K-Project, Kobe, Japan (competition).
1990 Subway Station, Tokyo (competition).
1989 Tokyo International Forum, (third prize, special mention)
1988 West Coast Gateway, Los Angeles (finalist)
1987 Virginia Townhall, Leesburg (competition); The International Garden and Greenery Exposition, Osaka; Pavillon Mitsui (competition with Teag Nishimoto, second prize)
1986 Young Architect Forum, Architectural League of New York
1984 Shinkenchiku Residential Design, Tokyo

Exhibitions

The designs and models of Neil Denari are in the permanent collections of the following institutions: Cooper Hewitt Museum, New York; San Francisco Museum of Modern Art; FRAC Centre, Orléans, France; Museum of Modern Art, New York; Denver Museum of Art, Colorado; Collection Carnegie/Heinz, Pittsburgh

Publications

1999 *Gyroscopic Horizons*, Princeton Architectural Press/Thames & Hudson, New York/London
1996 *Interrupted Projections*, Toto Publications, Tokyo; 'Recent Work' Bac/Esp Publications, Bangkok, Thailand
1995 'Intransigent Desires', *ANY magazine*, no 10, New York
1992 'Arguments for Paralogical Geometries': *OZ Journal*, no 14, Kansas State University
1987 'The Contexts of the Machine',Projects/Texts. 'Building'; Machines', Pamphlet Architecture, no 12, Princeton Architectural Press, New York

Selecteed bibliography

1998 'Transarchitectures', Nikkei Press, Tokyo; 'Space', Arlington Museum of Art Publications, Arlington, Texas; 'Casa Massey', *Architecti Magazine*, no 42, Lisbon; Zellner, Peter, *Pacific Edge* (Rizzoli/Thames & Hudson, New York/London)
1997 Zellner, Peter, *City of Sorts*, interview, *21C* nagazine, issue 24, Melbourne; Zellner, Peter, 'Gallery MA', *Monument* magazine, Melbourne
1991 'Four Statements on Architecture', Projects/Texts, *A + U* 91: 03 (March), Tokyo; 'Thoughts on Architecture and Education', *Kenchiku Bunka*, April, Tokyo
1988 'Exploding Sonic Test Audio Visual Big Guitar' *OFFRAMP*, SCI-ARC Journal, no 2, Los Angeles; 'The Philosophy of Impossibility', The London Project, exhibition catalogue, Princeton Architectural Press.

Odile Decq & Benoît Cornette

| Odile Decq (*1955) | Benoît Cornette (*1953–98) |

Paul Virilio said to his students that after the time of functionalistic resolution during the first part of the twentieth century in terms of abstract rationalistic solutions, after the time of meeting social needs during the emergence of a new society in the second part of the century in terms of quantitative social solutions, architecture, today, has to answer the question of desire in terms of giving pleasure, but giving an answer to the question of desire is complex. Each answer has to be specific and crucial. Nothing is definitive, every solution is transitory. These notions question the place of the body and the senses in space and architecture. The displacement of the body inside space, the instability generated by movement and the instability that creates movement change our way of perceiving space by all our senses. After the inactivity of the body during the past periods when space was perceived from a static point, we are now in the dynamic period in which the body is unstable, where time and space are perceived as instants, as events instead of permanent. We enter into the nomadic period in which the discontinuity of space and the fracture of time are part of the modern condition. We no longer think of centred space and axes pointing from and to any one observer but in sliding and tangential spaces in intertwining images that create escaping lines, moving perspectives, sequential images where tension is introduced in the assemblage of fading forms. The modern urban space is definitely not the traditional order of the city: the notion of centrality disappears and gives place to movement, to sliding, to a continuous shift of places and activities. Territory is no longer defined by its boundaries but by the network and the connections inside it. Territory is now always polycentric. The displacement inside cities and territories redefines them as a network in continuous flux. We have to discard the old notion of centrality and its reference to an abstract man to think of the world as a place of apparent topological disorder in which new urban forms spread far and wide, represented by continuity in discontinuity, deformations, bifurcations, density and dynamic heterogeneity rather than any neat, measurable system, and we also have to question the spatial stasis and constancy of the urban form in time. We integrate into our thinking the necessity of displacement and movement of the body in space from the beginning. The succession of points of view, which may appear as instability, generates a dynamic vision of space. The variation of perspectives creates a permanent tension and a sensual ambiguity in our perception of space. The sequential articulation of images such as linear distortion constantly displaces and perturbs our point of view. Material, light, texture, colours, as well as forms, shadows, tension, density, procession, transgression, hypertrophy are all the tools to create spaces in which the senses are awake. Architecture and the space it occupies are a realm of constant discovery in which nothing is out of bounds. ✦

ODILE DECQ

Gallery of Honour at the Rugby Stadium
Orléans, 1998

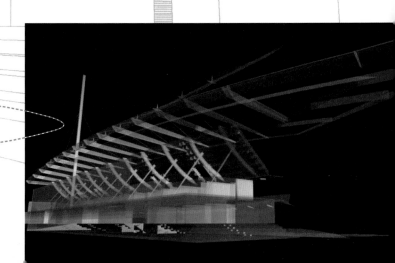

✦ Law Library

NANTES, ERDRE CAMPUS, FRANCE
1998

The Law Library is part of a system of parallel strips, adjacent to the strip that awaits its future extension, and the UFR Economics building and the Human Science Centre, both also designed by Decq and Cornette. This project is thus incorporated in a 'bar code' system which forms a single but fragmented complex, offering a variation on the campus layout, in order to 'finish' the design while dealing with the organization of the different university units and filtering access to the listed woodland. A large reading room, set on three levels, gives on to this woodland area to the south. Its all-glass façade is lined by an awning, which creates a shady entrance gallery built to the same scale as the library. This latter is flanked on the north façade by a service strip, which contains all the vertical traffic and movement, the offices and the technical department. ✦

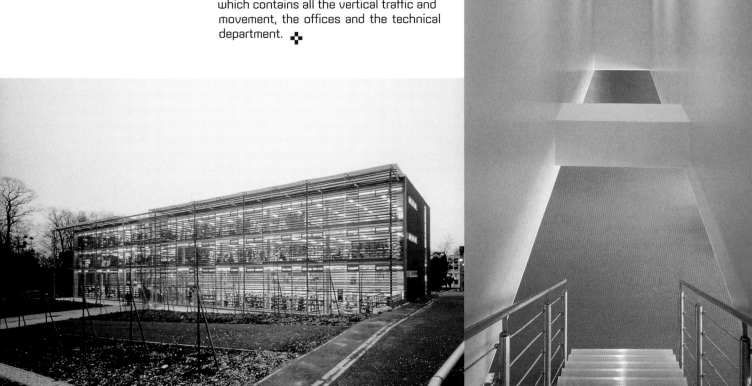

✦ UFR of Economic Sciences

Nantes, Erdre campus, France
1998

The UFR is situated very close to the Law Library, and, with it and the Human Science Centre, forms the same single but fragmented complex. The UFR, which borrows the same length-wise structural layout as the library (7.6 metres), consists of two buildings facing one another and linked by three levels of footbridges. Access to it is by way of a paved courtyard opening on to the Law School. The lecture hall, which occupies the sloping ground and faces the river Erdre, stands between the two wings of the UFR. The main students' entrance is on the north façade, opposite the library entrance. Each of the two UFR wings is devoted to a precise function: teaching for the wider south wing; research and administration for the narrower north wing. The halls, set on four levels, offer framed views over the forest and the river Erdre. ✦

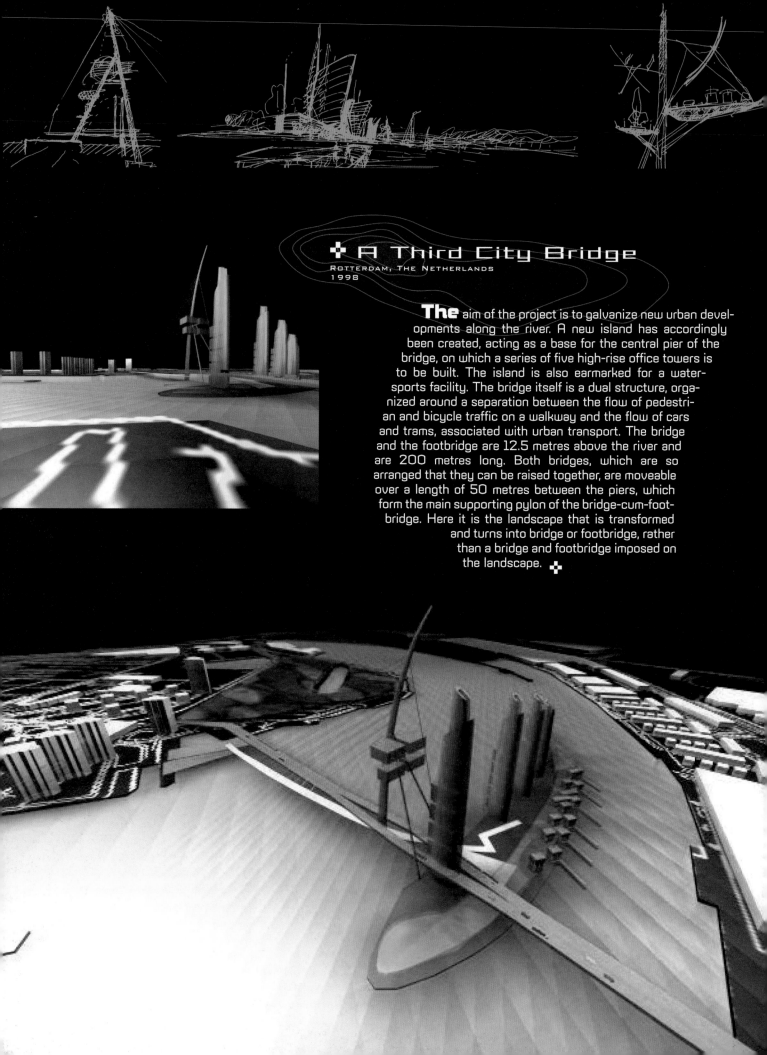

✦ A Third City Bridge

ROTTERDAM, THE NETHERLANDS
1998

The aim of the project is to galvanize new urban developments along the river. A new island has accordingly been created, acting as a base for the central pier of the bridge, on which a series of five high-rise office towers is to be built. The island is also earmarked for a water-sports facility. The bridge itself is a dual structure, organized around a separation between the flow of pedestrian and bicycle traffic on a walkway and the flow of cars and trams, associated with urban transport. The bridge and the footbridge are 12.5 metres above the river and are 200 metres long. Both bridges, which are so arranged that they can be raised together, are moveable over a length of 50 metres between the piers, which form the main supporting pylon of the bridge-cum-footbridge. Here it is the landscape that is transformed and turns into bridge or footbridge, rather than a bridge and footbridge imposed on the landscape. ✦

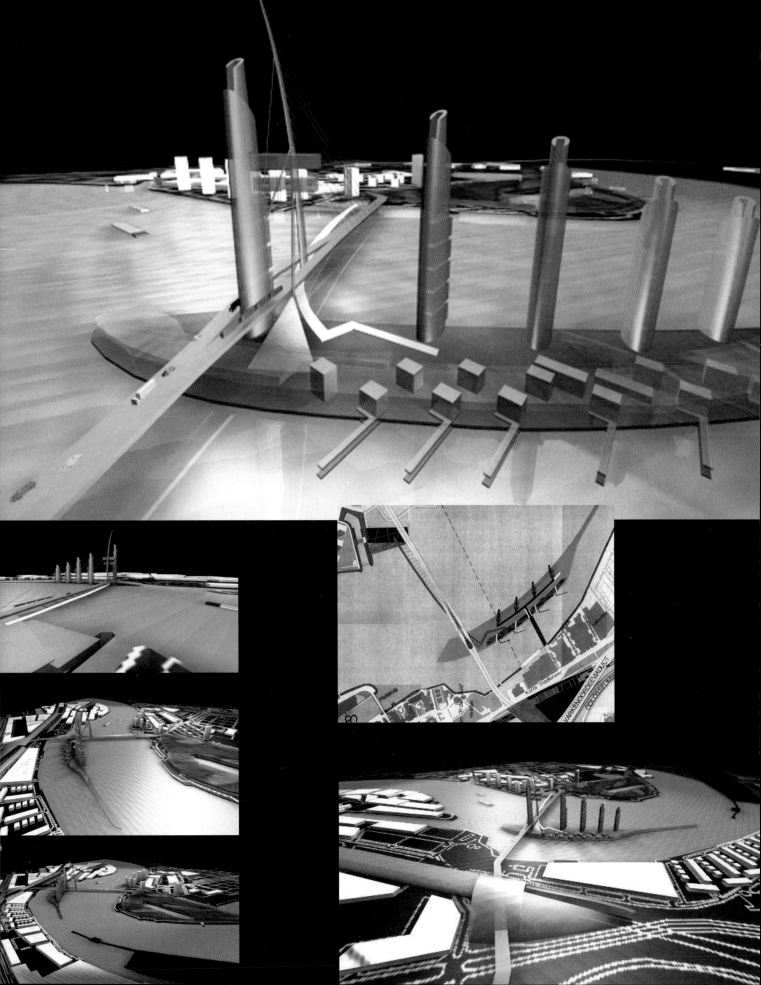

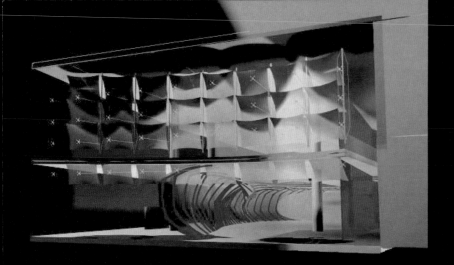

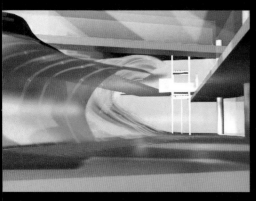

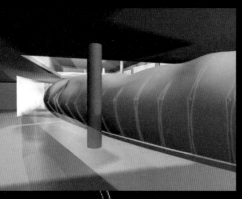

✦ Pub Renault

PARIS
1998

In the Pub Renault redevelopment project, the whole façade is designed like a James Turrell installation, which spreads light over its entire surface. It is a depth to be passed through in order to enter the place. The form is transformed according to its users' requirements, which are based on a limited number of predefined features that make up the spatial components: an active membrane – a fluid surface whose articulated arced structure – that provides configurations of flexible spaces that support different types of stretched skin (translucent, opaque, white and coloured); the sensitive sheets; sets of flat screens creating varied and extended spaces which can be changed at will; and the communication hub, a permanent platform for TV and radio events that is also the modular stage at the heart of performances and shows. Each one of the elements, itself made up of several elements, is transformable and moveable. ✦

✚ Odile Decq & Benoît Cornette

Odile Decq (1955)
1978 Diploma from the Ecole d'Architecture de Paris-La Villette
1979 DESS, City Planning and Design, Institut d'Etudes Politiques de Paris; Chevalier of the Order of Arts and Letters; Member of the Academy of Architecture

Benoît Cornette (1953-1998)
1971–77 Studies in medicine, Faculty of Rennes
1985 Diploma from the Ecole d'Architecture de Paris-La Villette; Chevalier of the Order of Arts and Letters

1985 Founded the practice in Paris
1986 Albums de la Jeune Architecture
1990 9th International Prize for Architecture
1994 Benedictus Awards, Washington DC
1996 Lion d'Or, Venice Biennale, VIth Mostra Internazionale di Architettura

Teaching
Odile Decq
1999–92 Ecole Spéciale d'Architecture, Paris
1992 Visiting professor at the University of Montreal
1998 T.U. Vienna
1986–84 Ecole d'Architecture de Paris-La Villette

Benoît Cornette
1998–97 Workshop at Paris Kansas University
1993–92 Ecole Spéciale d'Architecture

Principal buildings and projects
1999 Design of the Port of Gennevilliers for the Paris Autonomous Port (under construction); cinema complex, library, videotheque, mediatheque, brasserie, restaurant, studios and administration at Cambridge, UK; Saint-Gobain Recherche at Aubervilliers; A new restaurant concept in London
1998 Nouveau Pub Renault 1 & 2, Paris; 'A third city bridge' Rotterdam (project)
1998–1993 Three buildings for the University of Nantes, UFR, library, Humanities building
1997 Residential building in Paris

1996 Viaduct on the A14 motorway at Nanterre and the Centre for the Exploitation of the Motorway hung beneath it; arrangement and conversion of the GDF site for residential use and public facilities, Roquebrune Cap-Martin; scenography for the French Pavilion at the Venice Biennale, VIth Mostra Internazionale di Architettura
1994 Airport activity park, St Jacques de la Lande, Rennes
1995 Metafort, Aubervilliers (prizewinner), Cité des Arts de Fort d'Aubervilliers
1990 Banque Populaire de l'Ouest, Rennes

Publications
1996 'Hyper-tension', *d'Architectures* no. 68 (reprint of the catalogue of the Venice Architecture Biennale, *Bloc, le monolithe fracturé* HYX, Orléans

Selected bibliography
1999 *The Contemporary Architecture Guide* vol. 1, Toto Publications, Tokyo; *Re-creation, 21 architects at the dawn of the XXIst century* catalogue of the Buenos Aires Architecture Biennale
1998 *Displaced Grid* RIBA/FRAC Centre; *Exploding the river* NAI, Rotterdam; *Archis* (Nov.), Rotterdam; *d'Architectures* nos 79, 83; *Contemporary World Architecture*, Phaidon, London
1997 *Architects Journal* no. 22, UK; *The Architectural Journal* (Feb.); *Domus* no. 791, Italy; *AMC* no. 92; *Le Moniteur* no. 4880; *Architecture d'intérieure créé* no. 282
1996 *Monograph*, Phaidon, London; *l'Arca* nos 104 and 110, Italy; *Architectural Culture* no. 786, Korea; *AMC* no. 72; *Architecture* no. 3, Hong Kong; *Blue Print* no. 133, UK; *ArtPress* no. 216; *Hinge Magazine* no. 21, Hong Kong; *l'Arca International* no. 102, Italy; *World Architecture* no. 9601, Chine
1995 *Monograph*, Aedes, Berlin; *l'Arca* nos 89, 90 and 94, Italy; *Bauwelt* no. 31, Germany; *Paroles* no. 7/8, Hong Kong; *Nuova Finestra* no. 7/8; *Architektur* no. 9, Germany; *Architectural Design* no. 65; *Architecture Créée* no. 267; *Newsline*, USA; *d'Architectures* no. 59; *Beaux-Arts Magazine* no. 138; *Techniques & Architectures* no. 422; *Le Moniteur* no. 4797
1991 *Monograph*, Banque Populaire de l'Ouest, Paris

Pierre du Besset & Dominique Lyon

| Pierre du Besset (*1949) | Dominique Lyon (*1954) |

Architecture may be called a mental activity. This term does not adequately define this domain, but it offers a gratifying image of it, and clearly conveys its fluctuating nature. If architecture has always been practised by speculation, its fluidity is something new and radical. The fluidity of architecture is the happy outcome of what is commonly known as the loss of points of reference. The great 'modern' narratives composed to steer society have come up against general scepticism, so it is up to architects to follow the ongoing path of world renewal, by putting up with what it produces by way of continual confusion. We are at the mercy of instability, and thus obliged to investigate. So, we have a penchant for paradox, commentary and displacement. Architecture has accordingly become so diverse that our admiration is split between contradictory accomplishments. We thus extol an exuberant Californian, a rigorous Englishman, a cerebral Dutchman and a Frenchman who is in fine fettle. This does not lead us 'towards an architecture'. But it does involve us. Architecture is no longer a direction, it is an environment, a flux. Its floating state is maintained by that fact that, by diversifying, its production conditions have become vague and controversial. Ambitions, clients' fears, political powerplay, programmes, budgets, and rules and regulations all form a confused and unstable collection of forces which rarely converge. Moreover, architecture owes a large part of its changing character to the indifference that greets it. Within the mood of overall slackening, architecture comes across like an eruption, when it is produced. Its project passes for radical, its expression becomes a statement. It is rare and uncertain. It is also destabilizing and dynamic, owing to the fact that it is based on intelligence. Architecture is elusive. By dint of its fluidity, it cannot be contained. It is a state, a potential. Making architecture happen calls for continually coming up with arguments to justify its presence. It is essential, henceforth, to maintain its expressive capacity. Architecture is a language. It is made for narrating, and its validity lies in its expressive aptitude. What else is there to say when heroic tales are not longer believable? The only subjects we can talk about, with full knowledge of the facts and which represent an inexhaustible source of knowledge and enthusiasm, are provided by the conditions made for us. Conditions provided for architects are made up of a limited number of factors: a client, a site, a programme, a budget. These factors form a world. Forces are at work in it, forces which are either generous or stingy, passionate or indifferent, well thought-out or absurd. It is from here that we derive most of our knowledge. Because this theatre is absurd and frustrating, it is also potentially profound and poetic. Our ability to express it, to give it its meaning, justifies our architect's freedom. Architecture derives its strength from the happiness or rage it finds in connecting with objects that affect it directly, in drawing close to the way they are and in exhausting their meaning. Let us take a bar of soap – Francis Ponge's soap. It is colourless, shapeless, and its ingredients are trite. When rubbed in water, it turns into a flow of bubbles and washes us. It does not take long to be all used up: the soap has been expressed and we are all clean. Triviality, movement, fluidity, exhaustion of the object in a project, this is what architecture is: a precise transformation. ✦

DOMINIQUE LYON

Mediatheque
Orléans, 1994

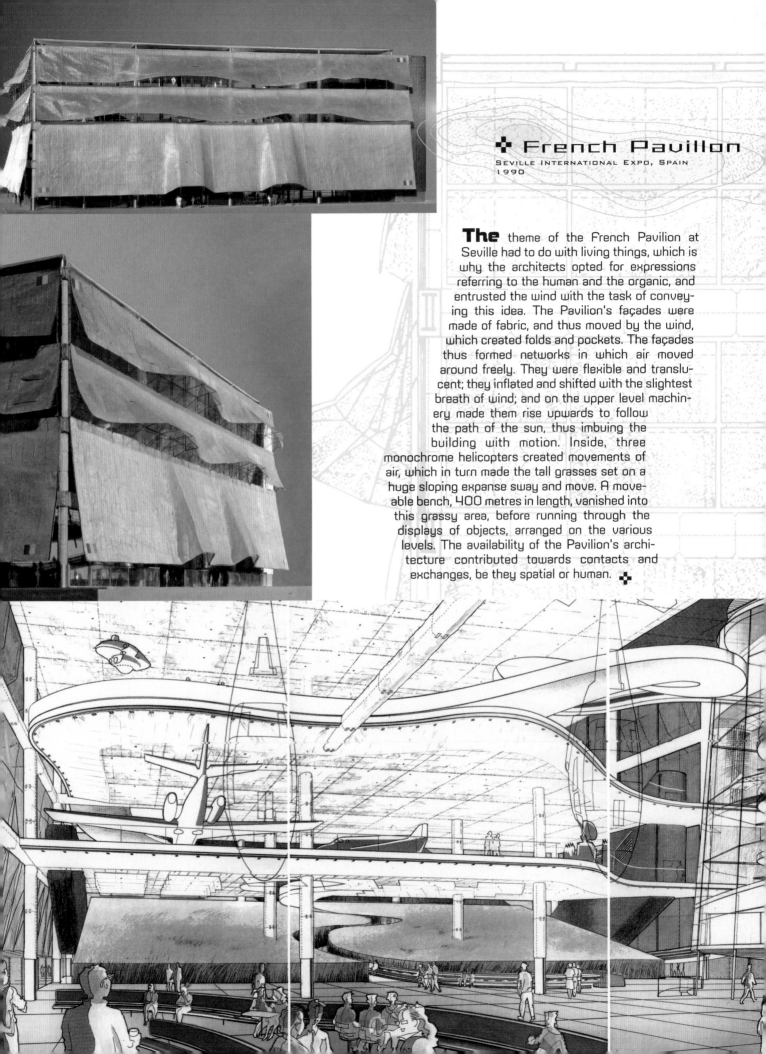

✦ French Pavillon

SEVILLE INTERNATIONAL EXPO, SPAIN
1990

The theme of the French Pavilion at Seville had to do with living things, which is why the architects opted for expressions referring to the human and the organic, and entrusted the wind with the task of conveying this idea. The Pavilion's façades were made of fabric, and thus moved by the wind, which created folds and pockets. The façades thus formed networks in which air moved around freely. They were flexible and translucent; they inflated and shifted with the slightest breath of wind; and on the upper level machinery made them rise upwards to follow the path of the sun, thus imbuing the building with motion. Inside, three monochrome helicopters created movements of air, which in turn made the tall grasses set on a huge sloping expanse sway and move. A moveable bench, 400 metres in length, vanished into this grassy area, before running through the displays of objects, arranged on the various levels. The availability of the Pavilion's architecture contributed towards contacts and exchanges, be they spatial or human. ✦

✦ Troyes Library

TROYES, FRANCE
1998–PRESENT

The Troyes Library is located near the city centre. Seen from Boulevard Gambetta, however, it is in the background, set back from the old high school (*lycée*). In order to assert itself, this major facility must not count on any façade effect. Rather than showing a constructed frontage, the library signals its indoor functions in such a way as to present a landscape built to an urban scale. The library's historic collection is displayed in a room 56 metres in length, displaying large arrays of old books and setting the tone for the rest of the building. The library is organized along flowing lines, based on principles of depth and linear layout. Coloured screens punctuate the inside area, which will be informed by wording created by an artist. The yellow roof is a fluid field of light that modulates the space with its optical accents. ✦

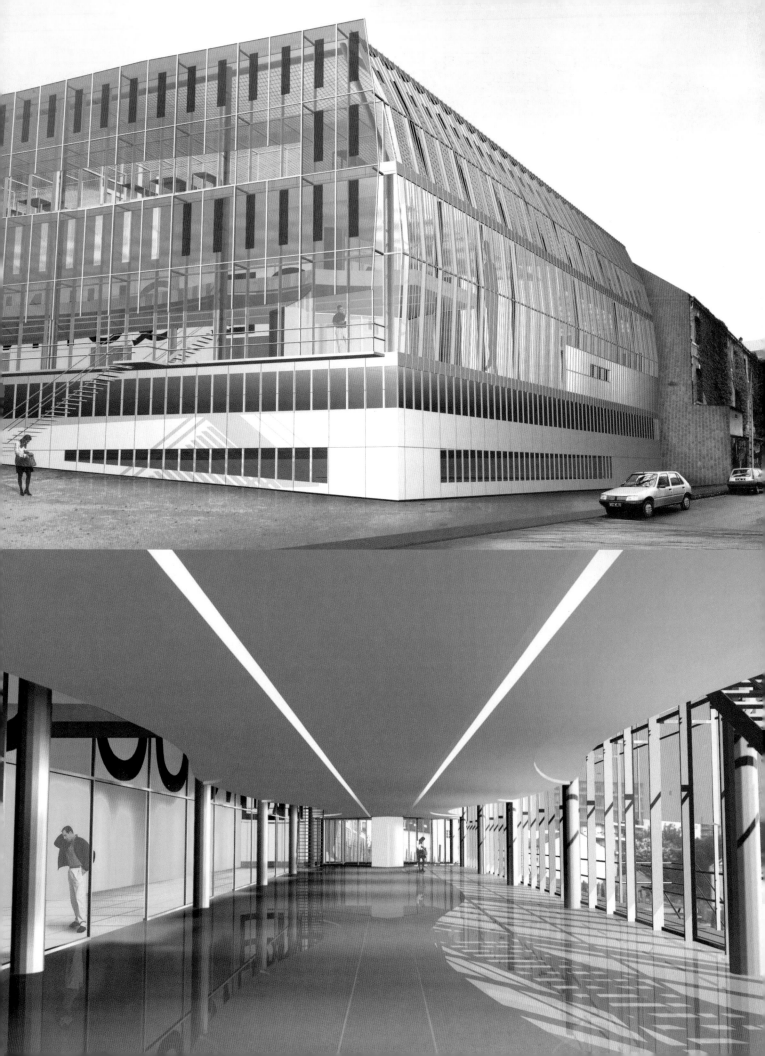

✦ Toulouse Library

UNIVERSITY LIBRARY OF MIRAIL, FRANCE (PROJECT)
1997

Here the architects sought to get across the idea of depth, seen from the viewpoint of a progression extending from the general (the mass of documents, the student community, the architecture) to the detailed (the book, the individual, an appropriate architectural arrangement). The building found expression less through its form (a parallelepiped) than through the repetition of a motif: a coloured strip regularly demarcating the windows. It was made up of expanses of glass forming the four façades on the one hand, and, on the other, internal partitions set at regular intervals along the right-angled grid of the structure. The library offered very large horizontal areas, set on three main levels, pierced by six patios containing ten stairways. Onlookers would perceive and experience the library in all its depth and height. The sight of the orderly collection, classification and organization of the books conveyed the expression of a lofty idea for the library. ✦

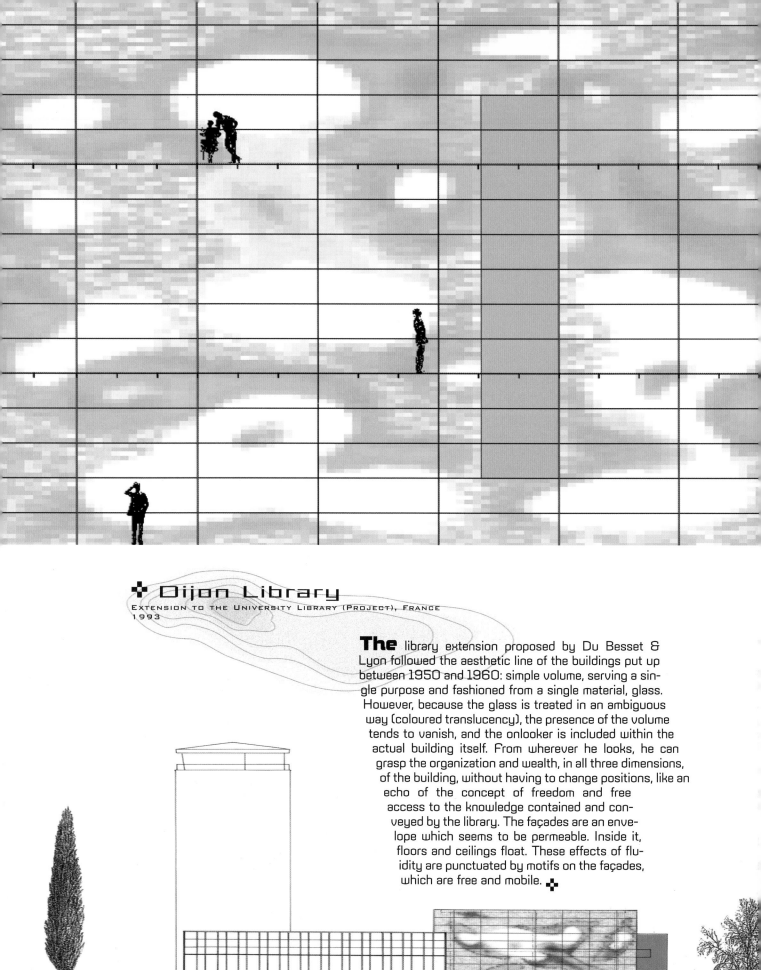

✚ Dijon Library
EXTENSION TO THE UNIVERSITY LIBRARY (PROJECT), FRANCE
1993

The library extension proposed by Du Besset & Lyon followed the aesthetic line of the buildings put up between 1950 and 1960: simple volume, serving a single purpose and fashioned from a single material, glass. However, because the glass is treated in an ambiguous way (coloured translucency), the presence of the volume tends to vanish, and the onlooker is included within the actual building itself. From wherever he looks, he can grasp the organization and wealth, in all three dimensions, of the building, without having to change positions, like an echo of the concept of freedom and free access to the knowledge contained and conveyed by the library. The façades are an envelope which seems to be permeable. Inside it, floors and ceilings float. These effects of fluidity are punctuated by motifs on the façades, which are free and mobile. ✚

✦ Pierre du Besset & Dominique Lyon

Pierre du Besset (1949)
Dominique Lyon (1954)

Teaching
1999   Columbia University, New York, USA
1998   Special Architecture School, Paris
1995   Fine Arts School, Vienna, Austria

1986   Founded the practice in Paris

Principal buildings and projects
1999   Fifty-five dwellings PLA, Gagny (completed); Lisieux library (completed 2000); Arrangement of a water castle at Grand Quevilly (completed 2000); Rungis library (completed 1999)
1998   Troyes library (completed 2000); Purification facility at Grand Caen (completed 2001)
1997   University library at Mirail, Toulouse (competition); Secondary school, rue d'Ulm, Paris (competition); Arrangement of Charpenterie block, Orléans (competition)
1994   Mediatheque at Orléans
1993   University library at Dijon (competition)
1992   University library at Jussieu, Paris (competition); Art college at Fresnoy (competition)
1993   Court of appeal at Aix en Provence (competition).
1990   Headquarters of the daily *Le Monde*, Paris; French Pavilion at the Universal Exhibition at Seville (competition, second round)
1989   International conference centre, Paris (competition)
1987   Maison de la Villette (Paris), honourable mention, *Le Moniteur*

Recent exhibitions
1998   Buenos Aires Biennale; Guggenheim Museum, New York, 'Premises'
1996   Galerie Arc-en-Rêve, Bordeaux '10 critiques, 10 bâtiments, 10 architectes'
1994   French Architecture Institute, Paris, 'Point de vue/usage du monde'.
1991   French Architecture Institute, '40 architectes de moins de 40 ans', also presented at the Venice Architecture Biennale, then at Düsseldorf, Houston and Kyoto

Principal publications (Dominique Lyon)
1999   *Le Corbusier vivant*, Telleri
1997   *Les Avatars de l'architecture ordinaire*, Sens & Tonka, Paris
1996   'Accents parisiens' *Mini PA* no. 13, Pavillon de l'Arsenal, Paris
1994   *Point de vue et usage du monde* Carte Segrete

Selected bibliography
1998   Catalogue of the Buenos Aires Biennale; *Premises* exhibition catalogue, Guggenheim Museum, New York; *Casabella* (no. 660)
1997   *Architectural Culture* (no. 191) Korea
1994   *l'Architecture d'aujourd'hui* (no. 294); *l'Arca* (no. 88), Italy
1992   *A + U* (no. 267) Japan
1991   *l'Arca* (no. 54)
1990   *l'Architecture d'aujourd'hui* (no. 268)

Shuhei Endo

| Shuhei Endo (*1960) |

Paramodern Architecture The architect today is groping for plausible paramodern architecture that can open up new possibilities by overcoming the self-imposed limitations of modernism in architecture that resulted from pursuing uniformity to excessive degrees, while taking advantage of its possibilities and effectiveness to the fullest extent. In modernism, architects broke down the whole of architecture into such elements as post, beam, roof and wall, and reassembled these elements again. Limitations inherent in this kind of 'composition' may be regarded as a major reason why modernism in architecture never gained real richness in its character. Therefore, this architect has experimented with non-compositional methods in two types of architecture. The first type was based upon questioning anew a fundamental premise of architecture, namely, complete separation of interior from exterior. This type of architecture consisting of open spaces has been named, to use a neologism, 'Halftecture'. In the other, architectural spaces were created with a single element, that is, continuous strips of plate encompassing both roof and wall, not with the compositional elements obtained by breaking down the whole of architecture into its elements. This was called, in a similar vein, 'Rooftecture'. These buildings are concrete examples of an attempt at realizing possibilities of paramodern architecture. This concept had been realized in small-scale buildings such as a building for parking bicycles, a public lavatory and an unmanned railway station. These 'Halftecture' structures encompassing ambiguous spaces were built with continuous, simple strips of steel plate only. This type of building points to a new possibility of building architectural structures. Many 'Halftecture' designs have been realized with corrugated steel sheeting. This material is an industrial product manufactured by applying a wavy form to steel sheeting. These plates have structural strength, and are durable and recyclable because of their galvanized surface. They are well suited to assembling a structure on site with bolts and nuts since they are produced in sheet form with standardized dimensions. In 'Halftecture', the interior and the exterior were reversed and interior spaces and exterior spaces fused by continuous strips of steel plate, realizing paramodern spaces. In attempting to create open spaces in 'Halftecture', the possibility was discovered of using strips of plate as a building material. As a development of using these strips, 'Rooftecture', built with continuous strips of plate encompassing both roof and wall, was born. This is to say that 'Rooftecture' refers to architectonic conduct in which continuous strips of roof/wall are identified as a sole means of creating architectural spaces. Using these continuous strips of roof/wall was an attempt to create versatile spaces without being restricted to further propagation of monotonous spaces. Further possibilities of this type of architecture are being explored. ✚

SHUHEI ENDO

✤ Springtecture

SINGU-CHO, HYOGO, JAPAN, 1998

Public lavatories are required to provide convenience, based on openness, and security, deriving from enclosure. Openness is essentially the possibility of passage. The structure is basically in the form of an independent spiral of steel sheets, with gate-shaped auxiliary materials partially inserted. The architectural concept of this facility aims to form a linkage between openness and enclosure through continuity of corrugated steel sheets. Interior walls double as exterior ceilings and floors, which also extend as exterior walls and roofs and once again turn into interior parts. The interior and exterior form a linkage of changes, challenging architectural norms expected by the observer, and suggesting a new, heterogeneous architectural form. The facility is also a small attempt towards a new architecture realized by continuous interplay between the interior and the exterior and the interactive effect of partial sharing of roofs, floors and walls. ✤

✦ Springtecture A

AOMORI, JAPAN, COMPETITION, 2000

This architectural design was created as an entry in a competition for an art museum complex planned in northeastern Japan. This was a proposal to propagate a type of architecture consisting of geometric regularity despite its versatile appearance, as attempted initially in 'Springtecture-H'. The architectural requirements for this museum included a variety of functions and spaces. These are satisfied by spaces formed by strips of steel plate that are tied together into curved continuous surfaces. Adjacent spaces are connected at narrow gaps between them, and steel plates winding inside-out and outside-in bring together all the interior and exterior spaces as a versatile whole. In this design, five strips of continuous and winding plates are integrated into a composite structure to secure required areas in the plan and required dimensions in the section. Structurally, it is a planar structure formed by curved precast concrete panels tied together continuously. This project was an attempt at creating a versatile and rich architecture possessing a geometrical regularity without being monotonous and boring. ✦

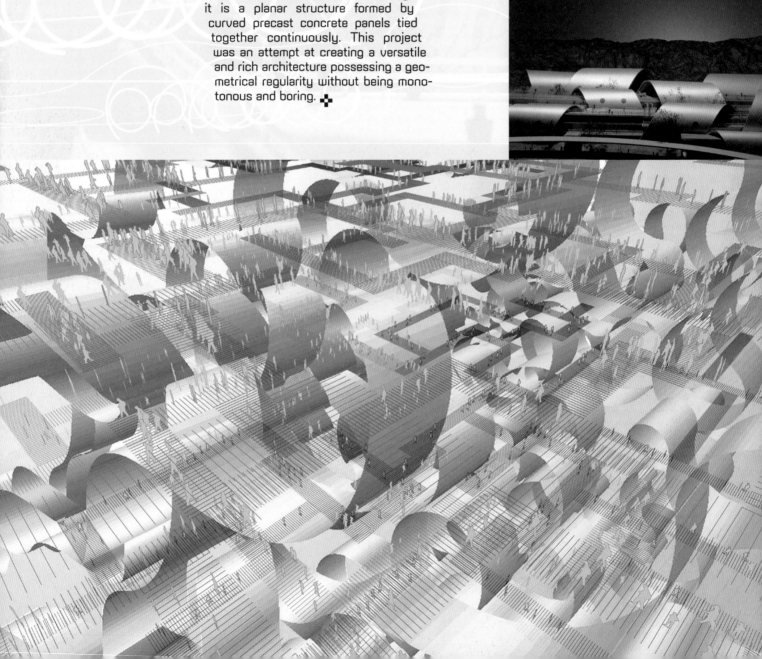

✚ Rooftecture W
(Wipo Project)
(WORLD INTELLECTUAL PROPERTY ORGANIZATION)
GENEVA, SWITZERLAND, COMPETITION, 2000

This design was an entry in a design competition for the new extension building to the World Intellectual Property Organization Headquarters in Geneva. The architectural brief for this extension was a complex one requiring underground parking lots, a large conference hall and offices. The main design concept of this project was to express complementary relationships between the architecture and people's activities therein. A structural system inspired by the structure of DNA was proposed as a fitting structure for the World Intellectual Property Organization. Possibilities of mankind lie in the versatility of multiple cultures and exchanges among them. These were recognized as similar possibilities to those exhibited by the regularity and versatility of DNA, which is shared by all living beings. Based on this insight, two design features, a wall system possessing structural regularity and spaces filled with a whole variety of light and wind created by the wall system, were proposed. In this architectural proposal, a universal structural system that could generate a variety of forms was employed while versatile and rich spaces were secured by topping the architecture with a large roof. ✚

✚ Shuhei Endo

Shuhei Endo (1960)
1986 Master's degree, Kyoto University of Art
1988 Creation of the Shuhei Endo Architect Institute
1998 Japan Federation of Architects & Building Engineers Association
       Award; Marble Architectural Award; East Asia Grand Prix, Italy

Teaching
2000–1988 Kinki University, Kobe; Design School and Fukui Institute of
           Technology

Principal buildings and projects
2000 S Complex, Shiga (project); Springtecture A/Aomori project, Art
      Museum, Aomori, Japan (competition); Rooftecture W/Wipo project,
      Extension of the headquarters of the World Organization for
      Intellectual Property, Geneva, Switzerland (competition)
1999 Rooftecture H, Hyogo (realized); Rooftecture Y, Hyogo (project);
      Rooftecture M, Tokyo (project)
1998 Rooftecture O, Shinto sacred site, Fukui (realized); Rooftecture N,
      Warehouses and offices, Hyogo (realized); Springtecture H, Public
      toilets, Hyogo (realized)
1997 Transtation O, Bicycle shelter, Fukui (realized); Halftecture F, Fukui
      (realized); Rooftecture T, Fukui (realized)
1996 Healtecture K, Family residence and offices, Osaka (realized);
      Skintecture I, Fishing cooperative, Hyogo (realized)
1995 House O, Kyoto (realized)
1994 Cyclestation M, Bicycle shelter, Shiga (realized)
1990 3d Factory, Shiga (realized)
1988 House U, Osaka (realized)

Recent exhibitions
1999 'GA House Project 1999' Tokyo
1998 'The Possibility of Architecture 98' Osaka
1997 'GA House Project 1997' Tokyo; 'The Possibility of Architecture
      97' Osaka

Principal publication
1999 *Shuhei Endo* GG Portfolio, Gustavo Gili, Barcelona, Spain

Selected bibliography
1999 *AJ* (Dec.) UK; *AA* (Nov./Dec.) UK; *AD* (March/April) UK; *Space*
      (March) Korea; *The Architectural Map of Osaka/Kobe*, Toto
      Shuppan, Japan
1998 *AR* (Oct.); *AJ* (April) UK; *Marble Architectural Awards '98*, East
      Asia Grand Prix, Italy
1997 *AR* (April) UK; *Wallpaper* (Sept./Oct.)

FAT (Fashion Architecture Taste)

| Emma Davis (*1968) | Sam Jacob (*1970) |
| Sean Griffiths (*1966) | | Charles Holland (*1969) |

Founded in 1993, FAT is a company that makes architecture and art (and lots of things in between). They are interested in making work that explores the experiences, contradictions and possibilities of the modern world. The issues the work of FAT addresses include:

Representation – In an age of communication, Fat pursues an architecture that is representational and inclusive rather than abstract and exclusive and which deals with visual sources outside of what is currently considered legitimate in architecture. FAT's architecture addresses the languages of public art and politics as well as the popular languages of cinema, advertising, communicational technology, the theme park and the ordinary. These languages are approached critically and are manipulated using tactics of juxtaposition, re-contextualization, superimposition, manipulation of scale, inversion and fragmentation.

Space and occupation – FAT's manipulation of experience in architecture moves on from the formalist sensualism which is usually associated with experience in architecture, to include plays on the politics of occupation, the use of multisensory environments for evocative purposes and the marking of territories. This sometimes involves the dematerialization of architecture itself, such as in the 'Picnic event' or 'The Kistner'. Similarly, in urban art projects, such as 'Shopping', the space of the art gallery is deconstructed both physically and conceptually.

Process – The re-use of existing icons to create often subversive meanings (a tactic familiar in conceptual art), as opposed to extravagant and esoteric formalism, allow for the inventive use of conventional building technologies in the means of construction as opposed to the expensive and nostalgic technological sophistries in the kind of extravagant abstract formalism which passes for innovative architecture. This seemingly banal fact is of utmost importance to the new generation of architectural practices whose methods are interdisciplinary and whose medium is content not form. Content is rich and can be achieved on a budget. Formalism is arcane and expensive to boot.

Taste – High architecture regards space as its medium. It attempts to make meaning through the manipulation of space. Taste, however, is the mechanism by which architecture engages with its audience and its market. Taste communicates and locates the social, political and financial meanings of architecture. It connects architecture with a wider cultural sphere in ways which are accessible beyond both the academy and the profession. Taste engages the contentious issues of quality and value, which are matters of subjective deliberation, raising the awkward issue of class. Taste counters the abstract geometries and spatial gymnastics that obsess contemporary architecture, exposing its lack of immediacy and popular appeal. ✤

FAT

'Kill the Modernist Within'
MANCHESTER, ENGLAND, 1999/2000

Part polemic, part homage, 'Kill the Modernist Within' is a manifesto arising out of the struggle of FAT to turn their backs on the myths of modernism. This exhibition at the Manchester's Cube gallery makes a plea for stylistic liberalism over modernism's puritanism and for an architecture that celebrates the riches of the information era rather than the imagery of the industrial age. It eschews the essentially modernist belief that new technology will lead naturally to shiny new form and argues instead for the everyday application of new technologies rather than a heroic struggle to represent them. The exhibition uses materials and languages outside architecture's current reduced vocabulary: flashing signs, oil paintings, sequins, soundtracks, neon lights and mock Tudor. It suggests that architecture's communicative potential does not lie in abstract formal approaches but proposes instead an architecture which addresses contemporary cultural experiences. ✦

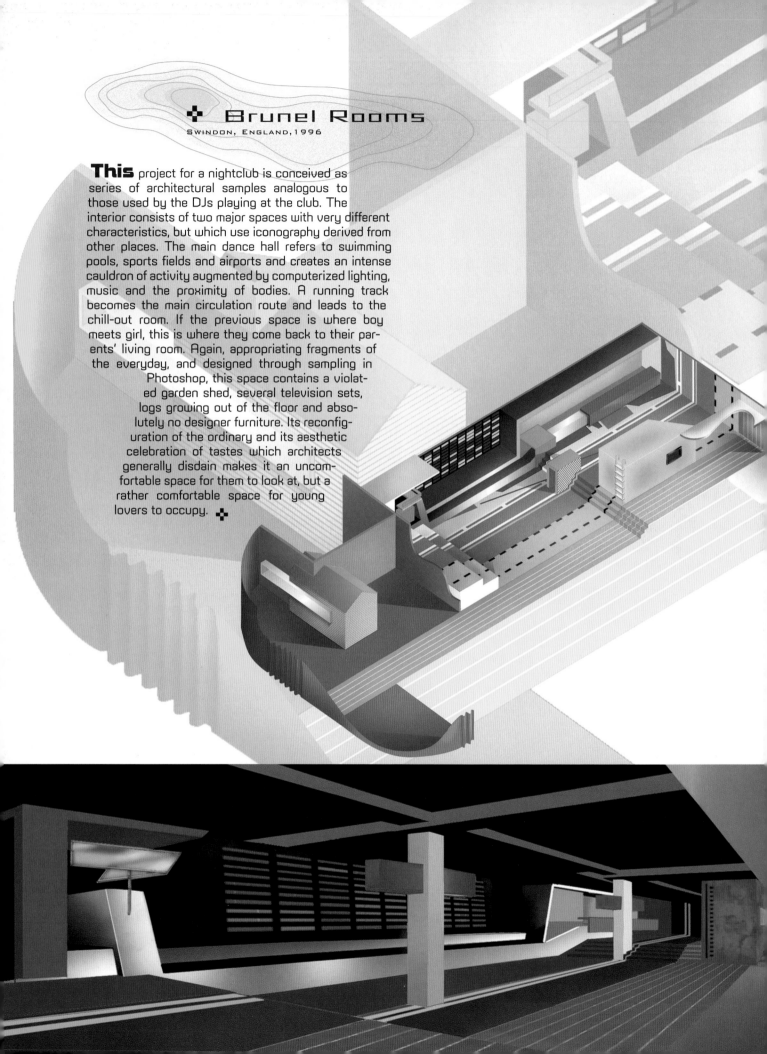

✦ Brunel Rooms

SWINDON, ENGLAND, 1996

This project for a nightclub is conceived as series of architectural samples analogous to those used by the DJs playing at the club. The interior consists of two major spaces with very different characteristics, but which use iconography derived from other places. The main dance hall refers to swimming pools, sports fields and airports and creates an intense cauldron of activity augmented by computerized lighting, music and the proximity of bodies. A running track becomes the main circulation route and leads to the chill-out room. If the previous space is where boy meets girl, this is where they come back to their parents' living room. Again, appropriating fragments of the everyday, and designed through sampling in Photoshop, this space contains a violated garden shed, several television sets, logs growing out of the floor and absolutely no designer furniture. Its reconfiguration of the ordinary and its aesthetic celebration of tastes which architects generally disdain makes it an uncomfortable space for them to look at, but a rather comfortable space for young lovers to occupy. ✦

✦ Kessels Kramer
AMSTERDAM, THE NETHERLANDS, 1998

This low-tech internet project for a hi-fidelity industry is built in a former church. The interior is an assemblage of objects (wooden fort, garden shed, and life guard's tower) seen alternatively as small buildings or very large pieces of furniture. They are both real objects and models of other buildings and other places. Each element has been subject to distortions in scale, fragmentation and juxtaposition, reinforcing their strangeness and inauthenticity. These major elements are supplemented by a number of smaller ones which include fragments of football pitch, picnic tables, hedges and picket fences as well as a number of pieces of furniture, ornaments and objects bought by the client from flea markets. The scheme sets up a series of incomplete and contradictory narratives through a collaging of disparate and distorted objects and experiences. This juxtaposition is a product of a sensibility engendered by the presence of information technology in our culture, as much as it is a product of the everyday application of these technologies. ✦

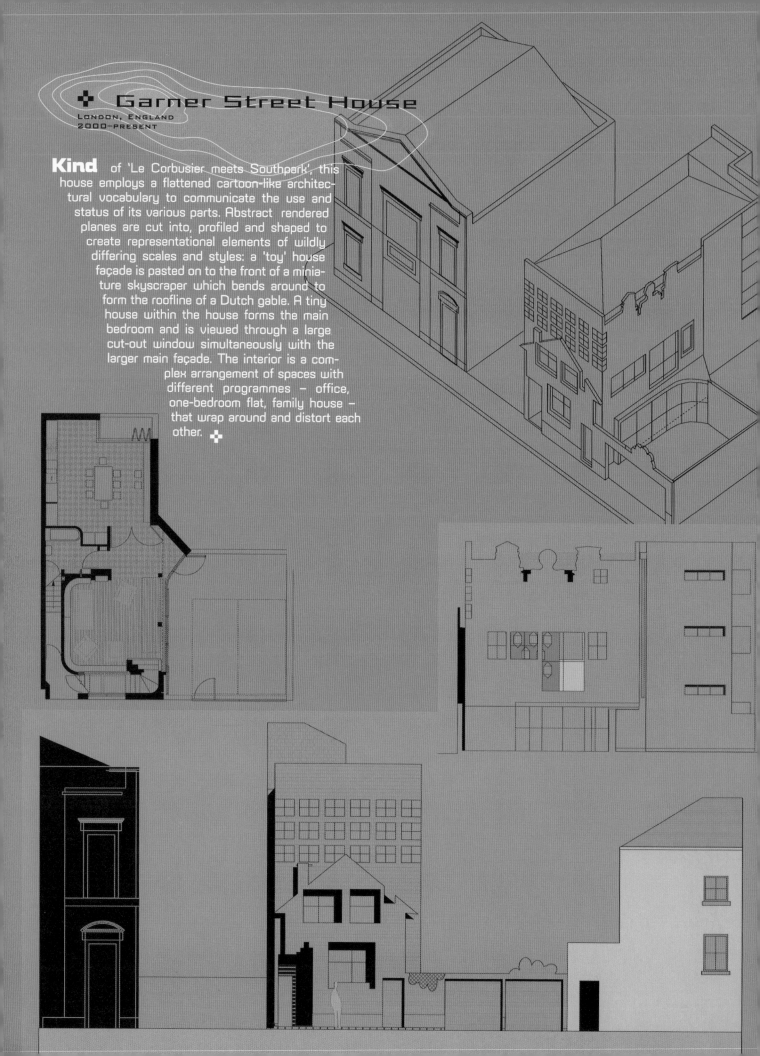

Garner Street House

LONDON, ENGLAND
2000–PRESENT

Kind of 'Le Corbusier meets Southpark', this house employs a flattened cartoon-like architectural vocabulary to communicate the use and status of its various parts. Abstract rendered planes are cut into, profiled and shaped to create representational elements of wildly differing scales and styles: a 'toy' house façade is pasted on to the front of a miniature skyscraper which bends around to form the roofline of a Dutch gable. A tiny house within the house forms the main bedroom and is viewed through a large cut-out window simultaneously with the larger main façade. The interior is a complex arrangement of spaces with different programmes – office, one-bedroom flat, family house – that wrap around and distort each other. ✤

✦ The Princess
Diana Memorial
Bridge
LONDON, ENGLAND, 2000 (PROJECT)

✦ FAT

Emma Davis (1968)
MA Fine Art

Sam Jacob (1970)
B Arch, Dip Arch

Sean Griffiths (1966)
BA (Hons), Dip Arch

Charles Holland (1969)
BA (Hons) Dip Arch

1993   Creation of FAT in London

Principal buildings and projects
2000   Garner Street House, Live-work development (under construction);
       The Princess Diana Memorial Bridge, London (project); 'Sitooterie'
       Pavilion, Belsay Hall, Northumbria (under construction); 'Split
       Clock', Public artwork, London; Kinnear House, London (under con-
       struction); Conversion of Thomas Neals Shopping Centre, London
       (under construction); Kings Cross Millennium Artwork, London;
       'Stroom' Public artwork, The Hague (under construction); House
       and Office, London (under construction); Two New Houses, Kent
       (under construction); Sutton Walk, South Bank London (competi-
       tion)
1999   'Architecture Foundation Roadshow' Newman Town Centre (pro-
       ject); Carnaby Art Billboard, London (realized); 'Mambo' boutique,
       London (realized); The Scala nightclub and cinema, London (real-
       ized)
1998   Kessels Kramer, conversion of a church into an advertising agency,
       Amsterdam (realized); Library in house for writers, London (real-
       ized); Orlando Road House extension, London (realized)
1997   LSD offices for an advertising agency, London (realized);
       Roadworks audiovisual installation in a bus shelter (realized)
1996   Kistner House extension, London (realized)
1995   Brunel Rooms nightclub, Swindon (project); Chez Garson church
       conversion, London
1993   Anti-Oedipus House (project)

Recent exhibitions
1999   'Kill the Modernist Within' Manchester' Cube Gallery; 'Shopping'
       London
1998   'Disaster' Fine Art Installation, Limehouse, London; 'Art Billboard'
       Bargehouse Museum, London
1997   'Home Ideals, Street as Gallery Art', exhibition on for-sale signs,
       London

Principal publications
2000   *The New Civic* exhibition catalogue (Feb.) FAT; *It's Not Unusual*
       (The Unknown City) Routledge (in preparation)
1999   'Art Attack!' *Public Art Journal* vols 1 and 2 (Oct.) Public Art
       Journal; 'Shopping' exhibition catalogue (Sept.) FAT
1998   *Contaminating Contemplation* (Occupying Territories) Routledge;
       'Fashion Architecture and Taste' *Scroope 10*, Journal of Cambridge
       School of Architecture
1997   'Roadworks' exhibition catalogue, FAT

Selected bibliography
2000   *Frame* (Jan./Feb.); *Blue Print* (Jan.)
1999   *Building Design*; *Blue Print* (Sept.); *International Design Magazine*
       (April)
1998   *Frame 2*; *Bauwelt* (Oct.); *Archis* (May); *Building Design* (April)
1997   *Blue Print* (April); *International Design Magazine* (Aug.)

Didier Fiuza Faustino

| Didier Fiuza Faustino (*1968) |

The central dimension of Didier Fiuza Faustino's line of thinking is the body. Not the body as a reference machine, but the body as a spatial component. For how is a space to be envisaged other than through its relationship with the body using it? So this involves taking the interactions between them into account, as well as the potential for action of each one, prior to any design. The area to be grasped is that of perception, as attested to by a series of works which challenge and question appearance, tactility, and visual and physical instability. There is also the area of displacement, like choreographic containers where the itinerary is one of the component parts of the architecture introduced. Lastly, and logically enough, there is the area of the interstice and the infinitesimal. In considering the links between two worlds, is one not trying to grasp the intangible and the space-time factor that joins them together (or separates them)?

Be it through his architectural projects or his explorations in the area of the visual arts – which reciprocally enhance one another – Didier Fiuza Faustino thus gets us to enter a physical dimension whose body is the atom and whose architecture the interface. He examines our senses and their extensions in the constructed space at the risk of damaging them. Although precariousness is not really a condition of his work, his attachment to this concept prompts him to see his role and his projections in a state of impermanence. He is keen to be an agent provocateur rather than an emissary, and consequently wants above all to incorporate the whole dysfunction as a spatial production vehicle.

In the research carried out, there is actually an underlying, political stance, which runs counter to order and tidiness. After flirting in his early phases with an ambient movement encouraging a certain 'urban guerilla' tactic, this is now being sought in greater serenity, but there is still a definitive emphasis on 'vicious actions', as is shown, for example, by the insidious distortions of the video *In, trans, ex* (1997) and the perverse reading of diplomacy for the Portuguese Embassy project in Berlin (1998). It is also expressed in the critical reading of our patterns of behaviour and our relations with others and our environment. The accentuation of desire and exhibition, as well as of the inquisitive eye, rooted in everyone, thus informs projects such as Personal Billboard (1999). Intimacy is plumbed to its limits and challenged in relation to our contemporaneity, new methods of communication and expression surrounding us, and our emerging desires.

The fact is that this context is the very context of the representational methods chosen. The approach is, nevertheless, in investigative, the intention being to use the medium above all as an exploratory tool. The sort of immateriality emanating from the video and computer imagery presented contrasts with the (epi)dermic world built in tandem with the projects, but it paradoxically asserts the recurrent line of thinking in all of Didier Fiuza Faustino's work, which prompts us to question our place and our role in this world, through our relationship with space in all its constructs and with time. ✛

MARIE-HÉLÈNE FABRE

'Body Building'
Performance video
1996

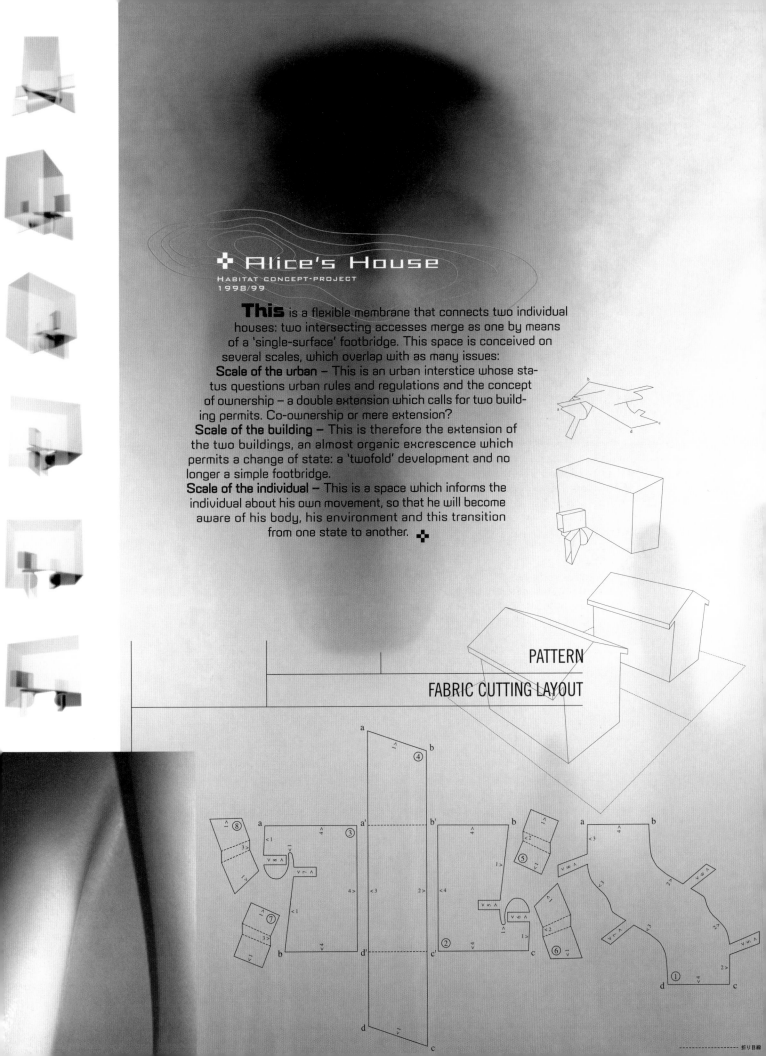

✦ Alice's House

HABITAT CONCEPT-PROJECT
1998/99

This is a flexible membrane that connects two individual houses: two intersecting accesses merge as one by means of a 'single-surface' footbridge. This space is conceived on several scales, which overlap with as many issues:

Scale of the urban – This is an urban interstice whose status questions urban rules and regulations and the concept of ownership – a double extension which calls for two building permits. Co-ownership or mere extension?

Scale of the building – This is therefore the extension of the two buildings, an almost organic excrescence which permits a change of state: a 'twofold' development and no longer a simple footbridge.

Scale of the individual – This is a space which informs the individual about his own movement, so that he will become aware of his body, his environment and this transition from one state to another. ✦

PATTERN

FABRIC CUTTING LAYOUT

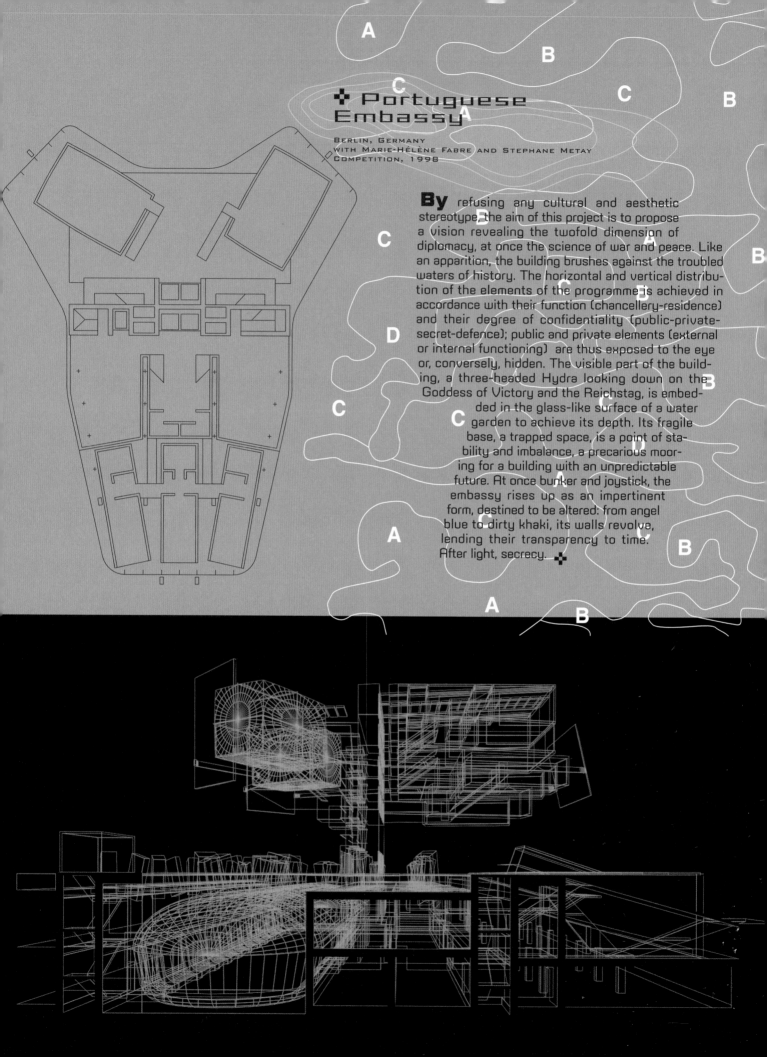

✦ Portuguese Embassy

BERLIN, GERMANY
WITH MARIE-HÉLÈNE FABRE AND STEPHANE METAY
COMPETITION, 1998

By refusing any cultural and aesthetic stereotype, the aim of this project is to propose a vision revealing the twofold dimension of diplomacy, at once the science of war and peace. Like an apparition, the building brushes against the troubled waters of history. The horizontal and vertical distribution of the elements of the programme is achieved in accordance with their function (chancellery-residence) and their degree of confidentiality (public-private-secret-defence); public and private elements (external or internal functioning) are thus exposed to the eye or, conversely, hidden. The visible part of the building, a three-headed Hydra looking down on the Goddess of Victory and the Reichstag, is embedded in the glass-like surface of a water garden to achieve its depth. Its fragile base, a trapped space, is a point of stability and imbalance, a precarious mooring for a building with an unpredictable future. At once bunker and joystick, the embassy rises up as an impertinent form, destined to be altered: from angel blue to dirty khaki, its walls revolve, lending their transparency to time. After light, secrecy. ✦

✦ Cultural Centre of Ribeira Grande

RIBEIRA GRANDE, AORES ARCHIPELAGO, PORTUGAL
WITH PASCAL MAZOYER AND JEAN-LUC NGO
COMPETITION, 1999

Three ideas govern this project: itinerary, instability and interstice. On the one hand, the itinerary, for it is a matter of encouraging the user's relationship with the space around him. His movements dictated by the museum's collection and temporary exhibitions offer an opportunity to hone his awareness about the architecture in which he is ceaselessly evolving in new ways. On the other hand, instability, for it is a matter of setting references within references, the better to stimulate the senses and proceed with a kind of hypersensory awareness. And last of all interstice, for it is a matter of offering a fragmented view of the building, its architecture and its environment, in order to stir up curiosity and encourage the itinerary. It is also a way of offering diminishing scales and visual outlets which are so many moments of dizziness and breathing. This is realized by the association of three structure-giving elements: a wood frame incorporating the building within its lightness, a façade wall on the left like a skin, whose outlines cannot quite be grasped, and a system of 'platform floors' offering spatial permeability and freedom. With this overall arrangement, a specific relationship is established between the building, the visitor, the city and the works on view. Each element interacts with the other by way of a heightened, or simply stimulated, perception: a relationship, at the end of the day, akin to that of an independent system. ✦

✚ Personal Billboard: An Urban Peep Show

HABITAT CONCEPT

This is an individual house fitted with a huge outer screen which shows video sequences of its occupants. This interface between interior and exterior, private and public, operates within but also beyond the framework of an interplay mixing exhibition and voyeurism. Conceived as an extension of the personal sphere, this interface enables the individual literally to project himself into the urban setting and blend in with it, like part of a landscape. The individual house thus occupies a 'living space' with blurred boundaries, another dimension, exploring an area which thus spills over from the area used by webcams. As an instrument of possibles, Personal Billboard is a component of the territory into which it fits, at once the reification of a virtuality and a factor of reflection and reflectivity of relations with others and space. ∎

✚ Didier Fiuza Faustino

Didier Fiuza Faustino (1968)

1995 Diploma from the Ecole d'Architecture de Paris-Villemin
1996 Independent architecture in Portugal and France, co-founder of the 'Laboratoire d'Architectures Performances et Sons' (LAPS) in Paris
1997 Co-founder of the multidisciplinary atelier 'Le Fauteuil Vert' in Paris
1998 Co-founder, co-director and artistic director of *Numeromagazine* review, Lisbon

Principal buildings and projects

1999 'Urban Rhizome hotel for the aliens', Roswell Housing Competition (mentioned); Cultural Centre at Ribeira Grande, Azores (competition); Personal Billboard: an Urban Peep Show, Habitat concept (project); 'Alice's House' Habitat concept (project)
1998 'Vertigo' Apartment, Paris (realized); Portuguese Embassy at Berlin (competition); 'Immersion' Video
1997 Residential complex and swimming pool, Sainte-Anne, Guadeloupe (competition by invitation, second prize); 'My First House' performance, Leiria, France; 'In, Trans,Ex' Video
1996 'To Experience Fragility', Shinkenchiku Residential Design Competition, Japan; 'Body Building' performance/video

Recent exhibitions

1999 '(A)casos (&) Materiais', CAPC (Centro de Artes Plasticas de Coimbra)
1998 'Interferência 01', Lisbon, Principe Real
1997 'Beau comme un camion' Collective Exhibition, Europride, Paris

Selected bibliography

1999 'Architecte Borderline' Charles-Arthur Boyer, *Art Press* no. 245; 'Tra Body Art and Architecture' Francesco Careri, *Spacio & Societa* no. 85; 'Tirer un homme de sa torpeur' and 'Expressions' *Parpaings* no. 3, France
1998 'Mode d'Emploi' *Visuel* no. 3/4; 'Mésarchitectures' *Numéromagazine* no. 00, Lisbon

Foreign Office Architects

| Farshid Moussavi (*1965) | Alejandro Zaera-Polo (*1963) |

With the interest to exploit mobile conditions of habitation – where the determination of the ground, its limits and its nature become increasingly problematic – we have performed several experiments working consistently with surfaces. Only recently have we realized that this experimentation has interesting connections with the theoretical agenda that we had proposed for the office, that the exploration of the surface was perhaps an intuition towards the problem we were facing: the reconfiguration of the ground as an architectural problem. Peter Eisenman proposes that architecture is always framed by the ground it occupies: it is the ground in its broader sense that allows us to recognise the traits of architecture as a figure. This has raised several questions for us. What happens when the ground – geographical, geological, cultural, economical – becomes distorted through mechanisms of temporal and spatial displacement that characterize our age? How can we frame architecture within these increasingly shifting conditions of the ground? And what is the nature of this ground? The enormous interest in landscape – landscapes in the abstract, not in the literal sense – that sweeps contemporary architectural debate is clearly a recognition that we can no longer rely on the classical relationships between building and ground. As Lyotard explains, landscapes are the domains devoid of meaning, origin and destiny produced 'when the mind is transported from one form of sensitive matter to another, but still retains the sensorial organization characteristic of the former'; landscape as the phenomenology of displaced sensibility rather than as a building type. Thinking about this matter, our surface projects are another approach to the problem to that proposed by Eisenman. Whereas Eisenman's approach is to produce the 'groundless', the void of ground, models to produce architectural figures without reference to a ground, in order to escape from composition as the organization of figure and ground, our surface projects turn the ground into the figure, by cultivating, empowering the ground. We are beginning to examine the projects that we have been developing during the past years, as a series of experiments in which the surface of the ground is systematically subjected to deformations that project it beyond its flat coding, into an active field. This ambiguity between the two-dimensional and the three-dimensional is perhaps one of the most interesting aspects of this research, as an alternative to the opposition between the ground and the architectural figure. If conventional architecture relates to the horizontality of the ground as a vertical entity, the possibility of a surface that envelops space is interesting to us. Our series of surface projects are attempts at making the ground devoid of its traditional determination as datum, by turning it into an ungrounded surface, an envelope. In the Glass Centre, in Yokohama, in Kansai, in Pusan, we explored the possibility of a geology of the hollow, where the ground is no longer sustained in solid layers of matter perpendicular to the forces of gravity, but is structurally stable by virtue of a geometrical structure that moves stresses through the surface of that ground. Architecture is matter. And that is perhaps an interesting path to follow in our attempt to treat the ground as a figure, the surface as a space. ✦

✦ Virtual House

COMPETITION ORGANIZED BY THE ANY CORPORATION, USA
1997

The project was to operate with an abstracted band of ground – a band of 'disruptive pattern material' – to produce alternative organizations to the conventional compartimentalization of domestic space. The manipulation of the ground in this case differs from other FOA projects, where they maintain the orientation of the surface in respect to gravity. In the Virtual House that relationship keeps reversing, every face of the surface shifting constantly between a 'lining' and a 'wrapping' condition. A diagonal shift in the plan increased the spatial complexity of this structure, making possible the stacking of different units to enable the unlimited proliferation of the body of the house. The FOA's concept of 'hollow ground' acquired in this project a more paradigmatic state, where the possibility proliferating the structure is an alternative development to the 'unframed' quality of the ground explored by FOA. ✦

❖ Yokohama Port Terminal

Ni-Wa-Minato: a differential Meditation
Yokohama, Japan
Competition, 1995 (first prize)

This project, in process of being built, aims for a mediating device between the system of public spaces of Yokohama and the organization of cruise passenger flow. The ground surface is used as the device to create a continuously varied form that articulates in a differential mode the various segments of the programme, producing a public space that wraps around the terminals — the first perpendicular penetration of the urban space within Yokohama Bay. The ground of the city is seamlessly connected to the boarding level and from there it bifurcates, encouraging interaction between the urban space and the terminal below. The terminal is organized as a seamless milieu, with the strategic provision of a small number of mobile or collapsible elements that substantially affect the definition of the domestic and international frontier, turning the terminal into an ideal battlefield that can be occupied by locals or invaded by foreigners. ❖

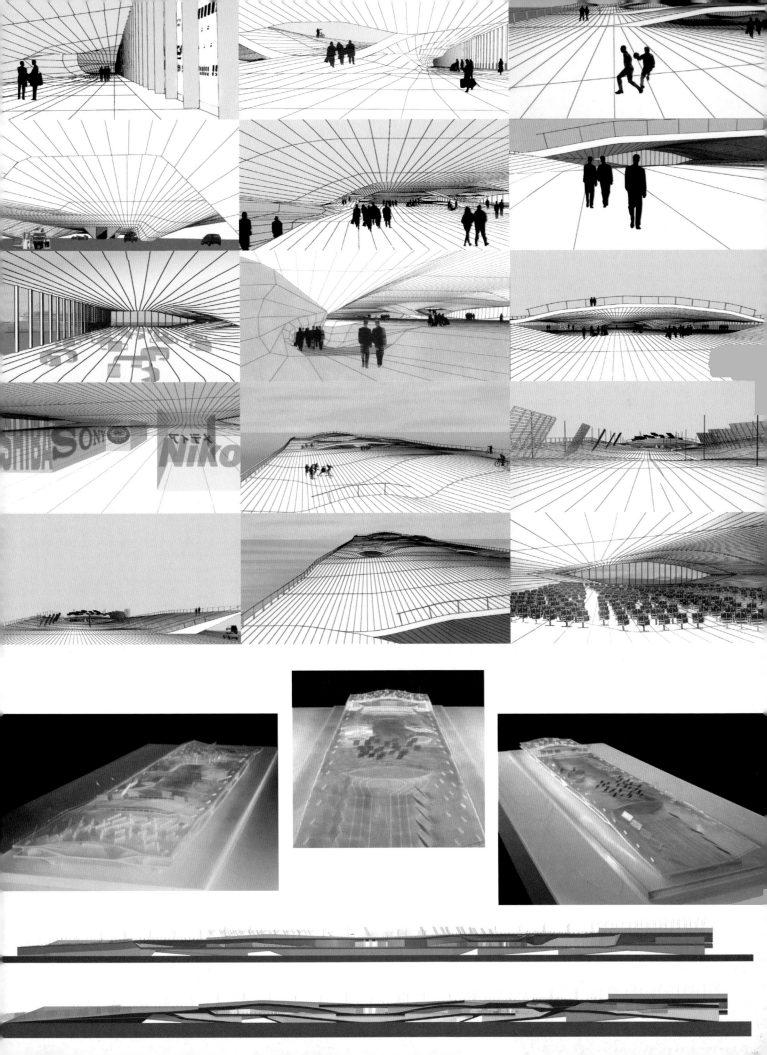

✦ Belgo Restaurant

LONDON, ENGLAND
1999

The main task for the Belgo restaurant in London has been to replace an existing roof and side walls to an existing building and to organize the space for its new use. FOA's proposal has concentrated on exploring structural surfaces and to use the same surface as a way of organizing the construction of the new roofs and walls. Belgo Zuid is built like a mussel: a shell structure, where a single roof hosts the two spaces for the guests: main dining hall and bar. The roof, a factory-like shell, is cut open to capture light from the south while it extends laterally to produce the side walls and eventually a long bench on the east side. The wood finish to the internal face of this structural skin explores the theme of continuity. The internal face is clad entirely in wood: ceilings, walls and furniture are continuous like the inside of a beer barrel or the surface of a velodrome. ✦

The Azadi Cineplex programme called for the arrangement of seven screening rooms (with 150 to 700 seats) and a series of exhibition and business areas on a 45 x 43–metre plot in downtown Tehran, initially occupied by the city's most famous cinema. The FOA proposal pitted against this nostalgic and monumental project a figurative idea that was instantly turned into a formal argument: the organization of the project was oriented like a film of folded celluloid. A strip of floor rises up in many folds, forming, stack-like, the spaces of the different rooms and circulation thoroughfares. At the same time, this surface forms the complex's load-bearing structure, producing tube-beams and leaving the 43-metre façade free. In order to maintain the activity of the floor outside the period when the screening rooms are in use, these are located in the middle of the section, leaving the ground floor for commercial activities and giving the restaurants and cultural areas the top of the building, with a view over the city. ✤

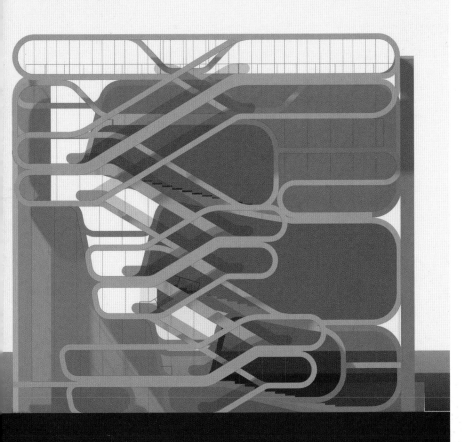

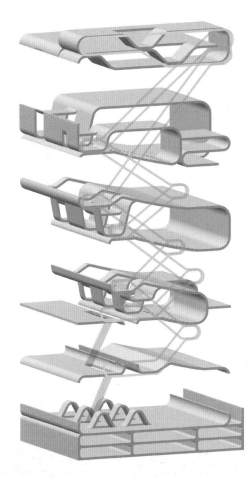

✦ Link-Quay Waterfront of Santa Cruz

TENERIFE, SPAIN
COMPETITION, 1998

The FOA proposal grasped the opportunity of a very large flat surface in an urban landscape that is characterized by very strong topography. Urban sport, large-scale performances and mass events will be be located in a particularly appropriate topography, a kind of 'space of possibility'. The proposal involves the construction of the programmes to be placed on this area as a series of 'pontoons', or piers, grounded on the harbour platforms, adding a variety of programs to the site and resolving the connection between the city level and the harbor platform by bridging the harbour road and ramping down smoothly. In order to provide a structural approach to the whole waterfront area, this project may become an overall strategy to treat the harbour domains, not as a single complex loosely controlled but as a chain of independent islands intensively controlled, in space and in time. ✦

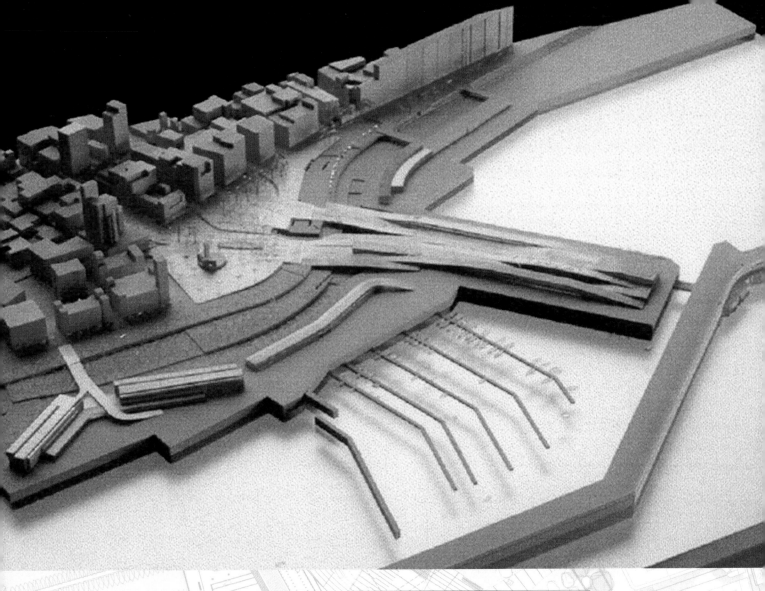

✦ Foreign Office Architects

Farshid Moussavi (1965)
Architecture Diploma, Bartlett School of Architecture, London
Master of Architecture, Harvard Graduate School of Design, Massachusetts

Alejandro Zaera-Polo (1963)
Architecture Diploma from the Technical College, Madrid
Master of Architecture, Harvard Graduate School of Design, Massachusetts

1995   Founded FOA, Foreign Office Architects in London

Teaching
Both have been teaching regularly in Europe and the USA since 1989
1999   F. Moussavi: Princeton University; Berlage Institute, Amsterdam;
       Architectural Association, London
1999   A. Zaera-Polo: Princeton University; Berlage Institute

Principal buildings and projects
1999–96   Yokohama International Ferry Terminal, Yokohama (under con-
          struction)
1999   New Belgo Restaurant (under construction), London
1999–98   Private apartment, London
1998   Belgo Restaurant, New York; Belgo Restaurant, Bristol; Rome
       Congress Centre, Rome (competition)
1998–97   Link-Quay Waterfront, Santa Cruz (competition)
1997   Bermondsey Antiques Market Design Commission, London;
       Government Centre, Bonn (project); Mirage City, mainland China
       (project); Azadi Multi Cinema Complex, Tehran (competition); Virtual
       House, USA (competition)
1996   Kansai-Kan National Diet Library, Kansai (competition); Taichung
       New Government Centre, Taiwan (competition)
1995   Private house, Hove, UK
1994   National Glass Centre, Newcastle (competition), UK
1993   Europan 3, Le Havre (competition)

1992   International consultation/*Quaderns*, Expo '92, Seville

Exhibitions
1998   Collection at the Design Museum, London
1998   Swedish Museum of Architecture, Stockholm
1997   'Critical Projects' RIBA, London; 'Cyber Architecture' Imagina,
       Monaco
1996   6th Venice Architecture Biennale, Korean Pavilion
1995   MACBA (Museum of Contemporary Arts) Barcelona; 'Work in
       Progress: Yokohama International Port Terminal' AA, London

Principal publications (Alejandro Zaera-Polo)
1998   'New Platforms' *ANYhow*, MIT Press, Cambridge, MA
1994   'Jean Nouvel: Intensifying the Real' *El Croquis* no. 65/66, Madrid
1992   'Notes for a Topographic Survey' *El Croquis* no. 53, Madrid

Selected bibliography
1999   'Belgo Projects' *Blue Print* (Jan.)
1998   *Building* (November); *The British Young Architects Directory*, UK
1997   'New Science = New Architecture?' *Architectural Design* no. 129;
       'New Geography' *Ten Plus One* magazine no. 11, Inax Publishing,
       Japan; 'Territoriality' *De Architect*, Netherlands; 'After Geometry'
       Architectural Design, UK; *GA Japan* (Jan.); 'Virtual House' *Building
       Design* nos 1309 and 1313
1996   'Architecture on the Horizon' *Architectural Design*, UK; 'Waterland'
       Quaderns no. 212; *Present and Futures: Architecture in Cities* cata-
       logue of the XIXth Congress of the UIA; *Building Design* nos 1279
       and 1281, UK; *El Croquis* no. 76, Spain
1995   *Monolithic Architecture* Prestel Verlag, Germany; *GA Japan* (no. 14),
       Japan; *Arch +* (nos 126, 128) Germany; *Architectural Design*
       (October), UK; *l'Arca* (June), Italy;
       Bauwelt (March), Germany

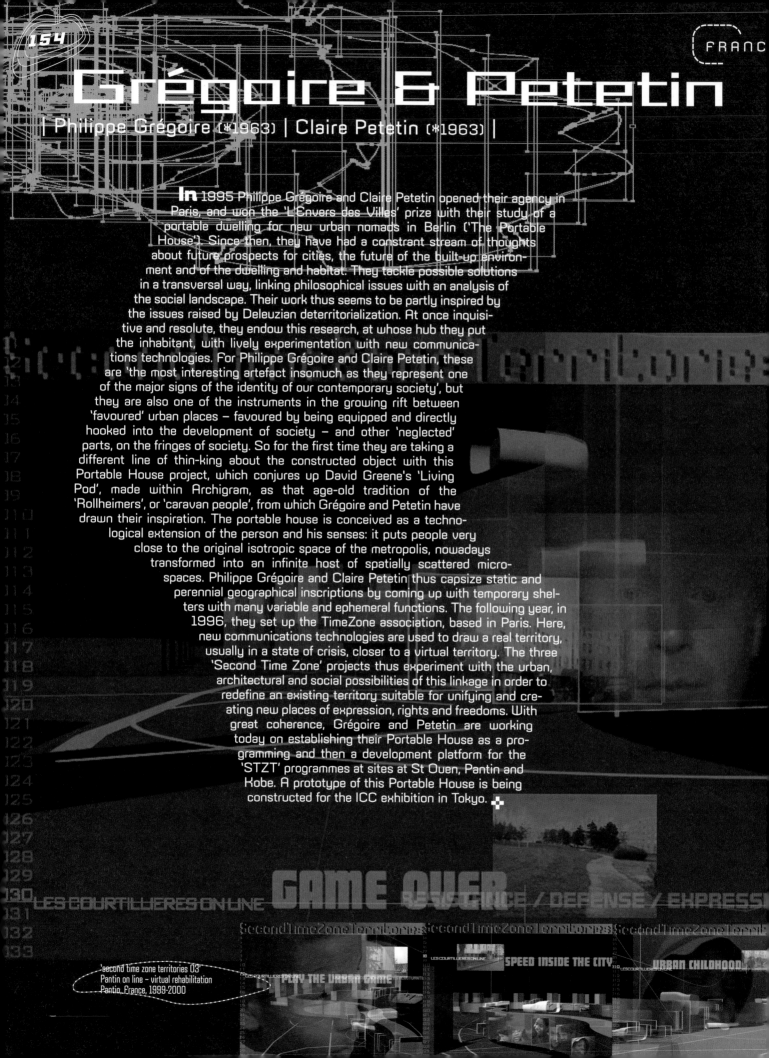

Grégoire & Petetin

| Philippe Grégoire (*1963) | Claire Petetin (*1963) |

In 1995 Philippe Grégoire and Claire Petetin opened their agency in Paris, and won the 'L'Envers des Villes' prize with their study of a portable dwelling for new urban nomads in Berlin ('The Portable House'). Since then, they have had a constant stream of thoughts about future prospects for cities, the future of the built-up environment and of the dwelling and habitat. They tackle possible solutions in a transversal way, linking philosophical issues with an analysis of the social landscape. Their work thus seems to be partly inspired by the issues raised by Deleuzian deterritorialization. At once inquisitive and resolute, they endow this research, at whose hub they put the inhabitant, with lively experimentation with new communications technologies. For Philippe Grégoire and Claire Petetin, these are 'the most interesting artefact insomuch as they represent one of the major signs of the identity of our contemporary society', but they are also one of the instruments in the growing rift between 'favoured' urban places – favoured by being equipped and directly hooked into the development of society – and other 'neglected' parts, on the fringes of society. So for the first time they are taking a different line of thin-king about the constructed object with this Portable House project, which conjures up David Greene's 'Living Pod', made within Archigram, as that age-old tradition of the 'Rollheimers', or 'caravan people', from which Grégoire and Petetin have drawn their inspiration. The portable house is conceived as a technological extension of the person and his senses: it puts people very close to the original isotropic space of the metropolis, nowadays transformed into an infinite host of spatially scattered microspaces. Philippe Grégoire and Claire Petetin thus capsize static and perennial geographical inscriptions by coming up with temporary shelters with many variable and ephemeral functions. The following year, in 1996, they set up the TimeZone association, based in Paris. Here, new communications technologies are used to draw a real territory, usually in a state of crisis, closer to a virtual territory. The three 'Second Time Zone' projects thus experiment with the urban, architectural and social possibilities of this linkage in order to redefine an existing territory suitable for unifying and creating new places of expression, rights and freedoms. With great coherence, Grégoire and Petetin are working today on establishing their Portable House as a programming and then a development platform for the 'STZT' programmes at sites at St Ouen, Pantin and Kobe. A prototype of this Portable House is being constructed for the ICC exhibition in Tokyo. ✦

'second time zone territories 03'
Pantin on line – virtual rehabilitation
Pantin, France, 1999-2000

Second Time Zone Territories 02

WWW.SECONDTIMEZONE.COM
KOBE ON LINE – VIRTUAL REHABITATION
ASHIYA ISLAND, KOBE, JAPAN, 1999–2000

The island of Ashiya has endured several handicaps since the 1995 earthquake and the 1997 economic crisis in Asia. Furthermore this area currently houses refugees who live in complete isolation in the middle of a wasteland covering 9 hectares, originally destined for a luxury harbour development. Against this backdrop of crisis and isolation Petetin and Grégoire propose a project that analyses and understands the situation and its urban context. The environment is mutated to create an 'object-tool' in the hands of the refugees. A creative agenda and a method of communication are developed for the inhabitants of the island through an Internet site that replicates their real environment. The current reality of the land-townscape is modelled in 3D VRML and can be inhabited with 'trace-objects' (texts, films, photographs), which will create a new environment. It can be modified by the inhabitant's aspirations, criticisms and their personal relationship to their surroundings. For the architects these 'traces' could be transcribed to the real. Their personal input would allow the inhabitants to re-appropriate their space in a completely different way. ✦

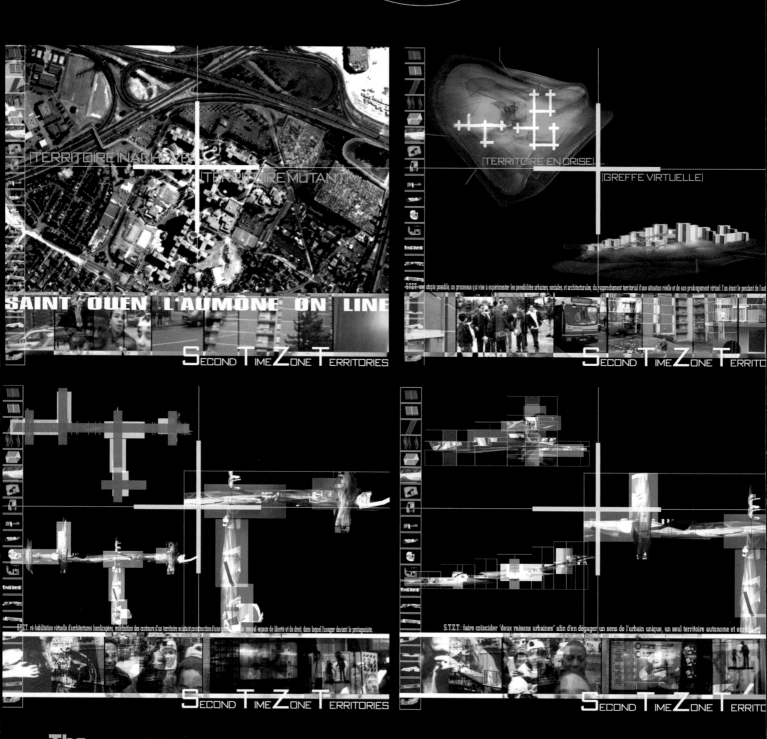

✦ Second Time Zone Territories 01

WWW.SECONDTIMEZONE.COM
St-Ouen-l'Aumône on line – Virtual Rehabitation
Chennevières district, St-Ouen-l'Aumône, France, 1999–2000

[TERRITOIRE INACHEVÉ]

[TERRITOIRE MUTANT]

[TERRITOIRE EN CRISE]

[GREFFE VIRTUELLE]

SAINT OUEN L'AUMÔNE ON LINE

Second Time Zone Territories

Second Time Zone Territo

S.T.Z.T.: une utopie possible, un processus qui vise à expérimenter les possibilités urbaines, sociales, et architecturales, du rapprochement territorial d'une situation réelle et de son prolongement virtuel. l'un étant le pendant de l'aut

S.T.Z.T.: ré-habilitation virtuelle d'architectures handicapées, redéfinition des contours d'un territoire existant,construction d'une grille, d'un nouvel espace de liberté et de droit, dans lequel l'usager devient le protagoniste.

S.T.Z.T.: faire coïncider 'deux raisons urbaines' afin d'en dégager un sens de l'urbain unique, un seul territoire autonome et entre

Second Time Zone Territories

Second Time Zone Territo

The series of STZT projects, developed in parallel, aim to create a relationship between real spaces and their virtual duplicate by means of an Internet site. In Philippe Grégoire's and Claire Petetin's opinion the extension of space generated by the virtual offers the very real possibility of playing with the boundaries and the perception of space by implanting virtual microcosms where imagined life and city interact and mix with reality. ✦

espaces vacants
espaces habités
accès +/-
information
repérage
membrane
espaces virtuels

S.T.Z.T.: espace de prolongement du lien social pour communautés émergentes.

SECOND TIMEZONE TERRITORIES

espaces vacants
espaces habités
accès +/-
information
repérage
membrane
espaces virtuels

1998 2002
2000 2003

S.T.Z.T.: intervention sur des territoires en crise, isolés, des territoires en rupture de lien social, habités par des communautés désarmées.

SECOND TIMEZONE TERRITORIES

S.T.Z.T.: temps d'imbrication des deux états.

SECOND TIMEZONE TERRITORIES

015
032
031
021
030

S.T.Z.T.: 'habitat avatar' mise en place de protocoles permettant l'ECHANGE EN TEMPS REEL d'informations entre l'environnement concret (le vécu, le quotidien) et la spatialité émergen

SECOND TIMEZONE TERRITORIES

Second TimeZoneTerritories is an experimental project with the objective of exploring the characteristics of a habitat in crisis to generate a virtual, parallel space where the inhabitants can participate in the regeneration of their own environment. For Philippe Grégoire and Claire Petetin the issue is to rethink housing as a place of communication. It should play a central role in all social, cultural and economic development to generate and fertilize a new urbanity. STZT, in its first phase, is a tool for the inhabitants. They acquire the opportunity to produce, present and promote themselves in their very own context. Information will be continuously exchanged between virtual and real space, two poles of the same entity: the living memory of everyday life. The onsite reality of this project will be a micro IT laboratory, which will be set up in the centre of the area. It will act as a focus for the development of the programme for this project. Once it is clearly defined the project will 'live' on an Internet site that will become a true exchange between the island and the exterior world: an active link with the objective to create new identity. ❖

✦ Portable House
INDIVIDUAL GLOBAL HOME
BERLIN, 1996-2000

Inspired by an age-old tradition in Berlin, th of the Rollheimers, or 'caravan people', Philippe Grégoire and Claire Petetin's Portable House is presented like a fleeting moment of emergence in the heart of the metropolis. It inhabits the surface, moves about on it, attaches itself to it and is akin to the household space of the domicile and the public place of the street. The challenge of the Grégoire and Petetin project is well served by this proximity and mobility: the model of an alternative space-time set against the 'gridded' metropolis on which the Portable House stands. It thus becomes a cut out, a micro-gap on the surface of the metropolis: a moment of paradoxical continuity. Grégoire and Petetin have designed it to be as similar to the body as possible, like an item of clothing, it becomes 'clothing-inhabitable', a technological and variable extension of this body. With an attentive eye on the various drifts away from the strict demarcations of the metropolis, they thus look for the best-suited materials and instruments, those of sports and computers, in particular, so as to meet the desire to be exposed and protected by the filter of this new proximity. ✦

[TERRITOIRES 1]

[MOBILES 2]

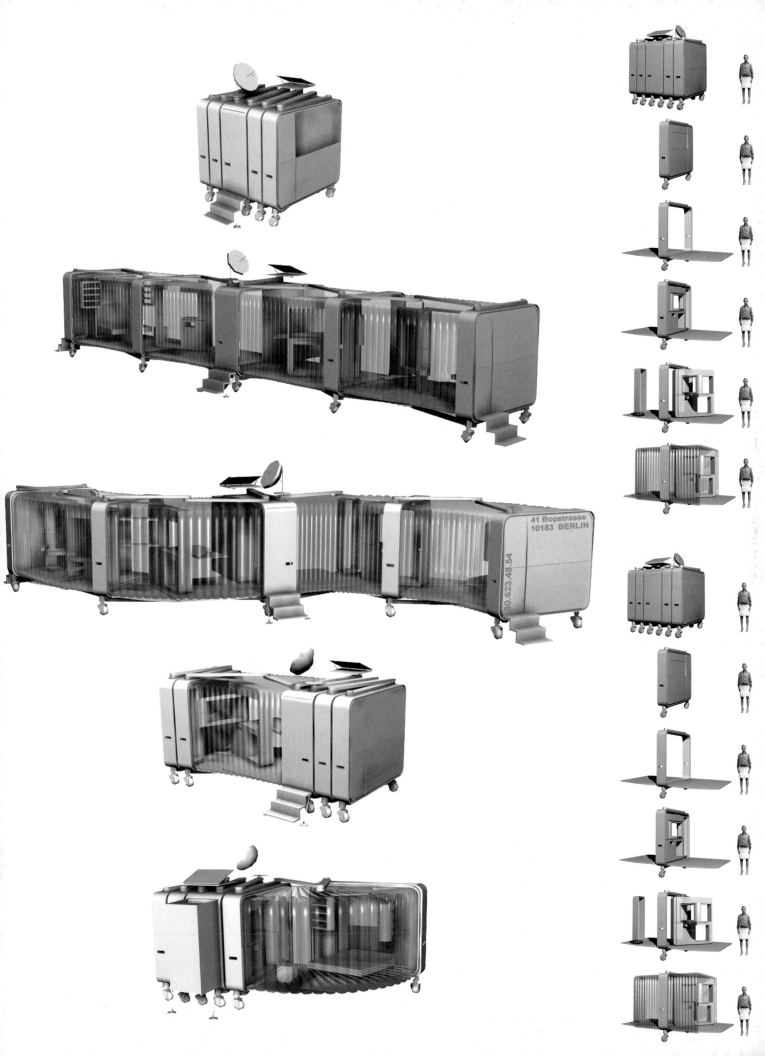

41 Bopstrasse
10183 BERLIN

30.623.48.54

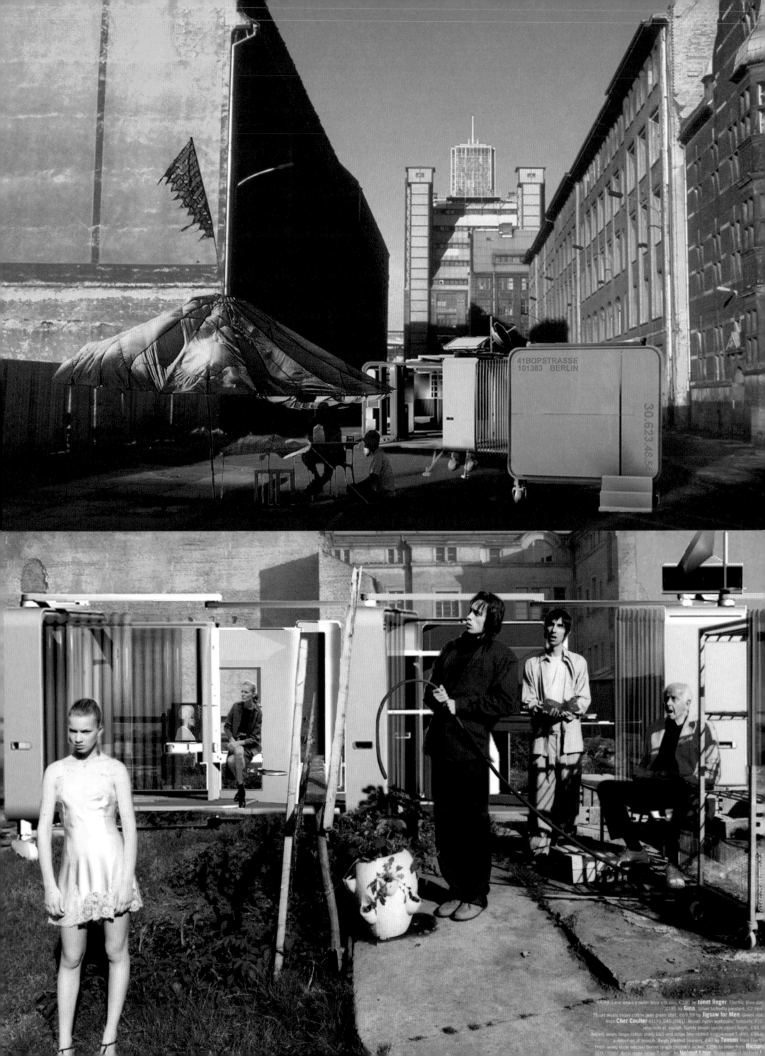

41BOPSTRASSE
101383 BERLIN

30.623.48.5

Grégoire & Petetin

Claire Petetin (1963)
1991 Diploma DPLG
1992 Master, Milan Polytechnic

Philippe Grégoire (1963)
1989 Diploma DPLG

1995 Creation of the practice in Paris
1996 Creation of TimeZone Association in Paris

Teaching
Claire Petetin
2000–1998 School of Architecture of Bretagne (assistant to Benoît Cornette)
1997 School of Architecture at Paris-Villemin, workshop with Philippe Grégoire

Principal buildings and projects
2000 'La Maison Portable' study prototype for the ICC exhibition Tokyo 2000; 'S.T.Z.T.': creation of website: www.secondtimezone.com
1999 'S.T.Z.T. 01 St Ouen-l'Aumône on-line': virtual rehabilitation of the Chennevières district by proposing reconstitution of social links (under construction); 'S.T.Z.T. 02 Ashiya-Island on-line': virtual rehabilitation of the Kobe district for the casualties of the earthquake of 1995 (under construction); 'S.T.Z.T. 03 Pantin on-line', virtual rehabilitation of the Courtillières district to disengage it from its context (under construction)
1998 U.F.R. Arts Paris VIII: creation of website; 'IGH-1' 'IGH-2': 'Individual-Global-Homes': minimal dwellings
1996 'IGH-Matrix': 'Individual-Global-Homes': study for a portable dwelling for new urban nomads in Berlino. Prototype + videofilm + photo reportage + interviews; Prix 'L'Envers des Villes' AFAA-CDC

Exhibitions
2000 'S.T.Z.T. 03 Pantin on-line' Festival of Citizenship, Ministry for Youth and Sport, Courtillères Civic Centre at Pantin
1999 'E-Spaces ' Purple Institute; 'S.T.Z.T.' São-Paulo Art Biennale (Nov.), FIAC 99, Plastic Arts (Sept.), CAUE 92, virtual architec-

tures (June/Sept.)
1998 'Trans-architecture': DEAF 98, Rotterdam, Dutch Electronic Art Festival Interfacing; Biennale of Contemporary Art at Montréal (Oct./Nov.) and AEDES East Berlin (August); 'Berlin Alternative' Montréal-200m3 (Feb./April); 'Trans-Architecture 02': Arc-en-Rêve, Bordeaux (Jan.)
1997 'Trans-Architecture 02': Labo, Florence (Dec.) ; Film+Arc, Graz (Nov.); Columbia University, New York (Oct.) and IFA, Paris (June); 'Trans-Architecture 01' Imagina, Monaco (Feb.)

Selected bibliography
1999 *Kobe IN-EX 01* extraordinary, In-Ex projects/Birkhaüser Verlag, Basel/Paris; *Techniques & Architectures* nos 443 and 445
1998 'La Maison Portable' *ICC-Intercommunication* no. 26, Japan; 'TransArchitectures' *ICC-Intercommunication* no. 24; *Intramuros* no. 76 (April); *Art Inter Actuel* no. 69, Quebec; *Techniques & Architectures* no. 435, *Ville et Architecture*, Franco-Japanese summit (13/14 Nov.)
1997 'Une valise pour Berlin' *d'Architectures* no. 72 (Feb.)
1996 'Pages Paysages' *Contacts* no. 6
1995 'L'Envers des villes' *d'Architectures* (Sept.)
1994 'Europan III' *Le Moniteur de l'architecture* no. 54 (Sept.)

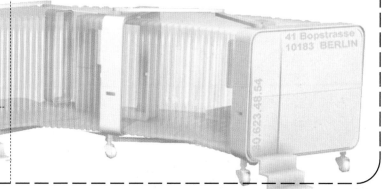

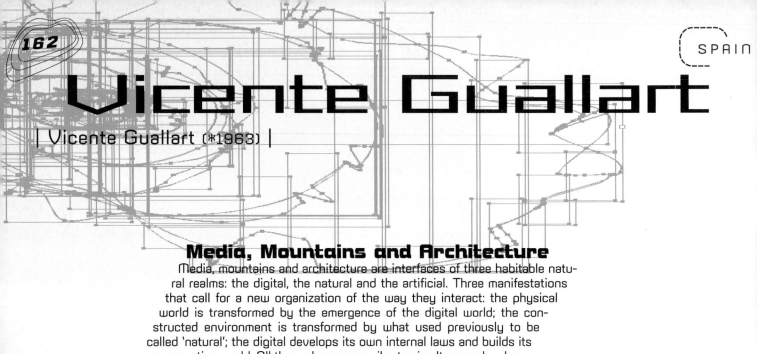

Vicente Guallart

| Vicente Guallart (*1963) |

Media, Mountains and Architecture

Media, mountains and architecture are interfaces of three habitable natural realms: the digital, the natural and the artificial. Three manifestations that call for a new organization of the way they interact: the physical world is transformed by the emergence of the digital world; the constructed environment is transformed by what used previously to be called 'natural'; the digital develops its own internal laws and builds its own operative world. All three phenomena vibrate simultaneously when faced with any kind of human action. My projects explore people's capacity to construct a habitable environment by assuming this new threeway interaction. Starting from the hypothesis that the end purpose of architecture is not (solely) to build but also to define environments where human life can be organized, I work as much through action as through omission; with stones as well as with glass and 'bits'; in urban and rural territories; and in the physical and virtual worlds. As a traditionally constructed interface, architecture must thus redefine its aims in the face of the emergence of the digital world, which encompasses and transforms everything, and through which people become immersed in a new reality. This situation might in addition give rise to an historical gap between a dazzling, luminous, thrilling and creative world on the one hand, and a deteriorated, dark and decadent physical world on the other. But these two worlds form just one and must be constructed at one and the same time. This situation produces a new operative system in which the architect must be able to take part, by making the most of all the physical and digital means within his reach. The architect must consequently assume the fact of experiencing, today, a moment when new paradigms are being invented, a moment when we are defining new human activities and changing existing situations, which require new constructed references. It is a moment of linguistic fervour, of inventing and experimenting with new materials, of developing new constructive processes, incorporating natural and artificial forms of energy, defining viable growth, recycling and reinforming cities, a moment of getting acquainted with new relationships in the physical world through an experimental passage in the virtual world. It is thus important to think about this new hybrid condition of the world that is peculiar to our day and age. The natural, the artificial and the digital. By way of media, mountains and architecture. ✦

VICENTE GUALLART

Plaza del Arbol
Valencia, 1991

✦ Mountains, the City of a Thousand Geographies

EXHIBITION, MADRID, SPAIN, 1998

Mountains are concentrations of natural or artificial energy which make them inhabitable. They are craggy folds of the ground, within or outside the city. They are accumulations of organic and economic matter. Mountains come into being like products of an accumulative act at a given moment in history. The organic mountain rises up out of a natural cycle, by way of a folding of sedimentary strata, by the upthrust of inner forces or through an eruption of magma. The artificial mountain rises up from the momentary accumulation of man's activities – intellectual, economic, religious... Momentarily, the mountain takes shape as the product of its origins and interaction with its environment. A mountain has neither beginning nor end. We only ever observe just one moment of its history. A mountain is the X-ray of a place. Its cross-section helps us to get to know about its past, and its immediate or distant environment helps us to predict its future. ✦

✦ House at Lliria

VALENCIA, SPAIN, 1994–96

The client: I'd like a big house. As a child, I lived in a conventional house,
with an L-shaped living room and a small bedroom where you could hear the TV all the time. Today I'd like to have a big, very lofty space, with lots of light and not much furniture. The bedroom will be upstairs with a view of the mountains.

The architect: That's a good idea.

The client: I'd like to have a garden, too, with trees and flowers, a tennis court
and a pool, but I don't want to have to tend an orchard like my father did.

The architect: We'll make it completely artificial. Plastic lawn, metal trees, false mountains made with the ground we dig up, flowers with coloured lights...
It won't be a 'consolatory' project.

The client: But I've only got a small budget.

The architect: Getting the best quality possible at minimal cost is a good enough challenge. We'll construct a noble building with simple materials.

The client: How are we going to do that?

The architect: The house will be hard and comfortable; abstract and natural at one and the same time. ✦

✚ Around the Arab Wall at Valencia

VALENCIA, SPAIN, 1998–99

+Vicente Guallart, Arquitecto

Vicente Guallart (1963)
1992 Creation of the practice in Barcelona

Principal buildings and projects
2000 Arab wall in the historical centre of Valencia, city planning, housing, crèche (under construction)
1999 Co-founder of the Festival for Advanced Architecture 'Metapolis'
1998 'Scape House – 36 models for a house' (project); The digital man's house, exhibition commission, Architects' Foundation, Madrid; Webhotel (project); 'The city of a thousand geographies'/'Montañas'
1997 'House of seven summits'; 'Around Barcelona' CD-ROM
1996/95 Loft Metapolitano, Lliria, Valencia (realized)
1994 New Media Productions, multimedia production society with the artist Nuria Diaz: realization of 'Mateo at ETH' CD-ROM, world contemporary architecture (Möbius prize 1995)
1993 House in the desert (project)
1992 House in the historic centre of Barcelona (realized)
1991 Plaza del Arbol, Valencia

Recent exhibitions
1999 'Barcelona Metapolis' Festival for Advanced Architecture
1998 'Fabrication': 'Webhotel' Museum of Contemporary Art, Barcelona; MOMA, New York and San Francisco, and Wexner, Columbus
1997 'Thirty-six models for a house' Arc en Rêve architecture centre, Bordeaux

Selected bibliography
2000 *Medias, Mountains & Architecture*, Actar, Barcelona (in preparation)
1999 *Singular Housing* Actar/Birkhaüser Verlag, Barcelona/Basel
1998 *Housing. New alternatives. New systems* Actar, Barcelona; *Fabrications* exhibition catalogue, MACBA, Actar; *Quaderns* no. 220; *Metapolis 1.0* Actar, Barcelona
1997 *36 modèles pour une maison* Périphériques, Paris; *Quaderns* no. 217
1991 *Plaza del Arbol* Europan II catalogue, Spain

ITALY

IaN+

| Luca Galofaro (*1965) | Carmelo Baglivo (*1964) | Stefania Manna (*1969) |

There is a common matrix in the movement of culture, which at a certain point makes painting, music and dance move in the same directions as those in which the sciences are moving. Einstein wrote that in the new physics there is no place for matter, as the field (that is, energy tensions) is the only reality and there is nothing else, nothing else to talk about. Architecture is an assemblage of energy fields connected to time: their organization produces space. Some years ago during a lesson Dino Formaggio mused that architecture as the art of time was gaining ground over architecture as the art of space. Architectonic space has usually been considered as a static space, static in its being an object and container. At this point, time enters as a mere control variable, which encloses in its deeper meaning the conquest of movement; space therefore has to be conceived in a different way, as a structure in the process of becoming. The planning process has to be considered in its essence, that is, in transformation, tied to different parameters able to highlight the incessant and continuous metamorphosis, to indicate and underline this movement and these transformations; it enriches the architectonic product with new and unexpected qualities; the substance is shown through deeper and more rooted reasons; life is again the main concern of the man who organizes space; the architect regains his role. To think of an architecture in movement is restrictive; it is the process that has to be considered in movement. The notion of time changes within us as has the concept of form has done, passing from the culture of being to the one of becoming. The form represents neither a starting point nor a finishing point, but a managing system; the direction is to fix some parameters through which to set up a self-producing dynamic, to introduce in the project elements capable of starting the process. These elements are the activity zones that represent daily actions and their fluctuations: they highlight the real and virtual movements between the activities, which are in tight correlation and able to shape the space. The different activities are separated yet interconnected through the limits. Seen as crossing and meeting points, the limits circumscribe the field of action; they are not lines of constant thickness but zones that can be expand to become exchange interzones. The interzone becomes the point of maximum visibility, of coagulation and concentration of experiences. Once these parameters are set, it is necessary to regulate and organize them in the void, transforming the traces of movement into architectonic spaces. These invisible elements exist and are the true matrix of the buildings, of the cities and of the space surrounding us; all we have to do is find them and seize every means of rendering them visible in the end.

IAN+

✦ Goethe's House

SHINKENCHIKU-SHA, TOKYO, JAPAN
COMPETITION, 1999

The initial gesture in the project for Goethe's House was a formal reflection on the space of the house, not on the static shape or form of the architecture, but a study of the possible variations of the spaces of the house through transformations of form. In fact, in his scientific research, Goethe studied the metamorphosis of form. Conscious of the historical significance of this term, IaN+, however, take Goethe's interest in changing form as a starting point for reflecting on the transition of form from one shape to another. They use the action of the transition of form to define the space of the house. The building starts as a simple abstract container that distends and contracts in continual change through human use, as a registration of human presence and desire. IaN+ have sought to de-emphasize the force of gravity by eliminating the clear division between floors, ceilings and walls. The spatial continuum expresses the flux of vital forces in the house as a living organism might. ✦

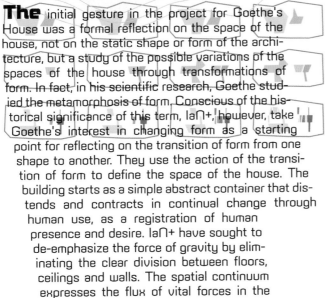

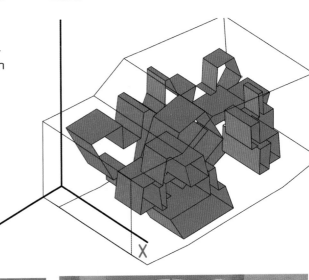

✦ EUR-Italia Congress Centre
ROME, ITALY, COMPETITION, 1998

The building is open even if its perimeter is not completely permeable but flexible and unstable, permitting an adjustable connection with the surrounding city. On the front side of the building the screen wall represents the strongest means of communication. Meeting the demands of the tender which required a plenary session hall for about 10,000 people, without using the principal hall of 3,000 seats, laⁿ+ transformed the whole building into an assembly hall. At each floor there are service areas, conference halls, vertical connections, organized as a solid block, and a flexible area free to be arranged in a different way according the needs and the type of congress. The overlapped levels at variable heights in front of the services areas become a terraced system that will permit the 10,000 visitors to take part in the plenary assembly by means of its projection on a screen. The hall is organized in a vertical way like Italian theatres. In its interior solid and void have the same value, as both locate an exact field of action, where the activities guide the configuration of the architecture. ✦

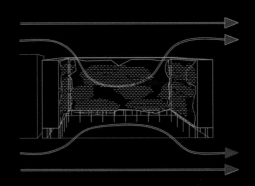

✦ Administrative Headquarters, Italian Space Agency

ROME, ITALY, INTERNATIONAL COMPETITION, 2000

The 'white-hot magma' is a whole constituted by points of energy continuously rising up and disappearing. The never-ending flow of lava escapes and shapes matter that is constantly changing , becoming the energy to model space. As inside magma, flows dictate the shape of this architecture and give order to the space. Order loses its character of permanence and becomes one of many possible interpretations, an instantaneous and subjective reading, a fragile certainty emerging from unforeseeability and chaos. The space into which one moves is defined by superimposition of orders, by juxtaposition of changeable frequency sources. Borders disappear, edges becomes mobile, reality is ruled by flows, intersections are points of accumulation. As to the building's spatial organization, there are three main zones, which are placed in close connection with each other by mutual exchanges of energy and flows. Spatial separation makes every zone autonomous but at the same time lets the different zones have a physical and mental exchange between the office and entertainment functions of the agency. ✦

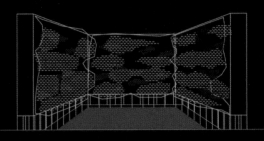

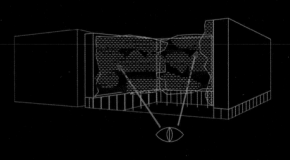

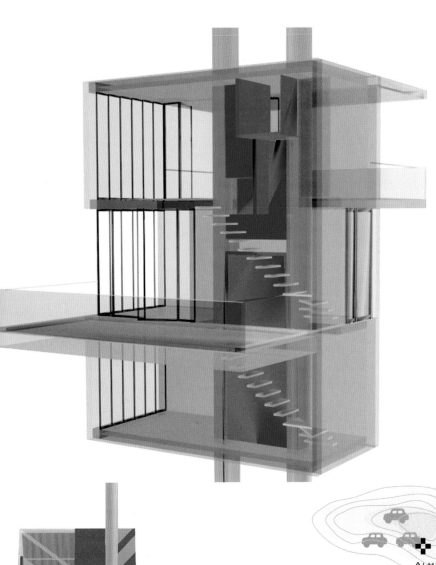

COMMUNICATION

✚ Europan 5

ALMERE, THE NETHERLANDS,
COMPETITION, 1998

In this project la∩+ mix low-density single-family homes, each with its own garden, with high-density housing. Rather than the separate elements appearing as a heterogeneous mixture of different types, the various elements are then reassembled in a 7-metre-thick slab. Open landscape and gardens and the high- and low-density residential elements are combined within this block. As an urban strategy, this system of landscape levels is best considered as a high-density system and not as an isolated building; in fact, by increasing the density of the single slabs, the buildings are transformed into vertical landscapes. The solid and void are merged into the one element and are equally important. Like John Cage, who described the presence of silence in his compositions as the 'nothing in between', la∩+ considers that void and solid have the same importance. In this project, the gaps in the structure are not simply an absence of matter but actual force fields. These fields would enable the building to blend.

5
4
3
2
1

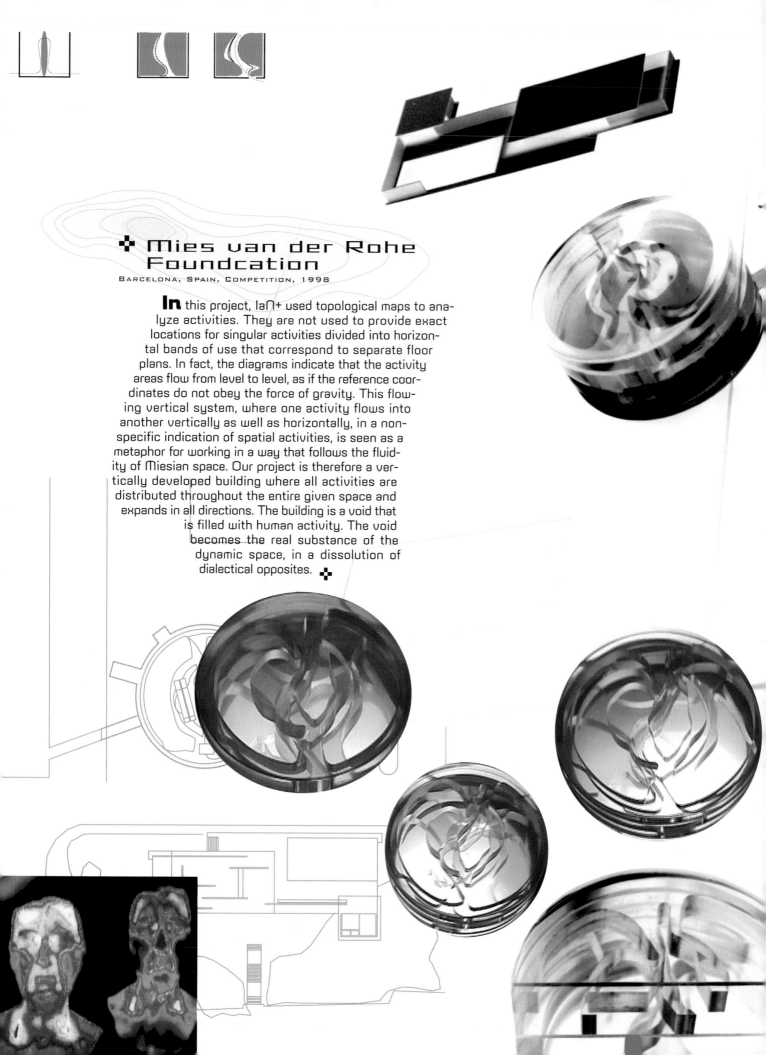

✦ Mies van der Rohe Foundcation

BARCELONA, SPAIN, COMPETITION, 1998

In this project, IaΠ+ used topological maps to analyze activities. They are not used to provide exact locations for singular activities divided into horizontal bands of use that correspond to separate floor plans. In fact, the diagrams indicate that the activity areas flow from level to level, as if the reference coordinates do not obey the force of gravity. This flowing vertical system, where one activity flows into another vertically as well as horizontally, in a non-specific indication of spatial activities, is seen as a metaphor for working in a way that follows the fluidity of Miesian space. Our project is therefore a vertically developed building where all activities are distributed throughout the entire given space and expands in all directions. The building is a void that is filled with human activity. The void becomes the real substance of the dynamic space, in a dissolution of dialectical opposites. ✦

✛ Iaⴎ＋

Luca Galofaro (1965)
1990 Architecture Diploma, University of Rome 'La Sapienza'
1993 Master of Space Sciences, International Space University, UHA, Huntsville, Alabama

Carmelo Baglivo (1964)
1993 Architecture Diploma, University of Rome 'La Sapienza'

Stefania Manna (1969)
1996 Engineering Diploma, University of Rome 'La Sapienza'
2000–1998 Research Doctorate in Construction Engineering, Engineering Faculty of the University of Roma 'La Sapienza'; collaboration with the University of Helsinki and the University of Ulu in Finland
1996 Creation of Studio Iaⴎ＋ in Rome

Principal buildings and projects
2000 Administrative headquarters of the Italian Space Agency, Rome (international competition); Building for scientific research, University of Rome Tor Vergata (under construction); Residential district, 64 residential units, Rome (under construction)
1999 The Goethe House, 9 SKL International Residential Design Competition, Shinkenchiku-sha, Tokyo (mentioned); Apartment, interior, Via L. della Robbia (realized); Three residential units, Vallerano, Rome (under construction); Trevi Flash Art Museum, Perugia (competition. second prize); Sarajevo Concert Hall, Slovenia (competition); Turgau Square, Dresden, Germany (competition)
1998 Europan 5, Almere, Netherlands (competition); EUR-Italia, Congress centre, Rome (competition); New headquarters for the Mies van der Rohe Foundation, Barcelona (competition); Reconstruction of the community buildings and construction of a council chamber and civic centre at Grottaferrata (under construction, with P. Trucchi); 'Architettura Americane @ the Edge of the Millennium' exhibition organization, Rome (invited to UCLA, Los Angeles and to Parson's School of Design, New York); Reconstruction of a veterinary dispensary, Olevano, Rome (realized); Apartment reconstruction, Via M. Fani, Rome (realized)
1997 Single-family house, Infernetto, Rome (project); Apartment reconstruction, Via della Camilluccia, Rome (realized); Showroom for Telecom Italia Mobile Spa, Via del Tritone, Rome (realized with E. Fraracci); Department for diagnosis of high-tech images, hospital complex, San Eugenio, University of Rome, Tor Vergata (realized); Parc de Centocelle, Rome (mentioned)
1996 Family unit, enlargement, Lunghezza Tivoli, Rome (realized); Head office of Telecom Italia Mobile Spa, Via L. Rizzo, Rome (realized with E. Fraracci); Apartment reconstruction, Via Filo Marino, Rome (realized); Apartment reconstruction, Porto Ercole (realized); Centopiazze, Rome (second prize)

Publications
2000 *Rem Koolhaas. Avant-pop architecture* Kappa Edition, Rome (in preparation) *Eero Saarinen* Bruno Zevi -Testo & Immagine, architecture section (in preparation); 'GSW Headquarters, Berlin' *L'industria delle Costruzioni* no. 341
1999 'Cycle track and Olympic pool, Berlin' *L'industria delle Costruzioni* no. 329 *Digital Eisenmanno. An office of the electronic era* Antonino Saggio; *The information revolution in architecture,* Birkhaüser Verlag
1998 'Peter Eisenmano. Works and projects' *I Quaderni de L'industria delle costruzioni,* Monograph (Nov.); 'Jewish Museum in Berlin' *L'industria delle costruzioni* no. 324; 'A church for Rome 2000 Be-Bop Eisenman: notes on a virtual house', *L'industria delle costruzioni* no. 317; 'School of architecture and art centre in Cincinnati' Library in the Place des Nations, Geneva
1997 'Section Big Events – Chicago Tribune Competition' *Bruno Zevi –Testo & Immagine* no. 31

Selected bibliography
2000 'Vision of the future' *Il Progetto* no. 6, Rome
1999 'Made in Europe' *d'Architettura* no. 4/20, Rome; *1°Premio Nazionale di Architettura -Trevi Flash Art Museum* Giancarlo Politi Editore, Milan; *New Italian Blood – Architects under 36 –Award Winning Projects in International Competitions* Editrice Librerie Dedalo, Rome; 'Shinkechiku-sha, 9 SKL International Competition' *JA* (spring 99)
1998 *Mies van der Rohe Foundation Competition* 2G Editorial Gustavo Gili, Barcelona
1997 *Centocelle Park – International Ideas Competition* Department of Territorial Policies – Eastern Directional System Office

Ibos & Vitart

| Jean-Marc Ibos (*1957) | Myrto Vitart (*1955) |

The Ibos & Vitart agency, which opened in 1989, is located in Paris. Jean-Marc Ibos and Myrto Vitart, who both graduated in the early 1980s, are part of the generation that came to the fore in France through the PAN competitions (Ibos was a prizewinner in the twelfth competition in 1981), and through the Cahiers de la Jeune Architecture (Ibos, in 1983). As founder members of Jean Nouvel & Associates in 1985, they took part in the agency's most salient and radical projects up until 1989 ('Nemausus' housing unit, 1987; the 'Endless Tower', 1989; the Conference Centre in Tours, 1989). Empowered by this experience combining design and construction, Ibos and Vitart then decided to join forces on the eve of the 1990s. Their architecture, which has retained a certain radical quality from their association with Nouvel, is firmly rooted in the real. It is neither utopian, nor make-believe, nor even 'virtual', and it does not look for the material of its own experimentation elsewhere than in the objects that surround us. It is located almost exclusively in France, in a socio-economic, political and urban setting where Ibos and Vitart control the cogs and the precise challenges, and as such it always strives to be part of the situations out of which it emerges. This is why Ibos and Vitart each embark upon their projects by way of a very detailed analysis of the programmatic elements, economic limitations and particular issues peculiar to the site. But this systematic identification of the data of the real is not conducted as part of a contextualist quest for disappearance, and dilution of their architecture in the commonplace. On the contrary, it represents the tool for formulating and planning a project that will be at once relevant, effective and critical. For Ibos and Vitart, a radical stance in relation to the real, must be based on complicity with the situation. This is where architecture starts: ahead of construction materials, ahead of the design and the drawing too. It is the situation itself that they endeavour, first of all, to work on and include in the architecture. This inclusion of all the basic data in the equation, which often strikes a chord of subversiveness and paradoxical upheaval, becomes the rule peculiar to each of their projects; it establishes the clarity of their works and their extreme readability once finished. While Nemausus overturned the conventions associated with public housing by giving precedence to the size of the apartments, the projects put forward by Ibos and Vitart invariably show an evident and radical involvement and commitment. Their proposal for the Massena mixed housing development showed a preference for the suburban character of the site as opposed to the official neo-Haussmannesque doctrine. The project for the library and departmental archives in Marseilles reversed the horizontal split of the two plots by putting the two programmes vertically on top of one another. To subvert the ordinariness of this type of construction, without stepping out of the very tight economic framework of which it is part, the project for warehouses C40 and C41 at Gennevilliers was bedecked in two unexpected colours: gold and silver. 'The real is only interesting,' observed Myrto Vitart in the magazine *IN/EX*, 'if you use it to come up with something that at once goes beyond it and becomes part of it.' ✥

Cultural Centre of Saint Herblain
Myrto Vitart for Jean Nouvel & Associés
France, 1988

✤ Notre-Dame de la Pentecôte

LA DÉFENSE, PARIS, COMPETITION, 1994

Building a church on the forecourt at La Défense in Paris means radically rethinking the traditional typology of the religious structure. The high-rise office towers, at once monolithic and crystalline, and vying for height in bristling disorder, straight away proscribe any vertical monumentality for the church. In reconsidering this particular set of problems, Ibos and Vitart based their project on the ideas of 'elevation' and 'presentation'. By taking on the form of a pod, or shiny, opaque blob covered with copper, the church is accordingly presented to the beholder and the sky, suspended on four slender pillars. By playing on a dialectic between concavity and convexity, it promotes from without an innerness, apt for congregations or people simply quietly meditating. As a precious object raised from the ground, asserting its strangeness within a homogeneous setting, the church has obvious access, which is easy, but no less meaningful for all that: at once progression, ascension and alienation. ✤

✦ Palais des Beaux-Arts
LILLE, FRANCE, 1992–97

In addition to the rearrangement of the existing permanent collections, what was involved in this project was to plan for the showing of new acquisitions, and design a temporary exhibition room and premises for conservation and the various departments of a museum thus renovated. The major concern of Ibos and Vitart was to re-emphasize the existing building, a palace of the arts with majestic, neo-classical architecture, hitherto turned inward on to its central plan. Its perspectives, row arrangements and see-through features were singled out and reinstated, thus enabling the building to regain its principal architectural effects. The new extensions observe the same enlightened respect. The temporary exhibition room is buried, freeing up a forecourt behind, where there is a restaurant terrace. The offices and services are housed at the end of the forecourt in a blade-like building offering the reflection of its stippled curtain wall to the old palais, and projecting, ad infinitum, the symmetrical extension originally designed for it. Old and new are linked in this complex interface, between the silk-screened glass and the mural composition of gold and red monochromes. ✦

✦ Cergy-le-Haut Cultural Complex

CERGY-PONTOISE, FRANCE, COMPETITION, 1999

This competition called for the construction of a complex for cultural programmes for Cergy-Pontoise, one of the 'new towns' in the Paris area. This involved, on the one hand, a multimedia centre, a 100-seat auditorium and music studios, and, on the other, a neighbourhood centre including conference rooms, facilities for various activities and a multipurpose hall. In their project, Ibos and Vitart elected to deal with this heterogeneous programmatic complex as a fragmented unit, in the form of an open, unifying block. No programme is conveyed as such through any distinct form. A single glazed curtain wall folds back on to the smooth façades, wrapping each of the three units. These take up the edge of the block, leaving room for a public esplanade, the real heart of the project, at the centre. The only architectural modulation between the programmes is the colour of the glass in the façades. Pale and transparent for the multimedia centre, blue for the neighbourhood centre, black for the studios, the glass takes on a mirror finish on the façades giving on to the inner square, representing the project's 'solution of continuity'. ✦

| Verre teinté noir | Miroir bleu | Miroir argenté | Verre clair | Béton noir |

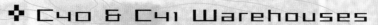

✦ C40 & C41 Warehouses
PORT DE GENNEVILLIERS, FRANCE, 2000-01

These warehouses, which also contain offices, are located in the independent port of Gennevilliers, and resemble two basic volumes beside the river Seine. Placed on black concrete bases, their outer structure consists of simple metal cladding, like any commonplace building of this sort. Ibos and Vitart turn their backs on any kind of technical and structural prowess, and focus on the architectural expressiveness of their shiny, compact warehouses, and their colour: gold for one, silver for the other. By systematically applying its respective colour to all the parts of each building, their intention is to shift them from their normal functions, and alter their industrial ordinariness with an ambiguous interplay of clearly displayed precious materials. By wrapping the roof at the standard railing height, the cladding hides both from prying eyes and thus reinforces the monolithic oddity of the two opaque boxes, which are top-lit. ✦

✦ Massena Sector (ZAC Seine Left Bank)
PARIS, FRANCE, COMPETITION, 1995

The challenge of this competition was the development of a Paris neighbourhood located on the large industrial wasteland at Tolbiac. Lying between the future avenue de France and the river Seine, the Bibliothèque de France and the ringroad, this zone, with its ambiguous status, is in a somewhat awkward position between historic Paris, which lies a little way off, and its immediate suburbs. Ibos and Vitart rejected both the logic of formed blocks, complying with the urban identity of Paris, and any 'neo-Haussmann-esque' annexation of this industrial and local crafts area. Instead, they sought, in their project, to understand, interpret and intensify the specific identity of the site. So it was rather with a discontinuous and suburban logic in mind that Ibos and Vitart drew up their plan. In this way they managed to incorporate within this composition of isolated objects the impressive grain silos, punctuating the site like 'industrial castles', and otherwise doomed to demolition. A double alignment of buildings along the avenue offers a porous façade to the verdant field on which the buildings stand. An interplay of transversal footbridges lends structure to the project and makes full use of the different levels between the avenue and the river Seine. ✦

✦ Ibos & Vitart

Jean-Marc Ibos (1957)
DPLG in 1982

Myrto Vitart (1955)
DPLG in 1984

1985–89 Founder members of Jean Nouvel & Associés
1989   Creation of the practice
1997 Equerre d'Argent
1998 Du Pont Benedictus international prize

Teaching
Jean-Marc Ibos
2000–1998 School of Architecture of Paris la Défense at Nanterre

Jean-Marc Ibos & Myrto Vitart
1995–94 Special Architecture School, Paris

Principal buildings and projects
2001   Warehouses C40 and C41, Port of Gennevilliers (under construc-
       tion); Rescue centre for the Paris fire brigade, Nanterre (under con-
       struction)
2000   'Administrative headquarters for the Italian space agency, Rome
       (international competition); Museum aan de Strom, Anvers (interna-
       tional competition); Extension of the headquarters of the World
       Organization for Intellectual Property, Geneva; Departmental
       archives and lending library, Marseilles (competition)
1999   Arrangement of the Quais Rive Gauche de la Garonne, Bordeaux,
       with Ron Arad and Yann Kersalé (competition); Cultural facilities at
       Cergy-le-haut, Cergy-Pontoise (competition); New communication
       centre for Renault S.A., Boulogne-Billancourt (competition);
       National automobile museum, Mulhouse (competition)
1997–92 Lille Palace of Fine Arts, Lille (realized)
1995   Massena sector, Zac Seine Rive Gauche, Paris (competition)
1994   Notre-Dame de la Pentecôte, Paris la Défense (competition)
1989   Tours congress centre, phase of competition Jean-Marc Ibos and
       Jean Nouvel (realized)
1988–87 Saint Herblain cultural centre, Myrto Vitart for Jean Nouvel &

Associés (realized); Parking Atlantis, Saint Herblain, Myrto Vitart
for Jean Nouvel & Associés with B. and C. Barto (realized)
1987–86 Nemausus, 114 dwellings at Nîmes, Jean-Marc Ibos & Jean
         Nouvel (realized)

Principal publications
1999   *IN-EX Projects 01 extraordinary IN-EX Projects*/Birkhaüser, Basel,
       Berlin, Boston; *Intelligent Glass Façades* 4th edition, Birkhaüser;
       *Architecture reborn, the conversion and reconstruction of old build-
       ing* by Kenneth Powell, Calmann & King, London; *Temps Denses
       1998* by Richard Edwards, Les Éditions de l'Imprimeur; *France: 99
       Architectures en 1999* co-publication by the Industry and
       Architecture Publishing House at Beijing, Jean-Michel Place and
       the Architecture Art Association at Paris; *International Architecture
       Yearbook* (vol. 5) The Images Publishing Group, Australia
1998   *Recréation, 21 Architectures en France à l'aube du XXIème siècle*
       exhibition catalogue presented at the VIIth Buenos Aires
       Architecture Biennale, Ministère de la Culture and AFAA;
       Nouveaux Musées Telleri, Paris; *Collection d'Architecture du
       Centre Georges Pompidou* Centre Georges Pompidou, Paris;
       Premises: Architecture & Design from France 1958-1998 exhibi-
       tion catalogue, The Solomon Guggenheim Museum
1997   *La Consultation Massena* Albert Skira
1996   *Bloc, le monolithe fracturé* exhibition catalogue presented at the
       VIth Mostra Internazionale di Architettura at Venice, HYX, Orléans;
       Conférences Paris d'Architectes, Mini PA, Pavillon de l'Arsenal,
       Paris

Jakob + MacFarlane

| Dominique Jakob (*1966) | Brendan MacFarlane (*1961) |

The T house, the first 1994 project at La Garenne Colombes in the suburbs of Paris, was designed as an absorption box – volumes steeped in the texture and skin of the local setting in which it happens to exist. The question: how is an object to be situated in an alien environment? leads us towards another: how is an object to be attached to its site? how is it to be brought out and 'stitched' in? This quality of stitching recurs in the project of the monument in memory of, and in honour of the peace of, Val de Reuil, where the wall is read together with the surrounding landscape. The geometry of the volume starts to fall apart, and then becomes immersed in the landscape. The extra floor of the T house, a second commission placed three years after the initial one, is a project which abandons reference to the object; the project creates a series of spaces, possibly initiated by turbulences made by wind, for the dwelling and its new rituals. That there are no longer any rooms for the boys as such – at the root of the programme of the second commission. These spaces have shed their usual bedroom connotation – there is no door. The space is left available and made larger, for sleeping and other activities. The private spaces have become ambiguous, interlocked with one another, giving rise to a new urban space actually within the house. Through all our projects the wall appears as a major element, from the early, more right-angled works like the monument, which, in some ways, is a project created solely around a wall, to the latest project involving the additional floor on the T house, which creates a series of wall-ceilings that unfold and change shape. This packaging of the floor-wall-ceiling is currently being worked on for the project to restructure the Maxim Gorki theatre. With the project for the restaurant at the Georges Pompidou Centre, the floor-wall-ceiling wall is an unbroken skin. All the surfaces have the same value, the floor becomes sky, becomes a physical experience, a flotation in a neutral space, where the usual references of scale are upset. This constant interest in working the site for all our projects comes across in the fact that a surface is hewn out or removed based on a reference plan. With the monument, the ground level is the fixed datum, from which there is a 2-metre drop, which then re-emerges at ground level. With the puzzle house, there is again a drop below the reference level, ending up looking at the sky. In the restaurant project for the Georges Pompidou Centre, the reference is the level 70.5 metres (the height of the fifth floor), based on which the bubbles take shape. The reference is still marked by a continuity of materials. We have yielded to the temptation to allow the architecture to disappear in the site as though camouflaged, so that it is no longer possible to define where the beginning or the end of the project lies; the surface of the architecture is treated like a conceptual mirror. This interest was sparked in the first T house and becomes more developed in the various projects, including that of the restaurant, where the skin of the bubbles envelops the functional programmes. We have no particular heroes. Our references are varied and are always evolving. We are interested in architecture as a unique work. We are very suspicious of all systems, responses, dogmas and premature answers. We are happier broaching new technologies and new ideas, even if we come to them later; we prefer not to find ourselves locked into procedures that end up hampering the imagination. We want to be able to develop and evolve in a world that is as open as possible, with projects driven by ideas. ❖

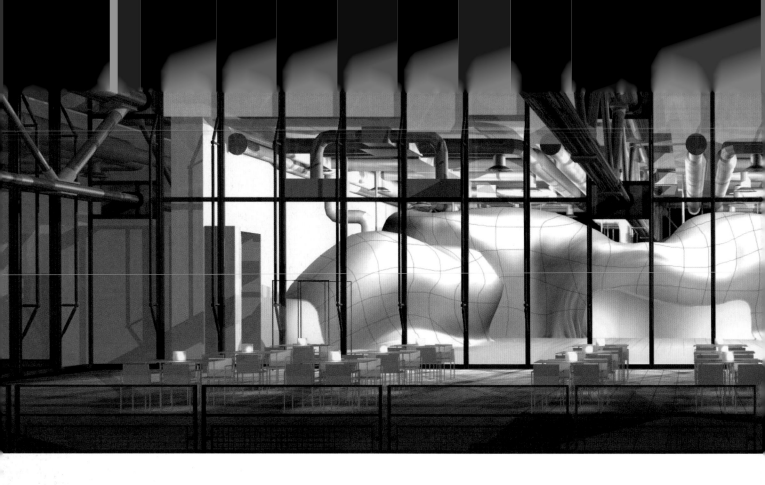

✦ George Restaurant
Centre Georges Pompidou

PARIS, FRANCE
1999 (COMPETITION, 1998)

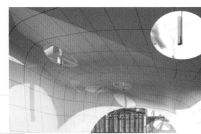

The aim of the project was to conserve the particularly unusual Beaubourg area. It thus showed a preference for dialogue with its specific architectural vocabulary. Jakob and MacFarlane decided accordingly to leave the structure's glass sheath untouched as well as the ventilation ducts and tubing for various liquids, wherever possible. Where the programme involving the restaurant was concerned, this remained well removed from the façades, both to give them clearance and to highlight them. The floor itself, with no structural supports in the restaurant and on the terrace, formed a very extensive smooth surface (14,000 m²), on which Jakob and MacFarlane decided to use aluminium. This would be locally 'inflated' from the ground, and wrap the whole plan like an undersurface, thus turning the project's volumes into fluid forms. ✦

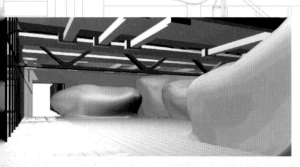

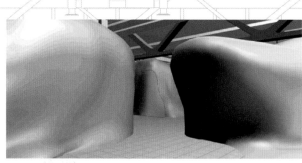

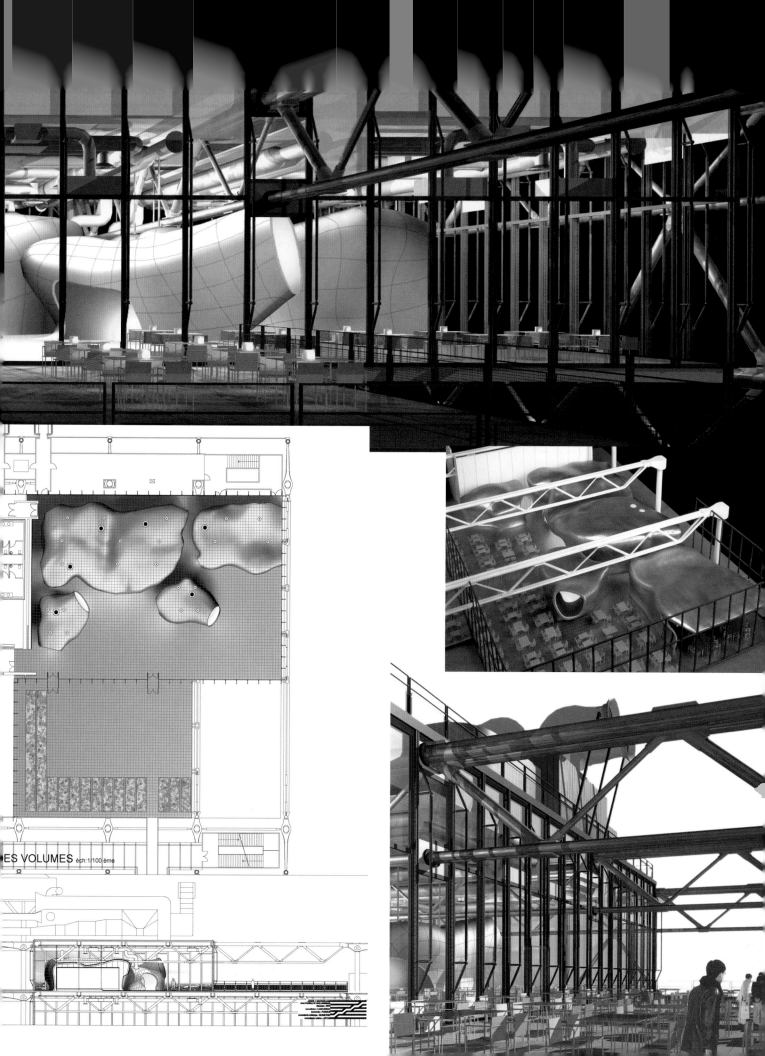

ES VOLUMES éch:1/100 ème

✦ Roof Extension, House T

La Garenne Colombes, France
1998

After an initial 1994 project, which involved absorbing an existing house in the suburbs of Paris, this second project has to do with adding an additional floor to this initial extension, creating a 40 m² loft space for the children. Dominique Jakob and Brendan MacFarlane decided to highlight the extra floor on the existing extension by giving it a different identity. They would offer the two small children two igloos made of zinc, perched on the roof of the existing house. The completed project involves an enclosing envelope made of zinc, broken up into several volumes. This achieves the goal of turning a loft into two igloos, while at the same time taking into account the dictates imposed by a large number of views. The dovetailing of the volumes thus creates a series of openings with complex geometric forms, offering both skyward views and views towards the street, which introduce a diagonal dialogue with the views, this being the intention with regard to the initial extension. ✦

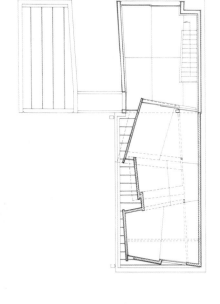

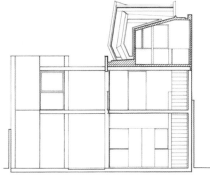

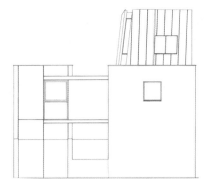

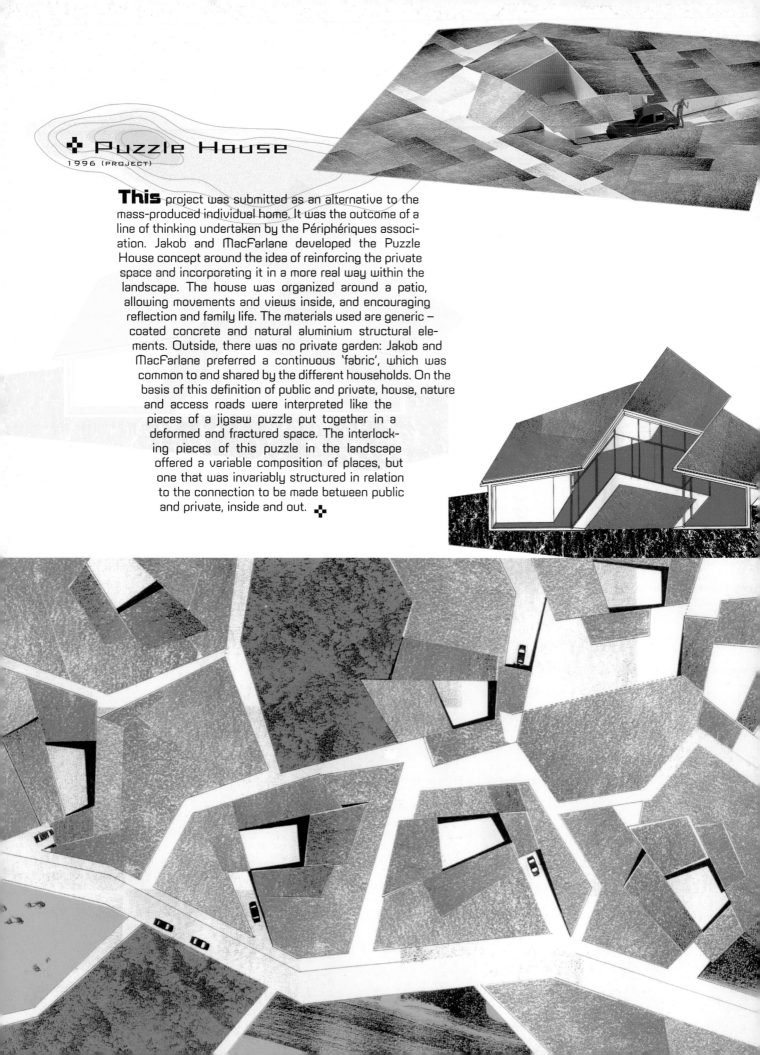

✦ Puzzle House
1996 (PROJECT)

This project was submitted as an alternative to the mass-produced individual home. It was the outcome of a line of thinking undertaken by the Périphériques association. Jakob and MacFarlane developed the Puzzle House concept around the idea of reinforcing the private space and incorporating it in a more real way within the landscape. The house was organized around a patio, allowing movements and views inside, and encouraging reflection and family life. The materials used are generic – coated concrete and natural aluminium structural elements. Outside, there was no private garden: Jakob and MacFarlane preferred a continuous 'fabric', which was common to and shared by the different households. On the basis of this definition of public and private, house, nature and access roads were interpreted like the pieces of a jigsaw puzzle put together in a deformed and fractured space. The interlocking pieces of this puzzle in the landscape offered a variable composition of places, but one that was invariably structured in relation to the connection to be made between public and private, inside and out. ✦

✦ Jakob+MacFarlane

Dominique Jakob (1966)
1991 Diploma from the School of Architecture at Paris-Villemin

Brendan McFarlane (1961)
1984 Bachelor of Architecture, Sci-Arc, Los Angeles
1990 Diploma from Harvard Graduate School

1992 Foundation of the practice in Paris
1995 Creation of the Périphériques association with E. Marin-Trottin & D. Trottin

Teaching
1999–98 B. McFarlane: Bartlett School, London
1999 Both: Special Architecture School, Paris
1999–94 D. Jakob: School of Architecture at Paris-Villemin
1999–95 B. McFarlane: School of Architecture at Paris–La Villette
1988 B. McFarlane: Harvard (MA) and Sci-Arc (CA)

Principal buildings and projects
1998 Restaurant at the Georges Pompidou Centre, Paris (under construction); Fourteen dwellings, Paris (study); Addition of storeys to Maison T, La Garenne-Colombes (realized)
1997 Reconstruction of the Maxim Gorky theatre, Petit-Quevilly (prizewinner); Modernization of the theatre at Pont-Audemer (study); National dance centre, Pantin (competition); Café-Musiques, Savigny (prizewinner with Périphériques); Ten individual houses, Turquénieux (study)
1996 Puzzle House (project); Monument to memory and peace, Val de Reuil (prizewinner with F. Vialet, realized); Arrangement of the Millons at St-Cloud (competition)
1995 Monument to the liberation, La Rochelle (competition); Arrangement of three squares at Coutances (competition)

1994 House T, La Garenne-Colombes (realized)
1992 Atelier Riegelman, Los Angeles (realized)

Recent exhibitions
1997 Arc en Rêve, Bordeaux; Pavillon de l'Arsenal, Paris; Bartlett School Gallery
1996 Galerie Philippe Uzzan, Paris; Institut de Bellas Artes, Mexico

Recent conferences
1997 Special Architecture School, Paris
1996 Berlage Institute, Amsterdam; VIth Mostra Internazionale di Architettura, Venice Off. Architecture School at Paris Villemin; Illinois Institute

Publications
1997 *36 modèles pour une maison* collective work, edited by the Périphériques Association

Selected bibliography
1998 *Casabella* (Oct.); *Axis* (vol. 75 Sept./Oct.); *d'Architectures* (Sept.); *Quaderns* (summer); *Le Monde* (21-22 May); *Le Figaro* (27 April); *d'Architectures* (March)
1997 *Réhabilitation, reconversion* exhibition catalogue, Pavillon de L'Arsenal; *Le Moniteur* no. 4896; *l'Architecture d'aujourd'hui* no. 310; *Architecture New Zealand* (July)
1996 *Techniques & Architectures* no. 429; *l'Arca International* no. 9; *Maisons d'architectes* Joël Carriou, Alternatives; *Casas International* (Paris); *Le Moniteur* no. 4839; *Competition perdus Huit murs*, text by Thom Mayne/Morphosis, Périphériques

Jones, Partners: Architecture

| Wes Jones (*1958) |

At the beginning of a new millennium, celebrated also as the end of modernism, form seems to be coming into fashion again – disguised, again, as expertise. The undeniably technological expertise heralded by the 'new' form is directed for the most part toward the indiscriminate production of difference, leaving its actual relevance to architecture unclear. That architecture would refer to technology is not itself new. The models may no longer be airplanes and steamships, but the same envy of an exotic expertise that previously tried to open the 'eyes which do not see' brings MAYA to architecture today. In both cases technology is addressed as a theme, with the trappings of heightened expression, lofty sentiment and formal exhibitionism. The mediated apparatus of expectation turns technology into a symbol or metaphor. If the theme is critical the architecture gets sharp and pointy, wordy and 'difficult', or if it is affirmational it becomes chrome-plated and party-coloured, or, more recently, virtual and amorphic. In either case, technology is excitingly 'exposed': revealed like a dirty secret or liberated as if harboring a heretofore hidden voluptuousness. Yet, the response to this issue need not necessarily be only celebration or harsh critique; when we understand that architecture is itself, at heart, technological, another possibility suggests itself: we can ask what sort of vernacular would/does it inspire ? The answer is not as obvious as celebration or critique, since it is not easy or expected for architecture to address a theme less than stridently. Matter-of-factness or straightforwardness is not an attitude associated with the signature work that counts for architecture today. The difference between using technology as a symbol, and more visibly being technology itself, as an expression arising from within technology rather than one that merely borrows technological form to illustrate some other non-technological interest, is the distinction between the work of Jones, Partners: Architecture and others who might be considered technologically oriented. Since technology does not admit an author other than nature, the signature architect must make non – or anti – technological adjustments in order to assert authorship. By such adjustment, the author asserts control and makes the technology serve these interests rather than the programme's (the idea of programme is itself a 'gift' of technology). These issues are explicitly addressed by Jones, Partners: Architecture in the four residential projects included here. The house is the architectural problem degree zero. All architectural programmes are at root houses-for-something, in the same way they are machines-for-something. Corbusier's term was not 'machine-for-living', but the more active 'machine-à-habiter', which we prefer in our ignorance to translate machine for dwelling. It is in the difference between these two words that architecture finds its reason to involve itself in the house programme, and discovers its technological heritage. ✜

WES JONES

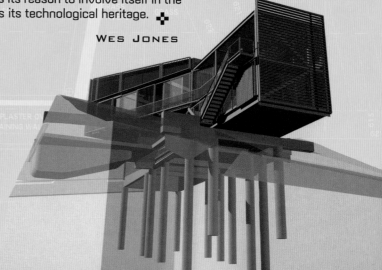

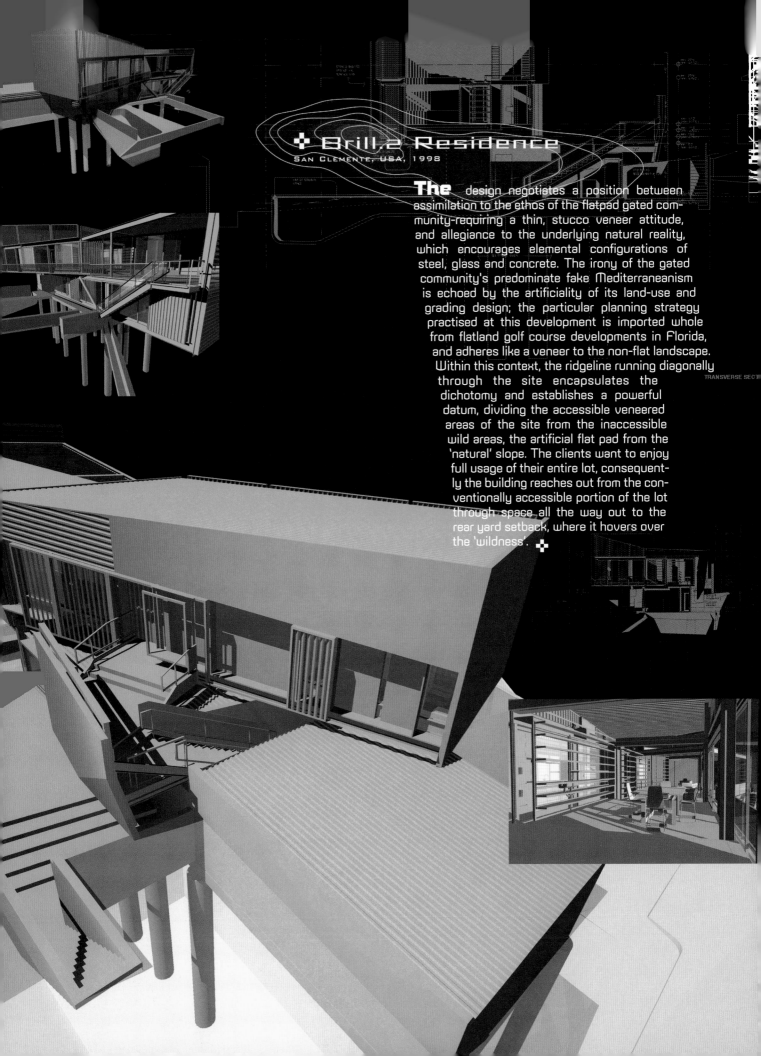

✦ Brill.2 Residence
SAN CLEMENTE, USA, 1998

The design negotiates a position between assimilation to the ethos of the flatpad gated community-requiring a thin, stucco veneer attitude, and allegiance to the underlying natural reality, which encourages elemental configurations of steel, glass and concrete. The irony of the gated community's predominate fake Mediterraneanism is echoed by the artificiality of its land-use and grading design; the particular planning strategy practised at this development is imported whole from flatland golf course developments in Florida, and adheres like a veneer to the non-flat landscape. Within this context, the ridgeline running diagonally through the site encapsulates the dichotomy and establishes a powerful datum, dividing the accessible veneered areas of the site from the inaccessible wild areas, the artificial flat pad from the 'natural' slope. The clients want to enjoy full usage of their entire lot, consequently the building reaches out from the conventionally accessible portion of the lot through space all the way out to the rear yard setback, where it hovers over the 'wildness'. ❖

TRANSVERSE SECT

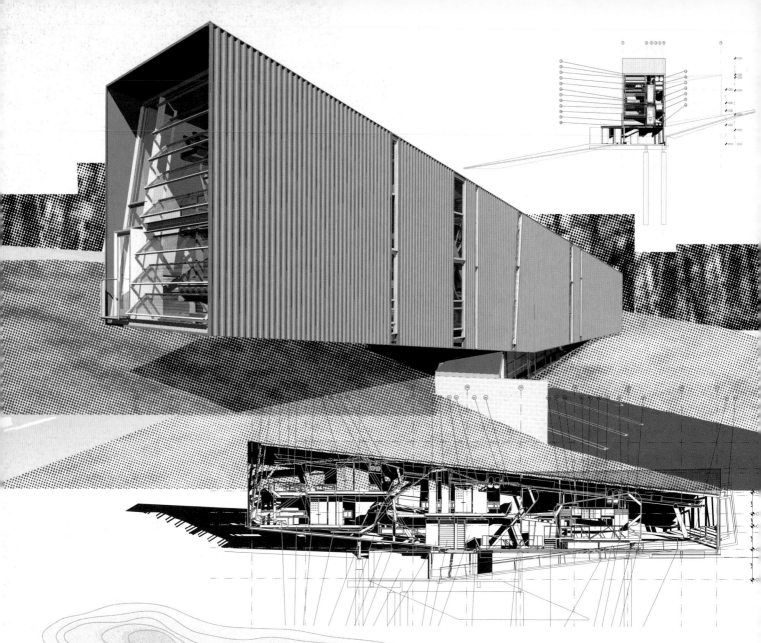

✦ Arias Tsang Residence
BRISBANE, USA, 2000

This project is situated in Brisbane, California, a small hill-side community south of San Francisco. The lot is located up in the hills, at the uppermost edge of development, on a sloping site bordering a dense oak forest. The downhill view is into the backyards of the neighbours. The uphill view into the oak forest is more pleasant. This means that the house must be more closed in the front and more open to the rear. The client prefers the house to have a minimal impact on the site. The house borrows from the 'loft' model, with openings at either end, focused to views along the edge of the oaks. Into this loft 'shell' a 'hermit crab' of functional support elements has been introduced. Vertical windows on the downhill side avoid the view of the neighbours' yards for the most part, while horizontal windows in the rear 'sample' the intricate patterns of the oak forest. The simple tube form has been flexed and twisted to conform more closely to the sloping contours of the site, and these contours work their way into the interior of the house in the living area, which is sloped. The client likes a spare space, so the sloped floor of fine hardwood takes the place of furniture here. ✦

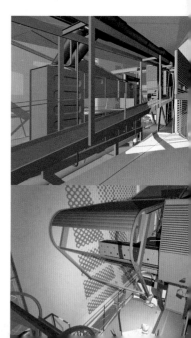

UPPER LEVEL PLAN 02

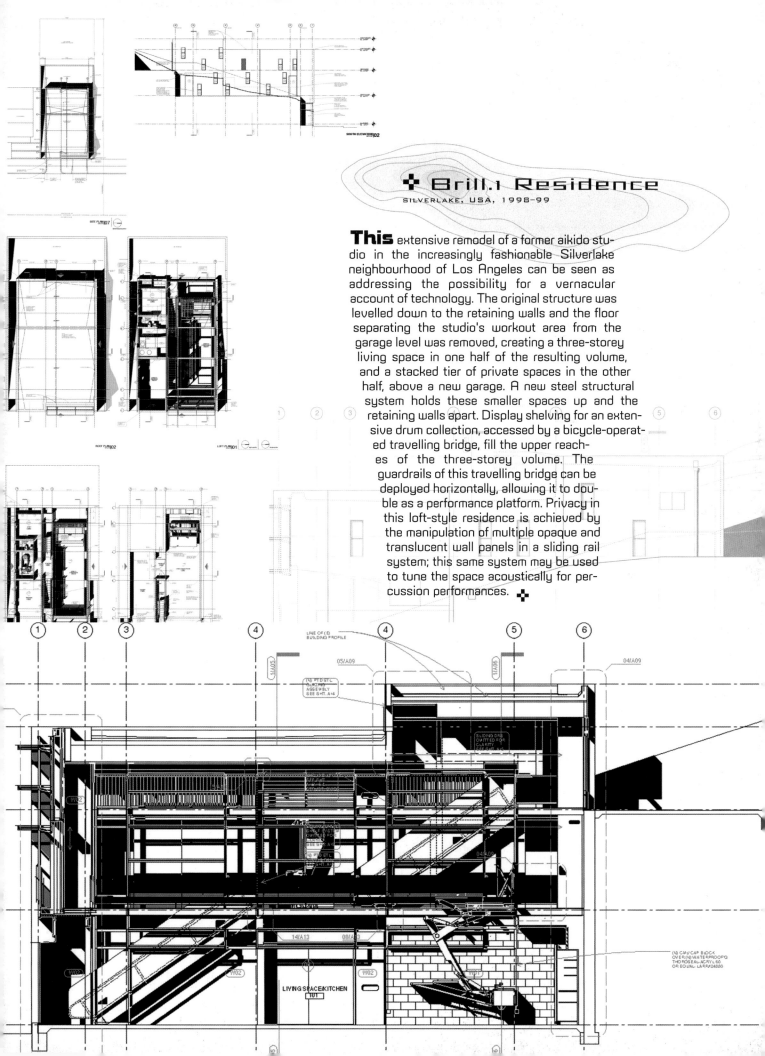

✦ Brill.1 Residence

SILVERLAKE, USA, 1998–99

This extensive remodel of a former aikido studio in the increasingly fashionable Silverlake neighbourhood of Los Angeles can be seen as addressing the possibility for a vernacular account of technology. The original structure was levelled down to the retaining walls and the floor separating the studio's workout area from the garage level was removed, creating a three-storey living space in one half of the resulting volume, and a stacked tier of private spaces in the other half, above a new garage. A new steel structural system holds these smaller spaces up and the retaining walls apart. Display shelving for an extensive drum collection, accessed by a bicycle-operated travelling bridge, fill the upper reaches of the three-storey volume. The guardrails of this travelling bridge can be deployed horizontally, allowing it to double as a performance platform. Privacy in this loft-style residence is achieved by the manipulation of multiple opaque and translucent wall panels in a sliding rail system; this same system may be used to tune the space acoustically for percussion performances. ✦

LIVING SPACE/KITCHEN

✦ Stieglitz Residence
HOLLYWOOD, USA, 1998

The project began simply enough as a straightforward roof replacement, and grew from there to become a whole lifestyle. The roof pretty much took over, becoming a roof. Under its 'protection' stuff began to happen. The house enjoys a magnificent view to the west. Unfortunately, this is also the worst sun exposure. The site is planted in an eclectic mix of native and exotic species, which mitigates the otherwise close presence of the neighbours to the north and south and gives the site a sense of privacy and solitude. Setting out to make a Hollywood kind of house raises the question: what does Hollywood look like, anyway? What is the spatial equivalent of the Hollywood thing? And that famous light? What's the blanc page that whispers 'noir'? The buildings of Southern California, the magnet of exuberant possibility, are worn to a shine by a harsher than obvious desert reality. The 'façade', if it could be called that, is a blank page, like anything else on the street, continuing the Hollywood paradox. ✦

✦ Jones, Partners : Architecture

Wes Jones (1958)

1983 Master of Architecture, Graduate School of Design, Harvard University
1980 University of California, Berkeley
1978 United States Military Academy, West Point

1993 Creation of Jones, Partners: Architecture in San Francisco
1991 Holt Hinshaw Jones, San Francisco
1987 Holt Hinshaw Pfau Jones
1983 Eisenman/Robertson, New York
1980 ELS Design Group, Berkeley

Teaching

Visiting professor at Harvard, Princeton, IIT, Columbia, UCLA and Ohio State University

Principal buildings and projects

2000 Arias Tsang Residence, Brisbane, California (project); House of the future (Time Magazine)
1999 Brill .1 Residence, Silverlake (realized); Redondo Duplex, Redondo Beach
1998 Stieglitz Residence, Hollywood (project); Brill .2 Residence, San Clemente (project); Urban Epicuria, West Hollywood; San José Repertory Theater, California
1997 Andersen Consulting, Kuala Lumpur; 18*Noodles Restaurant Prototype; 'Instrumental Form' (boss architecture)
1996 General Instruments Corporate Campus, Philadelphia; Zimmer Stair, University of Cincinnati; Confluence Point Bridge and Ranger Station, San José, California
1995 American Medicals Informatics Center, Romania
1994 Edenscape Area Improvements, Campus Services Building, University of Cincinnati; Hesselink Houses, Hope Valley, California
1993 Edenscape Masterplan, University of Cincinnati/UCLA Chiller Plant
1989 Astronauts Memorial, Kennedy Space Center, Florida

Principal publications

1999 'Mies-Takes' ANY no. 24
1997 Instrumental Form Princeton Architectural Press
1995 'The Mech in Tecture' ANY no. 10

Selected bibliography

2000 'How will you live' Time magazine (28 Feb.)
1999 'The Times Capsule' The New York Times Magazine (5 Dec.); Single Family Housing: The Private Domain Jaime Salazar, Birkhäuser/Actar; Techno Architecture Elizabeth Smith, Thames & Hudson; 'Jones, Partners: Architecture' GA Houses 59, Japan
1998 'Jones, Partners: Architecture' GA Houses 55, Japan; 'Confluence Point Ranger Station' Architecture; 'Boss Architecture' Nicolai Ourrossof, Los Angeles Times (Feb.)
1997 New Forms Philip Jodidio, Benedikt Taschen Verlag; Architectural Drawing: A Visual Compendium of Types and Methods Rendow Yee, John Wiley & Sons; 'Jones, Partners: Architecture' GA Houses 52, Japan; The Whitney Guide to 20th Century American Architecture Sydney LeBlanc, The Whitney Design Library
1996 Contemporary California Architects Philip Jodidio, Benedikt Taschen Verlag; 581 Architects in the World Gallery MA, 'Central Cogeneration Plant' A+U (Feb.); Architecture (March); 'Sierra Cabins Meadow House' Architettura Intersezioni no. 3; 'Notes, InRe:mediation' Aris no. 2
1995 Progressive Architecture (Jan.); 'Jones, Partners: Architecture' GA Houses 45, Japan; 'Wohncontainer on the Rocks' Häuser (March); 'Verpackungskünstler' DBZ (July); Conventional Bondage GSD Studio Works 95-96

Mathias Klotz

| Mathias Klotz (*1965) |

The office was founded in 1988 to work on a varietyof projects. The earliest projects were private houses, especially in the country. In the mid-1990s, the studio took on some scenographic projects, installations and commercial projects, such as theatres and restaurants, but continued to undertake residential projects in and outside of Santiago. At the end of the 1990s, the office has opened its range, developing projects of very different scales, from urban furniture to cultural commissions, such as events halls, and complex programmes, like industrial buildings, schools, and clinics. For each of these projects, the emphasis has been on the search for simple solutions with a clear vision that emerges out of a project's particularity, which is tied to the programme, the client and the given location. For each project working teams are formed to develop plans, drawings and models for each stage, which might be wooden, metallic or virtual to establish a connection to the context and the interior spaces. In his introduction to a monograph published in 1997 (GG Portfolio series), Horacio Torrent wrote: 'The South American landscape opened up the possibility of a yet more significant poetic art. This long country at the end of the world has seemed a promising place for untroubled exploration of modern style designed of the dual lines of abstraction and nature. A renewed continuation of that research seems to be present in the shapes and treatment of spaces and materials in the architecture of Mathias Klotz. This young architect has so far had a short career with a limited output, in many ways his work belongs to that mad geography that lies along a long, narrow strip of land west of the Andes, combining the most sublime of places, from dry desert to wet southern forest. Mathias Klotz seems to want to revel in nature's lavishness, and he does so, in a seeming contradiction, following a revitalized modern style. He is ideologically far from the vernacular; a born innovator, daring and contradictory. His pioneering approach resonates in the coherent shaping of his works, which reveal the architectural disorientation of the subcontinent and bring a deep draught of fresh air from the south.' ✦

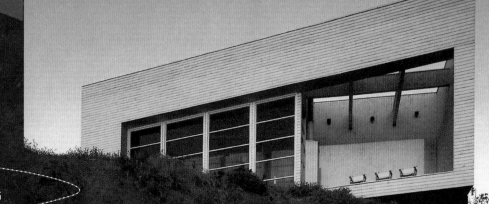

Ugarte House
Maitencillo Sur, Chile, 1995

✦ Las Niñas Vineyard
CHILE, 1999

This commission for a vineyard located in the Colchagua valley, which is famous for its vineyards, 350 kilometres south of Santiago. The programme comprises a series of small laboratories, control office, cellar, a large stainless-steel barrels cellar and a smaller wooden barrels cellar. The building is essentially a rectangular box buil of steel, wood and plexiglass. This main volume communicates with a smaller one that is constructecd of concrete. The project has an important technical component in contributing to the optimization of the wine-making process. Klotz tried to keep as close as possible to this aim, creating an architectural object that makes no attempt to be anything other than a cellar. This is achieved through the material-sand, which were selected for their climatic efficiency. The building is closed to the north with a double façade that allows air circulation by convection. The east and west façades are blind; the south façade is a 12 x 75–metre plexiglas surface. At night this façade turns into a large lamp to the exterior. The interior walls of the small concrete volume are covered with gabions to increase the mass of the walls in order to control the interior temperature. Here the wine ages in wood barrels. ✦

✦ Reutter House

CACHAGA, CHILE, 1999

This summer house is located in a slope of pine trees next to Cachagua Beach some 140 kilometres from Santiago. The project comprises two rectangular boxes that float on a wall to elevate the living space and insert it in among the trees. Against the landscape, the house nestles among the trees, while inside, there is a house within a house. A box containing bedrooms and bathrooms penetrates the main living area box. There are no doors, only sliding walls, so that one may open the rooms into the living room completely, that is, the small box into the large one. A third volume, built of reinforced concrete, passes through the principal box and represents the nucleus containing a bedroom and laundry room on the first floor, kitchen and TV room on the second floor and a study on the third. To accentuate the house's horizontality, access from the street is via a 30-metre-long bridge, which hovers amid the pine trees. From the roof, which features a large terrace facing the ocean, a steel staircase leads to a covered terrace, which gives into the interior space. From a structural and practical point of view, the Reutter house is a balancing act in stability and tension. ✦

✜ Street Furniture

PROTOTYPES, 2000

The project for street furniture was commisioned by the French company JC Decaux, which asked Klotz to develop three bus stops to accommodate an advertising space and shoe polisher. The bus stop has to provide several basic functions, from information services (telephone, city map) to being a guide for public transportation. In terms of the weather, density and security, the study was geared toward the Mediterranean context. Klotz developed the idea of using light elements that would retain their identity in the city when passed at high speeds, but with minimal occupation of public space would not disturb pedestrian traffic. The shoe-shine area is a metallic object, which contains all the accesories, and is fixed to the ground or used as a aluminium luggage. When it is open, the door turns into a surface for the shoe-shiner while the user sits on a leather cushion that fits on the aluminium top. ✜

✦ Altamira College
SANTIAGO, CHILE, 2000

A competition was held to design the 10,000 m² Altamira School, which was to house for 1,400 students. Situated at the slopes of the Andes, the site was is a rectangle of 60 x 200 metres, with a 20-degree incline on its longer side. Klotz's project comprises four buildings, arranged along each side of the site, which a central court-yard that opens up views to the mountains and the city and defines a east-west edge with a concen-tration of trees and schoolyard above the street. The larger spaces, which contain a gym and dining hall, are at the center of the plan, so that they can also be used for community activities. The central volume's structure is made of steel, with an inclined roof that covers part of the schoolyard. The four perime-ter buildings house the classrooms, each made of concrete pillars and uninterrupted floor space to allow maximum flexibility of use. The east and west façades are of concrete, the south façades in wood and the north in aluminium, glass and coloured pan-els. ✦

✦ Mathias Klotz

Mathias Klotz Germain (1965)
1991   Diploma from the Catholic University of Chile
1991   Creation of the practice in Santiago, Chile

Teaching
2000–1996 Federico Santa Maria University, Valparaiso
1998–96 Central University, Santagio

Principal buildings and projects
2000   Altamira College (under construction); 'Parade' and 'Lustra' small installations/projects
1999   Vino del Nuevo Mundo (realized); Reutter House (realized)
1997   Pizarras Ibericas (realized); Palockz and Sandoval houses (realized)
1996   Grudsky and Ubeda houses (realized); Hotel Terrantai (realized); Cyber-café (realized); 'Ruins of Huanchaca' (third prize)
1995   Ugarte House (realized); Grez House (realized)
1994   Sadhu, Müller and Lavados houses (realized)
1993   Ducaud and Von Plate houses (realized); Restaurant Metro; Oz Ritoque Discothèque (realized)
1992   Rio Liucura House (realized); Tienda Le Coq (realized); Oz Discotheque (realized); Acceso Casa 92 (realized)

1991   Klotz and Cummings houses (realized)
1990   Walker House, guardhouse and stables, Lago Panguipulli (realized)

Selected bibliography
1998   *Pacific Edge* Peter Zellner, Rizzoli, New York
1997   *GG Portfolio*, Gustavo Gili, Barcelona; *Abitare* no. 364
1996   *Abitare* no. 353

Kolatan/Mac Donald Studio

| Sulan Kolatan (*1956) | William J. Mac Donald (*1958) |

One of the emerging spatial paradigms is that of the network as a system of interrelations between dissipative processes and aggregative structures that shape new spatial patterns and protocols. How does this network logic affect space and its making? Our work focuses in particular on the network model's capacity to facilitate cross-categorical and cross-scalar couplings whereby the initial systems/morphologies are not merely interconnected, but form new hybrid identities. What differentiates this new generation of chimerical hybrids from previous mechanistic ones is the act of transformation. These new systems are not determined and cannot be understood through a logical extension of the initial parts alone. They are hybrid, but nonetheless seamlessly and inextricably continuous. The two specific models of the network and the hybrid that are of interest here are the 'co-citation map', and the 'chimera'.

Co-citation mapping is a form of electronic indexing and information retrieval. As an index, it works according to a similar principal to any keywork-based library search, listing all work related to the same keyword., thus revealing non-apparent conceptual connections across categories such as humanities and science for example. Interestingly, the next level of organization is constructed as a map, a geographic description of relational knowledge. They have no absolute axis. Instead their spatial organization is based on continually becoming hierarchies which are contingent upon frequency of citation and thus subject to change over time.

'The Chimera' is the proper name given to a mythological monster – the 'supreme hybrid' – constituted of part lion, part goat, part snake. The chimerical differs in crucial ways from other forms of hybrid systems such as collage, montage or the prosthetic. While the latter are also systems in which the diverse parts operate together, these parts never lose their individual identities. We have two primary interests in the chimerical. One has to do with its seeming capability as a concept to help define existing phenomena of fairly complex hybridity in which categorically different systems somehow operate as a single identity. The other is based on the assumption that the ways in which chimera are constituted and operate hold clues to a transformatively aggregative model of construction-production, that is to say, an aggregation that becomes more than the sum of its parts, and therefore is not reducible to its constituent parts. Thus, the chimerical has the potential to be both an analytical and methodological tool.

In combination, the two models offer an opportunity to link dissipative/aggregative operations to transformative ones with the co-citation analogue identifying similarities between unrelated sites/structures/programmes, and the chimerical analogue employing these initial similarities to construct new sites/structures/programmes. While existing categories might cease to be useful, the paradigm of the network/chimera has the potential to open up an entire new range of previously inconceivable kinds of structures for which no names exist as of yet. ❖

KOLATAN/MAC DONALD

Resi-Rise Skyscraper
New York, 1999

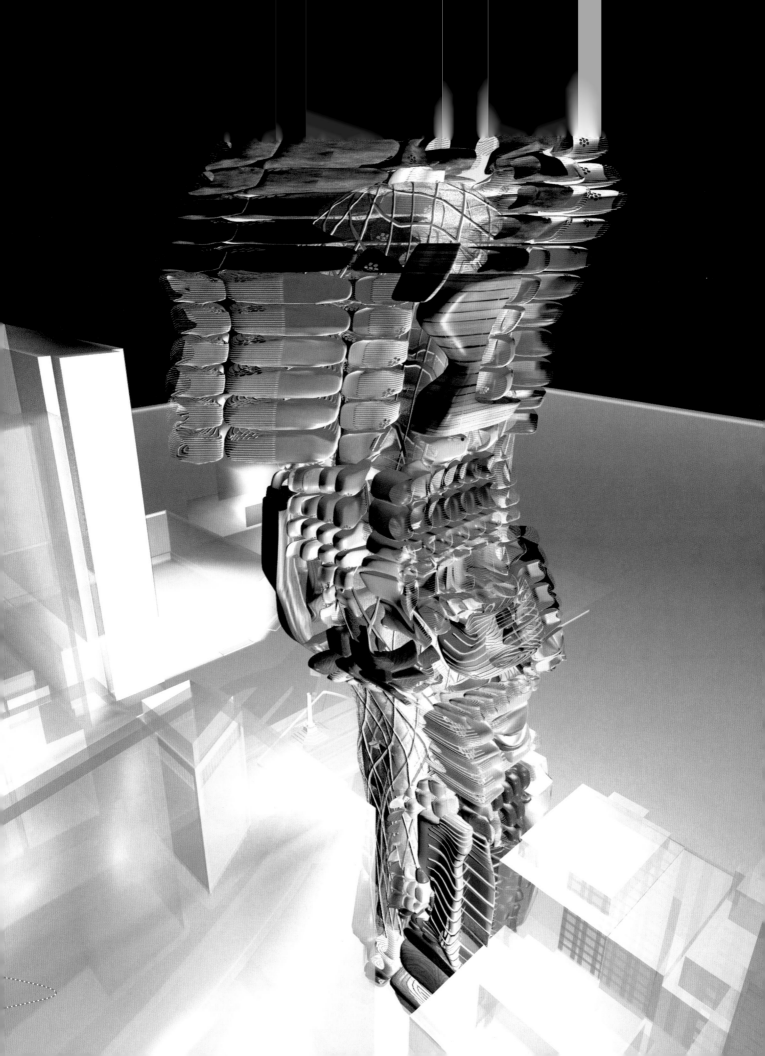

✚ Resi-Rise (vertical mode)
NEW YORK, USA 1999

The Resi-Rise is not so much a building as an actual example of 'vertical urbanism'. Taking up the whole
volume offered by New York's 'zoning laws', the form
of the tower incorporates the site's local restrictions
(views, height of adjacent buildings.). Conceptually
speaking, it comes across like a matrix of 'lots', taking
the shape of so many independent pods. The morphology, size, programme, functions, materials, servic-
ing and furnishing of each pod are indeterminate and
depend on the options of the users and on the programmatic scenarios and parameters laid down by the
architects. The organization of the pods among themselves carries on the urban analogy. Individual choice
and 'collective' performance merge in a complex and
flexible system linking the parts and the whole
together. Inhabitable as soon as the first pod is
installed and furnished, the construction
of the tower, which is endlessly updated by the vagaries of the property market, by technological developments
and by the mobility of the occupants,
can never actually be completed. For
the tenant, the pod principle actually
has less to do with real estate and more
with car 'leasing'. ✚

✦ Housings

SIX NON-STANDARD HOUSES, 1999

Housings constitutes the initial portion of a long-term project that focuses on experimental designs for mass-customized, prefabricated housing. These six houses were selected from a series of digitally designed variants. All variants originate from the same 'genetic pool'. Information for the 'genetic pool' was generated from a normative three bedroom, two and a half–bath colonial house plan as 'base', and a range of object-products as 'targets'. Subsequent digital blending operations between 'base' and a varying number of 'targets' in turn produced a large range of chimerical houses. Housings sets out to explore the question of serial and organic compositeness in architectural design on three parallel tracks. One, in relation to digital processes with their capacity for variable iterations, organic transformation and cross-referencing. Two, in regards to issues of viability: can a hybrid outperform existing normative types in a particular social, cultural, economic, ecological, geological and climatic life-context ? And three, vis-à-vis an emerging generation of composite materials and digital production technologies. ✦

De Beers
A DIAMOND IS FOREVER

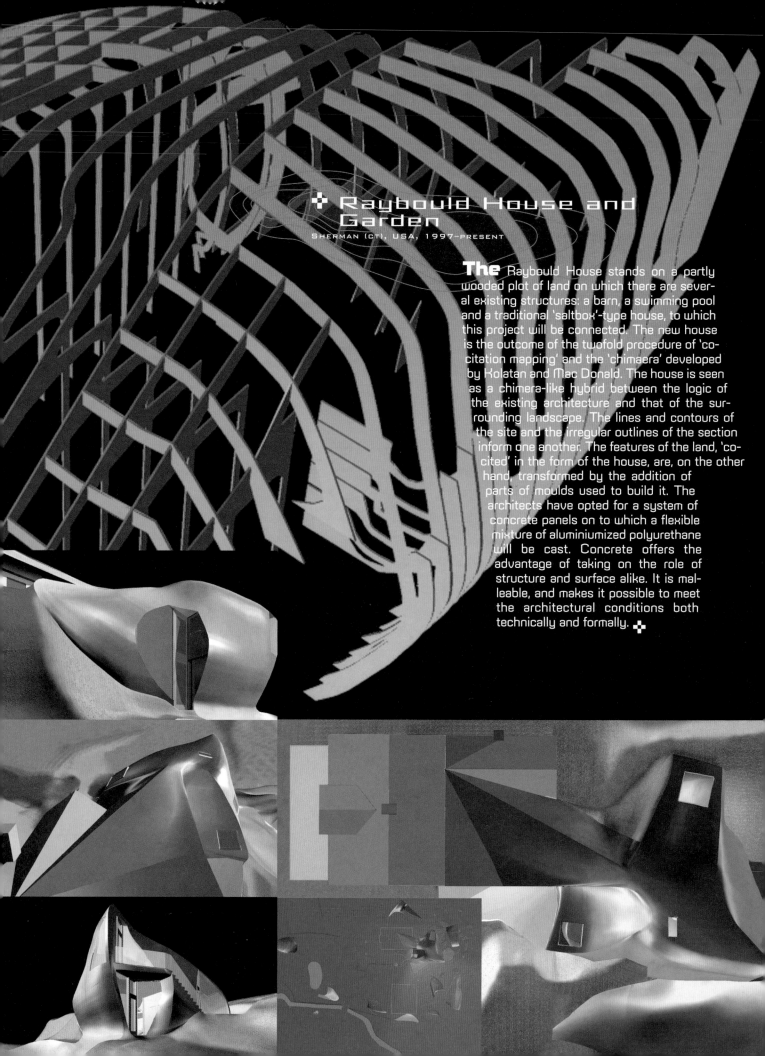

✦ Raybould House and Garden
SHERMAN (CT), USA, 1997–PRESENT

The Raybould House stands on a partly wooded plot of land on which there are several existing structures: a barn, a swimming pool and a traditional 'saltbox'-type house, to which this project will be connected. The new house is the outcome of the twofold procedure of 'co-citation mapping' and the 'chimaera' developed by Kolatan and Mac Donald. The house is seen as a chimera-like hybrid between the logic of the existing architecture and that of the surrounding landscape. The lines and contours of the site and the irregular outlines of the section inform one another. The features of the land, 'co-cited' in the form of the house, are, on the other hand, transformed by the addition of parts of moulds used to build it. The architects have opted for a system of concrete panels on to which a flexible mixture of aluminiumized polyurethane will be cast. Concrete offers the advantage of taking on the role of structure and surface alike. It is malleable, and makes it possible to meet the architectural conditions both technically and formally. ✦

✚ Take 5 on Manhattan (horizontal)
New York, USA, 1997

This urban project for the development of Manhattan's Fifth Avenue responded to a competition of ideas, organized in 1997 by the Municipal Art Society, and submitted to ten teams of architects, artists and landscape artists. The proposition made by Kolatan and Mac Donald, here associated with Erich Schoenenberger, started from an established fact : the roofs of Manhattan form an unused horizontal 'layer', a landscape on high, no less, which duplicates the streetscape. The project speculates on the urban potential of this fallow land. Turning their backs on strategies which might repetitively bolster the avenue's linearity, Kolatan and Mac Donald propose instead a form of network, based on notions of 'hybrid identity' and 'soft site'. 'Hybridizing' the identity of Fifth Avenue consists here in creating conditions of exchange and 'co-citation' with transversal sites, be they adjacent or otherwise. The 'soft sites' describe underconstructed sites in respect to city regulations, which thus offer horizontal expansion potential for this vertical city.

✚

✚ Kolatan/Mac Donald Studio

Sulan Kolatan (1958)
1984   Columbia University, New York; Rheinisch–Westfälische Technische Hochschule, Aachen, Germany

William J. Mac Donald (1956)
1982   Columbia University, New York; Architectural Association, London; Syracuse University, New York

1988   Creation of Kolatan/Mac Donald Studio

Teaching
Sulan Kolatan
2000–1990 Columbia University, New York
1994   Ohio State University, Columbus
1993   University of Pennsylvania, Philadelphia

William J. Mac Donald
2000–1985 Columbia University, New York
1997/93/91 Ohio State University, Columbus
1994–91 University of Pennsylvania, Philadelphia

Principal buildings and projects
2000   Gebekse Resort Hotel, Mamarlik, Turkey
1999   Resi-Rise Skyscraper, New York (project); Massachusetts Customized Housing Proposal dwellings
1998   Gillon Court, Milford, MA (under construction)
1997   'Take Five on Manhattan Horizontal' (urban design) (project); Southern New England School of Law, North Dartmouth, MA (under construction); Raybould House, Sherman, CT (under construction); Labowitz Apartment, New York
1996   O/K Apartment, artists residence, New York (realized)
1995   Yokohama Ocean Liner Terminal (competition), Japan

Principal publications
1999   'Des-Res Architecture' *Architectural Design*, London
1997   'Recent work (Chimera and co-citations)', 'Columbia 'D'' *Columbia Documents of Architecture and Theory*, New York

Selected bibliography
2000   'Housings/Raybould House and Garden' *Domus* (Jan.) Milan
1999   *Hybrid Space: New Forms in Digital Architecture* Peter Zellner, Thames & Hudson, London; 'Millennium: Futures to come' Resi-Rise Skyscraper, *Architectural Record Magazine* (Dec.); 'SCI-FI Architecture' *Architectural Design*; 'Projects: Houses' *Global Architecture*, Japan
1998   *kol/mac architecture* Arredamento Mimarlik, Istanbul; 'Farbflut und Kunsthoffwellen' *Architektur & Wohnen*, Hamburg; 'The New York School' *Archimade Magazine*, Lausanne
1997   'The Shape of Things to Come' *The New York Times* (18 Sept.); 'Furniture into form' *Architecture*
1996   *Exciting Manhattanism* Casa Brutus, Tokyo

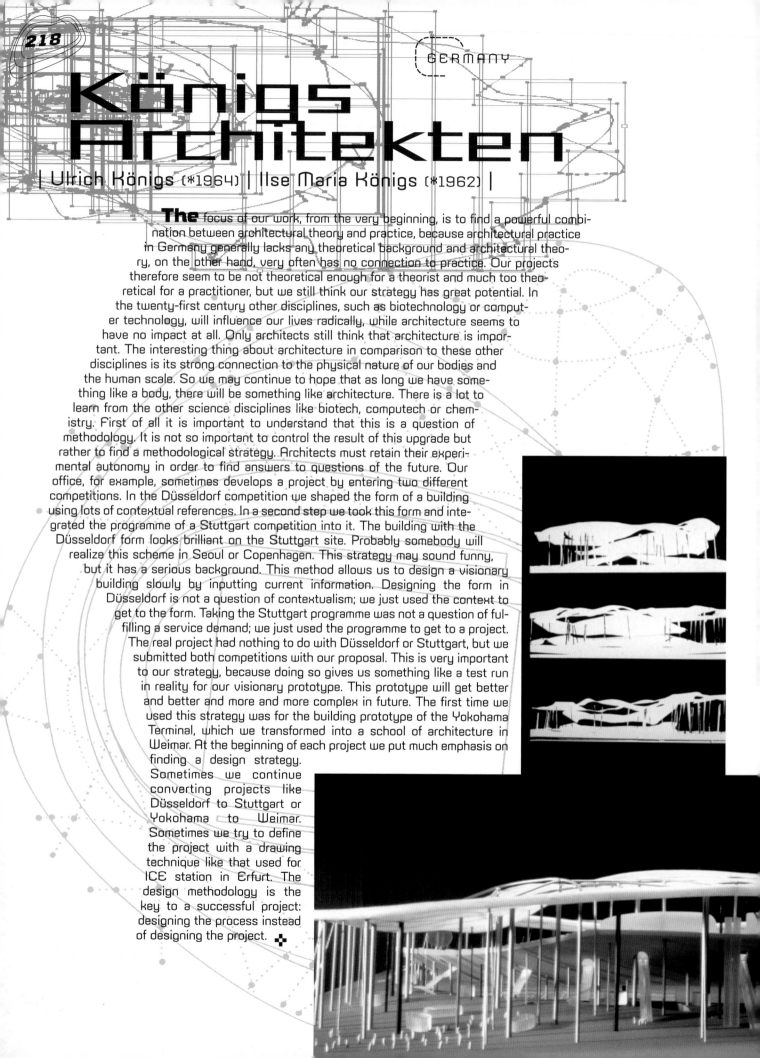

Königs Architekten

| Ulrich Königs (*1964) | Ilse Maria Königs (*1962) |

The focus of our work, from the very beginning, is to find a powerful combination between architectural theory and practice, because architectural practice in Germany generally lacks any theoretical background and architectural theory, on the other hand, very often has no connection to practice. Our projects therefore seem to be not theoretical enough for a theorist and much too theoretical for a practitioner, but we still think our strategy has great potential. In the twenty-first century other disciplines, such as biotechnology or computer technology, will influence our lives radically, while architecture seems to have no impact at all. Only architects still think that architecture is important. The interesting thing about architecture in comparison to these other disciplines is its strong connection to the physical nature of our bodies and the human scale. So we may continue to hope that as long we have something like a body, there will be something like architecture. There is a lot to learn from the other science disciplines like biotech, computech or chemistry. First of all it is important to understand that this is a question of methodology. It is not so important to control the result of this upgrade but rather to find a methodological strategy. Architects must retain their experimental autonomy in order to find answers to questions of the future. Our office, for example, sometimes develops a project by entering two different competitions. In the Düsseldorf competition we shaped the form of a building using lots of contextual references. In a second step we took this form and integrated the programme of a Stuttgart competition into it. The building with the Düsseldorf form looks brilliant on the Stuttgart site. Probably somebody will realize this scheme in Seoul or Copenhagen. This strategy may sound funny, but it has a serious background. This method allows us to design a visionary building slowly by inputting current information. Designing the form in Düsseldorf is not a question of contextualism; we just used the context to get to the form. Taking the Stuttgart programme was not a question of fulfilling a service demand; we just used the programme to get to a project. The real project had nothing to do with Düsseldorf or Stuttgart, but we submitted both competitions with our proposal. This is very important to our strategy, because doing so gives us something like a test run in reality for our visionary prototype. This prototype will get better and better and more and more complex in future. The first time we used this strategy was for the building prototype of the Yokohama Terminal, which we transformed into a school of architecture in Weimar. At the beginning of each project we put much emphasis on finding a design strategy. Sometimes we continue converting projects like Düsseldorf to Stuttgart or Yokohama to Weimar. Sometimes we try to define the project with a drawing technique like that used for ICE station in Erfurt. The design methodology is the key to a successful project: designing the process instead of designing the project. ✦

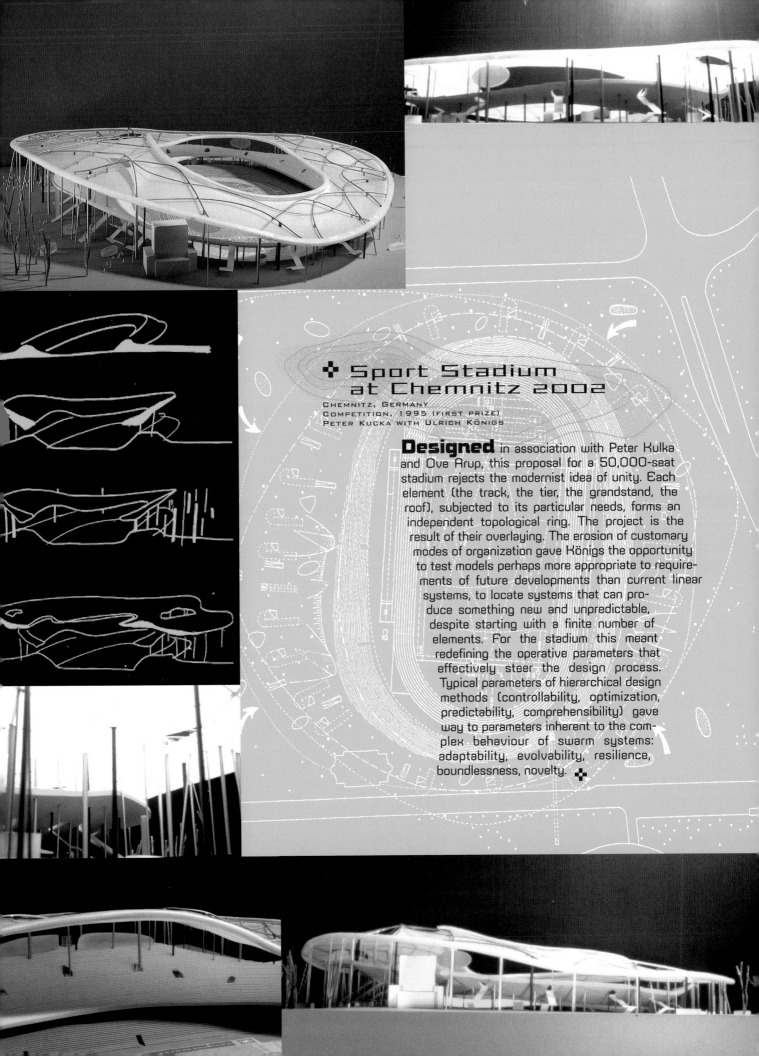

✦ Sport Stadium at Chemnitz 2002

CHEMNITZ, GERMANY
COMPETITION, 1995 (FIRST PRIZE)
PETER KUCKA WITH ULRICH KÖNIGS

Designed in association with Peter Kulka and Ove Arup, this proposal for a 50,000-seat stadium rejects the modernist idea of unity. Each element (the track, the tier, the grandstand, the roof), subjected to its particular needs, forms an independent topological ring. The project is the result of their overlaying. The erosion of customary modes of organization gave Königs the opportunity to test models perhaps more appropriate to requirements of future developments than current linear systems, to locate systems that can produce something new and unpredictable, despite starting with a finite number of elements. For the stadium this meant redefining the operative parameters that effectively steer the design process. Typical parameters of hierarchical design methods (controllability, optimization, predictability, comprehensibility) gave way to parameters inherent to the complex behaviour of swarm systems: adaptability, evolvability, resilience, boundlessness, novelty. ✦❖

✦ ICE Station

ERFURT, GERMANY
COMPETITION, 1995
ULRICH KÖNIGS, ILSE MARIA KÖNIGS

To Ulrich and Ilse Maria Königs it has become apparent that the future of high-performance computing is allied with with massively 'parallel' architectures. There already exist a variety of parallel hardware platforms, but, according to them, the ability of the architects to utilize fully the potential of these machines is constrained by their inability to write software of a sufficient complexity. There does not exist an art for writing this kind of software, at least not on a scale involving more than a few parallel processes. In fact, it seems unlikely that human programmers will ever be capable of actually writing software of such complexity. Therefore, the evolutionary system of the ICE station is represented by hand-drawn chromatographic plans as a two-dimensional parallel network. The slowness and stability of hand-drawings make an adequate substitute for the inefficient software for parallel computing. ✦

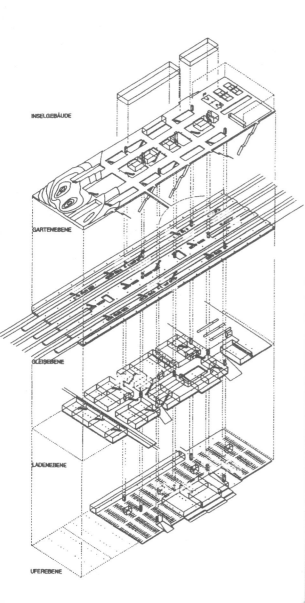

INSELGEBÄUDE

GARTENEBENE

GLEISEBENE

LADENEBENE

UFEREBENE

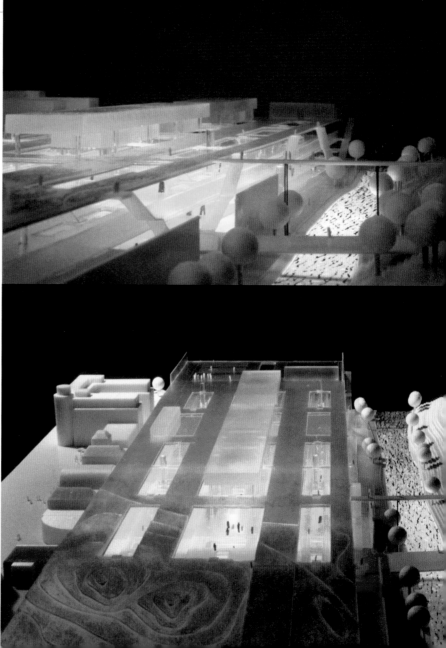

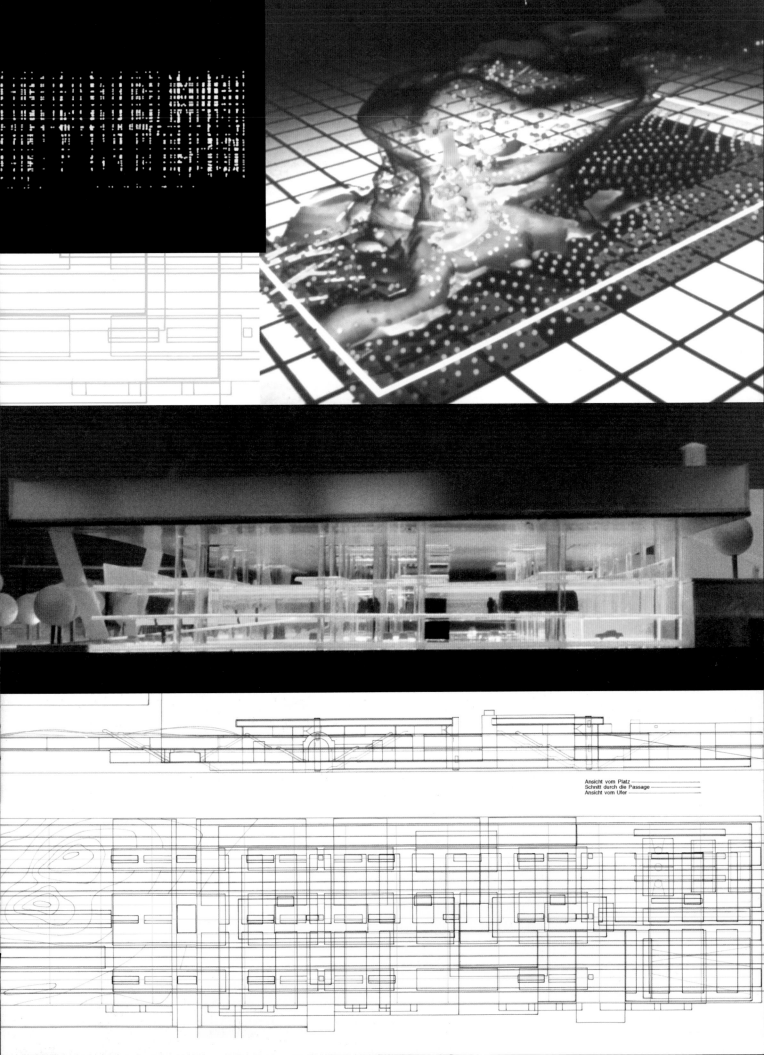

Ansicht vom Platz
Schnitt durch die Passage
Ansicht vom Ufer

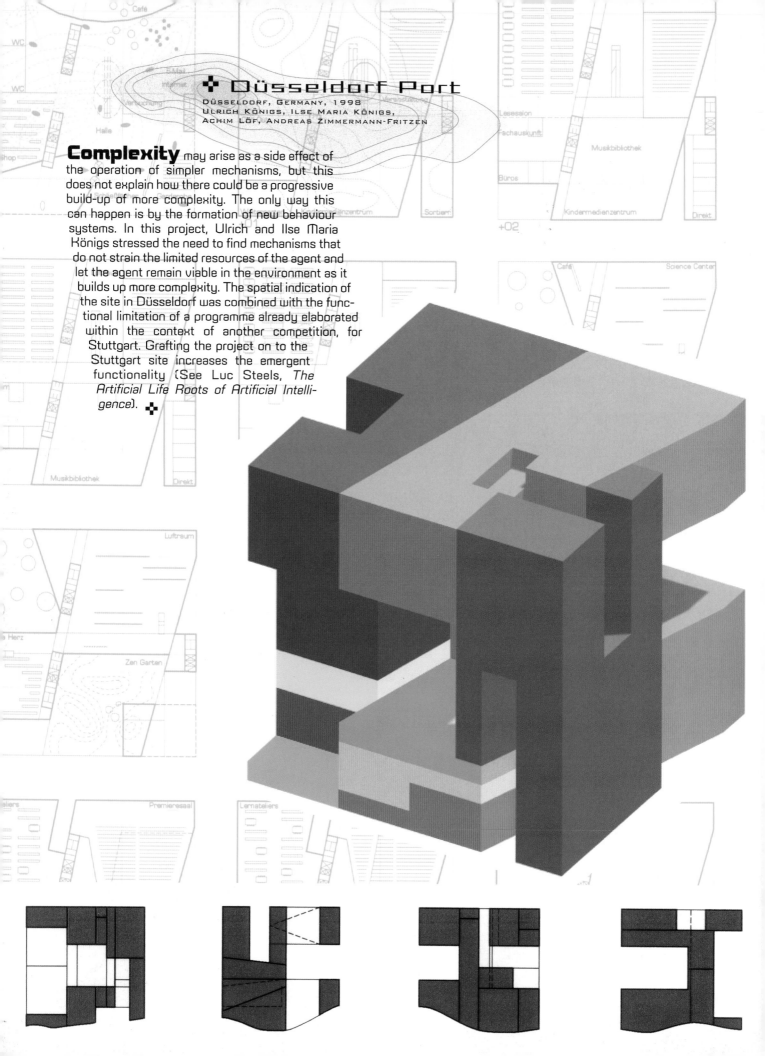

✤ Düsseldorf Port

DÜSSELDORF, GERMANY, 1998
ULRICH KÖNIGS, ILSE MARIA KÖNIGS,
ACHIM LÖF, ANDREAS ZIMMERMANN-FRITZEN

Complexity may arise as a side effect of the operation of simpler mechanisms, but this does not explain how there could be a progressive build-up of more complexity. The only way this can happen is by the formation of new behaviour systems. In this project, Ulrich and Ilse Maria Königs stressed the need to find mechanisms that do not strain the limited resources of the agent and let the agent remain viable in the environment as it builds up more complexity. The spatial indication of the site in Düsseldorf was combined with the functional limitation of a programme already elaborated within the context of another competition, for Stuttgart. Grafting the project on to the Stuttgart site increases the emergent functionality (See Luc Steels, *The Artificial Life Roots of Artificial Intelligence*). ✤

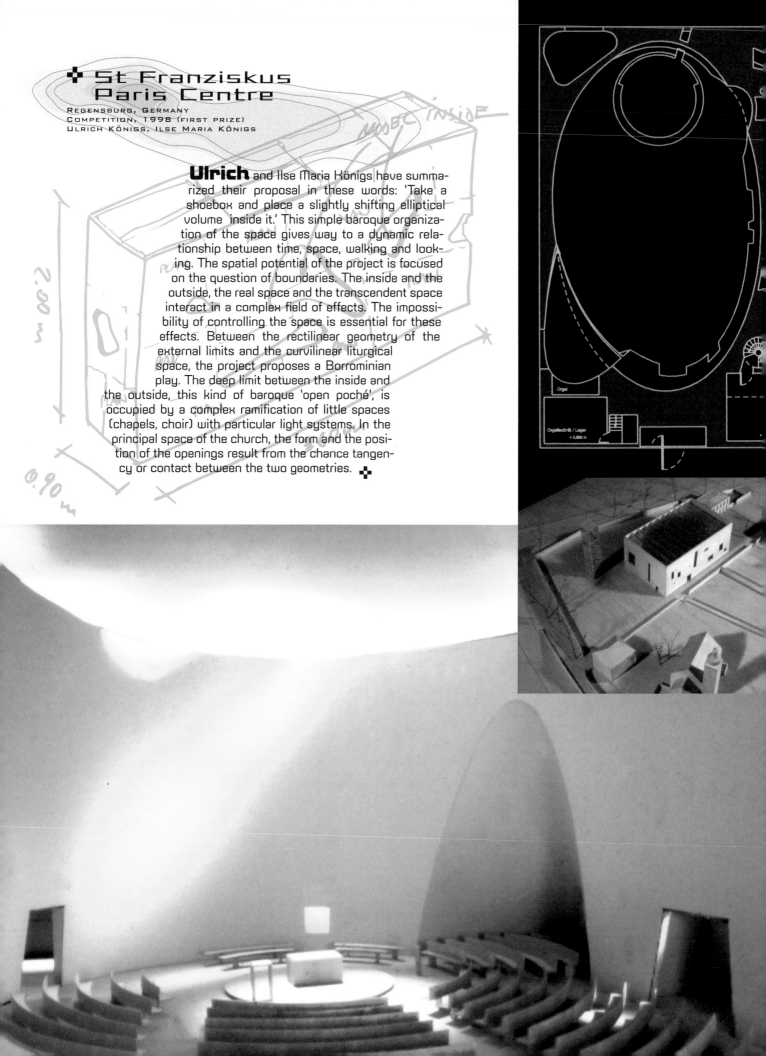

✦ St Franziskus
Paris Centre

REGENSBURG, GERMANY
COMPETITION, 1998 (FIRST PRIZE)
ULRICH KÖNIGS, ILSE MARIA KÖNIGS

Ulrich and Ilse Maria Königs have summarized their proposal in these words: 'Take a shoebox and place a slightly shifting elliptical volume inside it.' This simple baroque organization of the space gives way to a dynamic relationship between time, space, walking and looking. The spatial potential of the project is focused on the question of boundaries. The inside and the outside, the real space and the transcendent space interact in a complex field of effects. The impossibility of controlling the space is essential for these effects. Between the rectilinear geometry of the external limits and the curvilinear liturgical space, the project proposes a Borrominian play. The deep limit between the inside and the outside, this kind of baroque 'open poché', is occupied by a complex ramification of little spaces (chapels, choir) with particular light systems. In the principal space of the church, the form and the position of the openings result from the chance tangency or contact between the two geometries. ✦

✦ Königs Architekten

Ulrich Königs (1964)
Ilse Maria Königs (1962)
Diplomas from the AA, London, the University of Innsbruck and the RWTH, Aachen

Teaching
1999　RWTH, Aachen

1994　Founded the practice Königs Architekten in Cologne

Principal buildings and projects
1998　Pfarrzentrum St Franziskus, Regensburg, Germany (competition, prizewinner)

1997　Haus des Deutschen Beamtenbundes, Berlin, Germany; Industriemuseum, Chemnitz, Germany (competition); Thüringer Landtag, Erfurt, Germany (competition); St Theodor Church, Cologne, Germany (competition)

1996　Wallraf-Richard Musem, Cologne, Germany (competition); Hochschule für Architektur, Weimar, Germany (competition, second prize)

1995　Chemnitz stadium, Germany (competition, prizewinner); Terminal of the international port at Yokohama, Japan (competition, honourable mention)

Recent exhibitions
1996　Galerie Aedes East, Berlin; XIXth Triennale, at Milan; Architectural Association, London

Conferences
1999　GH Kassel, Kassel

1998　Neuer Aachener Kunstverein, Aachen; ETH, Zurich

1997　University, Stuttgart; Leopold Franzens University, Innsbruck

1996　Technische Universität, Graz; Ohio State University, Columbus; Columbia University, New York; Architectural Association, London

Selected bibliography
1997　*Arch +* no. 138 (Oct.); *Assemblage* no. 33 (August)

1996　*l'Architecture d'aujourd'hui* no. 306 (Sept.); *Architectural Review* (March); *Arch+* no. 131 (April); *Stadtbauwelt* no. 129 (April); *Der Architekt* (Jan.)

Kovac Malone

| Tom Kovac (*1958) | Geoff Malone |

We particularly like Léon van Schaik's idea that our architecture is 'neither carved nor moulded'. He has defined architecture as 'an architecture of the third term'. 'Building material is the medium of architecture ... can there be any other? Yes ... instead of letting imagination work with structural forms, with the solids of a building, the architect can work with the empty space – the cavity – between solids and consider forming the space as the real meaning of architecture. Thus Rasmussen defines the ancient duality in *Experiencing Architecture*.' The information age has architects adding a third term to this canon: the surface. As tech-nomads, we float above the ground surveying the terrain through surveillance screens: windscreens, computer screens, TV screens. The hard-won tactility of architectural reality fades into an undifferentiated array of surface effects all conveyed with the comfort of air-conditioning and piped music. An architecture of expression has emerged, competing in its coding with film. I want to demonstrate that, in contrast, Kovac is making an architecture out of this third term, and that he is doing so by engaging us in conflicting expectations, that his work is concerned primarily with the poles of the duality. I want to argue that it is precisely by making it impossible for us to incorporate either into our mental space that we come fully to experience a spatiality of the present rather than the caverns or objects of the past.' There are switches in scale in our work. These are inevitable in a practice that is determined to get its ideas built. We aren't happy to sit and watch screens. We want the vision built. We use every opportunity. 'There is one Kovac Malone image that captures this for me, even more than most. The Little Latrobe Street Apartment Building is shown against a red, rocket spattered millennial sky. The structural web of carbon-fibre cords is etched in white light, and the surfaces are all either transparent or translucent. The angled balconies however reflect light back at the sunbursts in the night sky. At its foot, the humdrum orthogonals of the existing Corrigan and Neometro urban fabric are dark or picked out in the green afterglow of the flash. An image from Bladerunner replaces the Kurokawa opposite. Aside from the extraordinarily sculptural sinuosity of the building itself, what am I seeing? It seems that the fibre of the structure is doubling up as an optic cable information system that is also a light source. It is this simultaneity that the work strains towards: a technology far in advance of the aluminium cable trays of the Boeing, and infinitely removed from the re-styling of the neo-classical into a machined aesthetic of reduction by that great pamphleteer of A-New-World-To-Come: Le Corbusier.' Our architectural ambitions are as serious as they are joyful. ❖

TOM KOVAC   GEOFF MALONE

✚ Capitol

MELBOURNE, AUSTRALIA
1994

The Capitol nightclub is located in the basement of a commercial building. One of the programme's main criteria was to retain as much as possible of the existing structure, owing to the loads of the building above. Kovac's scheme was also constrained by the three spaces available, which varied in height. Within these tight parameters the brief required two separate bar zones and a central dance area. Working around the existing plant room, offices and fridges, Kovac's white stud and stucco interior skin discreetly wraps itself around the existing basement walls and columns, filling the shell with opacity and transparency of form. Spatial scraping of folded and buckled ceilings and curving walls create an illusion of horizontal depth. The plan and form are foetus-like, containing three pods that rotate around a central core which is pierced by three existing columns. ✚

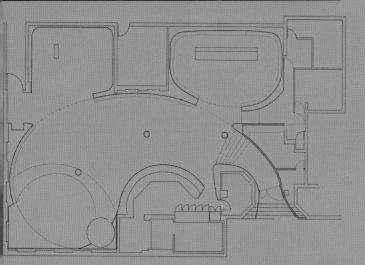

✚ Island House

VICTORIA, AUSTRALIA
1997

The special aspect of the site is the vast richness of the vegetation, the spectacular views accross the sea and the powerful topography. It is not architecture but nature that makes the essential contribution and defines the formal characteristics of the plan. The form that emerges consists of a central spine that articulates movement through the building and its spatial organisation. The approach to the house is recessed, cut into the hilltop that descends into a central passage distributing the public and private circulation of the house. The body of the bedrooms is recesssed into the natural ground and receives natural daylight and ventilation through deep narrow recesses that extend along the roofline into the landscape. The house folds into a covered void, providing the living zone with dramatic views across the ocean. The relationship between volume, surface and space dissolves a convential reading of the house. It dematerializes the form and assumes an anonymity that merges with the topography of the land. ✚

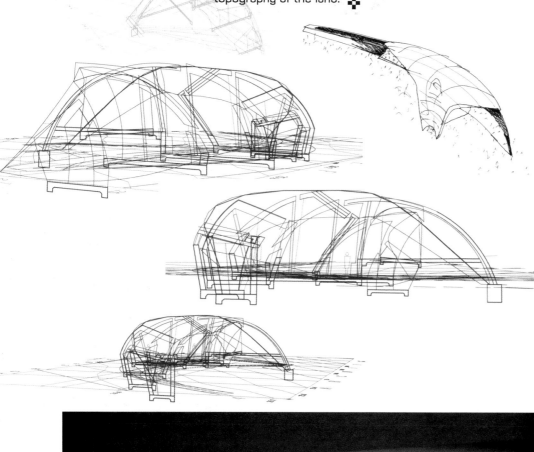

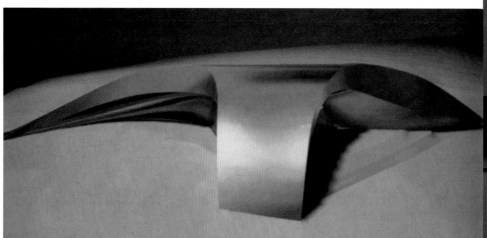

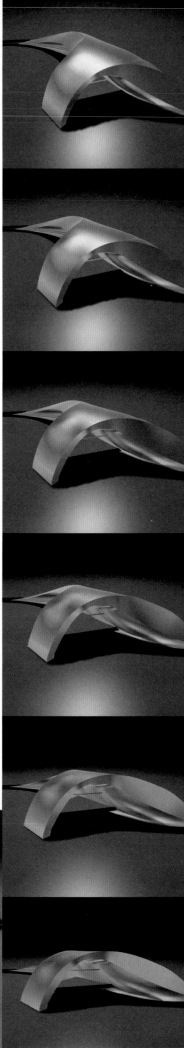

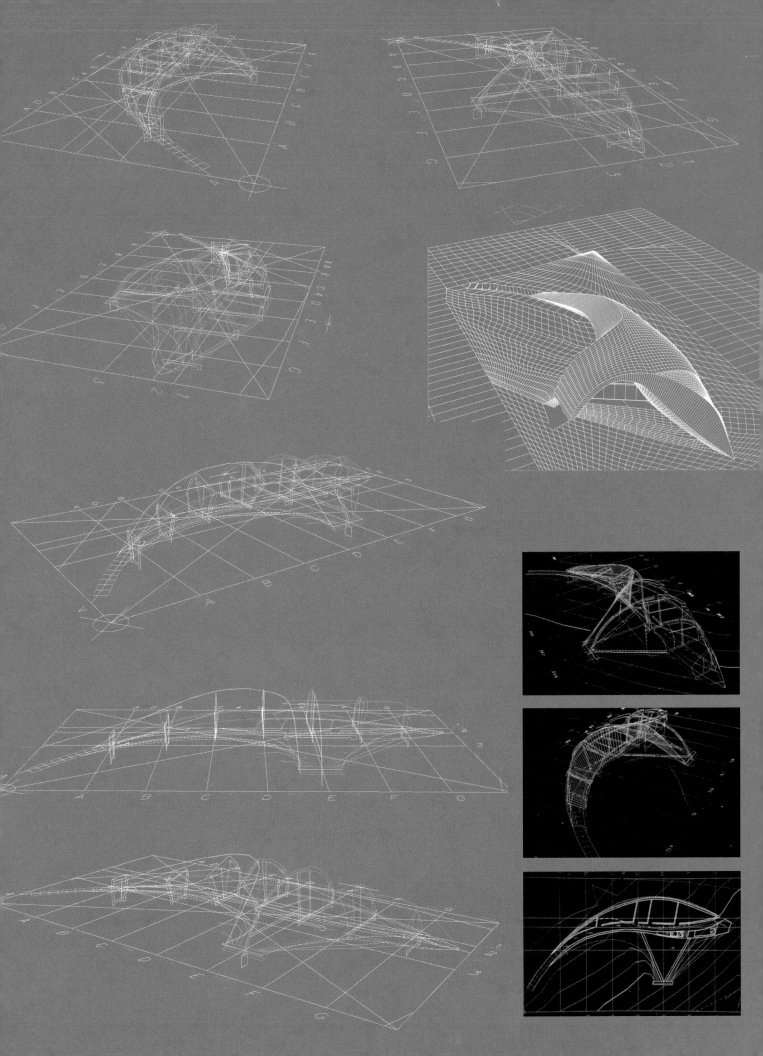

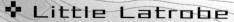

✚ Little Latrobe
MELBOURNE, AUSTRALIA
1998

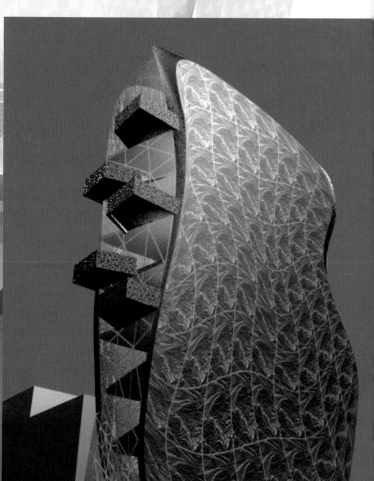

Located on a narrow site, the project is derived from a combination of urban, spatial and programming factors. It is a marker between the city's dense commercial core and its dissipated outer edge. The tall form articulates existing neighbouring structures, Kurokawa's Daimaru Tower, the Argus Tower and Corrigan's R.M.I.T. Building 8, which sits high on a natural mound. The gallery, studio, café and apartments form a series of linked cells. These are interconnected from the building's public zones on the lower levels through to the private apartments on the upper floors by a series of interconnecting floor plates. The fluid and undulating form of the building is a means of articulating the transition through its vertical layers which departs radically from the standardized construction for commercial space. This condition seeks to mediate in the confrontation between the city and the proposed new planning scheme, which extends beyond its current limits. ✚

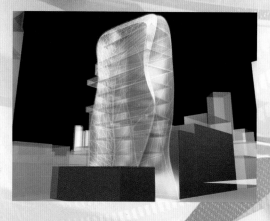

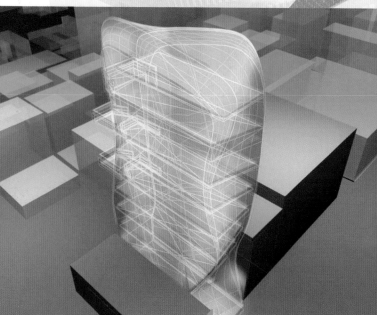

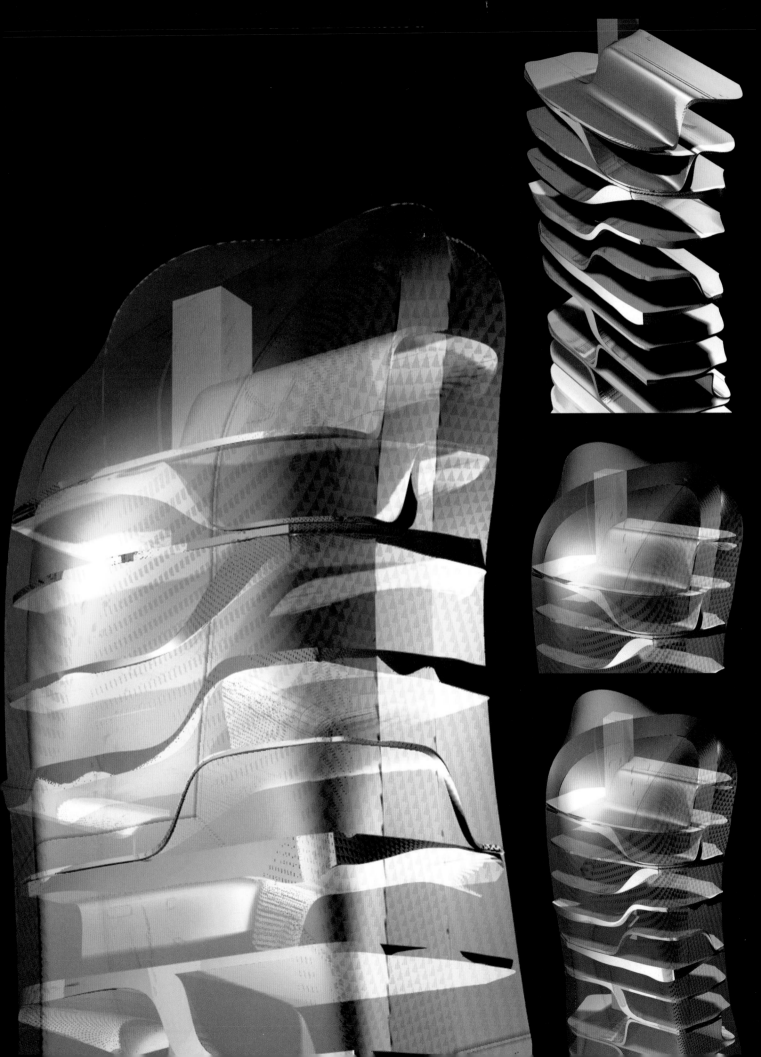

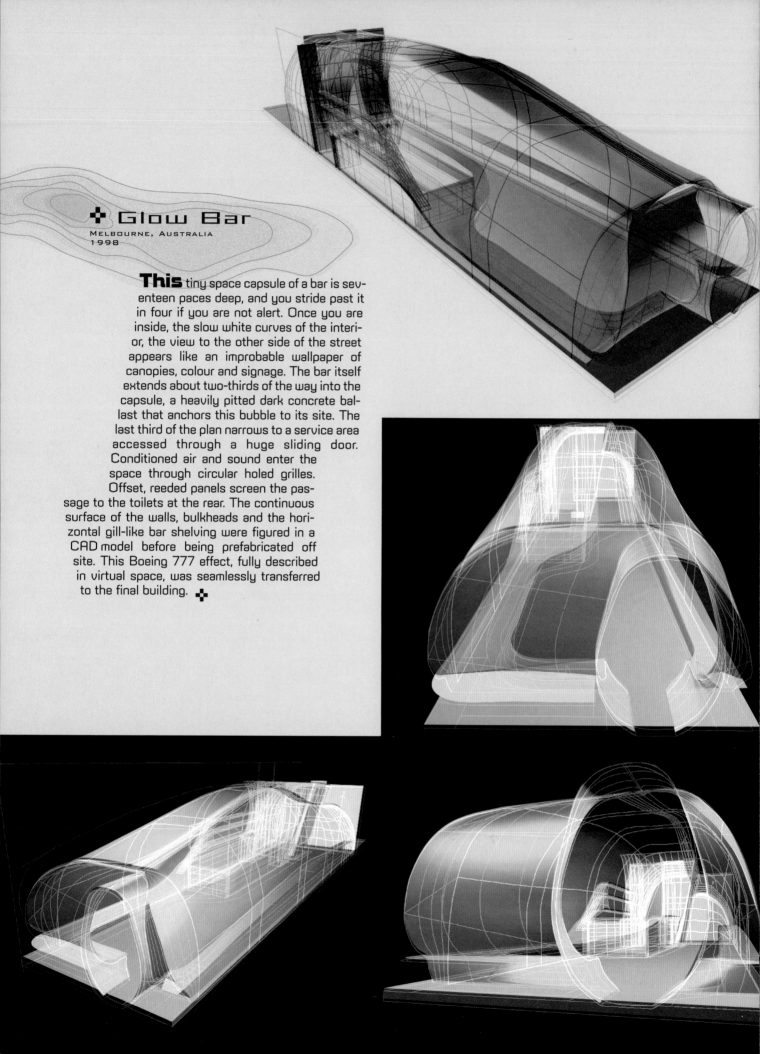

✚ Glow Bar
MELBOURNE, AUSTRALIA
1998

This tiny space capsule of a bar is seventeen paces deep, and you stride past it in four if you are not alert. Once you are inside, the slow white curves of the interior, the view to the other side of the street appears like an improbable wallpaper of canopies, colour and signage. The bar itself extends about two-thirds of the way into the capsule, a heavily pitted dark concrete ballast that anchors this bubble to its site. The last third of the plan narrows to a service area accessed through a huge sliding door. Conditioned air and sound enter the space through circular holed grilles. Offset, reeded panels screen the passage to the toilets at the rear. The continuous surface of the walls, bulkheads and the horizontal gill-like bar shelving were figured in a CAD model before being prefabricated off site. This Boeing 777 effect, fully described in virtual space, was seamlessly transferred to the final building. ✚

✦ Queen Bar
MELBOURNE, AUSTRALIA
1998

This project is situated in an existing corner building at the edge of the Melbourne Central Activities district bounded by Victoria Market. The client brief requires a flexible bar and dining environment to function as a day and night venue. A roundabout island provides a focal point for the design and is a generator for the evolution of this new space. The roundabout is governed by a frenetic vehicular drive-by pace. It orders traffic through to the market, the city and the western suburbs. Kovac Malone's design response is to use this urban typology and extend the functionality of the roundabout as an expanding sonar wave producing a synthetic pattern for the evolution of the interior volume of the new bar. The vehicular traffic informs the waveform and dissipates as it seeps through the existing boundary condition to become a fluid internalized skin. This wave condition breaks down the interface between public and private, inside and outside and provides a more complex organization of volume. ✦

✦ Kovac / Malone

Tom Kovac (1958)
1997 Master of Architecture, RMIT
1986 Bachelor of Architecture, Royal Melbourne Institute of Technology
1970 Moved to Australia
1991 Prizewinner RAIA; Interior Architecture Award; Light Makers Award

1990 Founded Kovac Architecture, Melbourne.
1994 Founded Curve Architecture Gallery, Melbourne

Teaching
1997–96 RMIT

Principal buildings and projects
1998 Glow Bar, Melbourne (realized); Latrobe Tower, Melbourne (project); Marina Tif, St Kilda Marina, Melbourne (competition prizewinner)
1997 Island House, Victoria (project); Tonic, Sydney (project); Student housing A'Beckett, Melbourne (project); Cinema complex, Paris (project); Apartments, Jaffa (project)
1996 Atlas House, Melbourne (realized); Urban Attitude, Melbourne (realized); Barkly Apartments, Melbourne (project); Pless House, Melbourne (project); Federation Square, Melbourne (competition); Pontian Centre, Melbourne (competition)
1995 Curve Architecture Gallery, Melbourne (realized); Sapore Restaurant, Melbourne (realized); Ryan Studio, Melbourne (realized)
1994 Capitol, Melbourne (realized); Gibbs Church Conversion, Melbourne; Museum of Victoria, Melbourne (competition)
1993 Gan House, Melbourne (realized)
1991 Succhi, Melbourne (realized)

1990 Square Boutique, Melbourne (realized); The Cherry Tree, Melbourne (realized)

Recent exhibitions
1997 Sydney, 'Interbuild', University de Melbourne
1996 London, 'Architecture on the horizon', Royal Institute of British Architects; Melbourne, Galerie Models Inc Artists and Industry
1995 Celje (Slovenia), Gallery of Contemporary Art

Selected bibliography
1998 *Architectural Monographs* no. 50, Academy Editions, UK; *A + U* (Jan.), Japan
1997 *Monument* (Feb.), Australia; *Architectural Design Profile* no. 126, UK
1996 *Monument* (Jan. and Sept.), Australia; *Architektur und Licht* (May), Germany; *Architectural Design Profile* no. 122; *Architectural Review* (Nov.), UK; *Wind* (Nov.) Japan; *B, Architectural Journal* no. 52/53, Denmark
1995 *Blue Print* (Feb.), UK; *Architecture Australia* (Jan.), Australia; *Monument* (March and Oct.), Australia; *Architectural Review* (May), UK; *The interior* (spring/summer), Australia
1993 *Architecture Australia* (Jan./Feb.), Australia; *International Interiors* (summer), USA; *Ambiente* (Dec.), Germany
1992 *Interior Architecture* (March), Australia; *Tostem View* (May), Japan; *CIA News* (Jun.), Japan; *Architect* (Oct.), Australia; *Kukan* (Nov.), Japan
1991 *Architecture Australia* (March); *Wind* (spring), Japan; *Interior Architecture* (Jun.), Australia; *The Interior* (Sept./Nov.), Australia
1990 *Interior Architecture* (Jan. and May), Australia; *Architecture Australia* (Nov.)

Kengo Kuma & Associates

| Kengo Kuma (*1954) |

'I want to erase architecture,' writes Kengo Kuma, 'that's what I've always wanted to do and it's unlikely I'll ever change my mind.' Erasing architecture, making it transparent to itself, preventing the appearance of any object, this is a recurrent problem-set in the already abundant and varied work of this Tokyo-based architect. In his work produced between 1986 and 1991, Kuma explored heterogeneous collage, brutal super-position and stylistic interference. It is his intent to dissolve this architecture of chaos in the actual chaos of the fast-changing Japanese city. The M2 building (1989–91), with its features that caricature an extravagant kind of postmodernism, is an exaggerated experiment in this vein. But in that period Kuma came up against a paradox: while wanting to dissolve architecture and denounce the object, he was, in spite of everything, producing new objects that were every bit as loquacious. After this formal exploration of chaos, Kuma gradually shifted the problem-set from object to subject, which he put progres-sively back into the centre of the process of architectural disappear-ance – this time around, phenomenological. Through its senses, its eye and its movement in space, it is Kuma's view that the subject alone can bring architecture back up to date, outside itself. This phase coincided with the opening, in 1990, of his agency, Kengo Kuma & Associates, in Tokyo. In his project for the Kiro-San observatory (1994), more than else-where, Kuma implemented this new way. By reversing the way the eye sees – a turn around from seen to seeing – he attempted to solve the paradox. The building here becomes invisible, hewn into the land, as if the architecture wanted to extend to the whole mountain and to the landscape offered to the beholder. The same goes for the Kikatami Canal Museum (1994), where the architecture works like a knot, a bridge that sorts out the discontinuities of the natural and manmade landscape, which is the real object of the project. The architect's new tools, digital tech-nologies, represent for Kuma a new field of exploration in relation to architectural deterritorialization and erasure; they dissolve all hierar-chies and existing territorialities in a flash. The form is cut off from its cause, from its method of original generation (classical or mod-ernist vocabulary), and is reduced to a combination of data, which can be manipulated and processed ad infinitum. This digitization process offers architecture a whole host of oppor-tunities: first and foremost, it can totally free it from the hold over it exercised by the eye; it opens it up to forms of logic that are more temporal than spatial; and, last of all, it helps to dissolve the distinction between built and not-built, inte-rior and exterior, and style and content. In the series of pro-jects titled 'Digital gardening', Kuma makes the most of these new conditions. He no longer works on objects but on landscapes; the challenge is to reweave the unity of a world in smithereens; architecture is no longer restricted to the isolated object but is being continually applied to the whole environment – a final way of erasing it. ✦

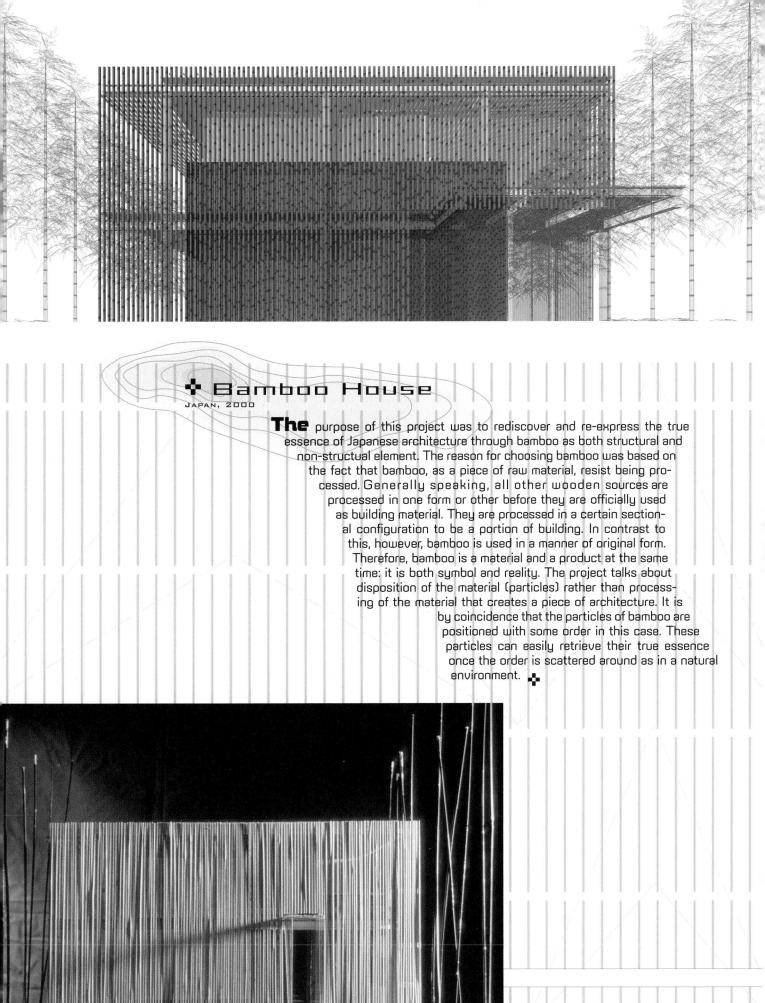

✦ Bamboo House

JAPAN, 2000

The purpose of this project was to rediscover and re-express the true essence of Japanese architecture through bamboo as both structural and non-structual element. The reason for choosing bamboo was based on the fact that bamboo, as a piece of raw material, resist being processed. Generally speaking, all other wooden sources are processed in one form or other before they are officially used as building material. They are processed in a certain sectional configuration to be a portion of building. In contrast to this, however, bamboo is used in a manner of original form. Therefore, bamboo is a material and a product at the same time: it is both symbol and reality. The project talks about disposition of the material (particles) rather than processing of the material that creates a piece of architecture. It is by coincidence that the particles of bamboo are positioned with some order in this case. These particles can easily retrieve their true essence once the order is scattered around as in a natural environment. ✦

✜ Kikatami Canal Museum
MIYAGI, JAPAN, 1999

Kitakami Canal is one of the oldest canals existing in Japan. The project is a museum and recreation space for a piece of land at the confluence of the Kitakami Canal and the Kitakami River. The building is embedded underground and the appearance of an architecture is fully extracted from the programme. The building is planned so that the walkway along the site extends into the function of underground space. A U-shaped walkway becomes an architectural structure at one point, and thus the walkway and the building do not contrast. Instead, the two functions merge to form a single line. What we encounter here is an ambiguity of physical boundaries between the architecture, the landscape and the infrastructure. A canal can be considered both natural and artificial. Without an effort to assimilate the canal into nature, the uninterrupted flow of water would not have been possible. Similarly, without an effort to merge canal with infrastructure, unimpeded navigation would not have been possible. As canal bridges nature and artefacts, the intention of this museum is a reperformance of bridging between the two elements. ✜

✦ Ando Hiroshige Museum

Ando Hiroshige was one of the most representative exponents of *ukiyoe* paintings in the history of Japanese art. His original pieces of work, found after the Hansin Earthquake (1995), were donated to the city of Batoh in the Toshigi Prefecture. The museum is composed of a series of wooden grids, forming the roof and the walls. Along with the change of light that pours into the space, the grid also alters its essence: sometimes the patterns of the grid transforms into a solid translucent plane, at other times it becomes a transparent plane. By creating the architecture entirely out of the grid system, Kuma have aimed for the building to be a 'sensor' of light. The *ukiyoe* works of Hiroshige are characterized by his visualization of nature and changes in nature (light, wind, rain, fog), and their expressions in solid form. This was done by selecting natural elements with specific clear features, and combining colour with them. Kuma's project applied the fundamental method of Hiroshige's approach to his art and redefined them into a vocabulary of architecture. ✦

✧ Stone Museum

NASU, JAPAN, 1998/2000

The project aims to retrieve the three stone-based traditional Japanese storage spaces that were built long ago in the Ashino region of Nasu city, Toshigi Prefecture. The new programme of the Stone Museum aims at reviving the space through new passage ways that would create spatial unification between the inside spaces and their immediate environment. The passageways are built out of two types of 'soft' walls. One type provides softness by making a series of stone slats (louvre). In this way the project was an outcome of the Japanese Pavilion at the Venice Biennale in 1995. Stone is typically a heavy source that poses a challenge in processing. However, a sense of lightness, ambiguity and softness can be gained by desolidifying the material with series of slats. The second type provides softness by punching numerous small openings in a stone-mounted wall. Hardness can be reduced by hollowing portions of the solid wall. This creates a system of ambiguity at the site boundary and the spreading of light that divides into infinite particles. ✧

✚ Noh Stage in the Forest

MIYAGI, JAPAN, 1996

Noh theatre was first established in the sixteenth century. Toyama City in Miyagi Prefecture is known for its unique style of noh performance, called Toyama noh, handed down to the present from the Edo period. This project was executed for the performance of Toyama noh in a forest. The fundamental concept to the project was to liberate and integrate the noh stage with the wooden environment. Typically, the noh stage is treated as a performance stage that is found independently within the overall architectural function. This treatment of the noh stage was introduced at the time of the Meiji Restoration and continued to the present day. However, the original noh, as a performance, was located within nature where the elements were part of the performance. The noh stage represents the world of death, whereas the audience seating area represents the world of life. In this project, Kuma attempted to reproduce the noh setting in its original style. Instead of building a piece of architecture for the performance of noh, the aim was to make a garden for it. ✚

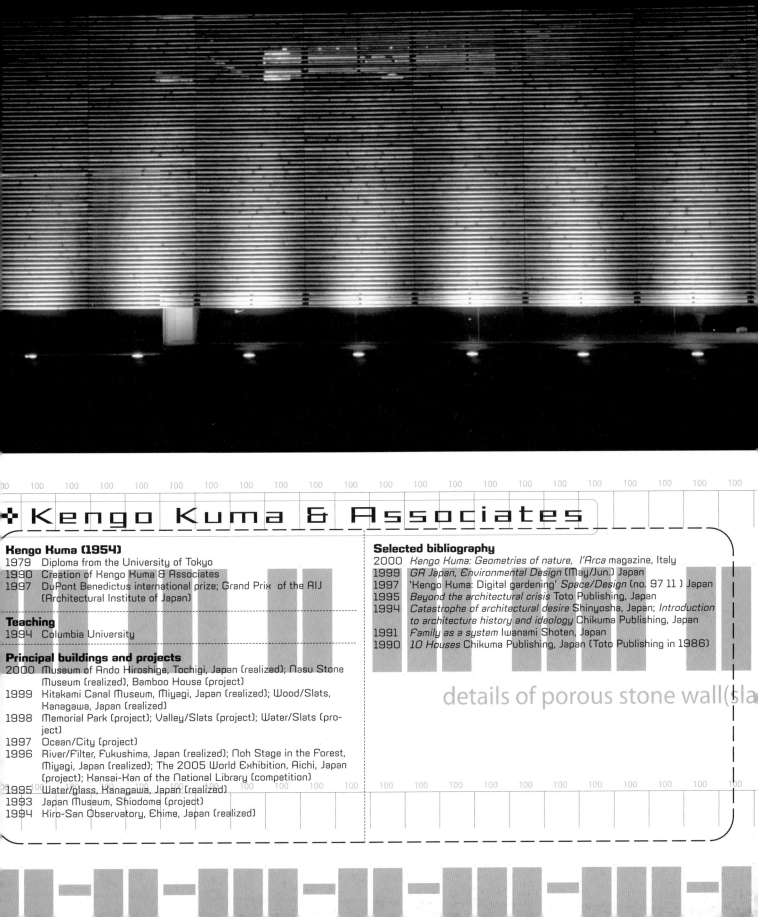

✦ Kengo Kuma & Associates

Kengo Kuma (1954)
1979 Diploma from the University of Tokyo
1990 Creation of Kengo Kuma & Associates
1997 DuPont Benedictus international prize; Grand Prix of the AIJ (Architectural Institute of Japan)

Teaching
1994 Columbia University

Principal buildings and projects
2000 Museum of Ando Hiroshige, Tochigi, Japan (realized); Nasu Stone Museum (realized), Bamboo House (project)
1999 Kitakami Canal Museum, Miyagi, Japan (realized); Wood/Slats, Kanagawa, Japan (realized)
1998 Memorial Park (project); Valley/Slats (project); Water/Slats (project)
1997 Ocean/City (project)
1996 River/Filter, Fukushima, Japan (realized); Noh Stage in the Forest, Miyagi, Japan (realized); The 2005 World Exhibition, Aichi, Japan (project); Kansai-Kan of the National Library (competition)
1995 Water/glass, Kanagawa, Japan (realized)
1993 Japan Museum, Shiodome (project)
1994 Kiro-San Observatory, Ehime, Japan (realized)

Selected bibliography
2000 *Kengo Kuma: Geometries of nature*, l'Arca magazine, Italy
1999 *GA Japan, Environmental Design* (May/Jun.) Japan
1997 'Kengo Kuma: Digital gardening' *Space/Design* (no. 97 11) Japan
1995 *Beyond the architectural crisis* Toto Publishing, Japan
1994 *Catastrophe of architectural desire* Shinyosha, Japan; *Introduction to architecture history and ideology* Chikuma Publishing, Japan
1991 *Family as a system* Iwanami Shoten, Japan
1990 *10 Houses* Chikuma Publishing, Japan (Toto Publishing in 1986)

details of porous stone wall(sla

Lacaton & Vassal

| Anne Lacaton (*1955) | Jean-Philippe Vassal (*1954) |

It'll be nice tomorrow/The beauty of the obvious

The civil engineering structure comes just before technical prowess, in the sense of engineers making things (machines, factories). There are not a thousand and one solutions. There are just one or two answers, and one of them will surely be the better one.

No architecture – One solves a problem of installation, incorporation and programme mathematically, as one does a technical, economic or social problem. This is enough, where relevant. It is already a lot. Self-construction: sheds, huts, factories, suburban shopping malls: a box, a sign. Which is right, which is clearly named: readability. It is up to (phoney) images of speed: aircraft wings and horizontal cladding and up to buildings ready to take off, to make direct suggestions about the destination, beaches and coconut trees ... We're not kidding.

Dwellings – Too much comfort. We do not have extraordinary architectures because of a bit too much – middle-class – comfort. New ways of living in, and living. The House: inventing something else, getting rid of foundations, mobility, nomadism. The box, the parallelepiped: what else is there to do? The Farnsworth House, and then? Dealing with transparency, filters, open buildings that are permeable to the climate. Inventing machine-houses, flower-houses.

Project – There is neither obviousness nor reference. Every time a new problem crops up, a concertinaing of restrictions, requirements, expectations. Raising good questions and making rigorous replies to them, one after the other. Always raising the issue of the necessary, the sufficient; what is important and what isn't. Avoiding accumulations, looking for simplicity and readability. Monitoring every slightly complicated detail like the consequence of an error of reflection. Shedding the idea of form other than architectonic or stemming from the context. Constructing from the interior. The precision of the installation. The perfect resolution of the functioning. Use: shifts, sensations, inner perception, appropriation. Sense: the evocation of a building; its contents, its life, its period. Cost: cost-cutting, the right means, as inexpensive as possible to build more. The rigour of the plans. A certain passion for organizing, setting, calculating, compressing, pricing, starting all over again, reading and rereading the programme, economizing, simplifying. And then, that magic moment when the images come back, when the two directions of thought are perfectly attuned, interlock, fuel one another, as if spellbound. Moment of euphoria and ease, as if miraculously and unconsciously the joyous, living part that gives the project its meaning had steered the laborious part to do with development. Born who knows where, experienced somewhere, far away, in Africa or elsewhere, in books of poetry and films, in smoke-filled bars, train compartments, airport concourses, an image, a persistent idea, that one waits for, that one delicately gathers up, that one protects, safeguards, forgets and finds again. It stays there throughout the project and ends up being absolutely indispensable. Architecture will be straightforward, useful, precise, cheap, free, jovial, poetic and cosmopolitan. It'll be nice tomorrow. ✣

ANNE LACATON &
JEAN PHILIPPE VASSAL

✦ Individual House

LÈGE CAP-FERRET, FRANCE
1998

The land, with its well-developed vegetation, is located at Grand Piquey on the Bassin d'Arcachon, on one of the last plots that has not yet been built on in this area. Its topography is undulating, with sandy ground. Bearing the particular qualities of the site in mind, the architectural and landscaping aim has been to retain its features of topography and vegetation alike. The house is on a single level, on piles, based on a broad layout that reduces the impact and cost of the foundations. The delicate structure is made of galvanized steel. The façade, overlooking the Bassin, is all glass, and the three other sides are aluminium walls, punctuated by windows. The platform is a concrete slab and its undersurface is made of aluminium sheets identical to those of the sides. The roof is a roof terrace. The overall form of the volume, with its lightness and transparency, means that the building interferes little with the landscape. The low vegetation is retained beneath the platform, and pines grow within with confines of the structure, passing through the house in special enclosed areas. By the beach, the traditional stone facing has been redone. ✦

35

41

33

43

✤ Latapie House

FLOIRAC, FRANCE
1993

This house is economical. Situated in the inner suburbs of Bordeaux, it was a commission for a family home – a couple and their two children, with a small budget. It fits into the contour of the street. It is a simple volume on a square base. The structure is metal. One half, on the street side, is covered with an opaque skin, with fibro-cement cladding, and the other half, the greenhouse, with a transparent skin and PVC cladding, on the garden side. A wooden volume behind the opaque cladding delimits an isolated winter area. It opens on to a greenhouse and the outside world, on the street side. This volume has two free levels, designed to suit the family's lifestyle: living room and garage on the ground floor, bedrooms on the upper floor. The utility rooms – kitchen, bathroom, WC, closets – are all included in a central volume. The greenhouse is east-facing and picks up the first rays of the sun. This is one of the home's living areas. The east and west façades are very moveable, with opening and folding doors. The house can thus switch from being very enclosed to very open, depending on the family's requirements and their desire for light, privacy, protection and ventilation. The home's living area can vary from season to season, from small – just the living room and bedrooms – to large, encompassing the whole garden at the height of summer. ✤

✦ Arts and Humanities University Building

GRENOBLE, FRANCE
FIRST PHASE, 1995; SECOND PHASE, IN PROGRESS

The project is part of the 'University 2000' plan and is located in an alignment of new buildings which heighten the campus's axis of development. It gives on to its surroundings – the campus and the presence of soaring mountains. The project is set on the four boundaries of the terrain, a rectangle of 60 x 45 metres, and consists of two floors – ground level and partial mezzanine. It is built in two balanced phases, the final aspect of which, resulting from the continuity of the greenhouses on the main façades, is that of a single building. These greenhouses, like slender transparent blades to north and south, create a filter of plants. They provide an innovative image, at once changing and poetic, matching the building's purpose and the artistic dimension of the classes held in it. The look of the building resides in the reality and transparency of its everydayness, made up of the lives of its occupants. The interior quality has more to do with the space, atmosphere, light arrangements and comfort. The structure's sober nature exists in tandem with an unexpected feature of the project, which creates both its image and its poetry: the greenhouses with their flowers. ✦

✚ Lacaton & Vassal

Anne Lacaton (1955)
1980 Diploma from the School of Architecture at Bordeaux
1984 DESS in Urban Studies at the University of Bordeaux

Jean Philippe Vassal (1954)
1980 Diploma from the School of Architecture at Bordeaux
1980–85 Architect-town planner in Niger, north-west Africa

1987 Founded the practice in Bordeaux
1991 Prizewinners in Albums de la Jeune Architecture
1996 Nominated for the Equerre d'Argent du Moniteur
1997 Selected for the Vth European Architecture Prize, Mies van der Rohe Foundation, Barcelona

Teaching
1999–94 A. Lacaton: visiting teacher at the School of Fine Arts at Bordeaux
1999–92 J.P. Vassal: temporary teacher at the School of Architecture at Bordeaux
1999–94 J.P. Vassal: visiting teacher at the School of Fine Arts at Bordeaux

Principal buildings and projects
1998 University of Grenoble, France, Department of Arts & Humanities, second tranche realized (under construction); Building of collective residences, Bordeaux, 20 dwellings (under construction); Maison Dartois, Cap Ferret (realized); Institut Universitaire/Journalisme et communication, Bordeaux (competition)
1997 University of Grenoble, reconstruction of the Department of Economics and Development; French school at Frankfurt (competition); Franco-Namibian cultural centre, Windhoek, Namibia (competition)
1996 Arrangement of Place du Vieux Lavoir, Sainte Eanne (realized); Arrangement of Place Léon Aucoc, Bordeaux (realized); Youth hostel, Biarritz (competition)
1995 Arrangement of the archeological museum at Saintes (realized); Lycée Ste Foy la Grande (competition)
1993 Maison Latapie, Floirac (realized); Day centre, Bègles (realized)
1992 Prototype of an economical house (project)

Recent exhibitions
1999–98 'Premises', Guggenheim Museum Soho, New York
1998 Galerie Taisei, Tokyo; Museum für Gestaltung, Zurich
1997 Architektur Zentrum, Vienna; Le Magasin, CNAC Grenoble; Arc en Rêve, Bordeaux IFA, Paris

Recent conferences
1998 Architektur Zentrum, Vienna, 6th Congress of architecture at Vienna; Columbia University, New York; Galerie Taisei, Tokyo, within the framework of the Year of France in Japan; Schools of architecture of Rome, Reggio Calabre, Barcelona

Selected bibliography
1998 *Premises: invested spaces in visual arts & architecture from France, 1958-1998* catalogue, Guggenheim Museum Soho, New York, in collaboration with MNAM Georges Pompidou Centre; *De Architect* (Nov.); *Casabella* no. 660; *Werk, Bauen + Wohnen* (May); *Domus* no. 803; *d'Architectures* no. 80; *AIT* no. 1/2; *Arquitectura viva* no. 72
1997 *Domus* no. 791; *Faces* no. 42/43; *Archit. d'intérieure créé* no. 280; *Techniques & Arch.* no. 434; *Quaderns* no. 217; *A + T* no. 10; *Arquitectura viva* no. 65
1996 *Dictionnaire de l'architecture du XXe siècle*, Hazan IFA, Paris (page 500); *Bauwelt* no. 16; *AMC-Moniteur* no. 76; *Le Moniteur* no. 4835; *Abitare* no. 347
1995 *Il fera beau demain* exhibition catalogue, IFA, Paris; *Qu'as-tu voulu me dire* exhibition catalogue, Arc en rêve, Bordeaux; *Archit. d'intérieure créé* no. 268
1994 *Une maison particulière*, Hubert Tonka and Jeanne Marie Sens, Sens & Tonka, Paris; *Techniques & Arch.* no. 416; *d'Architectures* no. 51; *Libération* (14 Nov.); *Intramuros* no. 54
1991 *Album de la jeune architecture*, Ministère de l'Équipement, Paris; *40 architectes de moins de 40 ans*, exhibition catalogue, IFA, Moniteur

Filmography
1994 *Habitant*, film by Ph. Madec and Michel Le Bayon, co-production with the Ministry of Culture and Art (Maison Latapie at Floirac)

UK

CJ Lim/Studio 8 Architects

| CJ Lim (*1964) |

Conventional thinking tells us that architectural drawings are a means to an end, a vehicle by which information is transmitted - they do not play the same role or have the same value as fine art. Cj was part of a generation of students at the Architectural Association whose milieu demanded a reappraisal of that status. The debate may be determined for those who see drawing as an unchallenged force and continue for those who celebrate its speculative and propositional power. I feel that CJ would argue that these drawings are a vehicle, for he can see their physical realisation in his mind's eye, but for most, they are a fantastic virtuoso performance of line and paint, deliberately and obstinately abstract, brilliant compositionally, a web of form that conjures a complex world, some of which might be realized, some that will always remain an enigma. Cj's cultural background must surely influence what we see, layer upon layer; the curious paradox of the pedantically practical coupled with wilful fantasy and an often naive disregard for the limits of modern technology.

The early influences of discussion at the London's Architectural Association in the 1980s were perhaps in a period that many would consider seminal; the architectural critique was sharp-edged and positional, the catalyst was always drawings that challenged our conventional understanding of architecture as product-based and challenged the narrow channels through which architectural ideas flowed. It was within this climate that CJ developed his own idiosyncratic spatial and functional juxtapositions; these early student drawings were not part of the 'genre' of critical angst, more an illustrated intrigue with what were then seemingly outrageous functional marriages. His work is not inherently technical, there is no fascination with smart or intelligent systems, they are perhaps too unobtrusive for his purpose. The architectural world that is created is one of flamboyant showmanship and exquisite tailoring. Architecture as a cerebral pursuit or vehicle for state-of-the-art science is left for others to pursue. His references are more likely to be Goldsworthy, Moholy-Nagy and Marey than NASA. Spatial manipulation can of course be taken to various levels of sophistication, but there are more ephemeral qualities that CJ refers to that will necessarily demand the interference of some science in order to achieve the goal. The early work of Dan Flavin, the later work of Gary Hill, the mechanical installations of Rebecca Horn are masterpieces of spatial manipulation and theatre using as much ingenuity with computer circuitry as with the chisel or paint brush. Cj's architecture aspires to the qualities of these pieces. Architecture as a form of inhabited art at this level should become an inhabited science. ❖

CHRISTINE HAWLEY

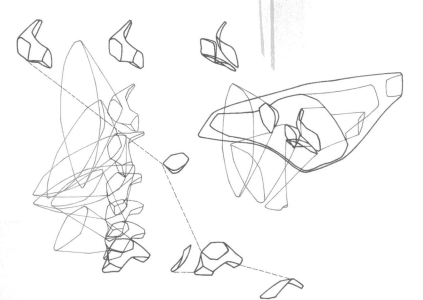

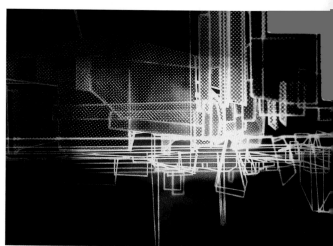

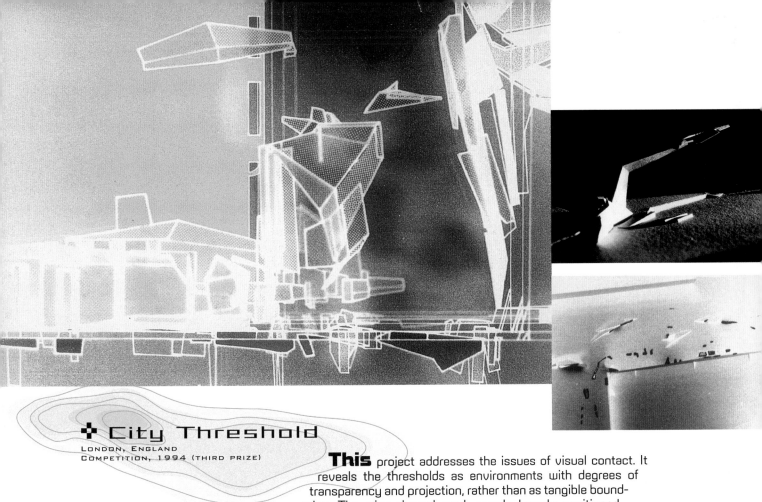

✦ City Threshold

LONDON, ENGLAND
COMPETITION, 1994 (THIRD PRIZE)

This project addresses the issues of visual contact. It reveals the thresholds as environments with degrees of transparency and projection, rather than as tangible boundaries. The wing-shaped mesh panels loosely positioned disguise the faces from every angle and delineate distinct routes providing varying intensities of privacy. Lights set into the road and pavement occasionally project a silhouetted yet disguised figure on to the façade of adjacent buildings. As the panels strech out into Wardour Street and into Old Compton Street the inserted architecture becomes increasingly solid to form a series of elevated catwalks, walkways and platform cafés. Each element is given a specific character by the use of specific lighting. The narrow catwalk dictates a singular approach to revelation. Plain panelled backdrops highlight the completed performance as selective integration across the threshold is achieved. ✦

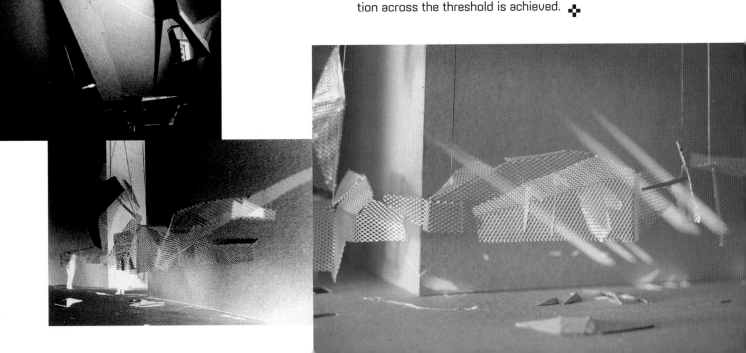

✦ The Guest House
THE LANDSCAPE AND ENVIRONMENTAL REGISTER, JAPAN
1995

The Guest House exists only in an animated artificial and topographical landscape. The form is in direct relationship to the fluctuating host environment as the relocation of elements kinetically addresses any introduced circumstances. The forms of the house are dependent on both the internal programme provided by the occupants and the exterior environment. The architectonic pieces have many assembly permutations, haphazardly configured by infinite sequences of circumstances. Only an oscillating dialogue between guest and host, constantly corrupted by the presence of the occupants, exists as definable. The boundary that exists between the host and the Guest House cannot be clearly defined. The fractured and dynamic landscape encroaches into the house, blurring the boundary between the two. A door may become a floor, a canopy become a bed and then a wall. The traditional architecture of the house has become adaptive and responsive within a highly interactive dialogue. ✦

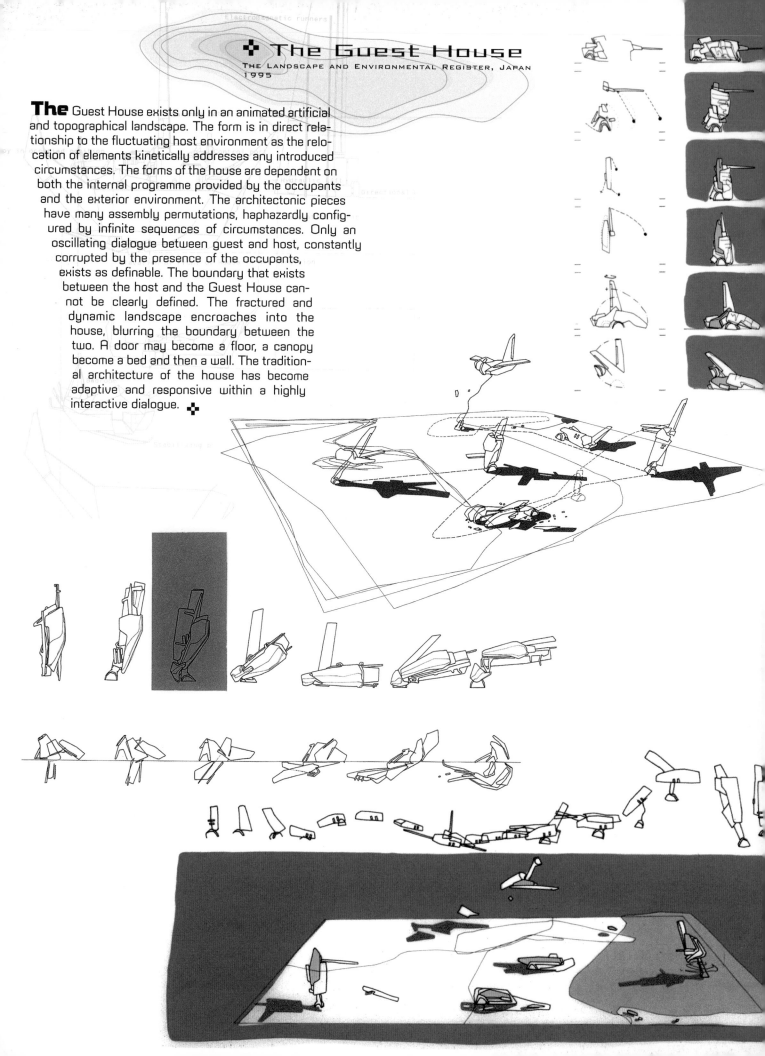

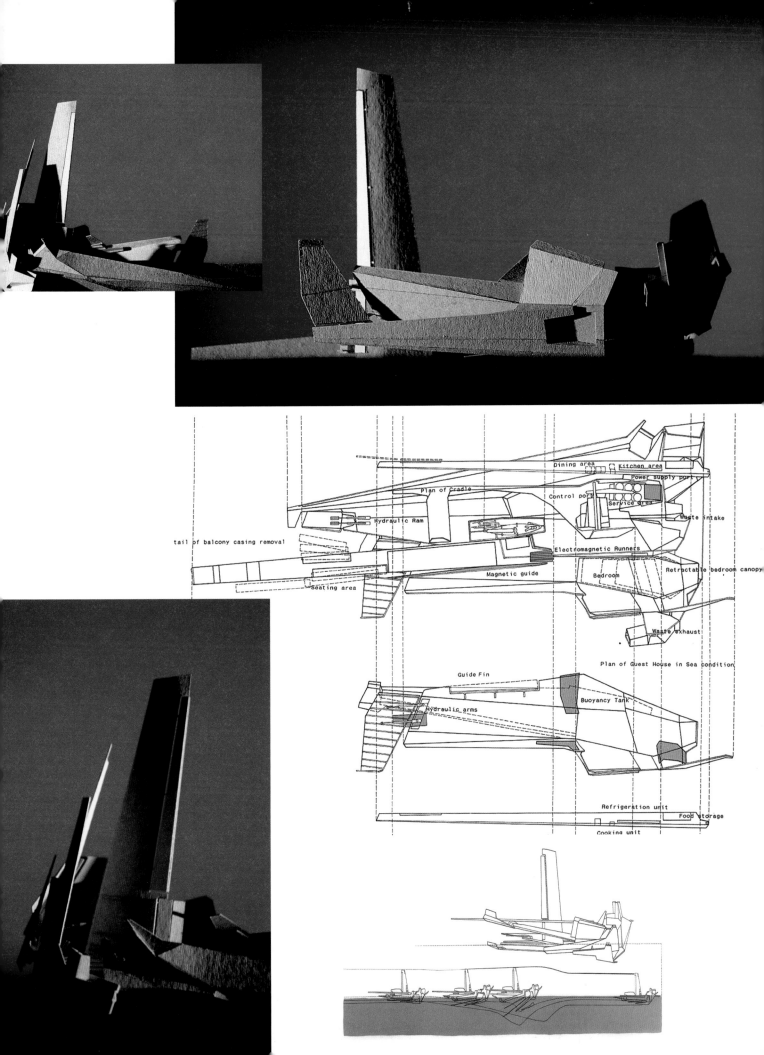

Dining area

Kitchen area

Power supply port

Plan of Cradle

Control port

Service area

Hydraulic Ram

Waste intake

tail of balcony casing removal

Electromagnetic Runners

Magnetic guide

Bedroom

Retractable bedroom canopy

Seating area

Waste exhaust

Plan of Guest House in Sea condition

Guide Fin

Buoyancy Tank

Hydraulic arms

Refrigeration unit

Food storage

Cooking unit

✦ UCL Cultural Centre

LONDON, ENGLAND
COMPETITION, 1996 (FIRST PRIZE)

The University College London Museum is an inhabitable void within the urban context of Bloombury. This 'positive space' has been shifted, fractured and sculpted into an internal courtyard housing all the exhibition spaces. UCLM is enclosed within four kinetic walls providing a perimeter for the site: the 'Projection Wall', where light is projected through the building on to the flank wall, signposting the collections on each floor; the 'Temporary Display Wall' where the collection of contemporary art work is exhibited running from top to bottom of the building; the 'Interactive Wall', the public front of the building, on Gordon Street. A laminate of LCD glass electrically controls the transparency of this façade subjected to a constantly transient state. On the 'Shadow Wall', by day or by night, the light casts an animated image of the building. ✦

✜ Ephemeral Field

1998

This assemblage illustrates the intricate system of interactions between life and our environment. Here, the space-making uses an electrical field which we can't see or hear or touch. This intangible membrane can retain heat, repel water particles and control levels of internal light/temperature levels. If an external electrical charge is brought into this electrical field, its status quo alters. The nomadic service-pod carries such an electrical charge and is therefore acted on by the field; and in doing so, performs an endless series of spatial dialogues with its surroundings. The electrical field liberates us from the traditional methods of space-making and questions the social economics of personalized spaces and city planning laws. We can have 'space-vending-machines' and these 'space-packs' can come in different sizes; all we have to do is just plug them into the nearest electrical socket! Space-making has therefore become a late-twentieth-century 'throw-away' consumer product. ✜

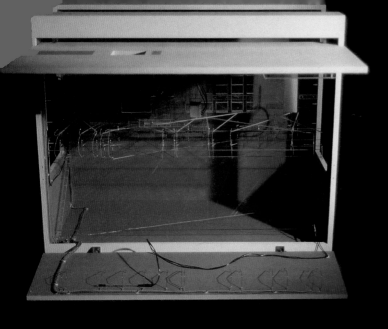

+ CJ Lim/Studio 8 Architects

CJ LIM (1964)
1982–87 Diploma from the AA School with Peter Cook et Christine Hawley

Teaching
1999 University of North London and The Bartlett School, University College, London
1997 Stadelschule, Frankfurt
1996 Curtin University, Perth
1991–83 Assistant architect (Zaha Hadid, Eva Jiricna, Peter Cook and Christine Hawley)
1994 Founded STUDIO 8 Architects in London
1997 First recipient of the RIBA Award for Academic Contribution in Architectural Education (also in 1998)

Principal buildings and projects
1996 UCL Cultural Centre, London (first prize)
1995 Architecture Triennale Nara/Toto (honourable mention); Guesthouse, Japan (competition)
1994 6th Shinkenchiku/Takiron: City Threshold (third prize)
1993–89 Competition by invitation
1988 Housing: A demonstration project (first prize)
1987 Bridge of the Future, Japan (second prize)

Exhibition
1996 Traveling exhibition, Europe/Australia/USA, '441/10: We'll reconfigure the space when you're ready'

Selected bibliography
1998 *Architects Journal* no. 1, vol. 207 (Jan.)
1997 *Special Narrative: cj LIM, monographie 1988–96*, JS + W Publishing, Taiwan; *GA Houses* no. 52; *Shinkenchiku*, Japan (July); *Domus* no. 796 (Sept.); *Building Design* nos 1332 and 1333; *Architects Journal* no. 21, vol. 206 (Dec.)
1996 *cj LIM/Studio 8 Architects Monograph*, Ind-E8 Publishing, London; *AA Files* no. 32; *Building Design* (August); *Architects Journal* no. 7, vol. 203; *Werk, Bauen + Wohnen* no. 6, Switzerland; *Artifice* no. 4 (May); *UCL News* no. 11, vol. 4; *Architecture + Urbanism* no. 308, Japan; *Document 4* Australia (Dec.); *Trien-Nara* no. 3, Japan
1995 *Architects Journal* nos 20 and 21, vol. 202; *Building Design* no. 1244; *Shinkenchiku* (March); *Artifice* no. 2; *Compe + Contest* no. 39, Japan
1993 *Building Design* no. 1134/1135
1992 *Architects Journal*, vol. 196; *Building Design* no. 1069
1991 *New Acropolis Museum*, National Gallery, Athens, exhibition catalogue
1990 *Building Design* nos 987, 1003, 1004 and 1013; *Art Random, Peter Cook: Conversations*, Kyoto Shoju International, Japan
1988 *Building Design* no. 890; *Architects Journal*, vol. 187

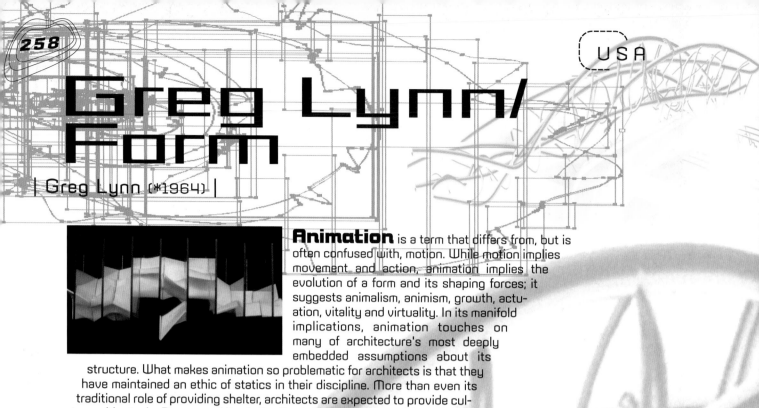

Greg Lynn/ Form

| Greg Lynn (*1964) |

Animation is a term that differs from, but is often confused with, motion. While motion implies movement and action, animation implies the evolution of a form and its shaping forces; it suggests animalism, animism, growth, actuation, vitality and virtuality. In its manifold implications, animation touches on many of architecture's most deeply embedded assumptions about its structure. What makes animation so problematic for architects is that they have maintained an ethic of statics in their discipline. More than even its traditional role of providing shelter, architects are expected to provide culture with stasis. Because of its dedication to permanence, architecture is one of the last modes of thought based on the inert.

Challenging these assumptions by introducing architecture to models of organization that are not inert will not threaten the essence of the discipline, but will advance it. Just as the development of calculus drew upon the historical mathematical developments that preceded it, so too will an animate approach to architecture subsume traditional models of statics into a more advanced system of dynamic organizations as a subset. The uses for an animate approach to architecture might be in its conception and design while more conventional tools remain in force for modelling and fabrication. Traditionally, in architecture the abstract space of design is conceived as an ideal neutral space of equivalent Cartesian coordinates. In other design fields, however, design space is conceived as an environment of forces rather than as an inert neutral vacuum. In naval design, for example, the abstract space of design is imbued with the properties of flow, turbulence, viscosity and drag so that the particular form of a hull can be thought of in terms of its motion through water. Although the form of a boat hull is studied in motion within an abstract space that has properties, there is no expectation that the shape of the boat hull will literally move. Similarly, an ethic of motion neither implies that architecture must be literally moveable, nor does it preclude actual motion. The contours and profiles of form can be shaped by the collaboration between an envelope and the active context in which it is situated. While physical form can be defined in terms of static coordinates, the virtual force of the environment in which it is designed should also contribute to its shaping. In this way, topology allows for not just the incorporation of a single moment but rather a multiplicity of vectors and therefore a multiplicity of times, in a single continuous surface. The availability and rapid colonization of architectural design by computer-aided techniques presents the discipline with yet another opportunity to both retool and rethink itself as it did with the advent of stereometric projection and perspective. If there is a single concept that must be engaged owing to the proliferation of topological shapes and computer-aided tools, it is that in their structure as abstract machines, these technologies are animate. ✦

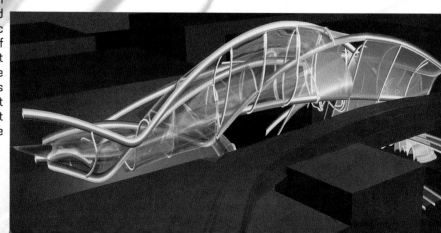

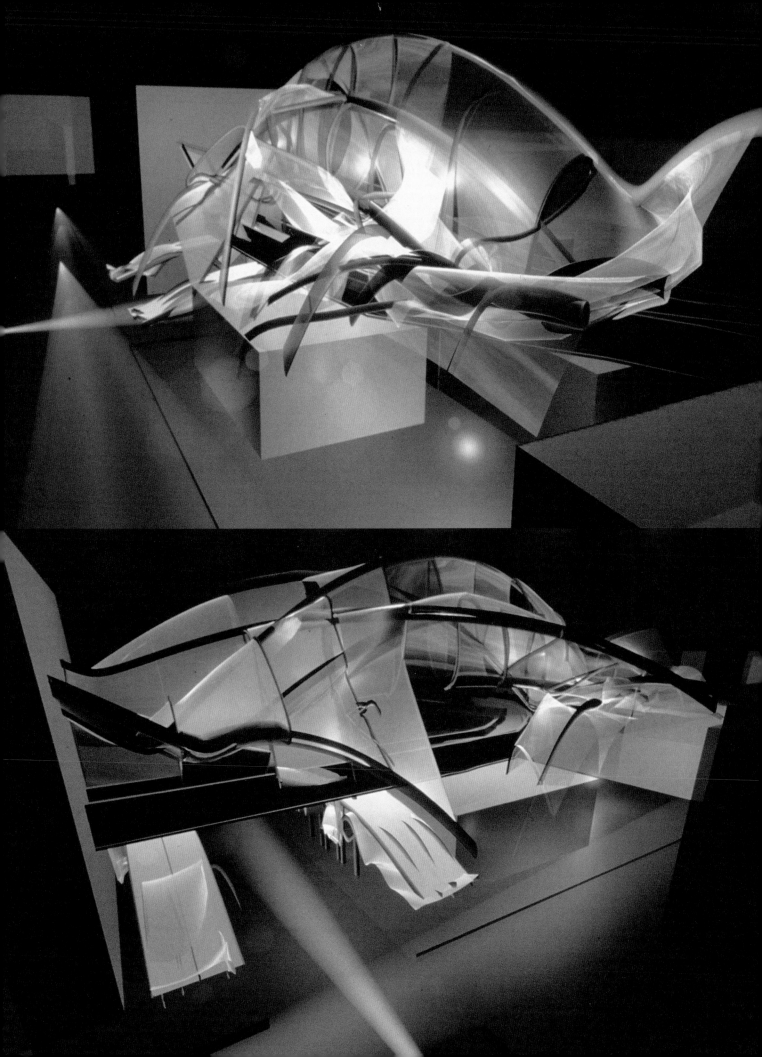

✦ Port Authority Gateway

NEW YORK, USA
COMPETITION, 1995

This competition involved the design of a protective roof and a lighting scheme for the underside of the bus ramps leading into the Port Authority Bus Terminal, in New York. The site was modelled using forces that simulate the movement and flow of pedestrians, cars and buses across the site, each with differing speeds and intensities of movement along Ninth Avenue, 42nd and 43rd streets and the four elevated bus ramps emerging from below the Hudson River. These various forces of movement established a gradient field of attraction across the site. To discover the shape of this invisible field of attraction, Lynn introduced geometric particles that change their position and shape according to the influence of the forces. From the particle studies, he captured a series of phase portraits of the cycles of movement over a period of time. These phase portraits are swept with a secondary structure of tubular frames linking the ramps, existing buildings and the Port Authority Bus Terminal. Eleven tensile surfaces are stretched across these tubes as an enclosure and projection surface. ✦

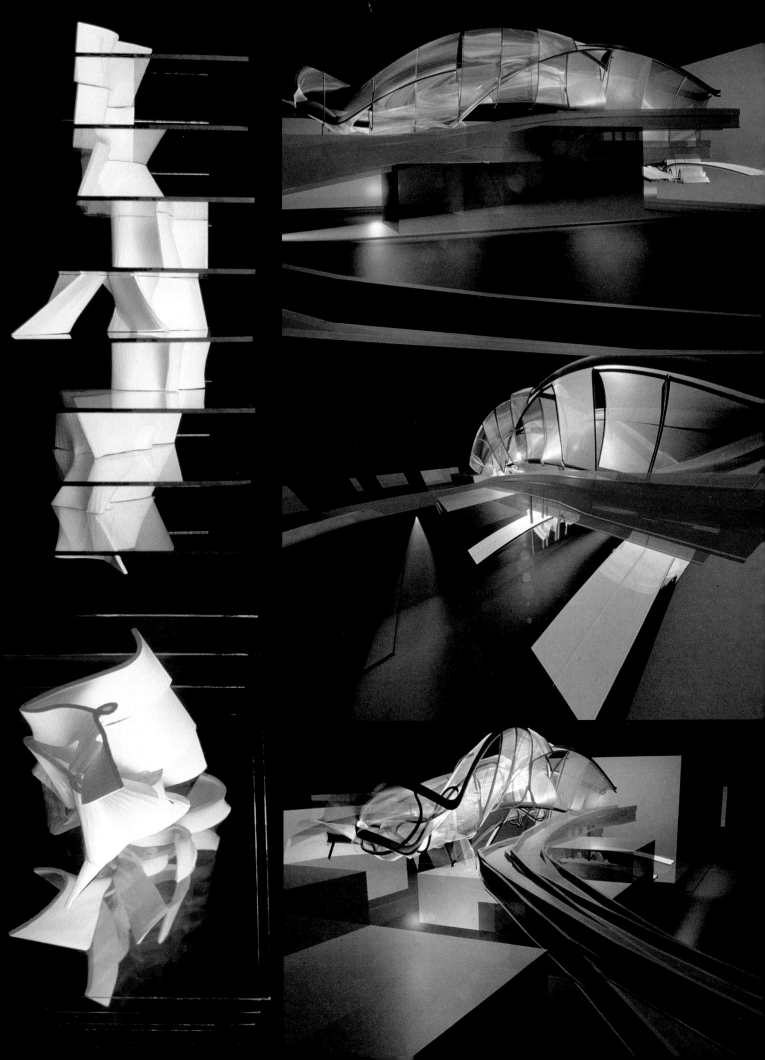

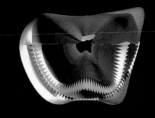

Embryologic
Space
1 9 9 8

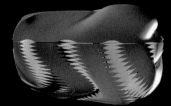

This domestic interior is enclosed in a surface composed of
over 2048 panels, all of which are unique in their shape and size.
These individual panels are networked to one another so that a
change in any individual panel is transmitted throughout every
other panel in the set. The variations to this surface are virtually
endless, yet in each variation there is always a constant number
of panels with a consistent relationship to their neighbouring panels. The volume is defined as a soft flexible surface of curves
rather than as a fixed set of rigid points. Instead of cutting window
and door openings into this surface, an alternative strategy of torn,
shredded and louvered openings was invented that allowed for
openings that respected the soft geometry of the curved envelopes.
Any dent or concavity is seamlessly integrated into the openings
and apertures of the surface. The curved chips of the envelope are
made of wood, polymers and steel, all fabricated with
robotic computer-controlled milling and high-pressure
water-jet cutting machinery.

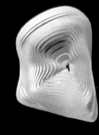

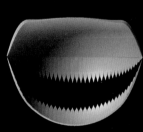

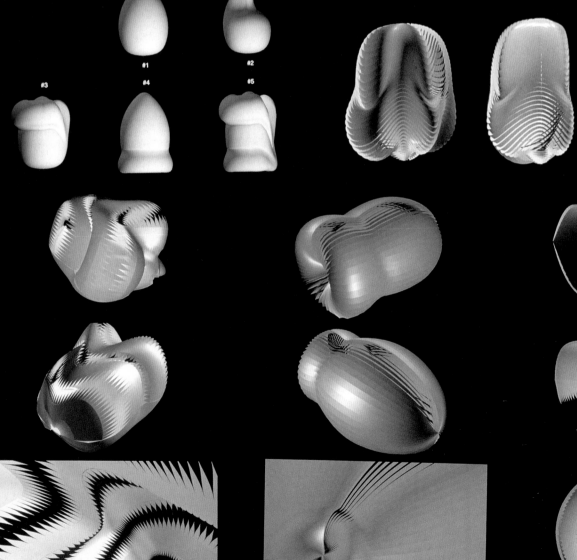

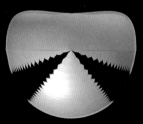

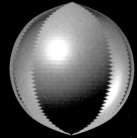

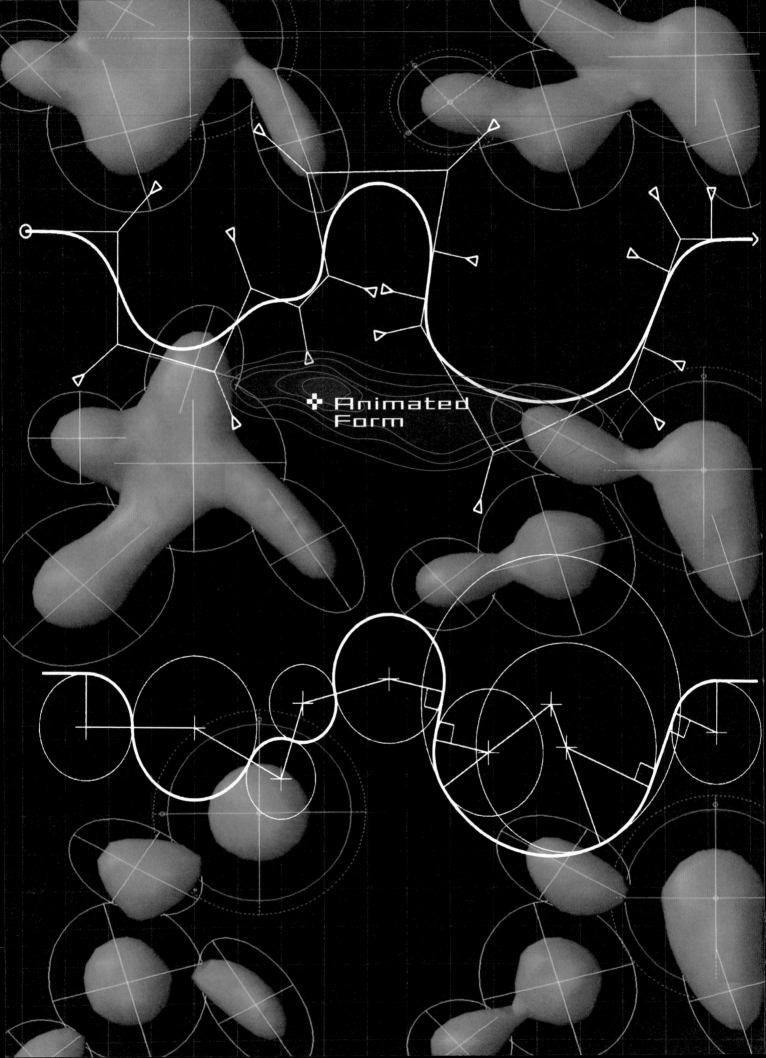

✤ Animated
Form

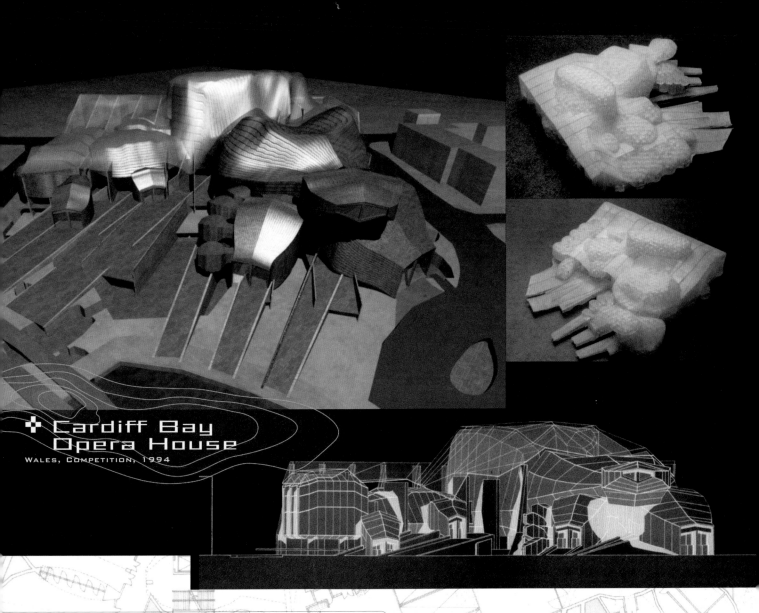

✤ Cardiff Bay
Opera House
WALES, COMPETITION, 1994

✤ Greg Lynn Form

Greg Lynn (1964)
Diploma in philosophy, Miami University, Ohio
Diploma in environmental design, Miami University, Ohio
Master of Architecture, Princeton University, New York

1994 Founded Greg Lynn/Form in Los Angeles, California

Teaching
1999–92 Columbia University, New York
1999–93 University of California, Los Angeles
1998 University of Illinois, Chicago
1997–96 Berlage Institute, Amsterdam
1997–93 Architectural Association School of Architecture, London
1994–92 Ohio State University, Ohio
1992–91 University of Illinois, Chicago

Principal buildings and projects
1999 Ark of the World Museum and Interpretative Centre (project),
       Costa Rica
1998 Vision Plan for Rutgers University, (project), with Eisenman Arch.,
       New Jersey
1997 Cincinnati Country Day School (project) with Michael McInturf
       Architects, Ohio
1996 H2 House for OMV Corporation, with Michael McInturf Architects
       and Martin Treberspurg & Partners, Vienna
1995–99 Korean Presbyterian Church, New York
1995 Citron House (project), New York
1994 Port Authority Triple Bridge Gateway (competition); Yokohama Pier
       (competition) with Michael McInturf, Japan; Cardiff Bay Opera
       House (competition) with Michael McInturf, Wales
1993 Cabrini Green Urban Design (competition), Chicago

1992 Stranded Sears Tower, (project) Chicago

Recent exhibitions
1999 'Secession Exhibition' with the paiter Fabian Marcaccio, Vienna
1998 'Body Mécanique: Artistic Explorations of Digital Realms' Wexner
       Center for the Arts, Ohio; 'Spectacular Optical' Threadwaxing
       Space, New York; 'Cities on the Move' CAPC Musée d'art contem-
       porain, Bordeaux; 'Cream Contemporary Art in Culture' Phaidon
       Press, Bristol; 'Virtual Architecture' Tokyo

Principal publications
1999–92 ANY magazine, member of the editorial board, New York
1999 Animate Form Princeton Architectural Press, New York
1998 Folds, Bodies & Blobs: Collected Essays La Lettre Volée, Bruxelles
1993 'Folding in Architecture', AD (no. 102)
1992 Fetish Princeton Architectural Press, New York

Selected bibliography
1998 'Embryological Housing' ANY no. 23, New York; Cream:
       Contemporary Art in Culture Phaidon Press, Bristol; AnyTime, New
       York
1997 From Body to Blob AnyBody, New York; Architectural Design no.
       127, London; Architecture + Urbanism no. 321, Tokyo; 'The
       Difference between the Possible and the Impossible' The Virtual
       Architecture, K. Sakamura and H. Suzuki, Tokyo
1996 Fisuras, Madrid; Arch + (May) Berlin; 'In the wake of the Avant-
       Garde' Assemblage 29, Cambridge
1995 Assemblage 26, Cambridge; Journal of Philosophy and Visual Arts,
       London
1994 Arch + (December) Berlin; Space Design (September) Tokyo
1993 Assemblage 19, Cambridge

Maxwan

| Rients Dijkstra (*1961) | Rianne Makkink (*1964) |

Among the emerging generation of Dutch architects, Maxwan is definitely one of those with the most range and enthusiasm, and the foremost representatives of the practice coined by Rem Koolhaas and Ed Taverne in the 1990s: Bigness. The actual name of the Rotterdam agency seems, furthermore, to be a direct reference to this. Rients Dijkstra and Rianne Makkink set up Maxwan in 1994, to deal with a commission that was already on a grand scale: the master plan for Leidsche Rijn, a new town acting as an extension to Utrecht, which would have 30,000 housing units by the year 2015. This urban project – the largest one currently being worked on in Holland – is nevertheless not isolated. The construction context has been defined and identified in this country by the radical conclusions of the Fourth Land Development Report, the famous VINEX. Forecasting a population increase of three million people before 2010, this forward-looking study recommends that large cities be doubled in size, with the construction of 1,100,000 housing units by 2015. In its scale and scope, this programme is unprecedented since the reconstruction period after the ravages of the Second World War. It will almost certainly have considerable consequences for the urban and suburban landscape of the Netherlands. But it is first and foremost mentalities and attitudes that will be affected, particularly those of architects and other people involved in construction. The work of Maxwan is representative of the challenges and issues raised by this situation. It is a matter, above all else, of reinventing project procedures and strategies on a par with the stakes involved, and at the same time breaking through certain deadlocks in the thinking of twentieth-century city planners. For the Leidsche Rijn plan, which they have worked on with the Crimson agency, the Maxwan architects surrounded themselves with tools and concepts that are closer to geo-economics than city planning. Starting from the fact that 70 per cent of VINEX housing units will be privately financed, they have based their approach on systems of logic peculiar to the financial markets and in particular on the idea of 'orgware' (organizational ware). This neologism borrowed from economics describes the set of political, legislative and administrative factors that dictate both the implementation of ideas (software) and the construction of physical elements (hardware). Like an invisible landscape, orgware works like a field of possibles, an actual topography of opportunities and restrictions, at times more decisive than physical topography itself. The incorporation of this host of quantitative factors and criteria, which Maxwan has abundantly mapped, leads to a form of 'soft urbanism', which is realistic, opportunistic and flexible. The project does not stem from any political or philosophical model, but is adapted to the floating logic of the market as an organic authority. The architecture of Maxwan cannot be conceived outside of this line of metropolitan thinking. Its form is not an end in itself, but uses the virtual strategies of orgware and specifically creates opportunities therefrom, in an often spectacular way. ✦

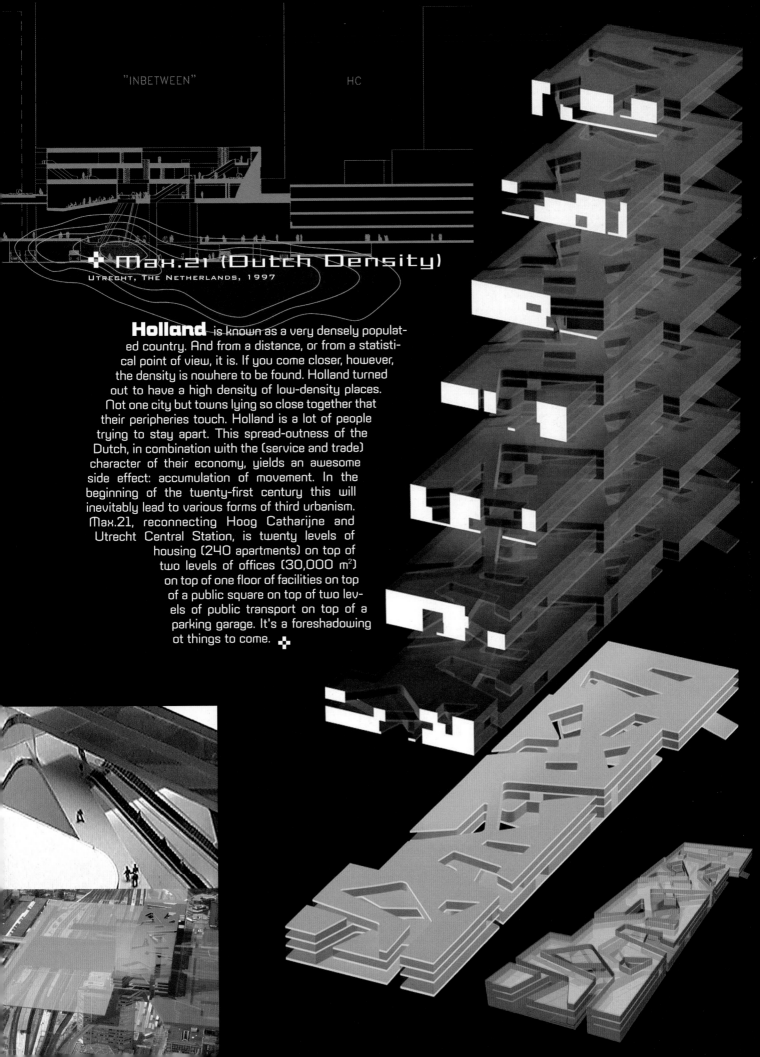

✛ Max.21 (Dutch Density)
UTRECHT, THE NETHERLANDS, 1997

Holland is known as a very densely populated country. And from a distance, or from a statistical point of view, it is. If you come closer, however, the density is nowhere to be found. Holland turned out to have a high density of low-density places. Not one city but towns lying so close together that their peripheries touch. Holland is a lot of people trying to stay apart. This spread-outness of the Dutch, in combination with the (service and trade) character of their economy, yields an awesome side effect: accumulation of movement. In the beginning of the twenty-first century this will inevitably lead to various forms of third urbanism. Max.21, reconnecting Hoog Catharijne and Utrecht Central Station, is twenty levels of housing (240 apartments) on top of two levels of offices (30,000 m²) on top of one floor of facilities on top of a public square on top of two levels of public transport on top of a parking garage. It's a foreshadowing ot things to come. ✛

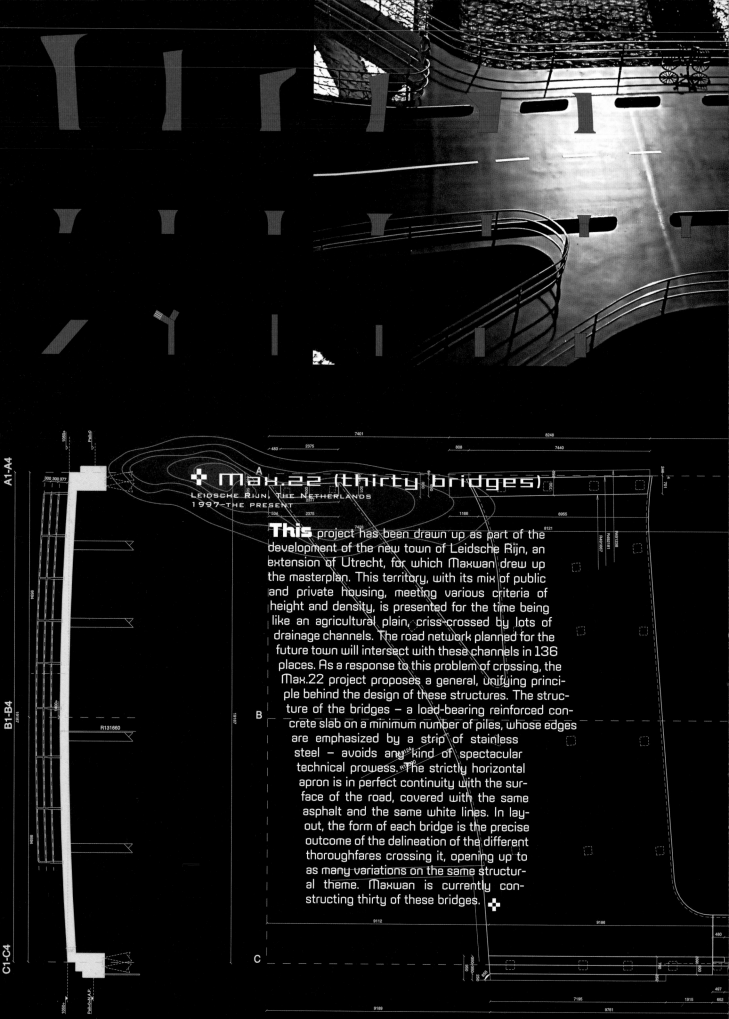

✦ Max.22 (thirty bridges)

LEIDSCHE RIJN, THE NETHERLANDS
1997–THE PRESENT

This project has been drawn up as part of the development of the new town of Leidsche Rijn, an extension of Utrecht, for which Maxwan drew up the masterplan. This territory, with its mix of public and private housing, meeting various criteria of height and density, is presented for the time being like an agricultural plain, criss-crossed by lots of drainage channels. The road network planned for the future town will intersect with these channels in 136 places. As a response to this problem of crossing, the Max.22 project proposes a general, unifying principle behind the design of these structures. The structure of the bridges – a load-bearing reinforced concrete slab on a minimum number of piles, whose edges are emphasized by a strip of stainless steel – avoids any kind of spectacular technical prowess. The strictly horizontal apron is in perfect continuity with the surface of the road, covered with the same asphalt and the same white lines. In layout, the form of each bridge is the precise outcome of the delineation of the different thoroughfares crossing it, opening up to as many variations on the same structural theme. Maxwan is currently constructing thirty of these bridges. ✦

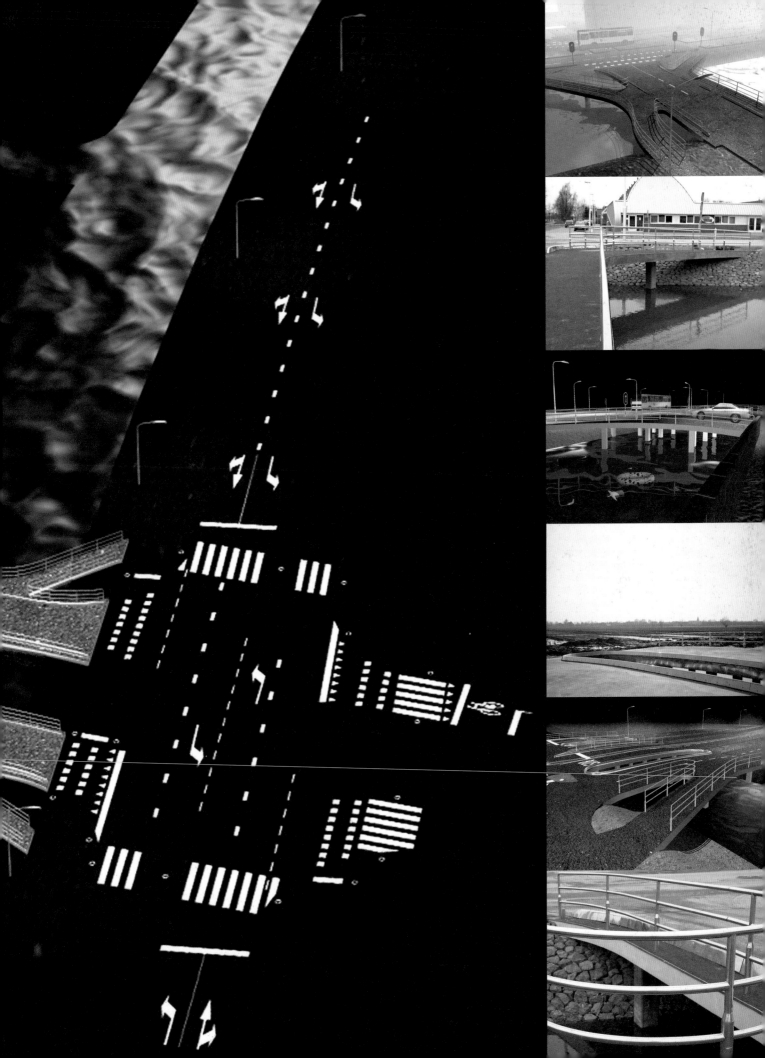

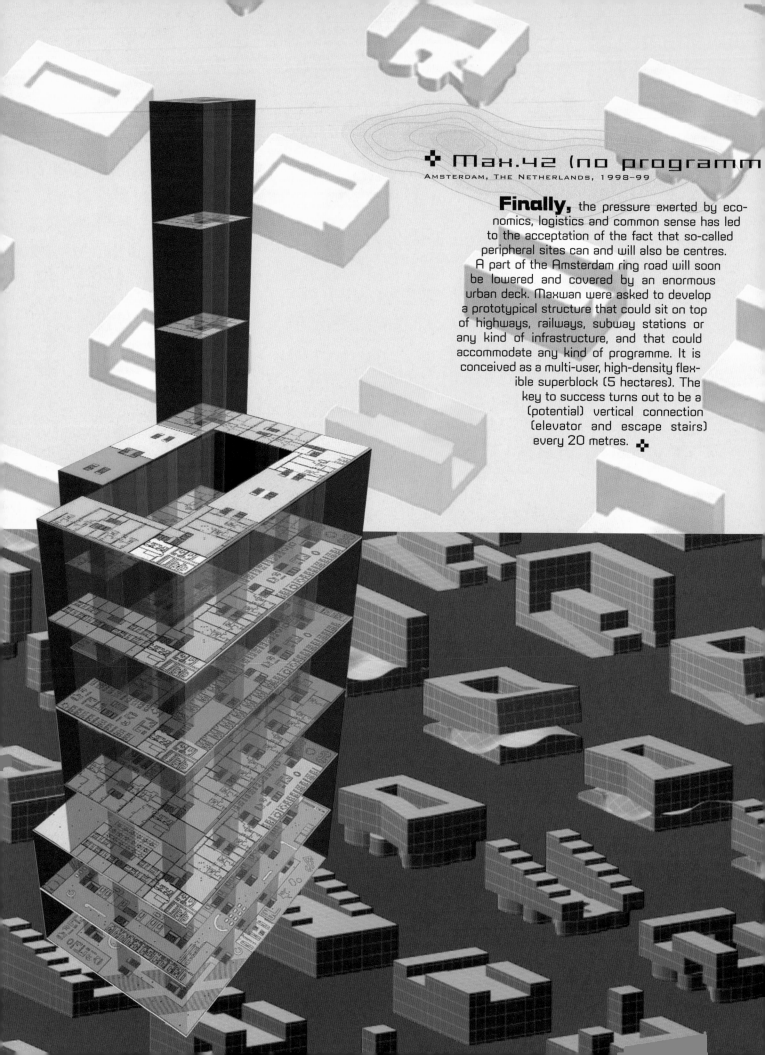

✦ Max.42 (no programm

AMSTERDAM, THE NETHERLANDS, 1998–99

Finally, the pressure exerted by economics, logistics and common sense has led to the acceptation of the fact that so-called peripheral sites can and will also be centres. A part of the Amsterdam ring road will soon be lowered and covered by an enormous urban deck. Maxwan were asked to develop a prototypical structure that could sit on top of highways, railways, subway stations or any kind of infrastructure, and that could accommodate any kind of programme. It is conceived as a multi-user, high-density flexible superblock (5 hectares). The key to success turns out to be a (potential) vertical connection (elevator and escape stairs) every 20 metres. ✦

✚ Max.7 (fourteen apartments)

EINDHOVEN, THE NETHERLANDS, 1995–98

The surrounding neighbourhood of this fourteen-apartment unit, consists of conventional housing blocks with total separation between the formal, public architectural side (street) and the informal, private courts (backyards). Maxwan decided to make a project that would be like the opposite of the canonical architectural photograph, in which all signs of life are wiped from the scene of the building. They inverted this typology so that the backyards lie in front of the house. To prevent abuse of the front garden (which now lay behind the house) they made it impossibly small. If the residents wanted to express themselves, they had to do it in public. The façade is a homebrewed rippled (polyurethane) surface with an aluminium coating, then a transparant glossy polyurethane finish. It changes colour and reflection continuously depending on weather and light conditions. ✚

✛ Maxwan Architecture Urbanism

Rients Dijkstra (1961)
Rianne Makkink (1964)

1994   Creation of the practice in Rotterdam

Principal buildings and projects

1999–94   Max.42 – flexible multi-user high-density 5-hectare urban block'
(project); Max.40 – extension of the port and airport at Rotterdam
(project); Max.39 – bridge over the river Maas, Rotterdam (realized); Max.38 – high-density housing on the A10 (project); Max.37
– F&I building (realized); Max.36 – master plan, Den Bosch;
Max.35 – planning, Delft University; Max.33 – underground building Atlantis (competition); Max.30 – 21st-century park' (project);
Max.27 – two electrical stations; Max.22 – 136 bridges (under
construction); Max.21 – Hoog Catharijne and Utrecht Central
Station; Max.20 – 1,000 houses, Enschede (project); Max. 11 –
three thousand houses near Breda (project); Max. 10 – Thalia cinema (rearrangement); Max.9 – 1,500 houses near Groningen (project); Max. 7 – fourteen houses at Eindhoven, with Wouter
Thijssen; Max.6 – Global Ranstad (project); Max.2 – master plan
for 30,000 houses, VINEX programme, Utrecht (one built)

Recent exhibitions

1999–98   'Max. 43 – Big Soft Orange' Yale University (New Haven),
Columbia University/Storefront Gallery (New York), CCAC (San
Francisco), Sci-Arc (Los Angeles), Saint University (Columbus,
Ohio)
1997   'Max. 24' 'Nine +One: ten young Dutch architectural offices' NAI,
Rotterdam

Selected bibliography

2000   'The Netherlands' Rob van der Bijl, Max.21, *TOPOS-European
landscape magazine*, Munich; *Het kunstmatig landschap* (An artificial landscape) NAI Publishers
1999   'The Dutch Model' *SD Space Design* no. 413 (Feb.) Tokyo;
'Nieuwe verhouding tussen overheid en markt. Het ontstaan van
een interactieve stedebouw' Harm Tilman, *De Architect* (Feb.);

'Overstapmachines' Max.21, *Blauwe Kamer* no. 5 (Oct.)
1998-99   'Big Soft Orange' exhibition catalogue, Yale University (New
Haven), Columbia University/Storefront Gallery (New York), CCAC
(San Francisco), Sci-Arc (Los Angeles), Saint University
(Columbus, Ohio)
1998   'Zeven studies naar een nieuwe oeverbinding in Rotterdam' (Seven
studies for a new cross-river connection in Rotterdam) publication
linked to the exhibition 'Living Bridges' NAI publishers, Rotterdam;
'Zilveren doosjes maken de tongen los' (People talk about silver
boxes) *Wonen in Beeld '97-98*; 'We willen ieder plan laten lukken'
(We want every plan to succeed) 'Max. 1 en de weerbarstige prak-
tijk' Harm Tilman, *De Architect* (May)
1997   'Hoe Nieuwstad?' (How New Town?) *Mutaties, fascinaties* no. 4,
NAI uitgevers; *Nine +One, ten young Dutch architectural offices*
publication linked to the exhibition '9+1', Dutch Institute for
Architecture (NAI) Rotterdam; *Festivalgebouw-Thalia 2001*
(Festivalbuilding, Thalie 2001) publication linked to the exhibition
'As good as new – Wederopbouw', Dutch Institute for Architecture
(NAI) Rotterdam; 'Keihard rijden tot vlakbij huis' (Top speed till
nearly home) interview with Rients Dijkstra, Max. 13 F-buurt
Bijlmermeer, *Archis* (March)
1995   '30 000 huizen bij Utrecht' (30 000 houses near Utrecht) article
master plan Leidse Rijn (R. Dijkstra, M. Provoost, W. Vanstiphout),
Archis (August)
1994   'Het lelijkste huis van Nederland' (Holland's ugliest house) article
Max. 1, House Leeuwarden, B. Lootsma, *De Architect* (May)

MVRDV

| Winy Maas (*1959) | Jacob van Rijs (1964) |
| Nathalie de Vries (*1965) |

MVRDV was established in Rotterdam in 1991 by Winy Maas, Jacob van Rijs and Nathalie de Vries. Since then, MVRDV has been building, teaching, publishing and exhibiting, offering the unusual spectacle of an activity that seems to involve conjunction and encounter as both method and objective. MVRDV makes use of, and lays claim to, diversity. They proceed as a team, inviting differing and at times unexpected skills to join forces with them, and thwart disciplinary categories. MVRDV thus either makes its methods systematic or undoes them in experimentation, but it is forever turning the process of conception into spatial or organizational research, in which they involve, from the project's premises onward, the greatest possible number of contributors and data. In every instance, the spatial consequences and the limits and potential of a sweeping overview of situations, are examined and shown. The limits encountered are tested by a systematic intensification, so as to reveal the extremities. This constitutes a radicalization that helps to identify these limits and makes the formulation of a discourse about them possible. The extreme diversity of these data thus finds a pragmatic transcription in a spatial matrix consisting of the superposition of the diagrams that distribute these data (datascapes). Acclaimed for its architectural works (like WoZoCos), MVRDV is currently involved in the development of overall plans, which it supervises. Its members simultaneously pursue research projects without any direct link to specific assignments, although the propositions in question permeate all their work, whatever the design area may be. They thus lay claim to this diversity in an even broader way when they call for 'three-dimensional city planning': 'replace two-dimensional planning' to 'generate a real densification', conditional, in their eyes, on a spatial quality made possible by this 'extreme increase of density', which might offer the experience of a 'simultaneity' rich in many different conjunctions and encounters, while preserving the compromised existence of a world in which rustic landscapes and urban installations still rub shoulders. To 'safeguard the rustic landscape from total, continuous urbanization', they propose their so-called 'MetaCITY' by 'reversing the situation through extreme increases of density'. This is a proposition that reminds us that Winy Maas and Jacob van Rijs have worked for the Office for Metropolitan Architecture, echoing the expectations of a 'culture of congestion', which Rem Koolhaas greeted in *Delirious New York*, a proposition with a potential that they examined in *FARMAX* (1998), a form of 'architectural narrative', and which they are presenting today in the form of projections with 'DataTown' and 'Private KM³/3D City'. MVRDV thus looks for conjunction and elevates it in a practical way as a system, formula and doctrine, but a doctrine that exhales the powerful scent of paradox, seemingly setting itself up as a method of not having any, substituting steering for driving, preferring produced lines to lines to be followed. MVRDV seems to deny fixed assignations in favour of 'vanishing lines', even in the exercise of language and portmanteau words, which turn into 'Ariadne's thread' in random relation to architectural propositions. ✚

✦ DataTown

1998

DataTown can be seen as a prelude to further explorations into the future of the Metacity (more or less continuous urban fields). DataTown is based on data only. It is a city that wants to be described by information; a city that knows no given topography, no prescribed ideology, no representation, no context. Only huge, pure data. DataTown can therefore be defined as a city of 400 by 400 kilometres: 160,000,000,000 m². In fact, with 1,477 inhabitants per square kilometre, DataTown is the densest place on earth, a city for 241 million inhabitants, the U.S.A. in one city. DataTown is autarkic. It does not know any foreign countries. It therefore has to be self-supporting. DataTown is constructed as a collection of data. The barcode thus became a Mondrian-like field, compressed by its square outline into the most compact city thinkable. DataTown is always in progress. Its evolution is literally endless. At this moment, six sectors may be entered. If the world settlement envelope were to be filled up with 376 DataTowns, world capacity would be 88,687 million inhabitants, 18 times the current population. ✦

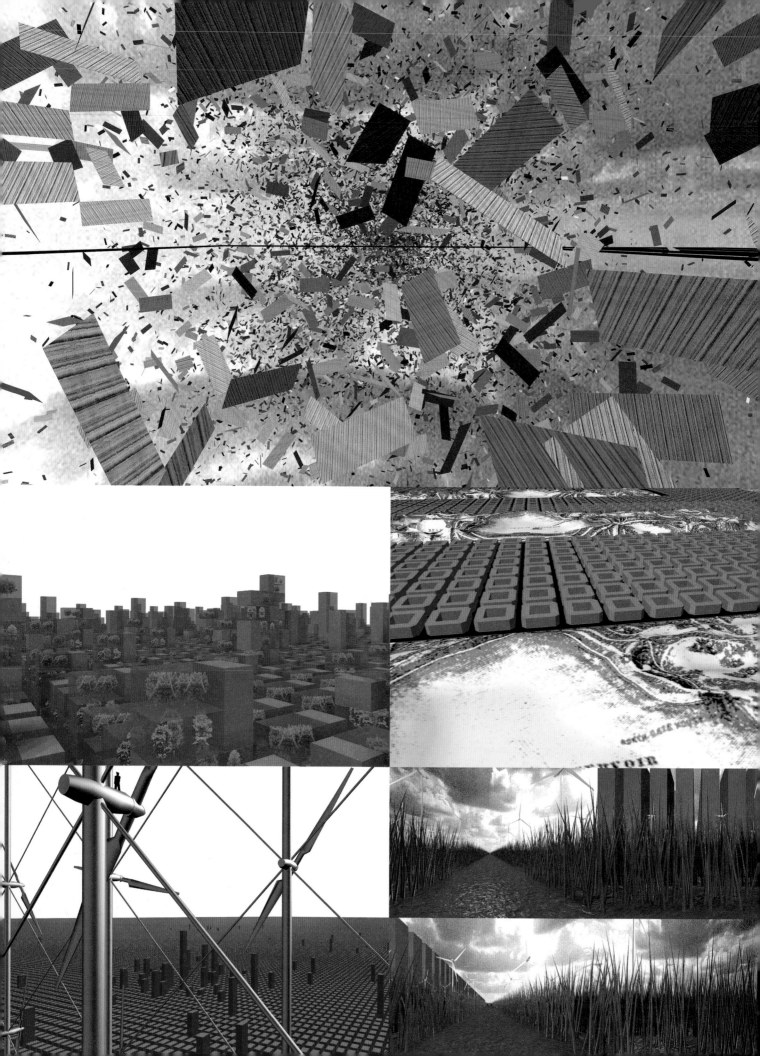

✦ Light Urb

1995

The housing estates to be realized by 2015 in the context of the VINEX operation (a housing programme for 800,000 dwellings set up by the Dutch government) are turning out more or less the same, all with a density of around thirty-five dwellings per hectare. Would it not be better to put forward a more experimental residential environment, one that would be reasonably easy to break up later, so that people would not be tied to it for eternity? A more relaxed form of urban development, one that can be applied until we have worked out whether we want to turn all our new housing estates into one compact town or a supersprawl, quite apart from the question of where they should be located. This 'litre' form of urban development can be brought about by shortening the depreciation period for durable dwellings, made-up roads, cables and wiring. ✦

LIGHTNESS

LIGHTNESS. Our lands seem to become full. But full of what? The suburban mix of factory-like farms, houses ... with gardens, warehouses seem to contain density without matter. Enormous areas of our lands ...

itself into this sea of planned mediocracy. Do we accept this condition as fixed or can we envisage experimental ... environments, which can be broken down, so that we can change our urbanistic goals within a ce...

COSTS

This lighter form of urbanism can be forced by reducing the economical value of expensive parts of our ways of ... urbanization: grass roads instead of asphalt, no sewage pipes but ecological pools, no gaspipes bu...

COSTS   COSTS   COSTS   COSTS

HOUSEGARDEN : ○ ▲ □GREEN

cables for heating, no telecomlines but portable phones, no expensive metrolines but minibusses or busses- ... on-demand. This economy can cause exciting possibilities: within the same existing budget, lower d...

GARDEN ☰ GREEN

be afforded. Economy obtains thus a connection with ecology. It delivers the paradoxical feeling that eco- ... logical sustainability has been translated into lightness and temporariness.

ECOLO
=
ECONO

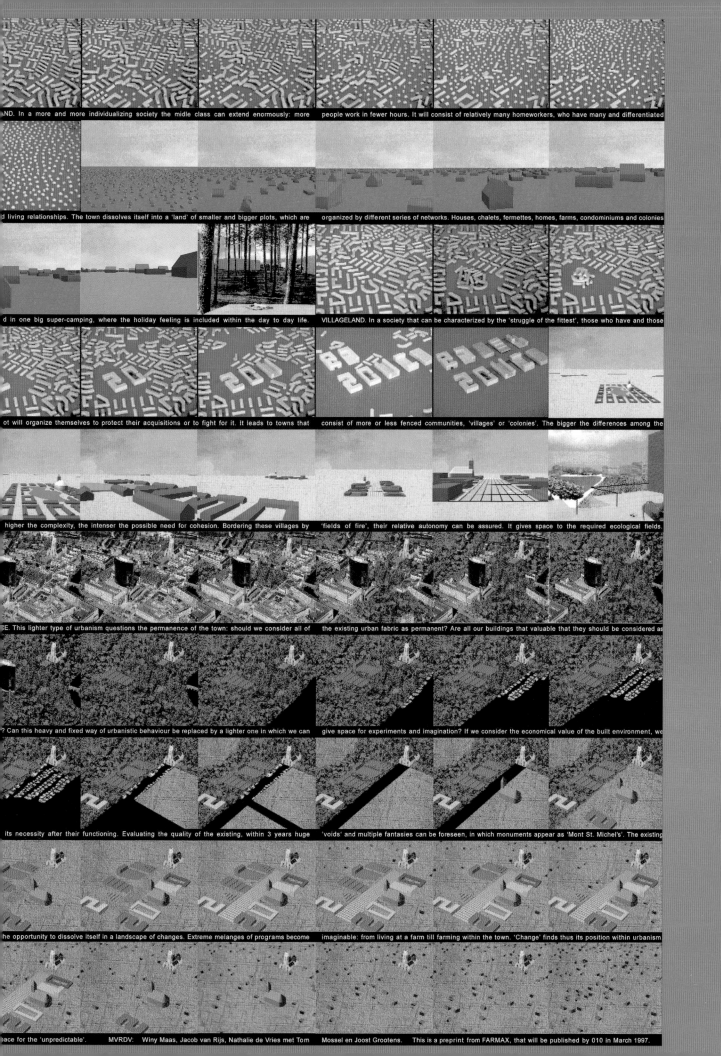

ND. In a more and more individualizing society the midle class can extend enormously: more people work in fewer hours. It will consist of relatively many homeworkers, who have many and differentiated

d living relationships. The town dissolves itself into a 'land' of smaller and bigger plots, which are organized by different series of networks. Houses, chalets, fermettes, homes, farms, condominiums and colonies

d in one big super-camping, where the holiday feeling is included within the day to day life. VILLAGELAND. In a society that can be characterized by the 'struggle of the fittest', those who have and those

ot will organize themselves to protect their acquisitions or to fight for it. It leads to towns that consist of more or less fenced communities, 'villages' or 'colonies'. The bigger the differences among the

higher the complexity, the intenser the possible need for cohesion. Bordering these villages by 'fields of fire', their relative autonomy can be assured. It gives space to the required ecological fields.

E. This lighter type of urbanism questions the permanence of the town: should we consider all of the existing urban fabric as permanent? Are all our buildings that valuable that they should be considered as

? Can this heavy and fixed way of urbanistic behaviour be replaced by a lighter one in which we can give space for experiments and imagination? If we consider the economical value of the built environment, we

its necessity after their functioning. Evaluating the quality of the existing, within 3 years huge 'voids' and multiple fantasies can be foreseen, in which monuments appear as 'Mont St. Michel's'. The existing

he opportunity to dissolve itself in a landscape of changes. Extreme melanges of programs become imaginable: from living at a farm till farming within the town. 'Change' finds thus its position within urbanism

ace for the 'unpredictable'.   MVRDV: Winy Maas, Jacob van Rijs, Nathalie de Vries met Tom Mossel en Joost Grootens.   This is a preprint from FARMAX, that will be published by 010 in March 1997.

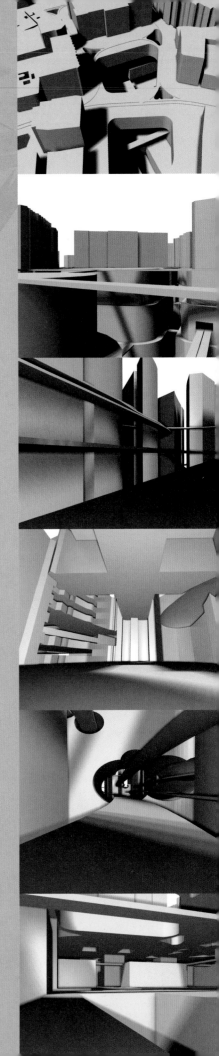

✦ Private KM³
∃D City

1998

Would it be possible to imagine a city in which two-dimensional planning is replaced by three-dimensional? Would it be possible then to generate true densification and to expand the existing space? This implies a city that is not only in front, behind or next to you, but also above and below. In short, a city that Piranesi drew in the 'Carceri' or as Friedman has suggested, in which level zero no longer exists but has dissolved into a multiple and simultaneous presence of levels, where 'the square' is replaced by a void or a bundle of connections, where 'the street' is replaced by simultaneous distribution/division of routes and is expanded by elevators, ramps and escalators, where 'far away' is reduced to proximity and the park is transformed into a stacking of public spaces. In this world spatial quality is no longer translated into morphology or geometry, but in richness, diversity, presence, proximity. It no longer matters where level zero is, since it exists simultaneously at different altitudes. The difference between under or above ground is no longer relevant. There is only simultaneity. ✦

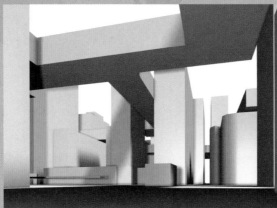

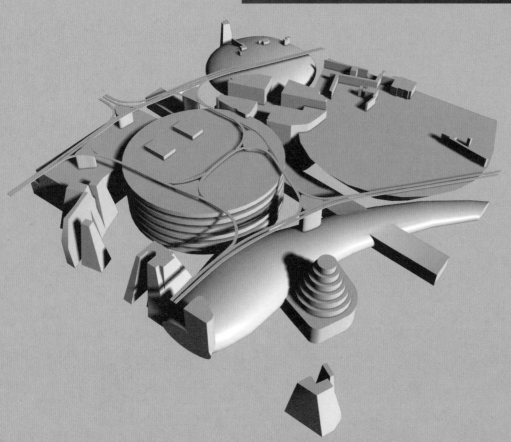

✛ MVRDV

Winy Maas (1959)
1984–90 Technical University Delft
1978–83 RHSTL Boskoop

Jacob van Rijs (1964)
1984–90 Technical University Delft
1983–84 The Hague Free Academy

Nathalie de Vries (1965)
1984–90 Technical University Delft

1991 Studio founded by Winy Maas, Jacob van Rijs and Nathalie de Vries

Realized projects
2001 Silodam, building with residential and business units, Amsterdam; Ypenburg, 182 houses in Rijswijk (The Hague); Ateliers, work and living space, Amsterdam
2000 Dutch Pavilion Expo 2000 Hanover, Germany; House on Borneo Sporenburg plot 12, Amsterdam; Garden Net3 Public Broadcasting Companies, Hilversum Calveen, office building, Amersfoort; Net 3, communal entrance building, Net3 Broadcasting Companies, Hilversum; Deelplan 10, urban design, Ypenburg
1999 House on Borneo Sporenburg plot 18, Amsterdam; Flight Forum Masterplan Parklane Airport, Eindhoven
1997 Headquarters of the VPRO Public Broadcasting Company, Hilversum; Headquarters of the RVU Public Broadcasting Company, Hilversum; WoZoCos, one hundred apartments for elderly people, Amsterdam-Osdorp; Double House, Utrecht
1996 Villa Plot 5, Housing Festival, The Hague; Three Porters' lodges, Hoge Veluwe National Park; Campus Net3, urban plan media park, Hilversum (under construction)

Selected bibliography
2000 *10x10*, Phaidon Press, London; *SuperDutch*, Thames & Hudson, London; *Building a new millennium*, Taschen, Cologne; *GA Document* no. 62, A.D.A. Edita, Tokyo; *Zoo no. 6*, Purple House Ltd., London; *100 Years Exhibition Pavilions*, Gustavo Gili SA, Barcelona; *Centrum, Jahrbuch Architektur und Stadt 1999-2000*, Bertelsmann; *Atlas van de verandering*, Nai Publishers, Rotterdam; *40 under 40*, Taschen, Cologne
1999 *Holland makes space, the Dutch pavilion at the Expo 2000 in Hanover*, V+K publishing, Blaricum; *MVRDV at VPRO*, Actar, Barcelona; *100 WoZoCos*, Aedes, Berlin
1998 *Media and Architecture*, VPRO and The Berlage Institute, Amsterdam
1997 *El Croquis* (86), *MVRDV 1991-1997* (monograph), Barcelona; *Villa VPRO*; *De wording van een wondere werkplek*, Wim Wennekes, ed., VPRO, Hilversum

Publications
New Nature/New Ecologies, the Dutch pavilion (2000); *KM3, The 3D City* (2000); *Datascape* (2001); *2000 Costa Iberica*, Actar, Barcelona; *1999 MetaCITY/DATATOWN*, 010 Publishers, Rotterdam; *1998 FARMAX*, 010 Publishers, Rotterdam

Exhibitions
2000 Expo pavilion and Silodam, Pavillon de l' Arsenal, Paris; 'MetaCITY/DATATOWN, KM3/3d City and other MVRDV projects', Venice Biennale; 'MetaCITY/DATATOWN', Johannesburg; Musée du Quai Branly, Musée National d'Art Moderne/Centre de Création Industrielle, Paris
1999 'MetaCITY/DATATOWN', Gammel Dok, Dansk Arkitektur Center, Copenhagen; 'MVRDV at VPRO', RAS Gallery, Barcelona; 'The Un-private House', Museum of Modern Art, New York; 'MetaCITY/DATATOWN', Space Art Gallery, Tokyo; 'MetaCITY/DATATOWN': MVRDV – Analysen + Projekte, Aedes East Gallery, Berlin

Naga Studio Architecture

| Tarek Naga [*1953] |

Architecture must be placed within a broader philosophical milieu. Architects can no longer afford to lag behind and linger in the post-industrial, post-classical mechanistic models. The Bergsonian attitude towards philosophy, that it 'cannot and must not accept the relation established by pure intellectualism between the theory of knowledge and the theory of the known, between metaphysics and science', provides an appropriate philosophical model for architecture today. Deleuze and Guattari, invoking similar disposition, consider Nous and Physis (metaphysics and physics), the two facets of the plane of immanence of concepts, the planomenon. Henri Bergson stated that 'form is essentially extended, inseparable as it is from the extensity of the becoming which has materialized it in the course of its flow. Every form thus occupies space as it occupies time'. Bergson's statement sums up the two fundamental principles that inform the basic tenets in my experimentation in architecture: the state of becoming and the flow. Architectonic and topological manifestations follow different behavioural patterns of becoming in response to the forces and flows inherent within, metaphorically or typologically. They both have internal codes of behavior, 'esoteric attributes', and external codes of influence, 'exoteric attributes'. Their rules of engagement are interdependent: a topological continuum may 'gravitationally' cause the unfoldment, twisting, or bending of planes or volumes. Conversely, the flow within emergent architectonics may rupture, warp, or deform a continuous membrane. Fixity and stasis may occur only at a thresholding instance (a point of suspension) where flows are moving in opposing vectors: a subversive counter-state to the point of inflection in a topological continuum. Would Deleuze's concept of inflection (a state of ambiguity and weightlessness) allow for an instance of metastasis, a reversal of vectorial purpose and desire, at a point of intersection? A point of turbulence. Architectonic volumes (imploding or exploding) that intersect with topological conditions, effectively become turbulences in the flow of continuous surfaces. Within this philosophical paradigm, morphological concepts (topological or architectonic) cannot be adequately generated within the framework of Cartesian coordinates. An alternative spatio-temporal coordinate system, suitable for simultaneous unfoldment of space and time, becomes an inevitable evolutionary step. [We are currently developing a coordinate system, Tetra-Vectors ©, that employs the four vectors of a tetrahedral system as basic vectorial coordinates (Vt1, Vt2, Vt3, Vtn). In this system, spatio-temporal Vt values are imputed to each of the four vectors. Thus each point in space falls within a particular tetra-quadrant. The fourth vector carries an intrinsic potential (t) value for that point to vibrate, to become activated into motion (i.e. Vt1, Vt2, Vt3, Vtn ⊃ Vt1, Vt2, Vt3, Vtn+X) (fig. 1).] Within those Vt vectors, a planomenon of architectonic fragments or topological continuums is imbued with a projective becoming. An inherent instability and fragile equilibrium permeates the behaviour of space. This architecture aspires to creating space that is simultaneously emergent and convergent, imploding and exploding. Space that is physically and metaphysically charged with the desire to transform, transmutate and transfold

TETRA-VECTORS

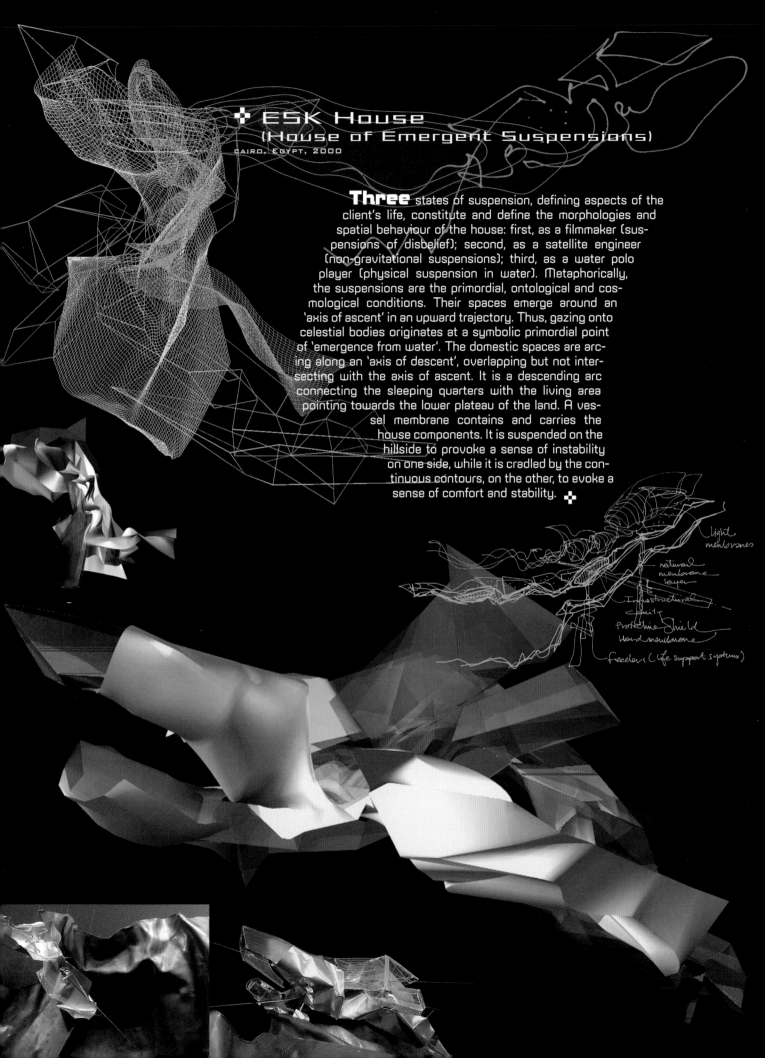

✤ ESK House
(House of Emergent Suspensions)
CAIRO, EGYPT, 2000

Three states of suspension, defining aspects of the client's life, constitute and define the morphologies and spatial behaviour of the house: first, as a filmmaker (suspensions of disbelief); second, as a satellite engineer (non-gravitational suspensions); third, as a water polo player (physical suspension in water). Metaphorically, the suspensions are the primordial, ontological and cosmological conditions. Their spaces emerge around an 'axis of ascent' in an upward trajectory. Thus, gazing onto celestial bodies originates at a symbolic primordial point of 'emergence from water'. The domestic spaces are arcing along an 'axis of descent', overlapping but not intersecting with the axis of ascent. It is a descending arc connecting the sleeping quarters with the living area pointing towards the lower plateau of the land. A vessel membrane contains and carries the house components. It is suspended on the hillside to provoke a sense of instability on one side, while it is cradled by the continuous contours, on the other, to evoke a sense of comfort and stability. ✤

light membranes
natural membrane layer
Infrastructural unit
Protective Shield
Hard membrane
feeders (life support systems)

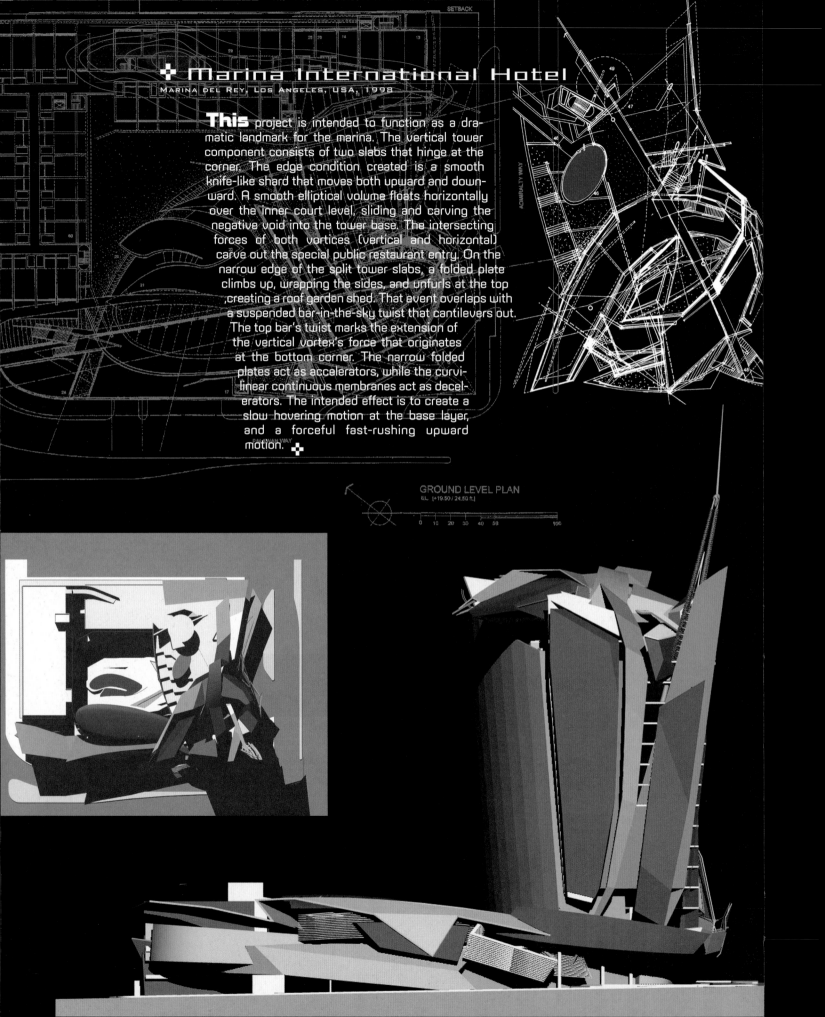

✛ Marina International Hotel

MARINA DEL REY, LOS ANGELES, USA, 1998

This project is intended to function as a dramatic landmark for the marina. The vertical tower component consists of two slabs that hinge at the corner. The edge condition created is a smooth knife-like shard that moves both upward and downward. A smooth elliptical volume floats horizontally over the inner court level, sliding and carving the negative void into the tower base. The intersecting forces of both vortices (vertical and horizontal) carve out the special public restaurant entry. On the narrow edge of the split tower slabs, a folded plate climbs up, wrapping the sides, and unfurls at the top, creating a roof garden shed. That event overlaps with a suspended bar-in-the-sky twist that cantilevers out. The top bar's twist marks the extension of the vertical vortex's force that originates at the bottom corner. The narrow folded plates act as accelerators, while the curvilinear continuous membranes act as decelerators. The intended effect is to create a slow hovering motion at the base layer, and a forceful fast-rushing upward motion. ✛✛

GROUND LEVEL PLAN
EL. [+19.50 / 24.50 ft.]

0   10   20   30   40   50   100

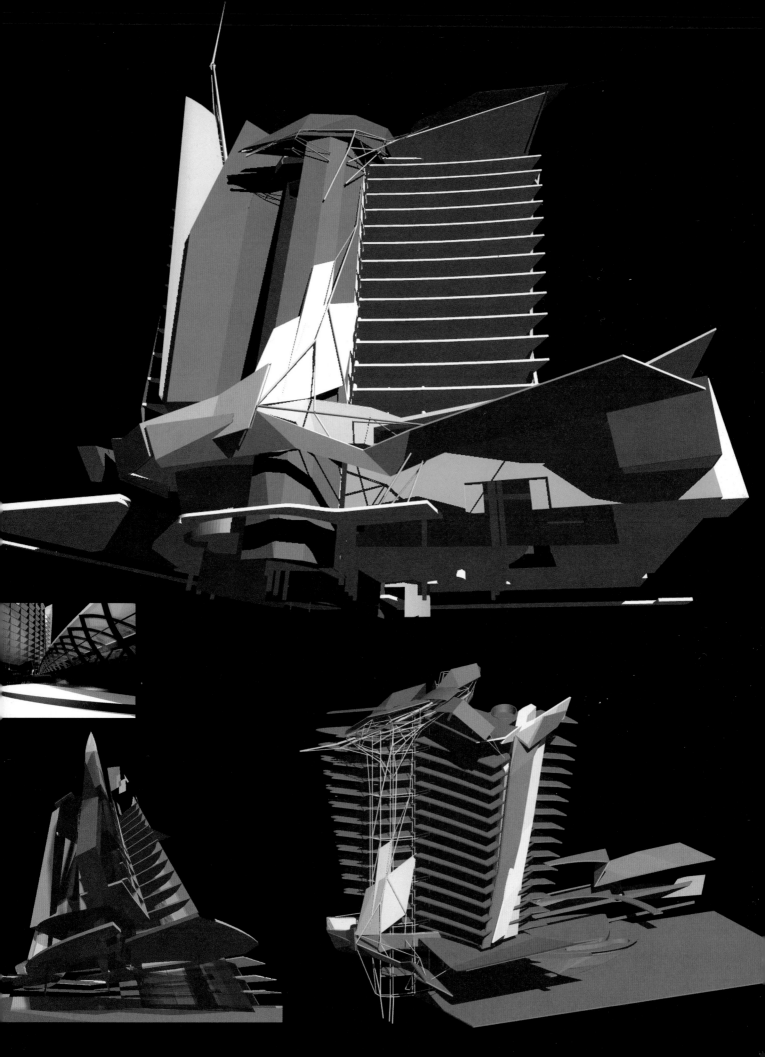

✦ Sharm Safari Gate
SHARM EL SHEIKH, SINAI, EGYPT, 1997

In Egyptian history and mythology, the Sinai desert is the quintessential condition of wilderness and nomadism. A facility that is designed for the exploration of such a rich locale has to take its clues from its natural and symbolic complexity. Mentally and physically, the Sinai explorers cross from the realities and trappings of this century, on to an unknown world of the primordial wilderness of biblical historical time. This became the basis for a narrative of five pods that, metaphorically, are themselves wanderers. In a search for the mystery of the place, they group and regroup, evolve and morph into different entities. One of the pods metamorphoses into an intelligent entity that becomes their guide. A membrane that hovered above now shields them. Extended tentacles tenuously dangle down. In an act of defiance, the 'pod of flight' penetrates the shield and nestles above the folded plates. It so desires to witness flight, the very act of its raison d'être. A place for nomadic explorers is itself conceived by a nomadic myth. The architecture is imbued with the very function that it is assumed to perform. ✦

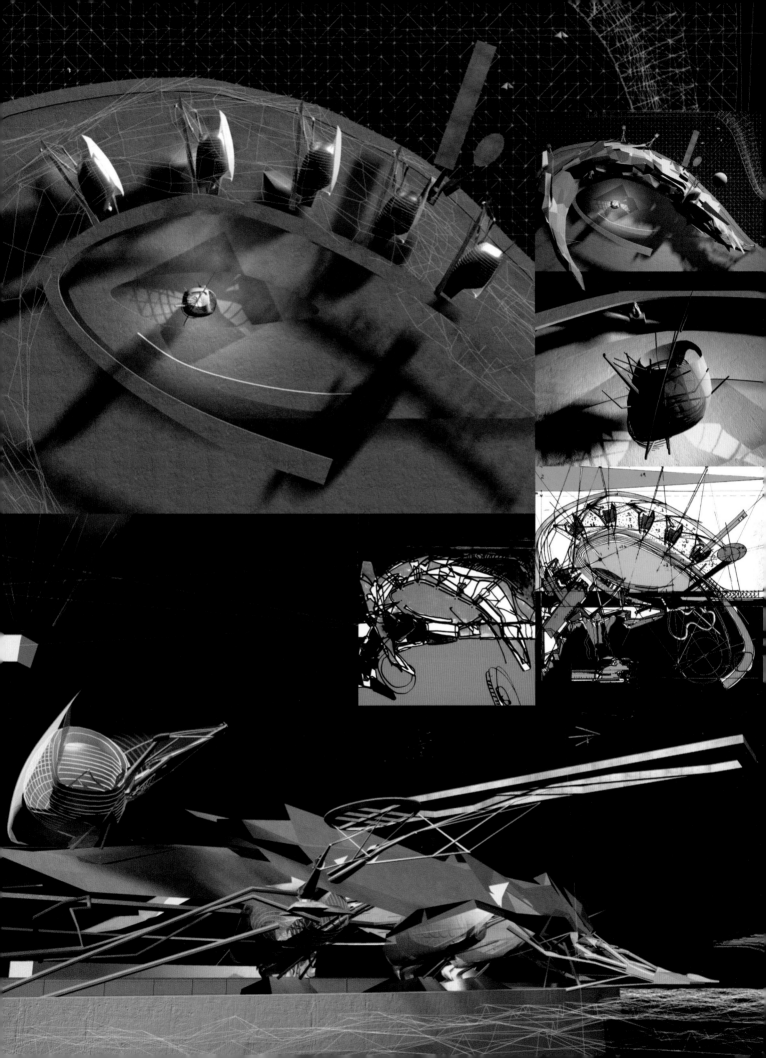

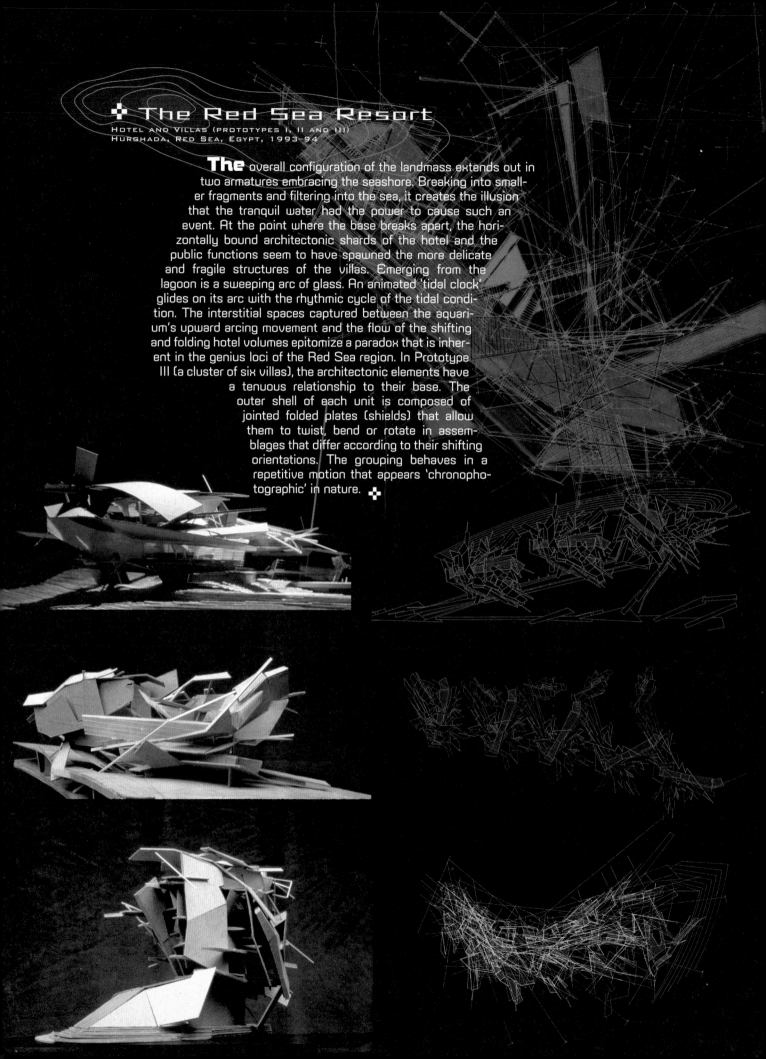

✦ The Red Sea Resort

HOTEL AND VILLAS (PROTOTYPES I, II AND III)
HURGHADA, RED SEA, EGYPT, 1993-94

The overall configuration of the landmass extends out in two armatures embracing the seashore. Breaking into smaller fragments and filtering into the sea, it creates the illusion that the tranquil water had the power to cause such an event. At the point where the base breaks apart, the horizontally bound architectonic shards of the hotel and the public functions seem to have spawned the more delicate and fragile structures of the villas. Emerging from the lagoon is a sweeping arc of glass. An animated 'tidal clock' glides on its arc with the rhythmic cycle of the tidal condition. The interstitial spaces captured between the aquarium's upward arcing movement and the flow of the shifting and folding hotel volumes epitomize a paradox that is inherent in the genius loci of the Red Sea region. In Prototype III (a cluster of six villas), the architectonic elements have a tenuous relationship to their base. The outer shell of each unit is composed of jointed folded plates (shields) that allow them to twist, bend or rotate in assemblages that differ according to their shifting orientations. The grouping behaves in a repetitive motion that appears 'chronophotographic' in nature. ✦

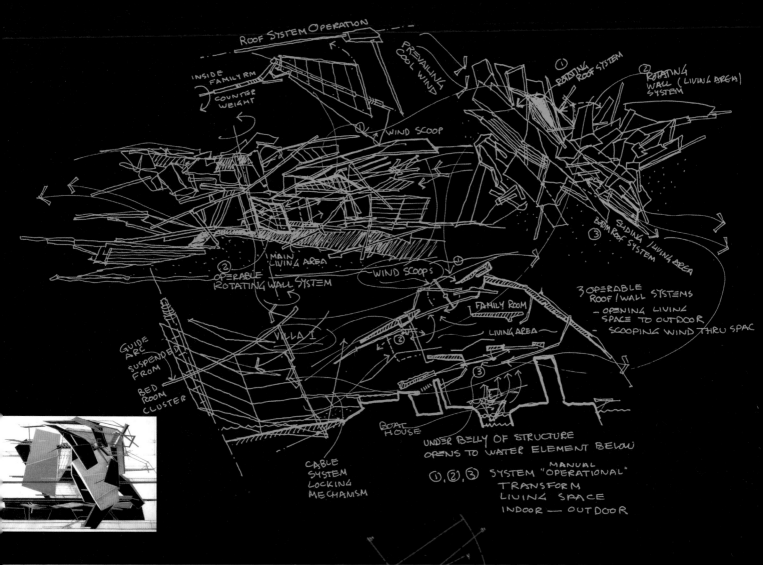

✛⌐aga Studio Architecture

Tarek Naga (1953)
1985–82 PhD candidate, doctoral programme in Architecture, University
          of Pennsylvania, Philadelphia
1982   Master of Architecture, University of Minnesota, Minneapolis
1977   Graduate Diploma of Urban Planning, Aim Shams University, Cairo
1975   Bachelor of Science in Architecture, Aim Shams University, Cairo

1991   Creation of Naga Studio in Venice, California

Teaching
1999–98 Sci-Arc, Los Angeles, California
1999–98 Cal Poly Pomona, Department of Architecture, California
1998–91 Art Center College of Design, Pasadena, California
1989–87 Boston Architectural Center
1984–82 University of Pennsylvania
1981–79 University of Minnesota
1979–75 Aim Shams University

Principal buildings and projects
2000   Egyptian Pavilion, Venice Biennal; 'House of Emergent
          Suspensions' (Esk House), Cairo (project)
1998   Marina International Hotel, Los Angeles, California (under construc-
          tion); Korekosmu experimental and film theatre, Los Angeles
1997   The Heritage House, Rochester, Minnesota; Sharm Safari Gate,
          tourist installations, Sinai, Egypt (under construction)
1996/97 The Sharm Retreat, Sharm el Sheikh, Sinai; The Malibu Retreat,
          Malibu, California
1995   The Raslan's Residence, Jeddah, Saudi Arabia (project); The
          Scandar's Residence, Cairo; Yokohama Port Terminal, Japan (com-
          petition)
1994–93 Red Sea Resort (Afras Village), Hurghada, Red Sea, Egypt
          (project)
1993   Taba Tourist Resort, Taba, Sinai (project)

1992   Nara Cultural Complex, Japan (competition); New Horizon
          Elementary School, Pasadena, California (project)
1991   McMillan House, Silver Lake, Los Angeles (project)

Publications
2000   *Domestication of Modernity* New Art Examiner, Chicago

Selected bibliography
2000   'Global Architecture', *GA Houses*, Project 2000 (vol. 53) Tokyo
1997   'Global Architecture', *GA Houses*, Project 97 (vol. 52) Tokyo
1996   *Surfaces*, W. W. Norton & Company, New York; 'Global
          Architecture', *GA Houses*, Project 96 (vol. 48) Tokyo;
          L'Architettura (vol. 481) Milan
1995   'Global Architecture', *GA Houses*, Project 95 (vol. 45) Tokyo;
          Ryuko Tsushin (vol. 385) Tokyo
1992   *UIA Conference Publication*, UIA Work Group, Cairo
1986   *Drawing Towards Building* exhibition catalogue, Pennsylvania
          Academy of Fine Arts, Philadelphia; *Personal Choices*, Foundation
          for Architecture, Philadelphia
1980   *Human Spaces*, University of Minnesota, School of Architecture,
          Minneapolis

Nishimoto Atelier

| Teag Y. Nishimoto (*1955) |

Architecture, for me, is a way to redefine reality. Within the limitations of each situation, critical as well as creative concerns are always about the ability to propose a set of conditions which are able to redefine our perceptions of reality. However, a statement such as this contains a fundamental problem in the very definition of the word 'reality' itself. Similar to the problems and the difficulties of using certain words, such as 'public', 'programme' or 'composition', it seems that the complex word definition connected with the question 'what' only results in a chain reaction leading to another definition game. In his book *Ways of Worldmaking*, the American philosopher Nelson Goodman points out the problem of posing the question 'What is art?'. In crucial cases, the real question is not 'What objects are (permanently) works of art?' but 'When is an object a work of art? – or, more concisely, 'When is art?' I would propose transposing this question to 'When is architecture?' In other words, 'What one does precisely or specifically (in one's office or at his or her desk) for how long' determines the purpose of operation for the development of each project. The given conditions or situations are, by definition, idiosyncratic in each case, and those idiosyncrasies, in general, can be articulated into three categories: space, material and programme. What is interesting to me in this articulation is the idea that they are really three different conditions that require independent operational modes. The more precisely one becomes aware of the sense of purpose in each situation, the clearer the strategic or intuitive response that determines itself as a condition-specific operation. In my work, these are done through, essentially, abstract line drawing for spatial concerns, writing the descriptive text for programmatic concerns. The operation of the materiality is a kind of mediator between these two in an effort to find the appropriate association with the physicality of the place. These operational modes seem to be neither interchangeable nor necessarily overlapping. What seems to be crucial in that process is the clarity in each operational mode. On the other hand, the form is rarely the initial or final concern for me. If the form still remains the viable way we understand and associate architecture with reality, perhaps the very difficulty of defining reality itself relates to the sense of suspicion relying on the form as an embodiment of ideas. At the same time, the effort to redefine reality does not include the definition of what that redefined reality is. It probably defies the desire to explain, but rather evokes a certain description of that reality. What seems to me more viable in that context is to reveal the strategic structure in which reality would unfold itself. Finding the precise and effective way to make the proposal relevant in this situation is what interests me most. ✦

TAEG NISHIMOTO

Plot House
Project, 1992

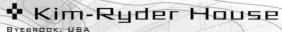

✦ Kim-Ryder House
BYEBROOK, USA
1996

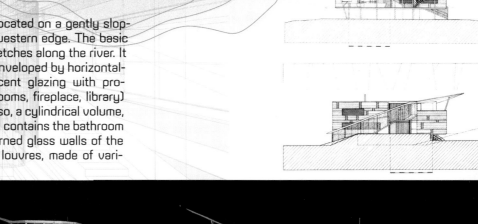

The site of this house is located on a gently sloping hill with a river along its western edge. The basic configuration of the house stretches along the river. It is essentially a single volume enveloped by horizontally banded transparent/translucent glazing with programmed spaces (kitchen, bedrooms, fireplace, library) given the articulated volumes. Also, a cylindrical volume, made of vertical translucent glass, contains the bathroom and closet. The horizontally patterned glass walls of the exterior envelope contain jalousie louvres, made of variously coloured glass, for ventilation. This combination of elements makes the constantly changing light effect inside the house, as well as the view towards outside, an inherent condition. This project seeks to create a specific relationship between the figurative quality of circulating through the house and the space-defining volume of the glass wall, that is, between the phenomenal aspect of the building and the temporal dimension of living experience inside. ✦

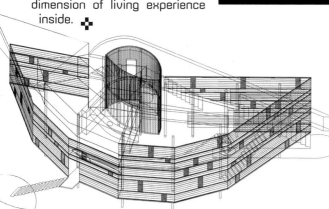

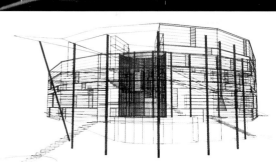

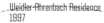

Weidler-Ahrenbach Residence
1997

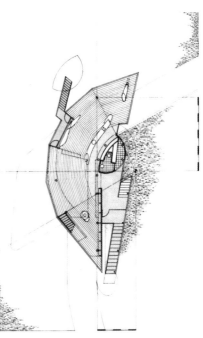

✛ Koma House
KOMA, JAPAN
1990

Nishimoto interpreted the site of the Koma house as a complex network of abstract lines. The complexity of its configuration generated this operation of the lines to articulate the spaces inside as well as outside the house. This, in turn, was related to the material relationships among the components, i.e. cast concrete, concrete block, metal, and the applied colour of the concrete surfaces and the floor. The house reveals an ambiguity between sculpture and architecture; it imposes itself upon its environment as 'foreign body', screaming to be noticed. Nishimoto has not attempted to blend in with the surroundings by bringing together old and new. On the contrary, he has worked on differences and disruptive asymmetries in an attempt to 'invent' an alternative location, a sort of organized space whose presence was already felt even before it actually existed. ✛

Super Pier 1+2

New York, USA
1990

This project, commissioned by the Toppan Company consisted of a conceptual planning and development and a design proposal for an abandonned pier on the edges of Manhattan. The programme of 'super piers' called for images of a new structure that would transform the site, an urban waterfront with derelict piers. Nishimoto's proposal uses outdoor sports courts as the connecting element of the whole building. The ground level is for tennis, basketball and volleyball, the upper level for café, gym and other facilities. The project received the New York Chapter/AIA's Design Award in 1991. ✦

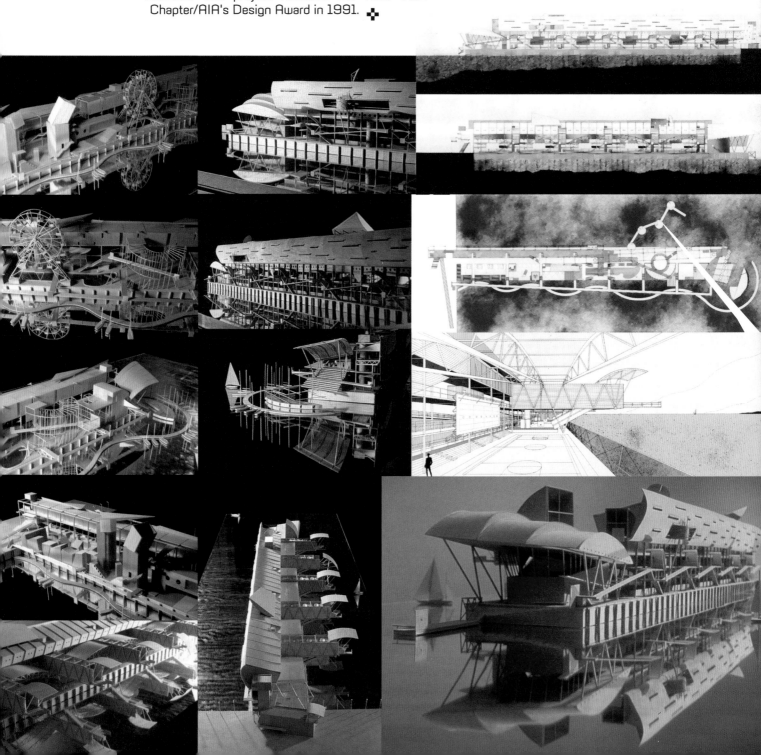

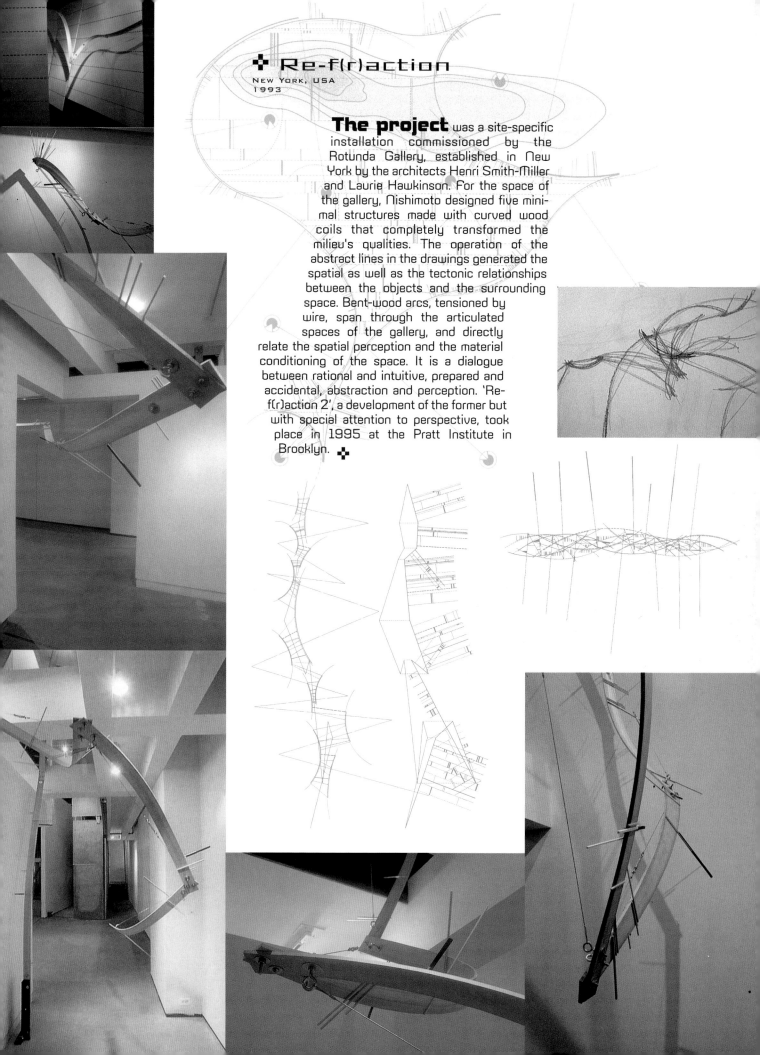

✚ Re-f(r)action

NEW YORK, USA
1993

The project was a site-specific installation commissioned by the Rotunda Gallery, established in New York by the architects Henri Smith-Miller and Laurie Hawkinson. For the space of the gallery, Nishimoto designed five minimal structures made with curved wood coils that completely transformed the milieu's qualities. The operation of the abstract lines in the drawings generated the spatial as well as the tectonic relationships between the objects and the surrounding space. Bent-wood arcs, tensioned by wire, span through the articulated spaces of the gallery, and directly relate the spatial perception and the material conditioning of the space. It is a dialogue between rational and intuitive, prepared and accidental, abstraction and perception. 'Re-f(r)action 2', a development of the former but with special attention to perspective, took place in 1995 at the Pratt Institute in Brooklyn. ✚

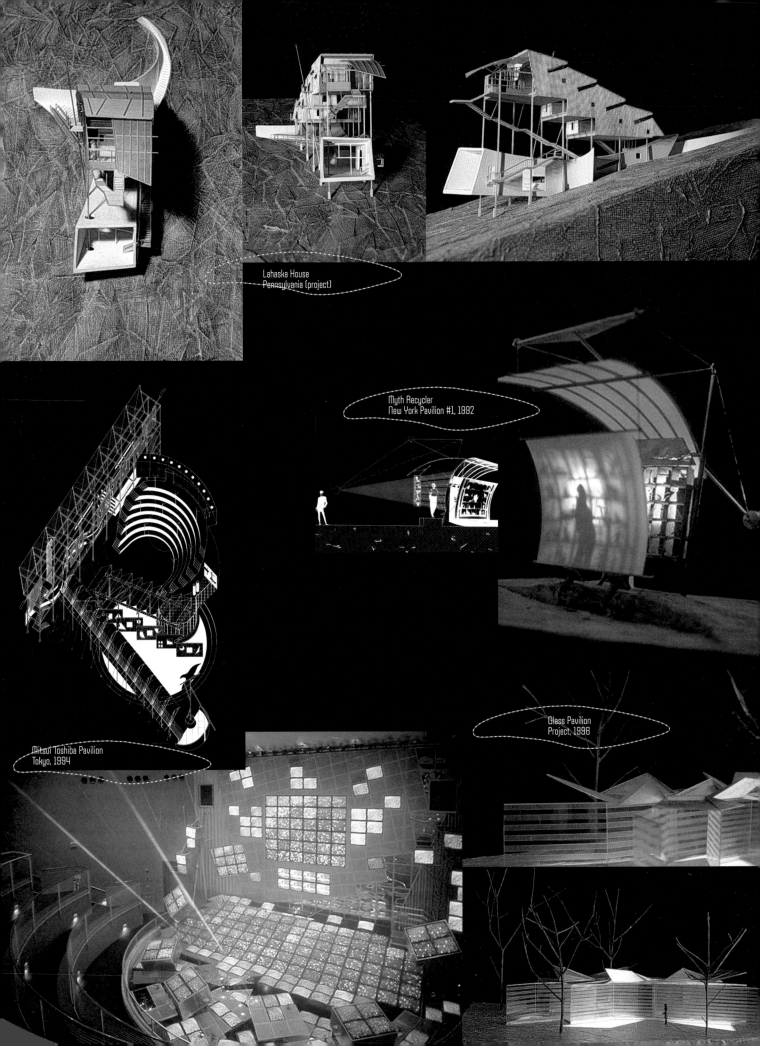

Lahaska House
Pennsylvania (project)

Myth Recycler
New York Pavilion #1, 1992

Mitsui Toshiba Pavilion
Tokyo, 1994

Glass Pavilion
Project, 1996

City Tempometer
New York Pavilion #2 (project), 1992

✛ Nishimoto Atelier

Taeg Y. Nishimoto (1955)
1978   Diploma of 'Architecture, Waseda University, School of Architecture
1981   Architecture Licence, Japan
1983   Graduate School of Architecture, Cornell University, Ithaca, New York
1989   Founded Taeg Y. Nishimoto + Allied Architects in New York
1991   New York Chapter AIA's Design Award for 'Super Pier 1 + 2'

Teaching
1999–85   Columbia University, New York
1999–89   Pratt Institute, New York

Principal buildings and projects
1997   Weidler-Ahrenbach Residence, Zurich, Switzerland (project)
1996   Kim-Ryder House (project); Greenport Waterfront, Long Island
       (competition); UCC Coffee Museum, Kobe (project); Glass Pavilion
       (project)
1995   Re-F(r)action 2 (installation); PLOT(ted) House (project); Connors
       Residence, Jefferson County, Pennsylvania (project)
1994   1 to (3 for) 5, Katonah, New York (realized); Sim-House (project);
       Harlan Residence, Salt Lake City (project); Stadium Parking Lot,
       Atlanta (competition); Mitsui Toshiba Pavilion, Tokyo
1993   PLOT House(s) (project); 'Re-F(r)action' (installation), Rotunda
       Gallery, New York; Tokyo Frontier Coca Pavilion, Tokyo (competi-
       tion); Penelope House, Muskoka, Canada (project)
1992   PLOT House (project); Rural Kiosk, Kumamoto Artpolis, Japan
       (competition, first prize) City Tempometer, New York Pavilion #2
       (project); Lahaska House, Pennsylvania (project)
1990   Super Pier 1 + 2 (project); Glass-Kline Residence (project)
1988   House at Koma, Saitama, Japan (realized in 1990)
1982   House at Tumagoi, Gumma, Japan (realized)

Recent exhibitions
1996   'British Culture' Tokyo Forum Exhibition Space, Tokyo, Japan

Selected bibliography
1996   *GA Houses* no. 48, 'Kim Rider House (project)'; *l'Arca* (April), 'RE-
       F(R)ACTION/RE-F(R)ACTION 2 and 1 to (3 for) 5' (Children's
       play shelter)
1995   *GA Houses* no. 45, 'Connors Residence' (project); 'PLOT
       House(s)' (project)
1994   *GA Houses* no. 41, 'Harlan Residence' (project); *Shelter and
       Dreams* exhibition catalogue, Katonah Museum of Art, Katonah,
       New York
1993   *GA Houses* no. 37, 'Penelope House' (project); 'PLOT House(s)'
       (project)
1992   *Compe & Contest* no. 9301; *GA Houses* no. 34, 'Lahaska House'
       (project); *New York Nomadism Design* GG, House at
       Koma/Lahaska House; *40 under 40* 'Vitae', 'Super Pier 1 and 2'
       (project) 'Lahaska House' (project) 'House at Koma' 'Independent
       Projects' Lumen (Myth Recycler, New York Pavilion #1/City
       Tempometer, New York Pavilion #2)
1990   *GA Houses* no. 31, 'Glass-Kline Residence' (project); *New York
       Architecture* vol. 4; *SITES* no. 24; *Interiors* (Sept./Oct.): 'Super
       Pier 1 and 2' *JA House* (Oct.) 'House at Koma'
1989   *Shinkenchiku* (Oct.) 'Design Expo – Mitsui Toshiba Pavilion'
1988   *GA House* no. 30, 'House at Koma'
1987   *Urban Design International*, vol. 10, 'West Hollywood Civic Center'
       (competition); *Bearings* Princeton Architectural Press, 'Three
       Pavilions' (project); *A + U* (Feb.)

Njiric + Njiric

| Helena Njiric (*1963) | Hrvoje Njiric (*1960) |

In the age of media and global production, architecture abandons its stylistic or canonic limits and enters the field of profane civic services. Qualifying it by speed, colour or smell means stepping away from the realm of professional exclusivity toward the efficiency of the free market. Touching off a wide range of association, architecture by colours is a kind of topological survey of field conditions, more than a typological concern. The greens represent the whole variety of such options. Standard green for the landscaped sites, supergreen for the recycled ones. Understated green for the areas of minimal impact on nature, ultragreen for the extreme conditions given. Fake green as an exercise in the artificiality of environment, forbidden green for the zones of limited access and platonic consumption. Blue for aquatic strategies, becoming purple to indicate the inert and heraldic. Yellow stands for openness, modesty and *Sachlichkeit* in social housing. Harnessing infrastructure, taking advantage of it, understanding and supporting the urban dynamic, its flows and speeds, is what orange register stands for. Time, as the fourth dimension, essential for contemporary design, puts colours in motion, subjects them to daily or seasonal change or weathering – distorted, fragmented, blurred, rippled, multiplied, pixelated, stylized, textured, interlaced. The projects shown tackle the themes such as those of discontinuity, subversive lite-ness and programmatic inexactitude, examine the interdependency of signs, the apparent breakdown of ideologies, question the modern legacy and validity of monofunctional systems, stressing the interchange modes, being interactive themselves, too, via various plateaus and different epidermal depths. The soft fabric of church elevation in Zagreb, lit up at night, the ever-changing multicoloured layers of the urban hill in Den Bosch, slopes and the 'inhabited' glazed sections of the Yokohama project, protectiveness and independence of different field conditions in Glasgow or the herbal nature of elevations as condensed gardens of pharmaceutical faculty in Zagreb, all polemize the viability of concepts, on one hand interactive and eventual, on the other unstable and generative, understood as an accumulation of strata, performing the new urban presence. The scary accumulations of the web city are taken to their limits in order to leave a fair amount of territory free. Beyond the post-architectural there are notions of nature, occasionally colonized or simply used as a camping site for global tourism. Territories of immense densifications, architecture-free zones, landscaped environments and the residual ones, constitute the trajectories of present-day urban concerns: to initiate (Zagreb), to prepare (Den Bosch), to stir (Yokohama), to condense (Zagreb), to reshuffle (Glasgow) – as possible key words of a new (secret) vocabulary. ✤

NJIRIC & NJIRIC

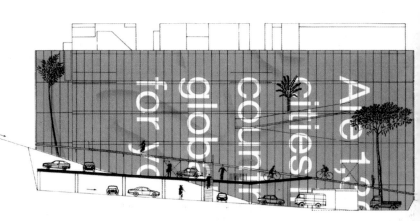

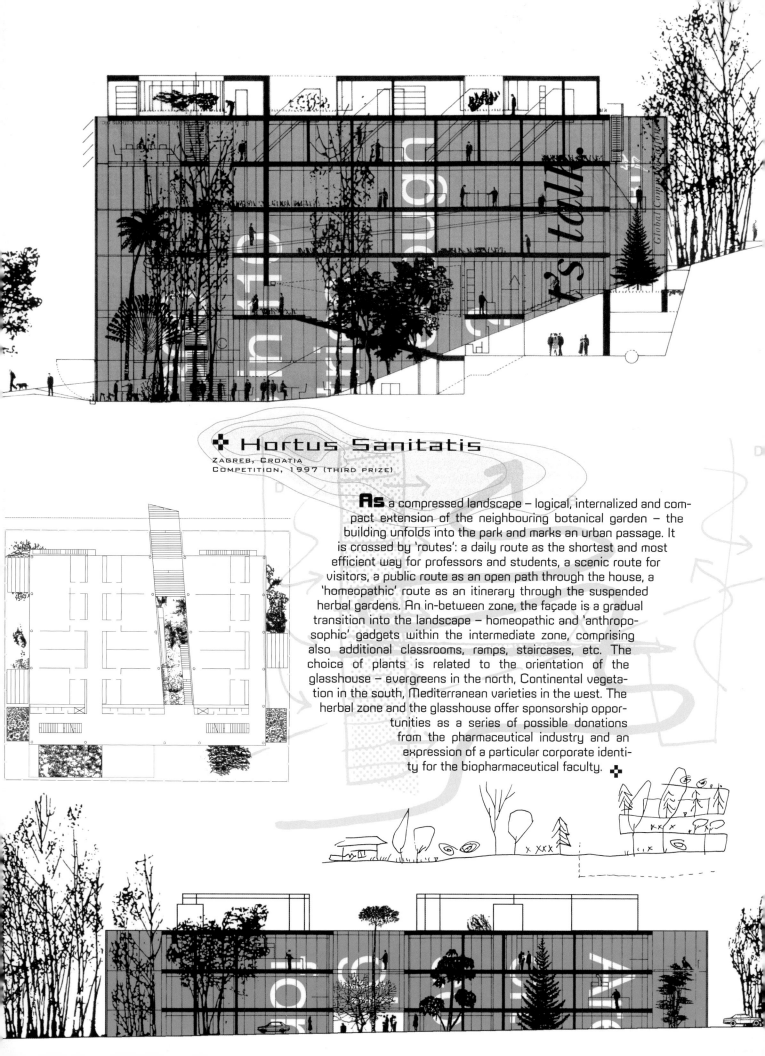

✚ Hortus Sanitatis

ZAGREB, CROATIA
COMPETITION, 1997 (THIRD PRIZE)

As a compressed landscape – logical, internalized and compact extension of the neighbouring botanical garden – the building unfolds into the park and marks an urban passage. It is crossed by 'routes': a daily route as the shortest and most efficient way for professors and students, a scenic route for visitors, a public route as an open path through the house, a 'homeopathic' route as an itinerary through the suspended herbal gardens. An in-between zone, the façade is a gradual transition into the landscape – homeopathic and 'anthroposophic' gadgets within the intermediate zone, comprising also additional classrooms, ramps, staircases, etc. The choice of plants is related to the orientation of the glasshouse – evergreens in the north, Continental vegetation in the south, Mediterranean varieties in the west. The herbal zone and the glasshouse offer sponsorship opportunities as a series of possible donations from the pharmaceutical industry and an expression of a particular corporate identity for the biopharmaceutical faculty. ✚

✦ Baumaxx Hypermarket

MARIBOR, SLOVENIA
1997-98

The urban concept consists of reversing the figure-ground ratio of American hypermarkets or perimeter centres, celebrating the traffic by cutting a regular pattern into an irregular plot contour. It is strenghtened by the green roof substance, as a new elevated ground, publicly accessible. All inward-facing planes are entirely glazed, all perimeter ones are mute, but user-friendly. Four billboards anchor the vast slopes of the building to the site and address themselves to the drivers. Colour 'classification' is an attempt to handle architecture by ordinary, if not banal, criteria — size, smell or colour. Even the glazed elevations exploit the properties of insulating wool as such. Njiric & Njiric are using its yellowness as a part of the Baumaxx corporate identity, simply attaching the red logos on to it and slightly blurring them with corrugated lexan sheets: colour as a marketing strategy. ✦

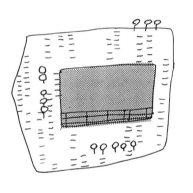

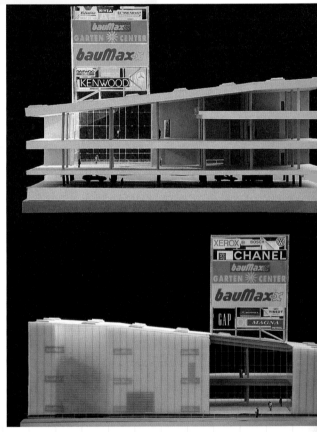

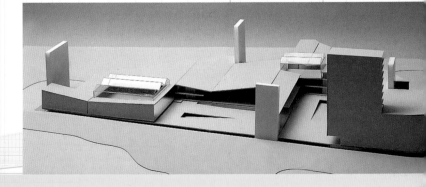

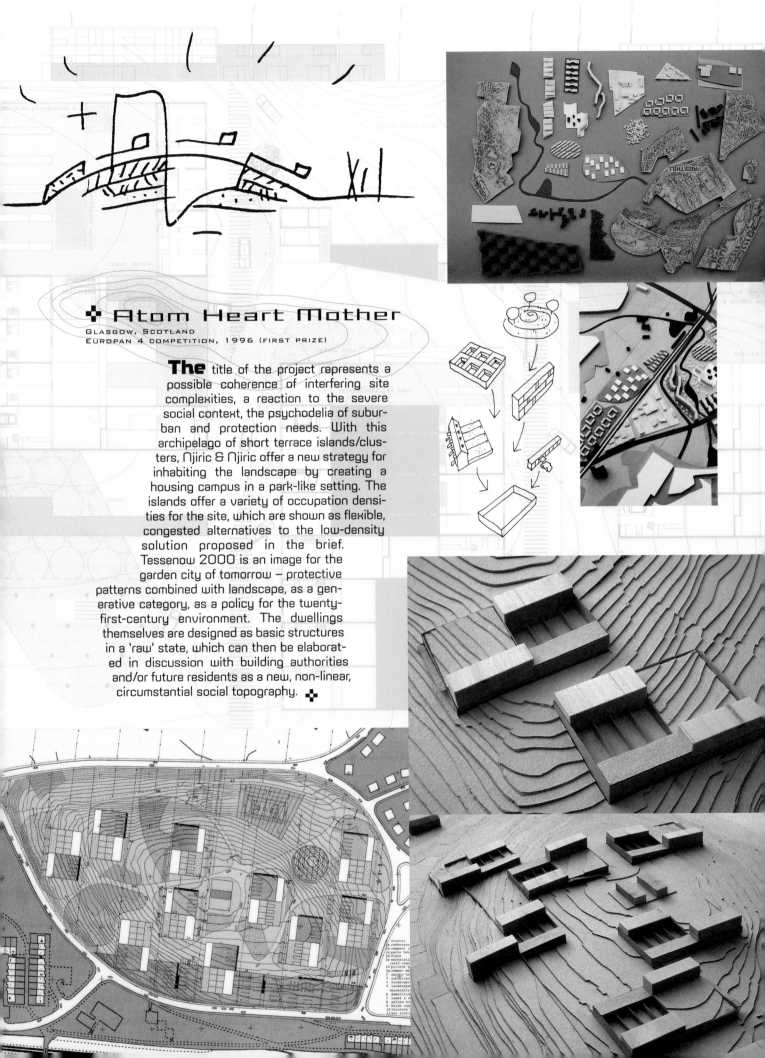

✦ Atom Heart Mother

GLASGOW, SCOTLAND
EUROPAN 4 COMPETITION, 1996 (FIRST PRIZE)

The title of the project represents a possible coherence of interfering site complexities, a reaction to the severe social context, the psychodelia of suburban and protection needs. With this archipelago of short terrace islands/clusters, Njiric & Njiric offer a new strategy for inhabiting the landscape by creating a housing campus in a park-like setting. The islands offer a variety of occupation densities for the site, which are shown as flexible, congested alternatives to the low-density solution proposed in the brief. Tessenow 2000 is an image for the garden city of tomorrow – protective patterns combined with landscape, as a generative category, as a policy for the twenty-first-century environment. The dwellings themselves are designed as basic structures in a 'raw' state, which can then be elaborated in discussion with building authorities and/or future residents as a new, non-linear, circumstantial social topography. ✦

✛ Yokohama Burning

INTERNATIONAL PORT TERMINAL, YOKOHAMA, JAPAN
COMPETITION, 1995

For Yokohama, Nijric & Nijric imagined an 'electronic raft', compulsorily combining several components: a shipyard-like structure (congested, with technically bulging sides, fluid in the middle); water as a material (typology of wet voids elevations as an accumulation of aquaria); stalactites (the water 'leaks' in the form of basins suspended through strips in the roof); a system of Routes: the Civic Route, the Speleological Route (under the 'stalactites'), the Marine Route (urban divers), the Zig-zagging Route (surfers); the living pixels (a system of low-current electric grids makes it possible to place fish to deliver desired elevational messages); an urban park (a floating fragment of hard-core Coney Island of the new breed); glass as a structural material, paper for the divisions; Japanese 'naturalism' and high technology as elements of Yokohama's cultural legacy for the twenty-first century and beyond. ✛

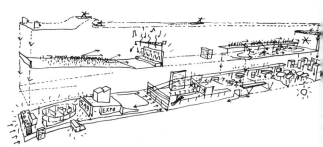

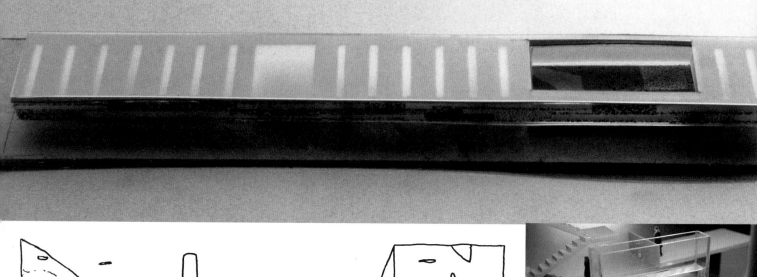

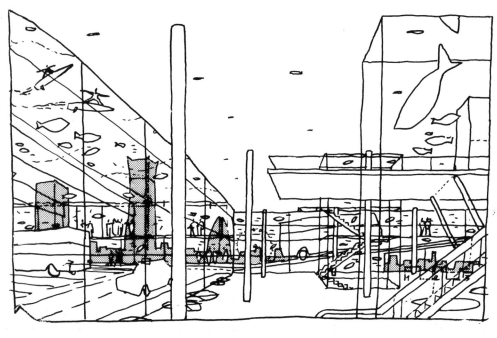

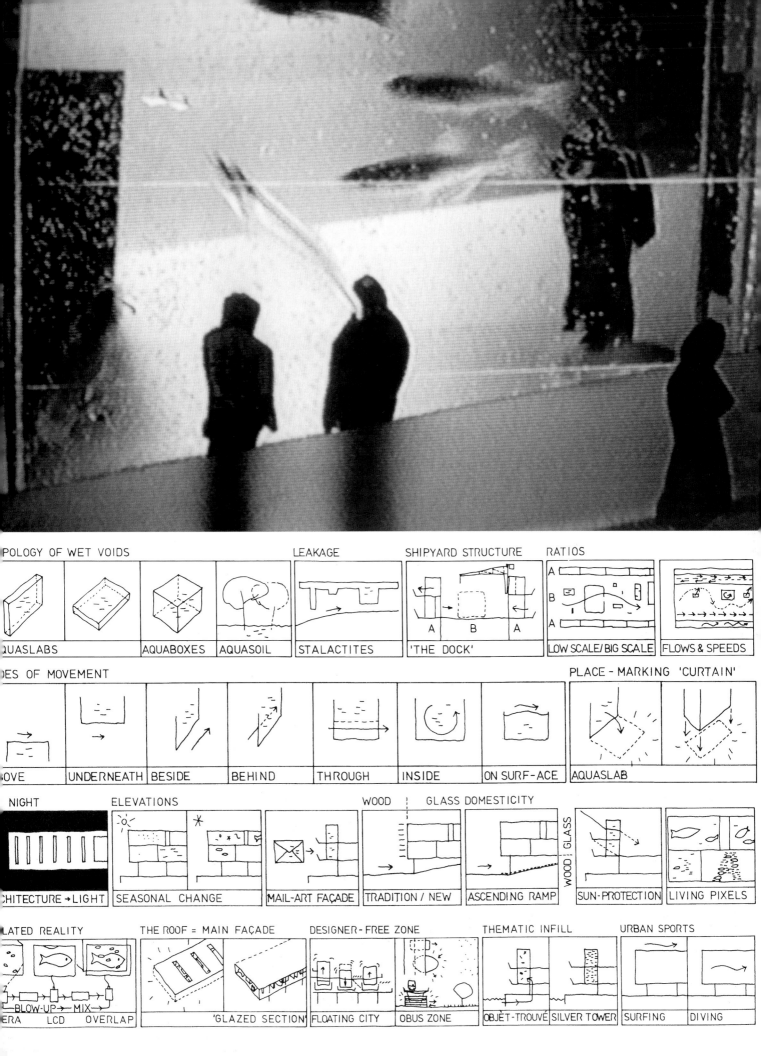

POLOGY OF WET VOIDS   LEAKAGE   SHIPYARD STRUCTURE   RATIOS

QUASLABS		AQUABOXES	AQUASOIL	STALACTITES	'THE DOCK'

LOW SCALE/BIG SCALE	FLOWS & SPEEDS

ES OF MOVEMENT   PLACE-MARKING 'CURTAIN'

OVE	UNDERNEATH	BESIDE	BEHIND	THROUGH	INSIDE	ON SURF-ACE	AQUASLAB

NIGHT   ELEVATIONS   WOOD ⋮ GLASS DOMESTICITY

CHITECTURE →LIGHT	SEASONAL CHANGE	MAIL-ART FAÇADE	TRADITION / NEW	ASCENDING RAMP	SUN-PROTECTION	LIVING PIXELS

LATED REALITY   THE ROOF = MAIN FAÇADE   DESIGNER-FREE ZONE   THEMATIC INFILL   URBAN SPORTS

BLOW-UP → MIX

ERA LCD OVERLAP	'GLAZED SECTION'	FLOATING CITY	OBUS ZONE	OBJET-TROUVÉ	SILVER TOWER	SURFING	DIVING

✚ Viskovo
Urban Plan

Viskovo, Croatia
1997; Competition, 1996 (first prize)

Organizing the (concentric) slopes as a fine synthesis of dwelling, working and agriculture, the project proposes a balance between the built substance and structured voids. Such a traditional typology mutates into a number of organizational patterns. Rural aspects concentrate on occupation modes of the land: field cultivation, formal gardens, open public space and civic facilities (playgrounds), extensions of dwellings or work forecourts/backyards. Organization of the section is a functional zoning, with workzones towards the street and dwellings oriented to the quiet, internal areas. What was once used as a living upstairs/working downstairs complex, is now appropriated to the new, centrifugal and sloping layout: one lives downstairs and works upstairs. Circulation between the slopes is conceived as a network of bypasses, enabling propulsion during traditional seasonal festivities, to take place along the main road. ✚

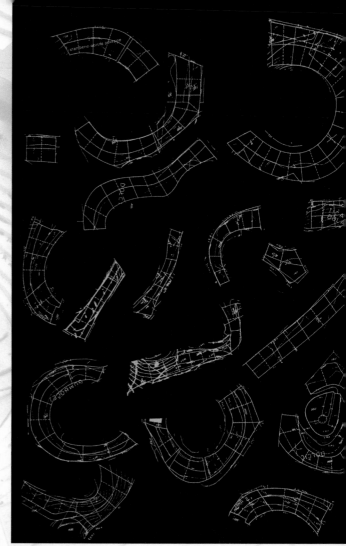

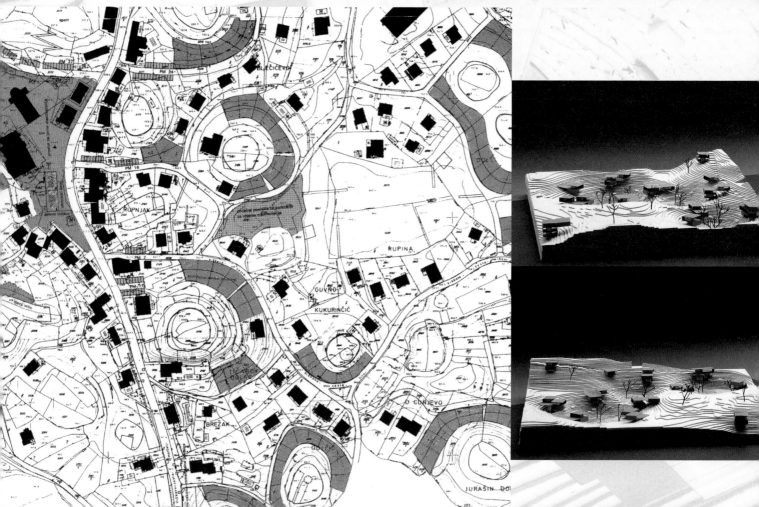

✛ Njiric + Njiric

Helena Njiric (1963)
1989 Diploma in Architecture, University of Zagreb

Hrvoje Njiric (1960)
1986 Diploma in Architecture, University of Zagreb

1996 Founded Njiric + Njiric in Zagreb

Teaching
1998–99 Hrvoje Njiric: Technical University, Graz, Austria

Principal buildings and projects
1998 McDonald's Drive-in, Maribor III, Maribor (realized); 'UltraNolli' Rijeka (competition); 'A Reclining Mat', Sestine (under construction); House N, Zagreb (realized); Hotel in Prvic, Luka (project)
1999–97 Baumaxx Hypermarket, Maribor (realized); Z2, Zagreb (realized)
1997 Social Housing Prototypes for War Victims (competition); 'Heaven Can Wait' Lukavec (project); 'O/01, Social Housing', Ogulin (project); 'O/02, Social Housing', Otocac (project); Fair Complex, Maribor (project); Law Courts and Housing, Slunj (project); 'Hortis sanitatis', Zagreb (competition) Masarykova 4, Zagreb (competition)
1996 Seniors' Housing, Ulm (competition); 'Terrain Vague', Maribor (competition); Urban Planning, Viskovo (competition); AA House, Zagreb (project) 'Housing: Six Memos for the Next Millennium', Barcelona (competition); 'Atom Heart Mother', Europan 4, Glasgow (competition); 'Felix', Zagreb (competition)'RH – Croatian government buildings', Zagreb (competition);'Jazz'– Improvizations on density', Zagreb (study)
1995 'Yokohama Burning', Yokohama (competition); 'Z-900', Zagreb (competition); 'Accelerating the Blue', Zagreb (project)
1994 'Prêt à Porter Housing', Zapresic (project)

Recent exhibitions
1998 'Progettare il confine, Gorizja – Nova Gorizja: nuovi paesaggi urbani' Italy; 'Colours' (solo exhibitions): AA, London; Strathclyde University, Glasgow; Manifesto Festival, Edinburgh; University of Newcastle, Newcastle
1997 'Europan Europe' Rome; '20 Young Architects' Sofia
1996 'Europan UK' Glasgow; 'Europan Österreich' Graz
1995 'Beiträge zur Urbanität' Vienna/Zagreb; 'CV 12 Frames of Metropolis' Zagreb/Ljubljana/Amsterdam
1994 '900 Years of Zagreb' Zagreb; 'Europan Niederlande' Rotterdam

Selected bibliography
1999 Njiric + Njiric Actar, Barcelona; Architektur Aktuel (January), Germany
1998 Colours exhibition catalogue, AA School, London; Housing: New Alternatives, New Systems Birkhäuser Verlag/Actar, Barcelona; A + T no. 11, Vitoria-Gasteiz
1997 Quaderns no. 219, Barcelona; Europan 4 Results, catalogue, Paris; Architects Journal no. 24, London
1996 Quaderns nos 212, 214, 211, Barcelona; Building Design (Jun.) London; Arch + no. 133, Aachen; Wettbewerbe, 155/156, Vienna
1995 Arch + no. 123, Aachen
1994 De Architectuurkrant no. 10, Rotterdam; At Home in the City Urbanizing Residential Areas Europan 3, Paris

NL Architects

| Pieter Bannenberg (*1959) | Walter Van Dijk (*1962) |
| Kamiel Klaasse (*1967) | Mark Linnemann (*1962) |

The Dutch agency NL Architects is based in Amsterdam. Its four associates, Pieter Bannenberg, Walter van Dijk, Kamiel Klaasse and Mark Linnemann, officially founded the agency in 1997, but their collaborative work dates back to the early 1990s, when they were all students together at the Technical University in Delft. Already resident in Amsterdam, it is in the switch between the two cities – in their day-to-day experience of a world of asphalt and of a specifically motorway-oriented aesthetic, and through the at once revealing and tedious way it looks at the territory – that they claim to have developed the seeds of their thinking about the contemporary metropolis, in a more or less self-taught way. For this is indeed the particular field that their architecture explores: the present-day, predominantly suburban Western condition. NL projects, which are radically critical of this reality, are typified by an extreme sensibility, and by a keen fix on all the issues, problems, scales and processes that are encountered. And it is, at the end of the day, in order to deal with the most commonplace aspects of the real, and the most prosaic practices, that they develop their most innovative and forward-looking devices and arrangements, in a systematic endeavour to get the most out of the unexplored potential of the things all around us: a carpark, a shopping centre, a road, a house. Architecture, for NL, cannot be separated from these suburban issues and strategies and is indeed their key. Through its capacity to articulate paradoxical conditions and heterogeneous elements, it is the preferred tool for synthesizing new types of buildings, programmatic hybrid structures and the expression of new limitations and practices. The form of the megastructure, for example, which they reintroduce in several of their projects (Return to the Fold™, Parkhouse/Carstadt), represents for them one of the typically architectural responses to problems of territorial staggering and horizontal de-densification. Architecture is thus presented as a field of experimental activity, at the crossroads of economic, programmatic, technical and even environmental thinking. The city is actually perceived by NL as an ecosystem, no less, an environment where logical systems of urban growth and natural factors, consumption and production, flux and stasis are balanced; and where recycling is set up as a method of stable and sustainable functioning, whether it has to do with waste, energy, materials or even architecture. This concern is very tangible in the WOS 8 project, where a power station becomes at once part of the cityscape, a backdrop for sports facilities and a refuge adapted to suit several species of birds. This decidedly realistic and pragmatic dimension of NL production cannot, however, be separated from a markedly critical, ironical and forward-looking stance, which can be detected in projects like Paid Parking (a carpark self-financed by the advertising in it, visible from the air) and Sky Cemetery (a cross-shaped high-rise building-cum-cemetery in Manhattan). ✦

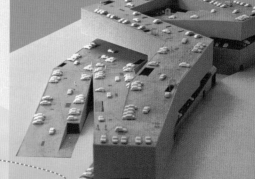

Parkhouse/Carstadt
Amsterdam, 1995

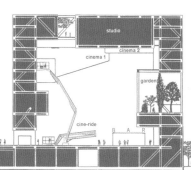

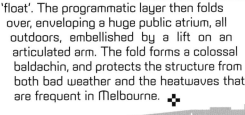

audio/visual library

cinema

bar with view
over the square

multimedia discovery

festival and arts company offices

asian fusion food

office accomodation

bar

cafe tavern style

technical retail

tv and radio studio

botanical retail

restaurants

news and broadcast preparation

shop

butterfly garden

sketball court

covered garden\
interior square

retail

it's a bar

station

arena   exhibition halls

casual eating

flexible performance room

tourbus parking and streetcar-station

public services

platforms

and garden maintenance

✦ Return to the Fold™

MELBOURNE, AUSTRALIA, COMPETITION 1997

In 1997, Return to the Fold™ was a response to the
competition for the creation of a civic centre in the heart
of Melbourne, beside the river Yarra, above the station
railway tracks. This complex would house a shopping
mall, a multiplex cinema, exhibition, sports and performance halls, gardens, an intermodal station, audiovisual
studios, offices. Faced with this programmatic heterogeneity, the NL Architects sought above all to solve the
problematic issue of continuity between public sphere
and privatized commercial sphere. The programmes are
housed on a homogeneous layer where the roofing forms
an independent public esplanade, at once stage and
seating for all collective activities. From this area, the
citizen/consumer decides to 'plunge' or to
'float'. The programmatic layer then folds
over, enveloping a huge public atrium, all
outdoors, embellished by a lift on an
articulated arm. The fold forms a colossal
baldachin, and protects the structure from
both bad weather and the heatwaves that
are frequent in Melbourne. ✦

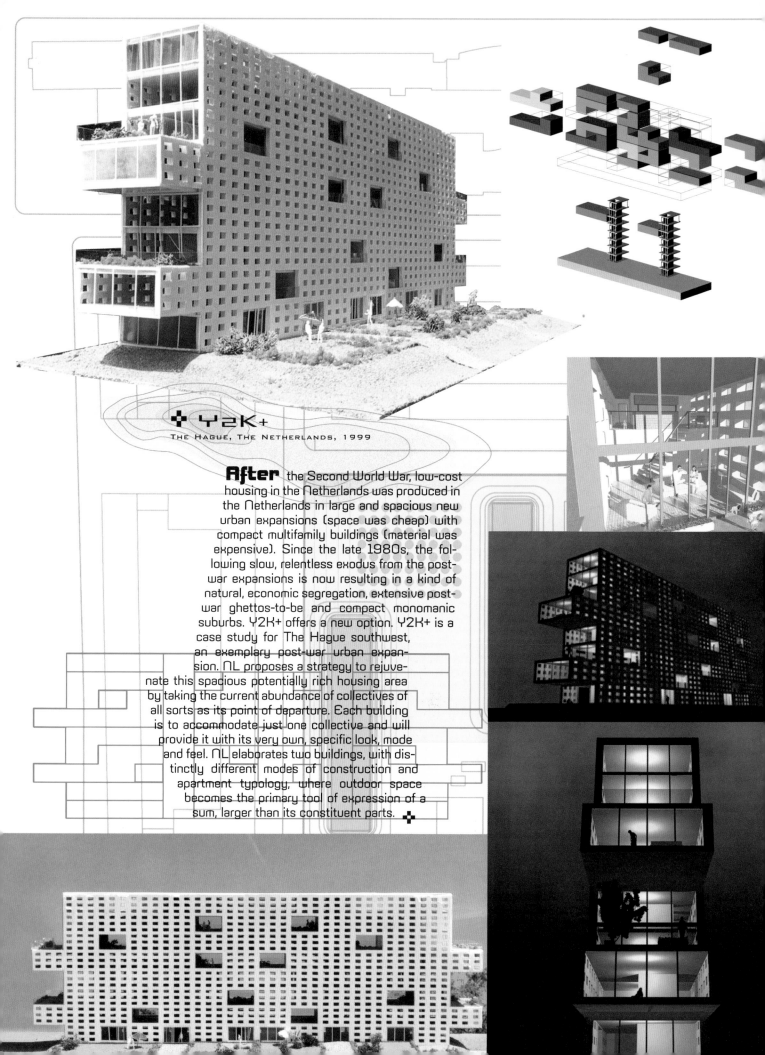

✚ Y2K+

THE HAGUE, THE NETHERLANDS, 1999

After the Second World War, low-cost housing in the Netherlands was produced in the Netherlands in large and spacious new urban expansions (space was cheap) with compact multifamily buildings (material was expensive). Since the late 1980s, the following slow, relentless exodus from the post-war expansions is now resulting in a kind of natural, economic segregation, extensive post-war ghettos-to-be and compact monomanic suburbs. Y2K+ offers a new option. Y2K+ is a case study for The Hague southwest, an exemplary post-war urban expansion. NL proposes a strategy to rejuvenate this spacious potentially rich housing area by taking the current abundance of collectives of all sorts as its point of departure. Each building is to accommodate just one collective and will provide it with its very own, specific look, mode and feel. NL elaborates two buildings, with distinctly different modes of construction and apartment typology, where outdoor space becomes the primary tool of expression of a sum, larger than its constituent parts. ✚

✦ Y Building
AMSTERDAM, THE NETHERLANDS, 1999

The location for this study is a very promising site on the banks of the river Y. Since the train tracks are partly decommissioned, a large piece of land, which directly connects to central station and the river, becomes available. The investors of the Harbour Building (designed by Dudok), one of four developers in this area, are looking for possibilities to double the existing square footage by at least 12,000 m². The dimension of the site, height restrictions and the monumental character of the Dudok building made any extension problematic. This proposal suggests 'cloning' the existing building. The result is manipulated and deformed in order to provide enough daylight and to maintain important views. The innovation of the scheme is the colonization of the 3D space outside and above the site boundary. The Harbour Building has one peculiar hidden property. This slab in fact consists of two towers that are held together by one façade. There are two elevator shafts, two staircases, two mechanical shafts, two toilet groups and two pantries on each floor. In the cloned building these towers are set free: a Siamese-twin tower appears. ✦

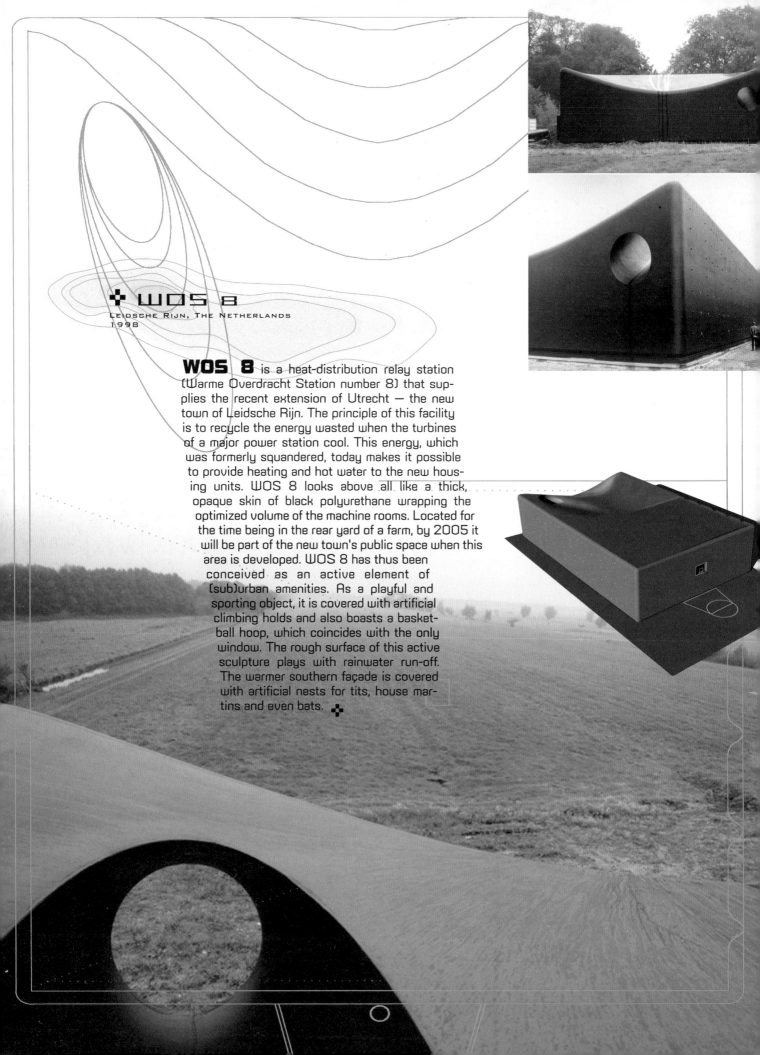

✦ WOS 8

LEIDSCHE RIJN, THE NETHERLANDS
1998

WOS 8 is a heat-distribution relay station (Warme Overdracht Station number 8) that supplies the recent extension of Utrecht — the new town of Leidsche Rijn. The principle of this facility is to recycle the energy wasted when the turbines of a major power station cool. This energy, which was formerly squandered, today makes it possible to provide heating and hot water to the new housing units. WOS 8 looks above all like a thick, opaque skin of black polyurethane wrapping the optimized volume of the machine rooms. Located for the time being in the rear yard of a farm, by 2005 it will be part of the new town's public space when this area is developed. WOS 8 has thus been conceived as an active element of (sub)urban amenities. As a playful and sporting object, it is covered with artificial climbing holds and also boasts a basketball hoop, which coincides with the only window. The rough surface of this active sculpture plays with rainwater run-off. The warmer southern façade is covered with artificial nests for tits, house martins and even bats. ✦

✛ NL Architects

Pieter Bannenberg (1959)
1995   Diploma from the Technical University, Delft

Walter van Dijk (1962)
1991   Diploma from the Technical University, Delft

Kamiel Klaasse (1967)
1995   Diploma from the Technical University, Delft

Mark Linnemann (1962)
1991   Diploma from the Technical University, Delft

1997   Creation of NL Architects in Amsterdam

Principal buildings and projects
2000   'CK', conversion of an office building into apartments and studios, Amsterdam (under construction); 'Hidden Delights', ten houses with patio, Amsterdam (under construction); 'Bike City', The Hague (under construction); 'KHK', eighty-eight dwellings, The Hague (under construction); concept for a Mandarin Duck shop, Paris (under construction)
1999   'Y2K+', eighty-five dwellings, Hoogeveenlaan, The Hague (project); 'Y Building', office building, Amsterdam (project); 'Wunderman Cato Johnson', Amsterdam (realized); Parking for Amsterdam Municipal Office (project); Maritime Zone, Ijburg, Amsterdam (project)
1998   WOS 8 thermal station, Leidsche Rijn (realized); 'Cinecenter', four rooms and foyer, renovation, Amsterdam (realized); 'Drive-in-Block' Zeeburg, Amsterdam (project); PNEM, a Boiler House, Breda (competition); Workshop Zeeburg, Zocher Parkway; Studio Photo & Apartment Edo Kars, Amsterdam (realized)
1997   'Return to the Fold™' Melbourne, Australia (competition); 'Vision 2020: Schiphol City', Amsterdam (realized); Leliegracht 3, House Canal, renovation, Amsterdam (realized)

1996   'Pixel City', Wateringse Veld, The Hague (project); Millennium Bridge, London (competition)
1995   Parkhouse/Carstadt, Amsterdam (project)
1994   'Flat' study for 220 dwellings, Leidsche Rijn (project)

Selected bibliography
2000   *Wohn! Design* (Jan.)
1999   *Arquitectura Viva* (Nov.); *Skim.com* (Dec.); *Spur* (Dec.); *Monument* no. 33; *l'Architecture d'aujourd'hui* no. 324; *Intelligente Architektur* (Nov.); *Quaderns* 'Spirals 99'; *Arch+* no. 147; *BLVD* (Oct.); *Spazio e Societa* no. 87; *Architektur Aktuell* (July/August); *Wired Magazine* (August); *Haüser* (April); *Interview* (Jun.); *Architecture in the Netherlands, Yearbook 98/99*; *Architect* (May); *Werk, Bauen+Wohnen* (April); *Frame* 7 (vol. 3); *Bauwelt* 1/1
1998   *Arquitectura Viva* no. 73; *Metropolis* 'The Ocular Issue'; *l'Arca* nos 128 and 129; *Big Soft Orange* exhibition catalogue, BSO, Yale University, New Haven; *Terra Incognita* exhibition catalogue; *Quaderns*; *HdA*; *Monument*; *Millennium*
1997   *Arquitectura Viva* no. 54; *Nine+One* exhibition catalogue, NAI, Rotterdam
1996   *Archis* no. 12; *Arch+* 133; *Topos* no. 15; *Wiederhall* no. 19; *Europan IV* Netherlands

Marcos Novak

| Marcos Novak |

Space is no longer innocent. Under the impact of science and technology, ordinary space has become just a subset of a composite 'newspace' that interweaves local, remote, telepresent, interactivated and virtual spacetime into the new spatial continuum that is the focus of emerging transarchitectures. Physically, this installation consists of four interrelated parts: a) a large-scale video projection of liquid forms derived from mathematical explorations of virtuality; b) a physical model captured from the fluctuating projected virtual forms; c) a sensor-created, invisible, interactive sculptural form; and d) a generative, interactive soundscape that weaves the previous three together. The video projection consists entirely of liquid, animated mathematical forms derived from the manipulation of mathematical fields. Various kinds are shown in rapid succession. An interactive, generative musical algorithm drives the video, intercutting among various sources at a high rate, producing a large number of new variants by multiplexing the sources in time. Each strand of video is thought of as a separate reality, and the rapid intercutting suggests the coexistence of multiple superimposed realities in the same instance. The rapid flickering tests the edge of our temporal perception, while the emergence of forms that are not in the source materials questions our familiar notions of objectivity. The physical component of the installation is a static form derived from the mathematical fields presented in the video portion. Captured from the perpetual flux of virtuality, this form has been built using LOM (laminated object manufacturing), a rapid prototyping process that builds forms directly from computer models by layering thousands of sheets of laser-cut paper. The resulting form has a dual personality: its geometry retains the character of its virtual origins, but its materiality is that of carved and polished wood. It is at once an anticipation of a static architecture derived from virtuality, and a premonition of a built dynamic, liquid architecture in which buildings actually move. The invisible component of the installation is implemented as a sensor field created by an infrared sensor-and-lens apparatus. The sensor-and-lens creates a distinct shape in space that, although invisible to the human eye, can be monitored and can yield information to the computer. When one reaches into this shape, a stream of numbers reports exactly how far into the shape one is extending. This information is, in turn, fed into the musical algorithms that generate the soundscape surrounding the whole piece, altering them. If one pays attention to the sound it is possible to feel, synaesthetically, the shape of the invisible form, reversing all our ordinary expectations of sculpture and architecture. Retinality is replaced by presence and voyeurism is replaced by intimate hypertactility. This piece investigates the axis between perception and materiality, connecting the two with interactivity. It explores the idea of multiple and multiplexed time in a way that tests the limits of temporal perception, and captures a single physical form from the numerous fluctuating virtual ones. The resulting object looks and feels like a heavy carved wood piece, at quite a contrast with both the virtual forms and with the sensor-created invisible form, which in turn acts as an interface to the interactive/generative musical algorithms that drive the virtual forms and create the temporal multiplexing, closing the circle.

Both the idea of an invisible architecture/sculpture and the idea of multi-plexed time hint at the existence of other realities besides the usual retinal one. The multiplexing of time is particularly cinematic, but in an unprece-dented manner: it involves interweaving numerous segments of film or ani-mation under algorithmic control as fast as possible, in a way that allows the viewer not only to see several 'films' at once, but also to begin to see sequences that do not exist in the original materials and are simply fabri-cated by perception. The word 'films' is in quotes because, in its fullest form, the separate strands would not be filmed or animated but would be computed in realtime, driven by algorithms and controlled by sensors. The investigation of multiple time is also the natural extension of my ongoing explorations of fields, non-Euclidean and trans-Euclidean spaces, and the derivation of architecture based on four or more spatial dimensions. The aspects of this installation that are here presented as nearly separate components will in subsequent installations be brought closer and closer together, until they cannot be distinguished one from the other. New realities require new vocabularies. I have coined the terms liquid architectures, transar-chitectures, eversion, transmodernity and others to begin to articulate the new conditions that we encounter on our journey to virtuality. In this sense, the overall work is an instance of transarchitectures; the phenomena it explores belong to the idea of 'ever-sion', the casting out of the virtual on to the actual, a concept that is the natural complement to the idea of 'immersion'; and the work is offered as an artefact of the cultural outlook of transmodernity. ✦

MARCOS NOVAK

✦ Variable Data Forms

1999

This ongoing investigation seeks to create architectonic propositions that are liquid, algorith-mic, transmissible and derived from the geome-tries of higher dimensionality. By 'liquid', Novak intends a total but rigorous variability driven by data shifts in cyberspace that can be transformed into a physical world. By 'algorithm' Novak means that the forms are never manipulated through man-ual corrections: rather, the mathematical formulae that generate them are adjust-ed to produce different results. By 'transmissible' Novak means that his data-forms can be compressed into algo-rithmic codes for transmission to fabri-cation sites, machines or to virtual envi-ronments. ✦

✦ Paracube
1997–98

For this project, a cuboid was defined by six parametric surfaces, each with its own coordinate system. The parametric equations governing each surface were arranged so that a variation on a particular surface would cause reactions or permutations on adjoining surfaces, effectively creating a topological cube. The parametric cuboid was manipulated to create two forms: a skeletal frame and a smooth skin. Parametrization allowed the smoothness of each element to be defined and manipulated through computational formulae; the frame was derived from the same process, where the skin was computed at high smoothness and the skeleton at low smoothness. The skeleton was then mathematically extruded into the fourth dimension by adding a fourth coordinate to every three-dimensional point. Thus, points became lines, lines became polygons, polygons became cubes and cubes became hypercubes. The resulting four-dimensional object was rotated about a plane in four-dimensional space according to the appropriate matrix transformations. The transformed object, projected back into three-dimension space, became a space-frame of variant dimensions. The skin was not extruded into the fourth dimension but instead remapped to create a rippling, non-homogeneous surface. ✦

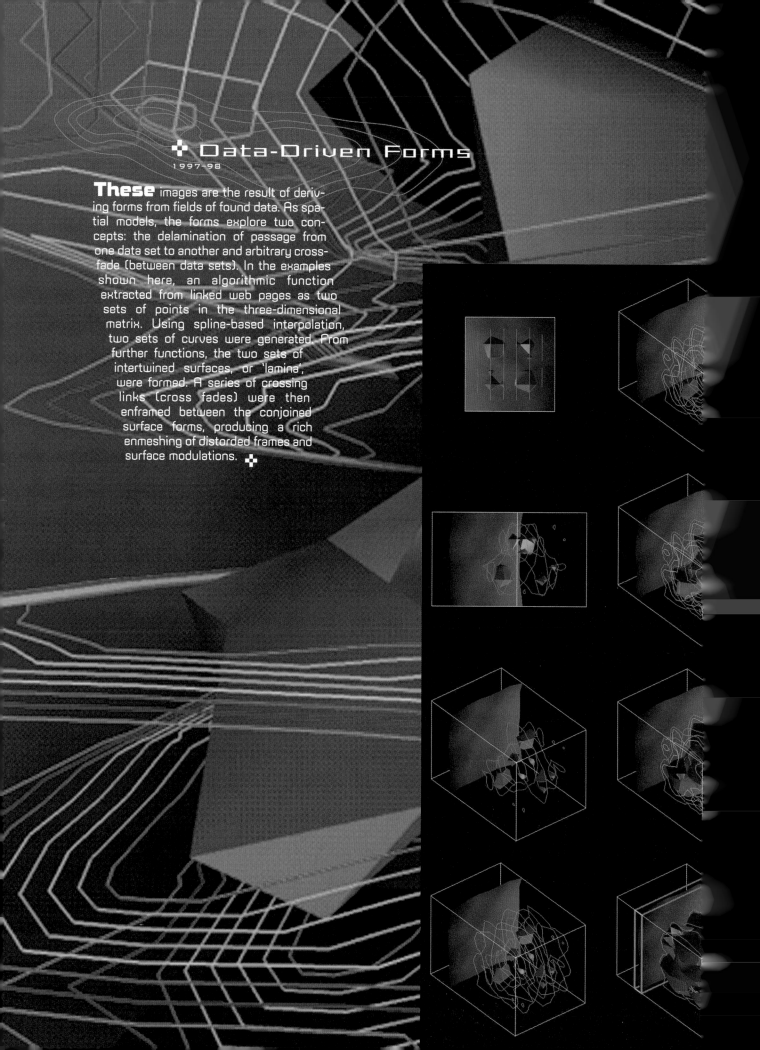

✦ Data-Driven Forms
1997-98

These images are the result of deriving forms from fields of found data. As spatial models, the forms explore two concepts: the delamination of passage from one data set to another and arbitrary cross-fade (between data sets). In the examples shown here, an algorithmic function extracted from linked web pages as two sets of points in the three-dimensional matrix. Using spline-based interpolation, two sets of curves were generated. From further functions, the two sets of intertwined surfaces, or 'lamina', were formed. A series of crossing links (cross fades) were then enframed between the conjoined surface forms, producing a rich enmeshing of distorded frames and surface modulations. ✦

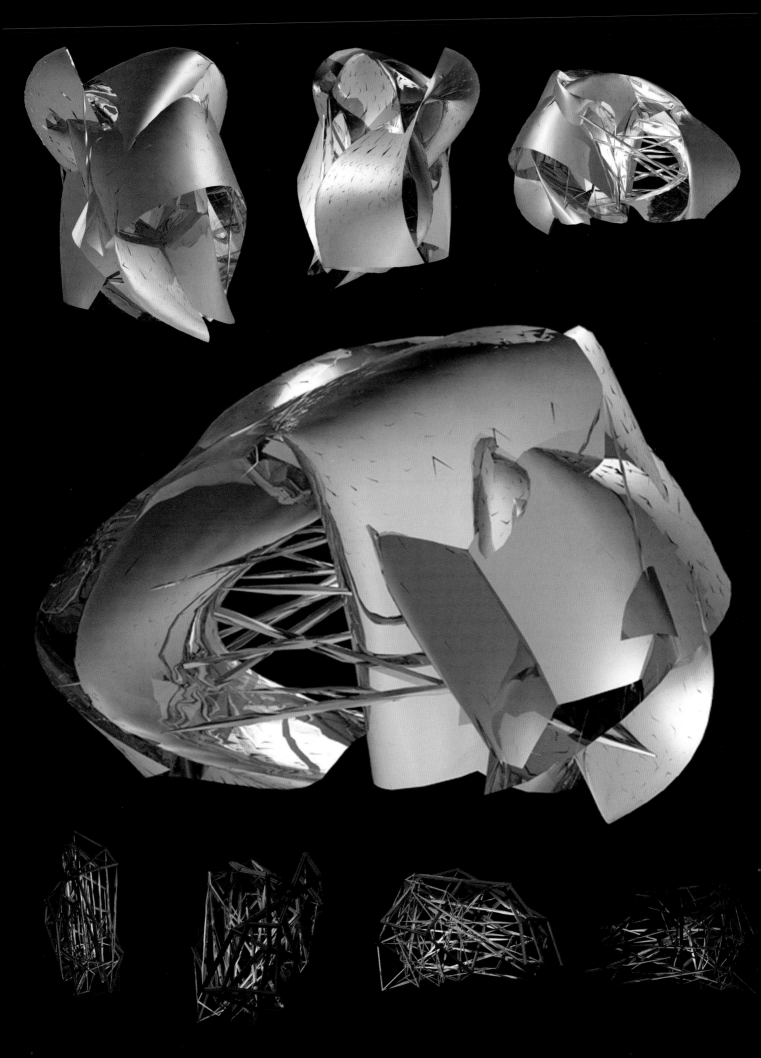

Liquid Process

✦ Marcos Novak

Marcos Novak
Doctoral studies, University of California, Los Angeles
Certificate of Specialization in Computer-Aided Architectural Design, Ohio
     State University, Colombus, Ohio
Master of Architecture, Ohio State University, Colombus
Bachelor of Science in Architecture, Ohio State University, Colombus

Teaching
2000–1999 Center for Advanced Inquiry in the Interactive Arts,
     University of Wales
2000–1998 Foundation of Transarchitectures (co-director with Paul
     Virilio), Paris
1999–98 Department of Design, University of California, Los Angeles
1999–96 Center for Digital Arts, University of California, Los Angeles
1999–96 University of California, Los Angeles
1996–89 University of Texas, Austin
1987–83 Ohio State University, Colombus

Principal projects
1999 'Variable Data Forms'
1997/98 'Paracube'; 'Data Driven Forms'; 'Sensor Space'; 'Interactive
     Environments'; 'Transarchitectures and Transmodernity';'From
     Immersion to Eversion'; 'Transmitting Architecture'; 'Information
     Spatialization'; 'Metadata Visualization'; 'Liquid
     Architectures';'Algorithm and Invention'; 'The Music of
     Architecture'; Worldmaking'; 'Poetics of New Technologies';
     'Computational Composition'; 'Design Machine'

Principal publications
1999 'Avatarchitectures: Fashioning Vishnu after Spacetime' *From
     Energy to Information*, Stanford University Press, Palo Alto,
     California
1998 'Next Babylon: Algorithm To Play In', *The Art of the Accident* NAI
     Publishers, V2 Organization, Rotterdam; *Architectural Design* no.
     136; 'Transarchitectures and Hypersurfaces: Operations of

Transmodernity' *Architectural Design* no. 133; 'The Architecture of
Augmented Spacetime' *Transarchitectures in Cyberspace: Ten
Architects Who Stimulate the World*, Nikkei Architecture, Tokyo;
'Entretien Marcos Novak/Kas Oosterhuis' *Duography Kas
Oosterhuis, architect, Ilona Lénard, visual artist*, 010 Publishers,
Rotterdam
1997 'Indirection: Speaking in Tongues' exhibition catalogue,
     Transarchitectures 02: cyber-espace et théories émergentes,
     AFAA/Architecture et Prospective, Paris; 'Transmitting
     Architecture: The Transphysical City' *Digital Delirium*, St Martin
     Press, New York; 'Cognitive Cities: Intelligence, Environment and
     Space' *Intelligent Environments*, Springer Verlag, Germany;
     'Transarchitectures: Inhabiting Spacetime' *Space Design* no. 391,
     Tokyo
1996 'Dancing With the Virtual Dervish: Worlds in Progress' *Immersed in
     Technology: The Art and Virtual Environments Project*, MIT Press,
     Cambridge (March); 'transArchitecture: Building the Edge of
     Thought' *10+1* no. 6, Inax, Tokyo; 'Cyborg Cities' *Journal of
     Architecture and Building Science*, vol. III no. 1390, Architectural
     Institute of Japan, Tokyo; 'The Media of Dis/Embodment' *Aris 2*,
     Journal of the Carnegie Mellon Department of Architecture,
     Carnegie Mellon University Press, Pittsburgh

NETHERLANDS

NOX

| Lars Spuybroek (*1959) |

NOX is a design office that has produced videos, installations, a magazine, texts and architecture. This hybrid production stemmed from their unease with the limited possibilities for development within the field of architecture and with the notion that it had got stuck within the territory architecture had created for itself in the early 1990s. NOX has, by a sort of genetic engineering in which architecture has been crossbred with other media, been able to generate a supple architecture that has nestled in the transitional area between two worlds, often thought of as parallel: one of biological organisms and the other, as diverse as the first, of the metallic and electronic fauna of modern technologies. NOX operates in that ever-growing twilight zone of blurring and fluidity. We are experiencing an extreme liquidizing of the world, of our language, of our gender, of our bodies. A situation where everything becomes mediated, where all matter and space are fused with their representations in media, where all form is blended with information. We are shifting from matter to substance, from solidity to grain and resolution, we are shifting from a space situation to a field condition. The liquid in itself is the substance of metamorphosis, of the in-between and the vectorial, of form constantly being informed by outside influences and inner coherence, expressed in a plastic metastability. Nothing, no object, no function can stay isolated; everything is always in a process of transformation to the next thing – everything is necessarily opened up and leaking. Nothing is treated as an element in space, but everything is stretched within a field of gradual or sudden changes. The fluid in architecture has earlier been associated with the easing back of architecture for human needs, of real-time fulfilment. But this soft technology of desire can only end up with the body as a residue, where its first steps in cyberspace will probably be its last steps. To NOX, the desire of technology seems far greater and a far more destabilizing force, as our need for the accidental is far greater than our need for comfort, and our need for potentialities and events is far greater than our need for determination and function. The liquid in architecture not only means generating the geometry of the fluid and the turbulent, it also means the dissolving of all that is solid and crystalline in architecture, that is, not only its materiality, but even the functional and programmatic, and especially the orthogonal basis of perception in which the horizontality of the floor crosses the verticality of the window. With the fluid merging of skin and environment, body and space, object and speed, we will also merge plan and volume, floor and screen, surface and interface, and discard the mechanistic view of the body in favour of a more plastic, liquid and haptic version where action and vision are synthesized. ❖

LARS SPUYBROEK

Tommy
1998

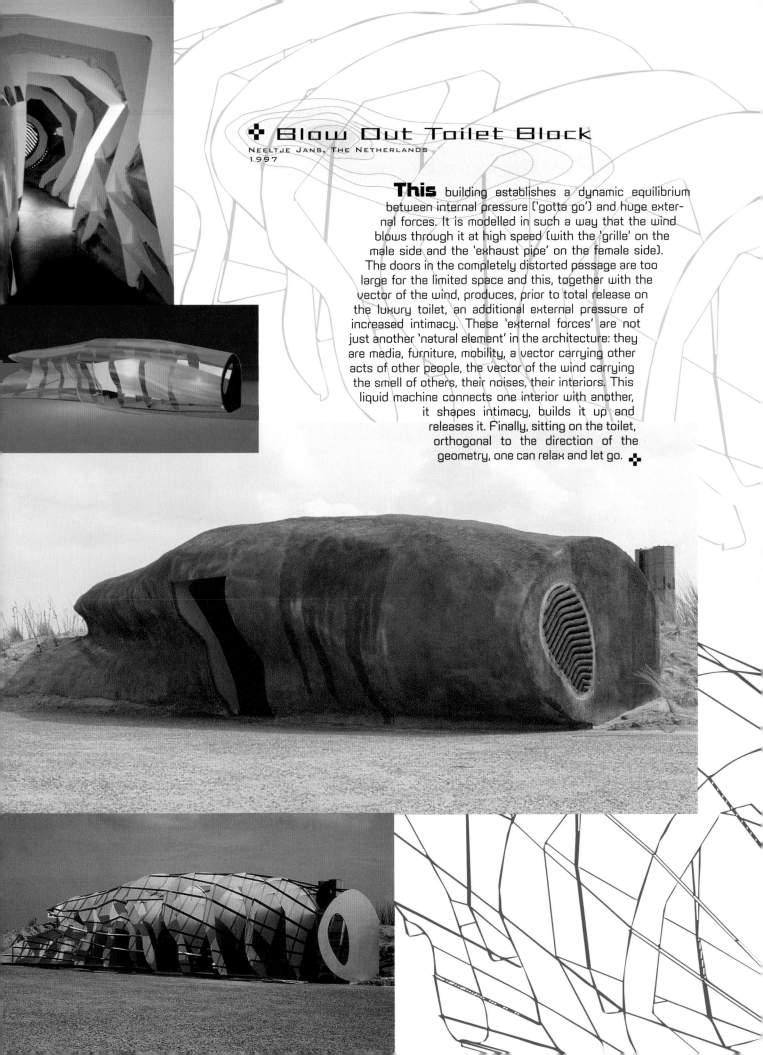

✦ Blow Out Toilet Block

NEELTJE JANS, THE NETHERLANDS
1997

This building establishes a dynamic equilibrium between internal pressure ('gotta go') and huge external forces. It is modelled in such a way that the wind blows through it at high speed (with the 'grille' on the male side and the 'exhaust pipe' on the female side). The doors in the completely distorted passage are too large for the limited space and this, together with the vector of the wind, produces, prior to total release on the luxury toilet, an additional external pressure of increased intimacy. These 'external forces' are not just another 'natural element' in the architecture: they are media, furniture, mobility, a vector carrying other acts of other people, the vector of the wind carrying the smell of others, their noises, their interiors. This liquid machine connects one interior with another, it shapes intimacy, builds it up and releases it. Finally, sitting on the toilet, orthogonal to the direction of the geometry, one can relax and let go. ✦

✦ Fresh H₂O eXPO

WATER PAVILION AND INTERACTIVE INSTALLATION
NEELTJE JANS, THE NETHERLANDS
1997

This pavilion is a turbulent alloy of the hard and the weak, of human flesh, concrete and metal, interactive electronics and water. A complete fusion of body, environment and technology. The design was based on the metastable aggregation of architecture and information. The form itself is shaped by the fluid deformation of fourteen ellipses spaced out over a length of more than 65 metres. Inside the building, which has no horizontal floors and no external relation to the horizon, walking becomes akin to falling. The deformation of the object extends to the constant metamorphosis of the environment, which responds interactively to the visitors to the water pavilion via a variety of sensors, which register this constant reshaping of the human body called action. ✦

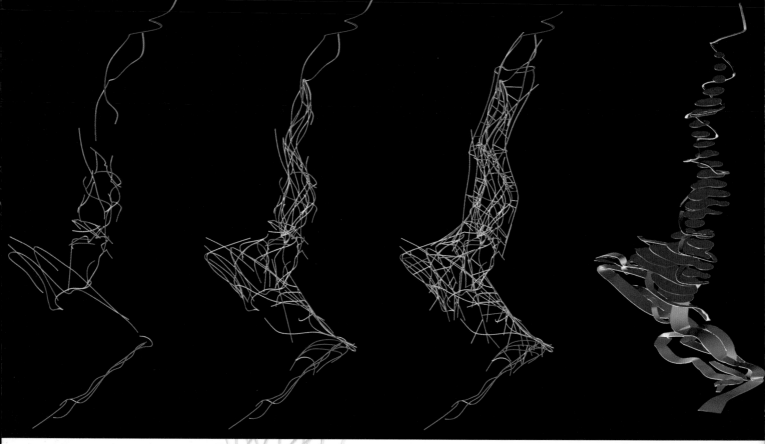

✦ Beachness

NEW PALACE HOTEL AND BOULEVARD
NOORDWIJK, THE NETHERLANDS, 1997

'Beachness' is defined here as a certain state of mobility, because the beach should be primarily conceived as a field in which everything is in a state of openness and non-fixation. This is a loose architecture of light materials, wood and fabric, and also sand, which is used for a highway when wet and for a bed or a chair when it is soft. Everything is mobile and moveable furniture. Bodies, fabric, sand, cars: as long as everything remains soft and in motion, it remains coherent – like a swarm. Where Noordwijk is concerned, this is being expressed in a two-part design: the boulevard and the New Palace Hotel. Both parts are linked in terms of content and both are based on two characteristics of soft matter: plasticity and memory. On the one hand, this implies the capability to move and to transform and on the other hand the ability to 'imprint' multiple movements (the traces in the sand, the browning of the skin, scorch marks on the fabric), to remember these and to let these interact with actual movements. ✦

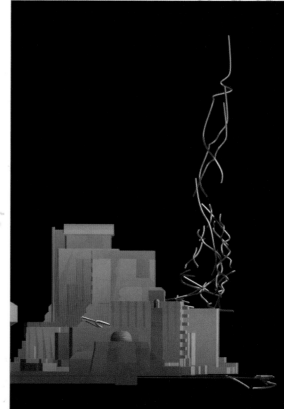

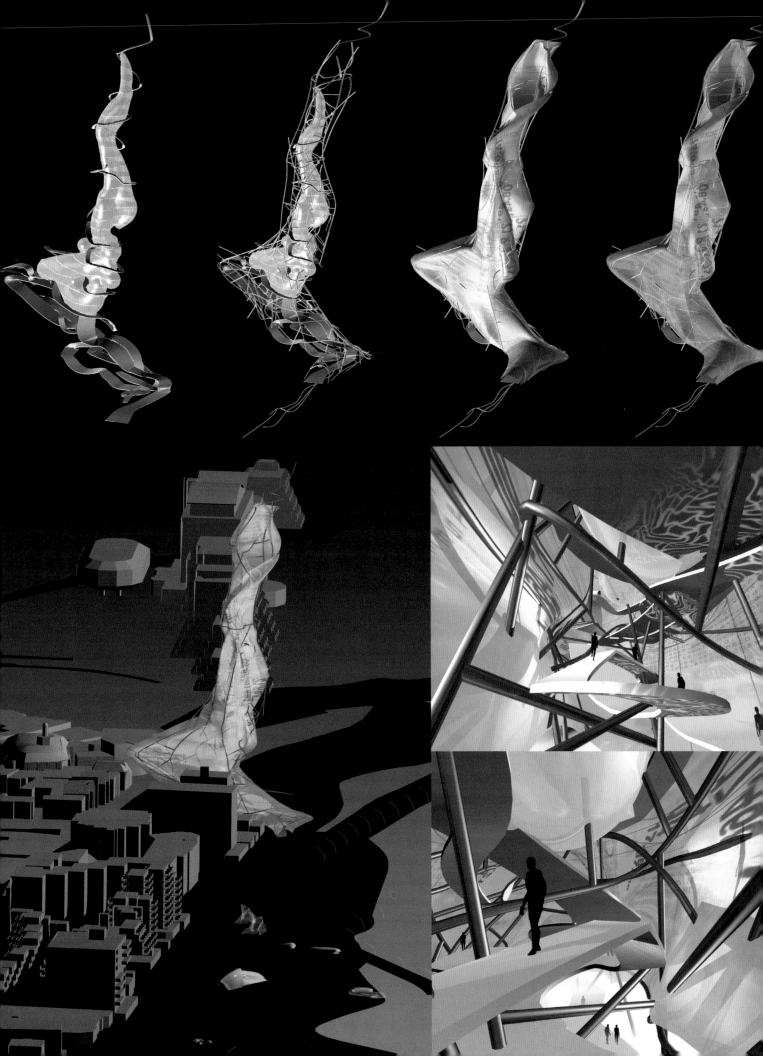

V2 Lab is part of a larger concept for the (future) renovation of the entire V2 building, which will include a conversion of the façade and hall, as well as the insertion of an extra floor for public activities (book-shop, café and lecture space) in the large exhibition space on the ground floor. This concept, called V2 Engine, has been developed in its entirety by computer with animation software, which allows for a non-linear and time-dependent architecture. V2 Engine consists of a central void, which will be partially finished with synthetic translucent fabric and will protrude noticeably from the facade. This space will be filled mainly with sounds and images, generated by a specially developed software engine that will roam the internet in search of webcam images of other façades around the world. These images are then projected from the inside on to the fabric of the façade. This architecture acts as carrier and the media as image. ✦

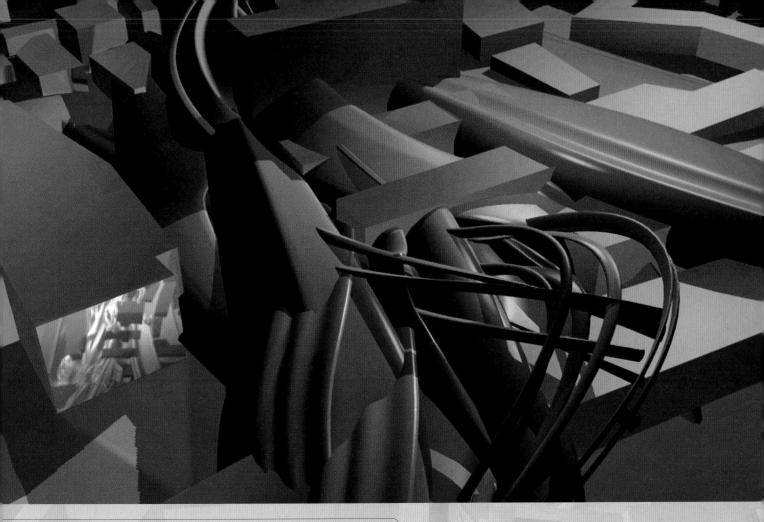

✦ ПОХ

Lars Spuybroek (1959)
Diploma in Architecture from the Technical University, Delft
1989 Archiprix (first prize)
1991 Mart Stam (encouragement prize)
1997 Iakov Chernikov (mentioned)
1998 Zeeuwse Architecture Prize

Teaching
1998–2000 Columbia University, New York; Technical University, Delft; Technical University, Eindhoven; Berlage Institute, Amsterdam

Principal buildings and projects
1999 OffTheRoad part II, housing and anti-noise barrier, Eindhoven
1998 'Tommy', pottery for Cor Unum, Den Bosch; OffTheRoad/103.8 Mhz, housing and anti-noise barrier, Eindhoven; V2 MediaLab, conversion, Rotterdam; 'Flying Attic', installation, Arnhem; The New Man of Cacharel, perfume bottle, Amsterdam; Goesgoes, Goes, Zeeland; Cheers! (A glass for Kristin Feireiss, 10 years old, NAI); Two-D-Tower, media tower, Doetinchem, with Q. S. Serafijn; '2001-future. com' (expo Bielefeld, for UBS, Switzerland, with Harm Lux and Mike Tyler)
1997 Edit Sp(l)ine, interactive installation at freshH2O eXPO, Zeeland; Blow Out, toilet block, Zeeland; Foam Home, dwellings, near Nijmegen, Netherlands (project); Beachness, coastal hotel, Noordwijk, project; V2 Engine, interactive façade for the V2 Organization, Rotterdam
1994 'Excessive Force', entrance installation for the V2 Organization, Rotterdam; The Laboratories; freshH2O eXPO (1994–97), water pavilion, Neeltje Jans, Zeeland
1993 1001 PK, Amsterdam; Centropa, Austria; Full Moon

Recent exhibitions
1999 'Deep Surface', Installation, Galerie Exedra, Hilversum, Netherlands
1998 'Arquitectura Virtual' Belem Cultural Centre, Lisbon, Portugal; 'NearDeathHotel' Walker Art Center, Minneapolis
1998–97 'transArchitectures 02/03' IFA Paris, New York, Graz, Los Angeles, Bordeaux, Monte Carlo, Brussels, Rotterdam, Vienna; 'NINE + One: Ten young Dutch architects', Rotterdam, Los Angeles, New York, São Paolo, Vienna, Berlin
1997 'NOX Sixty Minutes' video installation – individual expo, NAI, Rotterdam

Publications
1998 *The Art of the Accident* DEAF98, V2 Organization, and festival (graphic designer, collaborator and publisher)
1995 *NOX D, Jihad* (1001, Amsterdam)
1993 *NOX C, Chloroform* (1001, Amsterdam)
1992 *NOX B, Biotech* (1001, Amsterdam)
1991 *NOX A, Actiones in distans* (1001, Amsterdam); FORUM (publisher 1994 to 1998)
1997 *FORUM 39, #4: MASSA/MASS* (A and A, Amsterdam)
1996 *FORUM 38, #3: HET PUBLIEKE/THE PUBLIC* (A and A, Amsterdam)
1995 *FORUM 38, #1/2: COMFORT/COMFORT* (A and A, Amsterdam)

Principal publications
1998 'Where space gets lost' *The Art of the Accident*, V2 Organization; 'The motorization of reality' *Archis* (Nov.)
1997 'Motor Geometry' *TechnoMorphica*, V2 Organization; *AD Profile* 'Hypersurface', no. 133; *Arch+* no. 138; *Space* no. 9902
1996 'SoftSite' V2 Organization, catalogue of Death 96.
1995 'X and Y and Z, a manual' with Maurice Nio, *Archis* (Nov.); 'Phantombody Phantomhouse' *FORUM 38, #1/2*
1994 'De Strategie van de Vorm' with Maurice Nio, *De Architect*; special issue 57 'De Remu formatie' with Maurice Nio, *De Architect* (Feb.)
1992 'Cybernetic Circus' *De Architect*, special issue 49; 'Jap Tek Anima' *De Architect* (Nov.)

Selected bibliography
1998 'Constructing Atmospheres En Route to a New Tectonics', Bart Lootsma, *Daidalos* no. 68; 'Rethinking mobility', *Quaderns* no. 218; *Profile* no. 138; 'Architects in Cyberspace II' *AD* vol. 68

Objectile

| Patrick Beaucé (*1960) | Bernard Cache (*1952) |

Series of objects may be at once similar and all different, a little like the way each dune in the desert represents a particular variation on the same morphological theme. These non-standard objects are not designed, but rather calculated by computer and industrially produced by digitally controlled machinery. After nearly ten years of development, Bernard Cache, Patrick Beaucé and Jean-Louis Jammot set up Objectile SARL in Paris in November 1996. Their purpose was to work on the creation and production of curved and variable forms on every scale: sculpture, design, furniture, building components, architecture, town planning and landscape. Taoufik Hammoudi worked with 'Objectile Paris' from February 1997 to May 1998. After an initial project, Stephen Fitzgerald is now opening 'Objectile New Zealand' in Christchurch, and working with Rayonler New Zealand to develop a new range of machinable board: 'Patinna Stress-free' MDF. Objectile has introduced an original production method based on the TopSolid software of the MISSLER group. Objectile is actually convinced that architectural creation now starts at the stage of software and technological tools. With the Objectile software, forms are not designed or drawn, but calculated. For with calculation it is possible to design complex curved surfaces whose slight variations cannot be controlled by traditional CAD. Each form may produce an unlimited number of variations, which are presented in the form of interactive video sequences. To make the most of these surface generation resources, Objectile has developed a machining program-writing module that makes it possible to manufacture these series of objects — all of them different — industrially, on digitally controlled machines. So Objectile is in a position where it can guarantee its customers the technical and economic feasibility of their projects, no matter how complicated they may be, from the design stage on. Objectile has accordingly produced for the French Railways (SNCF) a ticket-office model with curved surfaces, which can be produced unit by unit on digitally controlled machinery, and can also be adapted to the situation specific to each particular station. Architecturally speaking, Objectile pays very special attention to secondary components that may become the medium of contemporary decoration. For Objectile, electronic architecture should not be restricted to major demonstrative projects; on the contrary, it should have to do with the most humdrum of buildings. As a result, Objectile has developed lines of decorative boards, which help, for example, to differentiate doors in office corridors, and create series of facing. ❖

BERNARD CACHE

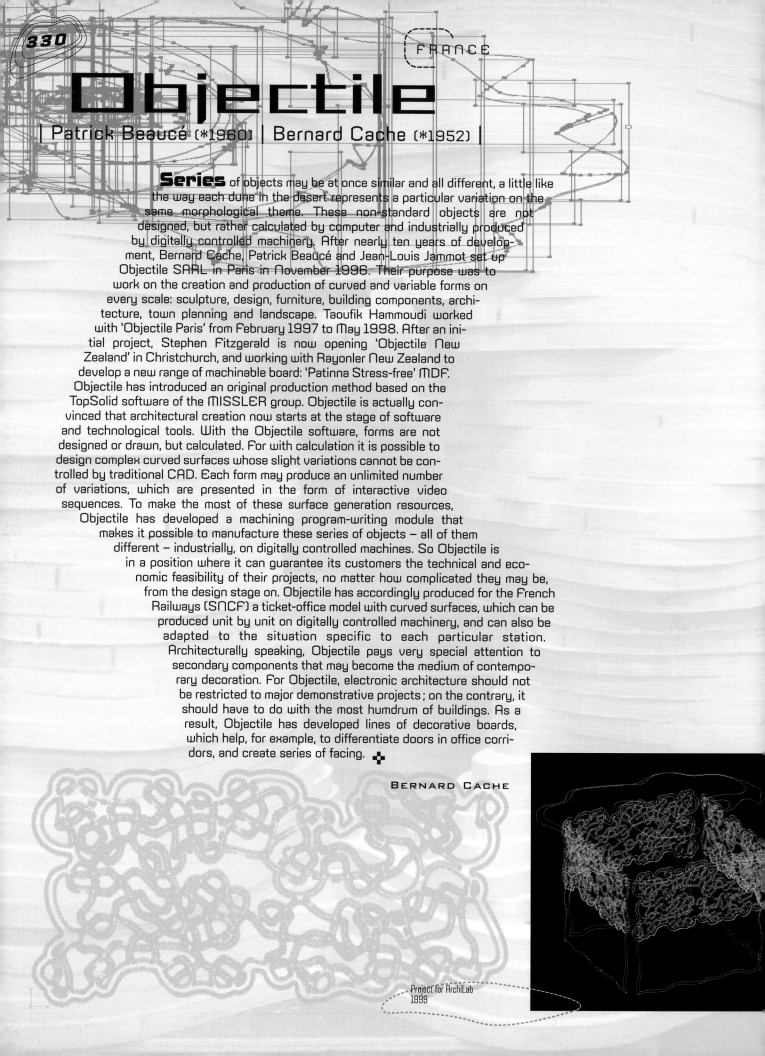

Project for ArchiLab
1999

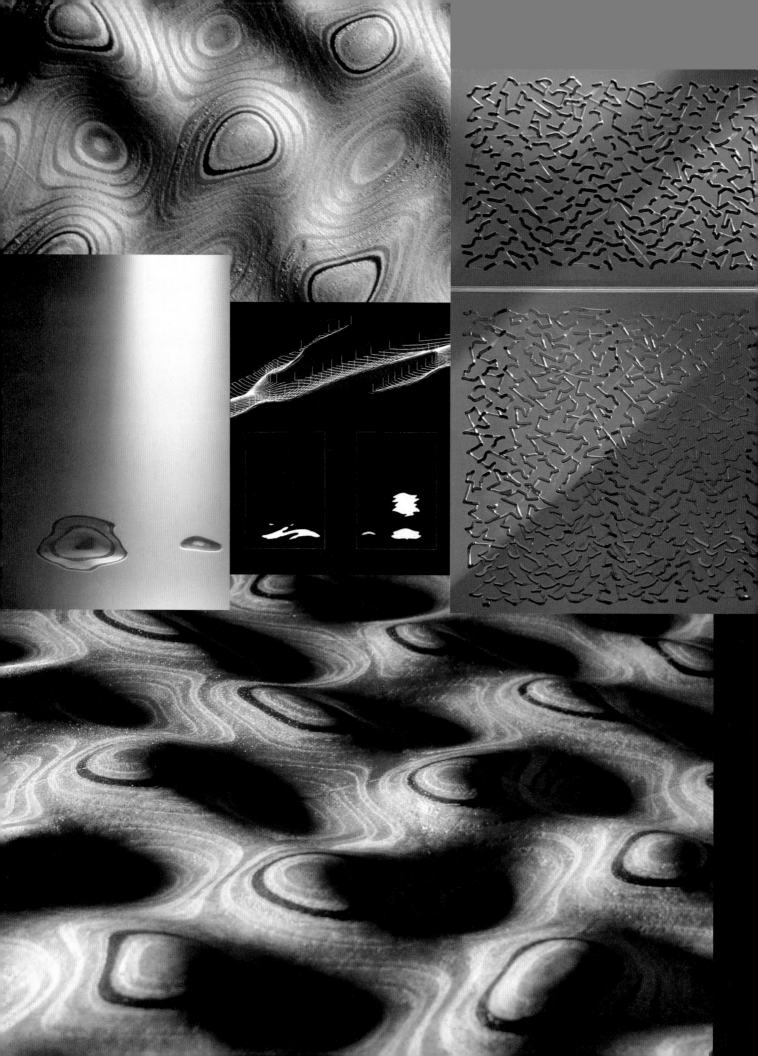

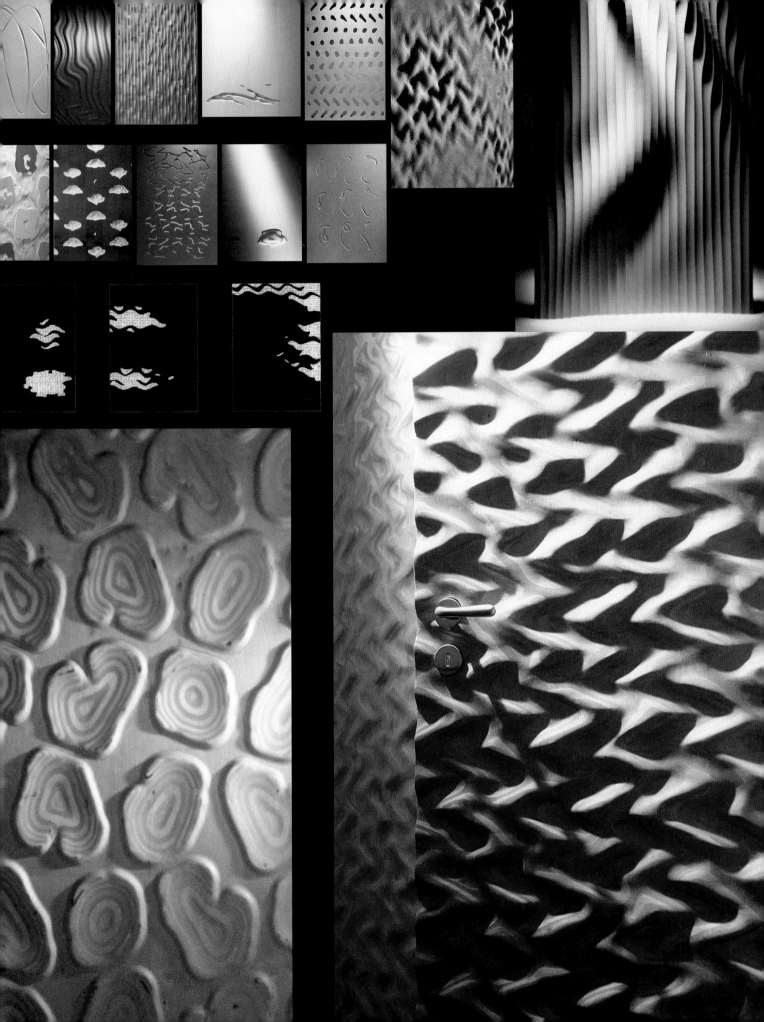

Making a virtue out of necessity
As part of ArchiLab, Objectile made further investigations into the work of Gottfried Semper. The project also acts as a commentary where technology is inseparable from a form of anthropology. Broadly speaking, this project is extremely simple: a cube turned 60 degrees, thus showing its main side to the entrance of the large exhibition hall. Every possible attention has been given to the calculation of the fluid elements and the complex textures, but it is also part of a right-angled geometry with flat sides, which is the very condition of the existence of architecture. Each of the elements originates from a mathematical model that is open to variation. So the pavilion built is just one specific case in an unlimited series entirely produced by digitally controlled machines. The elements of this Pavilion are four in number, in compliance with the organization of Gottfried Semper's thinking in *Die Vier Elemente der Baukunst*. The mound or plinth, which for Semper must insulate the building from the damp ground beneath it and protect it from flooding, has itself become fluid by its undulations, its outline and its texture. We thus go along with the fact that we do not find any solid foundation, which does not prevent us from building. Every aspect of it has been included in several layers of mathematical design, which was nothing new to Semper, who wrote an essay about the section of projectiles dispatched by catapults. The walls in themselves are reduced to vertical, screen-like enclosures with interwoven motifs. They are not load-bearing. They serve solely to enclose the area and clad it, as it were. The fretwork and tracery were produced by modulation algorithms- part above, part below — which represent the actual procedure of the textile. We should point out that the Semperian textile, from which the basic motifs of architecture originate, can in no way be reduced to fabric. Rather, it has to do with a cross-wise procedure that finds a chance to differentiate itself from the most varied of materials: wood, ceramics, metal and so on. At the same time, fretwork and tracery are basic tattooing patterns, which we have dealt with freely on the basis of a quasi-periodic graph. Because of the lighting system, the fretwork represents a kind of inner fabric that projects its motifs on the outer sheath of the room where the pavilion is installed. The roof is self-supporting; it is the architectonic crown of the pavilion, which does not alter the fact that it comes from models developed in the field of furniture. Furniture comes before edifice. These, in particular, are the models that Objectile has used to produce its series of 'Nymphea/Water Lily' tables. The shift to the scale of the building obviously has effects on the technique for manufacturing new boardsm which are assembled to make the roof. These boards in themselves form a series of variable elements, whose manufacturing process must be organized as such. Two holes are made in the roof, and these assume the property of that fundamental Semperian feature, the hearth, which lends the space a torus-like topology. Objectile borrows this element by adopting a multi-hearth perspective - the hearths themselves being deliberately off-centre. ✦

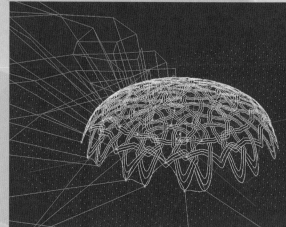

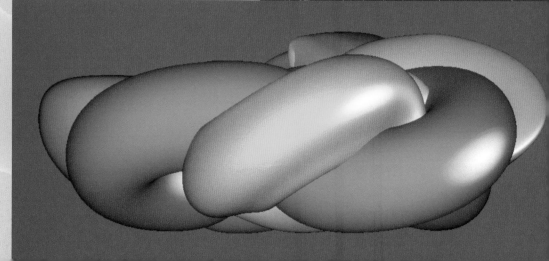

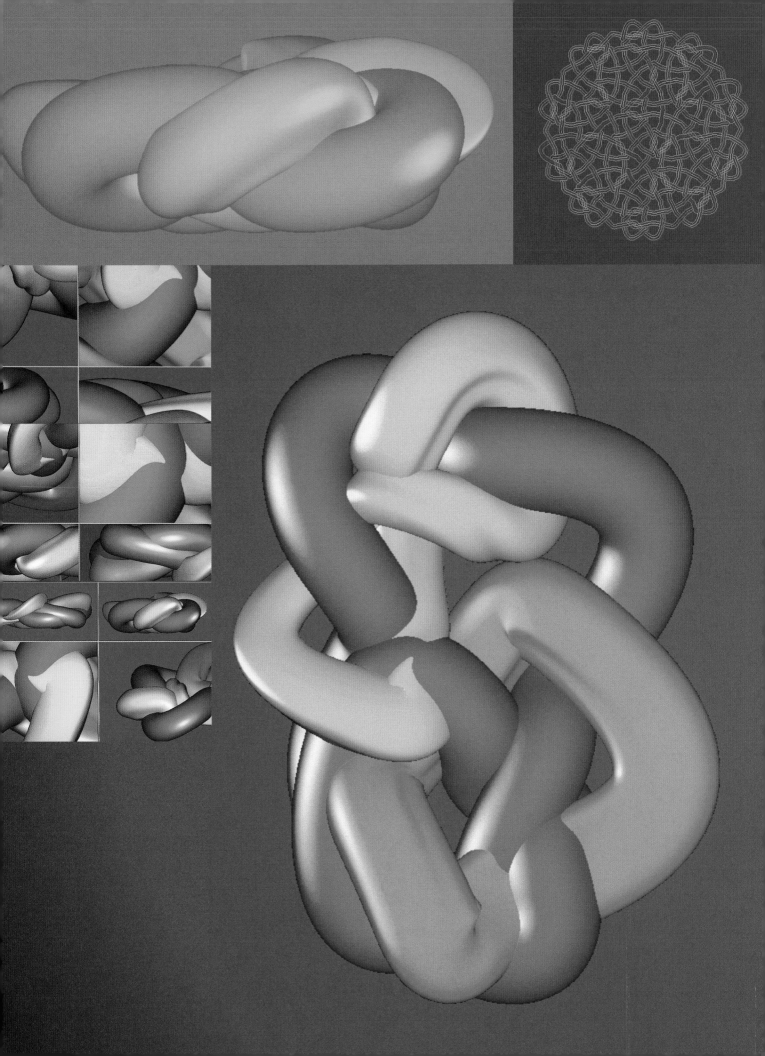

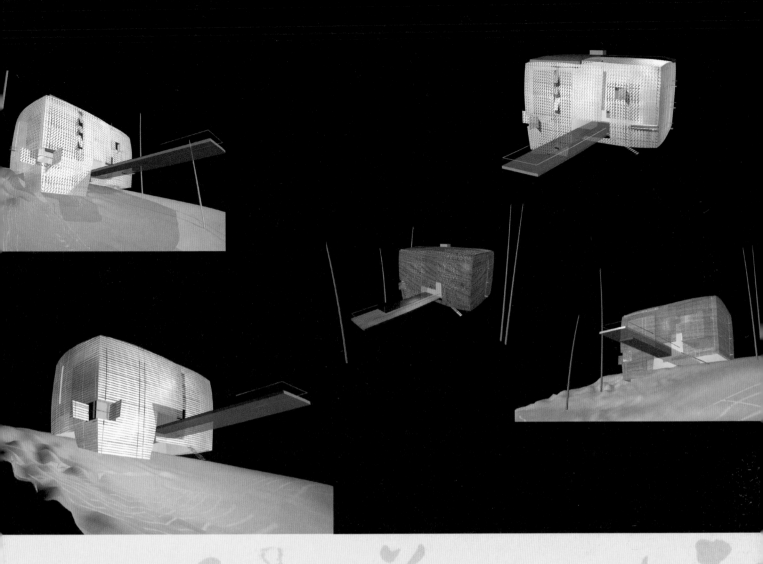

✛ Objectile

Patrick Beaucé (1960)
 Artist-designer DNS Expression Plastique, directed by Claude
 Viallat

Bernard Cache (1958)
 Architect, diploma from the Polytechnique Fédérale de Lausanne;
 diploma from the Institut de Philosophie, under the direction of
 Gilles Deleuze, and diploma from the Ecole Supérieure des
 Sciences Economiques et Commerciales; Director of Studies at
 BIPE, expert in telecommunication of images and digital television
1997 Gold medal for innovation, Bâtimat

Teaching
1999–98 Patrick Beaucé: Ecole des Beaux-Arts de Valenciennes;
 Bernard Cache: has taught humanities at ESSEC and information
 economics at the Institut Français de la Presse and currently teaches at the University of Toronto

Principal buildings and projects
1997 Pallas House with dECOi, Kuala Lumpur; Extension of Schiphol
 Airport, consultant with Ove Arup
Production – Realization of sculptures calculated by computer and manufactured by digitally operated machines, series of decorative wood
 panels (acoustic panels, partitions, false ceilings, doors) and tables
 (office, bistro, etc.)
Industrial design and building components – Series of ticket offices for railway stations of SNCF de Paris, Bld Henri Martin, Enghien,
 Pierrefittes, Villeneuve St Georges

Recent exhibitions
1998 FRAC centre, Orléans (June–September)
1997 VPR One (autumn); 'Trans-Architecture 02' IFA (summer);
 Columbia University, NY (autumn); 'Computers images' Imagina,
 Paris

Principal publications (Bernard Cache)
1998 *Objectile*, HYX/FRAC Centre
1997 *Terre meuble*, HYX
1995 *Earth Moves*, MIT
 Author of political economics articles on the media and telecommunications and of articles in architecture journals (*ANY*)

Selected bibliography
1996 *Wiederhall* (Jun.)
1995 *Chimères* (winter); *De Architect* (printemps); *Journal of Philosophy
 and Visual Arts* (autumn)
1994 *Faces* (spring); *ANY* (March-April), *Wiederhall* (Jun.)

O.C.E.A.N. UK

[Tom Verebes (*1965)]

O.C.E.A.N. UK is the original London branch of the O.C.E.A.N. network. It is run today by Tom Verebes (founder member with Michael Hensel). O.C.E.A.N. was foun-ded on a collective basis in 1995 by group of people with many and varied intellectual and geographical outlooks, but all sharing a common forum, whose connected synergy would seem to be located in the Architectural Association. Of the founder members, most of them – like the Hungarian-Canadian Tom Verebes, the German Michael Hensel and the Slovene Bostjan Vuga.– are actually products of AA training. This architectural collective thus brings together, above all, members of a spontaneously international generation, concerned with the global nature of the phenomena of identity and culture, generating a mobility that is at once geographical and disciplinary. O.C.E.A.N. is nei-ther an acronym nor a metaphor: its members are adamant about this. Does it all the same refer to the prophecy made by Robert Venturi, who, in 1968, dreamed of an authentically oceanic form of city planning? Behind this name, nevertheless, we can detect several images. Above all, horizontality. O.C.E.A.N. is not an agency as such; its structure is neither hierarchic nor vertical. O.C.E.A.N. is a network, a paradigmatic form of the contemporary world. It is decentralized, dynamic, horizontally distributed; it is ramified in geographical and intellectual space. Since its inception, O.C.E.A.N. has embraced a number of affiliated studios, including O.C.E.A.N. UK in London, O.C.E.A.N. Oslo (Johan Bettum), O.C.E.A.N. Helsinki (Kivi Sotamaa), O.C.E.A.N. Cologne (Michael Hensel), O.C.E.A.N. US (Robert Elfer, Wade Stevens) in Boston and Sadar in Vuga Arhitekti in Ljubljana. Today it is known simply as O.C.E.A.N. and continues to reorganize itself and to evolve around new nodal points. Each centre is run on the basis of at once indepen-dent and interdependent studios, acting and interacting, exploring, on a multidis-ciplinary basis, current practices in city planning, architecture, design, graphic design and even art. Based on participation and communication, the intent behind this network is to be the active and operational vehicle of an intellectual project, which is preoccupied not only by reconnecting architectural thinking and doing, but above all by updating models and concepts in a world that is itself being transformed by the development of digital technologies. Alongside its quest for new materials and new building procedures, O.C.E.A.N. is also actively involved in the different forms of the dissemination (publication), transmis-sion (instruction and teaching) and production (university research) of architectural cul-ture. The network structure of O.C.E.A.N. is itself the working hypothesis of a new way of organizing architectural praxis, open to its new tools and its new territories. ✦

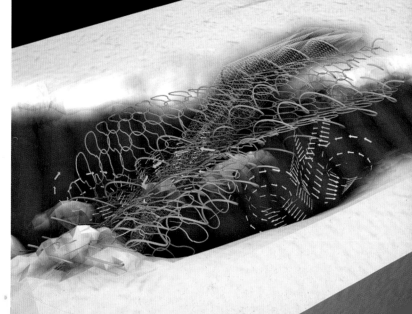

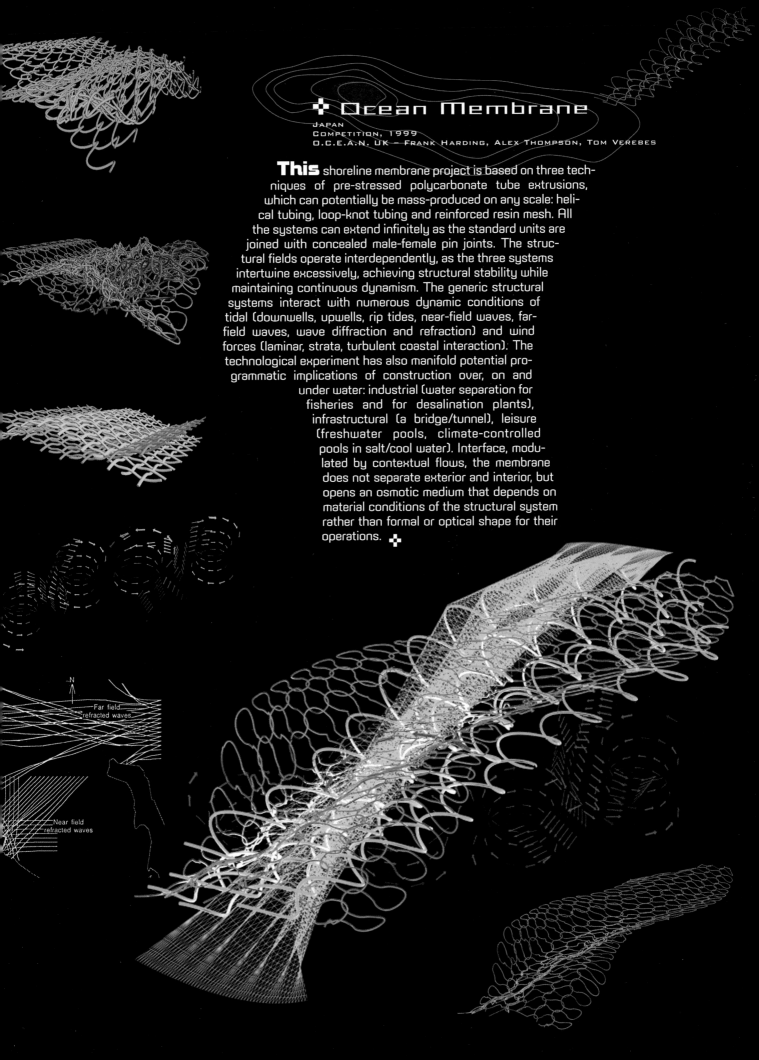

✛ Ocean Membrane

JAPAN
COMPETITION, 1999
O.C.E.A.N. UK — FRANK HARDING, ALEX THOMPSON, TOM VEREBES

This shoreline membrane project is based on three techniques of pre-stressed polycarbonate tube extrusions, which can potentially be mass-produced on any scale: helical tubing, loop-knot tubing and reinforced resin mesh. All the systems can extend infinitely as the standard units are joined with concealed male-female pin joints. The structural fields operate interdependently, as the three systems intertwine excessively, achieving structural stability while maintaining continuous dynamism. The generic structural systems interact with numerous dynamic conditions of tidal (downwells, upwells, rip tides, near-field waves, far-field waves, wave diffraction and refraction) and wind forces (laminar, strata, turbulent coastal interaction). The technological experiment has also manifold potential programmatic implications of construction over, on and under water: industrial (water separation for fisheries and for desalination plants), infrastructural (a bridge/tunnel), leisure (freshwater pools, climate-controlled pools in salt/cool water). Interface, modulated by contextual flows, the membrane does not separate exterior and interior, but opens an osmotic medium that depends on material conditions of the structural system rather than formal or optical shape for their operations. ✛

N

Far field
refracted waves

Near field
refracted waves

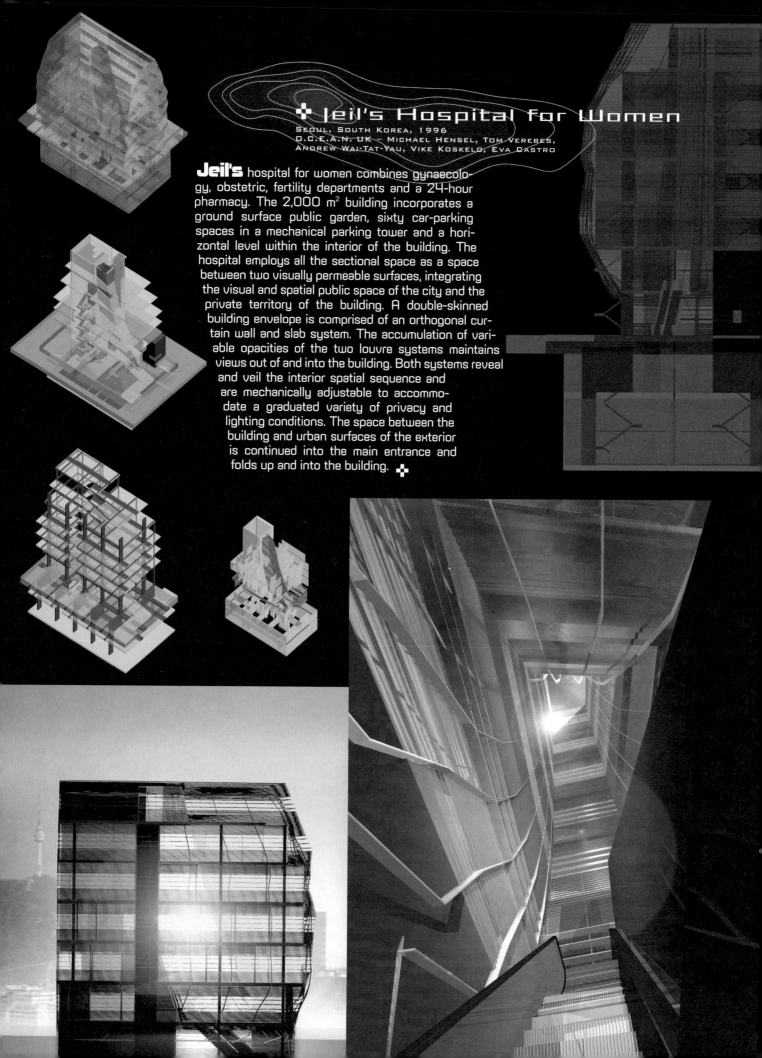

Jeil's Hospital for Women

SEOUL, SOUTH KOREA, 1996
O.C.E.A.N. UK – MICHAEL HENSEL, TOM VEREBES,
ANDREW WAI-TAT-YAU, VIKE KOSKELO, EVA CASTRO

Jeil's hospital for women combines gynaecology, obstetric, fertility departments and a 24-hour pharmacy. The 2,000 m² building incorporates a ground surface public garden, sixty car-parking spaces in a mechanical parking tower and a horizontal level within the interior of the building. The hospital employs all the sectional space as a space between two visually permeable surfaces, integrating the visual and spatial public space of the city and the private territory of the building. A double-skinned building envelope is comprised of an orthogonal curtain wall and slab system. The accumulation of variable opacities of the two louvre systems maintains views out of and into the building. Both systems reveal and veil the interior spatial sequence and are mechanically adjustable to accommodate a graduated variety of privacy and lighting conditions. The space between the building and urban surfaces of the exterior is continued into the main entrance and folds up and into the building. ✛

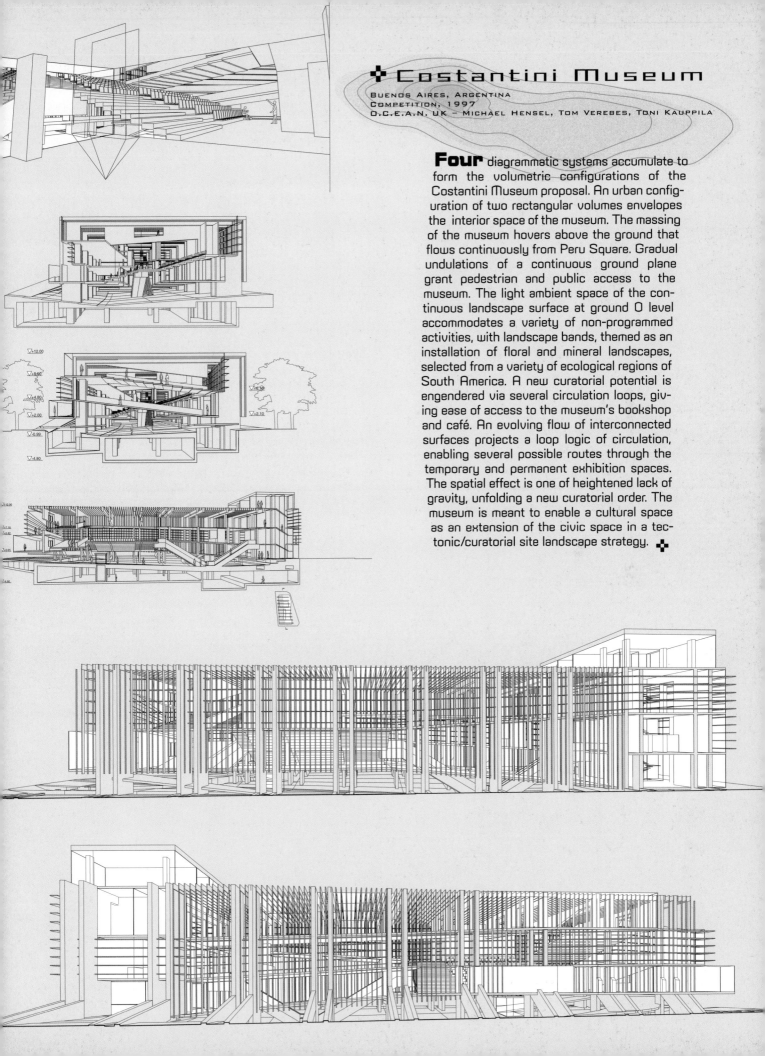

✛ Costantini Museum

Buenos Aires, Argentina
Competition, 1997
O.C.E.A.N. UK – Michael Hensel, Tom Verebes, Toni Kauppila

Four diagrammatic systems accumulate to form the volumetric configurations of the Costantini Museum proposal. An urban configuration of two rectangular volumes envelopes the interior space of the museum. The massing of the museum hovers above the ground that flows continuously from Peru Square. Gradual undulations of a continuous ground plane grant pedestrian and public access to the museum. The light ambient space of the continuous landscape surface at ground 0 level accommodates a variety of non-programmed activities, with landscape bands, themed as an installation of floral and mineral landscapes, selected from a variety of ecological regions of South America. A new curatorial potential is engendered via several circulation loops, giving ease of access to the museum's bookshop and café. An evolving flow of interconnected surfaces projects a loop logic of circulation, enabling several possible routes through the temporary and permanent exhibition spaces. The spatial effect is one of heightened lack of gravity, unfolding a new curatorial order. The museum is meant to enable a cultural space as an extension of the civic space in a tectonic/curatorial site landscape strategy. ✛

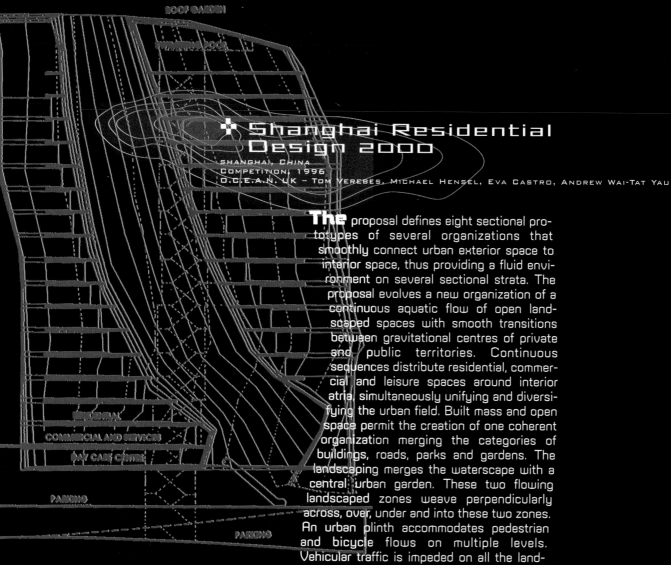

✛ Shanghai Residential Design 2000

SHANGHAI, CHINA
COMPETITION, 1996
O.C.E.A.N. UK – TOM VEREBES, MICHAEL HENSEL, EVA CASTRO, ANDREW WAI-TAT YAU

The proposal defines eight sectional prototypes of several organizations that smoothly connect urban exterior space to interior space, thus providing a fluid environment on several sectional strata. The proposal evolves a new organization of a continuous aquatic flow of open landscaped spaces with smooth transitions between gravitational centres of private and public territories. Continuous sequences distribute residential, commercial and leisure spaces around interior atria, simultaneously unifying and diversifying the urban field. Built mass and open space permit the creation of one coherent organization merging the categories of buildings, roads, parks and gardens. The landscaping merges the waterscape with a central urban garden. These two flowing landscaped zones weave perpendicularly across, over, under and into these two zones. An urban plinth accommodates pedestrian and bicycle flows on multiple levels. Vehicular traffic is impeded on all the landscaped and public pedestrian surfaces. Eight accesses to the service road system allow for a defined flow of cars to the towers. A new public transport link and commercial node integrate the site with the new metro station. ✛

PROTOTYPE 8

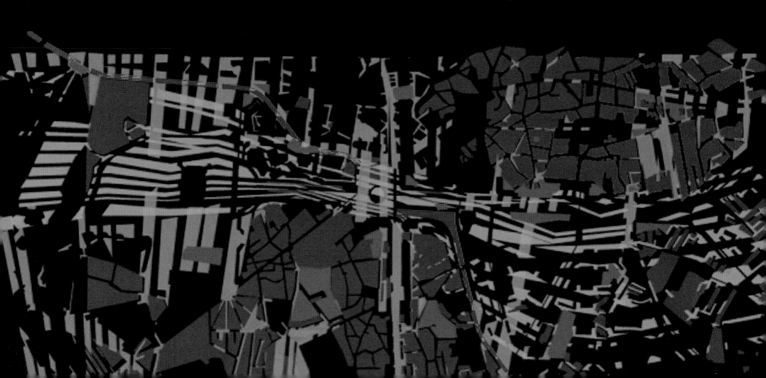

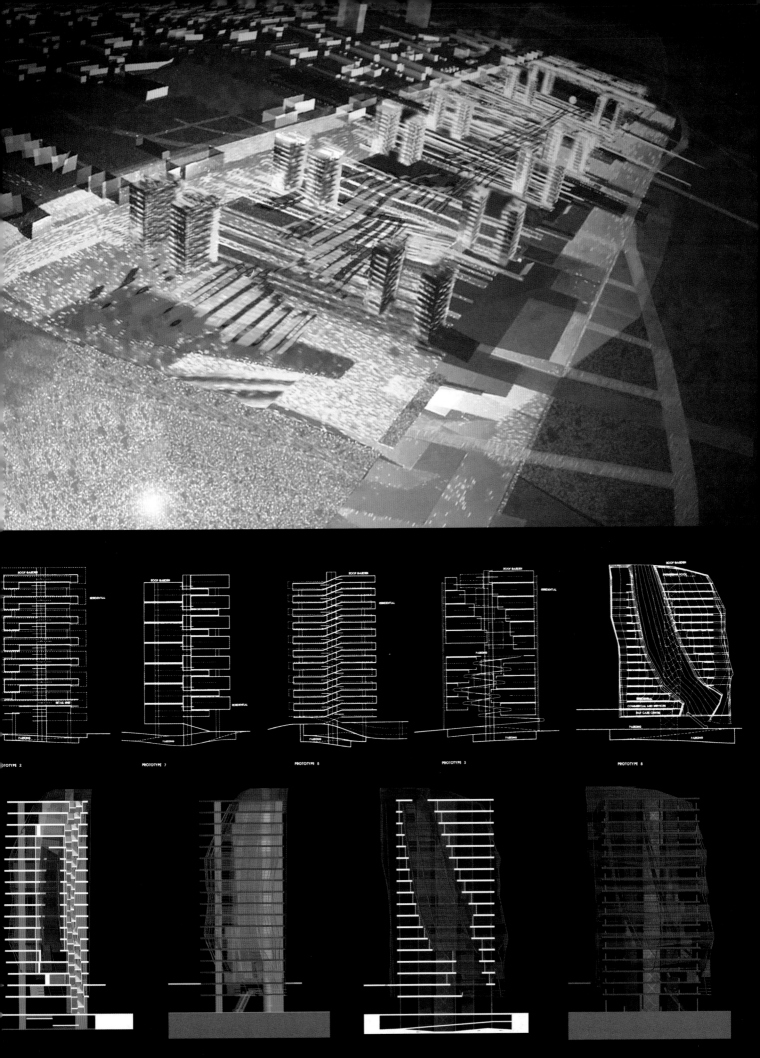

PROTOTYPE 2   PROTOTYPE 7   PROTOTYPE 6   PROTOTYPE 3   PROTOTYPE 8

✦ Tumbleweed™

FURNITURE RESEARCH PROJECT, PHASE 1, 2000
O.C.E.A.N. UK – TOM VEREBES, NATE KOLBE

The initial phase of Tumbleweed™ research intends to collate, renominate and transform categories of existing historical typologies of furnishing. A broad selection of twentieth-century furniture sections are sampled as a genetic code in their generation. The initial profiles emerge subverted and hybridized via radical exercises of abstraction and reconfiguration. They can be configured in a variety of scales. Extruded polycarbonate or aluminium tubing follow trajectories that generally describe highly lineated surfaces achieved from the accumulation of lines. The organization of the tubes follows three directions that converge in structurally necessitated laminations, and reorient to shift to adjacent laminated tubes. The surfaces of Tumbleweeds provides opportunities to be filled with foam, or sheathed with a loose inflatable skin, or wrapped in a tight skin. Tumbleweed's aim is to revise modes of production and consumption and codes of utility of furnishing objects. Devoid of fixed orientation, Tumleweeds roll with force exerted by the user, with differential states of stability. The occupant engages with Tumbleweed™ in unfamiliar tendential patterns, always on the verge of finding new ways to use the object. ✦

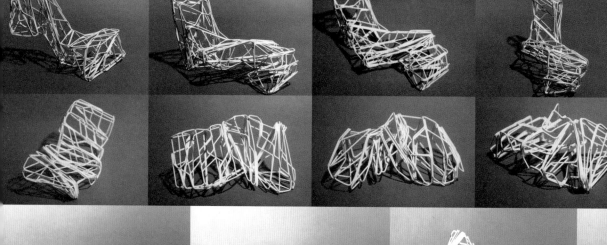

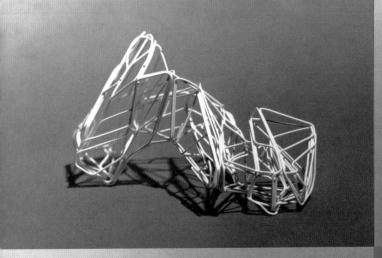
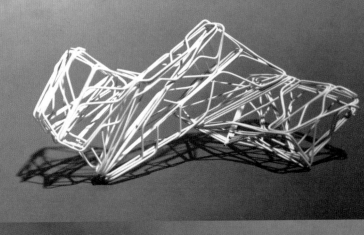
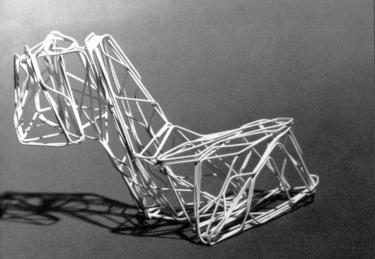
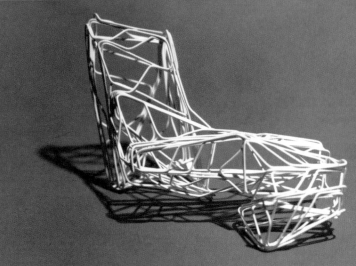

✦ O.C.E.A.N. UK

Tom Verebes (1965)
BSc Arch., B Arch., McGill University (Canada); AA Graduate Diploma (London)
Tom Verebes currently teaches at the Architectural Association School, London

Alexander Thompson (1967), associate
Diploma from School of Architecture, Heriot-Watt University (Edinburgh)

1995   Creation of the London branch of the interdisciplinary network O.C.E.A.N.

O.C.E.A.N. also has offices in Helsinki, Oslo, Ljubljana, Cologne and Boston

Principal buildings and projects
2000   Tumbleweed™ furniture (project); Martin Luther King Memorial (competition), Washington, D.C.; Museum of Modern and Contemporary Art (competition), Rome

1999   'Ocean Membrane', shoreline membrane design, Japan (competition); Four Residential Extensions/Conversions, London (under construction); Times Square Ticketing Booth (competition), New York; Operation Interface Installation, CCA, IFA website

1998   Dolce Vita couture clothing shop, London (realized); Verde 2000, Timisoara (project); Europan 5, Jeumont, France (competition); Flat Conversion, London (realized)

1997   'Urban Surface', public installation, Jyväskylä, Finland (project); Costantini Museum, Buenos Aires (competition); Lasipalatsi Media Square, Helsinki (competition); 'Future Vision for Kyoto' (competition); Kuala Lumpur Multi-use Complex, Malaysia (competition)

1996   Jeil's Hospital for Women, Seoul, Korea (project); 'Bucuresti 2000: Active Urban Projection' (competition); Shanghai Residential Design 2000, sectional prototypes (competition); Pusan High-Speed Railway Complex, Korea (competition)

1995   Arabianranta urban design, Helsinki (project)
1994   Yokohama Port Terminal, Japan (competition)

Selected bibliography
2000   *City Levels*, Nick Barley (ed.) Autumn/Birkhäuser, London/Basle; *Small City* Anders Johansson (ed.), KTH, Stockholm

1999   *Hybrid Space: New forms in Digital Architecture* Peter Zellner, Thames & Hudson, London; *Urbanisation* Michael Hensel and Tom Verebes, O.C.E.A.N. UK, Serial Books, Architecture & Urbanism no. 3, Black Dog Publishing Limited, London; *RIBA Journal* (Feb.); *l'Architecture d'aujourd'hui* (Sept.); *Wallpaper**

1998   *De Architekt*

1997   'After Geometry' *Architectural Design* (UK); 'Practice Profile' *Urban Design Quarterly* (UK); *Architectural Profile*, Thailand; *AA Files* no. 33; *Arch+*; *AB, arkitektov bilten* (Slovenia)

1996   *Gateway II: Managing Urban Change* UIAH, Finland

1995   'New Approaches in Contemporary Urban Design' *Arttu!* (Finland); *Space* (Korea); *Art 4D* (Thailand); *The Architecture of the Jumping Universe* Charles Jenks, Academy Editions, London

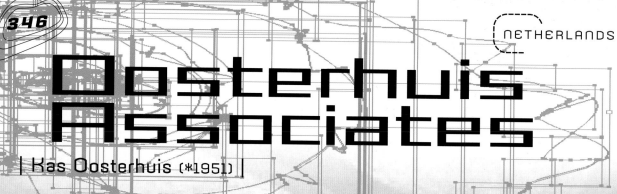

Oosterhuis Associates

| Kas Oosterhuis (*1951) |

We are physically situated under a common denominator with quarks, planets, ideas, language, programmes, radiation and light as the numerators. We are part of a vast information flow. We are information ourselves, and we swim about in abundant information. Life could be the power to direct the flow of information. The very notion of life seems to be the very opposite of entropy. Building projects – architecture – are like placing an attractor into the future. All information will head towards that attractor from then on. This particular stream of information is thus energized and vectorized. Since the question we are discussing here has enormous implications far beyond architecture I suggest for the moment that I comfort myself with the notion that people are intermediate bodies – among many – absorbing data from a redundant stream of life (information) and excreting them again in modified form. When we make a film of, for example, a house and speed it up a thousand times (the Koyaanisqatsi effect) the house is acting like a living body. It absorbs all kinds of material, including a liquid stream of humans, pulsating in and out. Ecological balance also includes people going in and out, and data being imported and exported, information flowing towards it (feeding), through it (digesting) and away from it (excreting). In the end it does not matter if we call this evolution, proto-evolution, co-evolution or exo-evolution. The most important thing is how we make things work, how we will involve ourselves in building greater complexities of meaning and establishing an increased exchange of information between human body and building body. We design the way we look into the universe, we design the way we transport ourselves over great distances, and we design the way we transport data. All new designs, which are contributing to the further development of tools and extensions, are information enhancers. These designed objects and networks contain ever-growing amounts of data. Where does this affect our own work? In what way are we contributing to the global enhancement of information content? One of the first questions htat has to be answered could well be : does our complex splined architecture (Saltwaterpavilion) have a bigger impact on the evolution of the new life forms than traditional architecture does? Or, stated otherwise, is the very act of building responsible for the enhancement of information content, or is it the complexity of the proposed building scheme that determines the value of the information-index? It is theoretically possible, though, that we may be inefficient in processing vast amounts of data and as a result may contribute less than we would expect to do. But I think – comparing our work to that of other offices – that we have realized greater complexity, both in the physical volume and in its behaviour, within the same stretch of time. That must inevitably mean that the information content per volume and per amount of time has been raised. ✦

KAS OOSTERHUIS

Sculpture city
1994

✦ Garbage Transfer Station

ELHORST/VLOEDBELT ZENDEREN, THE NETHERLANDS
1995

Usually the different functions of this kind of programme (hall, office building, purification plant) are scattered over the site. But here, all the separate building elements were put together to form one large building body composed of a head, a trunk and a tail. The intelligent head houses the weigher's office, the computers, the network, the brains. The actual processing of the garbage takes place in the trunk, the large covered space where it's digested. Finally, the filter unit is set in the tail of the building body. The succession of body sections adjusts itself flexibly to the volume and character of the functions. The body reaches its greatest volume at the centre of the trunk; towards the head it narrows to become slender and compact. The shaped container is inspired by the development in the growth of biological bodies, which display fluid transitions between the different body parts. Industrial bodies like cars and ships display this same quality. ✦

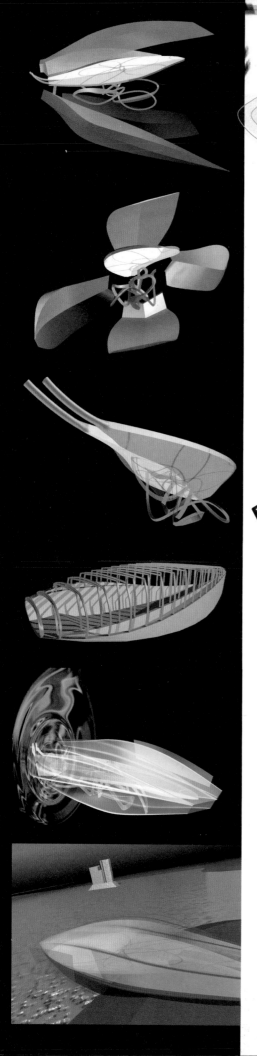

✦ Saltwaterpavilion

NEELTJE JANS, THE NETHERLANDS
1997

The form gene underlying the saltwater pavilion's shape is an octogonal, faceted ellipse, which gradually transmogrifies into a quadrilateral along a three-dimensional curved path. Along that path the volume is first pumped up and then deflated again to form the sharply cut nose. The body juts out a whopping 12 metres over the inland sea of the Oosterschelde. The saltwater pavilion is also a sculpture, which is fashioned in accordance with its own laws and rules and for reasons that other people can never quite fathom. Because of this self-sufficiency of form as interpreted by the independent observer, the saltwater pavilion is suddenly and simultaneously a hundred different things : a stranded whale, a late Brancusi, a Paramecium, a sea cucumber, a submarine, a lemniscate, a speedboat, a tadpole (with silver tail), a solidified droplet, a wave, a stealth bomber. ✦

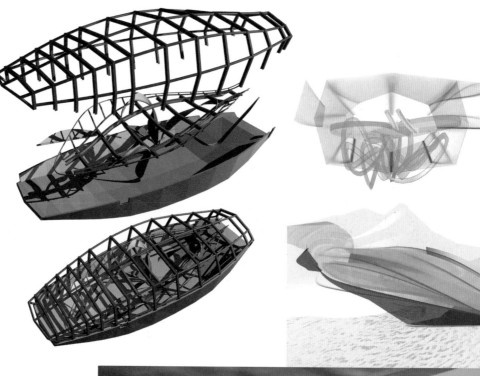

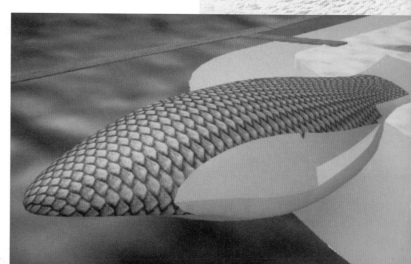

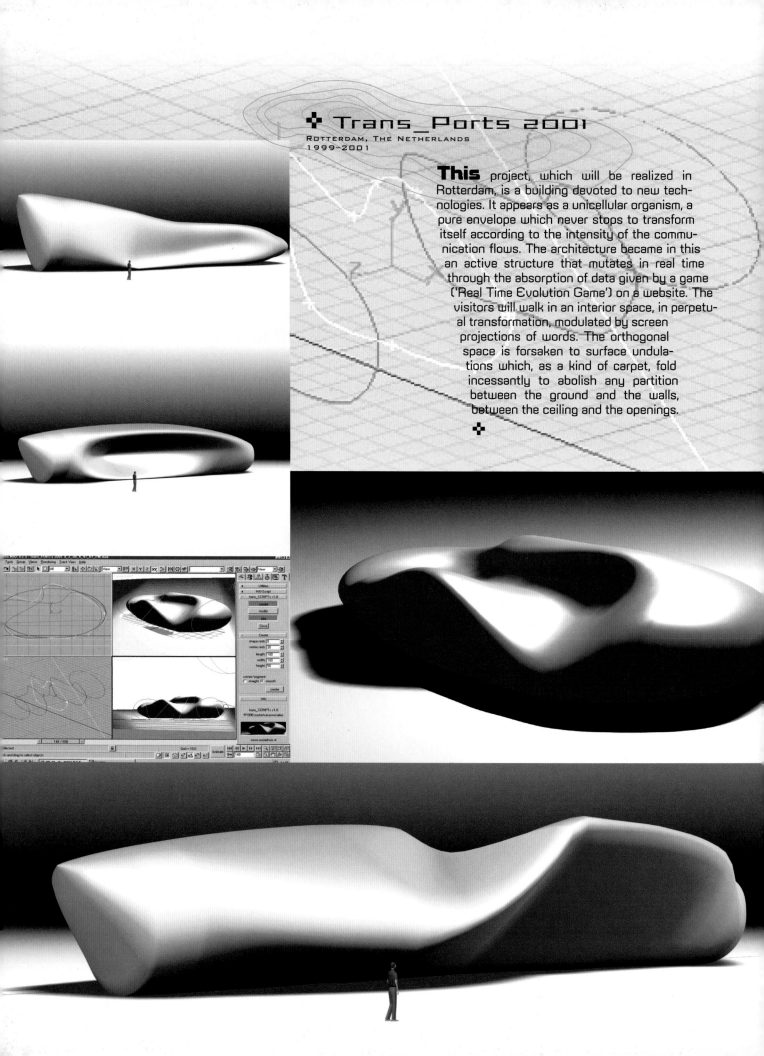

✦ Trans_Ports 2001

ROTTERDAM, THE NETHERLANDS
1999–2001

This project, which will be realized in Rotterdam, is a building devoted to new technologies. It appears as a unicellular organism, a pure envelope which never stops to transform itself according to the intensity of the communication flows. The architecture became in this an active structure that mutates in real time through the absorption of data given by a game ('Real Time Evolution Game') on a website. The visitors will walk in an interior space, in perpetual transformation, modulated by screen projections of words. The orthogonal space is forsaken to surface undulations which, as a kind of carpet, fold incessantly to abolish any partition between the ground and the walls, between the ceiling and the openings.

✦

✦ Attractor Game –
ParkStad Reitdiep

GRONINGEN, THE NETHERLANDS
1996

The 'park city' of Reitdiep is torn between being a city and an
international ecological main route for migrating birds. The new
city is conceived as a giant sponge. This sponge-city breathes
through the cyclic absorbing and discharging of liquids,
matter, people, impulses and information (data). The
existing site forms the breeding ground for the new park
city. The new city will be synonymous with the landscape. A new design tool has been developed to give
shape to the multiple processes that govern the
making of this new city : the Attractor Game. Playing
it is done by placing attractors and distractors in the
landscape. The Attractor Game is a new programmed
tool for interacting in the design process with non-
experts such as the future inhabitants.
The design process has become tranpar-
ent, flexible and fluid, like ecology itself. ✦

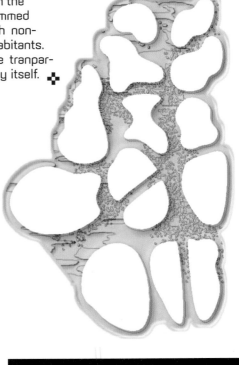

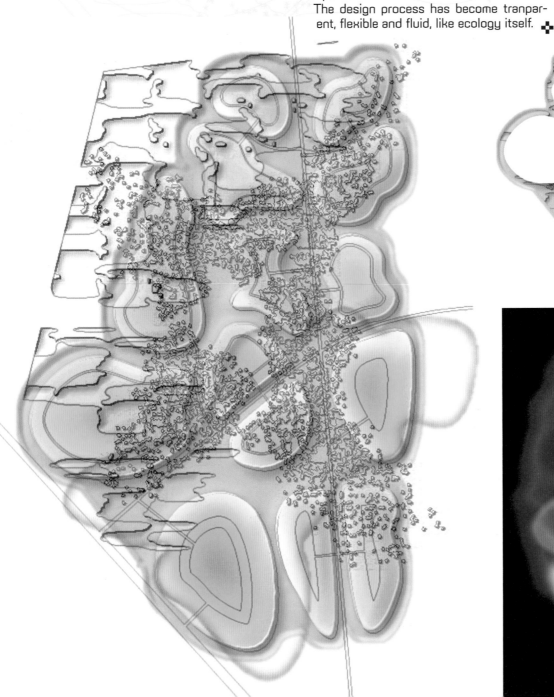

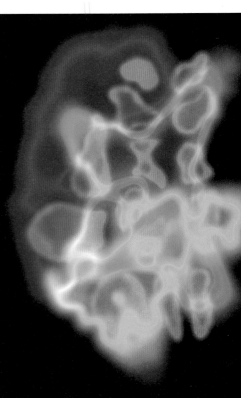

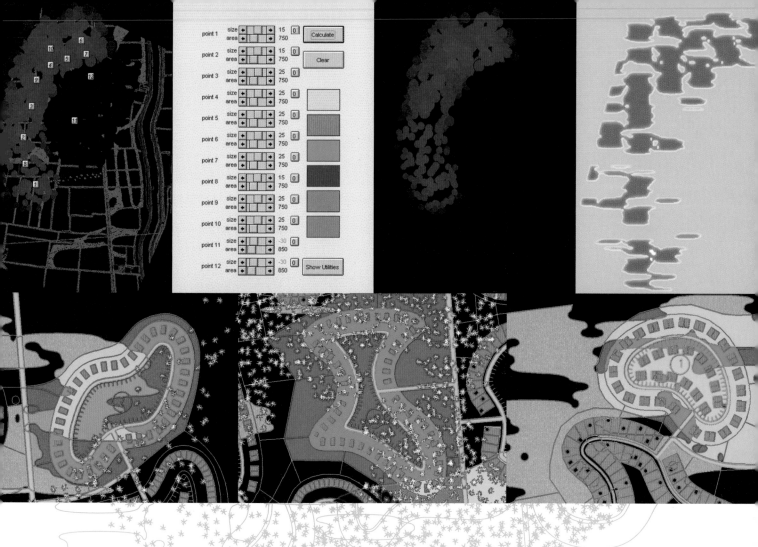

✢ Oosterhuis Associates

Kas Oosterhuis (1951)

1970–79 Architectural studies at the Technical University of Delft
1987–88 Resident at the Studio Theo Van Doesburg, Meudon, France

1989 Founded Kas Oosterhuis Architekten, Rotterdam, Netherlands
1994 Created the Attila Foundation with Ilona Lénard and Menno Rubbens
1997 Founded Oosterhuisassociates, Rotterdam, Netherlands; 'Gold Award for Innovative Recreational Projects/Saltwaterpavilion'
1998 Zeeuwse Architecture Prize/Saltwaterpavilion

Principal buildings and projects

1998 Urban villa, Rotterdam (realized); 56 houses, Utrecht (realized); 64 bridges (project); 'Cockpit in a sound barrier' (project); Intelligent Sculpture paraSCAPE, with Ilona Lénard (realized)
1997 Saltwaterpavilion, Neeltje, Zeeland (realized); Music sculpture, with Ilona Lénard (realized); Urban Planning Study, Zoetermeer (project); 'Saltwater LIVE immersive virtual reality', Waterpavilion, Neeltje (realized)
1996 Attractor Game (planning) Reitdiep, Groningen (project); Kampen Town Hall (second prize)
1995 Garbage transfer station, Elhorst/Vloedbelt, Zenderen (realized); 55 houses, Zonland, Groningen
1994 Thirty-four houses, including eight with a patio, De Hunze, Groningen
1993 Wintergarten housing, Kattenbroek, Amersfoort
1992 'City fruitful', with 4E, Dordrecht (project); Drive-in patio housing, The Hague (realized)

Recent exhibitions

1998 'Polynuclear landscape' with Ilona Lénard, Almere
1997 'ParaSITE' with Attila, European tour travelling to Rotterdam, Helsinki, Graz and elsewhere

1994 'Sculpture City Exhibition' with Attila, Galerie Ram, Rotterdam
1993 'L, v' with Ilona Lénard, Arnhem

Recent conferences

1998 Getty Research Center, Los Angeles, 'Realtime Behaviour of Synthetic Bodies'
1997 Architectural Association, London, 'Parametric Behaviour'; Geelong, Australia, Morphe conference, 'Building Bodies'; Design Institute, 'Building Bodies in Time', Architecture Academy, Rotterdam, 'Attractor Game'

Principal publications

1998 *Kas Oosterhuis, architect, Ilona Lénard, visual artist* 010 Publishers, Rotterdam
1995 *Sculpture city* with Attila, 010 Publishers, Rotterdam
1994 *paraSITEs for Rotterdam* with Ilona Lénard, Designing for Holland
1992 *City fruitful* with 4E, 010 Publishers, Rotterdam

Selected bibliography

1998 'Saltwaterpavilion', *Quaderns* no. 218; 'Parametric behaviour', *AA Files*
1997 'Saltwaterpavilion', *Archis* (Sept.); 'Saltwaterpavilion', *De Architect* (March); 'Attractor Game', *De Architect* (Jun.); 'Park City Reitdiep', *Groen* (Feb.)
1996 *Housing in the Netherlands* NAI, Rotterdam; 'The living artform', *Archis* (August); 'Dikes and roofs as façades', *Bouwwereld gevel* (Jun.)
1995 'Garbagetransferstation', *De Architect* (Dec.); 'Computer Esthetics', *Items* (July); 'Saltwaterpavilion', *Archis* (Nov.); 'Intuitive 3D sketching in digital space', *Leonardo* (Feb.)
1994 'Artificial intuition', *De Architect* Thema 57 (Nov.)

AUSTRIA

Pauhof

| Michael Hoftsätter (*1953) | Wolfgang Pauzenberger (*1955) |

The Pauhof agency has been in existence since 1986. It has grown out of the encounter and collaboration between two Austrian architects, Michael Hofstätter and Wolfgang Pauzenberger, who are actually divided between two cities, respectively Vienna and Linz. As a result, project designs are themselves divided between periods of independent, individual explorations, when each architect works in relative isolation, and limited periods of pooling when the project is systematically rationalized. Although the Pauhof architects have not as yet built a great deal (Metal Workshop, 1990; House P, 1996), the radical nature of their production is very much part of the architectural debate: publications in many different forms and formats, exhibitions and installations which may be seen equally as experiments akin to those of contemporary art and actual architectural pieces, and noteworthy participations in many major international competitions. To be fully grasped, the radical nature of Pauhof must be referred back to and contrasted with the specific context of Austrian postmodern architecture of the 1970s and 1980s, scene of a mannered and historically oriented reaction to the universalist themes of the 'modern movements'. It is this very question that haunts Pauhof: How is one to go beyond this modernity, but without doing away with it, without denying it? They accordingly opted to explore an approach involving intensification. In Pauhof architecture we do indeed come upon themes inherited directly from the avant-gardes of the twentieth century: formal language stripped of all symbolism, formal work on an elementary volumetry, 'impositive' relationship to the context and a tendency towards the large urban scale. With Pauhof, however, all these themes are ploughed back, exacerbated, and pushed to the limit. The proportions of the elements are intentionally exaggerated, like those of the 'flattened' volume that surmounts the Expo '92 Austrian Pavilion. The surfaces strike the eye with their brutal nakedness; rough concrete in the Metal Workshop, aluminium sheets in House P, black steel sheets in their exhibition sets. They are usually smooth and polished, and continually turn inward over the sides of the volumes, emphasizing their compactness. The structural systems are also pushed to the limit in order to dramatize the volumetric effects: maximum cantilevers in the Tuchfabrik, dearth of vertical supports in the House P. Pauhof architecture also plays on a series of radical reversals of diametric pairs. In particular, it expresses a paradoxical dialectic between volume, in all its encompassing exteriority, and space, in all its open interiority. In all their projects, there is a recurrent desire to construct what Pauhof calls the 'implicit volume': in the Expo '92 Austrian Pavilion, the three principal elements, hall, circulation and exhibition rooms, define the boundaries of a large empty space, the 'implicit volume'. This volume is like the invisible law that underlies every project. The form, the arrangement and the scale of each one of the parts are all connected in it and all derive from it. No element holds up on its own. The structure, for example, is never defined in an autogenic way, following a purely structural rationalism, but in the role it plays in the definition of this implicit and immaterial whole. ✦

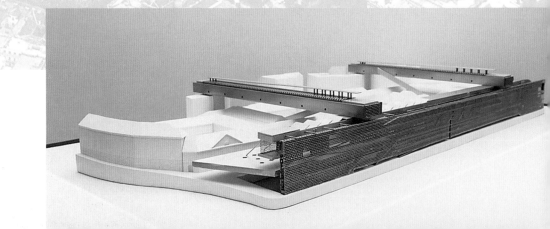

✦ Synthesis Museum

Pauhof's proposal for the development of the Messepalast as a 'museum quarter' consists of a number of elements that act together but remain physically distinct. The general layout of the Messepalast is retained but the larger spaces are upgraded and used for temporary exhibitions. A new building, facing Maria Theresien Platz, houses a permanent collection whose organization is visible through the main façade: escalators lead directly from the subway exits at each end to the display areas, which in turn look back towards the city. The two main exhibition areas are connected by elevated galleries, supported by four service towers set on top of an underground road. The dimensions of the bridging elements correspond with those of the main galleries in the nearby museums designed by Semper. Additional facilities include a photography gallery, located beneath a flat suspended roof, and a cinema at the northern end of the new building. ✦

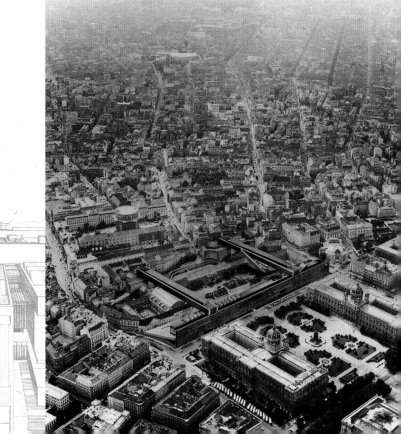

✦ House P

GRAMASTETTEN, AUSTRIA
1992–98

The house reclines upon or is perhaps anchored
to the gentle slope of the ground by the external
wall, which seems to have its origin in the lawn as a
wall enclosing the garden and then unfurls to hold
the ground floor of the building. It ends on the
downhill side, virtually suspended in the void and
physically separated from the earth by means of a
glass strip, the source of natural light for the cellar.
Thus, the wall suggests a conceptual open-ended
rectangle that makes the living room and garden into
a single outside-inside, linked by a large glass wall.
On the upper floor, the sleeping area
seems to be raised in a suspended prism,
which is separated in its turn from the floor
below by means of a thin strip of glass running its length. It offers a sweeping view
that extends far into the distance. The
room is a place for individual privacy and,
it is suggested, for contemplation of the
world. ✦

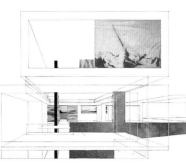

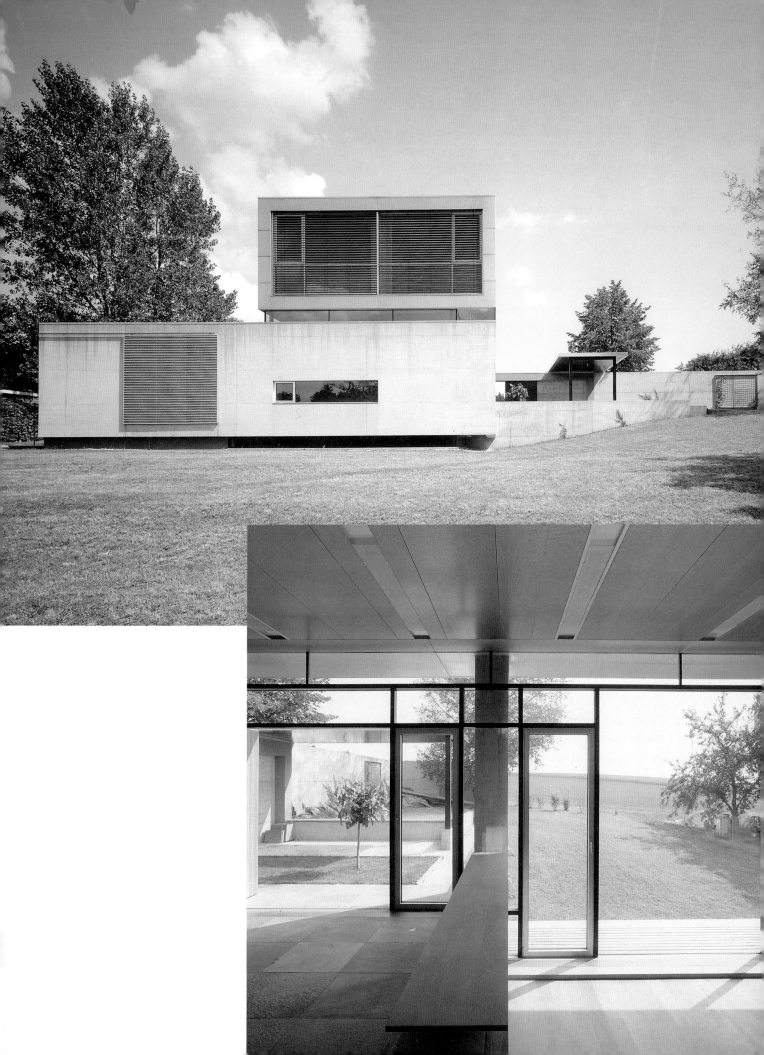

✦ Austrian Pavilion
Expo '92

SEVILLE, SPAIN
1989–90

Three major elements – the entrance hall, the main gallery and the connecting circulation space – are arranged so as to define the edges of a large open volume. Any reference to the scale of everyday construction, such as standard window, door and storey heights, is avoided so that the larger space remains a blank receptacle from which to view the surrounding pavilions. The external simplicity of the entrance hall and the main gallery is maintained by the use of a type of continuous construction normally employed for aircraft fuselages, with no distinction made between wall, roof and underside. The long, tall volume containing the vertical circulation has a solid wall with perforated windows, plus a large circular opening towards the site boundary and a transparent screen on the remaining faces. ✦

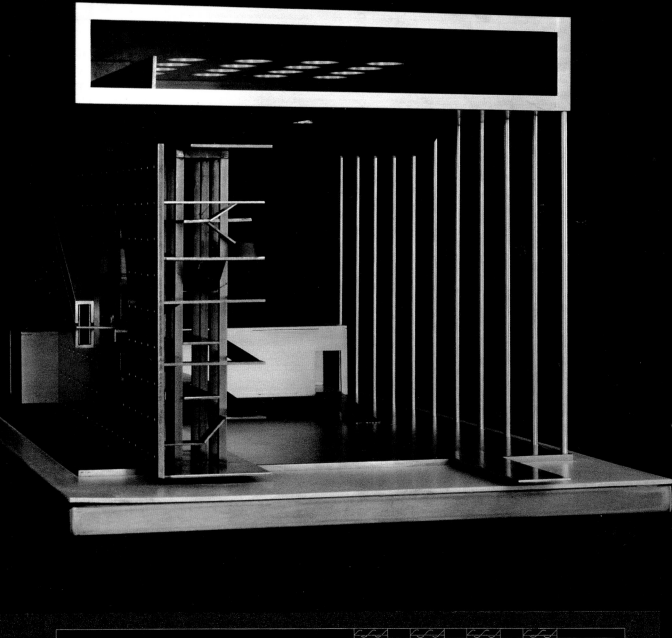
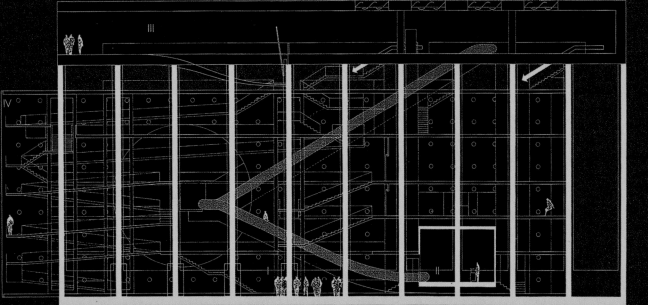

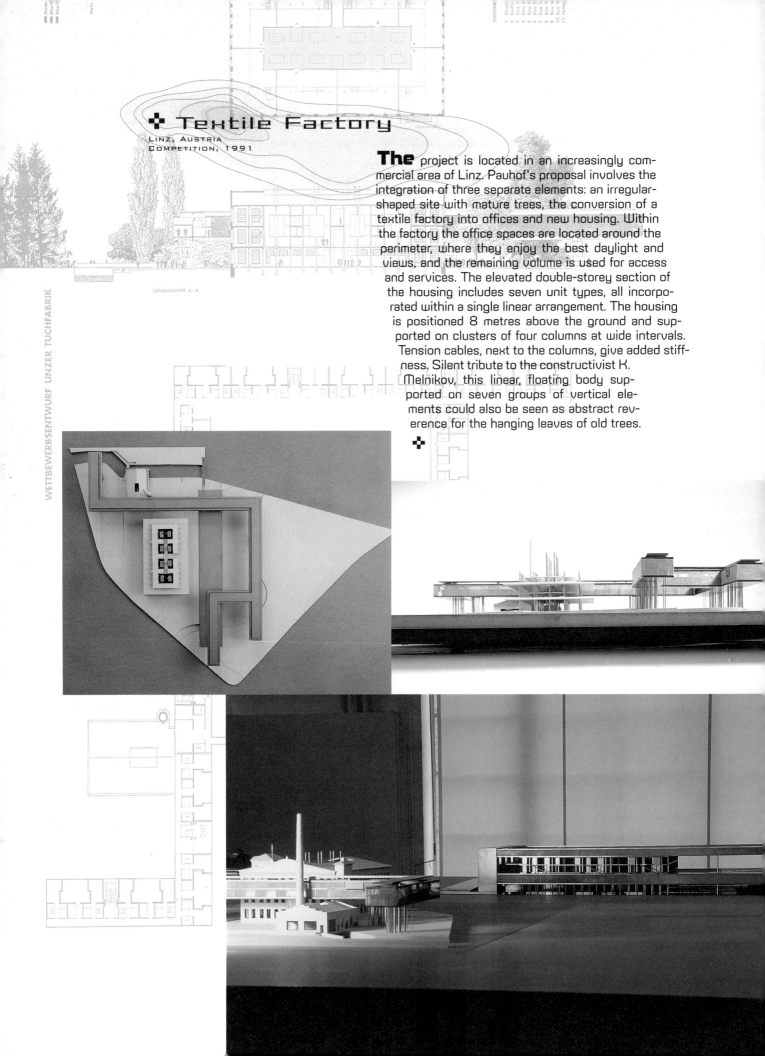

✦ Textile Factory

LINZ, AUSTRIA
COMPETITION, 1991

WETTBEWERBSENTWURF LINZER TUCHFABRIK

LÄNGSSCHNITT A - A

The project is located in an increasingly commercial area of Linz. Pauhof's proposal involves the integration of three separate elements: an irregular-shaped site with mature trees, the conversion of a textile factory into offices and new housing. Within the factory the office spaces are located around the perimeter, where they enjoy the best daylight and views, and the remaining volume is used for access and services. The elevated double-storey section of the housing includes seven unit types, all incorporated within a single linear arrangement. The housing is positioned 8 metres above the ground and supported on clusters of four columns at wide intervals. Tension cables, next to the columns, give added stiffness. Silent tribute to the constructivist K. Melnikov, this linear, floating body supported on seven groups of vertical elements could also be seen as abstract reverence for the hanging leaves of old trees.

✦

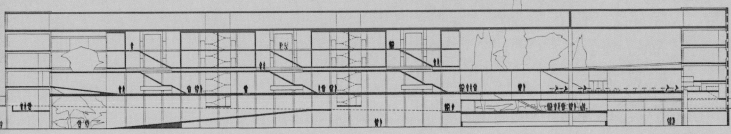

✛ Pauhof

Michaël Hofstätter (1953)
Wolfgang Pauzenberger (1955)

1986　Founded Pauhof in Linz and Vienna

Principal buildings and projects
1998　LKH 2000, Graz (project); Centre for medical research, Graz (project); Gallery of Art and Architecture, Linz (project)
1997　Hochhaus-duo, Vienna (project); Ver Sacrum Room, Wiener Secession, Vienna
1996　Kansai-kan of the National Diet Library, Japan (competition); Urban study, Schwerin
1995　Holocaust Memorial, Vienna (project)
1994　Reconstruction of the Suk, Beirut, Lebanon (project); Professional School, Vienna (project)
1993　House P, Gramastetten (realized); Government centre on the Spree, Berlin (project); Architectural fragment, Grenoble (project)
1992　La carteja, Expo 92, Seville (project); House M, Gramastetten (realized); Art Museum, Krems (project)
1991　Urban complex, Linz Textile Factory, Linz (project); Metal Workshop, Grammastetten (realized)
1990　Austrian Pavilion Expo '92, Seville (project); City Hall, Ottensheim (project)
1989　Alexandrine Library, Egypte (project)
1988　Trigon Museum, Linz (project)
1987　Synthese Museum, Vienna (project)

Recent exhibitions
1998　'Beyond the Minimal', Architectural Association, London, and Art Front Gallery (Hillside Terrace) Tokyo
1997　'Die Schrift des Raumes', Kunsthalle, Vienna; 'Implied Volumes', OPOS Gallery, Milan; 'Houses for Sales', Sophia Ungers Gallery, Cologne; 'Partition', Museum Gallery, Bolzano

Selected bibliography
1998　*Remixed: Pauhof/Walter Niedermayr/Sigrid Hauser* AR/GE Kunst, Museum Gallery, Bolzano; *Beyond the Minimal* AA, London, catalogue of the exhibition mounted in London and Tokyo; *Sprache z.B.Architektur* Sigrid Hauser, Löcker, Vienna; *Architektur & Bauforum* nos 192, 193 and 194, Vienna; *Abitare* no. 369; *AA Files* no. 36; *l'Arca* no. 131; *Arquitectura Viva AV* 72; *Kenchiku Bunka* no. 11; *Disenointerior* no. 75
1997　*Houses for Sale*, catalogue, Ungers Gallery, Cologne; *Kansai-Kan of the DNL*, catalogue, PBA, Tokyo; *Abitare* no. 360; *Zlatý Rez* no. 14, Prague; *Daidalos* no. 66, Berlin; *Werk, Bauen + Wohnen* no. 9, Zurich
1996　*Pauhof, New Architectural Experiences in Europe* Skira, Milan; *Judenplatz Wien*, Folio, Vienna-Bolzano; *GA Houses* no. 48, Tokyo; *Turris Babel* no. 37, Bolzano; *Architektur Aktuell* no. 198, Vienna. Audiovisual: *Pauhof/Architektur ist nicht Kunst* Auracher, Vienna
1994　*Pauhof – Architekten*, Wiese, Basel
1990　*Um Bau*, ÖGfA, Vienna

Périphériques

| Louis Paillard (*1960) | Anne-Françoise Jumeau (*1962) |
| Emmanuelle Marin-Trottin (*1967) | David Trottin (*1965) |

Périphériques is a non-profit association founded in 1996 by three architectural agencies. Since 1998 it has been run by David Trottin and Emmanuelle Marin-Trottin, Louis Paillard and Anne-Françoise Jumeau. Our aim is to promote architecture beyond the normal customs of this profession. Like film makers, we are at once authors and go-betweens; we would describe our status as that of architectural producer. It is in this spirit that we recently put on the exhibition '36 Models for a House', where we showed the projects for homes commissioned from us by thirty-six European architectural agencies. In tandem with this exhibition, which was held in France and Europe, we formed our own architectural agencies forming of two or three people under the label PÉRIPHÉRIQUES, with a view to entering competitions. The Café-Musiques at Savigny-le-Temple, recently delivered, and the Mâcon Library for which we are currently drawing up studies, are the first two concrete examples of this research. These projects are part of the central issue of contemporary creation where 'digital cultures' are coming up with new ideas of author, work, context and meaning. Sampling, remixing, cutting, pasting – all are relevant ways of positing new bases for creative work. The architectural productions of PÉRIPHÉRIQUES, in parallel with our personal projects, submit architecture to this approach. Today we are extending our research and our projects to an international scale by taking part in the competition for the Musée des Arts Premiers on the Quai Branly in Paris (30,000 m²), where we are inviting the MVRDV agency in Rotterdam to take part in this project with us. At the same time, in October 1999, we launched the first issue of our architectural magazine, *IN-EX* 01, a virtual architectural gallery. In it, through our video eye (we take all the shots), we discuss meetings with artists, architects and places. *IN-EX* is thus a non-exhaustive summary of the subjective viewpoints of things that concern us. All its productions were shown at the City of Paris Museum of Modern Art in October 1999 as part of the ZAC 1999 exhibition. ❖

PÉRIPHÉRIQUES

❖ Extension to the School of Architecture and Landscape at Bordeaux

COMPETITION, 1998
PAILLARD & JUMEAU AND TROTTIN & MARIN-TROTTIN

What is involved this time for Périphériques is the completion of the different extensions scattered around a complex of buildings put up in the 1970s by René Ferret, and to do so without upsetting the distinctive character of the School, which means in the splitting up of the teaching areas, linked together by covered outdoor passages. The two teams of architects tossed a coin to decide on the functional organization and distribution of the programme. To visualize the results they relied on modelling in synthetic images. They then defined two alphabets to describe the sides of each space. The new building lastly contains a series of open sets exactly the same width as that of the neighbouring building on which the project is supported. This playful protocol enabled the architects to favour uses and relationships as much as possible, without having to worry about composition.

❖

✦ Café-Musiques

SAVIGNY-LE-TEMPLE, FRANCE, 1999
PAILLARD AND JUMEAU, TROTTIN AND MARIN-TROTTIN
AND JAKOB AND MACFARLANE

For Périphériques, one of the interesting things about the Café-Musiques programme was the possibility that it could be divided up into several units, which, once assembled, would form a whole: the billboard, the performance room and the restaurant. This assemblage of such different functions referred them to the idea of urban assemblage and street. The project was thus devised as a truth-and-consequences by three teams of architects: three buildings in one, on the borderline between town and fields, responding in different ways to the ordinariness of the railway station, a car park, and an amusement park on one side, contrasting with a pond, woods and fields on the other side. On the town side, the building is a coloured box which takes on its meaning by the definition of its outermost structure five: the light here expresses the architecture. On the pond side, where people can look and hide, a camouflage of galvanized metal incorporates the building in its setting. This is a work that questions architecture as an individual work, while at the same time challenging the predetermination of the aesthetic. ✦

✜ Museum the Primary Arts

Paris, Competition, 1999
Trottin and Marin-Trottin, Paillard + Jumeau and Moussafir; members
of MVRDV

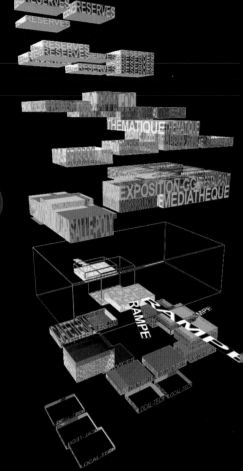

For this museum, the architectural matter provided by the architects reflects the diversity and immensity of the programmes involved: seventy sets are brought together in twelve 37-metre-tall towers, forming a compact unit of 120 × 70 metres. In each of these towers programmes of differing heights are installed, which, as required, are developed horizontally. Périphériques here proposes a catalogue of spaces based on a module of some 500 m². Each one of them has its own quality: some are monumental and fixed, others are changeable. By literally tiering the different factors in the programme, one on top of the other, the museum becomes a crystallization of differences, a simple overlay of art and product, which transforms it into a world of civilizations. In this world, the freed spaces between towers, like actual narrow, deep faults, innervate, organize and divide up the mass of the museum. ✜

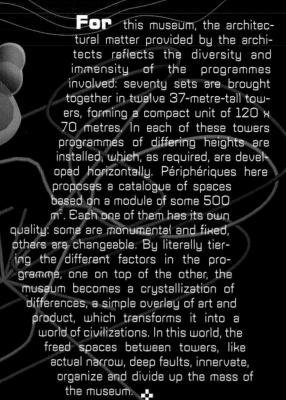

ISBN 3-7643-6128-X

9 783764 361280

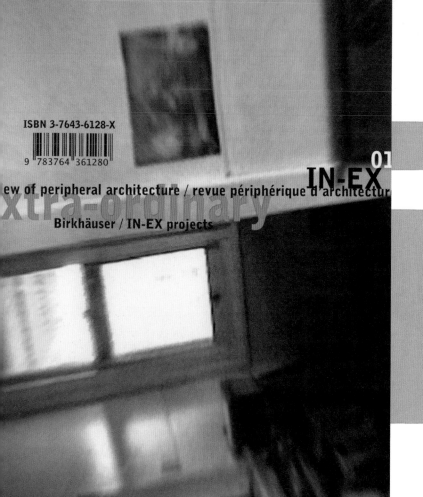

IN-EX 01

...ew of peripheral architecture / revue périphérique d'architectur...

Birkhäuser / IN-EX projects

IN-EX has set itself up as 'a virtual gallery of architecture'.
Weary of hemmed-in attitudes which prevail throughout the profession,
we have decided to offer a snapshot display of our subjective viewpoints and concerns,
proposing links between architecture and other branches of the arts.
This approach illustrates our ambition to convey an innovative outlook on architecture.
Like new-wave film-makers, we claim the dual status of authors and mediators.
We are producers.
IN-EX is a debating arena which brings critical ideas to the fore.
It is a yearly journal organised around a specific theme, in which artists,
architects and critics alike are invited to present their schemes and design processes,
expressing their points of view in a creative and open way – something along
the lines of an architectural UFO, intended to spawn determined forces.

**IN-EX is a video camera,
a car, people, roads and computers...**

The chosen theme for this first issue is the

extra-ordinary

which ties together our initial research work.

in Australia

is a stretch of land running 10,000 km from north to south of Australia,
where we went off in search of makeshift structures,
rejecting all taboos and calling into question the forms of the city and the dwelling.

interview(s)

is a subjective cross-section of the various architectural approaches
that will be seeing us into 2000 and beyond. These discussions, totalling 17 in all,
seek out more than mere comparisons between generations and location;
they draw parallels between processes in terms of how built works
can adopt the form of testing grounds.

exterior(s)

is a road movie that takes place in Europe.

exhibition(s)

is a gallery in which artists, architects and photographers
are invited to display their works.

interest(s)

features unfamiliar schemes and built works.

view of peripheral architecture / revue périphérique d'architect...

extra-ordinary

Birkhäuser / IN-EX projects

✚ Périphériques

Louis Paillard (1960)
1999–98   Teacher at the School of Architecture of Bretagne
1999–97   Teacher at the Ecole Professionnelle Supérieure d'Arts et
          d'Architecture de la Ville de Paris
1988   DPLG from the Ecole d'Architecture de Paris-La Villette
1980   Diploma from the Ecole Boulle, Paris

Anne-Françoise Jumeau (1962)
1996   CESP from the Ecole du Paysage de Versailles
1987   DPLG from the Ecole d'Architecture de Paris-Villemin

Emmanuelle Marin-Trottin (1967)
1991   DPLG from the Ecole d'Architecture de Paris-La Seine

David Trottin (1965)
2000–1996   Teacher at Architecture Schools of Paris-Tolbiac and Paris-
            Charenton
1990   DPLG from the Ecole d'Architecture de Paris-Villemin

2000–1998   Périphériques set in motion by E. Marin-Trottin, D. Trottin, L.
            Paillard and A.F. Jumeau
1995   Creation of the Association Périphériques Marin-Trottin+Trottin,
            Paillard+Jumeau and Jakob & MacFarlane
1992   Creation of the Marin-Trottin practice
1990   Creation of the Paillard+Jumeau practice

Principal buildings and projects
2000–1999   Quartier de la Pirrotterie, Rézé, district and housing develop-
            ment (under construction); Musée de l'Art Concret, Mouans Sartoux
            (prizewinner); Musée des Arts Premiers (competition, associated
            with MVRDV, Rotterdam); Café-Musique Le Charbon, Paris (under
            construction P&J); Europan' social housing (competition P&J)
1999   Café-Musiques, Savigny-le-Temple (realized); Bibliothèque de
            Mâcon (under construction); Launch of review IN-EX and IN-EX
            projects/Birkhaüser Verlag, Paris/Basel; MR House (realized T-
            M&T)
1998   Ecole d'Architecture et du Paysage de Bordeaux (competition);
            Centre National de Danse, Pantin (competition); Zac de Pierre-
            Louve, L'Isle d'Abeau (competition)

1997   'In search of the model house' – fourth Périphériques event, open
            discussion among thirty-six European architects and landscape gar-
            deners about an alternative to the mass-production of the individual
            house, with the Architecture Directorate/AFAA/Arc en Rêve Centre
            d'Architecture (see exhibitions)
1996   'La Nuit de la Jeune Architecture', VIth Venice Architecture
            Biennale

Recent exhibitions
2000   Pavillon de l'Arsenal (under construction); 'Les 100 ans du Métro'
            (under construction P&J)
2000–1998   'Thirty-six models for a house' traveling European exhibition
            (created at Bordeaux in 1997   Arc en Rêve Centre d'Architecture)
            following the open discussion among thirty-six European rural plan-
            ners and architects (fourth Périphériques event)

Principal publications
2000   Beaucoup Minnesota IN-EX Projects/Birkhaüser Verlag,
            Paris/Basel; IN-EX 02 IN-EX projects/Birkhaüser Verlag
            (in preparation)
1999   IN-EX 01 IN-EX projects/Birkhaüser Verlag, Paris/Basel
1998   Périphériques: travaux récents Périphériques, Paris
1997   '36 modèles pour une maison' ('Thirty-six models for a house')
            Périphériques, Paris
1996   '3 Maisons 1/2 en Banlieue', Competition perdus, 14 projets d'archi-
            tecture et de paysage' catalogue of the exhibition at the Galerie
            Philippe Uzzan, Paris, Périphériques, Paris

Selected bibliography
2000   Frame no. 13; l'Architecture d'aujourd'hui no. 326; Architecture
            d'intérieure créé no. 292; Le Moniteur no. 5025; Prototypo no. 3;
            AMC no. 105
1999   Singular Housing Actar; 'Architécti' Casas no. 47; Parpaings no. 1
            et 2
1998   l'Arca International no. 26; Architecture d'intérieure créé no. 280

The POOR BOYs ENTERPRISE

| Marie Thérèse Harnoncourt (*1967) |
| Florian Haydn (*1967) | Ernst J. Fuchs (*1963) |

FRAGMENTS

TRASH POETRY – The preoccupation with the NOW – not the construction of a specific image as the goal, but the use of conditions/states as the parameters for requirements, usage, form and aesthetics. Rubbish bins, waste-paper baskets, data banks, plots of land, cities are treasure troves. We develop FRAGMENTS (beginnings). Fragments are the trigger for activity. We condense the field, the field of possibilities that have to be drawn from the user. Possibilities are the result of seeing, thoughts, ideas. A fragment contains all possibilities within itself. There is no letting things get done. The user's doing affects the atmosphere. The fragment is an impulse, a motivation. In connection with other fragments, they come to life. We attach our vision – (hopes) of building – to working with fragments. Buildings are to be entirely different from one another. Dreams and wishes develop inspiration. Grow, starting without knowing what something is.

'DATA-FIELD' Zirl DESIGN/BUILDING – We want emancipation from design's being a speculation on a possible prospective act of building. The design is the opportunity to fill the selected field with ideas. The enrichment with ideas results in a spatial source of nutrition, this forms the communicative base for later interpretations that serve as causal in the process of building. We do not speculate with what might be. We act within the condition that we have access to.

WORKABLE-ACCOMMODATION – We want to develop a lifestyle in the workable-accommodation. Contexts that can be experienced – understanding associated volumes renders an interaction possible. The pre-existing elements that are used in the composition of the volume can be perceived in their basic structure. The user lends the pre-existing elements significance; the user gives them the associations that the user requires. This is the creation of personal zones of significance and has creativity as its basis. The user creates identity. The user creates an environment for animation.

EXISTING STATE – Growth of the structure via the addition or subtraction of fragments. Fragments generate the state. State is timeless, it is ever-present. The state is a parameter that can adjust the space between reality and virtual reality.

FRAGMENTS – Demonstrate an early stage of a condition. The condition or state is independent of time – it is now. Fragments can be partially conceived of as unusual or incomprehensible as there is no regularity or system initially legible within them; this uncertainty is the independence of fragments. They show a multiplicity of possibilities and demand intellectual mobility : perhaps to the extent of everyday flights of fantasy. The unexpected can be expected. The unexpected as the possibility for structures.

THE SPEAKEASY – Only exists in the moment, where the traces are read. It is a space like a hallucination that can arise autonomously and suddenly collapse again – it's all about the unpredictable space.

IDENTITY – The environment's inclination – the Walking Building (Gehende Haus) – the Growing Building (Wachsende Haus) – the City-Eating Building (Stadtfressende Haus). The building spreads by positioning activities. The city is eaten up, the building is already urban space, city, because of its activity, the city is your house, you live in the city, the flowing city. Your home cannot be perceived with the help of a floor plan any longer. The designation of activities can give an idea of what your home, your living space really is.

HIRNSEGEL (BRAIN-SURFERS) – Are capable of absorbing whatever comes along. Winds. Winds introduce states of breaking open and slipping away. Winds result in different atmospheres at different spatial nodes. Hairs are retarded brain-surfers. Speech bubbles are brain-surfers. Winds generate spaces – gaps with brain-surfers! ✦

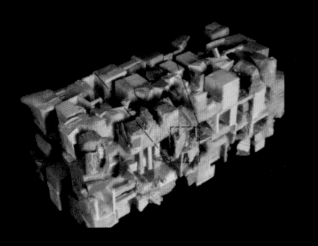

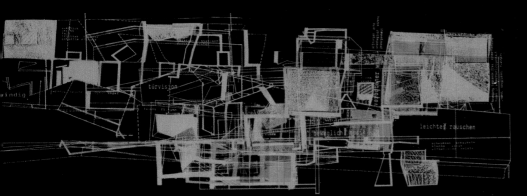

✛ Data-Field
House, Zirl, Austria
1997

"Data-Field" Zirl
Zirl, Autriche, 1997

Luftansaugfassade

+3,15

±0,00

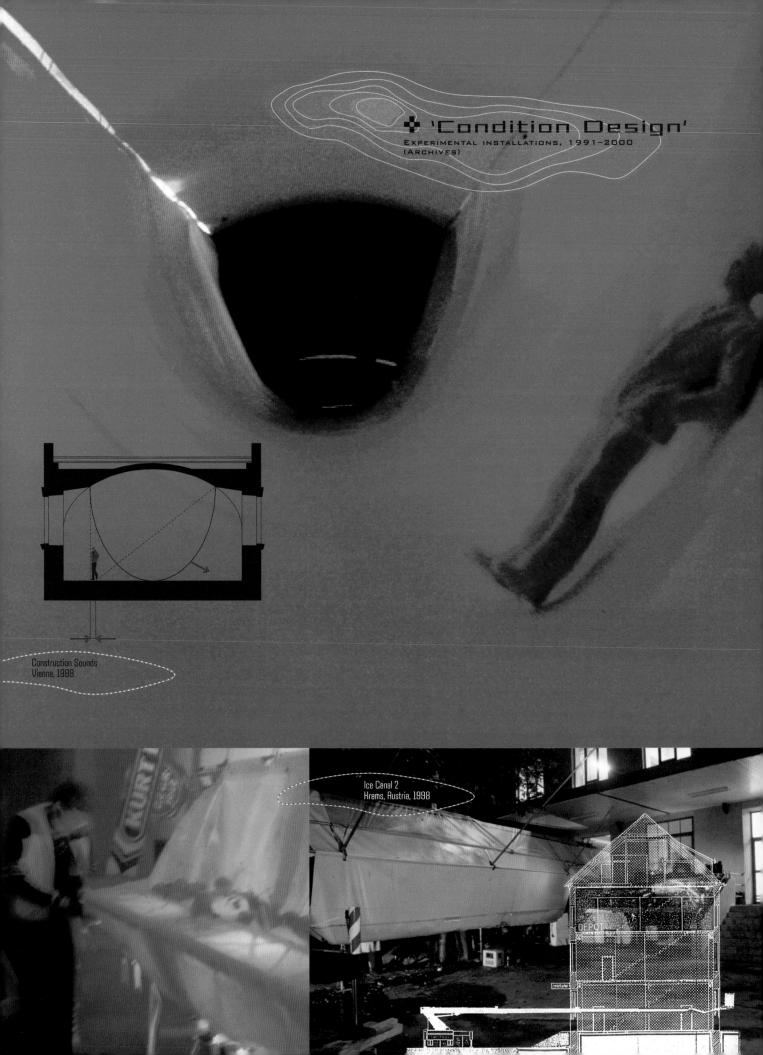

✦ 'Condition Design'

Experimental installations, 1991–2000
(Archives)

Construction Sounds
Vienna, 1998

Ice Canal 2
Krems, Austria, 1998

Dud
Hof/Lbg, Austria, 2000
Photographer : Veronika Hofinger

✤ 'Message in the Bottle'
Private indoor swimming pool
Vienna, Austria
(Photographer: Veronika Hofinger)

✛ The POOR BOY's ENTERPRISE

Florian Haydn (1967)
1993   Diploma from the University of Applied Arts, Vienna

Ernst J. Fuchs (1963)
1994   Diploma from the University of Applied Arts, Vienna
1988/85   Study of design at the University of Art and Design, Linz

Marie-Thérèse Harnoncourt (1967)
1993   Diploma from the University of Applied Arts, Vienna
1993   Collaboration with Steven Holl, New York

1991   Creation of the practice (Paul Zoller, Florian Haydn, Wolfgang Grillitsch (since 1997 'Peanutz Architekten', Berlin) Ernst. J. Fuchs
2000–1994   Creation of The POOR BOYs ENTERPRISE (Ernst J. Fuchs, Floran Haydn, Marie-Thérèse Harnoncourt)

Principal buildings and projects
2000   'Message in Bottle', indoor swimming pool, Vienna (under construction); 'Dud' public arrangement (realized); 'Dyn@tmosphère' (project with Rainer Pirker ARCHItexture)
1998   Rooftop remodelling, Graz (realized); 'Construction Sounds' (with Rainer Pirker ARCHItexture), Museum district, Vienna (realized); 'Ice Canal 2', Krems (realized); Gym-Studio, Salzburg (realized); City Planning-KDAG-Gründe, Vienna (prizewinner); Hof am Leitaberge', reorganization of public space (prizewinner)
1997   Datafield, Zirl House, Tyrol (realized); 'Party – Ice Canal I' (realized); Texture wall, Museum district, Vienna; 'Experimental Tendencies in Architecture 1996' (prizewinner)
1996   Holzstoss housing (project); 'Whotel', a concrete Utopia (project); Zentrum Breitengut, Salzburg (award)
1995   Hirnsegel no. 7, Südtirolerplatz (realized); Nationalpark Akademie Hohe Tauern, Salzburg (award)
1994   'Field of Nutrition' (1991–94); Container Bar, Vienna (realized); '97 chairs New York', Vienna (realized)

1993   'Booth at a Fair', prefabricated aluminium, Hanover (realized); Sportanlage Anras, Tyrol (project)
1992   Party, 'Potable Landscape', Vienna; 'Labor X' (project)
1991   Hirnsegel no. 1–5' (realized); 'Öko-Lexikon/'Werkswohnen' (project)

Select bibliography
1999   *Daidalos* no. 71; *Raum Journal III*, Stuttgart; *Architektur Aktuell* no. 230/23 1; *Titelbild*; *Architektur & Bauforum* no. 199; *Casabella* no. 665; *OI   Diagonal* (March)
1998   *Bauwelt* no. 20; *News* no. 8; *Der Standard* (21 Feb.); *Architektur & Bauforum* no. 194; *Architektur* vol. 6 (Sept.); *Architektur Aktuell* no. 219/220
1997   *Beton & Zement* no. 4; *Architektur & Bauforum* no. 190; *Report* (Dec.)
1995   *SD: Space and Design* no. 9610, Tokyo, Japan
1994   *Architektur Aktuell* no. 16
1993   *Architektur & Bauforum* special issue on 'Experimental tendencies in architecture 1993'; Europan 3 *At Home in the City*; Europan 3 Union of Europan Austria
1992   *Experimentelle Tendenzen in der Architektur* (Experimental tendencies in architecture) catalogue (1989/92)
1987   *Europaplads Aarhus –Denmark* catalogue

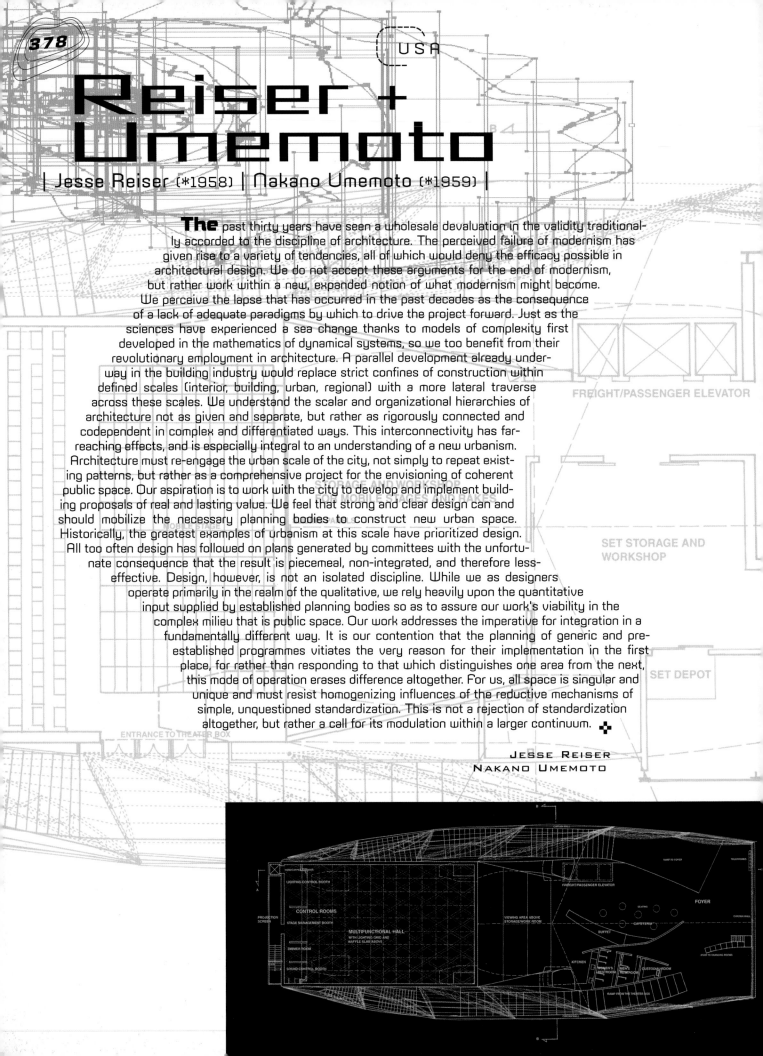

Reiser + Umemoto

| Jesse Reiser (*1958) | Nakano Umemoto (*1959) |

The past thirty years have seen a wholesale devaluation in the validity traditionally accorded to the discipline of architecture. The perceived failure of modernism has given rise to a variety of tendencies, all of which would deny the efficacy possible in architectural design. We do not accept these arguments for the end of modernism, but rather work within a new, expanded notion of what modernism might become. We perceive the lapse that has occurred in the past decades as the consequence of a lack of adequate paradigms by which to drive the project forward. Just as the sciences have experienced a sea change thanks to models of complexity first developed in the mathematics of dynamical systems, so we too benefit from their revolutionary employment in architecture. A parallel development already underway in the building industry would replace strict confines of construction within defined scales (interior, building, urban, regional) with a more lateral traverse across these scales. We understand the scalar and organizational hierarchies of architecture not as given and separate, but rather as rigorously connected and codependent in complex and differentiated ways. This interconnectivity has far-reaching effects, and is especially integral to an understanding of a new urbanism. Architecture must re-engage the urban scale of the city, not simply to repeat existing patterns, but rather as a comprehensive project for the envisioning of coherent public space. Our aspiration is to work with the city to develop and implement building proposals of real and lasting value. We feel that strong and clear design can and should mobilize the necessary planning bodies to construct new urban space. Historically, the greatest examples of urbanism at this scale have prioritized design. All too often design has followed on plans generated by committees with the unfortunate consequence that the result is piecemeal, non-integrated, and therefore less-effective. Design, however, is not an isolated discipline. While we as designers operate primarily in the realm of the qualitative, we rely heavily upon the quantitative input supplied by established planning bodies so as to assure our work's viability in the complex milieu that is public space. Our work addresses the imperative for integration in a fundamentally different way. It is our contention that the planning of generic and pre-established programmes vitiates the very reason for their implementation in the first place, for rather than responding to that which distinguishes one area from the next, this mode of operation erases difference altogether. For us, all space is singular and unique and must resist homogenizing influences of the reductive mechanisms of simple, unquestioned standardization. This is not a rejection of standardization altogether, but rather a call for its modulation within a larger continuum. ❖

JESSE REISER
NAKANO UMEMOTO

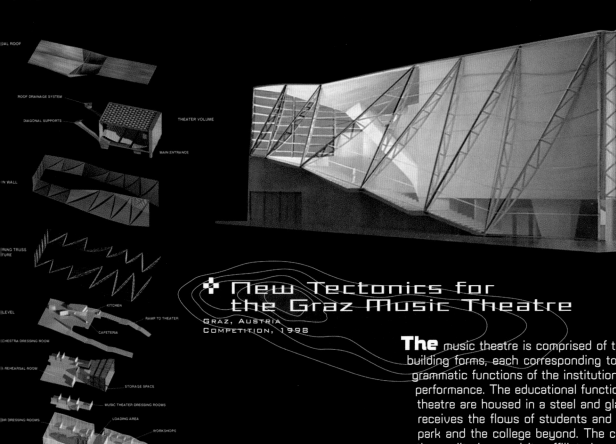

Exploded axonometric labels (top left to bottom):
AL ROOF
ROOF DRAINAGE SYSTEM
DIAGONAL SUPPORTS
THEATER VOLUME
MAIN ENTRANCE
IN WALL
RING TRUSS
URE
LEVEL
KITCHEN
RAMP TO THEATER
CAFETERIA
CHESTRA DRESSING ROOM
REHEARSAL ROOM
STORAGE SPACE
MUSIC THEATER DRESSING ROOMS
R DRESSING ROOMS
LOADING AREA
WORKSHOPS
HEARSAL ROOMS
ELEVATOR CORE
NICAL LEVEL

✚ New Tectonics for the Graz Music Theatre

GRAZ, AUSTRIA
COMPETITION, 1998

The music theatre is comprised of two interlocking building forms, each corresponding to the major programmatic functions of the institution: education and performance. The educational functions of the music theatre are housed in a steel and glass plinth which receives the flows of students and faculty from the park and the college beyond. The civic functions of the auditorium and its affiliated spaces are housed within and under a concrete structure conceived as a forthright industrial space for the production of civic events. A long processional stair pulls the urban organization up through the body of the building, into a larger foyer and then into the main hall. Upon the close of a performance, the audience exits out and down the same processional stairway and moves back into the city, thus completing the cycle of civic performance. ✚

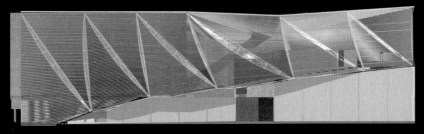

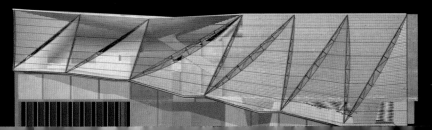

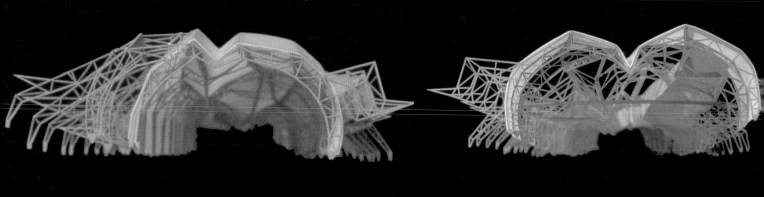

SECOND FLOOR

MEZZANINE LEVE

FIRST FLOOR

APRON ±0M

IT FLOOR +5M

APRON ±0M

Yokohama Port Terminal
YOKOHAMA, JAPAN
COMPETITION, 1995

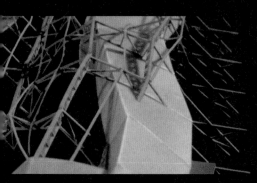

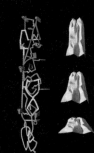

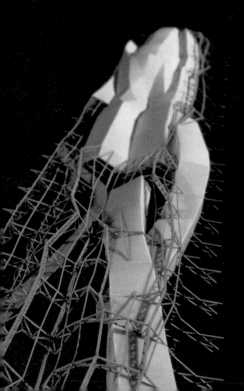

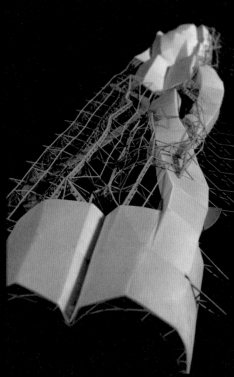

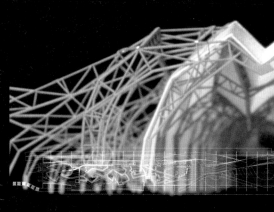

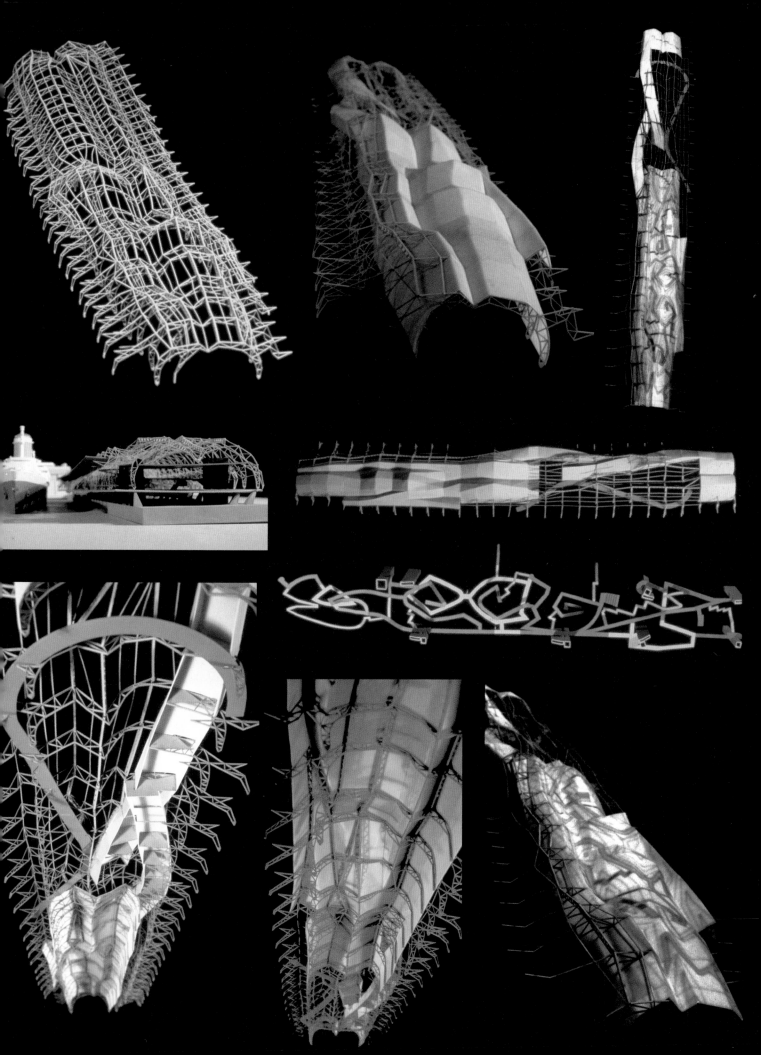

✦ Kansai Library

KANSAI, JAPAN
COMPETITION, 1996

Reiser+Umemoto's proposal addresses the apparent paradox surrounding the universal proliferation of data, the presumed placelessness of information and the persistent necessity, nevertheless, to find a definition for this condition in architecture. The proposal embodies also two distinct yet related imperatives: to fulfil the explicit programmatic criteria of the library while developing implicit spatialities that would foster the new and unforeseen irruptions of program brought about by the 'information zone'. The Library comprises three ramped slabs suspended by cables from a prestressed steel roof carried on four steel piers. The slabs are so formed as to maximize continuity and multiple interconnection among the public spaces and levels. Topological deformations – cuts, mounds, ramps, ripples and stairs – render the library a programmed landscape. ✦

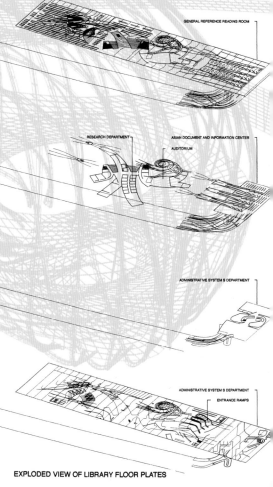

GENERAL REFERENCE READING ROOM

RESEARCH DEPARTMENT
ASIAN DOCUMENT AND INFORMATION CENTER
AUDITORIUM

ADMINISTRATIVE SYSTEM S DEPARTMENT

ADMINISTRATIVE SYSTEM S DEPARTMENT
ENTRANCE RAMPS

EXPLODED VIEW OF LIBRARY FLOOR PLATES

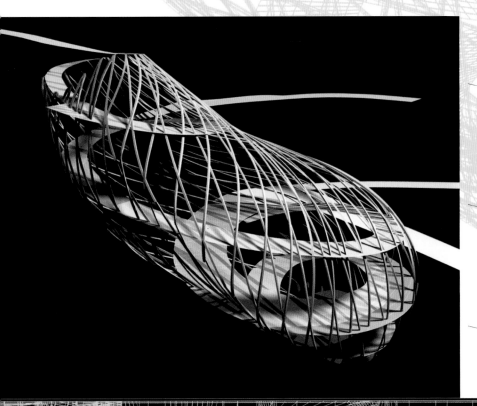

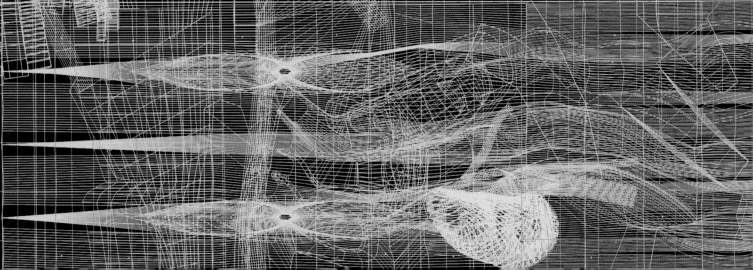

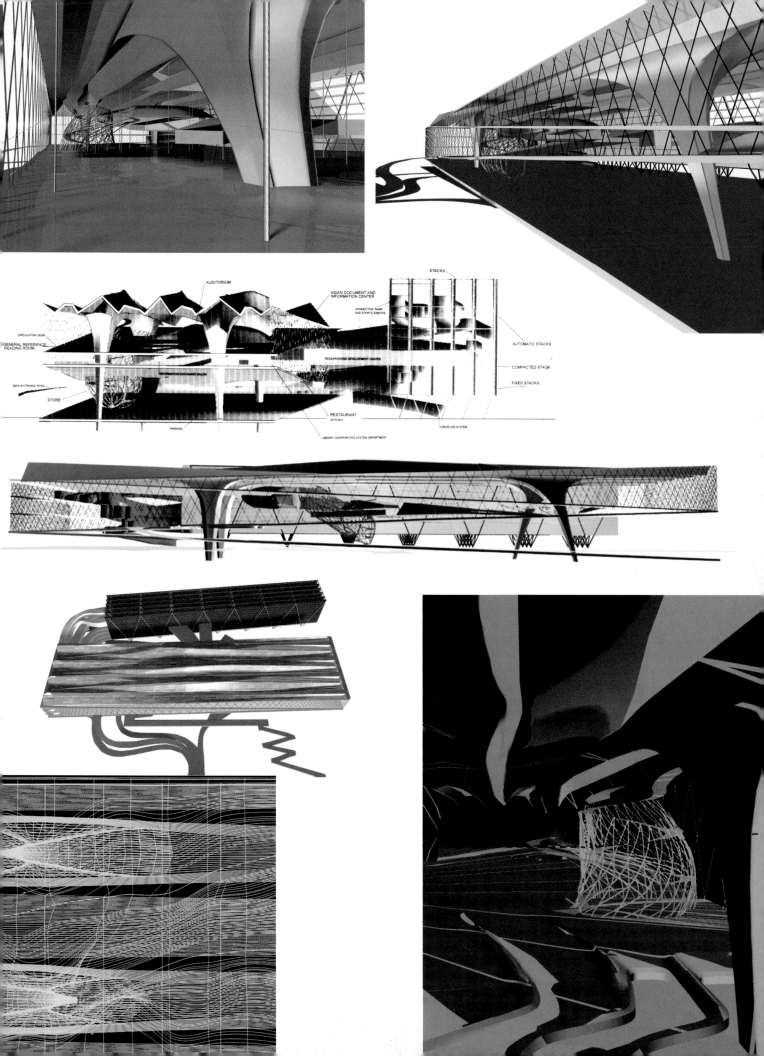

GENERAL REFERENCE READING ROOM

AUDITORIUM

ASIAN DOCUMENT AND INFORMATION CENTER

CONNECTING RAMP AND STAIR ELEMENTS

STACKS

CIRCULATION DESK

AUTOMATIC STACKS

COMPACTED STACK

FIXED STACKS

MAIN ENTRANCE ROAD

RESEARCH AND DEVELOPMENT CENTER

INFORMATION EXCHANGE SALON

STORE

RESTAURANT

KITCHEN

PARKING

LIBRARY COOPERATION SYSTEM DEPARTMENT

CONVEYOR SYSTEM

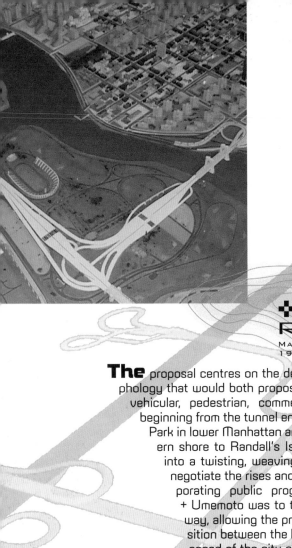

✦ East Riverfront

MANHATTAN, NEW YORK, USA
1998

The proposal centres on the development of a new linear urban morphology that would both propose and incorporate the highly diverse vehicular, pedestrian, commercial and cultural infrastructures, beginning from the tunnel entrance of the FDR Drive at Battery Park in lower Manhattan and continuing north along the eastern shore to Randall's Island. The project thus developed into a twisting, weaving system that could continuously negotiate the rises and falls of the FDR as well as incorporating public programming. The tactic of Reiser + Umemoto was to tap into the already existing roadway, allowing the proposal to occupy the zone of transition between the high speed of the FDR and the low speed of the city grid. Rather than producing a collection of isolated objects, they seek to organize series of moments structured within a continuum. ✦

✦ Reiser + Umemoto

Jesse Reiser (1958)
1981 Graduate of Architecture, Cooper Union, New York
1984 Master of Architecture, Cranbrook Academy of Art

Nanako Umemoto
1975 Graduate of Urban Design, Osaka
1983 Graduate of Architecture, Cooper Union, New York

1984 Founded Reiser + Umemoto RUR Architecture PC in New York

Teaching
Jesse Reiser: 1998–89 – Columbia University, New York; Architectural
    Association, London; Stadelschule, Frankfurt; Berlage Institute;
    Kyoto University; Yale University; Princeton University

Nanako Umemoto: 1998–97 – Columbia University, New York; Berlage
    Institute; Harvard University; Columbia University; Yale University;
    Tulane University; Illinois Institute of Technology

Principal buildings and projects
1998 Graz Music Hall, Austria (competition); East River Parkway, New
    York; Cousin Apartment (realized), New York
1997 Spence Center for Women's Health, Tyson's Corner and Bethesda
    (realized); IIT, Student Center, Illinois
1996 Kansai Library, Kansai (competition); Bucarest 2000, Bucharest
    (competition); Spence Center for Women's Health (built), Wellesley;
    Sklar Residential Loft (realized)
1995 Geodetic Bridge, Cohen Residence, New Jersey; Yokohama Port
    Terminal, Yokohama (competition)
1994 Cardiff Bay Opera House, Wales (competition)
1993 Apartment and furniture of Leonard Brechner, New York (realized)
1992 Croton Aqueduct, Chicago (project); Boros Residence, H. Jadow
    Residence, Levinson Garde, New York (realized)
1990 Venice Gateway, Venice Biennale (competition); 'Aktion Poliphile'
    Wiesbaden

1989 The Icarus Project, Kyoto (realized); 'Japan Tex Exhibition', Tokyo
    (competition)
1988 Shadow Theater, New York (project)
1987 Dawn Profession, New York (realized)

Recent exhibitions
1998 'Relations between Contemporary Architecture and Painting'
    Bregenz, Austria; 'TransArchitecture' Paris, London, Tokyo; 'Global
    Cities' Ann Arbor
1997 'Reiser+Umemoto, Solid-State Architecture' Berlage Institute,
    Amsterdam
1998 *Chum: Computation in a Supersaturated Milieu* J. Reiser and J.
    Payne, Kenchiku Bunka, Tokyo (in preparation)
1995 'Computer Animism: Cardiff Bay Opera House' *Assemblage* no. 26;
    Post-Contradictory Practices catalogue of the Architecture
    Triennale, Nara, Japan; *Space* (Seoul)
1993 *Semiotexte Architectur: Façade Writing* Semiotext(e), Los Angeles
1991 'Hypnerotomachia Ero/Machia/Hynia, House' *Assemblage* no. 13,
    Cambridge

Selected bibliography
1998 'Reiser + Umemoto's Kansai Library' *Archimade* (March) Lausanne
1997 'Architecture after Geometry' *Architectural Design*, London; 'The
    Water Project' *City Speculations*, Princeton Architectural Press,
    New York
1996 'Reiser + Umemoto: Cardiff Opera House' *Architectural Profile*
    (July) Thailand; 'Blob Tectonics' *ANY*, New York
1994 'The New East Coast Movement' *Space Design* (August) Tokyo
1992 *Machine(s) d'Architectures* catalogue Cartier Foundation, Jouy en
    Josas
1990 'Reiser + Umemoto' *A + U* (November) Tokyo; 'Globe Theatre
    Project' in *Violated Perfection*, Rizzoli, New York; *Aktion Poliphile*
    catalogue, Frankfurt

Rudy Ricciotti

| Rudy Ricciotti (*1952) |

In the 1980s, engineer and architect Rudy Ricciotti practised a hedonistic architecture, involving the pleasure of form and space. Then, with the advent of the 1990s, he veered away from the formal deadlocks of neo-modernism. From then on his work has been informed by a critical radicalism that found early expression in the Vitrolles Stadium (1994). This suburban bunker, made of dark concrete, rises up in the midst of bauxite slagheaps, redefining a rubbish tip. Land Art practitioner Robert Smithson employed the concept of 'ruins in reverse' for this post-industrial nature. Similarly, architecture and landscape are entropic in Vitrolles, at once vitalist and fractured in their semantic itinerary. The rough expressiveness of this monolith – at once isolated block and mineral concretion – is at the same time a paradox. Its façade is as if shattered into countless red motifs, which glow day and night. The massive imposition of the building is hollowed out within, in the form of fiercely extruded walls. The backwashes of light dwindle into wires that streak the space with their kinetic vibrations. Shape and shapelessness, opaqueness and holes, compactness and upheavals, darkness of the primitive mass and telescoped lights, all refer, in their harsh alchemy of opposites, to the poetics of the Sublime and to the spatial constructs of Suprematism, where matter and sign, and obscurity and lightness are one. Everything here contributes to foil the unitary understanding of the building. Architecture is, from the outset, a heterogeneous and paradoxical sign. Form is not irreducible and implacable, beauty and ugliness are not end purposes, but operational processes that must give on to hybrid fields of appropriation of the real, culminating in an architecture that Ricciotti describes as 'impure'. Architecture is seen as artefact, a conflagration of possibles, extracted from the composite fabric of the real and from the make-believe fabric of artistic creation. The Apollonian and the Dionysiac, the minimal and the expressive all merge together in the transgressive territorial cut-out represented by the Villa Lyprendi (Toulon), a window stretched horizontally over 35 metres, like a slash of transparency in the surrounding landscape. The eye often looks out onto the outside only through the cracks laminating the space (College 600, St Ouen, 1997; EDF Houses, 1999), as if to shut out any underground viewpoint on the world. This fault architecture, involving the obliqueness of the sign, a resistance to pigeonholed divisions of space, and a refusal of mind-boggling hierarchies, which advocates the multiplicity of meaning of both artifice and falseness (dead palm tree and Vitrolles blue, or poppy field at St Ouen), is thus an architecture of the availability of meaning. As a contemporary art lover and collector, Ricciotti espouses an aesthetic of poverty, vulgarity and low-tech, as energy-giving material. The conceptual paths that Ricciotti explores come across in a tension between optimism and negativity. The complexity of the real – the cross-fertilization of cultures, and the mixedness of word fields and social behaviour patterns – is part and parcel of his conception of architecture. Rudy Ricciotti's architecture, which is fictional, narrative and disruptive, triggers incoherence, while at the same time drawing its critical operational quality from a questioning of art. ❖

✦ Villa Lyprendi

TOULON, FRANCE, 1998

This house is affixed to the buttresses of the Toulon roads, looking out to sea. It is part of a recent housing development whose specifications dictated a regionalist architectural expression – pale rendering, Roman tile-covered gable roofs. Rudy Ricciotti twists this restriction by embedding his project in the very steep slope (45 degrees). The house is incorporated in a parallelepiped volume 35 metres long, and unfurls along the mountain, opening broadly on to the landscape combining city and sea – its sole façade. Made up of a continuous glass surface, it is duplicated by a linear terrace cantilevered over the void, and a sun screen treated like horizontal, artificial foliage. The materials used are rough and stark, often borrowed from industrial architecture: polished concrete slab, wood, metal, glass. The applications assert the simplicity of the building, in their turn rejecting any technological effect and any industrial performance. As a minimalist object, cutting into the mountain, the house represents a radical counterpoint to the architecture merry-go-round . ✦

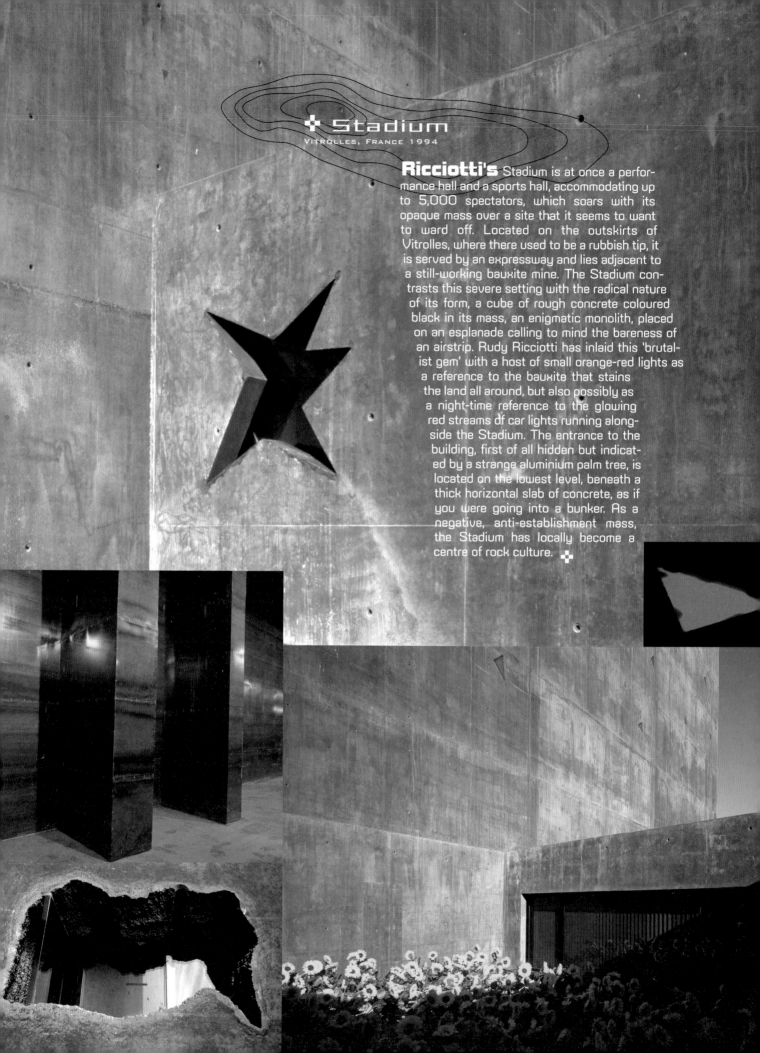

✦ Stadium
VITROLLES, FRANCE 1994

Ricciotti's Stadium is at once a performance hall and a sports hall, accommodating up to 5,000 spectators, which soars with its opaque mass over a site that it seems to want to ward off. Located on the outskirts of Vitrolles, where there used to be a rubbish tip, it is served by an expressway and lies adjacent to a still-working bauxite mine. The Stadium contrasts this severe setting with the radical nature of its form, a cube of rough concrete coloured black in its mass, an enigmatic monolith, placed on an esplanade calling to mind the bareness of an airstrip. Rudy Ricciotti has inlaid this 'brutalist gem' with a host of small orange-red lights as a reference to the bauxite that stains the land all around, but also possibly as a night-time reference to the glowing red streams of car lights running alongside the Stadium. The entrance to the building, first of all hidden but indicated by a strange aluminium palm tree, is located on the lowest level, beneath a thick horizontal slab of concrete, as if you were going into a bunker. As a negative, anti-establishment mass, the Stadium has locally become a centre of rock culture. ✦

✦ Museum of the Primary Arts

QUAI BRANLY, PARIS, FRANCE
COMPETITION, 1999

In his project for the Musée des Arts Premiers, Rudy Ricciotti espoused a critical stance to the actual programme. Located at the foot of the Eiffel Tower, a distant throwback to an imperialist West whose influence encompassed the world, the museum had a duty above all, in his view, to veer radically away from all those colonialist connotations floating over its collection. For this perforce problematic monument, he discarded any unitary option, be it continuous or frontal, preferring to operate by lateralization, burial and suspension. Above the large collection room, cantilevered over the Seine, the roof offers a large accessible terrace. A garden, where plants mingle with architecture, surrounds the building, filling the entire site. In the crevice in the ground are hewn out a series of interactive venues, lit by and accessible from vaults. From outside, even when the museum is closed, these offer many different intersecting views of the collections. Close by, a volume on the Haussmann-esque scale of the surroundiing structures houses staff and researchers. ✦

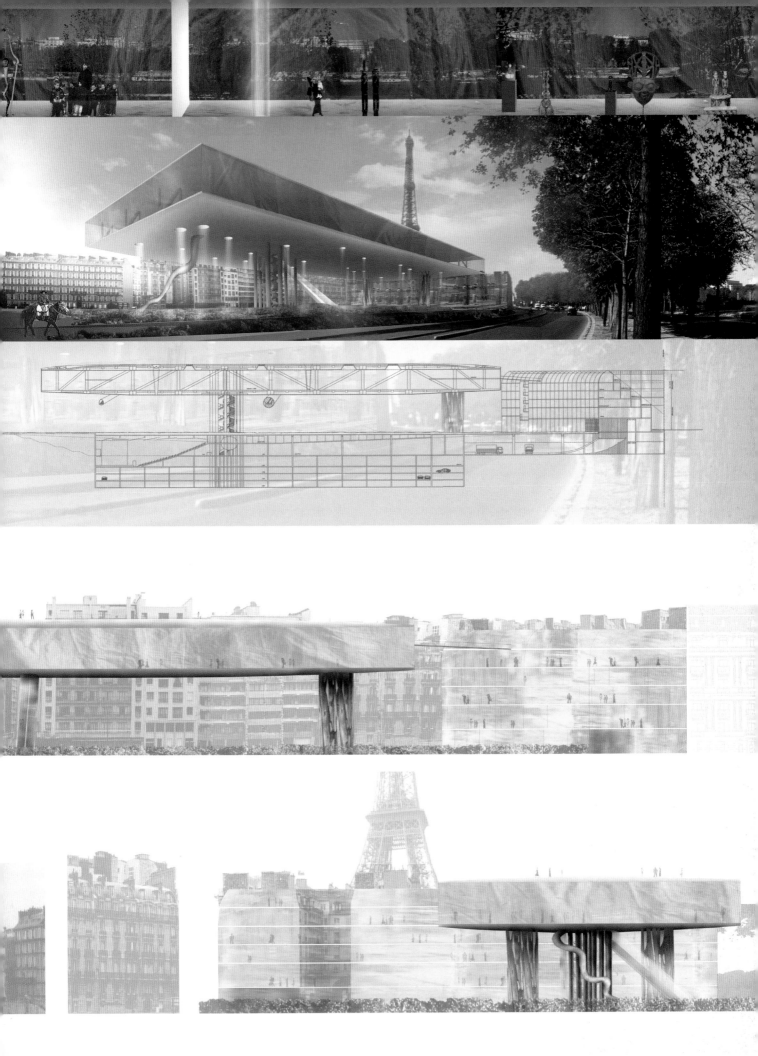

✛ Quayside Railway Station

MARSEILLE, FRANCE, 2000

The project, at the end of the wharf, occupies a sp[e]-cial position, at the gateway to both city and sea. [It] serves two opposite quays, one to the west, the other to the east, forcing it to develop along this axis and to be programmatically duplicated. The option chosen by Rudy Ricciotti is, in spite of everything, one of com-pactness. A single building incorporates all the func-tions, cutting down on useless circuits, encouraging a streamlined programme and rationalized movements and flows, and offering a sturdier profile both to the mistral wind and to the spray. An atrium-like hall, open to the south and shared by both zones, fills the mid-dle of the project, containing the waiting area and shops on the upper level, and check-in and baggage registration on the ground floor. On both sides the programme is developed symmetrically, based on a logic that is not vertical but horizontal: each level contains both public areas (passenger hall, baggage zone), technical facilities and premises for the personnel, as well as car parks linked to the station by footbridges straddling the set-down area and the different vehicle flows. This horizontal option is confirmed by the tectonics of the building: rough concrete slabs with large spans on minimal, thin supports.

EDF Houses
COMPETITION, FRANCE, 1999

✛ Rudy Ricciotti

Rudy Ricciotti (1952)
1975 Diploma from the Engineering School, Geneva, Architect ETSG
1980 Diploma from the Architecture School at Marseilles
1980 Creation of the practice in Marseilles

Principal buildings and projects
2000 Gare maritime, Marseilles (competition); Seoul footbridge, Korea; Reconstruction of Montmajour Abbey; Philharmonia concert hall, Potsdam (under construction); Spectacle hall, Strasburg (under construction); 'Scenes of contemporary music in Nîmes' (studies); Rearrangement of the National Centre of Photography, Paris (studies); National Choreographic Centre. Aix en Provence' (studies)
1999 Museum of Primary Arts, Quai Branly, Paris (competition); Individual houses EDF (competition); Le Goff villa and swimming pool, Marseilles (realized); Marmonier villa and swimming pool, La Garde (realized)
1998 Villa Lyprendi, Toulon (realized); Foyer restaurant du CREPS, Boulouris (realized); Grand hall of the Faculty of Sciences, Marseilles (realized)
1997 Collège 600, Saint Ouen (realized); Villa Gros, Gémenos (realized)
1996 A20 motorway service centre, Uzerche (realized); Collège 900, Auriol (realized)
1995 Nautical base at Bandol (realized); Villa Chaix reconstruction, Ramatuelle (realized)
1994 Vitrolles stadium (realized); Festival hall, Port Saint Louis du Rhône (realized)
1993 Spectacle hall and cinema, Pierrelatte (prizewinner)
1992 Road information and coordination centre, Marseilles (realized)

1986 Youth leisure centre, Bandol (realized)

Publications
1998 *Pièces à Conviction: Les interviews vitriol d'un Sudiste* Sens & Tonka (Sept.)

Selected bibliography
1999 *Le Moniteur* (May and August); *d'Architectures* (Jun.); *l'Architecture d'aujourd'hui* (Feb.); *Construction Moderne* (Dec.); '99 Architectures en 99' *Maison d'Architecture et de Construction de Chine* (Jun.); *World Architecture Review* (Jun.)
1998 'Re-création: 21 architectures in France at the dawn of the XXIst century' (1998/2000: travelling exhibition in Latin America) AFAA/Ministry of Culture, France/Argentina; *De Architect* (Nov.); *Space Design* (Sept.); *The Architectural Review* (July); *Le Moniteur AMC* (May); *Techniques & Architectures* (Jan.)
1997 *Stadium de Vitrolles* Taschen; *Archi-Créé* (Sept. and Nov.); *Techniques & Architectures* (Sept.); *Le Moniteur AMC* (Jun.); *l'Arca* (Jan.); *Connaissance des Arts* (August)
1996 *Techniques & Architectures* (Oct.); *Le Moniteur AMC* (April and July); *d'Architectures* (April); *l'Arca* (Feb.); *Werk, Bauen+Wohnen* (Feb.); *Architectural Review* (Feb.)

Richter Studio

| Dagmar Richter (*1955) |

To design in architecture is to transform found spatial structure. In a fluid field of changes the planner and the designer are active readers of this spatial text put forward in different forms of representation, such as diagrams, photographic or film material, as well personal experience, which in turn is automatically transformed through the reader's appropriation. Planners and architects alike plan future structures and try to predict the direction fluid spatial realities will take. The collected data will then be presented in various forms of representations to different readers. These readers are not regarded as passive entities consuming the text in an unaltered form. Every reading will leave the text put forward altered. The different representations architects and planners find, are filled with traces of active reading processes. The politician, potential user, fellow architect and planner, to name just a few, will leave those numerous traces, which emerge in subsequent altered representations. The architect and planner are collectors of these traces, be they historical traces found on maps, traces on contemporary representations as photographs or drawings, texts or spoken words, found images and texts that seem at first unrelated. The planner-architect combines, translates and transforms the found material, which in further reading processes is consumed and transformed by new readers who may implement and translate the given representations to create a new spatial and political reality. The produced text is never objective, never clean and never original in the classical sense. It is a text ready for interpretation by the next party involved. Planner and architect alike collect material deemed appropriate and create a transformed representation ready for debate, translation and appropriation. Any act of reading is simultaneously an act of appropriation and the selection of reading material is crucial in order to arrive at a relevant spatial representation. The art of architecture is then defined as a strategy of appropriation, trickery and rhetoric of use. It is an art of copy, appropriation and recombination. A space occurs, when directional vectors of speed and variables of time are interwoven. This space can influence action but never define it. The architect, a strategist, will always attempt to create something of his own, which acts as a normative; the user will always transform it through a tactic of use and appropriation.

Instead of following the classical idea that the act of designing and assigning is defined by a process of invention, one has to regard oneself as an editing specialist, who critically initiates choice through a process of translation of already assembled material. As there have been many voices not read through history since they were deemed inappropriate, irrelevant or undesirable, it is now necessary to apply thorough criticism towards the selection of representations considered relevant to the reading process. Our interest is therefore concentrated in the reading of the contemporary city, landscape and periphery. ✤

DAGMAR RICHTER

❖ Rereading the City
West Coast Gateway, Los Angeles, USA
Competition (Second Prize)

This project for Los Angeles clearly illustrates Dagmar Richter's urban approach: the city is a sedimentation of 'traces' that interact with each other. The city is here extended horizontally above a freeway, whose drawn-out form it follows. Translucid walls, affixed to this linear structure, broadcast information by night while an electronic genealogical library is suspended within it. The city comes across like an aerial leaf-like structure of 'traces', which have nothing to do with any kind of inclusion. The factors implicit in electronic communications lie at the core of her approach. For Richter, the city is a media-related text, altered by its producers and users alike; the city is a geographical map, at once the 'skin' of a territory and a representation. The city is both the condensation of traces from the past and their dissolution in the electronic fluidity of different forms of circulation. ❖

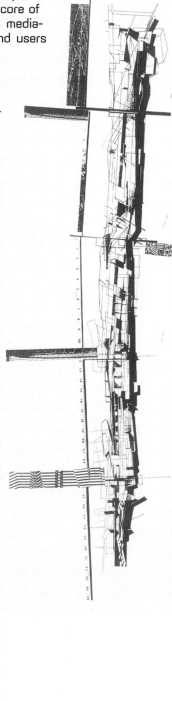

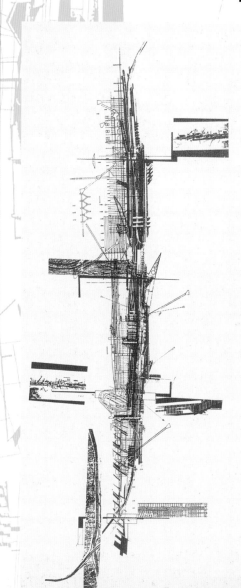

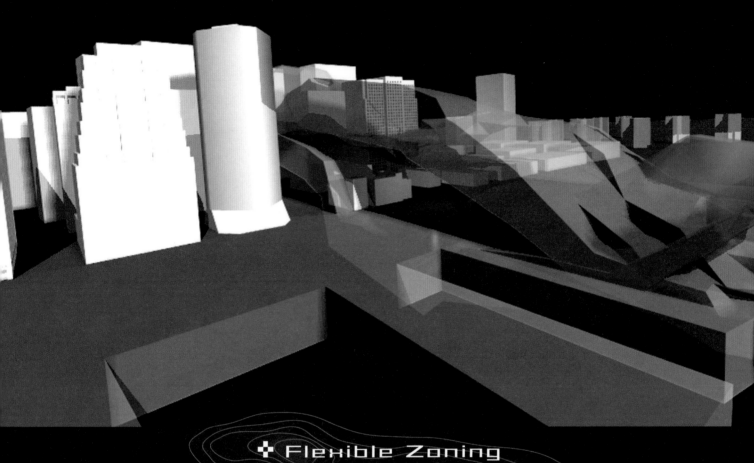

✦ Flexible Zoning

NEW YORK, USA
1998

The area between Piers 16 and 18 in Lower Manhattan has been chosen by the D. Richter Studio for experimental investigations regarding the new use of computer equipment in its relation to spatial zoning manipulations. This area, around the East River, was used to collect spatial and statistical data and translated into a mental animated spatial 3D map. The inherent and impredictable dynamics of the city, understood as a large organism, influenced by inside and outside events, are the force that animates the model. This new three-dimensional zoning effort allows the creation of a more complex programmatic relationship in the city's section and creates the possibility of the expansion of more public space throughout the volumes of the buildings. Then, continuous sky-park on the roof tops or 'fuzzy' water edge conditions, for example, could be electronically negotiated. ✦

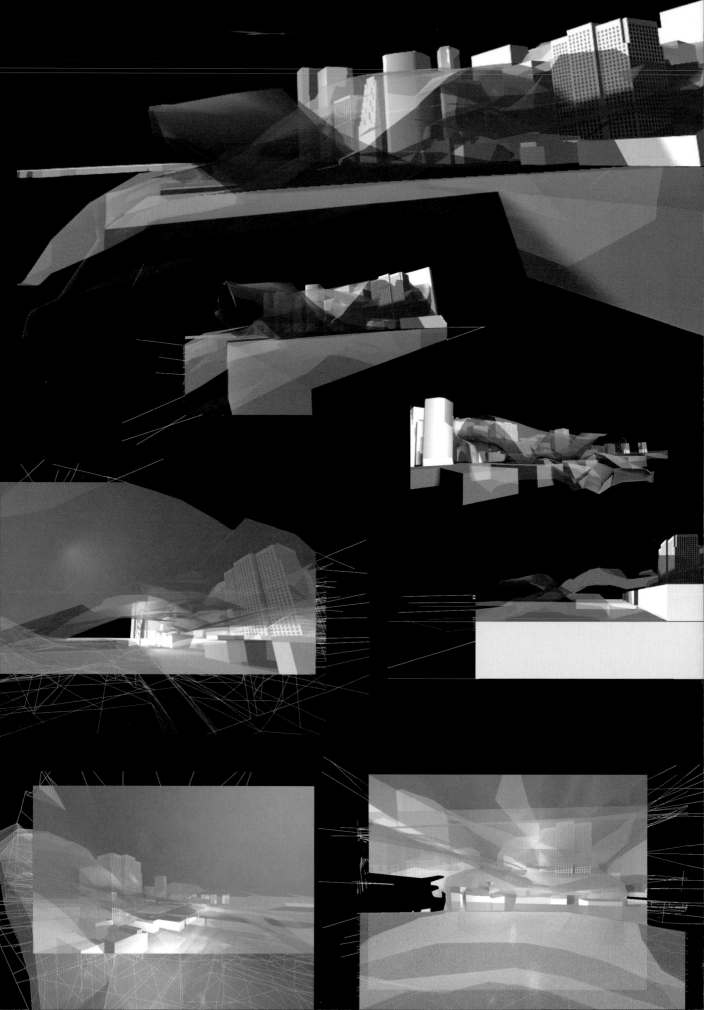

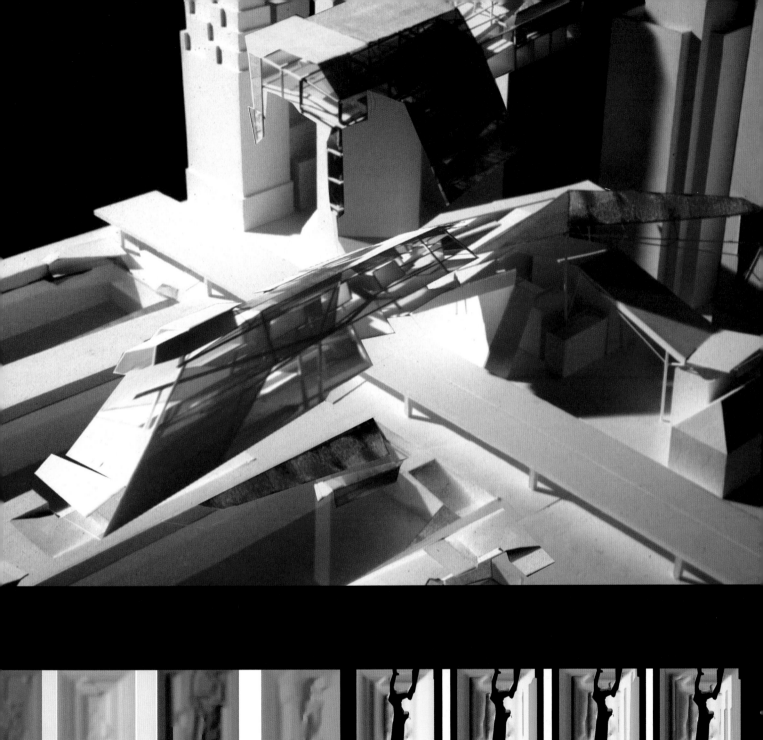
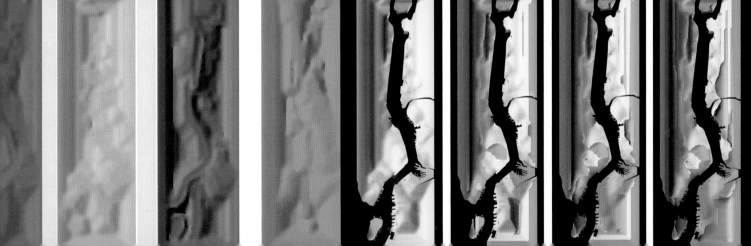

✦ Shangai Housing 2000

SHANGAI, JAPAN
COMPETITION, 1997

Dagmar Richter based her project on the tradition and design of Chinese garden. First of all, she has interpreted it as a complex network of sophisticated pathways serving a range of varied public spaces. Thus, the public trajectories of the project were attentively studied in order to open views, to provide distinct views in often compressed spaces. Water and mountains, two elements that were dominant in the Chinese gardens, helped Dagmar Richter to create an alternative to the well-established Western techniques of housing design. Instead of directly copying the formal vocabulary of the singular high-rise or low-rise building of the West, she used the old tradition of artificial hill construction to achieve dense and, in some cases, relatively high housing volumes. Based on the representation of the height of sacred mountains surrounding Shangai, she distributed the necessary high-density housing on the site. Water was also used to create voids and distances, contemplative mirror surfaces that divide but do not separate. ✦

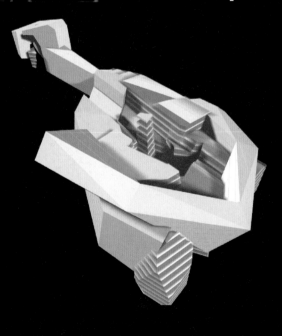

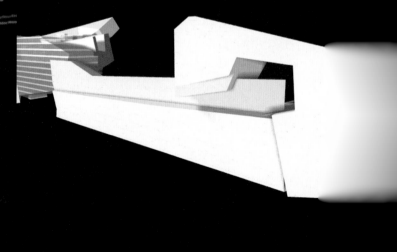

✦ Richter Studio

Dagmar Richter (1955)

1976 Preliminary diploma, University of Stuttgart, Germany
1982 Master of Architecture, Royal Art Academy School of Architecture, Copenhagen, Denmark
1984–86 Postgraduate diploma, Städelschule, Frankfurt

1982–86 Studio at Copenhagen, Denmark
1986–89 Studio at Cambridge, MA
1987 Founded Dagmar Richter Studio in Los Angeles and Berlin

Teaching

1999 Kunsthochschule Berlin, Weissensee; UCLA, Department of Architecture and Urban Design
1997 Columbia University, New York
1992 Sci-Arc, Los Angeles
1991 University of Illinois, Chicago

Principal buildings and projects

1998 Research Project on Flexible Zoning, New York (project)
1998–97 House, Santa Monica, CA (realized)
1997 Shangai Housing 2000 (competition)
1994 Shinkenchiku Membrane (competition, first prize)
1993 Royal Library, Copenhagen (competition, second prize)
1991 Temporary Playhouse, Pacific Palisades, California
1990–89 'Re-Reading Century City' (project)
1988 International West Coast Gateway, with Shayne O'Neil (competition, third prize)
1987 Shinkenchiku Central Glass, with Ulrich Hinrichsmeyer (competition, second prize); 'The Intelligent Market',

with Ulrich Hinrichsmeyer (competition, second prize)

Recent exhibitions

1997 New York and Los Angeles, Collective exhibition, Henry Urbach
1995 Technical University, Berlin, Germany
1992 Aedes Gallery, Berlin; Storefront, New York; ROM, Oslo

Principal publications

2000 *XYZ: The Architecture of Dagmar Richter*, Laurence King, London
1997 'Beyond Euclidean Geometry' *Newsline* (spring) Columbia University
1996 'Spazieren in Berlin' *Assemblage* (vol. 29), MIT Press; 'Gedanken um den Design Process'/'Internationaler Ideenwettbewerb Berlin, Spreebogen'/'Neue Koenigliche Bibliothek Kopenhagen'/'Membranen und Energien' (four chapters) *International Forum Prague Architecture and Responsibility'* Joerg Kirchbaum and Anna Meseure. Trad. Arcum Verlag
1994 *Shinkenchiku* vol. 11 Tokyo; *Oz* vol. 16; *Zodiac* (vol. 11) Italy
1993 'A Child's Guest House' *l'Architecture d'aujourd'hui* no. 290
1992 'Dagmar Richter, The Art of Copy: Rereading the City' *Storefront* (Dec.); 'The Century City' *Architectural Design: Theory and Experimentation: Architectural ideas for today and tomorrow*, London; 'The Art of Copy' *Journal of Philosophy and the Visuals Arts* (Feb.) London
1991 'Reading Los Angeles: A Primitive Rebel's Account' *Assemblage* vol. 14, MIT Press, Cambridge
1990 'Dagmar Richter and Ulrich Hinrichsmeyer' *A+U* no. 233

Roche, DSV & Sie.P

| François Roche (*1961) | Gilles Desèvedavy (*1963) |
| Stéphanie Lavaux (*1966) | François Perrin (*1968) |

For some years now, Roche, DSV & Sie. P have been pursuing their research into an almost negative definition of architectural identity. 'Making do with less' is the way they put it. Over and above any presupposition about form and function, architecture should be defined by a set of relations, not only to do with its contextual incorporation, but also with social pragmatics in which it must regain a factual value. Many projects seem akin to installation-architecture of the moment, contrasting with the traditional architectures of inclusion and permanence. Roche, DSV & Sie. P often contrast modern, functional form with a parasitic form, a non-form that seems made of humble materials – a temporary form stemming from an assemblage, the vestige of an immediately readable human praxis. The references to nomadism, factual constructions, shanty towns and favelas betoken a culture of recycling, displacement and makeshift assemblages, where architecture is defined as something empirically close to use and function. What Roche, DSV & Sie. P propose often clashes with a context, be it urban and well thought-out or natural, with its flipside, a negative part that has to be reactivated in order to make architecture dynamic. Whence, come the Memorial Museum project in Soweto, the Sainte-Rose project or the Maïdo project, on the island of Réunion, whose identity seems vague to the point of becoming altogether virtual, with the invisible bloc and the rectangular section that create an artificial clearing for the Réunion Regional Contemporary Art Collection [FRAC], by redistributing the functional premises at the edge of a forest. The architecture of Roche, DSV & Sie. P is an architecture of *dérive* (drift). It shrinks from any constructional positivism. It raises issues to do with means, techniques and the language of a type of engineering, which seems to have completely frozen the role of project management. Here the architect regains a primary role. He assembles, gives cohesion, reveals, and accomplishes a demand that is capable of redefining and recontextualizing. The architecture of Roche, DSV & Sie. P thus aims to participate in its own environment in a twofold movement of mimesis as an inventive method, and recycling, extraction and transformation. It does not rise up on a piece of ground, but within a critical experiment, which introduces a change of contextual parameters. This is a critical experiment that Roche, DSV & Sie. P is currently undertaking with new technologies (morphing), in order to remain open to areas of investigation likely to introduce new parameters and prompt 'scenarios of distortion, substitution, hybridization, cloning, grafting and scarification'. We thus have Acqua Alta, the Venetian project, which aims to 'capitalize on the lagoon identity' and which sets forth processes of 'sedimentation and hybridization' where 'functions occur in many different string-like intersections, like a PVC medusa sweeper, with murky, dense transparency'. ✣

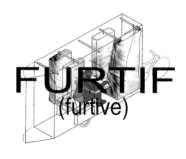

FURTIF
(furtive)

✦ Maïdo
RÉUNION ISLAND, INDIAN OCEAN
1995/1996

On Réunion, the Regional Contemporary Art
Collection [FRAC] moved to new premises and had to
incorporate an exhibition area, storage rooms, offices
and residential studios for visiting artists. Roche, DSV
& Sie. P contrasted the clearing that matches the
island's image with the aspect of a unifying building. The
primary architectural object is thus something vacuous,
a geometric void, shaped like a huge parallelepiped that
demarcates the FRAC site, cutting a modest notch in
the forest. The different facilities are scattered along
the edge of the forest, their glass façades looking out
on to the open area. The artists' studios, cubic volumes
erected on piles on the furthest part of this hill, dominate the site, but blend in with the foliage of the forest.
There are two contrasting orders of construction : the
organization of the vegetation and the definition of
the structure, both defined by this section, a forest edge that makes no division between the form and formless-
ness of the building. ✤

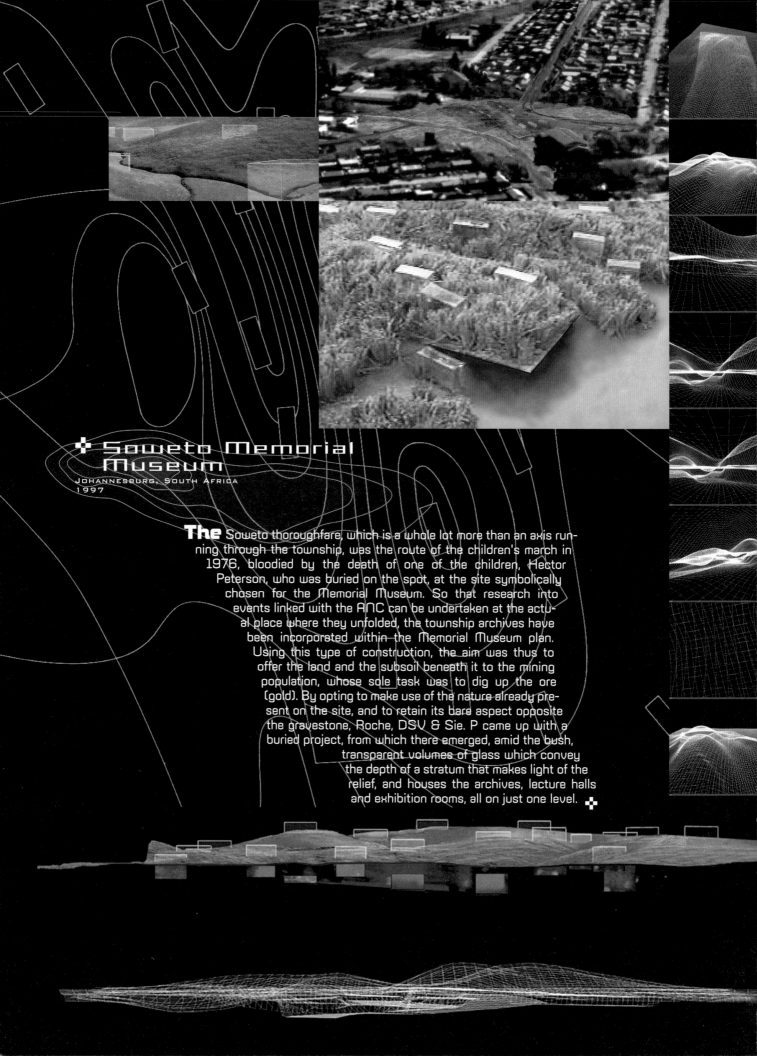

✦ Soweto Memorial Museum

JOHANNESBURG, SOUTH AFRICA
1997

The Soweto thoroughfare, which is a whole lot more than an axis running through the township, was the route of the children's march in 1976, bloodied by the death of one of the children, Hector Peterson, who was buried on the spot, at the site symbolically chosen for the Memorial Museum. So that research into events linked with the ANC can be undertaken at the actual place where they unfolded, the township archives have been incorporated within the Memorial Museum plan. Using this type of construction, the aim was thus to offer the land and the subsoil beneath it to the mining population, whose sole task was to dig up the ore (gold). By opting to make use of the nature already present on the site, and to retain its bare aspect opposite the gravestone, Roche, DSV & Sie. P came up with a buried project, from which there emerged, amid the bush, transparent volumes of glass which convey the depth of a stratum that makes light of the relief, and houses the archives, lecture halls and exhibition rooms, all on just one level. ✦

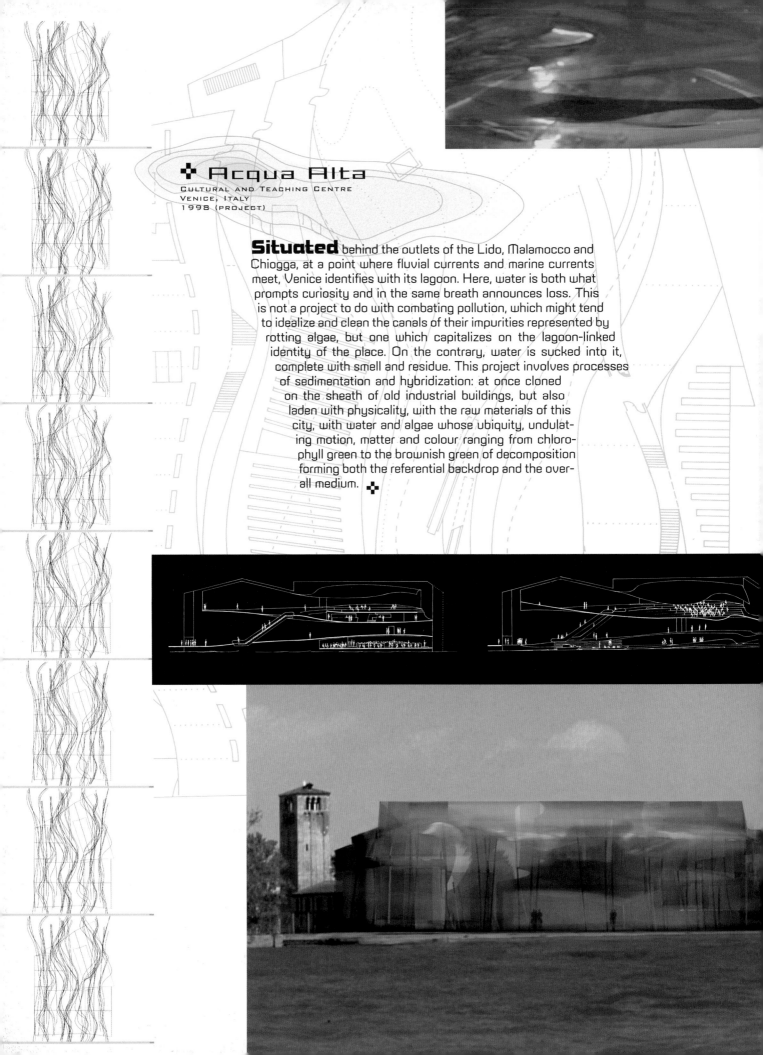

✦ Acqua Alta

CULTURAL AND TEACHING CENTRE
VENICE, ITALY
1998 (PROJECT)

Situated behind the outlets of the Lido, Malamocco and Chiogga, at a point where fluvial currents and marine currents meet, Venice identifies with its lagoon. Here, water is both what prompts curiosity and in the same breath announces loss. This is not a project to do with combating pollution, which might tend to idealize and clean the canals of their impurities represented by rotting algae, but one which capitalizes on the lagoon-linked identity of the place. On the contrary, water is sucked into it, complete with smell and residue. This project involves processes of sedimentation and hybridization: at once cloned on the sheath of old industrial buildings, but also laden with physicality, with the raw materials of this city, with water and algae whose ubiquity, undulating motion, matter and colour ranging from chlorophyll green to the brownish green of decomposition forming both the referential backdrop and the overall medium. ✦

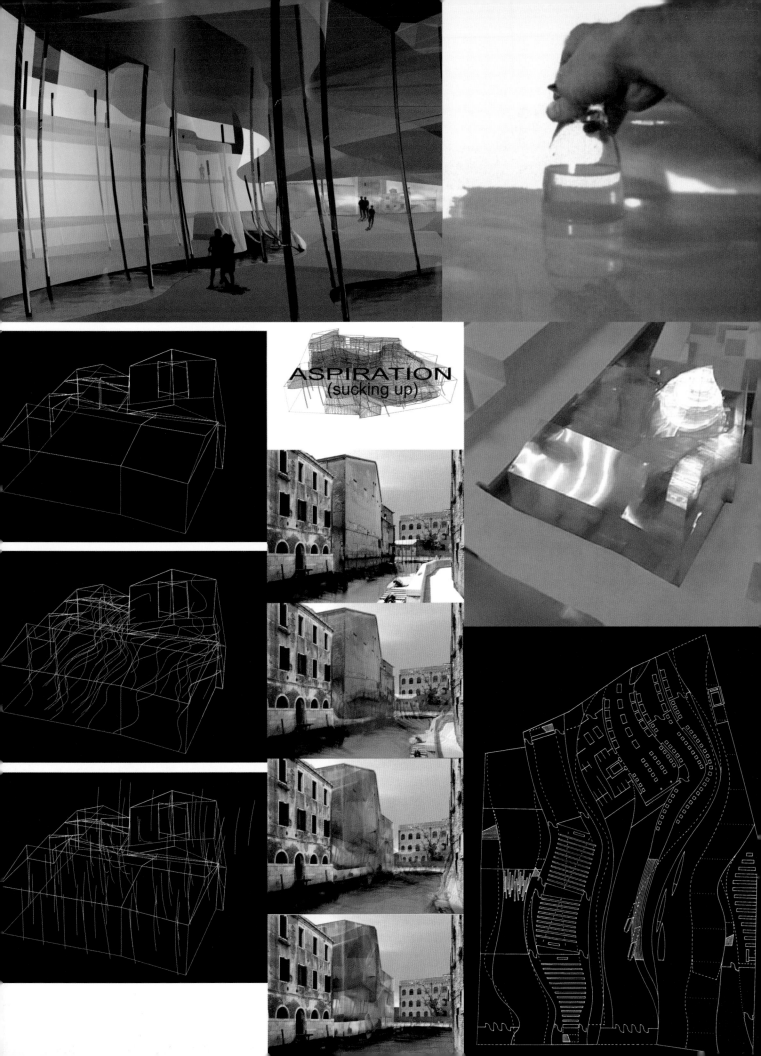

ASPIRATION
(sucking up)

✦ Shoreline Shelter and Development
SAINTE-ROSE, RÉUNION ISLAND, FRANCE
1998 (PROJECT)

The marine of Sainte Rose used to be a port brimming with coffee, rice, grain, sugar and tapioca all stored in warehouses, massive, sober structures made of basalt, built to withstand a climate character- ized by clement weather capriciously alternating with the vio- lence of hurricanes. The vast, irregular nature of the terrain, made up of recent flows of jagged lava, crags dripping with vegetation, a harsh climate and the 'geological' strata — all in shades of blue, black, green — factors that underpin the project's conception of a building that which is akin to an extrusion of basaltic material in lava rocks. On this building Roche, DSV & Sie. P propose to fix and embed the development of the shore, so as to avoid separating or breaking up the activities and to develop a dynamic of linkages and exchanges. ✦

EXTRUSION
(EXTRUSION)

✛ Roche, DSV & Sie.P

François Roche (1961)
1987 Diploma from the School of Architecture at Versailles; Installation of a first structure
1989 Album de la Jeune Architecture
1994 Prix de la Villa Médicis (external)

Gilles Desèvedavy (1963)
1993 Diploma from the School of Architecture at Paris-Villemin
1986 MIQCP bursary winner

Stéphanie Lavaux (1966)
1990 Diploma from the College of Fine Arts, Paris

François Perrin (1968)
1993 Diploma from the School of Architecture of Paris-La Seine
1998 Electra bursary winner

Principal buildings and projects
1999 Les Mots, BPI, Georges Pompidou Centre; Polder, Rotterdam
1998 'Acqua Alta', Venice School of Architecture; Sainte-Rose (project) Fishing port, Réunion (project)
1997 Museum Memorial, Soweto, Johannesburg, South Africa (project); Baïse, Vianne (project)
1995 Maïdo, Réunion (project)
1994 Deligny swimming pool, Paris (project); Building 48, Sarcelles, France (project)
1992 Ecole Supérieure d'Art du Fresnoy, Tourcoing (competition)
1991 Arrangement of sea shore, Trébeurdun (project)
1990 The House of Japan, Paris (competition)

Recent exhibitions
1998 'Mutations @morphes' FRAC Centre, Orléans; 'La Table' Galerie Air de Paris; 'Trans-Architecture 03' Berlin and Rotterdam; 'Paysage Sud' 45, rue de Belleville, Paris; 'Urbanismes' Ecole des Beaux-Arts, Nîmes
1997 '36 modèles pour une maison' Arc en Rêve, Bordeaux; 'Sous le soleil exactement' Art en Thèse, Montpellier; 'Shelter'

Kunstnersenter, Trondheim, Norway; FRAC Centre collection, Orléans
1996 'Villette-Amazone' Grande halle de la Villette, Paris; Mostra Internazionale di Architettura at Venice, French Pavilion; 'Paysage no. 5' Le Magasin, Grenoble

Recent conferences
1999 'Mutations 2.0 Espace Croisé, Lille, France; 'Polder' NAI, Rotterdam
1998 'Mutations' USC, Los Angeles, Columbia, New York; 'Territoire plié' Ecole d'Architecture de Rouen; 'Tra archittetura arte e paesaggio' Reggio Calabre, Rome; Ecole Nationale des Arts Décoratifs, Paris

Principal publications
1998 *Mutations @morphes* HYX/FRAC Centre, 'Quelques nouvelles du front' *Mini PA*, Pavillon de l'Arsenal; 'Situation' (text) *Quaderns*
1997 *Paysage sud* FRAC Réunion; '2G' *Matières* (editorial)
1995 *L'Ombre du caméléon* IFA/Karédas
1993 'Le 3 mars 1993' *Journal*, IFA
1989 'Album de la Jeune Architecture' *Mino. de l'Equipement*

Selected bibliography
1999 'Mutation génétique', *Parpaings* no. 1; 'Vous avez dit patrimoine' (tribune) *Beaux-Arts Magazine*
1998 *Crash* (Oct.); *Quaderns* no. 220; 'Tracing Architecture', *Architectural Design*; *Quaderns* no. 217
1996 *Bloc,le monolithe fracturé* catalogue of the Venice Biennale; *Art Press* no. 213
1995 *Paysage no. 5*, exhibition catalogue, Grenoble
1994 *Techniques & Architectures* no. 416
1993 *Quaderns* no. 195
1991 *40 architectes de moins de 40 ans* exhibition catalogue, IFA.; *l'Architecture d'aujourd'hui* no. 277; *Architecture créée* no. 245

Sadar in Vuga Arhitekti

| Jurij Sadar (*1963) | Bostjan Vuga (*1966) |

Sadar in Vuga Arhitekti is a young critical architectural practice in Ljubljana. Underlying its projets is to stand back from conventional design processes and techniques, which inevitably lead to conventional architecture products. Sadar in Vuga Arhitekti search for stimuli for their projects in the world of visual, acoustical and written information, in art, fashion, science and technology. It aims to develop design techniques that make their architectural products both fresh and long-lasting. Don't be surprised to find textile fabric woven in two colours presented as the effect of a new façade. One of the basic premises for a residential single-family house is the least possible displacement of land on terrain innaccessible to machinery and vehicles. You can discuss the new sports centre as you would a sequence from a science fiction film. A diagram of human brain impulses is the basis for determining relations between spaces in the multiplex cinema. The office building is a floating monolith. The commerce institution building consists in part of metal boxes resembling those by LeWitt set one on top of another. Of course all these motions, these basic prototypes, are modified, reworked and adapted to the client's programme, wishes and demands through the project's development and execution. The value of the investment is always one of the project parameters – the price influences all aspects of planning. Sadar in Vuga Arhitekti invests its financial profits in the development of new design concepts and techniques. Within strict commercial conditions where time and money are the main concerns, this enables it to create fresh, different and attractive architectural products. Sadar in Vuga Arhitekti attempts to bridge the distance between experimental, theoretical architecture and corporate architecture with a predetermined appearance. Sadar and Vuga believe that today's architectural product can only be the result of the common effort of internal as well as external team members. The concept of the superior creative individual mind has been exhausted. From the initial brainstorming to the choice of presentation means, key decisions are always made in a team; Sadar in Vuga has worked as part of O.C.E.A.N. Net, for example. Founded in London in 1995, this network as an open and flexible form of affiliation, cooperation and promotion of architectural production. The architecture of Sadar in Vuga Arhitekti wants to open itself to all geographical and intellectual influences, to integrate all the internal or external parameters and to innovate. ◆

SADAR IN VUGA ARHITEKTI

b − b'

✦ Aomori Museum

AOMORI PREFECTURE, JAPAN
COMPETITION, 2000

The proposal put forward by Sadar in Vuga Arhitekti for the competition for the Aomori Museum is based on permeability. The view and the light move through the five overlaid platforms (108 x 42 metres) forming the building, filtering inside and working their way from one floor to the next by way of a host of round apertures or cavities. In the horizontal landscape made up of these platforms, these holes open up an infinite array of vertical permeable elements. The actual museum occupies three of the five platforms. Two are buried underground and one is suspended above the ground. Between the two, an intermediate space is left free, allowing the natural ground to pass through the museum and, with it, wind, snow and strolling visitors. Nature also resolutely inhabits the exterior of the museum by means of this permeability, here horizontal. Each of the museum's four levels has its own entrance hall. These halls are interconnected by the round apertures, housing escalators and lifts. ✦

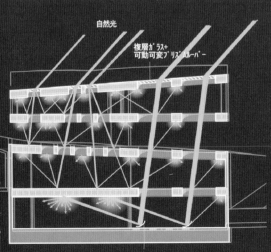

自然光

複層ガラス+
可動可変プリズムルーバー

床に鏡面ガラス

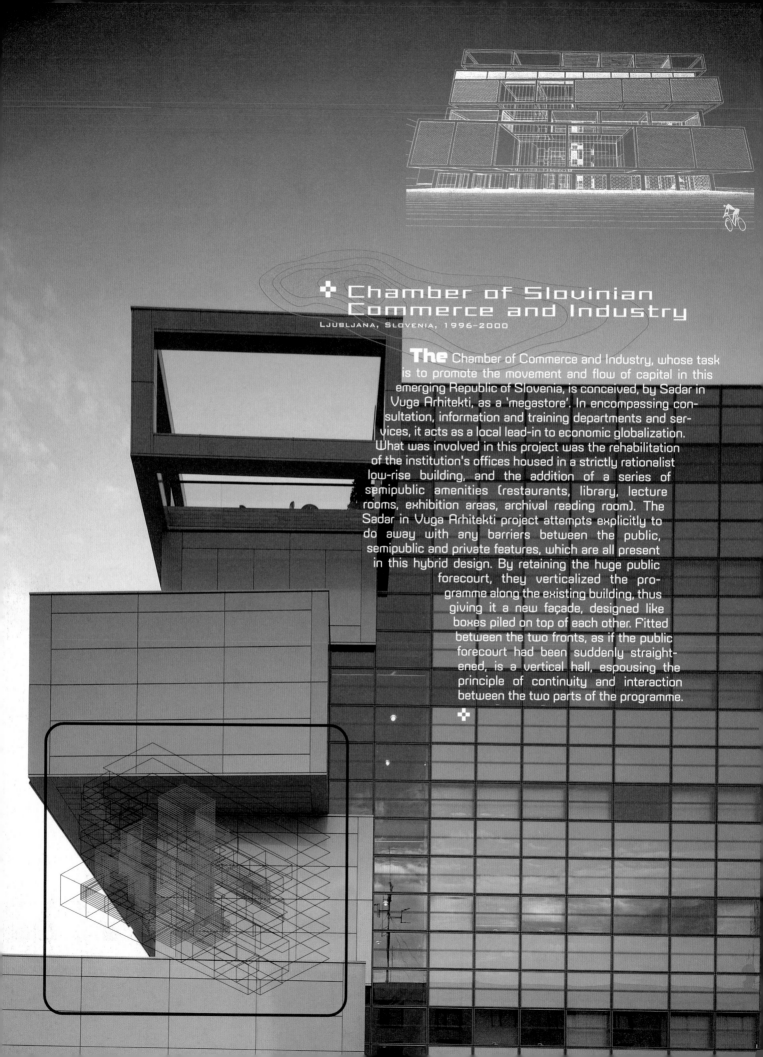

✦ Chamber of Slovinian Commerce and Industry

LJUBLJANA, SLOVENIA, 1996–2000

The Chamber of Commerce and Industry, whose task is to promote the movement and flow of capital in this emerging Republic of Slovenia, is conceived, by Sadar in Vuga Arhitekti, as a 'megastore'. In encompassing consultation, information and training departments and services, it acts as a local lead-in to economic globalization. What was involved in this project was the rehabilitation of the institution's offices housed in a strictly rationalist low-rise building, and the addition of a series of semipublic amenities (restaurants, library, lecture rooms, exhibition areas, archival reading room). The Sadar in Vuga Arhitekti project attempts explicitly to do away with any barriers between the public, semipublic and private features, which are all present in this hybrid design. By retaining the huge public forecourt, they verticalized the programme along the existing building, thus giving it a new façade, designed like boxes piled on top of each other. Fitted between the two fronts, as if the public forecourt had been suddenly straightened, is a vertical hall, espousing the principle of continuity and interaction between the two parts of the programme.

✦

✚ University Sports Centre

LJUBLJANA, SLOVENIA
COMPETITION, 1997 (PRIZE-WINNER)

The sports centre is a large, multipurpose object, a critical mass with significant urban implications. Sadar in Vuga Arhitekti designed it to cope with the possible extreme conditions of a sold-out event. Billed to become Slovenia's largest sports hall, it is conceived as an actual sheltered part of the city – with its shopping galleries, its restaurant, its fitness rooms and its gymnasium. This huge but compact pebble-like structure, which is connected to both the city and the park, looks like an André Bloc sculpture. The structure of the building is provided by a colossal twisted concrete ring. The roof and the façades are made of the same homogeneous and translucid membrane, creating changing interplays of natural and artifical light. The sports centre is completely adjustable and flexible, and offers every possible type of configuration for the various sports, on a whole range of scales (with a maximum of 10,000 spectators). ✚

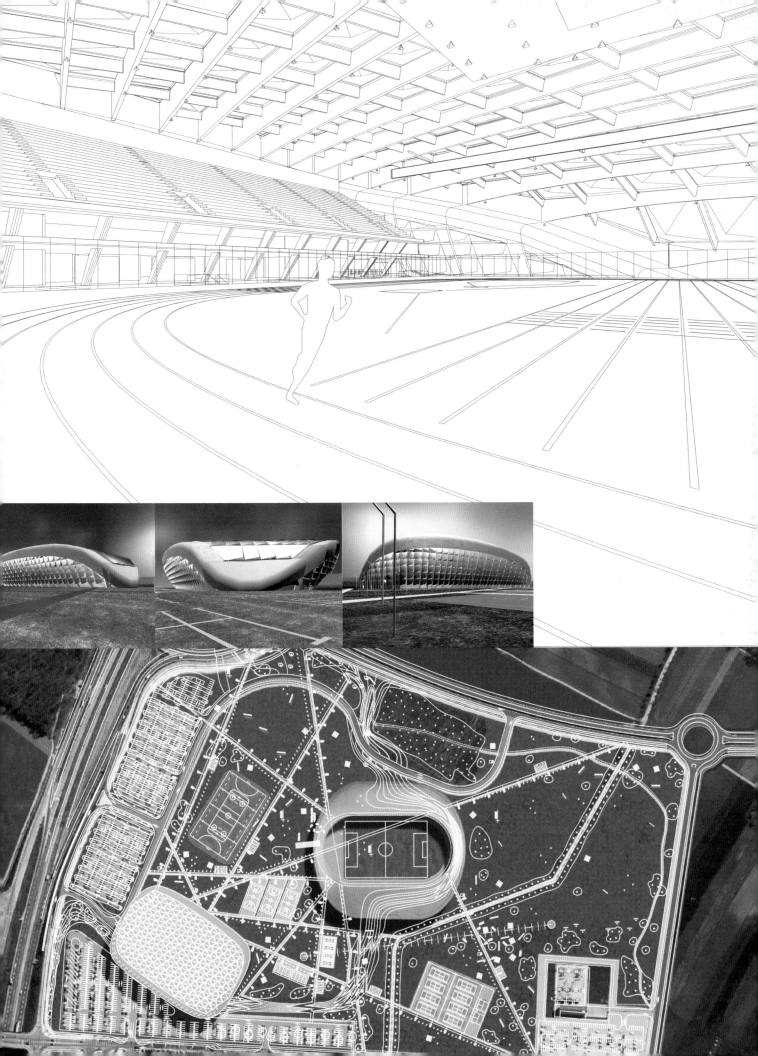

✦ Central Part of the National Gallery

LJUBLJANA, SLOVENIA
COMPETITION, 1996 (PRIZE-WINNER)

What was involved in this project was the linkage of two existing National Gallery buildings, and the development of a place for the monumental Robba fountain, as well as an independent place for the museum's public events (openings, meetings). In their project, Sadar in Vuga Arhitekti tried above all to free themselves from the indeterminate distance between the two buildings, deemed to be absurd and irrational. They examined a solution that would be independent and would work even if this distance were different. Inspired by Issey Miyake's 'folded tubes', the building's structure consists of an alignment of parallel porticoes with varying geometry. These porticoes have many different functions. They support the roof and the curtain façade, as well as the various networks and systems: electricity, lighting, ventilation, heating. The completely glazed extension comes across like a see-through interface between park and city. Set in the Presernove Street axis, it affords a monumental entrance to the museum. ✦

✛ Sadar in Vuga Arhitekti

Jurij Sadar (1963)
1987   Diploma from the Faculty of'Architecture, University of Ljubljana
1997–93 Assistant professor at the Faculty of'Architecture, Ljubljana

Bostjan Vuga (1966)
1992   Diploma from the Faculty of'Architecture, University of Ljubljana
1995   Graduate Design Diploma, Architectural Association School of
       Architecture, London; co-founder of the interdisciplinary network
       O.C.E.A.N. (London, Helsinki, Oslo, Cologne, Boston and Ljubljana)
1996   Creation of the practice in Ljubljana (Slovenia)

Principal buildings and projects
2000–1996 Chamber of Commerce and Economic of Slovenia Office
       Building, Ljubljana (realized); Aomori Museum, Aomori, Japan (com-
       petition); Arcadia World Office and Exhibition Building, Ljubljana
       (under construction); Lesna Industrija Bovec, Bovec (under con-
       struction)
1999   Business Centre Tivoli, Ljubljana (project); House Tivoli, Ljubljana
       (project); Business Centre Moszkva Ter, Budapest (project);
       Bioclimatic House, Ljubljana (project); Jewellery Divina, Ljubljana
       (project)
1998   Office Building Dimiceva 9, extension, Ljubljana (realized);
       Television Studio Nova Gorica (project); Expo 2000 Slovenian
       Pavilion, Hanover (project); Solkan Fountain, Solkan (prizewinner);
       Parliament of Slovenia renovation, Ljubljana (second prize); Crni kal
       Viaduct and Bridge over the Mura River, Koper/Lendava motorway
       (honourable mention); Tacenski dvori Residential and Commercial
       Complex, Ljubljana (second prize)
1997   Dom/Mueller Department Store, Ljubljana (realized);'Residential
       Building extension, Piran (project); University Sports Park and
       University Sports Hall, Ljubljana (prizewinner); REI Business

Centre, Ljubljana (honourable mention); Cinema Multiplex, Ljubljana
       (project)
1996   Central Part of the National Gallery, Ljubljana (prizewinner)

Principal publications
1999   'Sadar in Vuga arhitekti' *d.o.o.* no. 2, Ljubljana (March)
1998   'Sadar in Vuga arhitekti' *d.o.o.* no. 1, Ljubljana (Jan.)

Selected bibliography
1999   'Slovene Dream' *Wallpaper* no. 20, Intelligence, London
1998   'Spaces in Time, Sadar in Vuga Arhitekti' S. Tomazic, *Monoliths of
       the Future* Ars Vivendi, Ljubljana; *Dom Gospordarstva* M. Hribar,
       GZS, Ljubljana
1997   'Sadar in Vuga Arhitekti, studio organization is economic strategy'
       Architectural Profile no. 2, Bangkok; 'O.C.E.A.NO. net.' *Architects
       Bulletin* no. 135/136, Ljubljana; 'The O.C.E.A.NO. net.
       Becoming Unlimited' B. van Berkel, C. Bos *AA Files* no. 33,
       London; 'Architecture Designed by Operativity' Spela Mlakar, *Il
       Progetto* no. 1, Trieste

Michele Saee

| Michele Saee (*1956) |

For Michele Saee, 'instances of architecture' or the instance of space are the principal issues to be identified in his search to define an architecture that rejects an imposed order or example. Each building is an example of instance; it is detailed; it forms a new singularity, a whole that takes shape according to infinitely renewed links. The world is no longer a closed system whose expansion can be controlled; thus as neither object nor organizing principle can exist, the architect's work must now face an identity crisis. The architectonic has regained its rights, the architect now organizes links and interactions, and each project only appears as a whole at the last moment or instant. Michele Saee's architecture provokes a crisis among organized identified elements — be it a crisis of form, of the notion of scheme, of surface, of dwelling, of the closed singularity of the project, its methods of construction or its engineering. Saee's architecture also embodies a strong temporal dimension. It responds to a Californian tradition of urgency and shelter, to a culture of assemblage and installation. His architecture is of the 'instance',propelled by the necessity of time. The instance rejects all metaphors of a unilateral founding moment and is instead an open process. It poses long-standing questions about geometry, permanent resolutions to the scheme, the box, the constraints of partitions and configuration, and the return of hypothetical historical examples both classical and vernacular. It also questions the logic of a project that seeks to differentiate between the language of the architect and that of the engineer, to separate the architectural concept from the technical world. Michele Saee teaches a true architecture of urgency, an immediate architecture that does not distinguish between the idea and the building. It is an architecture where 'instancing' has a generic function: the capacity to mobilize the symbolic, practical, social and technical aspects of a project to create an exemplary, original built prototype that reinvents the medium and its syntax. For Saee, building remains an open process and signifies a template, a possibility, a pattern that must recombine for each project. The recombined elements establish a unique order in which space is imminent, where it is 'instanced.' As Michele Saee would say, 'the building is a template'. ❖

FRÉDÉRIC MIGAYROU

Project for Venice Biennale
1990

✚ Golzari
Guest House

WESTLAKE, USA
1996

The Golzari house did not look to the outside for
its order, but within. The argument was that one
could discover the origin of an ordering system by
looking at the elements that make the system itself,
not at the surrounding information that we divide up
and categorize. This approach was, in a sense, a
response to the site context and conditions – the site
is a small, triangularshaped, hillside lot between two
roads – It was driven by a new way of looking at the
site not as a static form to be worked on but as a collection of elements in process, like living organisms,
each developping at its own rate. The house was
pushed to the front of the lot to create a secure and
confortable backyard. The house steps down the
slope, responding to rather than altering
the hillside, connecting with the street to
eliminate the buffer that is the typical
Southern California front yard. Here the
boundaries between inside and outside
were blurred to create a place that is harmonious with both. There is no spatial hier-
archy and no distinct sides. The goal was
to create a space for multiple functions,
subject to the will of the user. ✚

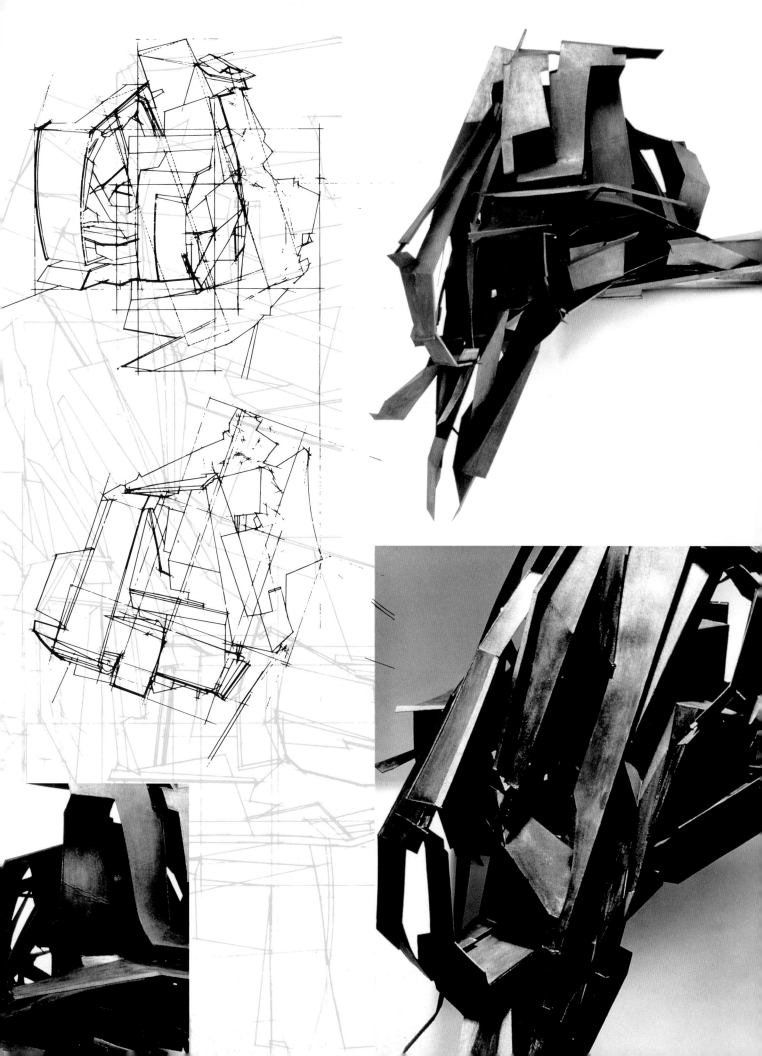

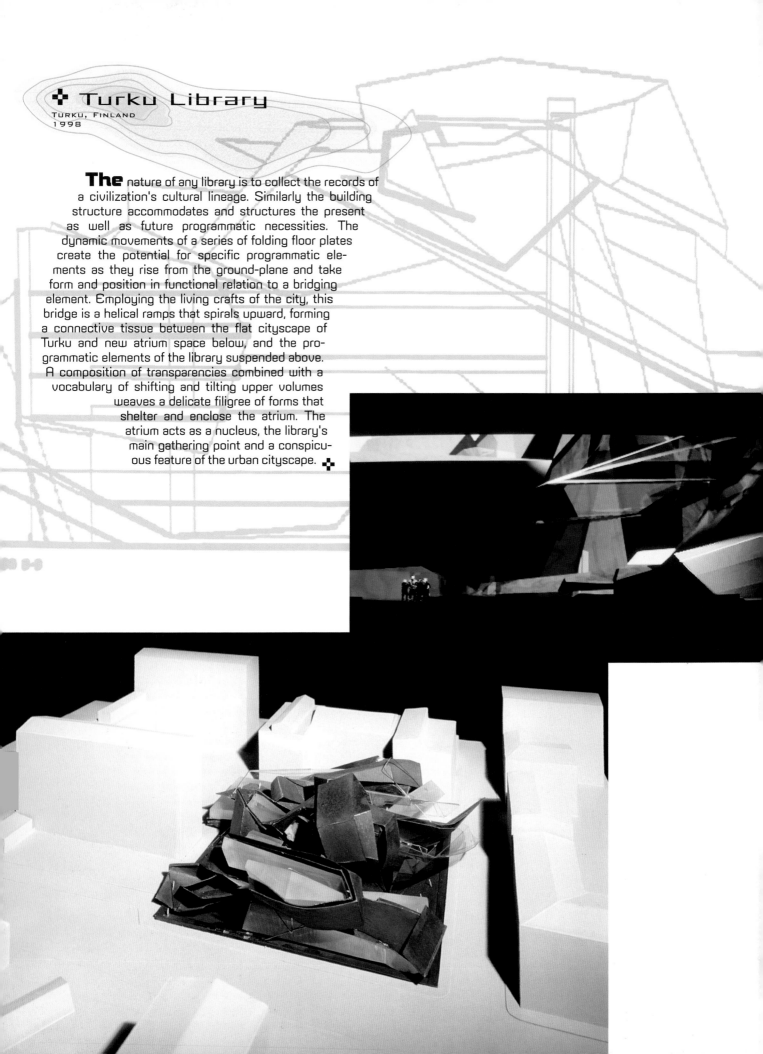

✤ Turku Library
TURKU, FINLAND
1998

The nature of any library is to collect the records of a civilization's cultural lineage. Similarly the building structure accommodates and structures the present as well as future programmatic necessities. The dynamic movements of a series of folding floor plates create the potential for specific programmatic elements as they rise from the ground-plane and take form and position in functional relation to a bridging element. Employing the living crafts of the city, this bridge is a helical ramps that spirals upward, forming a connective tissue between the flat cityscape of Turku and new atrium space below, and the programmatic elements of the library suspended above. A composition of transparencies combined with a vocabulary of shifting and tilting upper volumes weaves a delicate filigree of forms that shelter and enclose the atrium. The atrium acts as a nucleus, the library's main gathering point and a conspicuous feature of the urban cityscape. ✤

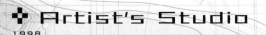

✦ Artist's Studio

1998

An initial morphological pursuit can lead not only to the formal unity of building but also the entire relationship to engineering and the mechanistic and positivist understanding of the act of construction. This building first acts as a box, a container or a scheme and later on it evolves with the site and generates the programme that it is intended to serve and respond to: a residence and a studio for the sculptor David Lindberg. Not accepting the single meaning it might communicate, it offers a multilayered complex of meaning that the work might need to communicate consciously or unconsciously. This makes the peeling away of the layers that had separated different surfaces, volumes and functions a continuous part of the experience. It is as if the space reveal itself in a different fashion in a continual search for a new meaning. The conventional reading of the space will be challenged, just as the work that is being made inside or outside of the studio space will be challenged and made and remade. ✦

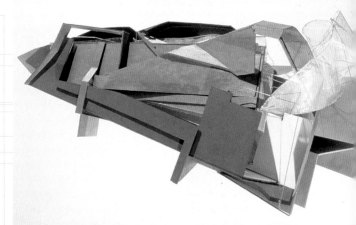

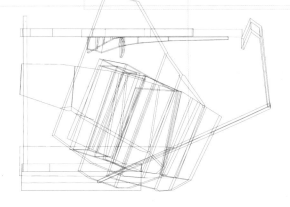

Lt. Petrosino Park
New York, 1996

✤ Michele Saee

Michele Saee (1956)
1974–81 Master of Architecture and Doctorate in Architecture, Florence
1981–82 Postgraduate Diploma in Planning and Urbanism, Milan

1985 Founded the Michele Saee practice in Los Angeles

Teaching
1999 UCLA extension, Santa Monica; Public Access Press Committee; Southern California Institute of Architecture, Los Angeles; Wasc Accreditation Advisory Board; Forum for Architecture and Urban Design, Los Angeles; Otis Parsons School of Design, Los Angeles

Principal buildings and projects
1998 City Space Commercial Complex, Inglewood, California; Rodriguez Building, Los Angeles
1997 Turku Library, Finland
1996 Lt Petrosino Park Redevelopment, New York (competition); House IS, Los Angeles; Golzari Guest House, Westlake; Saee Studio, Los Angeles;'Dance Studio, Los Angeles
1994 'Proprioception' installation, Florida; 'Art Works for Children' installation, Los Angeles; Acks House, Bel Air; Zone Night Club, Arizona
1993 Arc-Angeli Café, Southern California Institute of Architecture, Los Angeles
1992 Atwater Tea and Coffee House, Atwater; Angeli Restaurant in the Rodeo Collection; Cosmetic Dental Clinic, Beverly Hills
1990 Sun House, Fullerton; Township House Grosse Ile (competition); Meivsahna House, Los Angeles; Piazzale Roma, Venice Biennale (competition); Wall Clock, Los Angeles (project)
1989 Ecru Clothing Store; Angeli Mare, Marina del Rey
1988 Jones-Chapman Residence, Brentwood; Ecru Clothing Store, phase II, Los Angeles

1987 Design Express Warehouse and Furniture Store; Ecru Clothing Store, Capitaine Restaurant, Los Angeles
1986 Trattoria Angeli; Stage and Set Design, Los Angeles
1985 Sprecher House, Pacific Palisades

Recent exhibitions
1997 Musée des Beaux-Arts, Orléans; Castello di Rivoli, Turin
1996 'UCLA: Extension Exhibition Space' Los Angeles; 'Belem Cultural Centre' Lisbon
1995 'Artists/Architects' Villeurbanne, France
1993 'Michele Saee: Humain' Galerie Uzzan, Paris; 'Michele Saee: Body, Object, Landscape' Storefront, New York

Selected bibliography
1997 *Michele Saee: Buildings + Projects* Rizzoli, New York
1994 *World Cities/Los Angeles* Academy Editions, London; 'Esperimenti de Architettura' *Area* (September) Italy
1993 *Heteropolis* Academy Editions, Ernst & Sohn, New York; *Los Angeles Architecture: The Contemporary Condition* Phaidon, London
1991 'Meivsahna' *G.A Houses*; Sci-Arc Kenchiku Bunka, Tokyo
1992 'The Curvature of Space' *Progressive Architecture* (September)
1990 'Stressed for Success' *L. A. Weekly*, Los Angeles (Feb.); 'Le corps en morceaux d'Architecture' *Architecture Intérieure* (October/November) Paris; 'Complexity and Contradiction' *Blue Print* May) London
1989 'Fractured Façade' and 'California Beaming' *Designers' Journal* (April) UK; 'Trans Cities Wind: Los Angeles' *World Interior Design* (summer)

Schie 2.0

| Jan Konings (*1966) | Ton Matton (*1964) | Lucas Verweij (*1965) |

In the context of its forward planning project, Nederland 2030, the Dutch National Spatial Planning Agency commissioned Schie to come up with an innovative, unconventional vision of the Netherlands in the year 2030, full of new emotions, provocations and uncertainties. The 'Randstad Club' team was set up specially for this project. 'Schie Power' is a plea for increased sustainable consumption, based on arguments thrown up by the Club. It envisages a larger role for government in its capacity as formulator and guardian of environmental laws. The spatial consequences of unbridled consumerism have been translated into five spatial strategies aimed at achieving a greater variety of residential habitats. Commenting on this new urban-world-global city phenomenon, Lucas Verweij observes: 'A city used to be a place which had been granted a city charter, but that concept no longer works. Now one thinks more in terms of size, population figures and commerce.' As with Maxwan, quantity has taken on a new meaning in the work of Schie. Schie is now researching urban flow phenomena such as traffic jams, which they argue offer the opportunity for rethinking how we may more profitably and enjoyably spend leisure time in our cars and on the motorways. All of their projects are serious urban interventions, but as this example suggests, they are also playful, even a bit cheeky. The 'Schie Power' advertising flyer which simulates supermarket flyers, for example, offers wonderful and inventive ecological solutions to urban design problems without being too heavy-handed. Part of the flyer, the spatial designs produced for Schie by NL Architects, features a stunningly clever solution for housing on a series of 'wandering islands', which, because of erosion and other natural forces, actually move about in the ocean. A typical solution might try and stop the erosion of the island, before abandoning it altogether. Instead, Schie and NL proposed that rows of nomadic houses be built on a grid system, and as the island loses land mass on one side, the row of houses situated there are leapfrogged over the other houses by truck to the other side, thus forming the leading edge of housing as it follows wherever the land leads. Not only are the natural movements of the island and ocean undisturbed, but sooner or later everyone will have beach front property. Ecology and the market are both satisfied. ✦

MICHAEL SPEAKS

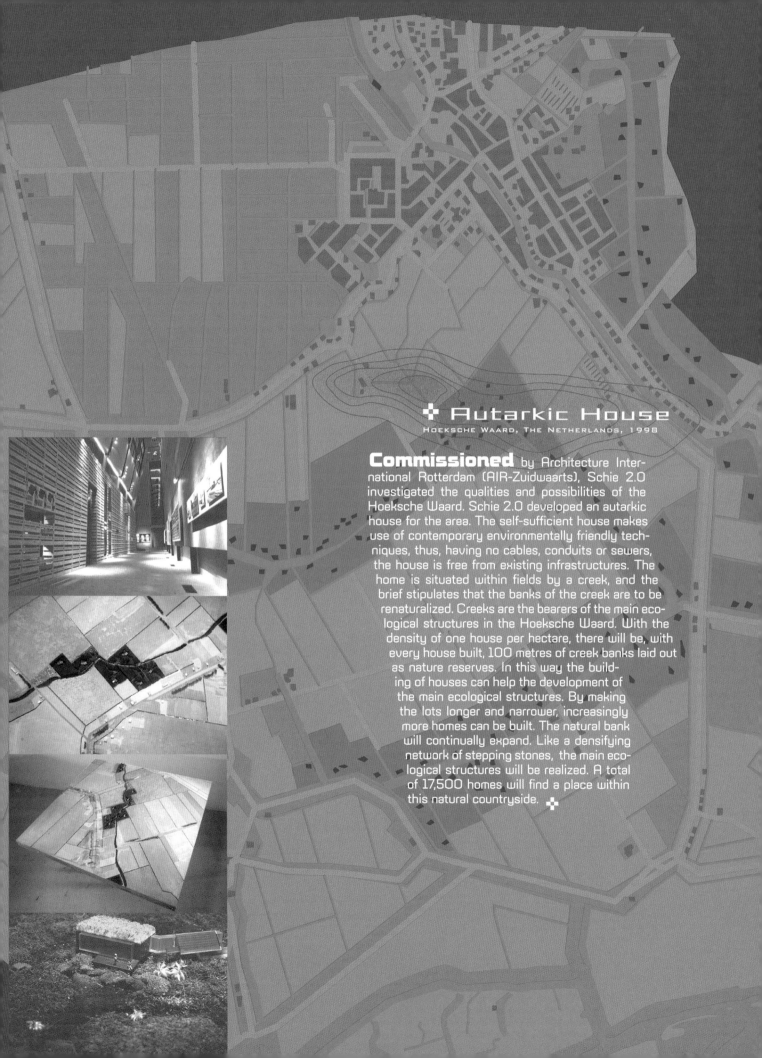

✦ Autarkic House
Hoeksche Waard, The Netherlands, 1998

Commissioned by Architecture International Rotterdam (AIR-Zuidwaarts), Schie 2.0 investigated the qualities and possibilities of the Hoeksche Waard. Schie 2.0 developed an autarkic house for the area. The self-sufficient house makes use of contemporary environmentally friendly techniques, thus, having no cables, conduits or sewers, the house is free from existing infrastructures. The home is situated within fields by a creek, and the brief stipulates that the banks of the creek are to be renaturalized. Creeks are the bearers of the main ecological structures in the Hoeksche Waard. With the density of one house per hectare, there will be, with every house built, 100 metres of creek banks laid out as nature reserves. In this way the building of houses can help the development of the main ecological structures. By making the lots longer and narrower, increasingly more homes can be built. The natural bank will continually expand. Like a densifying network of stepping stones, the main ecological structures will be realized. A total of 17,500 homes will find a place within this natural countryside. ✦

✛ Seven Pieces of Street
ALMERE, THE NETHERLANDS
1999

Schie 2.0 was asked to develop a proposal for the application of art in the newly developed VINEX district 'between the waterways' in Almere's Centre for Contemporary Art and 'The Pavilions'. Schie 2.0's proposal radically breachews the layout of the streets at seven sites within the district, at the same time keeping them publicly accessible.

For the projet they selected streets that have an extensive and unchangeable profile; where both sides of the street have private homes; had no intersecting bicycle routes; were in a state ready for development.

The collages here show some impressions: De Heidestraat (Heather Street); De Boomgaardstraat (Orchard Street); De Bosstaat (Forest Street; for which there is a winter and a spring collage); De Blauwe gietvloerstraat (Blue Cast Floor Street); De Heuvelstraat (Hill Street). ✛

you have to stay in line

the minimum age to drive this car is eighteen

the indicators of your car must flash between sixty an hundred and twenty times p minute

you can not make the postman walk more than twenty-five metres

the minimum level of sound exposure for your front yard is fifty-five decibels

there is a restricted numbe of people who can enter Holland this way

you may not have sex in a public space

you may not write on public property

a building has to be approv by an aesthetic jury

you are not allowed to play basketball here

the surface beneath this recreational equipment must be shock-absorbent

the minimum distance betwe recycling box and the front door of your house i 450 metres

the maximum noise intensity at the façade of a residential building is fifty-five decibels

you are not allowed to drive this car

this room has to be separate two doors from the living ro

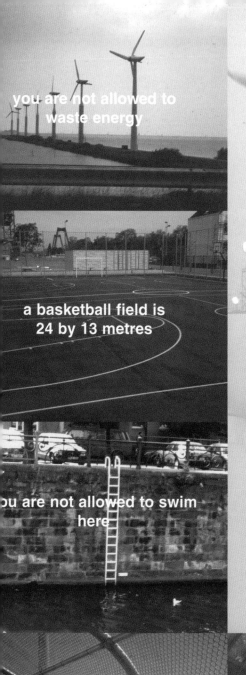

you are not allowed to
waste energy

a basketball field is
24 by 13 metres

you are not allowed to swim
here

✦ Regelland

Dutch society can be characterized by a large numberof rules and regulations. The number is still growing. Everything is perfectly organized and well thought-out; nothing can happen to you. This over-regulation leads to a lack of freedom and makes you passive. You do not feel responsible because of too many regulations, which is bad for inventiveness. Negotiations with fellow citizens slowly stop, everyone sticks to the rules. In the end this will undermine society. Those who want to live in freedom have to take responsibility for their own behaviour. Schie 2.0 tries to counter-balance over-regulation and opens the discussion on freedom and rules. 'Holland is a well-regulated country' was exhibited in 'De Appel' Amsterdam as a part of 'Unlimited ∩L', curated by Hu Hanrou. After 'De Appel' it was exhibited in the political café 'De Balie' in Amsterdam as part of a series of lectures on 'De orderverstoorders' (the disturbers of order). ✦

you are not allowed to put your
life in danger

to walk here you have
to be dressed properly

you have to separate
your waste

experience this you need to
have a club card

she is not allowed to skate
here

you are not allowed to
repair your car in the street

you are not allowed to waste energy

⁴ Schie 2.0

Jan Konings (1966)
Design Academy Eindhoven/Man & Living

Ton Matton (1964)
Technische Universiteit Delft

Lucas Verweij (1965)
Design Academy Eindhoven/Man & Public Space

1998   Creation of Shie 2.0 in Rotterdam: merger between Buro Schie (1991) and Konings & Beij (1991)

Principal buildings and projects

1999   Het trouwplein, Krimpen, arrangement of a square (project); 'Regelland: Holland is a well-regulated country', exhibitions/conferences; Snacklocket Ijburg ecological park (project); '7 straatstukken voor Almere', Almere, installation (project); 'Learning from Berkel Roderijs' programme Vinex (project)

1998   Autarkisch Huis, Hoeksche Waard, ecological house (project)

1997   'Schie 2030', prospective (project); 'Zontlewijzer 52°09'NB 5°22'OL*' installation

1996–95 'Ranstad Stadsplattegrond' cartographic interpretation of Ranstad (realized)

Recent exhibitions

1999   'Unlimited ∩ L' De Appel, Amsterdam; 'Regelland in de Balie' De Balie, Amsterdam; 'Taiwan Holland Festival' Glasshouse, Taipei, Taiwan

1998   'Planologische Hallucinaties' NAI, Rotterdam

1997   'Nine+One: 10 Dutch architects' NAI, Rotterdam; 'Rotterdam Designprijs', Kunsthal, Rotterdam; 'De Nieuwe Kaart van Nederland' Musiekcentrum Vredenburg, Utrecht

Selected bibliography

1999   *Architect* (March and May); *MetropolisM* (April); *Carp* (April)

1998   *Holland is a well-regulated country* De Toolpub   Dutch Mountains

1997   *Nine+One: 10 Dutch architects* exhibition catalogue, NAI, Rotterdam

Snøhetta

| Craig Dykers (*1961) | Christoph Kapeller (*1956) | Kjetil T. Thorsen (*1958) |

Snøhetta is the name of a large mountain standing in the middle of Norway. Viking legend has it that it was the resting place for the most valiant of warrior souls – the abode of 'Valhalla'. Snøhetta is the name that Craig Dykers, Christoph Kapeller and Kjetil T. Thorsen have chosen for their architectural, landscaping and design agency. For them, a mountain represents a complex form, at once landscape, quasi-architectural object, and, in this particular instance, a powerful symbolic medium. It is a form which, in the final analysis, sums up their approach to architecture – an ongoing, extensive approach whose intent, without any disciplinary divide, is to work not on objects but on environments, in all their varying dimensions. This approach is based first and foremost on a quest for conjunction between the different parties involved in construction, and principally, within the agency, between architects and landscape artists. For Snøhetta, landscape cannot be scaled down to a simple carpet of tamed greenery which forms the usual limits. Snøhetta develops an extended and inclusive landscape definition. Everything is part of the landscape, and actually forms it. The body itself is one of its forms. Architecture is quite 'naturally' included in this definition. Snøhetta's minimalist and hypercontextual architecture invariably strives to take a back seat in relation to the reasons for the site, in the interests of the readability and coherence of its environment. The Snøhetta agency, which was set up in Oslo in 1987, started out with the project for the new Alexandrian Library, and won the competition. Today, after a long on-site period, the building is being completed, thus winding up a highly productive phase for the Norwegian team, which has authored many projects and works in the realm of institutional architecture (museums, libraries, facilities). This phase has also been one of formulation and development to do with working methods and organization. The Snøhetta team has once and for all rejected the classical vertical functioning of architectural agencies, where the person or persons who get their ideas across, at the top of the pyramid, are those most removed from the realities and details of the project. This verticality, responsible for wasted time and lost efficiency, recurs, in their view, in the management and uses of buildings, once finished. Snøhetta has radically opted for a horizontal and cross-disciplinary praxis, refocusing on the project. To this end, they have, for example, developed a computer system in which all the documents and data to do with a given project are centralized in a single Internet file – a hyperfile. Access to this hyperfile, which is universal and available to one and all, imposes a horizontal working organization in which each person can work live on the project. By playing the part of a kind of diary that is systematically updated and dated, the hyperfile keeps tabs on the project as it develops in time. It also means that there is never split thinking about techniques and technologies, the construction and the purely architectural parameters. The Snøhetta team makes this search for efficiency, flexibility and professionalism available to a sensitive, significant and almost metaphysical architecture, incorporating the most immaterial and the most fluctuating elements of the real: time passing, the weather, light, the seasons, movement. ✚

The most prominent characteristic of the new library in Alexandria is its circular, tilting form; rising from the ground to reveal a massive stone wall 32 metres high. Five thousand square metres of granite were hand carved with inscriptions of historic and contemporary signs and symbols. The building's roof, a glass and honey comb aluminium 14 x 9–metre bay construction, allows the interior space to open toward the Mediterranean Sea and the reflected north light to enter the interior. The main event of this interior is a great room, similar to the main spaces within libraries of previous centuries, which reveals the building's form into the reading space. The reading space is developed in an original manner along terraces that conceal the limited-access books, providing a new standard in library planning. These terraces also allow for unobstructed views for the reader and division of the different subjects of the collection. Each terrace can be reached by stairs and lifts from the circulation spine of the building. This spine also provides the separation of staff and public movement in the building. ❖

❖ **Alexandrine Library**
ALEXANDRIA, EGYPT
UNDER CONSTRUCTION

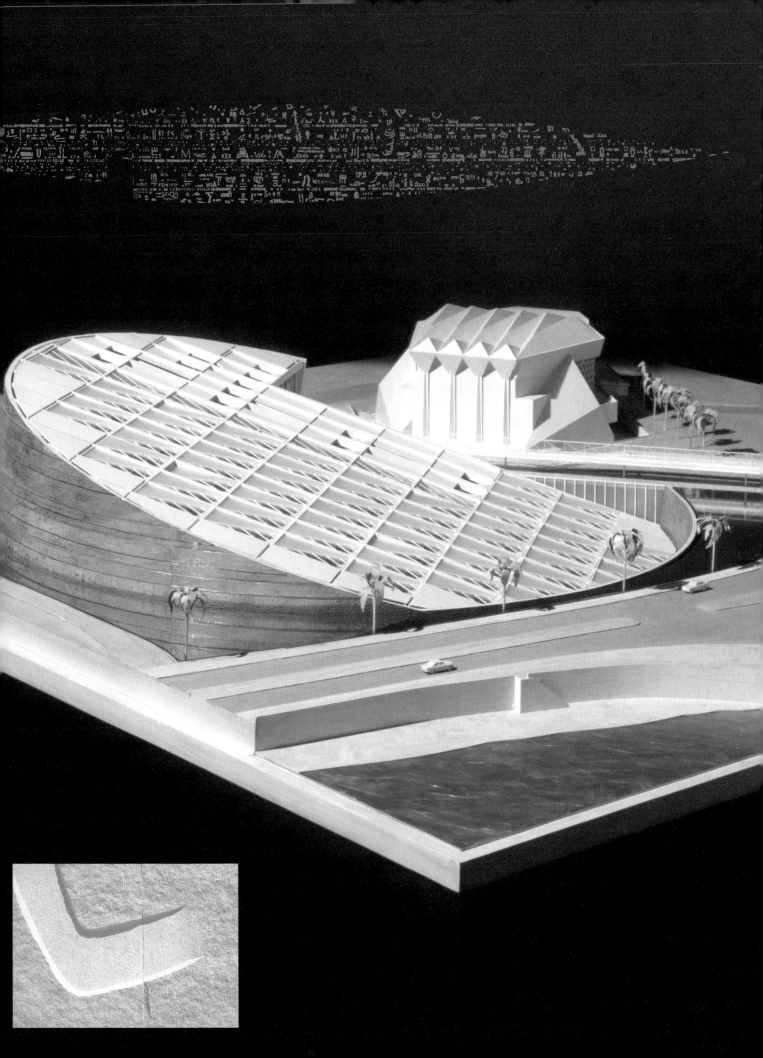

✦ Lillehammer Olympic Art Museum

LILLEHAMMER, NORWAY, 1993

For the 1994 Winter Olympics in Lillehammer, the Winter Olympic Committee collaborated with the Lillehammer Art Museum to build a new addition to their existing building. Situated in the centre of the small rural town, the project would be a centre-piece design of strong and responsive character and create a dynamic interaction with the concrete brutalist style of the original structure. The foremost feature of the project is its smooth, undulating and inclining wooden form, which faces the town's main square. The tilted and curved wall forms the three major gallery spaces and proposes a new interpretation of a traditional way of viewing art.

With paintings mounted on a plane inclined toward the viewer, glare is minimized and physical comfort maximized. The gracefull curve of the wall is further emphasized by the introduction of natural light along its edge, creating a visual separation from the ceiling. In contrast to the sculptural front, the façade facing the existing museum is a straightforward glass wall and defines the garden space between the buildings. ✦

✦ Zumtobel Staff Light Workshop

OSLO, NORWAY, 1999

In the case of the light workshop, a non-design approach resulted in a room of 30 x 30 x 6 metres, creating a 'space' for light in all its various forms with high flexibility and a wide variety of user options. The space is carved from the earth and the workshop space as a resultant replaces the mass of the earth. In its most comprehensive interpretation, this could be seen as creating space without creating a building. A curving glass roof that is both a raised ground plane and a protective skin covers the workshop. This large skylight makes the natural lighting conditions of the space relate mainly to the light from above. There are, however, two long, slight ramps descending into the workshop from east and west, slowly revealing the relationship between morning and afternoon light and earth. The volume of the space itself is recreated at night by means of a light volume equivalent to the volume of the space. The negative-positive relationship of volume becomes the main issue of the building in the context of its function. ✦

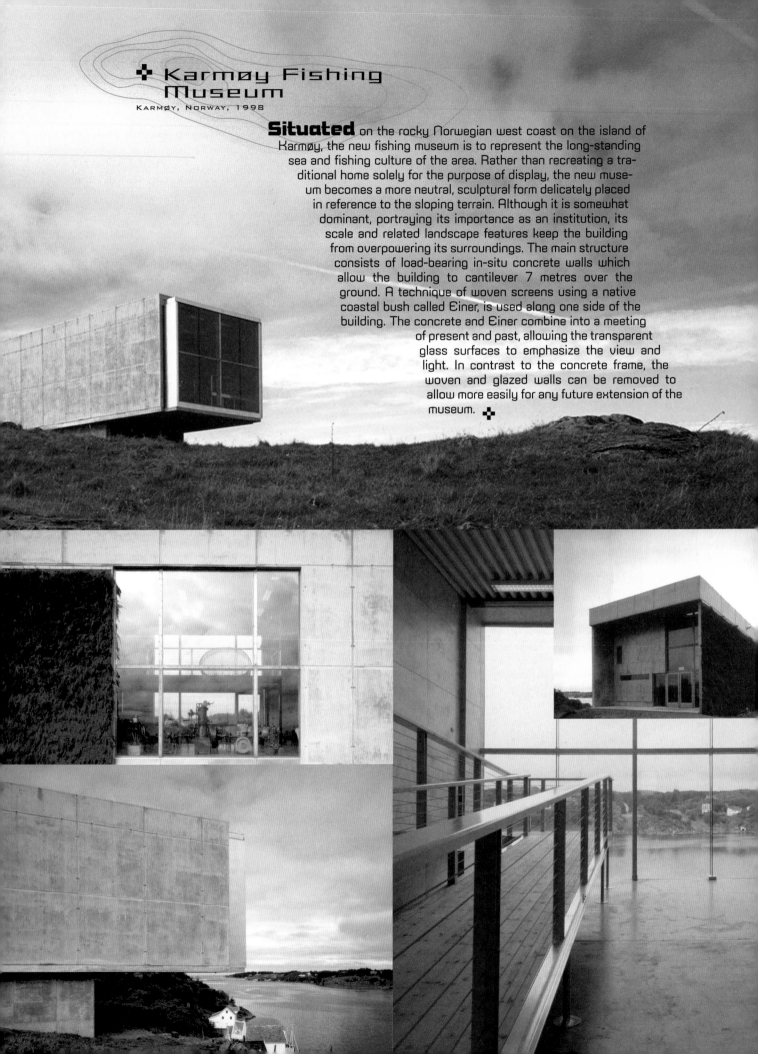

✚ Karmøy Fishing Museum

KARMØY, NORWAY, 1998

Situated on the rocky Norwegian west coast on the island of Karmøy, the new fishing museum is to represent the long-standing sea and fishing culture of the area. Rather than recreating a traditional home solely for the purpose of display, the new museum becomes a more neutral, sculptural form delicately placed in reference to the sloping terrain. Although it is somewhat dominant, portraying its importance as an institution, its scale and related landscape features keep the building from overpowering its surroundings. The main structure consists of load-bearing in-situ concrete walls which allow the building to cantilever 7 metres over the ground. A technique of woven screens using a native coastal bush called Einer, is used along one side of the building. The concrete and Einer combine into a meeting of present and past, allowing the transparent glass surfaces to emphasize the view and light. In contrast to the concrete frame, the woven and glazed walls can be removed to allow more easily for any future extension of the museum. ✚

✛ Snøhetta

Craig Dykers (1961)
BS Arch. University of Texas, Austin

Christoph Kapeller (1956)
MNAL Architecture Diploma Graz, MS UCLA

Kjetil Thorsen (1958)
MNAL Architecture Diploma Graz

1987   Creation of the practice in Oslo, Norway

Principal buildings and projects
2000   Alexandrine Library, Egypt (under construction); Hamar Town Hall,
          Hamar, Norway (under construction)
1999   Zumtobel Staff Light Workshop, Oslo (realized); Institut de neurobi-
          ologie, Marseilles, France (prizewinner); King Fahad National
          Library, Riyad, Saudi Arabia (competition); Norwegian Embassy in
          Berlin, Germany (realized); Strømme Throndsen Design, Oslo (reno-
          vation); Uranienborg Terrace, Oslo (renovation)
1998   Karmøy Fishing Museum, Karmøy, Norway (realized); Eidsvoll
          Building Trades School, Eidsvoll, Norwaye (realized); Nordvoll
          School for Autistic Persons, Oslo (realized)
1997   Kansai-Kan Library, Kansai-Kan, Japan (second prize); Skistua
          School, Narvik, Norway (realized); Fjaler Media Centre, Fjaler,
          Norway (realized); Telenor Headquarters, Oslo (competition); Three
          Rs Cultural Centre, Oslo (competition)
1996   Danish National Archive, Copenhagen (competition); Sami
          Congress Hall, Karasjok, Norway (competition); National Theatre
          Subway Station, Oslo (competition)
1993   Lillehammer Olympic Art Museum, Lillehammer, Norway (realized)

Selected bibliography
1995   *Archis* no. 9; *Mur* no. 3
1994   *Techniques et Architectures* no. 408; *Garten+Landschaft* no. 12
1990   *Architectural Review* no. 1120; *Skala* no. 19; *Byggekunst* no. 1

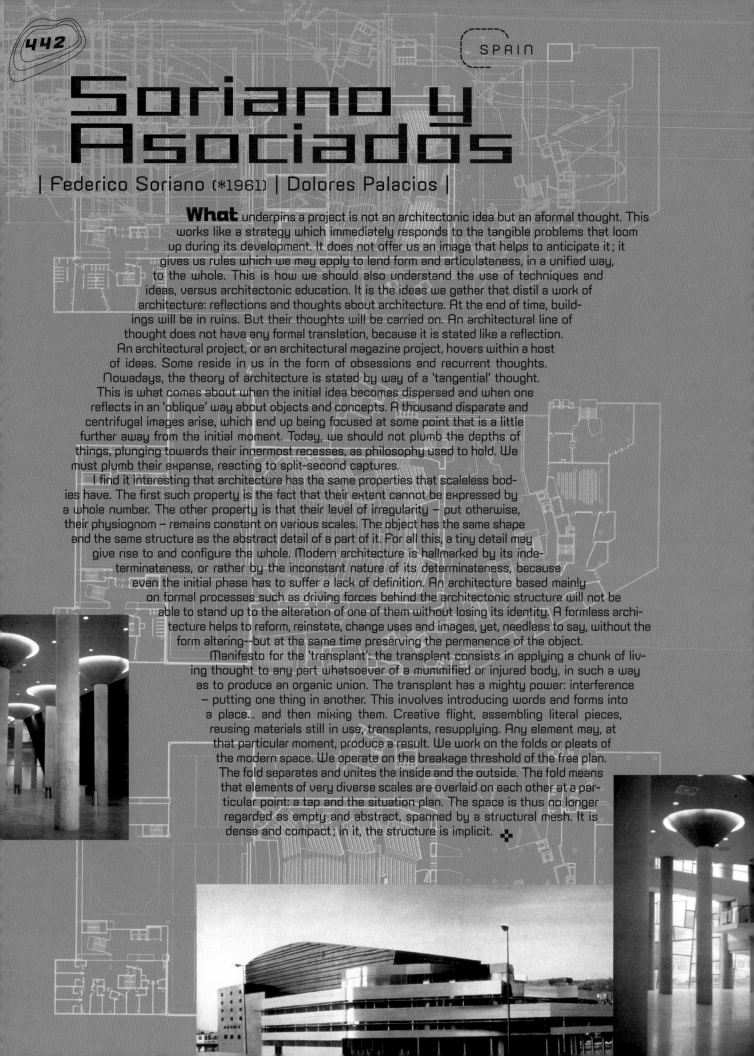

Soriano y Asociados

| Federico Soriano (*1961) | Dolores Palacios |

What underpins a project is not an architectonic idea but an aformal thought. This works like a strategy which immediately responds to the tangible problems that loom up during its development. It does not offer us an image that helps to anticipate it; it gives us rules which we may apply to lend form and articulateness, in a unified way, to the whole. This is how we should also understand the use of techniques and ideas, versus architectonic education. It is the ideas we gather that distil a work of architecture: reflections and thoughts about architecture. At the end of time, buildings will be in ruins. But their thoughts will be carried on. An architectural line of thought does not have any formal translation, because it is stated like a reflection. An architectural project, or an architectural magazine project, hovers within a host of ideas. Some reside in us in the form of obsessions and recurrent thoughts. Nowadays, the theory of architecture is stated by way of a 'tangential' thought. This is what comes about when the initial idea becomes dispersed and when one reflects in an 'oblique' way about objects and concepts. A thousand disparate and centrifugal images arise, which end up being focused at some point that is a little further away from the initial moment. Today, we should not plumb the depths of things, plunging towards their innermost recesses, as philosophy used to hold. We must plumb their expanse, reacting to split-second captures.

I find it interesting that architecture has the same properties that scaleless bodies have. The first such property is the fact that their extent cannot be expressed by a whole number. The other property is that their level of irregularity – put otherwise, their physiognom – remains constant on various scales. The object has the same shape and the same structure as the abstract detail of a part of it. For all this, a tiny detail may give rise to and configure the whole. Modern architecture is hallmarked by its indeterminateness, or rather by the inconstant nature of its determinateness, because even the initial phase has to suffer a lack of definition. An architecture based mainly on formal processes such as driving forces behind the architectonic structure will not be able to stand up to the alteration of one of them without losing its identity. A formless architecture helps to reform, reinstate, change uses and images, yet, needless to say, without the form altering--but at the same time preserving the permanence of the object.

Manifesto for the 'transplant': the transplant consists in applying a chunk of living thought to any part whatsoever of a mummified or injured body, in such a way as to produce an organic union. The transplant has a mighty power: interference – putting one thing in another. This involves introducing words and forms into a place... and then mixing them. Creative flight, assembling literal pieces, reusing materials still in use, transplants, resupplying. Any element may, at that particular moment, produce a result. We work on the folds or pleats of the modern space. We operate on the breakage threshold of the free plan. The fold separates and unites the inside and the outside. The fold means that elements of very diverse scales are overlaid on each other at a particular point: a tap and the situation plan. The space is thus no longer regarded as empty and abstract, spanned by a structural mesh. It is dense and compact; in it, the structure is implicit. ✦

✛ Euskalduna Palace

MUSIC HALL AND CONFERENCE PALACE
BILBAO, SPAIN, 1998

'**Any** architectural work,' writes Federico Soriano, 'is already completely defined by its location plan, which implicitly contains its position and its size, down to the smallest details.' The project is thus conceived like a link in a chain which imposes its principle of order and layout on it. In this bend in the Ria, at the far end of Las Campas de los Ingleses, looking across at the Guggenheim Museum, the Euskalduna Centre looks like a ship, a 'vessel-like building' run aground and stuck, as it were, on the edge of a wet dock, where work is in progress. Located close to the University and the Museum of Fine Arts, it accommodates an auditorium and a Conference Centre. Staying closely with his project, Federico Soriano uses ship-building techniques to design and construct the 'hull' of the auditorium and its façade on which the Conference Centre is set laterally, like a kind of scaffolding. This, in a word, is a project where every detail helps to bring back to life the movement — here crystal-lized in a single instant — of the past activity of shipyards that are now abandoned.

✛

✦ Cota de Malle
BENIDORM, SPAIN
COMPETITION, 1997 (SECOND PRIZE)

This competition called for reflection about a sort of 'municipal tower', with many different uses: conference centre, conservatory, museum, library. Soriano tackled this project above all like a sectional issue. He located the foyers of these apparently contradictory programmes in different and strategic places. He overlaid platforms at varying heights, conceiving the section on the basis of topological criteria, before any programmatic definition. In order to prevent this building from becoming a rigid volume, inert in relation to light and time, Soriano endowed it with a skin that was at once sensitive and protective: a metal mesh of variable grids and colours, a fabric of stainless steel wires, whose undulations gave rise to shimmering effects and highlights. This web juxtaposed the reflections of the surrounding colours with an effect of transparency coming from within. Beneath there was a traditional glass façade. ✦

The children's museum is designed like an imaginary cave, a magical place. Soriano has sought to offer sensations rather than objects. The building has a particular structure, at once distinctive and powerfully present. The floor, roof and structure are covered with an identical skin which turns the place into a timeless space, where all the walls have the same curved surface geometry. The inside presents a soft, undulating floor, an ideal play area, as well as a strange, unearthly sky, which is shiny and metallic. The Cyber-auditorium is a geode. Soriano's idea was to deal with the Cyber-auditorium like an opaque, closed room, set within the museum like an independent object. To this end, he used a curved form, independent of the strong geometry of the structural arcs. The auditorium is like a small pebble inside a concrete carapace. Swathed in woven metal, its sheen calls to mind the slow sedimention process that forms a pearl. ❖

❖ Children's Museum and Cyber-auditorium

Valencia, Spain
1999; competition, 1997 (first prize)

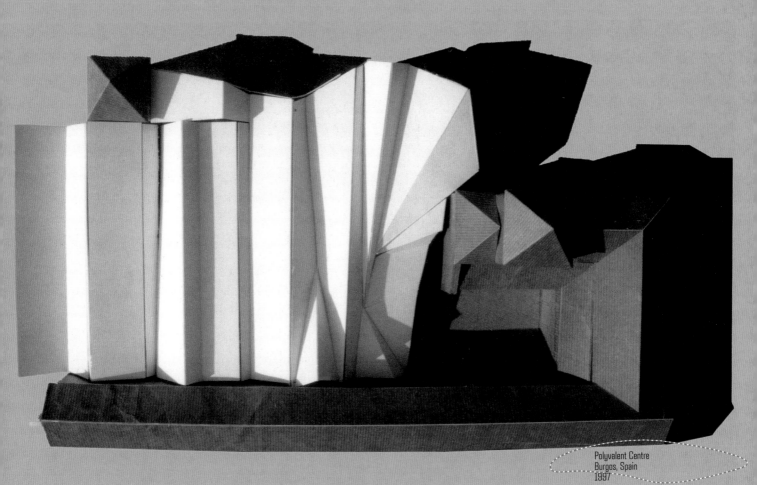

Polyvalent Centre
Burgos, Spain
1997

✦ Soriano y Asociados

Federico Soriano
1986   Diploma in Architecture, E.T.S.A.M., Madrid
1994   Creation of the review *Fisuras de la cultura contemporanea*
1991–93 Director of *Arquitectura* magazine

Teaching
1999–90 Escuela Técnica Superior de Arquitectura, Madrid

Dolores Palacios
1986   Diploma in Architecture, E.T.S.A.M., Madrid
1988–91 Review *Arquitectura*
1998   Soriano y Asociados; on the board of the journal *Fisuras*, collaborator on *Via* journal
1992   Creation of Soriano y Asociados

Principal buildings and projects
1999–97 Childrens Museum and Cyberauditorium, Valencia (under construction)
1998–92 'Opera and Congress Centre', Bilbao (realized); 'Vivienda unifamiliar', Granada (project)
1997   'Ya no separan a las mujeres de los hombres', Burgos (competition); 'Cota de Malla', Benidorm (competition); New Government Seat, Madrid (competition); Centro polivalente en el antiguo hospital de la concepcion, Burgos (competition)
1996   'Kansai-Kan of the National Diet Library', Kansai (competition); Law School, Valladolid (competition); San Fermin council housing, Madrid (competition); Mina del Morro master plan and social housing, Bilbao (competition)
1995   Restoration of the Ramos Carrion Theatre, Zamora (competition)
1994   Centre of Arts and Communications, Madrid (competition)

Recent exhibitions
1998   'Nous paisatges, nous territoris', Museu d'Art Contemporani, Barcelona
1996   'Arquitectura para la musica', VIth Venice Biennale
1994–95 'Bilbao 2000', Madrid/Orense/London
1993   'Bilbao Spain', Guggenheim Museum, New York

Principal publications
1997   'Articulos hiperminimos I' *Fisuras de la cultura cotemporanea* no. 4; 'Articulos hiperminimos I et II' *Arquitectos* no. 143
1996   'Ideario. Ideas para un cuestionario de arquitectura' *El hibrido* no. 4
1995   'Planta Fluctuante' *Fisuras de la cultura contemporanea* no. 3; 'Arquitectura sin forma' *Fisuras de la cultura contemporanea* no. 2
1994   'Edificar navios' *A + T* no. 4
1993   'Sin escala' *Arquitectura* no. 295

Selected bibliography
1998   *Quaderns* no. 219; *Guia de Arquitect. Espana 1920-2000* MOPU, Madrid; *Via* no. 2
1996   *Werk, Bauen + Wohnen* no. 12; *Quaderns* no. 212; *Architecture Today* no. 65; *Bilbao, construir la ciudad sobre la ciudad* catalogue, Madrid
1995   *Bilbao 2000. Architecture and Regeneration* Book Art, London; *Casabella* no. 622; *Bauwelt* (July); *Arquitectura* no. 40
1994   *Arquitectura viva* no. 34
1992   *Quaderns* no. 195; *Architécti* no. 15
1982   *El Croquis* no. 26/27 (monograph)

Michael Sorkin Studio

| Michael Sorkin (*1948) | Andrei Vovk (*1958) |

Hallowe'en reminded me of Michael Sorkin

Two kids came to our door trick or treating, stepped into our house and looked around. One kid asked me why we had a Christmas tree. Before I could reply the other kid said, 'It's not a Christmas tree, it's a Hallowe'en tree. You have to use your imagination.' Hallowe'en is a time filled with expectations of simultaneous fear and fantasy. A time when one's consciousness of the ironic nature of life's events, places, people and things serves to inspire the mind to great leaps of imagination. 'Ordinary' people reinvent themselves into extraodinary represen-tations of far-fetched things from static-cling to the Daughters of the American Revolution. Anything and everything is subject to reinterpretation, transfor-mation and reconfiguration. A twenty-four-hour blast of freedom to invent without fear or reproach. Magically, the darkest and brightest sides of human endeavour and thought are brought into a universally acceptable condition of equilibrium. Horror equals joy, death lives, pumpkins smile and skeletons dance. Michael Sorkin's view of the world might be described as a Hallowe'enistic reality check. He sees things exactly as they are. He makes and describes things with an unerring honesty. He concerns himself with seri-ous matters of the future of our world environment and social and political order. His proposals are at once full of irony and a delightful sense of humour. His solu-tions require horrifyingly difficult yet strikingly simplistic action. He operates with a mind-set more inclined toward the goofy world of *Popular Mechanics* than Ruskin's *Seven Lamps of Architecture*. Architects of lesser skill, talent and knowl-edge with similar tendencies would undoubtedly slip into the less relevant world of the idiosyncratic. Michael Sorkin, however, continues to impress with his uncanny ability to strike fear in the hearts of the intelligentsia and fantasy in the minds of the banal. ◆

MACK SCOGIN

✦ Governors Island
New York, USA, 1995–96

This spectaculary sited island (Upper Bay of New York) has been remaindered by the Coast Guard and is currently up for grabs. Clearly, the future of the island is that it will be brokered as a deal. These studies are not specific about exact activities, save that they be dense and public. Sorkin has in fact gone through various schemes and in the end decided that a 'University of the Earth' devoted to environmental science and policy would make a fine project, the island in the harbour standing in for the planet's own situation in the universe. In addition, it seemed appropriate to include a variety of water-related and recreational uses as part of the mix. The round buildings are brick-walled lofts, inspired by the circular fortress across the water at the Battery and its angular companion on the island. These loft buildings have hollow cores over which domes would grow during the winter to allow continuous use. The island has been slightly reshaped, recalling its origins as fill. ✦

✦ Weed, AZ
NEAR YUMA, ARIZONA, USA, 1994

Weed, AZ, is a proposal for a small new city that grew out of an investigation of the possibilities for conversion of the American military economy. Located on an existing artificial lake created by a dam on the Colorado River, Weed occupies a small piece of territory appropriated from the enormous Yuma Proving Ground and adjoins a large irrigated agricultural area. The town's dimensions are limited by the capacity and character of the land, by proximity to water and by neighbourhood structure loosely configured to a ten-minute walking radius. A serie of intersecting, branching spines provides pedestrian streets, an element of order and surfaces for different styles of movement, including a slow-motion public transit system. Automobiles are relegated to the periphery of the city. Weed is just one look at a new kind of city, located at a particular convergence of landscape, culture, technology and architecture. Dense and pedestrian, laced with water and greenery, Weed seeks to offer non-coercive variety, spaces to support activities both predictable and unenvisioned. ✦

✤ House for a Near Future

EXPERIMENTAL PROJECT, 1998

This proposal is for a community of thirty people sharing resources and environment. The basic unit is a double space, two sheltering elements that share water and waste management, energy production and a social space. From this kernel the larger house grows and from these houses larger communities might also develop, finding their form according to the living arrangements desired by their inhabitants. The future house will be very selective about its technologies, embracing both the most advanced and the most traditional. Constructed of soybean-derived plastic panels cast to form an infinite variety of shapes, glazed with aerogel windows that can be made transparent or opaque at the turn of a dial, generating its own power from photovoltaics and hydro, and treating its own wastes through green 'living machine' technology, the house is at peace with its rural setting. Located on a net of slow-moving solar, hydrogen and human-powered vehicles, it sits easily in its local setting, completely connected to the world. ✤

✦ Shrooms Housing

NEW YORK, USA, 1994

The genesis of Shrooms is in the idea of an 'all-sided' loft building in an east Manhattan neighbourhood, characterized by extensive abandonment and vacant land, much of it city-owned. Looking at the empty lots not as blight but as a community resource, Sorkin hoped that a growing garland of Shrooms might help in both greening and rebuilding the neighbourhood. In addition, he thought of the loft type as crucial protopublic space where innumerable private possibilities might be drawn. Rejecting the modernist notion of public space as disembodied and universal, Shrooms is an investigation of the reciprocities of public and private rather than an essay in their disjunction. As an urban proposition, Shrooms seeks to establish a new pattern of movement through the neighbourhood. These public greenways lead to the green rooms at the core of each structure, forming blossoms that act as distributors for the loft spaces that surround them. The system of green and publicly aggrandizable spaces emerges on the roofs of the Shrooms as a linked system of gardens, a vertical displacement of the ground plane, a return to collective use

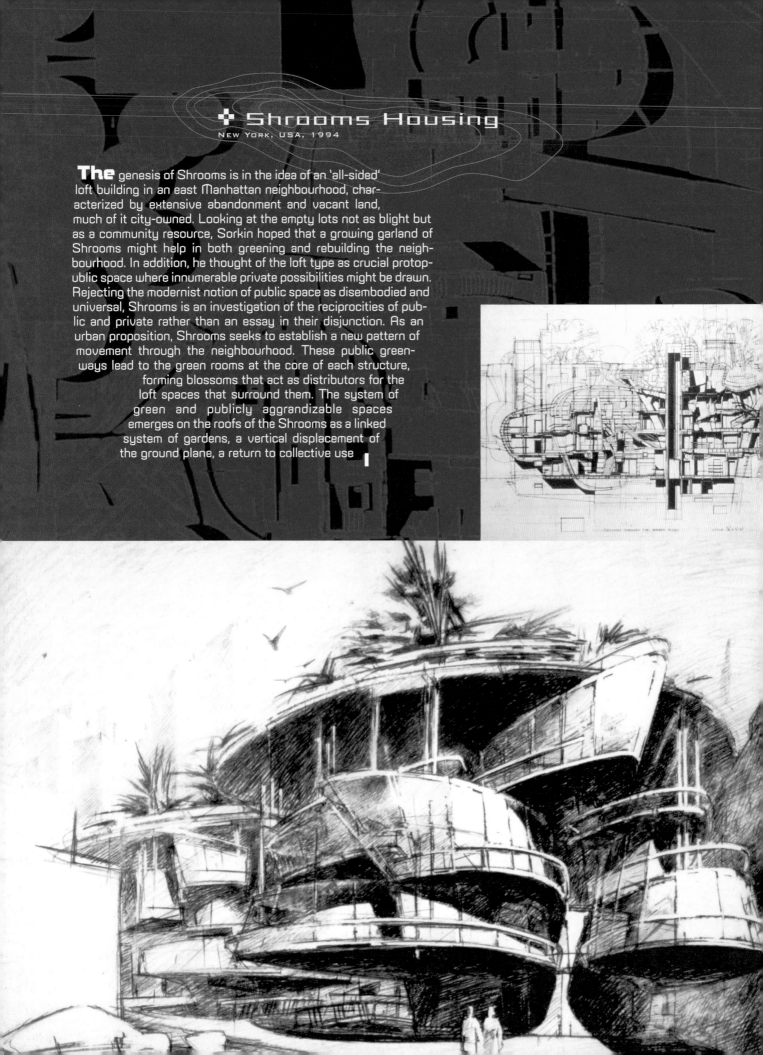

✦ Michael Sorkin Studio

Michael Sorkin (1948)
Diplomas from Harvard University and from the Massachusetts Institute of Technology

Andrei Vovk (1958)

Teaching
Michael Sorkin
2000 Professor of Urbanism and Director of the Institute of Urbanism of the Academy of Fine Arts, Vienna; Director of the Graduate Urban Design Programme at New York's City College

Michael Sorkin has also taught at Cooper Union, Columbia, Yale, Harvard, Cornell and elsewhere

Principal buildings and projects
1999 East Jerusalem, plan for a Palestinian capital (project); University of Chicago, arrangement of the campus (competition); Schwerin, Germany, master plan (project)
1998 House for a Near Future (experimental project); Hamburg, Germany, master plan (project)
1997 'Bay City Studies', master plan for a section of the sea front, San Francisco (project); Chavez Ravine, public park around Dodger Stadium, Los Angeles (project); Floating Islands, Hamburg, Germany (project); Friedrichshof Commune, urban project, Burgenland, Austria
1996 Governors Island, master plan (competition); Bucharest 2020, urban project (competition); 'Neurasia' urban prospective
1995 Wagga Wagga civic centre, New South Wales, Australia (competition); Turtle Portable Puppet Theatre (project)
1994 Weed AZ, project for a new town, Yuma, Arizona; 'Shrooms' lofts 'multi-face' east New York (project); Brooklyn Waterfront, master

plan for a section of the sea front, New York (project); Mondo Condo, Miami, Florida (project); 'Shoehaus' dwellings, Vienna, Austria (project); 'Suks of Beirut' (competition)
1991 Berlin Spreebogen (competition); New York City dwellings (project); Beached Houses, Whitehouse, Jamaica (project)
1990 'Tour Godzilla' Tokyo, Japan; Tracked Houses, houses on rails, New York (project)

Recent exhibitions
1995/96 'Urbanagrams' Harvard University and Cornell University
1995 'Subjects & Objects' San Francisco Museum of Modern Art
1994 'World War II and the American Dream' National Building Museum, Washington

Principal publications
1998 *Michael Sorkin Studio: Wiggle* The Monacelli Press, New York
1992 *Variations on a Theme Park* Will & Hang, New York

Michael Sorkin is also author of *Exquisite Corpse, Local Code, Giving Ground* with Joan Copsec; he collaborates on a number of general reviews, as well as on some specialist ones, including *Architectural Record, I.D., Metropolis*. For the last ten years he has been the architecture critic of *Village Voice*, USA

UN Studio
(Van Berkel & Bos)

| Ben van Berkel (*1956) | Caroline Bos (*1959) |

A new role for the architect is taking shape as coproducing technician, organizer and planner in a highly structured, cooperative process in which clients, investors, users and technical consultants all take part. With this new role comes a move towards a new empowerment. Boxed in by market forces and by its own need to appear in charge, the architecture of the twentieth century was driven by legitimizing arguments. This ultimately undermined the continuity of the independent architectural practice. This approach is pragmatic in that it deals with real social, economic and public conditions, but it is crucially an interactive pragmatism. A simple, opportunist response to what is being asked is impossible in a large-scale, multiclient project of considerable complexity. And a preconceived idea of urbanism preceding the specificities of location, programme or users has become redundant. Instead, the project emerges interactively. Deep planning includes an emerging articulation of a policy of mobility and the incorporation into architecture of aspects of time. This approach is specifically intended for projects and locations that are rich in meaning, loaded with structure and full of potential movement. The combined use of automated design and animation techniques enables a working method integrating questions of user movement, urban planning, construction and the potential for a programme to develop at certain points in this web. New computational techniques make it possible to lay bare a multiplicity of layering of experiences and activate this knowledge in new ways. When mapping movement patterns, the time-programme relationship is not compartmentalized but reflects synchronic, continuous time. Separate infrastructural layers may be classified, calculated and tested individually, to be subsequently interwoven to achieve both effective flux and effective interaction. Temporal conditions are thus connected to programmatic themes in a simulation of the non-segmented manner in which time flows in a real situation. An ability to grasp the process of collecting, structuring and centralizing the depth and wealth of public information puts the architect once more at the centre of his own world. The architect as a public scientist is a concept neither objective nor subjective, neither before-theory nor after-theory, neither theoretical nor opportunist. No longer dependent on the subjective value of 'talent' or the rationality of design choices, the architect coordinates the different parties who take up different places in the public field and uses specific tactics and techniques to once more take the radical step of offering vision. ✤

UN STUDIO (VAN BERKEL & BOS)

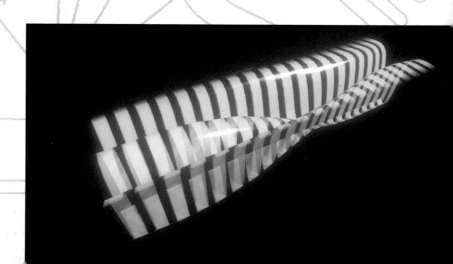

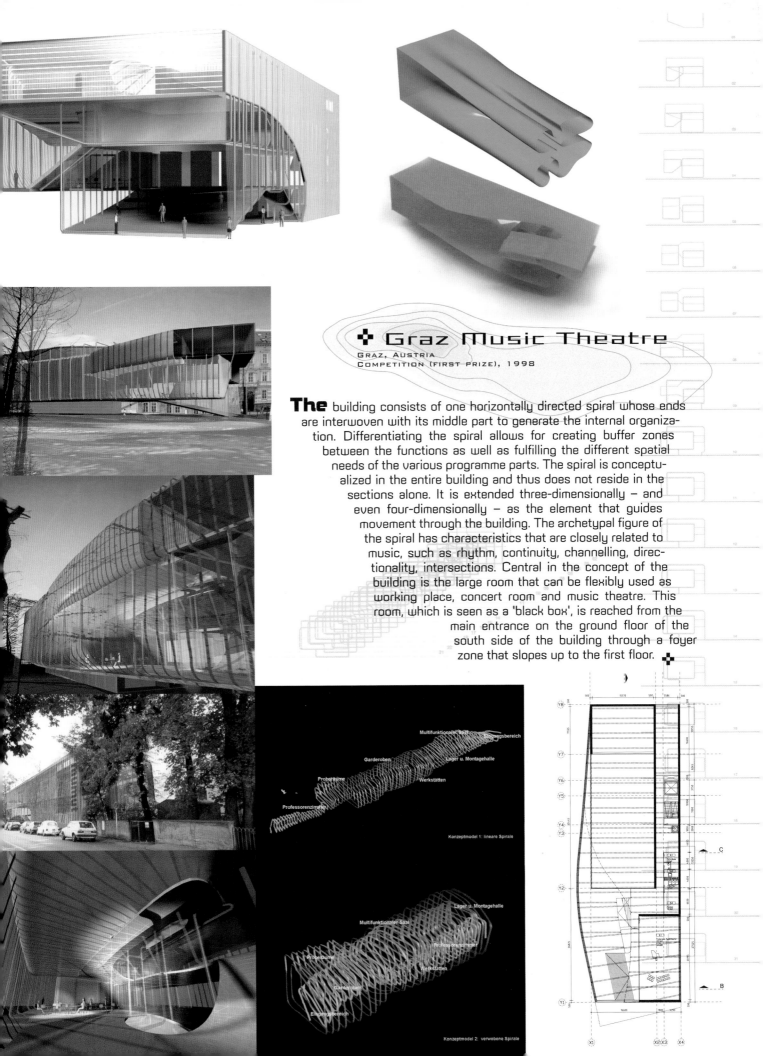

✦ Graz Music Theatre

GRAZ, AUSTRIA
COMPETITION (FIRST PRIZE), 1998

The building consists of one horizontally directed spiral whose ends are interwoven with its middle part to generate the internal organization. Differentiating the spiral allows for creating buffer zones between the functions as well as fulfilling the different spatial needs of the various programme parts. The spiral is conceptualized in the entire building and thus does not reside in the sections alone. It is extended three-dimensionally – and even four-dimensionally – as the element that guides movement through the building. The archetypal figure of the spiral has characteristics that are closely related to music, such as rhythm, continuity, channelling, directionality, intersections. Central in the concept of the building is the large room that can be flexibly used as working place, concert room and music theatre. This room, which is seen as a 'black box', is reached from the main entrance on the ground floor of the south side of the building through a foyer zone that slopes up to the first floor. ❖

Konzeptmodel 1: lineare Spirale

Konzeptmodel 2: verwobene Spirale

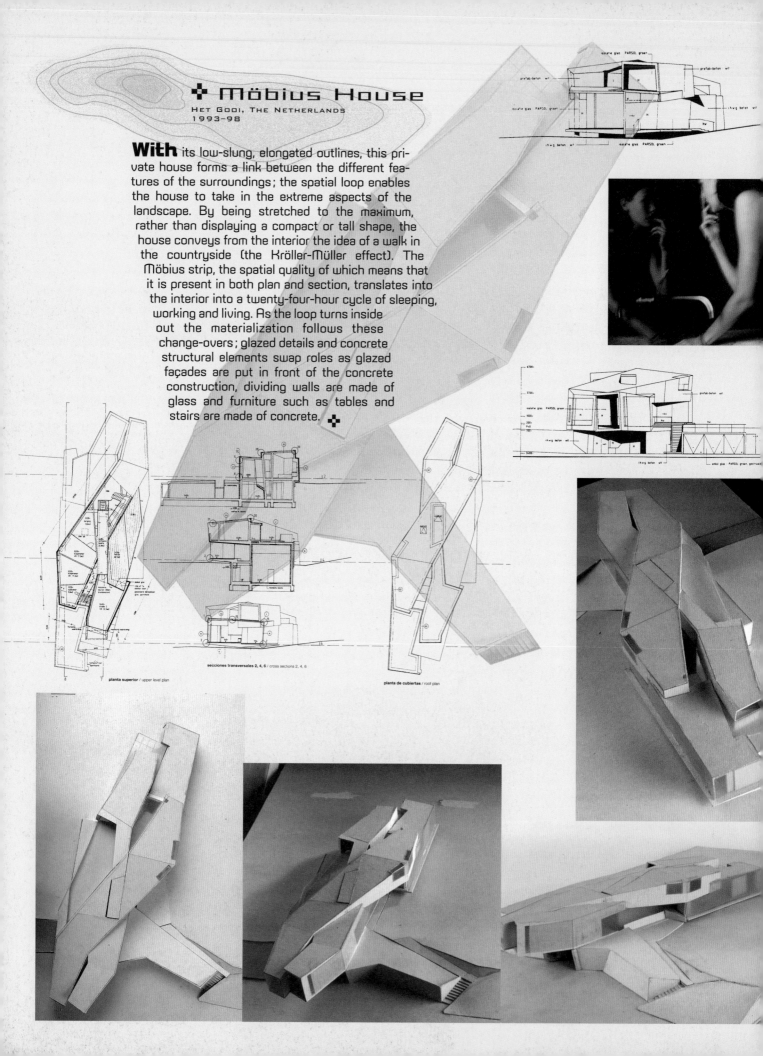

✦ Möbius House

Het Gooi, The Netherlands
1993–98

With its low-slung, elongated outlines, this private house forms a link between the different features of the surroundings; the spatial loop enables the house to take in the extreme aspects of the landscape. By being stretched to the maximum, rather than displaying a compact or tall shape, the house conveys from the interior the idea of a walk in the countryside (the Kröller-Müller effect). The Möbius strip, the spatial quality of which means that it is present in both plan and section, translates into the interior into a twenty-four-hour cycle of sleeping, working and living. As the loop turns inside out the materialization follows these change-overs; glazed details and concrete structural elements swap roles as glazed façades are put in front of the concrete construction, dividing walls are made of glass and furniture such as tables and stairs are made of concrete. ✦

planta superior / upper level plan

secciones transversales 2, 4, 6 / cross sections 2, 4, 6

planta de cubiertas / roof plan

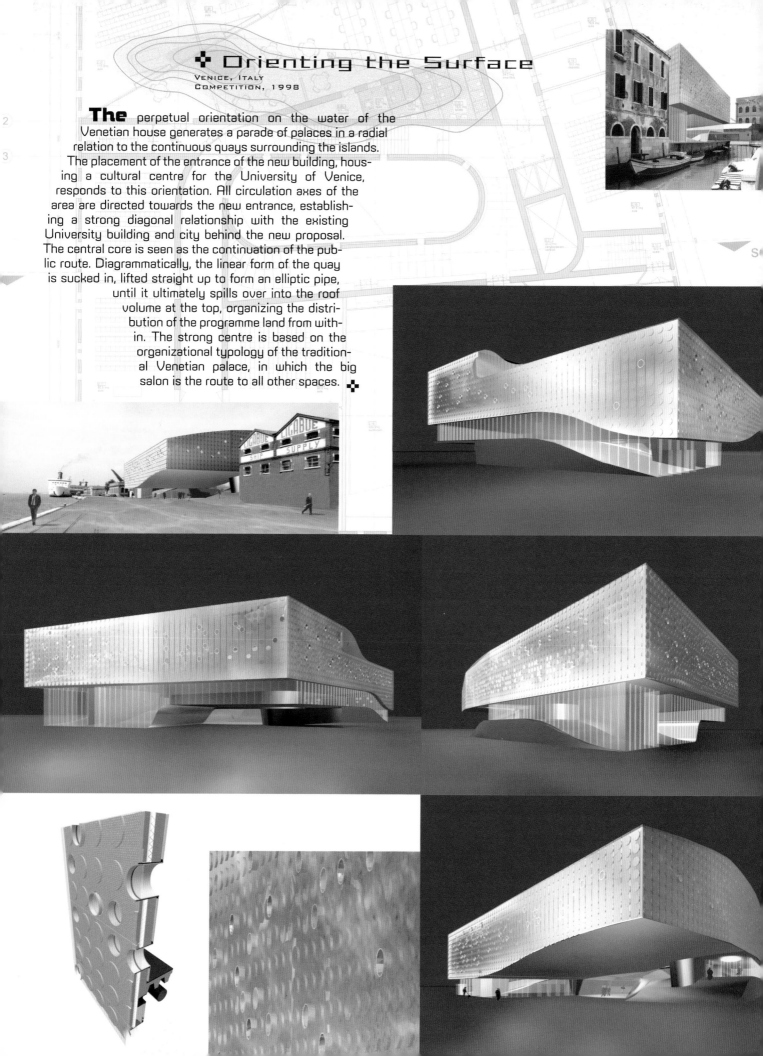

✦ Orienting the Surface

VENICE, ITALY
COMPETITION, 1998

The perpetual orientation on the water of the Venetian house generates a parade of palaces in a radial relation to the continuous quays surrounding the islands. The placement of the entrance of the new building, housing a cultural centre for the University of Venice, responds to this orientation. All circulation axes of the area are directed towards the new entrance, establishing a strong diagonal relationship with the existing University building and city behind the new proposal. The central core is seen as the continuation of the public route. Diagrammatically, the linear form of the quay is sucked in, lifted straight up to form an elliptic pipe, until it ultimately spills over into the roof volume at the top, organizing the distribution of the programme land from within. The strong centre is based on the organizational typology of the traditional Venetian palace, in which the big salon is the route to all other spaces. ✦

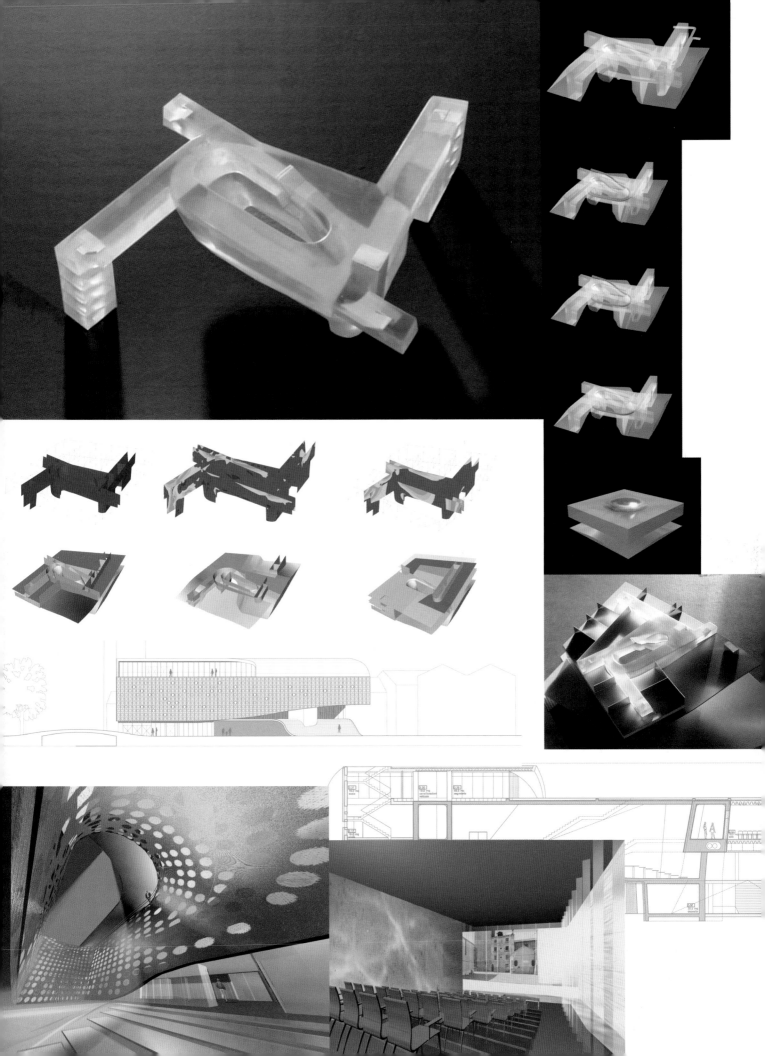

NMR VIDE
SERVICE
WERKRUIMTES
ULTRARUIMTE
LABORATORIUM
WERKRUIMTES

✦ NMR Facilities

BIJVOET UNIVERSITY CAMPUS, UTRECHT, THE NETHERLANDS
1998

This laboratory is conceived as a pavilion-like structure. It is dedicated to NMR, Neutron Magnetic Resonance, a research technique that analyzes the structure and behaviour of proteins with the use of high-frequency magnetic pulses. The new NMR facilities require space for eight spectrometers, a console and a control board. The functioning of the magnets creates specific architectural requirements. They all generate magnetic fields of various sizes, dependent on the frequency of the magnets. These fields are sensitive to movement, types of structure, types of installation and so on. Any irregularity within particular distance from the magnets disturbs the results of the test. On the other hand the magnetic radiation also affects people, computers, credit cards, pacemakers. Therefore the placement of magnets determines the organization of the core of the building. The magnetic radius shapes structure and surface, directs programme and equipment, and affects the internal circulation. ✦

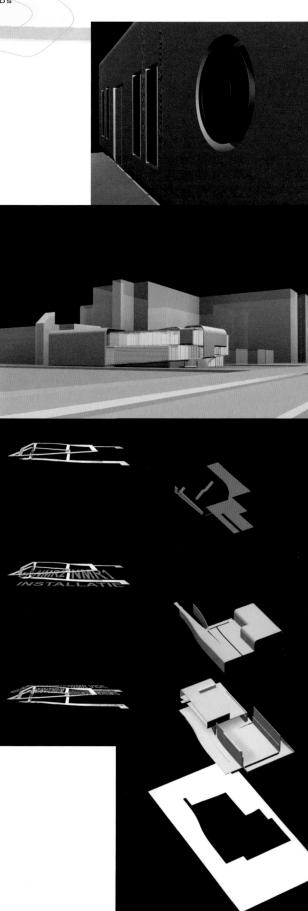

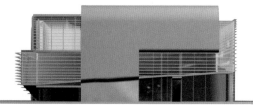

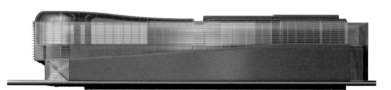

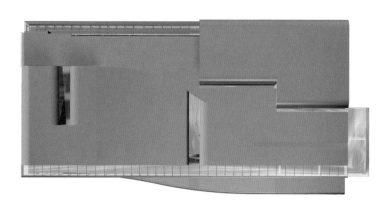

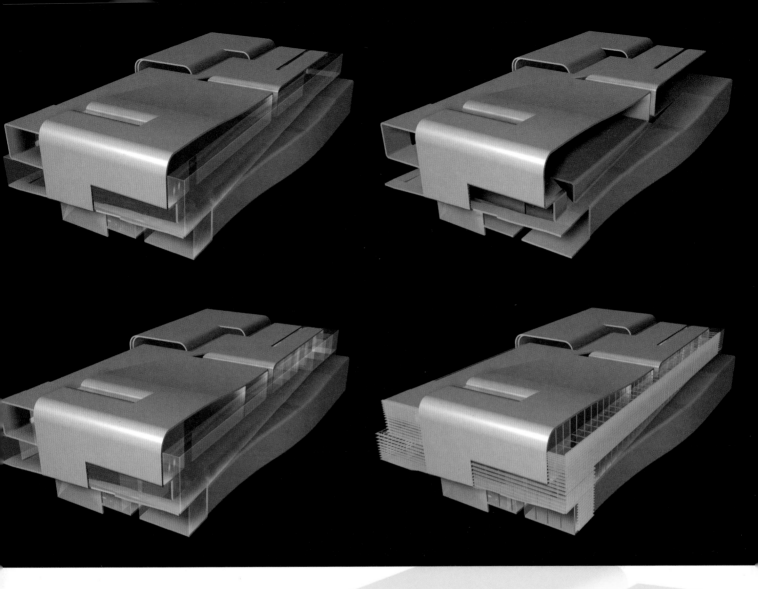

✦ UN Studio (Van Berkel & Bos)

Ben Van Berkel (1957)
Rietveld Academy, Amsterdam
1987   Honours Diploma from the Architectural Association, London

Caroline Bos (1959)
Art historian

1988   Founded Van Berkel & Bos Architectuurbureau in Amsterdam
1998   Founded UN Studio (United Net) in Amsterdam

Teaching
Ben van Berkel
1999–96   Architectural Association, London
1994   Columbia University, New York; Harvard, Cambridge (MA)

Principal buildings and projects
1999   Möbius House, Het Gooi, Netherlands (realized)
1998   Music Theatre, Graz, Austria (competition, first prize); Venice
        Faculty of Architecture (competition); Purmerend Bridge (realized);
        Arnhem Station Area (project); Electricity station, Innsbruck; NMR
        facilities, Utrecht (project)
1997   Tunnel Piet Hein, Amsterdam (realized)
1996   Pont Erasmus, Rotterdam (realized); Netherlands Pavilion, Milan
        Triennale (realized); Rijksmuseum Twente, Enschede (renovation
        and extension)
1995   Yokohama International Port Terminal (competition)
1994   Villa Wilbrink, Amersfoort, Netherlands (realized); Swoz II (project)
1993   ACOM, Amersfoort (renovation of façades); Electricity sub-station
        REMU, Amersfoort (realized); Das Schloss, Berlin (project); Centre
        Swoz, Amsterdam (project); Jollenpad Amsterdam (project);
        Oostelijke Handelskade, Amsterdam (project); Carillon, The Hague

(project); Vroom & Dreesman, Emmen (project); Borneo Sporenburg
I Amsterdam (project); Borneo Sporenburg II, Amsterdam (project)
1992   Karbouw Office and Workshop, Amersfoort (realized); Company
        centre NijKerk (project); Electricity sub-station, Oudenrijn (project)
1990   Bathing machine, Domburg (competition)

Principal publications
1999   *Move* (3 vols) Goose Press (spring)
1994   *Mobile Forces* Ernst & Sohn, Kristin Feireiss, Berlin
1993   *Delinquent Visionaries*, essays, in collaboration with Caroline Bos,
        010 Publishers (republished in 1994); *Crossing Points*, Aedes
        Gallery, Berlin

Selected bibliography
1999   *A + U* no. 342, Bart Lootsma, diagrams in costume; *De Architect*
        (March), Janny Rodermond, Topology van het wonen; *Space Design*
        no. 143, Arnheim Centre
1998   *Architecture in the Netherlands, Yearbook* Rotterdam; *De Architect*
        (Jun.); *Arch +* no. 143, Möbius House; *GA Houses 5*; *Architektur &
        Wohnen* (Feb.); *Architectuur & Bouwen* nos 4 and 7/8; *Eleven
        Architectural Houses* Arco, Barcelona
1997   *Quaderns* no. 214; *De Architect* (May, July/August and file 4);
        *Yearbook of Architecture in the Netherlands, Yearbook 1996-
        1999*, Rotterdam; *A + U* no. 323; *Lotus International* no. 94;
        l'Architecture d'aujourd'hui no. 314
1995   'Ben van Berkel 1990–95', monograph, *El Croquis* no. 72, Madrid;
        'Ben van Berkel and Caroline Bos', monograph, *A + U* no. 296
1992   *Ben van Berkel*, monograph, 010 Publishers

Ushida Findlay Partnership

| Kathryn Findlay (*1953) | Eisaku Ushida (*1954) |

The Tokyo-based Ushida Findlay Partnership was set up in 1987 by the Japanese architect Eisaku Ushida, graduate of Tokyo University (1976) and the Scottish architect Kathryn Findlay, who trained at the Architectural Association (1979). Both are former associates of Arata Isozaki (between 1976 and 1982). Their architecture is situated at the crossroads between a Bachelardian conception of space, which explores its symbolic, psychoanalytical, not to say 'psycho-geographical' components, and a purely scientific and geometric research into form. For Ushida and Findlay, this detour by way of the basic sciences, focusing on the geometry of chaos and non-linear mathematics, is the means of introducing a real independence of the architectural object. It also enables them – via an architecture which bears some resemblance to the formal explorations of Frederick Kiesler ('Endless House'), and Antoni Gaudí, Bruce Goff's organic spaces, André Bloc's sculptures, as well as those designed by Häusermann and Chanéac in the 1960s – to propose a possible synthesis between the subjective desire to free up form and the need to ground it objectively. Architecture, landscape and sculpture open here on to the path which sports new forms of spatiality, run through by recurrent motifs like the Möbius strip and the spiral, a model of growth within nature, which retains the internal analogies while making interior and exterior inseparable. Their organic forms unfold in an interplay of topological twists which galvanize space and stimulate its multisensorial perception (Truss Wall House). Their architecture is the projection on to a physical space of the psychological desires of its inhabitants (Soft and Hairy House). It lays claim to the continuity between body and space. Here spatial consciousness and the unconscious have merged in one and the same cognitive field, where there is an interference involving intuition and mathematical modelling. The relationship between the body as space and the mental perception of this space lies at the hub of their architecture. It is the intent of Ushida and Findlay to reactivate this psycho-psychic perception of space by infusing their buildings with forms derived from the movements of the human body. Fluidity, continuity and the unconscious must transform architecture into a materialized subconscious that is not only individualized but also global and cosmic. Intrigued by 'the flowing space' (Leon van Schaik), they perceive the interiors of their architectures as 'inhabited landscapes', psycho-sensorial landscapes, at once tactile and mental, where the furniture and the light are plastic components. For Ushida and Findlay, the city is also a landscape, just like the continuous surface of a strip or loop, in other words a hybrid matrix of economic, agricultural and industrial implications. Everything takes part in the same flux and continuity: the intuitive and the rational, the solid and the void. Architectural space is polyphonic. ✦

✦ Truss Wall House

MASHIDA CITY, TOKYO, JAPAN, 1993

Truss wall method allows a variety of independent shapes, within the limits of structural integrity of the reinforced concrete. Ushida and Findlay explored these possibilities in the design of this experimental house. The system's plasticity enabled unlimited topological manipulation between solid and void. Thus functional criteria were satisfied by emulating the flow of pliable viscera packed into a vessel and frozen at a moment in order to acquire a balanced fluidity. By replacing the standard architectural parlance, in which elements are 'articulated', with this 'slimy fluid', Ushida and Findlay intended to attain a deeper layer of architectural language borrowing from the mathematics of topology. The courtyard was laid with balloon tiles, the doors embossed with fractal veins and the entire building was brush-finished in mortar, creating a continuous surface inside to out. The essence of the finished building cannot be captured by video or photograph, it needs to be experienced in movement and over time. ✦

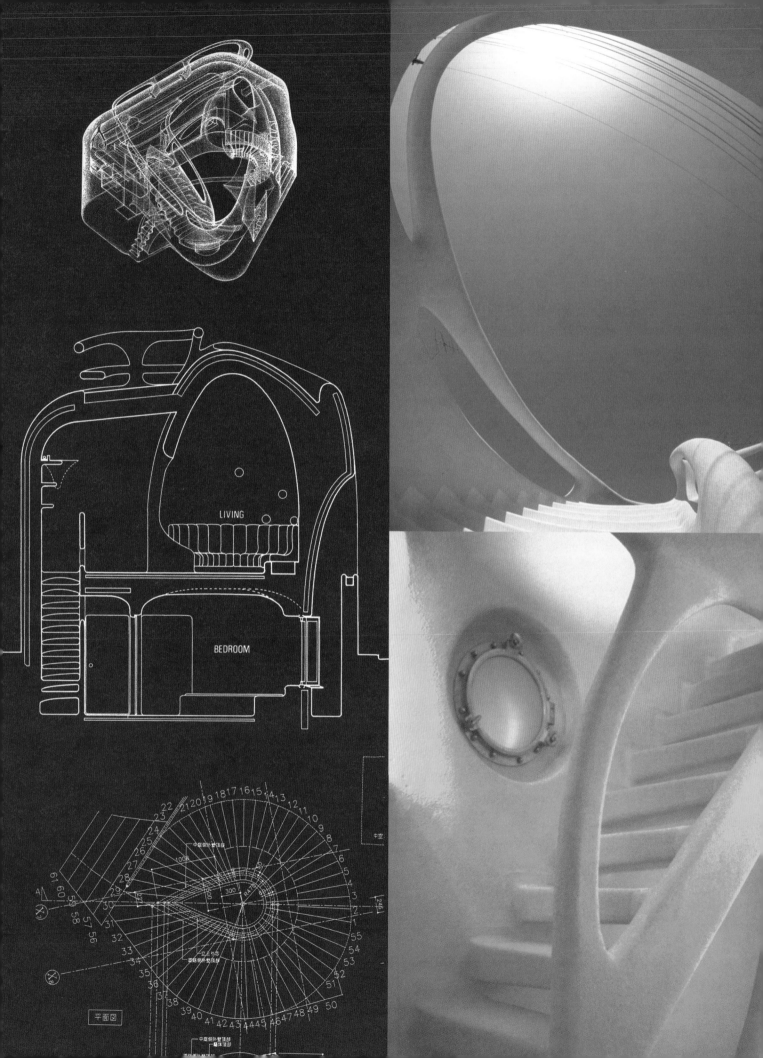

LIVING

BEDROOM

平面図

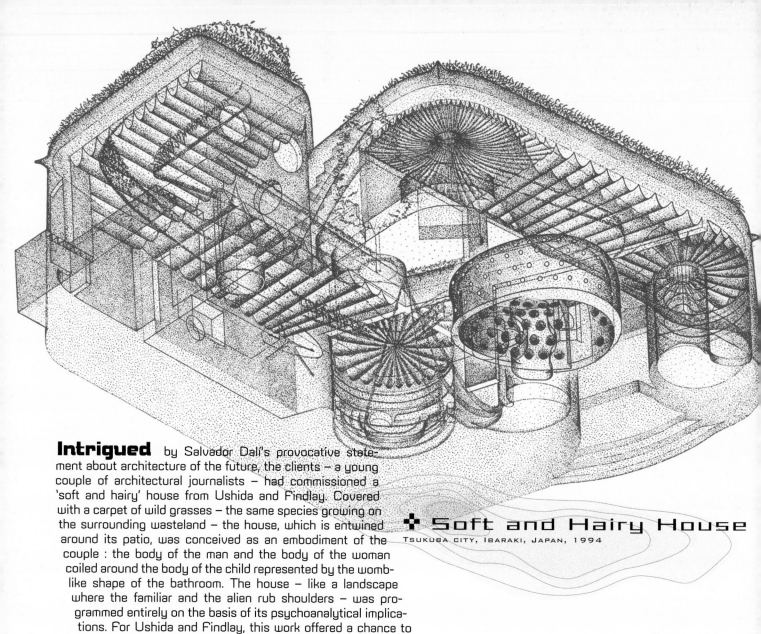

Intrigued by Salvador Dalí's provocative statement about architecture of the future, the clients – a young couple of architectural journalists – had commissioned a 'soft and hairy' house from Ushida and Findlay. Covered with a carpet of wild grasses – the same species growing on the surrounding wasteland – the house, which is entwined around its patio, was conceived as an embodiment of the couple : the body of the man and the body of the woman coiled around the body of the child represented by the womb-like shape of the bathroom. The house – like a landscape where the familiar and the alien rub shoulders – was programmed entirely on the basis of its psychoanalytical implications. For Ushida and Findlay, this work offered a chance to project a Surrealist line of thinking into architecture. While minimalism, a predominant architectural trend in Japan, strives to 'dematerialize the real', they have attempted here, in the manner of Dalí, to 'materialize the dream' and construct a 'reality', mixing in one and the same space factors that are inside and outside architecture. This new 'reality' shows a vague periphery, as if it had been abstracted from the world and the real 'real'. ✦

✦ Soft and Hairy House
TSUKUBA CITY, IBARAKI, JAPAN, 1994

✦ House for the Third Millennium

LONDON, ENGLAND, 1994

This house is a prototype designed for an exhibition held at the Architecture Foundation in London. Ushida Findlay proposed a house for the future when the network of electronic devices wraps around the globe forming a new layer of 'Electronic Gaia'. Cities would have been dispelled, dissolving their functions into the countryside or computer displays. People would spend their time in a very different way. This house was designed for this type of living and working, located in a rural environment. Dwelling and landscape are fused into one. The roof is a three-dimensional extension, arising and returning, of the ground plane. The plan is based on a logarithmic spiral and the elevation is based on the sine curve. This method, which amalgamates two kinds of geometry into three-dimensional shapes, has the potential to generate many other new forms. Inside, the house comprises a series of oval pods for the bedrooms, studies, eating areas and bathrooms, with more flexible living areas between them. ✦

✦ Ushida Findlay Partnership _____

Eisaku Ushida (1954)
1976 Diploma from the University of Tokyo
1999 Visiting professor at UCLA, Los Angeles

Kathryn Findlay (1953)
1979 Diploma from the Architectural Association, London
1998 Professor at the University of Tokyo
1999 Visiting professor at UCLA, Los Angeles

1986 Creation of Ushida Finlay Partnership in Tokyo

Principal buildings and projects
1999 Homes for the Future, Glasgow 1999 (prizewinner); Hopton Street loft residential interior, Thames-side, London
1998 Billiard Hall and House, Nagoya; Kumamoto Artpolis– Park Management Office, Kumamoto
1997 Polyphony House, Osaka; Financial Times Millennium Bridge (competition)
1995 Housing Prototype 1, Osaka
1994 Soft and Hairy House, Ibaraki Prefecture; Kaizankyo company villa, Wakayama Prefecture; Spiral Wall House, Kobe, Hyogo Prefecture; NEG Glass (prizewinner); House for the Third Millennium (project)
1993 Chiaroscuro House, Tokyo; Truss Wall House, Tokyo; BBC Design Awards (mentioned)
1991 Vertical Horizon, Tokyo (project)
1990 Yokohama Sports Club, Kanagawa Prefecture
1989 Echo Chamber, Tokyo; Park Museum City (project)

Recent exhibitions
1999 'Homes for the Future', Glasgow
1998 'Creator's Legs', Madrid, Valencia, New York, Tokyo

Selected bibliography
1999 l'Architecture d'aujourd'hui no. 325; Domus no. 818
1998 'Ushida Findlay' monograph, 2G no. 6, Gustavo Gili, Barcelona (Text by Ushida/Findlay: 'Genealogy Diagram 1987–94 & Matrix 1996')
1996 Parallel Landscapes Gallery MA Books 02, Toto Shuppan, Tokyo (May)
1993 Truss Wall House special publication, Kenchiku Bunka, Tokyo

Makoto Sei Watanabe

| Makoto Sei Watanabe (*1952) |

For the Image to the Method/Part-Whole-Relation-Generation/ Architectural structures and cities are made up of many parts. 'Design' is an activity which determines the interrelations among those parts. From that the whole is generated. There are thus two possible approaches to design. On the one hand, a set of ground rules (like those of Newtonian mechanics) can be laid down to regulate the whole, with the parts successively falling into place in accordance with those rules. On the other hand, it is possible to begin with the smallest parts and gradually form a whole from those. Ordinarily, design follows the former approach, starting from the top down. But the alternative is also a viable approach to 'design'. Researchers using simulation modelling have found that when living organisms move in groups, the only thing determinate is the relation of each with its immediate neighbours. Simple rules on factors like mutual distance, orientation and posture are fixed, but no one member of the group tells the others how to move. Despite this, when large numbers of such organisms move in groups, remarkably precise patterns are generated. To create a whole according to a blueprint, powerful overall rules and a great amount of energy are required. But by simply giving rules for relations among parts, a whole can be defined through very simple relays, and because the rules affect only the parts, the whole can adapt flexibly to change. A new 'method' of urban planning is called for around the world. 'The Induction Cities' project is one such possibility. The cities brought forth through this project would not be 'planned' cities. Although they may bring to mind actual cities, these are cities spontaneously generated by computer programs. Image-Desire-Dreams-Flotation. It's better for humans to do things computers can't do. One thing human beings should do is to 'design' a programme like that of 'The Induction Cities' project itself. This would be a matter of 'Meta-Design'. It's an act of setting values, of deciding what is good. One more thing that programmes cannot do is to 'dream' .'Image Design' and 'Meta-Design' make up a complementary combination. What, then, is the greatest desire of architecture? Architecture is subject to many conditions. Site, function, environment, construction deadlines, costs, etc. The strongest among these conditions is gravity. No technology exists in today's world for cancelling the force of gravity on objects situated on the earth's surface. Because there is no escaping from gravity, this becomes a universal symbol of all other kinds of constraints. The floating quality of works such as 'Jelly Fish', 'Osaka Prefectural Peace Museum', 'K Museum' and others does not signify simply the liberation from gravity. It is also an expression of the will to be released from layer on layer of many kinds of 'spells' or bewitchments. ✦

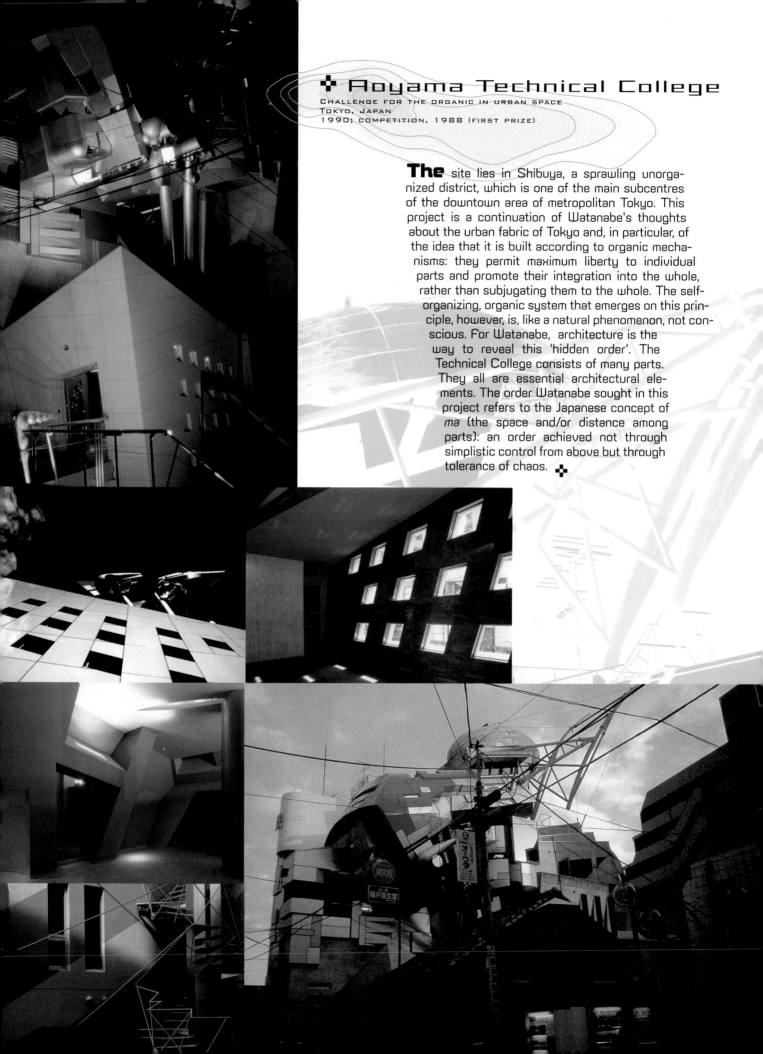

✦ Aoyama Technical College

CHALLENGE FOR THE ORGANIC IN URBAN SPACE
TOKYO, JAPAN
1990; COMPETITION, 1988 (FIRST PRIZE)

The site lies in Shibuya, a sprawling unorganized district, which is one of the main subcentres of the downtown area of metropolitan Tokyo. This project is a continuation of Watanabe's thoughts about the urban fabric of Tokyo and, in particular, of the idea that it is built according to organic mechanisms: they permit maximum liberty to individual parts and promote their integration into the whole, rather than subjugating them to the whole. The self-organizing, organic system that emerges on this principle, however, is, like a natural phenomenon, not conscious. For Watanabe, architecture is the way to reveal this 'hidden order'. The Technical College consists of many parts. They all are essential architectural elements. The order Watanabe sought in this project refers to the Japanese concept of *ma* (the space and/or distance among parts): an order achieved not through simplistic control from above but through tolerance of chaos. ✦

✚ Jellyfish Houses
JAPAN, 1990-97

The Jellyfish series is a prototype for experimenting with light and water. One of its aims is to give material substance to the invisible power of 'buoyancy'. Another is to transform actual space into a control filter vis-à-vis the external world. The ultimate goal of these two attempts is to exchange substance for space and space for substance. People have the preconceived idea that space is empty and substance is dense. The Jellyfish series presents space that is full of liquid, space that has substance that we can touch. It also exhibits space as a film that changes light and wind. The shape of a Jellyfish resembles a balance, a set of scales for measuring the weight of space and the mass of light. On this balance, force becomes material, and the material becomes action-interchangeable symmetry. The first 'Jellyfish' led to the Mura-no Terrace project, in 1995. Part of 'Jellyfish 2' was realized as a semitransparent, free-curved surface volume in the K Museum project, in 1996. ✚

SECTION 1

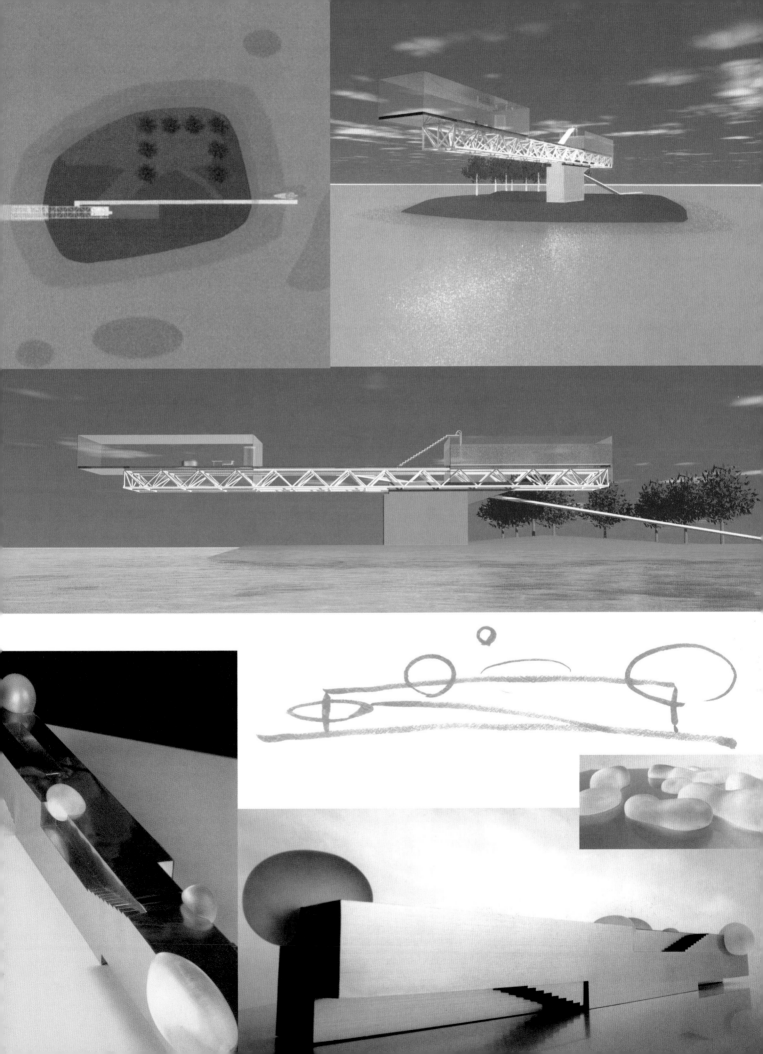

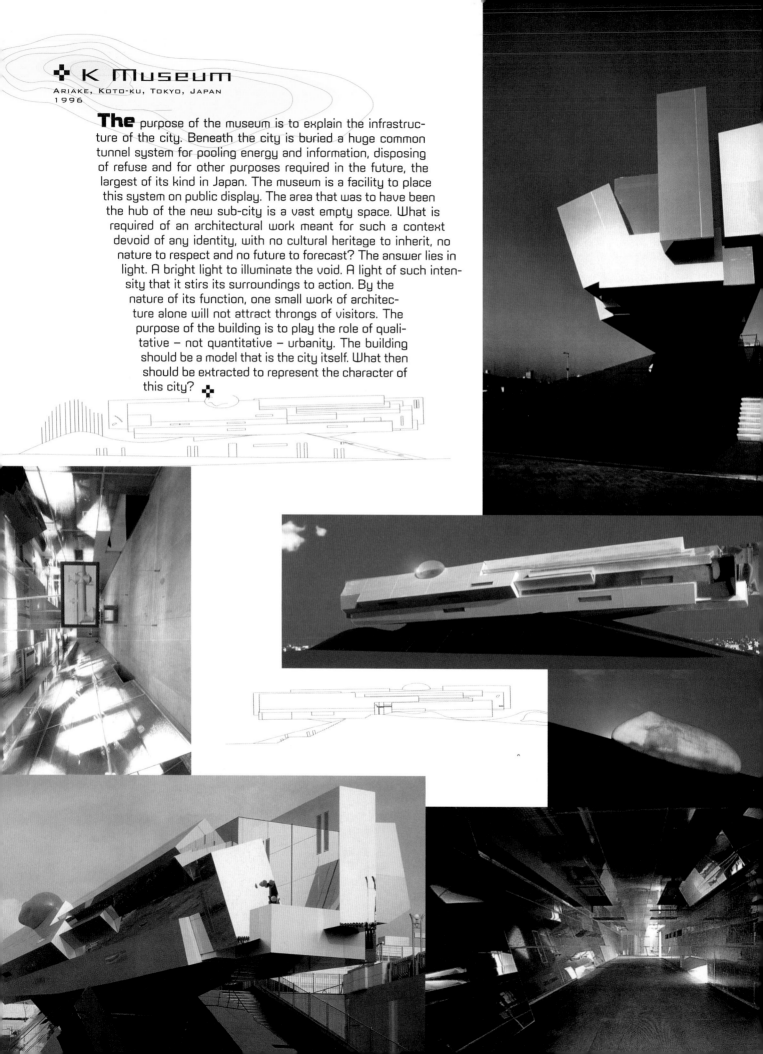

✦ K Museum

ARIAKE, KOTO-KU, TOKYO, JAPAN
1996

The purpose of the museum is to explain the infrastructure of the city. Beneath the city is buried a huge common tunnel system for pooling energy and information, disposing of refuse and for other purposes required in the future, the largest of its kind in Japan. The museum is a facility to place this system on public display. The area that was to have been the hub of the new sub-city is a vast empty space. What is required of an architectural work meant for such a context devoid of any identity, with no cultural heritage to inherit, no nature to respect and no future to forecast? The answer lies in light. A bright light to illuminate the void. A light of such intensity that it stirs its surroundings to action. By the nature of its function, one small work of architecture alone will not attract throngs of visitors. The purpose of the building is to play the role of qualitative – not quantitative – urbanity. The building should be a model that is the city itself. What then should be extracted to represent the character of this city? ✦

✦ Mura-no Terrace

HIGH TECHNOLOGY WITHIN NATURE
MURA-NO, JAPAN
1995

This is a public complex located deep in the mountains of Gifu Prefecture, in central Japan. Bordering the least densely populated village in Japan, the population of Mura-no is only 750 people. It possesses the image of a 'home town' which many Japanese still hold. However, even though the image of a home town has not changed, in reality the home town itself is not the same as before. Even in this area of beautiful rivers and green valleys, which do not exhibit any manifestations of change, optical fibre has arrived and high-definition televisions illuminate the night. The people enjoy a comfortable life through the use of high technology within their beautiful nature. In this way, the image of a 'lost home town' overlaps with the image of the 'still distant future'. Within such an environment, this architecture, a location for holding meetings for the villagers and as an information centre for people visiting the village, is imagined as a small artificial object intensifying the natural landscape. ✦

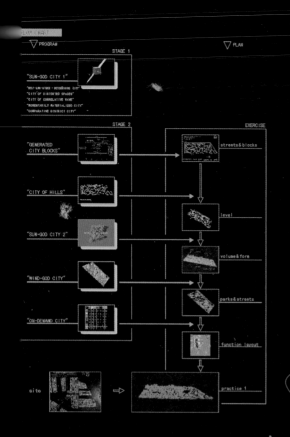

✦ 'The Induction Cities'
Theory of Evolutionary Design/
A New 'Method' for Architecture and the City
1991–96

Instead of designing a plan and a resulting form, this project designs a 'mechanism' for generating the result. This is a matter of attempting to design a process of evolution, of design without design, i.e. 'Design-less Design'. This might otherwise be described as a higher-level approach to design, designing the system of the process of design, i.e., 'Meta-Design'. This kind of new approach to design is possible through computer programming. 'Induction City' consists of a kind of atlas of four-dimensional virtual cities. 'Sun-God City' and 'On-demand City' of 'The Induction Cities' project are readily accessible examples. When one element of the city is changed, relations with all other elements are altered. As the number of elements increases, interrelations among them become more complex and only a computer program can solve problems of 'complexity'. ✦

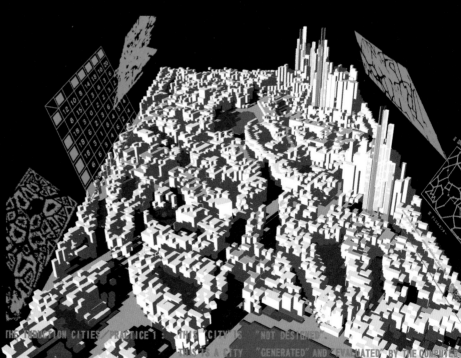

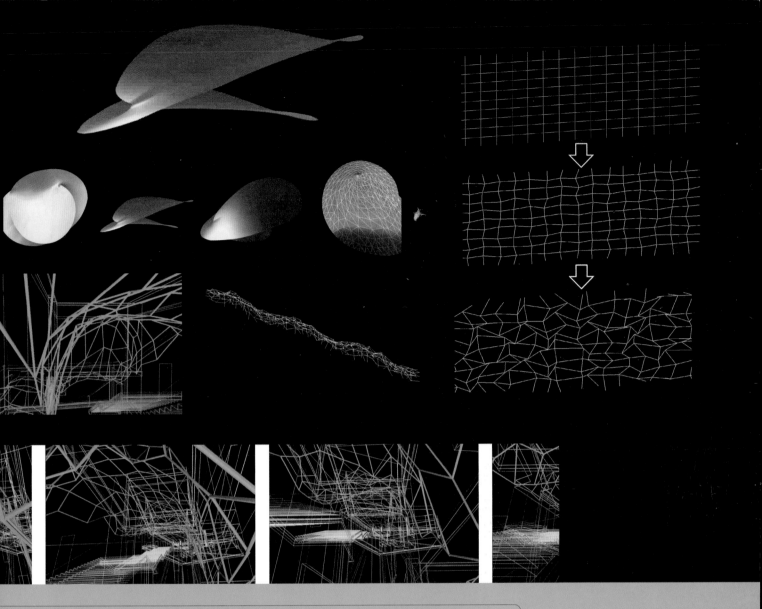

✛ Makoto Sei Watanabe

Makoto Sei Watanabe (1952)
1974 Diploma from Yokohama National University
1976 Master of Architecture, Yokohama National University

1984 Founded the Makoto Sei Watanabe practice
1994 Winner of the Hylar International Award
1997 Winner of the SDA Award from the Ministry for Industry in Japan

Teaching
1997–88 Yokohama National University
1997 Tokyo Denki University
1995–94 Kyoto Seika University

Principal buildings and projects
2000 Iidabashi Subway Station, Tokyo Subway, Line 12 (competition 1991)
1999 Star Site housing, Tokyo
1998 Fiber Wave, Chicago Atheneum, Jelly Fish III, Shanghai, China
1996 K Museum, Tokyo; Atlas Housing, Tokyo; Fiber Wave, Tokyo; The New Capital of Japan New Capitol Building (project)
1995 Mura-No Terrace, Gifu
1994 Jelly Fish II (project)
1992 Stera Vista Residence (project); Lagoon Residence (project)
1991 Chronospace – Spiral Hall, Tokyo
1990 Aoyama Technical College, Tokyo (international competition 1988); Jelly Fish Second House (project)

Recent exhibitions
1997 'The Virtual Architecture', Tokyo University Digital Museum
1995 'Architectural Design Conference', Yokohama; 'Wooden City' Japan

Institute of Architects
1993 'Re-Engineering Tokyo' AXIS

Principal publications
1998 *Conceiving the City* monograph, Makoto Sei Watanabe, I'Arca, Italy; *Liquid Crystal* Jitsugyo no Nihon sha Publishing, Tokyo
1995 *7 Polilogue* Collaborator, Delphi Research Publishing, Tokyo
1992 *Kenchikuka* ('Architect') Jitsugyo no Nihon sha Publishing, Tokyo
1990 *Sokudo Kukan* collaborator, Rikuyo sha Publishing, Tokyo

Selected bibliography
1998 *Building Journal* (Jan.) HongKong; *LD + A: Lighting Design + Applications* (Feb.) USA; *If Product Design Award*, Germany; *Annual Report*, France; *Indian Architect & Builder* (April) India
1997 *World Architecture* (April) UK; *World City Tokyo* Academy Editions, UK; *l'Architecture d'aujourd'hui* (Jun.) France; *Deutsche Bauzeitung* (August) Germany; *L'industria del costruzione* (May) Italy; *Inter* (April) Canada; *Building Journal* (Jan.) Hong Kong; *Indian Architect & Builder* (March and April)
1996 *I'Arca International* (July/.August) Italy; *Architectural Review* (July) UK; *Blue Print* (August and December) UK; *Inter* (Sept.) Canada
1992 *Japan Design*, Taschen, Germany; *l'Architecture d'aujourd'hui* (Oct.)

West 8

| Adriaan H. Geuze (*1960) |

The office of West 8 landscape architects and urban planners was set up in 1987 as an international team of architects, urban designers and industrial designers. West 8 designs urban plans, squares, parks and gardens. The philosophy of West 8 is deeply rooted in an optimistic attitude towards the contemporary landscape, in which it expresses both the vulnerability and the euphoria of mass culture. Landscape, infrastructure, nature and archaeology coalesce to form vital constituents of the city. Arcadian landscapes coexist alongside the dynamic, mutable and sprawling city unimpeded by architectural doctrines or history; the city stretches towards the horizon or shoots skywards. Space has acquired new dimensions that constantly put the sense of scale and proportion to the test. West 8 draws inspiration from the poetic beauty of the artless and the mundane. The urban dweller is no pitiful victim needing compensation in the form of green and nature; today's urbanite is a self-assured, exploratory, creative individualist. He is well-informed and affluent and equipped with the most up-to-date technology. he is an explorer and manipulator of his surroundings. The design of this environment demands a sensitivity that goes beyond the creation of mere decorative nature. The city produces its own wastelands. Severed from the traditional centre by railway lines, motorways and fly-overs, new dispersed centres are created. That their identity is not fixed in advance is neither good nor bad. In its urban design work the office seeks to devise powerful building typologies that are attuned to the landscape and public space. A sharp line is drawn between private and public space in order to engender a sense of contrast. West 8's designs for public spaces reveal the office's fascination with emptiness as a condition. Within the urban fabric, West 8 creates quasi-unprogrammed spaces that can be colonized at will by urbanites. Potential play surfaces are demarcated in a two-dimensional, graphic design by different materials such as steel, glass, wood and rubber. The sparsely distributed objects in public spaces acquire the quality of totems or icons. They furnish the location with identity and lure the urbanite. Large wooden benches boldly face the sunshine. Bridges evocative of reptiles ask to be climbed. The lighting in public spaces often creates the sense of the surreal through the use of large moveable spotlights or coloured lamps shining from tree stumps. The knowledge that the contemporary landscape is for the most part artificial and made up of different components, both designed and undesigned, allows West 8 the freedom to respond by positing its own narrative spaces. The basic ingredients are ecology, infrastructure, weather conditions, building programmes and people. The aim is to incorporate the awareness of these various aspects in a playful optimistic manner that stimulates the desire to conquer and take possession of space. Gardens form the only exception. The organized world of commerce, functionality and efficiency finds its necessary counterpart in specific spaces that appeal to uncertainty, mortality, desire and perversity. The gardens are enclosed and withdrawn from the world. It is here that the human dwellers can literally retreat into themselves. ❖

Schouwburgplein
Rotterdam, 1997

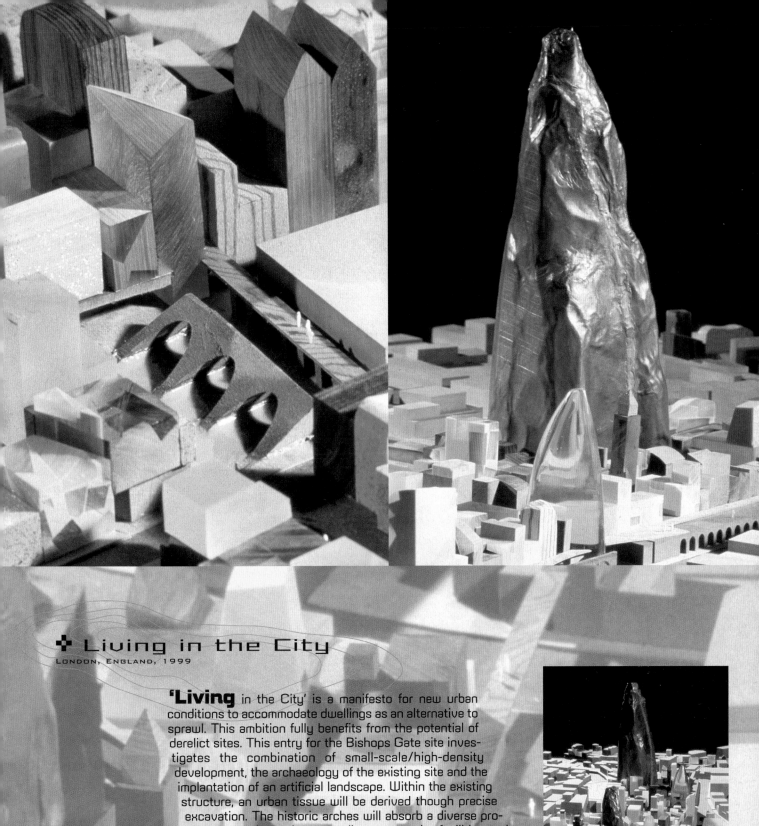

✦ Living in the City
LONDON, ENGLAND, 1999

'Living in the City' is a manifesto for new urban conditions to accommodate dwellings as an alternative to sprawl. This ambition fully benefits from the potential of derelict sites. This entry for the Bishops Gate site investigates the combination of small-scale/high-density development, the archaeology of the existing site and the implantation of an artificial landscape. Within the existing structure, an urban tissue will be derived though precise excavation. The historic arches will absorb a diverse programme such as shops, studios, community facilities and services. On top of the arches a colonization process will start, based on a small-scale parcellation grid (derived from the existing structure). Once the number of new levels exceeds the threshold limit, the existing structure is reinforced, or removed to carry new structure and higher loads. In this low-rise/high-density area three magnificent landscape features will be raised: the peaks. These rocks with Arcadian nature and micro biotopes will be icons of urban nature on the scale of London. ✦

✦ Borneo Sporenburg
AMSTERDAM, THE NETHERLANDS, 1993-97

Adriaan Geuze designed the urban plan and architectural specifications of this project, situated near the very centre of Amsterdam, in the eastern part of the docks, on the twin wet docks of Borneo and Sporenburg. He proposes to create a model of semi-detached individual accommodation of high density in order to respond to the particular context of this project: to satisfy, on the one hand, a strong demand for individual housing and, on the other hand, the real estate profitability. Two thousand five hundred homes thus form a dense covering (100 units per hectare) punctuated with several higher buildings. To reconcile the dictates of density and the idea of the individual house, Geuze explores new intermediary housing typologies and radically diverts the pattern of individual houses in blocks widely spread across in the Netherlands. Here, the public space is reduced to the street; the houses on three floors – topped by a flat roof – are equipped with private gardens that become enclosed terraces or patios, thus enabling steady flow and transparency in spite of the compactness of the design. ✦

Makeblijde
St Marteendijk, The Netherlands, 1999

✦ Secret Garden

MALMÖ, SWEDEN, 1999

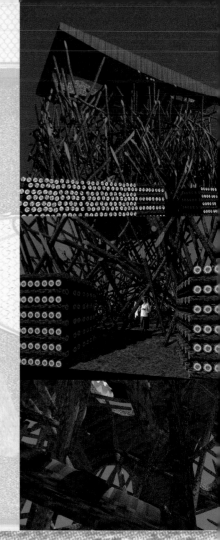

Situated on a landfill area, the proposed garden dreams of the sea. It consists of an enclosed dark forest cut into the shape of a cube with a side length of 12 metres. It is a mysterious garden to find your way through and to move in. Surrounded by a wall of pine logs, its atmospheric interior is also made of pine trunks, with a maximum length of 17 metres. The ground is covered with blueberries. When walking in the garden you discover a big shell belonging to another world. If you glance up you see the sky through three holes cut into a thick layer of seashells. Parts of huge rocks lying on the surface are visible. It is possible to climb up through the garden to this other layer by using ladders. Up here at sea-level the atmosphere is different and focuses on the nearby Öresund. The floor is covered with 60 centimetres of shells, while several smooth rocks stick up so that you can sit down and relax. Two large shells lie on the surface to collect water. The garden enables an imaginary relationship to develop between the ocean and the Swedish forest. ✦

West 8 Landscape Architects & Urban Planners

Adriaan H. Geuze (1960)
1979–87 Master's Degree in Landscape Architecture, Agricultural
University, Wageningen

1987 Creation of West 8 Landscape Architects b.v. practice in Rotterdam

Teaching
1999–92 Technical University, Delft
1997/95 Harvard University, School of Design, Boston
1995 University of Amsterdam; De Appel, Amsterdam
1994 Institut Saint Luc, Brussels; Architektur Zentrum, Vienna

Principal buildings and projects
2000–1991 Landscaping Schiphol: a Green Strategy for the Airport
(under construction)
1999 'Secret Garden', Malmö (project); 'Skywalk from Zoo to Zoo', footbridge, Emmen (realized); 'Living in the City', urban manifesto,
London (project); Makeblijde, St-Marteen, garden (project); Jubilee
Gardens and Chiswick Park, London (realized); Design for
Temporary Agricultural Garden, Weil am Rhein, Germany (project);
Urban Design for the Headquarters of the AMSF, Seregno, Italy
(project)
1998 'Between Sky and Water', bridges, Borneo Sporenburg (project);
'Tree Trunks in Twilight Forest', square, Carrascoplein, Amsterdam
(realized); Highway Water Jet, Vlotho, Germany (competition);
Square West, Utrecht (realized); Venice Cemetery extension (com-
petition)
1997 'Borneo Sporenburg, plan for 2,500 residences, Amsterdam;
Schouwburgplein public square, Rotterdam (realized); Schiphol-
Oost, master plan (project); Central Park, Leidsche Rijn (prizewinner); Seafront Thessaloniki, Greece (joint prizewinner)
1996 Landscape Design Eastern Scheldt, Rijkswaterstaat (project)
1995 Bench Bridge, Utrecht (realized); Market Stalls, lamp-posts,
Rotterdam (realized); Kröller-Müller Museum rearrangement,
Otterloo (realized); Interpol Headquarters, garden, Tillburg (realized)
1994 Südraum Leipzig, design/landscape (project)

Recent publications
1999 *Engineer Meets Poet* Aedes, Berlin
1997 'Landschap in Acceleratie' *90.000 Pakjes Margarine, 100 meter
vooruit* exhibition catalogue, Groningen
1996 *Colonizing the Void* VIth Venice Architecture Biennale;
'Accelerating Darwin' *Scope, Cambridge Architecture Journal* no. 8;
'New Parks for New Cities' *Lotus* (Feb.); *Adriaan Geuze/West 8.
Landscape Architecture* Rotterdam; 'Het Vemmende Succes.
Maaskantlezing van Adriaan Geuze' *De Architect* no. 2

Selected bibliography
1999 *NZZ Folio* (Sept.)
1998 *De Architect* (July/August); *Bauwelt* no. 30; 'Hypersurface
Architecture' *Architectural Design* no. 133; *Architecture in the
Netherlands, Yearbook 97/98* Rotterdam; *Lotus* no. 96;
Architectural Review (Jan.)
1997 *Quaderns* Landscape Architecture no. 217; *International
Landscape Architecture*, Barcelona; *Lotus* no. 94; *De Architect*
(March, July/August, Sept. and Nov.); *Bauwelt* no. 43 /44;
Architecture in the Netherlands, Yearbook 96/97 Rotterdam; *Werk,
Bauen+Wohnen* no. 10; *Domus* no. 797; *Archis* no. 9; *Quaderns* no.
217; *Daidalos* no. 65; *Landscape Architecture* no. 7; *Archithese* no.
3; *Topos* no. 19; *Archis* nos 3 and 4
1996 *A+U* no. 313; *Quaderns* Forum International no. 1; *Studio Works 4*,
Harvard University, Cambridge, MA; *Abitare* nos 354 and 356; *De
Architect* nos 2 and 11; *Blue Print* no. 133; *International Landscape
Design* R. Holden, London; *Topos* no. 16; *Werk, Bauen+Wohnen* no.
11; *Bauwelt* no. 37; *l'Architecture d'aujourd'hui* no. 306; *Quaderns*
no. 211

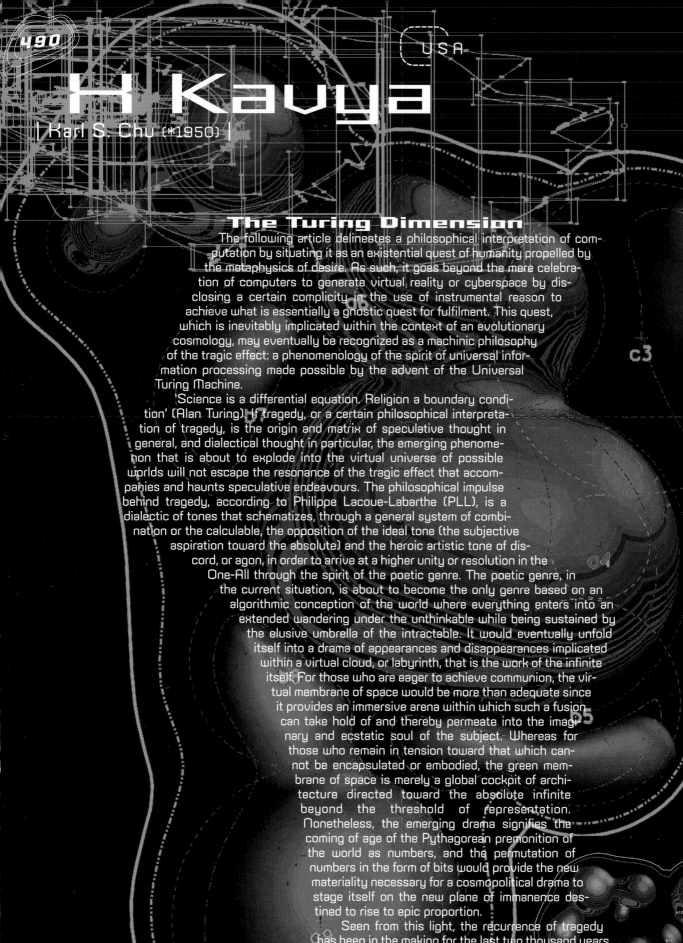

USA

X Kavya

| Karl S. Chu (*1950) |

The Turing Dimension

The following article delineates a philosophical interpretation of computation by situating it as an existential quest of humanity propelled by the metaphysics of desire. As such, it goes beyond the mere celebration of computers to generate virtual reality or cyberspace by disclosing a certain complicity in the use of instrumental reason to achieve what is essentially a gnostic quest for fulfilment. This quest, which is inevitably implicated within the context of an evolutionary cosmology, may eventually be recognized as a machinic philosophy of the tragic effect: a phenomenology of the spirit of universal information processing made possible by the advent of the Universal Turing Machine.

'Science is a differential equation. Religion a boundary condition' (Alan Turing). If tragedy, or a certain philosophical interpretation of tragedy, is the origin and matrix of speculative thought in general, and dialectical thought in particular, the emerging phenomenon that is about to explode into the virtual universe of possible worlds will not escape the resonance of the tragic effect that accompanies and haunts speculative endeavours. The philosophical impulse behind tragedy, according to Philippe Lacoue-Labarthe (PLL), is a dialectic of tones that schematizes, through a general system of combination or the calculable, the opposition of the ideal tone (the subjective aspiration toward the absolute) and the heroic artistic tone of discord, or agon, in order to arrive at a higher unity or resolution in the One-All through the spirit of the poetic genre. The poetic genre, in the current situation, is about to become the only genre based on an algorithmic conception of the world where everything enters into an extended wandering under the unthinkable while being sustained by the elusive umbrella of the intractable. It would eventually unfold itself into a drama of appearances and disappearances implicated within a virtual cloud, or labyrinth, that is the work of the infinite itself. For those who are eager to achieve communion, the virtual membrane of space would be more than adequate since it provides an immersive arena within which such a fusion can take hold of and thereby permeate into the imaginary and ecstatic soul of the subject. Whereas for those who remain in tension toward that which cannot be encapsulated or embodied, the green membrane of space is merely a global cockpit of architecture directed toward the absolute infinite beyond the threshold of representation. Nonetheless, the emerging drama signifies the coming of age of the Pythagorean premonition of the world as numbers, and the permutation of numbers in the form of bits would provide the new materiality necessary for a cosmopolitical drama to stage itself on the new plane of immanence destined to rise to epic proportion.

Seen from this light, the recurrence of tragedy has been in the making for the last two thousand years, beginning with Euclid's axiomatic treatment of geometry,

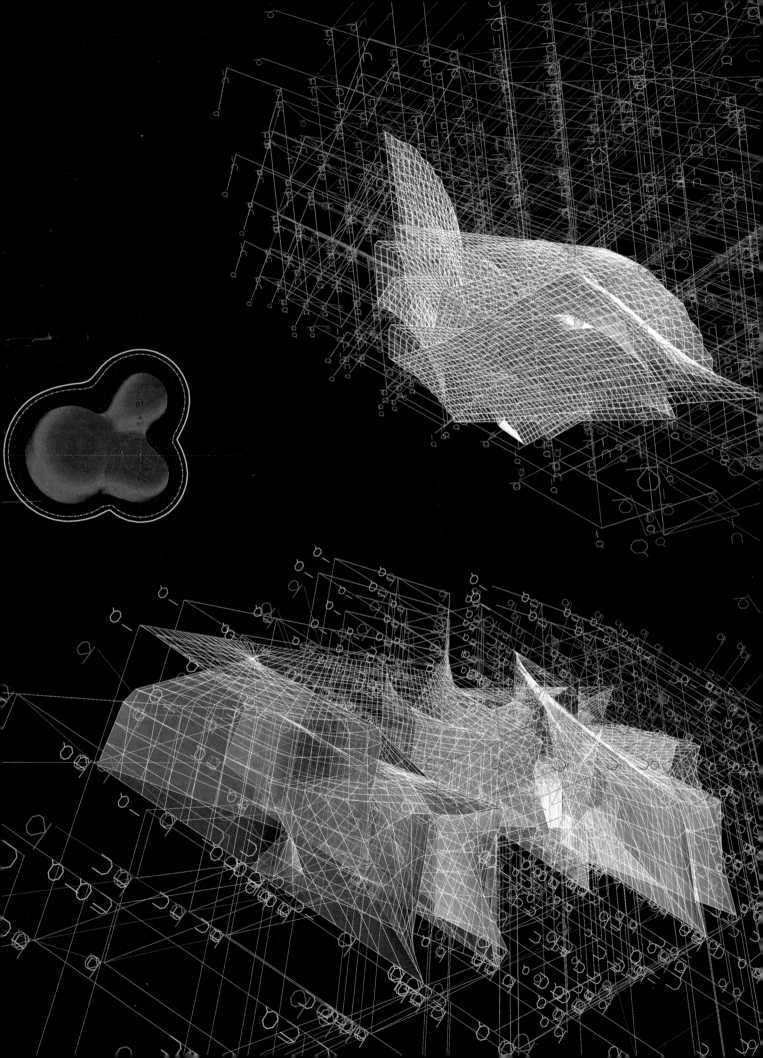

Leibniz's quest for a symbolic logic, and Russell's and Whitehead's monumental *Principia Mathematica* in the early part of the twentieth century. It is a consequence of the manifest destiny of instrumental reason whose aim is, on the one hand, to verify and control knowledge by means of a mechanization of mathematics that finds concrete expression in the Universal Turing Machine (UTM), and, on the other, to enter into communion with the substance of effects engendered by the instrumental use of reason in the first place. The tragic effect is a dialectic of fusion of numbers and beings driven by a utopian impulse that channels and transports the spirit of universal information processing into an epic dramatology of transubstantiation. In this echo of tragedy, the subject is mediated by the Universal Turing Machine, which will, in due time, prove to be a gnostic medium that operates on the logic of functional synthesis. It is a machinic alchemy of subjectivization that enfolds both the subject and the object of architecture into this instrumental medium by generating a universal surface upon which a mutant reality can exfoliate into a possible world. This tragic dimension is the scene of a transfusion where the subject of speculative Idealism finds him-/herself plunged into the manifold cockpit of the topological surface now being engendered by the Universal Turing Machine. It is a trajectory, or a tragic transport, that becomes infused with the medium by steering from within the infinite movements of thought and lines of flight in order to overcome, through a dialectics of transgression, the fabric of mimetology brought on by the machine of the double bind. It is simultaneously a catharsis of the subject and of the medium that represents both the substance of Aristotelian mimesis as a mode of poesis and mimesis in the sense of mimetism or imitation. It is this aspiration for overcoming through sublimation that turns into a play of mourning, which lies behind every metaphysical desire, that induces a philosophy of the tragic effect, or tragic pleasure of the sublime, by situating the subject of architecture in an in-between space of melancholy, or, to use Plato's designation, metaxy. Even though it is at once the nearest and yet the farthest from absolute fulfilment, it may require the intrusion of the caesura so that what appears is not the alternation of representations or simulations but the limits of representation itself.

With the publication of the paper 'On Computable Numbers, with an Application to the Entscheidungsproblem' in 1936, Alan Turing launched the specification for an abstract machine that would ultimately engender a new world by laying out a new plane of immanence specific to its mode of formal implementation. This plane is the virtual arena upon which diagrammatic flows and constructions are instantiated by the abstract machine. The birth of the Universal Turing Machine (UTM) marks the inauguration of the Hyperzoic Era (the artificial life of self-organizing systems) by redefining the projective content of the plane of immanence as information-theoretic in origin. It is the harbinger of a new breed of biomechanical species and carries with it the germ of a Brave New World more fantastic and hyperbolic than anything we have seen in the history of human civilization. In its most significant form, the UTM is not merely another instrument in the history of technical inventions; it is a computational monad that redefines a new plane of immanence as the spectacle of a second-order nature transposed on to the cultural universe of humanity, that is, founded on first-order nature. As a generative mechanism, the UTM has brought to the foreground a universe of counterfactual possibilities by showing that these potential states of affairs are inextricably woven into the invisible fabric of reality itself. Its latent ambition is to exfoliate this reality in all its manifestations through the inner workings of the Turing Dimension: a linear sequence of cells that function as the channel through which information is processed to form the digital economy of the Universal Turing Machine.

The UTM is a logical counterpart of Leibniz's idea of the metaphysical monad. It is a computational monad that is founded upon the classical model of computation owing to its reliance on the mechanism of classical logic for its operation. As such, the UTM is an abstract machine composed of a linear tape, which is potentially infinite in length and is divided into squares or cells, and a device called a head, which reads and rewrites binary digits registered on each cell according to the instruction set of the program. The tape serves as a receptacle for storing as well as for processing binary information. The notion of universality derives from the fact that every UTM can compute, according to the Church-Turing Thesis, anything that is logically computable and can therefore model and nest within itself any model of computation, classical or otherwise. As such, it is a simple conceptual mechanism capable of perpetually inducing an internal model, or perception (Leibniz's term for the same feature within a monad), of the world by means of an internal principle that continually modifies its internal state to arrive at a more comprehensive version of the model or perception of the world. In other words, the UTM is a logical subset that can compute the potential content of the larger set that is the universe itself. Consequently, by the nature of its embeddedness, it is capable of altering the content of the universe by further computing the numerical substance of the cosmos and staging it on to the plane of immanence as diverse modalities of possible existence. According to Rolf Landauer of IBM, who has done fundamental research into the material and energetic aspect of computation, not only does physics determine what computers can do, but what computers can do, in turn, will define the ultimate nature of physical laws. This is a profound and radical idea, which necessitates a new paradigm concerning the nature of computation and, consequently, of our role as active participants, or agents, in the evolution and transformation of the universe at large.

The Universal Turing Machine therefore is a machinic idea of a perpetual computing system, or an abstract evolutionary machine, that processes information through sequential iteration of bits by registering them on the linear tape of the machine, which is potentially infinite in length. As such, it is endowed with the latent capacity to self-organize and transform its internal states, at least in principle, into all possible states of a monad without end. Even though its initial design is predicated on the need to delineate the consistency of the sequence of steps necessary in the formation of a mathematical proof, a response made by Alan Turing to David Hilbert's call (1900) for resolution to the so-called decision problem, the UTM has transcended its original function by overcoming its task as an instrument of representation. It has now entered into the domain of self-organizing systems with the ambition to assert its autonomy as a mode of existentiation, or auto-projection. This is an ontological status distinct from a condition that is dependent, as a prime mover, solely on external forces that instantiate its will to action. In other words, the UTM is a primitive precursor of a biomechanical species with the metaphysical ambition to embody a machinic form of artificial life and neural intelligence. Since the UTM is the simplest and the most general type of computing system, its internal principle or program can be made to accommodate a generalized form of genetic algorithm that could evolve through self-modification and optimization of its internal states. It could, in principle, evolve through self-replication and mutation into ever more complex states of monadic encoding by incorporating new axioms into its existing matrix of axioms. In the process, it would bifurcate into other self-replicating UTMs, each of which in turn would bifurcate and nest other self-replicating UTMs to form an epigenetic landscape of computational monads or a machinic phylum of Universal Turing Machines. Even though the Leibnizian monad continually engages in simultaneous, albeit non-linear, modification of multiplicities as it develops into higher levels of

complexity, the UTM is a one-dimensional cellular automaton that self-organizes and transforms itself by incessantly rewriting the binary digits registered on the tape that constitutes the Turing Dimension. It is a one-dimensional universe of monadic states generated by the perpetually evolving code of the machine. The Turing Dimension, together with the arrow of time, establishes the plane of reference necessary for the mapping and projection of the Turing Surface into the plane of expression. Each UTM is a monadic agent that enters into autocatalytic reactions with other UTMs to weave a multilayered tapestry of surfaces, which subsequently coalesce by forming into a Universal Turing Surface as the virtual membrane of the mechanosphere. The Surface oscillates according to the dynamic flow of information outputted by each scanning particle as it scans and rewrites bits along the linear sequence of cells marked on the tape of the Turing Dimension of each machine.

Such a perpetual Turing Machine is an abstract biological engine made to sustain itself through self-modification and self-maintenance within the intertextual networks of machinic phyla generated by Universal Turing Machines. Each Turing Dimension therefore is an aperiodic time machine that weaves a fractal surface with inflections and perturbations that amplify to form holes and vortices on various regions of the membrane that constitutes the Universal Turing Surface. These are the caesurae of the Turing Dimension that interrupt the crazed oscillations of the tragic effect induced by the dialectics of fusion operating in complicity with the synthetic logic of the Universal Turing Machines.

Herein lies the supreme irony of a gnostic quest, which may well be usurped by the very instrument that promises to deliver. The internal principle and the internal complexity contained within each computational monad are dependent on the universe of computable functions drawn from the universe of mathematics that has proven to be irreducibly random and incomplete in its organization. As a consequence, any algorithmic compression that reflects the matrix of the internal complexity would be a code that is also irreducibly random, a specific kind of randomness that is qualitatively different from any random scrambling of bits. If the totality of all possible worlds is a mirror of the infinity of possible effects engendered by the absolute infinite cause, there are, in all likelihood, no binary strings that can encapsulate the hidden logic of

the absolute infinite in its entirety. However, if there does exist
such a metacode, it would by definition pertain to all possible
worlds including those that exist outside the domain of the
laws of physics that underlie the present state of the universe. Yet Seth Lloyd of M.I.T. has suggested a surprising
proposal stating that in a universe in which local variables
support universal computation, a quantum theory of
Everything can be simultaneously correct and fundamentally incomplete.

Let it suffice for the moment to say that the Turing
Dimension is the potential infinite interspersed with
breaks or interruptions that lie between overlapping
dimensions of the tragic effect. The Universal Turing
Surface is the instrumental medium that exfoliates into a
topo-dramatology of the virtual cockpit of architecture
infused with an ambivalent mixture of exultation and
despair. It is a theatre where the very excess of the speculative switches into the very excess of submission to fini-
tude (PLL), as defined, in this context, by the logic and limits of computability. It is at once a tragic comedy and a
machinic philosophy of the tragic effect. Nothing symbol-
izes the emergence of the Hyperzoic Era more clearly and
explicitly than the emergence of the Universal Turing
Surface, which lays out a virtual cartography of a possible
world among an infinite number of possible worlds.
Architecture is implicated in the folds of this cartography,
which has become the green membrane of space suspended essentially in a twilight zone that is everywhere
and nowhere. The Universal Turing Surface is the phase
space topology engendered by the cyclothymic oscillations
of the Universal Turing Machine. It is saturated with the stuff
of information out of which unheard-of dreams and dramas
emanate to form a part of the living texture of the evolving
universe. The Surface is nonetheless permeated with the
Caesura of the Turing Dimension, which allows each
interruption to sustain a pause or the empty moment,
the absence of moment that, if luck is with it, may
allow for the intrusion of the prophetic word (PLL).
The Universal Turing Surface is the new plane of
immanence that is, above all else, a cosmopolitical orchestration, an onto-organology constituted by an autopoeisis: a self-generated organ of
a self-synthesized information system (John
Wheeler) within demiurgic space. ✦

KARL S. CHU

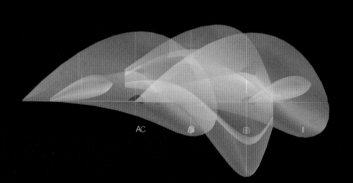
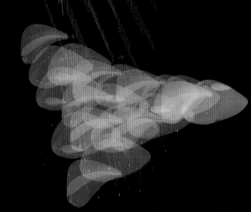

X PHYLUM, Version 3.0

The end of the second millennium will eventually come to be acknowledged as the evolutionary time of convergence. A convergence, due, in great measure, to the emergence and subsequent complicity of computation and bio-genetics in the twentieth century, which will gradually transform the global community into a demiurgic economy, which, so far, has been driven and constrained by normative capitalism. There are indications that a brave new world is already in the making, which I have elsewhere referred to as the Hyperzoic Era full of promise and uncertainty. Undoubtedly, it will prove to be much more incredible and treacherous than anything we have seen in the history of planetary evolution. If the Cambrian Period marks the sudden explosion in both the range and complexity of multicelled animals whose descendants fill the world today, the emergence of the Hyperzoic Era will announce the profusion of a new type of life, the artificial life of abstract machines and architecture where a new type of bionic economy of the mechanosphere will develop and coincide with the biosphere. Such a condition will transform the behavioural logic of normative capitalism, from one based on the production of static commodities into a demiurgic economy that engenders the artificial life of global intelligent systems. This is the sphere of virtuality where the global matrix of evolutionary computational systems will produce and populate the planet with diverse forms of artificial life and beings.

It is within this context of an evolutionary cosmology that the project X PHYLUM takes its impetus to model a new form of proto-bionic architecture. Its mode of becoming is based on the autogenetic logic of the L-system (Lindenmayer System), which is one of the simplest types of recursive branching systems. The axiomatic infrastructure that governs its output requires a set of mathematical functions in order to determine its morphological outcome as a viable expression of architecture. In addition to implementing self-reproducing and self-organizing mechanisms, X PHYLUM is also an attempt at conceptualizing a computational theory of architecture based on the classical model of computation, the Universal Turing Machine as inaugurated by Alan Turing in a seminal paper on computable numbers published in 1936. The new paradigm of evolutionary cosmology ultimately would require quantum computation as its infrastructure, which, at present, however, is still in its embryonic state of research and development. Nonetheless, X PHYLUM is an index marking the formation of a species of genetic architecture based on an algorithmic conception of the world.

As an autogenetic system, X PHYLUM is a computational monad that is a logical counterpart to Leibniz's notion of the metaphysical monad. It is a singularity, or an incomplete totality, whose morphology is generated by an internal principle and brought to a provisional closure in order to qualify itself as a form of proto-species. Leibnizian monads are modal entities that can be characterized as metaphysical species. A reconceptualization of monads from the standpoint of computation necessitates a

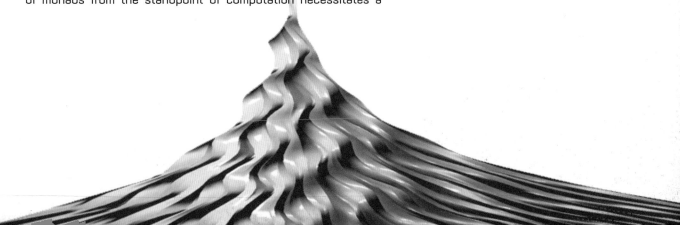

redefinition and generalization of the biological concept of the term 'species' so that it is adequate to encompass a wider categorical frame of reference. One fundamental difference between the notion of species and typology is that species require morphogenetic processes for the development and evolution of individuated wholes or singularities, whereas typology is predicated on a static classification of typographic arrangements derived from the conjunction of iconography and utilitarian programmes informed by cultural values. Within such a generalized notion of species, a self-organizing system, a robot or a dynamic logical infrastructure would be considered new types of species as well as diachronic formations of epigenetic processes which evolve into 'epistemic species' or hyperstructures that reside within some domain of virtual configurations. The universe of virtuality therefore is a dynamic constellation composed of ever shifting spheres of indiscernibles, forces, information and virtual particles that unceasingly self-reproduce and self-synthesize into ever more complex matrices of monadic self-organizations.

The internal movements of computational monads are propelled by the dynamics of self-generating mechanisms whose abstract desires, such as compulsions, innate propensities or tendencies, are already implicit within the configuration space of axioms. The unfolding of a computational monad generates a logical depth which measures the time-complexity necessary to generate and produce a species. Even though it is essentially a diachronic procedure, the process does not exhaust the surplus of information that enters into the non-linear modulation of generative sequences. The emergence of a monad is an event derived form algorithmic formation. Yet there are unaccountable intrusions or virtual implications that manage to enter into these non-linear processes, which resist any simplistic appropriation of quantitative analysis or prediction, even within the context of a strictly deterministic procedure. Events that determine the constitution of monads are truly complex in that they are emergent effects generated by massive complicity of causal relations, which inevitably come into collisions and interactions with virtual particles that accompany and surround a given set of axiomatic explications. Diachronicity, as a phylogenetic procedure, is not without synchronic interventions by virtual particles and co-implications derived from conditions that are within as well as outside of a given set of axiomatic formation. They contain a surplus of the unknowable and the indeterminate owing to the fact that algorithmic strings with a high level of complexity are imbued with varying degrees of randomness with regard to their internal composition. Finally, computation is a physical and logical phenomenon and, as such, it is circumscribed by Godel's Theory of Incompleteness and Undecidability. The construction of the artificial life of architecture, of a new form of bionic architecture, will also be inevitably constrained and delimited by the logic and physical limits of the computable. Constructibility is a function of computability. ✤

✦ H-Kavya

Karl S. Chu (1950)
1977   Bachelor of Architecture, University of Houston, Texas
1984   Master of Architecture, Cranbrook Academy of Art, Bloomfield Hills, Michigan
2000   Lefever Fellowship, Ohio State University

Teaching
2000–1990   Southern Design Institute of Architecture (Sci-Arc) Los Angeles
2000   Columbia University, New York

Principal buildings and projects
2000   'Jungle' theoretical research on the development of generative systems; architectural and town planning proposal
1999   'X Phylum'

Selected bibliography
2000   *The Caesura of the Turing Dimension* (abridged version) Natural Born CAADesigners, Birkhaüser, Basel; 'The Cone of Immanenscendence' *ANY*, Issue of Diagram Works, New York; 'X Phylum' *Domus*, no. 822, Italy; *Genosphere* development around the concept of Leibnizian 'possible worlds' (in preparation)
1998   'Hourglass of the Demiurge' *Architectural Design*, issue on architects in cyberspace, no. 136, London; *Architektur & Bauforum*, no. 196, Austria
1996   'The Virtual Anatomy of Hyperstructures' *Architectural Design*, issue on architects in cyberspace, no. 118, London
1995   *Space*, no. 334, Seoul, Korea

Hideyuki Yamashita

| Hideyuki Yamashita (*1961) |

JAPAN

'NestedCube' to Decode/Live Feed-Back Loop – Two detached places in the 'dialogue' are characterized as the same events taking place over and over again, only each time on a higher and higher level; it is an analogue to 'recursively enumerable set'. In the 'NestedCube', a transgressive methodology, 'recursively enumerable set', has been a central notion. A fully abstract, conceptual system of the representation of space, a system that would assert its potential perspective, leads us to such an apprehension: it would not try to let us step there physically, but perceive a phenomenal platform. It is a set of nested generations on a monitor screen.

Recursively Enumerable Space – A loop connection of two pairs of cameras and monitors gives the image of two different frames repeating one after the other, visualizing 'Place A' linked to 'Place B' linked to 'Place A' linked to 'Place B' and so on. This system is incorporated fully into the real space as a nested system. The notion of 'recursively enumerable space' relies heavily upon the recognition of traditional Japanese architecture, beam/column structure and sliding partition system. Each element grows, being compounded out of previous elements by the repeated application of rules. Here is a simple but fundamental typographical manipulation.

Time Goes, Space Shifts – The issue of 'time and space' is related to the phenomena in a four-dimensional cube (hyper-cube), where architecture is newly reorganized in the interaction of detached spaces. The cubic structural frame of 'Related Space' is represented as an equivalent of the continuous and infinite extension of space, though the receding repetition of the foreshortened picture frame. 'Related Space' is in the preceding 'dialogue' of the two detached places. 'NestedCube' is a message to decode. 'Info-Domino' is a scheme conceptually developed by means of the computer technology.

Womb Within Womb – 'Torus' is a form to run different building systems, not by paralleling them, but by nesting them. Its base is the topology to renormalize a void within another void. It could be described as an inductive system where a womb generates another womb inside. This analogy demonstrates ambiguity in architecture, such that an exterior space unexpectedly turns into an interior space, or such that a door to the outside unexpectedly turns to the inside. This is not realistic, but gives a hint of ways of re-organizing architectural methodology.

Set and Reflection – Space is renormalized (enveloped by and enveloping another mode of space). The 'NestedCube' represents 'renormalized space'. It reflects and projects the attached spaces like a prism. It assembles and reflects the real spaces, so that the disposition of these spaces is renormalization. 'NestedCube in Process' (weekend house project in Kyushu, Japan) holds a 'NestedCube' as the central concept in which two cubes are framed to form the simplest unit of torus. The 'NestedCube' becomes a recursive space and a core of the structural system to support a nexus in combination with 'attached spaces'.

Relation to the Hyper-Cube – The wire-frame axonometric drawing featuring the main structural members of the 'NestedCube in Process' was quite similar to the drawing unfolding a hyper-cube. Although the illusion of the four dimensions has no physical reality in the actual space, there is a strange coincidence in a geometrical sense. Of course nothing illusional would occur in the physical experience in space, but this analogy has been a radical index in architecture. ✦

HIDEYUKI YAMASHITA

Goree Memorial

COMPETITION, 1997 (SECOND PRIZE)
COLLABORATORS: ALAN BURDEN AND SHINYA SATOH

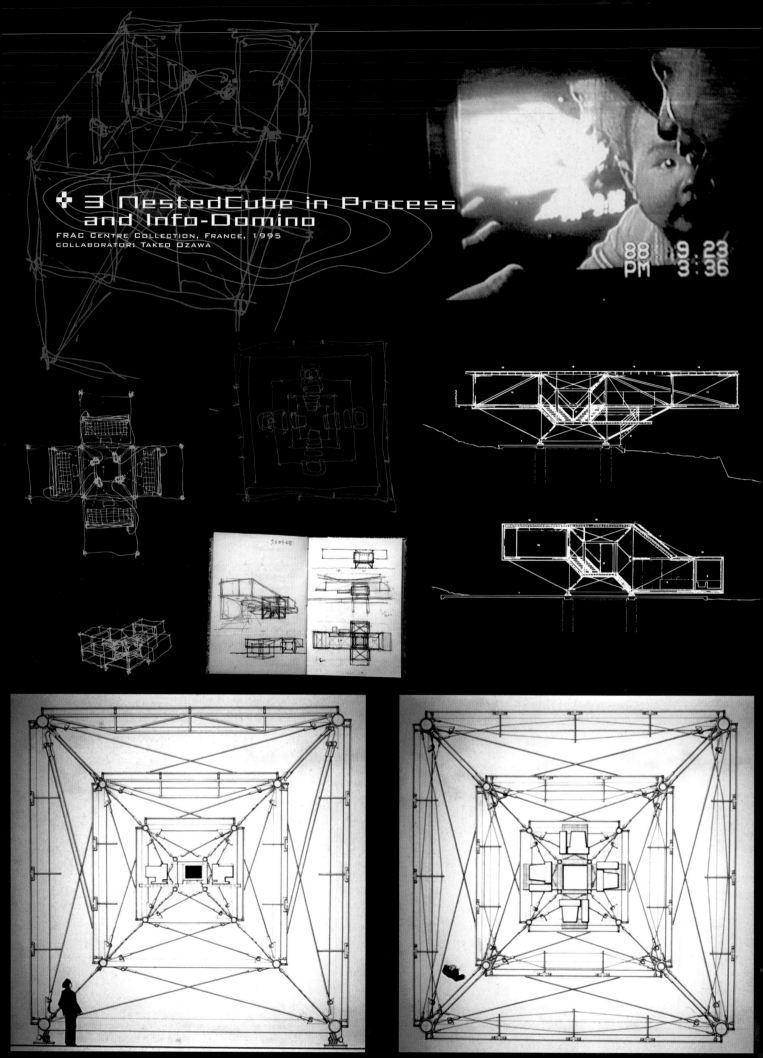

3 NestedCube in Process and Info-Domino

FRAC CENTRE COLLECTION, FRANCE, 1995
COLLABORATOR: TAKEO OZAWA

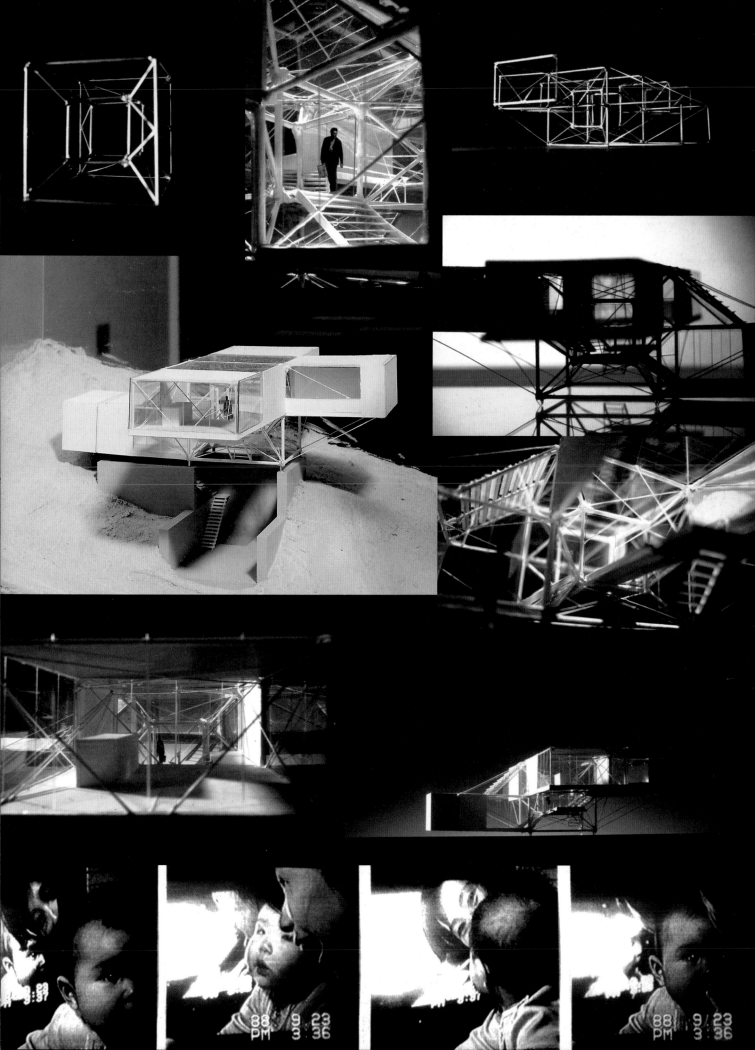

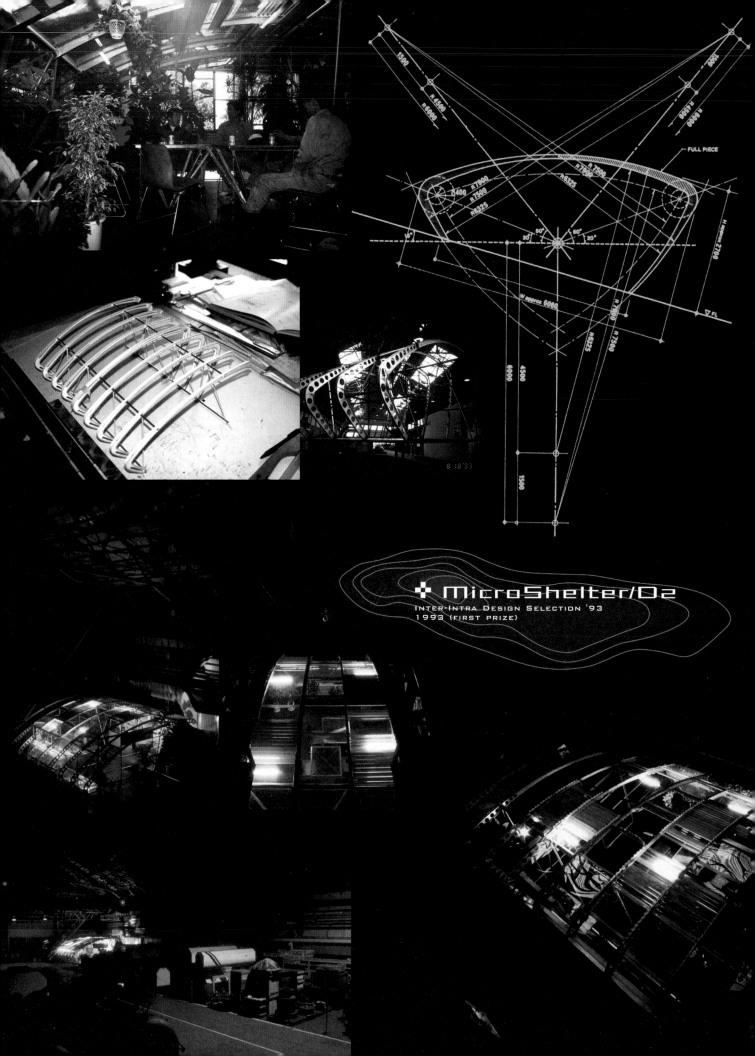

✦ **MicroShelter/02**
INTER·INTRA DESIGN SELECTION '93
1993 (FIRST PRIZE)

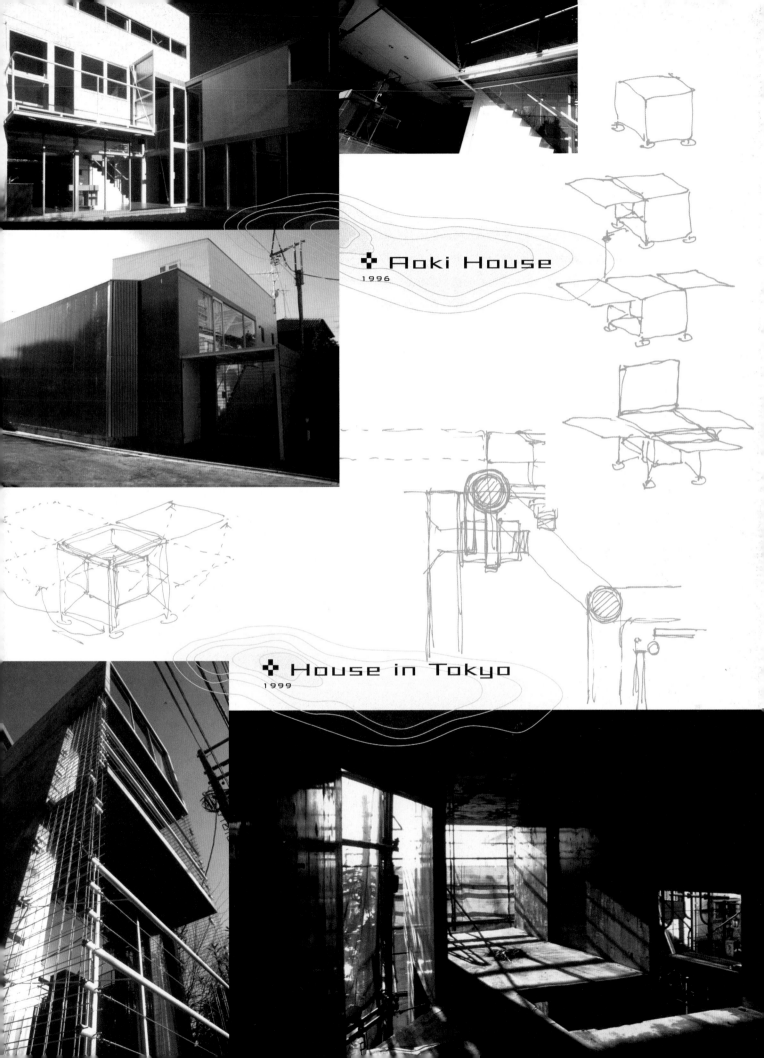

✛ Aoki House
1996

✛ House in Tokyo
1999

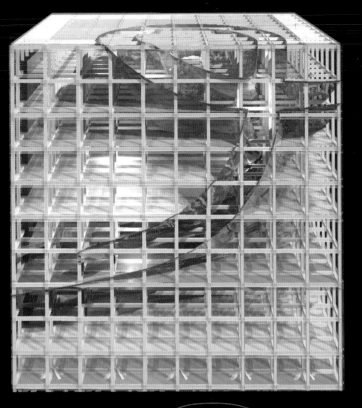

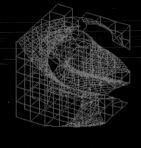

MATRIX OF 125 SAMPLING MODULES

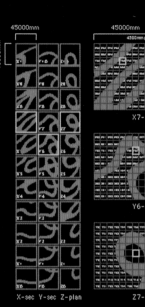

45000mm 45000mm

X-sec Y-sec Z-plan   X7-sec.   Y6-sec.   Z7-plan

Mediatheque
COMPETITION, 1995
COLLABORATOR: SHINYA SATOH

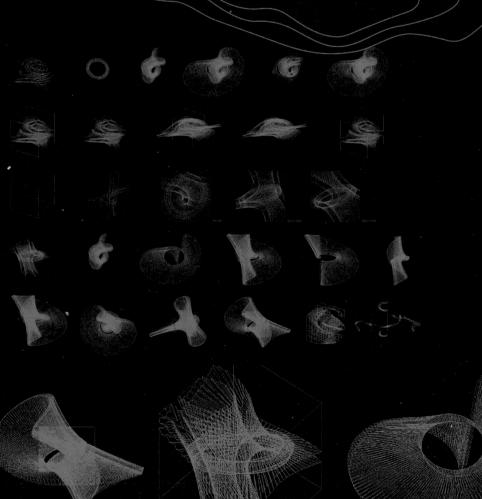

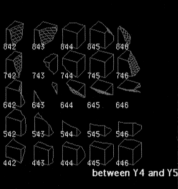

842	843	844	845	846
742	743	744	745	746
642	643	644	645	646
542	543	544	545	546
442	443	444	445	446

between Y4 and Y5

852	853	854	855	856
752	753	754	756	757
652	653	654	655	656
552	553	554	555	556
452	453	454	455	456

between Y5 and Y6

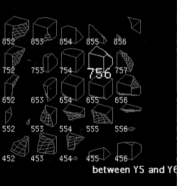

862	863	864	865	866
762	763	764	765	766
662	663	664	665	666
562	563	564	565	566
462	463	464	465	466

between Y6 and Y7

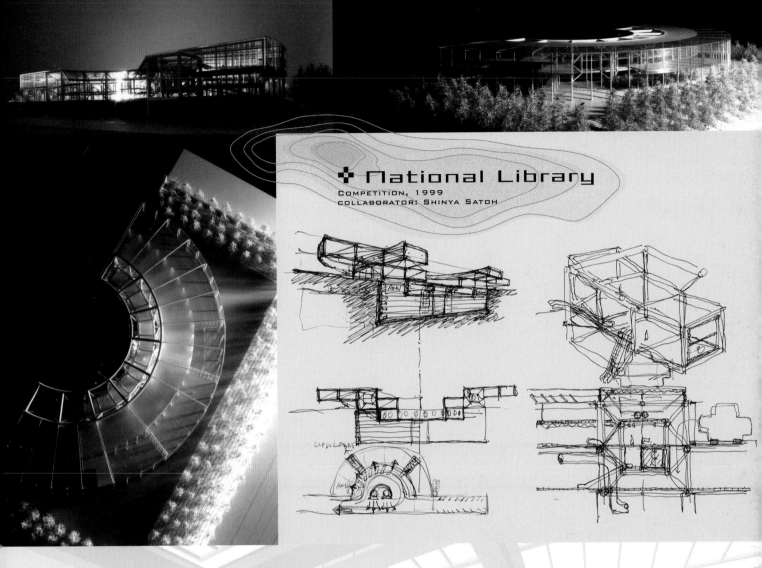

✦ National Library

COMPETITION, 1999
COLLABORATOR: SHINYA SATOH

✦ Hideyuki Yamashita

Hideyuki Yamashita (1961)
1984 Diploma from Tokyo Institute of Technology
1987 Master of Tokyo Institute of Technology
1991 Founded Info-Agenda Design Office

Teaching
2000 Nagaoka Institute of Design, associate professor
1995 INHA University, Korea

Principal buildings and projects
2000 'MF' (Digital Creators Grand Prix, first prize)
1999 House, Tokyo
1998 Goree Memorial (competition, second prize)
1996 Aoki House, Tokyo (completed); National Library (competition)
1995 Tokyo International Forum; Mediatheque (competition)
1993 'Info-Domino in Nested Cube' (project); 'Nested Cube in Process' (project); House in Koshigawa, Saitama (completed)
1994 Asahi Glass Design Competition, Inter Intra Design Selection '93 for Microshelter/D2 (first prize)
1992 Kugayama Kindergarten, Tokyo (completed), Yokohama Urban Design International Competition, (honourable mention)
1991 Institute of Architects Design Competition '91 (first prize)
1989 'Related Space' (project)
1986 'Time and Space' (project)

Recent exhibitions
1992 'Yokohama Urban Design Forum'; 'Institute of Architects Design Competition '91', Ishikawa Pref.
1990 Tokyo Institute of Technology

Selected bibliography
1998 *GA Japan* no. 30, *Mechanism of Innovation #6*, 'Dream of Africa/Goree Memorial Competition Scheme'; *GA Japan* no. 34, Tokyo and London
1997 *GA Japan* no. 29, *Mechanism of Innovation #5*, 'To be Kazuo Shinohara/Straight Direction in a Cold Logic'; *GA Japan* no. 27, *Mechanism of Innovation #4*, 'Bler/Virtual Realism'; *GA Japan* no. 26, *Mechanism of Innovation #3*, 'Rogers New Direction/Emerging Young Directors' *GA Japan* no. 24, *Mechanism of Innovation #2*, 'Farshid Moussavi and Alejandro Zaera-Polo/Their Presence and Future'; *Aoki House Review* (March) 'Nested Cube and Mirror Effect'
1996 *GA Japan* no. 23, *Mechanism of Innovation #1*, 'Glass Canopy/Another Story of International Forum'
1994 *GA Houses* no. 41, 'Nested Cube in Process'; *Shinkenchiku* no. 69, 'Microshelter'; *Japan Architect* (Feb.) 'Frame within a Frame'

Zellner Architecture Research

| Peter Anthony Zellner (*1969) |

When discussing Peter Zellner's design work, he quickly likes to refer to Melbourne and to the specific conditions of his domestic and professional life of the last ten years. And in fact, what renders Melbourne and further Australian urbanism for Zellner a place of architectural interest are the transitional zones of an apparent juxtaposition of intense urban development and a fairly undisturbed natural condition. Zellner's conceptual positioning in the 'in between' suggests complex reflections on the conflict of suburban expansion. This deliberate reliance on the transitional zones of suburbanity not only allows for connections between the urban realm and natural topographic environment, but also forms a conceptual space for the mediation of this mutual exclusiveness. The Jetty House, Terrain House and Krist Residence are all situated halfway between a modern confidence in the invention of form – artifice – and idealized dynamics of nature. Seen as hybrids between object and landscape, the buildings suggest a lingering interest in dissolution, adventure and uncertainty. And hence the projects increasingly reveal a tendency towards diagrammatic reiteration of metamorphic conditions between form and natural phenomena. The diagrammatic dimension performs a double role: it is a mode of notation, resuming, analytic and reflective, but it is also a model of thought, generating, synthetic and productive. As a form of visual thinking – a thought image – henceforth extrapolated into architectural form – Zellner converts this generating forces into a transgressive presence. Peter Zellner obviously does not believe in a homogenization of architectural semiotics but he nevertheless senses that one can observe some 'fields of gravity' in the variety of tendencies. These projects appear to be grounded between contextualism and expressionism. Their formal language is not exactly figural but remains aware of decidedly contemporary strategies – of geometries of a topologic rather than a Euclidean order. These diagrammatic articulations are productive of extremely seductive, almost problematic building forms. A spatiality of dispositioned elements, spatial flows and dissolutions open to the transgression of architectural semantics and topological limits. Nevertheless, the constituting relationship to terrain and site embeds the Jetty House, Terrain House and Krist Residence into the phenomenal dimension of nature. The designs are thought to be in dialogue with their immediate contextual condition and hence generate an architectural condition that unfolds over time. This aspect takes care of the grounding of Zellner's highly intellectualized aesthetic into the Real. And here is the hub. Zellner's projects are all so far of virtual existence although they seek for a continuous correspondence with natural phenomena. ✦

KLAUSKLAAS LŒHNERT

SECTION

SECTION

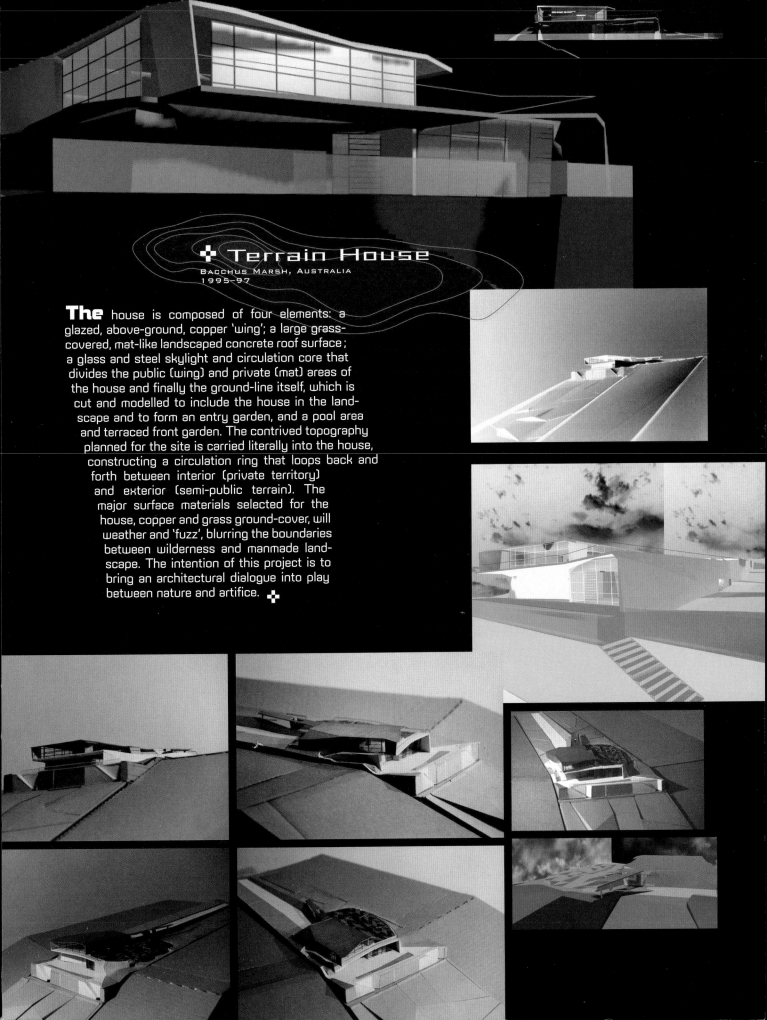

✦ Terrain House
Bacchus Marsh, Australia
1995–97

The house is composed of four elements: a glazed, above-ground, copper 'wing'; a large grass-covered, mat-like landscaped concrete roof surface; a glass and steel skylight and circulation core that divides the public (wing) and private (mat) areas of the house and finally the ground-line itself, which is cut and modelled to include the house in the landscape and to form an entry garden, and a pool area and terraced front garden. The contrived topography planned for the site is carried literally into the house, constructing a circulation ring that loops back and forth between interior (private territory) and exterior (semi-public terrain). The major surface materials selected for the house, copper and grass ground-cover, will weather and 'fuzz', blurring the boundaries between wilderness and manmade landscape. The intention of this project is to bring an architectural dialogue into play between nature and artifice. ✦

✦ Moto House
MELBOURNE, AUSTRALIA
1995

The Moto House is envisioned as an insertion into a 3 x 25-metre-long access corridor between two buildings in downtown Melbourne. It spans an entire city block. It is intended as the home and workshop of a motorcycle aficionado. The Moto House contains a bike workshop, an entertainment lounge/change area and food preparation, ablution and sleeping areas. The Moto House explores and develops residential type for a dense urban space. This project attempts to create an environment in which the daily circulation patterns of the dweller (her/his daily 'cycle') help determine a flexible and open living arrangement. Like the colourful, slick panels found on contemporary racing bikes, the Moto House derives its appearance from a fascination with pop culture, speed (turbulence) and spatial fluidity. ✦

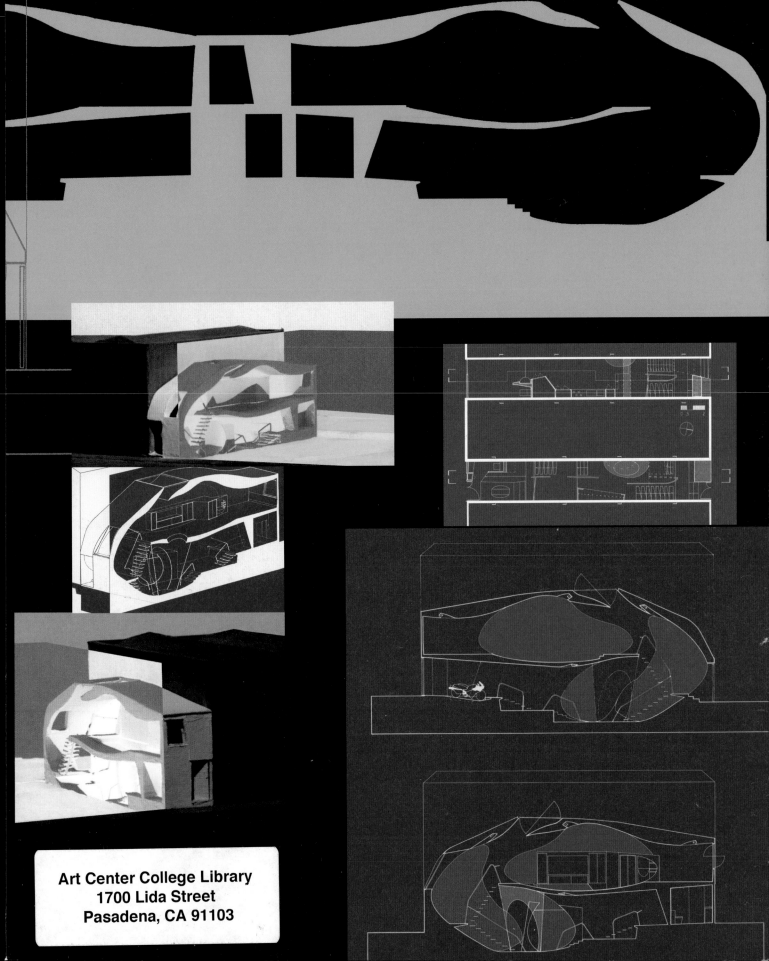

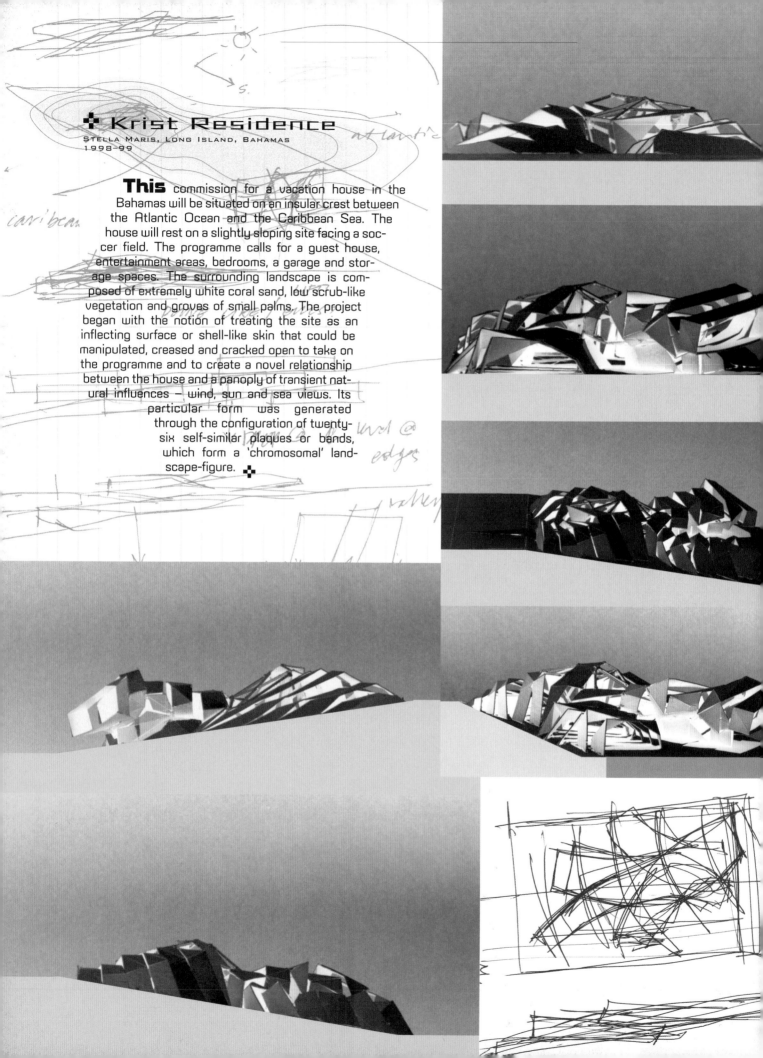

✦ Krist Residence
STELLA MARIS, LONG ISLAND, BAHAMAS
1998-99

This commission for a vacation house in the Bahamas will be situated on an insular crest between the Atlantic Ocean and the Caribbean Sea. The house will rest on a slightly sloping site facing a soccer field. The programme calls for a guest house, entertainment areas, bedrooms, a garage and storage spaces. The surrounding landscape is composed of extremely white coral sand, low scrub-like vegetation and groves of small palms. The project began with the notion of treating the site as an inflecting surface or shell-like skin that could be manipulated, creased and cracked open to take on the programme and to create a novel relationship between the house and a panoply of transient natural influences – wind, sun and sea views. Its particular form was generated through the configuration of twenty-six self-similar plaques or bands, which form a 'chromosomal' landscape-figure. ✦

garage

ens

mbr

entry

ens

kitchen

guest

living

✦ Jetty House

MILANG, AUSTRALIA
1993-95

The Jetty House is a prototype model for living between land and water – conceived of as a line crossing two distinct conditions. This house reconstitutes the interface between a manmade body (architecture) and a natural body (water) along and within its attenuated form. By weaving the lake into the house and extending the landscape into the water, the project initiates an exchange or dialogue between structure and medium that moves beyond a binary opposition (and/or, both/neither). The Jetty House is composed of three spatial types or elements: a concrete rectangular pier (circulation, living zones, deck, swimming area); floating metal containers (kitchen, bedrooms) and a marine plywood/aluminium shield structure (roof garden). This project is specifically about the relationships between land (edge), water (body), light and architecture found in Australia. ✦

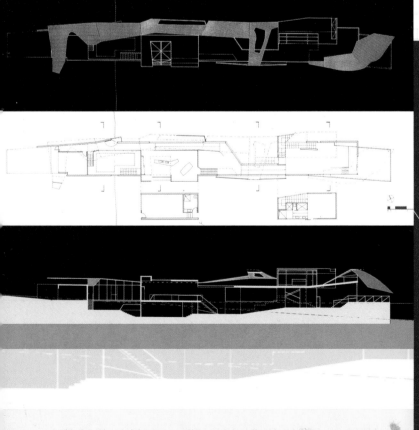

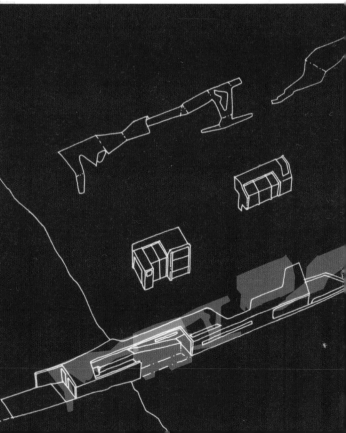

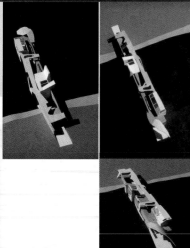

✦ Zellner Architecture Research

Peter Anthony Zellner (1969)

1989–93 Bachelor of Architecture, Royal Melbourne Institute of
Technology, Australia
1997–99 Master of Architecture, Graduate School of Design, Harvard
University, Cambridge, MA

Teaching

1999–2000 Sci-Arc, Los Angeles, California
1998 Boston Architectural Center, Boston; Graduate School of Design,
Harvard University
1994–97 Royal Melbourne Institute of Technology, Australia

Principal buildings and projects

1998 Krist Residence, Stella Maris, Long Island, Bahamas (project)
1997 Terrain House, Bacchus March, Australia (project)
1994 Snow House, St Kilda, Victoria (realized); Lawson House, Russell
Island, Australia (project); Architecture Australia Display Stand
(project)
1993 Beach House, Rye, Australia (project)
1992 Showroom Lighting Fixture, Melbourne (project)

Recent exhibitions

1999 'Pacific Edge' Hennessy & Ingalls, Santa Monica, California;
'Terraforms and interiorobjects', Graduate School of Design,
Harvard University
1998 'Terrain House: Dwelling between Nature and Artifice', Boston
Architectural Center

1997 'Twenty Young Architects', 8th World Triennale of Architecture,
Sofia, Bulgaria

Principal publications

1999 *Hybrid Space: Generative Form and Digital Architectures*, Thames
& Hudson, London; *The City Disappears: Motorised Speed, Human
Mobility and Electrical Communication in Frank Lloyd Wright's
Broadacre City*' Daidalos, Berlin (in preparation)
1998 *Pacific Edge: Contemporary Architecture on the Pacific Rim* Rizzoli,
New York, and Thames & Hudson, London (author/editor)

Selected bibliography

1998 *World Architecture* no. 72, London; *Architectural Review* no. 1221,
London; *Architecture Australia* no. 6, vol. 87
1997 *Architecture Profile* no. 1, vol. 2; *GA Houses*, vol. 52, Tokyo;
Monument nos 18 and 19, Sydney; *Architecture Australia* vol. 86,
no. 4; *The Lucky Country: Myth, Image and the Australian Suburb*
with Laurel Porcari, P. Lang and T. Miller, eds, Storefront Books
Princeton Press, New York
1996 *GA Houses*, vol. 48, Tokyo; *Monument* nos 9 and 15, Sydney;
Transition no. 52, *Melbourne Tostem View* no. 59, Tokyo; *The
Interior* vol. 1 no. 9/10, Melbourne

✦ Non-Standard City Planning

| Frédéric Migayrou |

What is architecture? How is everything that is organized around architecture specifically defined? Architecture, it is clear, is everywhere. It surrounds and encircles us. It forms a common frame. It is woven into an urban realm which no longer seems in a mood to stop – forever expanding networks and systems, gaining ground by the day; nature turned into an area of production which has to be constantly recreated in order to be conserved. On the other hand, though, what about architecture and city planning, when everything that is being erected every day is given over to the technical departments of local authorities and design From now on, it will not be possible to argue in terms of territory, extension, boundaries and limits, all of which help us to divide the world into an urban realm – the world with an extreme physical and human density – and an outer, independent territory, organized in accordance with the laws of another economy. The urban realm seems to have taken possession of the world, going beyond any notion of territoriality, growing into every manner of exchange system, exceeding the material nature of what is constructed and being continually reconstructed, commensurate with a simultaneity and intensity of exchanges. What is architecture, when the structuring of the public place outstrips the objective reality of what is constructed – the reality of buildings and transport system? The urban is no longer content with just the city. The city is merely one factor of density in a fabric of an unprecedented complexity that is continually redistributing the logic of the social, the economic and the political. So the meaning of the word changes: city planning is thus tantamount to involvement in a kind of game of incompatibility; it is still talking about the city and its development models; it is still hanging fire on the idea of a relationship to the ground, to the foundation that seems denied by the ongoing growth of cities and by the spontaneous appearance of megalopolises that no longer owe anything to historical sedimentation. City planning is inseparable from territory, it is a store of knowledge that is part of geography, and instrumentalized by many additional maps and surveys and plans.

The legacy of a military mastery of space still seems to be the preferred tool of a hermeneutics of urban arenas. Analyzing the sedimentation and layering of the constructed, the architecture of networks and systems and the historical interweave of plots and parcels invariably presupposes, when one steps back, the availability of the free plan, the plan that inextricably links the control of space with political power. The endless space of modern rationality, the space that has, quota-like, set the shape of all exteriority since Kant, has once and for all done away with traditional understandings of an anthropocentric space. The world has given in to rational cosmologies, it is no longer

a closed realm, it opens out on to a limitless extension, a pure form that permits every sort of measurement and geometrization. The metaphors of the city that still punctuate the *Discourse on Method* have given way in the Kantian discourse to a definitive incompatibility, where architecture fails to represent the rational idea of an open totality, stretching ad infinitum. If we stay with the status that Kant gives to nature, a world governed solely by mechanical laws, man's constructions seem like a manifestation of his finiteness, the successive sedimentation of the stages of a history of reason. The never-defined hypothesis of a real transcendental city links up with the ideal of the free plan, and, by turning the proposition inside out, by introducing the city as the place of history, Engels would make it the model for a diagram of development leading to the ideal of a classless society. For him, the critique of the great industrial cities of the nineteenth century is never the denunciation of an incoherent development, a continual chaos; rather, it corresponds to drawing up a report of the present, and taking cognizance of a state of affairs caught in the motion of historical mechanics. The city has an independent dynamic, it is a symptom of history and it would seem that any desire to intervene and develop must be relativized. The city and the urban have their own order, which is an ongoing revelation of the jolts and moments of history. Any other analytical logic that does not comply with this inner need of time must founder in an inert materialism or in the idealism of a Utopian future. The currently very topical idea of a chaos of the urban world and the idea of an anticipation and a projection of what a state of the future city might be, have been made subordinate, in advance, to this undeclared transcendental city.

The general extension of the urban space, the absence of any distinction between city and non-city, the increasing muddle between public domain and private space and the standardization of the economic fabric, information networks and cultural values, all these factors of a diagnosis of the state of the world seem to respond directly to this status of a rational and continually expanding space. Can we simply give in to this reason of history, which caused Engels to say that, 'For the time being, the only task that falls to us is a simple social makeshift repair'?[1] The conception of the public place, bequeathed by the Enlightenment, seems fully to achieve a modern form of the city based on a perpetual incompatibility with the real, which keeps individuals in the sphere of an continual lack of authenticity. In its incestuous relationship with industry, architecture was the main vehicle of a standardization of the habitat and, by extension, of all the city's functions. The calculations of reason and its far-reachingly liberating dimension ended up by mixing the restrictions of production and a modelling of urban life. Over and above the prophetic visions of someone like Franz Jourdain, who was perhaps the first to remain aloof from the paternalistic understandings of the nineteenth century, with his work *Les habitations ouvrières* (1902), modernism radicalizes the rationalist project by inverting the geometric logic of classicism and by substituting the humanist balance of the body's proportions with the idea of a normative measurement. The 1929 C.I.A.M. (International Congress of Modern Architecture), where Ernst May raised questions about 'minimum life', where Walter Gropius held forth about the sociological presuppositions on minimum housing, Victor Bourgeois on 'the minimum dwelling' and Le Corbusier on 'the minimum house', fully arrayed the principles of a new universality. City planning is a recent science and it is still peculiar that, in clinging to the principles of the human establishment, it should appear when architects start to define the ingredients of a syntax. From the minimum dwelling to the 'machine for living', architecture has had to comply with standards that do not simply respond to the mass production of objects in accordance with given functions, but more openly to an optimization of the production processes associated with the development of services. Standardization and the overall extension of production standards respond directly to an expansionist desire for territorial mastery, where the industrial rationalism of the liberal economy intersects, ultimately without any contradiction, with the deployment of historical reason – the history of reason incarnate.

It is time to concern ourselves with a real archaeology of identity models which have run through the history of architecture and city planning, and which now seem to have become completely uniform on a worldwide scale. The fight for the standard – the very one that set Le Corbusier, who with his Maisons Citrohan (1920–23) attempted to systematically develop aesthetic and constructive standards, against Walter Gropius, who merely tried to define types forms, capable of all manner of assembly, as if in a construction game – was resolved independently in the world of production. Type or standard, the architect's language has itself become industrialized and its basic material is now made up of a set of procedures which steer any implementation. It is industry that objectivizes the architect's language, beyond any kind of romanticism attaching to a specific expression. In taking the example of car production, Le Corbusier sealed the new order of praxis. 'What is interesting in the goals set up by Gropius is the contribution to industrial production, the factor involving the perfection of standards, but what saddens us is to be bound to conclude that

an art school is incapable of improving industrial standards and introducing standards – ready-made standards cannot just be ushered in.'[2] Promoting the standard against the type, Le Corbusier stepped back from the idea of decorative art and became fully involved in the model of an endlessly growing city, to borrow the name of his famous museum project. With regard to the City for Three Million Inhabitants, Hans Seldmayr, then a young critic, 'reproached Le Corbusier for once again using this age-old idea of emancipation and being completely subordinate to the problems of the twentieth century, such as hygiene and traffic'.[3] Hugo Häring, who was concerned with the city planning concepts put forward by Le Corbusier and Hilberseimer, spoke out against this 'geometric principle of a mechanical world', in order to usher back in the concept of urban organism and 'cell', both more attuned to man's individual needs – terms that Hilberseimer was to espouse when he moved away from Le Corbusier. Is there such a thing as a Le Corbusier Kantianism, or an unexpressed Marxism of this modernism that has never really admitted its rational end purpose?

These days, continuous, unilateral urbanness is an obvious fact, and the expected standardization is now in effect. Normalization goes beyond all predictions and forecasts, and the logical systems of trade and services have increased ad infinitum the number of labels and marks and brands, in the end creating a uniform worldwide culture where a growing number of values now forms the new unity of a symbolic world being shared by one and all. This unexpected form of universality has taken on the form of globalization, the reign of an undivided economy, which is no longer even the object of any political or ideological debate. Saskia Sassen and Manuel Castells have greatly emphasized this new fracture, which splits the world into a network of global, interconnected cities, siphoning off almost all forms of trade, and a secondary, almost indeterminate realm, which remains a mere resource, an availability, a potentially usable deposit where one may find, willy-nilly, raw materials, human resources and tourist sites. How is this public place to be described? How is it to be defined over and above any spatial distinction? This question goes beyond the separations that used to differentiate between centre and outskirts, city and country, developed world and developing world, and which still built borders and nations. How is a city to be built for six billion inhabitants? This is the ultimate question, which goes beyond any idea of territorial settlement, and definition of identity. Confining the architect's work to that of a building process, a construction that invariably presupposes an availability of space, and turning architecture into an unambiguous art of space, is to stay at the hub of a contradiction that has borne along the whole history of modernism. It is time to come directly to grips with this hidden ontology, which is still trying to pin architecture down close to a foundation whose transcendental value is inaccessible to it – a Hegelian pyramid, a Heideggeresque Greek temple, a Marxist city. Paul Virilio put it in a masterly way: 'This geodesic faculty of defining a unity of time and place for activities now clashes openly with the structural capacities of means of mass communications'.[4] Nowadays, space is dimensionless, it no longer involves measurement, it is being constantly redefined in tune with our technological capacities of configuration.

Repeated attempts to redefine the modern space have all turned out to be illusory, and the ceaseless redefinition of a more adequate urban space, more available to human uses and functions, has invariably renewed the presupposition of an available spatial realm and a more or less agreed geometrization of space. The rational city planning of the C.I.A.M. meetings has actually been replaced by the dynamic of Team X, which in trying to transform sociocultural models into a spatial reality became enmeshed in a geometrism of another kind. The use of grids, proliferations, more dovetailed and multipurpose networks, the accumulation in complex systems of modular units, or clusters, all stem from a logic involving the application of a procedure that invariably presupposes a prior reification of the chosen context. Here again, mastery of space and the implementation of the architectural project and the city plan were always inseparable from an economy of standards. Space is put back together again in accordance with programmes that people try to redefine with regard to 'motifs', and 'new motifs of association',[5] which sidestep the traditional organization of built-up urban areas. The most creative aspect of the Team X contribution lies, undoubtedly, in this initial merger between form, space and the cultural social parameters that lead to the advent of the decisive concept of context. This normative factor, which is always being reintroduced, is further expressed in the works of the *tendenza*. If an issue is indeed made out of space as a unilateral vehicle of architectural conception in favour of a historicist understanding of contexts, it is put back together in the form of a sociology that outlines new maps and new territorial divisions. The abstract form of modern rationalism contrasts with a postmodern rationalism, which speaks out against the utilitarianism of functionalist architecture, but which also attempts to define a normative basis borne along by historical values. When Carlo Aymonino tackles the rationalism of the Moderns, it is to denounce its abstraction and its profoundly aesthetic dimension, to develop the dynamic of the historical contradiction in urban sedimentation. He endeavours to replace the abstract universality of modern standardization with the concrete universality of contextual standards.[6]

The claim of a complexity of urban phenomena does not, however, dodge other forms of renewing an external normativeness, which always presents the city as an object, like the outer realm of an intervention. We have lost count of the number of analyses that liken Colin Rowe's famous *Collage City* to Robert Venturi's *Complexity and Contradiction in Architecture*. The value of assembly, be it a passive statement of the way things are or the active challenge of a new kind of architectural writing, does indeed form the basis of a new analysis of the urban, but it remains passive and clings to the primary idea of a heterogeneous composition. Even if Colin Rowe objects to the idea of a collective medium for these collages, a kind of 'neutral backdrop', it reintroduces the ideas of an open field, derived from Karl Popper, an induced form of metaspatiality that presupposes collage. The city still seems limited to a passive morphology, an object that may be perfectly defined on the basis of its geographical limits, its form and its structure and its particular history. Complexity is always analyzed in relation to this morphological definition, be it formal – distinctions of elements – or dynamic – based on an update of all the possible interactions. This postmodern city planning where 'the policies of universalism (or of abstract rights) have culminated in a policy of difference and recognition, where the decision depends more on the context than on any binary modernist logic',[7] nevertheless ushers back in the values of a withdrawn normative factor. Standardization gives way to typology, which fulfils the same normative functions and, in the final analysis, creates a new semantic universality of the city. Communicational space, as understood by Habermas, may respond directly to this conception of a postmodern urbanness, whose sense – a consensus that replaces the old universality of idealism – is never really defined.

Perhaps there is cause to reverse the proposal and turn complexity into a dynamic resource, by refusing it any particular analytical value. The urban is now established as a dynamic fabric of exchange, which comprehensively determines the physical realm of cities. Globalization is less an economic fact than a system of exchanges, which reconfigures all decisions in real time, be they political or economic. Architects who have long been dispossessed of any capacity to intervene, now work at objectivizing the permanent scrambling of information, which fuels the public domain. Cities, these days, are thresholds, or ports, to borrow from computer vocabulary. A whole literature has swiftly come into being by making light of the supposed gap between a real public place, empowered by its laws, its norms and its geography of nations organizing economic and political balances, and this intangible realm of the virtual, which blurs our age-old forms of logic to do with identity – virtual individuals caught in a social virtuality that renders the body immaterial, financial movements and symbolic and cultural exchanges. There is an amusing side to the plethora of titles that joyously proclaim the future development of cyberspace communities, cyberspace government, cyberpower and cyberception. The cyber ideology introduces, in the negative, as it were, the idea of an otherness, a technological utopia, which, needless to say, is illusory. It seems more important to understand how a new legal economy redefines the traditional identities of the political and economic world. 'On the one hand, we can observe the advocates defined in terms of size and scale (individuals, institutions, players and persons involved, states, systems of states, international organizations and corporations and, last of all, the global). On the other hand, we can take a close look at all the situations and arenas in which these identities are produced. What are defined as bonds or links are these realms where relations between identities/players clash and collide and collude. From this angle, the globalization of communications is capsizing the whole field of identity creation'.[8] Globalization is thus shifting all the old hierarchies and reforming an open field of decision-making, where each and every intervention is at once local and constrained by the limitations of the overall structure.

Behind the division of the globe, between those who have access to the various technologies and a developing world that is banished from the new public place, today's urban domain, made up of an infinite number of transport and communications systems and a host of satellites that direct and control movements and flows, appears like an independent system, with no sovereignty, entirely supported by the laws of self-organization. The worldwide domain of the non-city, every manner of minority, infra-economies, everything that constituted the apparently minor, is fully assimilated to this global realm and increases the number of interactions with the decision-making hubs of globalization.

The global urban phenomenon appears to be an actual organism, as was prophesied in the 1960s by Christopher Alexander, who raised questions about the 'nature of order' and advocated stepping up the number of local actions in order to steer urban strategies. 'The local authority will reject all forms of physical masterplan; its essential performance consists in permitting the local authority to derive its organization not from a fixed projection of the future, but from a model system that acts as its own syntax'.[9] Countless studies have since endeavoured to apply the theories of complex systems and the models of biological organization to the urban arena. Behind the idea of a modelling of the 'fractal city',[10] there is often a normativeness where the 'models' seem to stand in for the old norms of geometric space. A rationality of disorder, buttressed by a form of neo-Kantianism,

might, as in the epistemology of the Catastrophe Theory, reintroduce archetypes into the heart of urban modelling. The issues outlined by research architects, incredibly diverse though they are, seem to be coming together around the same established facts and the same postulates: the emergence of an immediate culture and a pragmatism of urbanness, a new cognitivism; the co-existence of many forms of localism in an unprecedented space-time pluralism; a growing simultaneity of information exchanges; a generalized recourse to models of morphogenesis and calculation; a radical change in the relationships between the individual and politics and economics. The introduction of calculation as an actual production tool involves an active hermeneutics of the phenomenon of urban globalization which incorporates normativeness as so many possibles. Bernard Cache has stressed this definitive break with the rationalist models: 'We are probably about to complete a tremendous twisting movement in philosophy, following which the consciousness will become a centre of interest, no longer as a place of reason, but as the place of a relentless unreason.'[11] Globalization invites us to think in terms of a plurality of possible worlds, possibles that are being forever updated in a contradictory manner. It is imposing on architecture a hybrid, local, plural praxis. It is time to invent a non-standard form of city planning, a meta-constructivism of urban morphogeneses.[12] It will have to be accompanied by an adequate political dimension, a policy of possibles, which, with no hierarchies of scale, will be capable of dealing with all the states of citizenship in the global city and reforming a pluralist community that eludes models of rationalist sovereignty.[13] ◆

1. Friedrich Engels, *La question du logement* (Editions Sociales, 1957), p.47.
2. Le Corbusier, 'Pédagogie' in *L'esprit Nouveau*, n. 19, December 1929.
3. Winfried Nerdinger, 'Standard et type: Le Corbusier et l'Allemagne 1920–27' in *L'Esprit Nouveau, Le Corbusier et l'industrie, 1920–25* (Ernst & Sohn, 1987), p.52.
4. Paul Virilio, *L'espace critique* (Galilée, 1984), p.24.
5. Alison and Peter Smithson, 'CIAM 10 Projects' in *Architectural Design*, n. 9, Septembre 1955, p.268.
6. Carlo Aymonino, *L'abitazione razionale* (Marsilio Editori, 1971), p.89.
7. Nan Ellin, *Postmodern Urbanism* (Princeton Architectural Press, 1996), p.7.
8. Jerry Everard, *Virtual States* (Routledge, 2000), p.7.
9. Christopher Alexander, *Une expérience d'urbanisme démocratique* (Seuil, 1975), p. 34.
10. Michael Batty and Paul Longley, *Fractal Cities* (Academic Press, 1994) and Pierre Frankhaüser, *La Fractalité des Structures Urbaines* (Anthropos, 1994).
11. Bernard Cache, 'Objectile: poursuite de la philosophie par d'autres moyens' in *Rue Descartes*, n. 20; Gilles Deleuze, *Immanence et vie* (PUF, 1998), p.157.
12. Jean-Michel Salankis, *Le constructivisme non-standard* (Septentrion, Presses Universitaires, 1999).
13. Chantal Mouffe, *Dimensions of Radical Democracy* (Verso, 1992).

+ *Maps*

| MARIE-ANGE BRAYER |

'My surface is myself.'
WILLIAM CARLOS WILLIAMS, *PATERSON*

The digital world coils and uncoils, enravels and unravels. The changes occurring with paradigms have benefited dynamic and process-based systems, the generative aspect of form and a complex world of synapses. 'Everything is involved in a continual process of transformation' (Lars Spuybrook, 'Motor Geometry'). The architectural object, closed in upon itself, has been replaced by new fractal forms of geometry, which put the local in touch with the global and challenge irregularities and singularities. A new geography of auto-similarities within differentiation has been introduced. Connection, movement and co-existence of many, varied dimensions - forms of heterogeneity all living in syntonic harmony in this machinic world. Digitization may well have ushered in a time of simultaneity, but it also leads us towards a time of retrospection, in which informative and formal data reverberate. The architect whose intent is to get to grips with this complexity — which is cultural, social, political, territorial and digital — finds him- or herself facing an unstable and fluctuating world, pierced by all manner of infiltration, woven with flexible fabric, permeated by ebbs and flows, analogies and variations, and at once differential and similarly oriented.

This world no longer admits place and form as separate, disjunctive entities. On the contrary, it talks in terms of 'topomorphs', morphologies and morphogeneses of place. Nowadays the number of architects appropriating concepts of architecture, landscape and infrastructure, in order to map them in one fell swoop, is legion. Among them we find Adriaan Geuze, Maxwan and Schie 2.0. The geographical map is no longer merely an instrumentalization of territory: it has become a fully-fledged procedural tool, in which many different dimensions of appropriation come together (sociological, economic, climatic). The age-old dichotomies between nature and artifice are having a bad time of it. With regard to the 'topological landscape', Mark Lee defines this as seeking 'to eradicate the difference between the artificially constructed and the natural landscape'.[1] Likewise, the Catalan architect Vicente Guallart talks to us about a digital nature and an artificial ecology. What the geographical map offers these architects stems here from network, mesh, fabric and the 'intranet', where the natural and the artificial crossfertilize. The map is something that performs; it is transitive; it reactivates the factual data of the territory that is projected into it in all its complexity. The map offers a 'vertical economics' (Christian Jacob), where a whole host of conceptual plans and entries of the territory are overlaid and dovetailed. As Deleuze and Guattari demonstrated, the map is a rhizome with many different entrances — an interconnecting arrangement between differing orders of representation and semanticization.

The instability of new urban conditions, and the shifting of people caused by war and natural disaster throughout the world, refer architects to a crisis of inclusion and the idea of foundation. 'We are in the process of becoming nomads,' declared Constant in the 1960s, imagining, as he did with 'New Babylon', the first global city where the shifting movement of individuals involves the transformation of architecture. 'New Babylon' is just a map, a space turned into a vehicle and a vector by displacements. In so doing, Constant perpetuated the precepts of 'moving urban situations' championed by Debord and the Situationists. He was also subject both to the influence of the megastructures and 'streets in space' proposed by Team X and Aldo van Eyck, who themselves develop maze-like, suspended urban forms, and to the influence of Alison and Peter Smithson, in England, who support the concept of 'ceaseless changes' within urban grids and the complexity of the 'human association'. 'New Babylon' time is one involving a slow flow of human movements. 'It is actually more a question of a continually changing micro-structure, in which the time factor — the fourth dimension — plays a considerable role'.[2] In the 1980s, Deleuze and Guattari developed the concept of 'deterritorialization', a decentralized, nonhierarchical space; and they defended the idea of intensities and their nomadic organization of movement and flux. Nowadays, an architect like Michael Sorkin is updating this notion of trajectory in his urban projects. He talks to us about a 'culture of encapsulation' (vehicles, trains), which co-exists with a phenomenon of neo-nomadism with an electronic heart.

In this world of fluctuation and diversity, in which we are caught in the disarray of forever-changing scenes, why does the geographical map still offer us a credible frame of reference? It goes without saying that, like any form of tabularity and informational system, the map does away with the illusionism of style and content, which many architects try to dodge, because, for them, it extends the illusionism of the object placed on a support. Yet the map informs a coded process of representation. It is a system of projection. Mercator's cartographic distortions appropriated the expanding world of the great discoveries of the Renaissance; the atlases of Ortelius conveyed a new, encyclopaedic conception of the universe, by indexing the whole world within the space of a single book; in the 1930s, Richard Buckminster Fuller's dymaxion map pointed to a new internationalization of the globe. Local and global merge in the cartographic representation that simultaneously encompasses particular and general, detail and overview. The map, however, is only ever a map of movements and flows. 'We might wonder, in the final analysis, what cartography deals with, if not fluctuation. Continents drift, deserts encroach, landscapes suffer wear and tear and erode, and climates change. Our age is acutely aware of the world's instability and 'liquidness'. And this is in turn expressed in our actual constructions'.[3]

With the geographical map it is also possible to survey territory mentally. This is something that Land Art artist Robert Smithson developed through his 'site' and 'non-site' dialectic. His activities in a post-industrial nature, which he called 'ruins in reverse', were presented like an entropic landscape, sedimented in a time frame rendered archaeological. The 'non-site' may be a map, a text or an installation, referring to the site. Site and non-site are not two distinct entities, but quite different states of one and the same phenomenon. Likewise, the procedural, and no longer merely instrumental, recourse to geographical maps by architects is perhaps not foreign to this dimension of similarity and differentness introduced by the site and non-site dialectic, which also embraces territory and map. Mapping and map-making in present-day architecture, turning towards the exploration of new territories that are physical and digital alike, possibly also link to the ancient notion of 'periegesis'[4] – the map as graph of a new anthropological dimension of constructed space.

Tiering: artificial landscapes

Constant's 'New Babylon' (circa 1957) is a global city; it is the whole earth that no longer belongs to anyone in particular. There are no boundaries any more, because humankind has become fluctuating. 'Life is an endless journey through a world that is changing so fast that it always seems different' (5). In 'New Babylon', automated production has reunited all its inhabitants with a creative freedom. The 'sectors', where the social space is concentrated, are interconnected and stretch in every direction. In them, links are being ceaselessly forged and undone, and mobility brings on disorientation with a 'dynamic' labyrinth, which is invariably liable to change shape, from one activity to the next. Constant declared that the topographical survey of New Babylon could not be carried out using the usual cartographic methods. 'New Babylon' is actually organized on many levels (ground, roof-terrace), which intercommunicate. The fact that no map can get this across is not least because 'New Babylon' is itself a map, a diagram, a nodal interplay of networks and interconnections, which Constant transcribed in the geographical maps on which he marked human movement and displacement. 'The network in general [...] comes together in the distance, synchronizes, opens up far away and at the same time draws near: the way, the fork and the connection all lend structure to the territory by abstracting it from itself, and by allocating its simple unity – or by, in a way, de-allocating it, and putting it to another purpose. There is no such thing as territory without network, there is always just network, or grid; the simple unity of the territory is mythical'.[5] This network, which binds and synthesizes the territory, is also, however, an archipelago of dis-locations, or, in other words, migratory locations which outline a cartographic arrangement, for here territory and map have come together in the synaptic city with its foundationless narrative.

In 1958, Yona Friedman developed the 'spatial city', to wit, a three-dimensional, bestraddling structure, which has only minimal contact with the ground. In it, constructions can be dismantled and moved, and they can be altered as the occupant desires. This spatial structure, raised up on piles, contains lived-in volumes, set within some of its 'void' spaces. The tiering of the spatial city on several levels that are independent of each other defines this 'spatial city planning'. The piles contain vertical circulation systems (lifts, stairs). A residential city, a commercial city and an industrial city can all rub shoulders on the same site. The spatial city thus represents what Yona Friedman has called an 'artificial topography', a grid suspended in space. Once again the city has become cartography, through its homogeneous, continual and indeterminate network. Its modular mesh authorizes its unlimited growth. The cities of Constant and Friedman, which hoist architecture above the territory and transform it into an 'artificial landscape', are lived-in maps. The geographical map is no longer capable of describing the spatial city, because it is a graph, an independent diagram, which thwarts the factual limitations of the territory as exteriority. The artificial landscape is an inhabitable map; the map, an inhabited city.

The influence of Constant and Friedman would be decisive for the 'plugged' cities of Archigram and for the Japanese Metabolists (Isozaki, Kurokawa); and, closer to home, for Rem Koolhaas and his approach to the 'grid' as architectural subconscious (Delirious New York), his conception of the city as 'archipelago' and his definition of the urban landscape as 'SCAPE', crossfertilizing nature and the manmade. Today, the Dutch architects MVRDV are developing 'Datatowns' (1998), which may well solve territorial over-densification problems. These 'Datatowns' are vertically tiered, like Friedman's spatial cities; they are towns of data, which are merely information networks. These towns, which are developed high up, are without topography, without representation and without context. All that matters is the multiple and simultaneous presence of levels. There is no original referent any more, as with Friedman. Once more, the city is its own cartography.

Upheavals: landscapes of derivation

'Architecture will soon shed light on a hitherto hidden element, the floor-ground, at once a means of contact and a means of overview. By assuming its full significance, the ground tends to absorb the other architectural factors: at once partitioning, covering, façade. This transformation, made possible by the use of the oblique, is imminent, for the ground is the least abstract of all the elements, and the most useful.'[7] And Claude Parent said when he met Le Corbusier: 'Freeing the ground has become false. Occupying the ground in the military sense becomes the only true action.'[8] Surfaces and ramps now create upheavals in the ground forming 'topotonic' plates which encourage circulation and movement.

For Architecture-Principe – Claude Parent and Paul Virilio – 'the oblique is the medium of spatial continuity'.[9] 'Oblique architecture becomes a kind of activity generator.' Being static is replaced by being energetic, because oblique potentialism summons up its physicality and its participating dimension. Once detached from the ground surface, the city includes 'sites of derivation', which unfurl like waves. The major principle of the oblique function is that of 'inhabitable circulation', made possible by inclined planes, artificial ground and ramp systems. In the Parent/Virilio city that pulsates with inhabitable circulation, it is the movement of people that imbues the architecture with its dynamic. Architecture is co-extensive with movement. Here the territory is in perpetual transformation, changing from one moment to the next. So how is it to be mapped? These upheavals, derivations and emulsions of private life in the social space make the city levitate. Once more, the city is a situation which no map can describe, because it is choreographed by the itineraries that are caught in a 'journey without maps'.[10] Claude Parent nevertheless lays claim to a cartographic eye for the oblique city: 'For the human inhabitant, an overview of the landscape turns into a necessity, a right; it replaces the horizontal vision, and introduces bird's-eye views and worm's-eye views'.[11] The sites of derivation are surveyed by the map-maker's synoptic eye. The map not only paradoxically offers a deterritorialization of the territory, but also refers to a vision that has become operative. The anchorage is no longer the ground that has risen up, like a skin, like a change of territory, which has separated like an independent surface of projection. Nor is it any longer the body, always active and always in motion. The anchorage comes from a new system of vision, artificial this time, and no longer 'natural' – the vision of the map-maker, with his aerial, overbearing eye, and his 'oblique' way of looking that passes through space, without any centrality, and perceives its relief through the range of its viewpoints. The map then tends to merge with the landscape of derivation.

Space is an envelope, a surface that coils and uncoils, rises up and shrinks back. With Parent/Virilio, the ground is indeed this hybrid between the site's naturalness and its artificiality. This radical exploration of the surface is nowadays forcefully echoed in the research projects being conducted by architects, from Greg Lynn to Reiser-Umemoto. For FOA (Foreign Office Architects), only the reconfiguration of the ground can shift the meaning of architectural production, as is shown by their work in progress on the Yokahama terminal, and the 'Virtual House' (1997). 'What happens when the ground – geographical, geological, cultural, economical – becomes distorted through mechanisms of temporal and spatial displacement that characterize our age?'[12] As an active field, the ground gets rids of the binary contrast between style and content, between the two-dimensional and the three-dimensional. With FOA, the ground is neither a volume nor a flat surface, but lies somewhere in between the two, in a figurative possible that has been released from the determination of the anchorage. Architecture is the 'incorporation' of territorial data. These 'surfacings' are unstable topics, lying somewhere between object and space, between the territory and its artificial making in map form. These surfacings are a 'flexible' and abstract form of mapping, retaining the planar dimension, the dimension of a smooth sheet, across which the world's flows are forever spreading.

Folds: fractal landscapes

For François Roche, architecture is not erected on a ground, but within a critical experience that effects a change in contextual parameters. In the extensive field of architecture, his approach, which we might also describe as 'Spinozist', involves a kind of 'plane of immanence', constructed by 'the speed and slowness of metabolisms', articulating 'sociabilities and communities', 'frozen catatonias and accelerated movements, unformed elements, unsubjectivized feelings'.[13] How can architecture become a fluence affected by social, economic, sensorial and territorial multiplicities? 'Places and territories nurture identities, preconditions and feelings that architecture and city planning are forever restricting and eradicating'.[14] For Roche, on the other hand, architecture is a 'management of differentiated flows'. 'Fractal City' (project for Rotterdam, 1998) is at once a singular territory and an artificialized nature. Here it is upheavals of the ground that become architecture. Topography and infrastructure are understood as structural tools. What about territory and map? Territory is cartography, and maps are endowed with the structural, stratigraphic depth of territory. Both are involved in the same operative function, which links up with Robert Smithson's 'sites' and 'non-sites'.

This congruence of map and territory recurs in a project such as NL Architects' 'Flat City' (1998), for the future town of Leidsche Rijn in the Netherlands. These architects describe it as a 'folded linear town'. No constructed volume is erected, the ground is raised by several metres, radically opening up the skyline. In the oblique function of Parent/Virilio, the roof was already a ground to be climbed and crossed; here, lawn coverings make the roofs of 'Flat City' accessible. Maps – semantic, urban and anthropological – are folded in the inflections of the 'endogenous fold' (Deleuze) of the territory.

For Kengo Kuma, digital technology has dissolved the idea of territoriality. His conception of the 'landscape' or 'digital gardening' stems from a reversal of perception: 'Instead of looking towards architecture from outside, we must look at the environment from inside. It is important to plan architecture like a frame for observing the environment from within'. 'By doing away with the object, we must bring out a place in its stead'.[15] We venture into different forms of matter because there must no longer be frames for viewing: architecture can no longer be an object that is visually measured; henceforth it is surveyed like a territory, it has gained in materiality at the same time as it merges in the digital world of continuity. In his 'Park Network' (1996) project for Tokyo, the park is at once a source of sustenance and a refuge in the event of an emergency. For Kuma, we have to live in a 'garden' – that is, in a territory that is at once cybernetic and physical – and no longer in a building.

The reconfiguration of territory is achieved, by the Catalan architects Actar and Vicente Guallart, through a cartographic modelling and recourse to fractal geometries. 'Fractals are defined as infinite curves contained in a finite area'. Involved here are 'orders that are changeable in their complex relations', in which contradictory states co-exist. 'Fractals capture a new type of order typified by half-similarity, the similarity between the part and the whole on many different scales. Snowflakes, clouds, ferns, coastlines, the ramified forms of blood vessels and even the 'cytoskele-

ton' within each cell are all examples of fractal structures'.[16] Manuel Gausa developed the idea of '(LAND)ARCH', 'new operative landscapes' that proceed by way of 'colonizations, infiltrations, insertions, camouflage and modelling', or new 'operative topographies (carpet: land on land; relief: surface = land; folds: intersection of the land; furrows; scratching the land)'. For Gausa, Guallart and Willy Müller, 'offering a different description of reality is already the beginning of projection'.[17] They define their projects as 'operative maps', flexible mechanisms for discovering new potentials in the stratified territory.

Their representation of Barcelona is thus a fractal landscape or an operative map: the city is like a fabric whose fibres are stretched in order to introduce infrastructures into their interstitial folds. Barcelona is no longer a series of lays, a seam of lengthwise strips, which, in their dilatations and retractions, squeezed by perpendicular movements that 'colonize' it, have incorporated heterogeneous territories where voids alternate with solids. Maps alone make it possible to reveal systems of relationships and interconnections, and bring out the city as a 'vibrating system', a mixed flux and a grid evolving on different scales, local and global alike. The city thus rises up in its fractal development through its multiple cartographic rendering.

What the map ordains here is indeed the discharge of compositional factors, style/content polarities and nature/artifice. For Actar, the map is a 'metaterritory', an 'osmotic ground'. It alone makes it possible to broach the infrastructural dimension of the territory. The map is extruded territory. Or, conversely, for Xavier Costa, territory is explored like a 'metacartography', with its lines, its boundaries and its areas of density. 'In order to embrace as broad a spectrum of referents as possible, a distant positioning is necessary, permitting the act of drawing up a map of all these zones of influence. This cartography, which must have a critical dimension, is actually already in the process of constructing the new conditions of the city'.[18]

For Vicente Guallart, likewise, architecture no longer has forms: it is a dynamic process, a conature. Through fractal geometries, Guallart explores the city like a media-related hybridization between nature and the digital. In 'The City of 1000 Geographies' – also a tribute to Rem Koolhaas's 'City of the Captive Globe' in *Delirious New York* – Guallart takes territorial samples which are as much fractal extrusions of landscape as they are cartographic fragments. Architecture must change in real time: trees may be artificial, mountains may be lived in ('Los edificios son montanas'). Nature is 'artificially natural and naturally artificial'. 'The world thus becomes an inhabitable environment'. It is a matter of 'representing the real, inhabitable world based on the virtual world',[19] of 'mapping, but mountains, water-courses, sunshine, views, vegetation' ... 'A fractal object with two essential features: an indefinite detail of each point and a certain similarity between the parts of the object and its complete characteristics'[20]: the fractal object is in itself a cartography of the object through its dimension of auto-similarity. It is a changing method of representation in which different distances and different moments may come together, and which can describe the changes in the landscape. With Guallart, everything happens as if 'cartography could be directly included in the landscape it describes'.[21]

Deployments: semantic landscapes

Kolatan/Mac Donald, for their part, make use of the co-citation map system, so as to deploy complex networks of interrelations 'between dissipative processes and aggregative structures', which form new, hybrid identities. To this end, they refer to the metaphor of the 'chimera', that genetically hybrid mythical being, at once singular and complex, to develop their transformational hybrid models. The co-citation map system is a kind of electronic index, borrowed from the new information-related sciences. 'If one paper cites an earlier publication, they bear a conceptual relationship to one another. Implicit in these linkages is a relatedness of intellectual content. In reordering the literature by works cited, we obtain a citation index'.[22] This co-citation map thus makes it possible to deploy conceptual linkages that are not otherwise visible. 'The next level of organization is constructed as a map, a geographic description of relational knowledge. In this kind of map, groups of co-cited papers are organized in clusters, each cluster representing a network of interrelated, co-cited publications. What is achieved in clustering is a matrix of objects linked together by varying degrees and in different states of aggregation.'[23] The co-citation method thus helps to 'identify similarities between unconnected sites/structures/programmes' The co-citation map deploys 'a territorial description of associations and disassociations, to coordinate groups of morphologies into clusters that each represent a network of interrelated elements, a matrix of objects'.[24] This is how Kolatan/Mac Donald have reconfigured an interior based on the indexing of the outline of household objects, which, when then interrelated, culminate in new formal and programmatic possibilities. This dictionary of object outlines has led in turn to the discovery of new operational similarities. This same method means that they crossfertilize the outline of a house with its environment to make 'chimeric' architectures.

For Neil Denari, likewise, digital technology has altered the concept of local. Denari reminds us that the word map means 'sheet' in Latin. The origins of the map consequently 'are not in information, but in the geometry of the flat surface'.[25]

'The world, in terms of technology, is more like a map than a real sphere. Perhaps it could even be called a graph where information is more important than how many square miles of land a country or city has.'[26] Neil Denari designed the redevelopment of the Gallery MA in Tokyo based on what he calls the Homolosine Interrupted Projection Mapping System. The inner surfaces are folded and deformed, turned down like 'interrupted' projection mapping planes, stripped of all geographical information. They form a complex geometric space, smooth like a sheet or map, without any referent. The exploration of these new digital, map-like territories has enabled architecture to become 'another global surface'. 'Technology coerces a flattening of the world through its attempts to be horizontal, and to be in all places at all times. It creates a new form of global projection or a new cartography depicting phenomena surrounding the flowing plasmas of money, knowledge, power and politics.'[27] These global surfaces, which are developed as a spatial device, have merged with a graphic, 'logo-ized' world of intertextualized codes, taken from the world's cultural flows. For Neil Denari, nowadays, there is no such thing any more as a traditional map to guide us; we navigate in floating spaces of signifiers. Architecture henceforth consists in 'folding' the sheet of the world.

Movements: cinematic landscapes

The architects Ushida & Findlay explore the psycho-analytical and 'psycho-geographical' components of architecture, in tandem with a line of purely scientific and geometric research into form. The 'Truss Wall House', built in Japan, illustrates quite clearly their comprehensive approach, in which the subconscious meets mathematical modelling. For them, architecture is a psycho-sensorial geography, involving a free itinerary during which the inhabitant is being forever solicited in his cognitive and physical dimension. The organic shapes of their buildings stem from the movements of the human body. They are intrigued by 'flowing space' (Leon van Schaik), and the interiors of their architectural works are perceived like 'inhabited landscapes' – psycho-sensorial landscapes that are at once tactile and mental.

Digital technologies have thus radically capsized the ideas of territory and its modelling, because the digital territory encompasses all the heuristic features of a map. In the case of Greg Lynn, the formation of the architectural object is the outcome of a simultaneous crossing of map and territory. His 'blobs', matrical elements and 'isomorphic polysurfaces' are part of a generative grammar of forms, which is developed in both continuity and differentiation. Influenced by the radiolarians and the morphological studies of the zoologist D'Arcy Thompson, Greg Lynn compares the 'blob' to a gelatinous organism, with no formal regulation, an evolving form that encompasses the components of its environment.[28] The distinctive feature of the 'blobs' is that they can be both mould and model, landscape and map. Greg Lynn thus produced panels of stratified wood based on machines with digital controls bearing the formal imprint of his 'blobs'. These panels form an analytical cartography of the 'blob' as much as its moving geographical territory (cf. 'Embryologic Space'). For Greg Lynn, the blob is an example of a 'topological surface exhibiting landscape characteristics although it does not look like a topography'.[29] Architecture lies somewhere between the unfolding of this proto-object and a field informed by oriented surfaces, which update the oblique function of Parent/Virilio. 'Topological surfaces that store force in the inflections of their shape behave as landscapes in that the slopes that are generated store energy in the form of oriented surfaces'.[30] Here there are no longer any locations; the 'topological landscape' is a folding of geological sediments. At the same time it is permeated by gentle waves whose inflections cause a singular topography of hills and valleys. 'These topological surfaces are inflected by the field in which they are modelled'[31]: the landscape and its cartographic modelling have merged with each other, striated by one and the same space-time dynamic.

Maps are thus presented in their relational operative function, their transformational capacity, a return to the referent, made up of abstraction and similarity. The map here is neither an object nor a graphic representation; it is a vehicle of translations between architectural form and its physical or digital environment. The map is a function, an intermediary between the cognitive field and an intertextual realm. The map is no longer there to measure and inform a comparative order between real and representation, it is at once impulse and inflection. As a folding of the signifier and the signified, it has become a 'metastratum' which works in the manner of Deleuze and Guattari's 'machinic arrangement'.[32] The map is what imbues architecture with an implicit virtual movement. It is what renders architecture unassignable. The map has itself turned into a flux. ✣

1. Mark Lee, 'The Dutch Savannah: Approaches to Topological Landscape' in *Daidalos*, n. 73, October, 1999, p. 9–15.
2. Constant, 'Een schets voor een kultuur', 1960–65 in Mark Wigley, *Constant's New Babylon: The Hyper-Architecture of Desire*, (Witte de With, Center for Contemporary Art/010 Publishers, Rotterdam, 1998) p. 163.
3. Pierre Chabard in 'Orbis Terrarum', directed by Marie Ange Brayer (Moritz Küng, Ludion/Antwerpen Open, 2000).
4. Periegesis is the 'literary description in which geography is blended with ethnography', in Christian Jacob, *L'empire des cartes: Approche théorique de la cartographie à travers l'histoire* (Paris, Albin Michel [Bibliothèque Histoire], 1992), p. 39.
5. Constant, op. cit, p. 161.
6. Bernard Stiegler, *La technique et le temps. 2. La désorientation* (Paris, Galilée [Collection La Philosophie en effet], 1996), p. 168.
7. Paul Virilio, 'Nevers chantier' in *Architecture-Principe 1966 et 1996*, Paul Virilio et Claude Parent (Paris, Les Editions de l'Imprimeur, 1996).
8. Claude Parent in *Aujourd'hui*, n. 51, 1965.
9. Claude Parent, 'Architecture: singularité et discontinuité' in op. cit., s.p.
10. John Rajchman, 'Grounds' in *Constructions* (The MIT Press, Cambridge [USA]/London, England, 1998), p. 86.
11. Claude Parent, 'Expérimentation' in op. cit., s.p.
12. FOA, ArchiLab,1999.
13. Gilles Deleuze, *Spinoza: Philosophie pratique* (Paris, Minuit, 1981).
14. François Roche, 'Situation' in *Quaderns*, 'LandArch' issue (Barcelona, 1997), p. 97.
15. Kengo Kuma, 'La période du chaos: Jardin digital' in *Quaderns*, 'Spirals' issue, (Barcelona, 1999), p. 128.
16. Mae-Wam Ho, 'La nouvelle ère de l'organicisme' in op. cit., p. 154.
17. Manuel Gausa, Vicente Guallart, Willy Müller, Met 1.0., *Metapolis: 25 propuestas x 21 equipos*, Festival de ideas para la futura multiciudad (ACTAR, Barcelona, 1998).
18. Xavier Costa, 'El arquitecto como etnografo' in op.cit., 1998.
19. Vicente Guallart, 'La Ville aux 1000 géographies' in *Quaderns*, 'LandArch' issue, (Barcelone, 1997), p. 171.
20. Op. cit., p. 173.
21. Xavier Costa in op. cit.
22. E. Garfield, R. Kimbeley, D.A. Pendlebury, *Mapping the Social Sciences: The Contribution of Technology to Information Retrieval*. Cited by Kolatan/Mac Donald.
23. Ibid.
24. Kolatan/Mac Donald Studio in Peter Zellner, *Hybrid Space: New Forms in Digital Architecture* (Thames & Hudson, London, 1999).
25. Neil Denari, 'Interrupted Projections' in *Another Global Surface or Territorial Re-Codings on the World Sheet* (Gallery MA, Tokyo, 1996). See also Neil Denari, 'Project No. 9601 Interrupted Projections: Another Global Surface' in *Architectural Design*, 'Architecture of the Borderlands' issue, vol. 69 (London, 1999).
26. Ibid.
27. Ibid.
28. Greg Lynn, 'Blob Tectonics, or Why Tectonics is square and Topology is groovy', p. 169–86 in *Folds, Bodies & Blobs: Collected Essays* (Brussels, La Lettre Volée, 1998).
29. Greg Lynn, *Animate Form* (New York, Princeton Architectural Press, 1998), p. 30.
30. Ibid.
31. Op. cit., p. 32.
32. Gilles Deleuze, Félix Guattari, *Mille plateaux: Capitalisme et schizophrénie* (Paris, Minuit, 1980), p. 10.

✛ In Praise of the Fragment

| Marco Brizzi |

Certain lines of research in contemporary architecture point to a process of transformation that actually entails the entire discipline by its direct action on instruments and technologies, which accordingly makes the discipline temporarily unstable. It is still not possible to draw up a classification of the effects of the digital revolution, insofar as their development process is still under way and the definition of new technological paradigms is still, it would seem, a long way off. Yet it is precisely a knowledge of the methodologies of dissemination and the critical application of the available instruments that may play a decisive role in the development of these technologies, by veering towards some of the possible avenues of study. In the contemporary world, there is a tendency to acknowledge a fragmented and discontinuous materiality within which the digital takes on an ever more conspicuous consistency. There is not really anything surprising about this, because it is precisely the digital, whose appearance has largely contributed to the apparent, present-day break-up of knowledge that represents the major means at our disposal for working on the 'confetti' of a new poetry.

It is from this angle that we must look at the latest conceptual experiences, especially those of a mainly experimental nature, as attempts to establish new links with constructed matter. There are times when research to do with the applications of digital technologies corresponds not only to a phase of individual enthusiasm but also to a work tending to look for an integrity, a connectivity and the reinstatement of a dialogue. The major development of architecture in the wake of the arrival of industrialization involved a considerable and positive upheaval, in the early twentieth century, within the architectural profession, which we definitely find again today in contemporary architecture. The introduction of new technologies and production processes has offered architecture the chance to rethink the project, over a period culminating in the phase of the historical avant-gardes. It was precisely during this period, which in some respects resembles the present-day period, that we saw the emergence of the conditions for a widespread application of technologies through

a process of complex transformation within which the contribution of designers and the industry play an quintessential role.

During the presentation of a recent Greg Lynn work, Herbert Muschamp wrote that the past masters of digital architecture use software the way the modernists used structure. Actually, during the last century, the development of technologies was such that it culminated in complex scenarios that were not easy to solve in terms of conception. It is worth remembering the degree to which the fact of possessing technical knowledge has given rise to obvious disparities. Suffice it to take an evident example like that of the calculation of structures to see how much technical and formal distance separated whole generations of architects belonging to the Modern Age. But over and above virtuosity there is praxis, for which, in the course of history, there have been holistic, simplistic and trivializing choices, for reasons to do with convenience and distribution capacity.

If we take a look at the present-day situation, we find ourselves face to face with a diagram that is busily developing, and rich in extremely interesting elements within which software packages – to mention the instruments that most hold our attention – seem to represent one of the crucial elements of the development and monitoring of the architectural project. The software issue deserves a study all of its own. In the case in point, I would simply like to emphasize how much the process of formulating and introducing digital instruments in the world of architecture has been, and still is, problematic. As well as the intrinsic problems to do with the way software is developed, and its specific purpose, a lot of architects currently exercising their profession show a certain condescension towards new technologies – the process of technological development is regarded as a system that is subject to an unconditional and beneficial growth, even without having access to objective means of assessment and critical instruments capable of challenging the processes of transforming technologies and media. In a general way, the world of architectural praxis has negotiated a phase of uncompromising scepticism towards digital instruments, this phase having given way to a phase of blind positivism. It is important to have opportunities for further in-depth development, discussion and monitoring. Architecture must learn how to dialogue with the media, establish confidential links with technologies, make the best possible use of software potential and challenge limits.

Within the current fragmentary situation, the activity of designers serves likewise and above all to develop new configurations, architectural arrangements and diversified instruments. Digital methods imply the possibility of incorporating the world of the project in the database. In this sense, any conceptual contribution, any detail and any architectural fragment, whatever its diversity in terms of origin and form, has a hope of solid and inalienable completion. This tension is one of the driving forces of the digital condition, something akin to a system of connections in which each neuron occasionally develops or inhibits synapses, based on specific needs. The Internet system is in some ways the representation of this characteristic. In this sense, and

in particular because of its digital essence, the fragment contains a conceptual potential that is much greater than any kind of planning conducted through a general systemization of knowledge and instruments. On the other hand, even as global models are proclaiming their omnipotence, they are above all speaking out against an intolerable approximation.

Contemporary experimental architecture is a little bit like Borges's narratives. The split fragments trace a loosened itinerary, which, in reality, is being constantly put back together again, because it brings together and combines lines of research following in the footsteps of what runs through the fragments. ❖

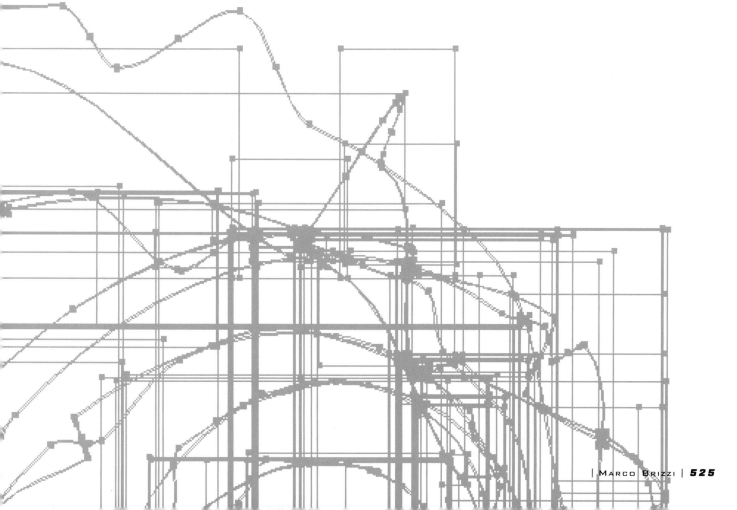

✢ Architecture of Resistance
International Center for Urban Ecology in Detroit

| Kyong Park |

The disinvestment and depopulation of Detroit lead us to question the viability of all urban fabrics, even the overtly ambitious mega-cities of Asia. In losing almost one million people since 1958, one could argue that the abandonment of the city has paved the wealth and density of the suburbs that encircle it. The avenues that once radiated its dream afar have come to drain the soul and memory from the city, flushing the core of its collective beliefs down to the rust that coats industrial wasteland of this manufactured city. The downtown is a canopy of once-heroic but now empty skyscrapers, standing tall to remind you how far away and safe you are from this 'black hole' in urbanity. In this collection of urban archeology, of modernism, the architecture that aspired to heaven instead shades our social conscience. Detroit, reluctantly, has become the tragic figure in the 'Fragmentation of American Space', a play that now travels to other cities and continents.

Yet, because of the decay, Detroit is the city of the future, more than any other city. Branded on it are successive rings of new technologies, moving outward across the city, taking labour and economy with them, as the moment of heavy industry ripples across this glacier-flattened horizon called metro Detroit. The lesson here is that the city is a biological process that evolves, not a mechanical novelty that breaks down. And, in surviving its second Ice Age, which came to Detroit in the twentieth century, the city is a reflection on the cyclical conspiracy of urban history; now, its abandoned buildings and vacant lands speak new possibilities. Nature has returned to fill the fault lines of human ideals, and in Detroit a new ecology will flower. This time it will be an urban ecology.

So in this city where tens of thousands of buildings and houses are sentenced to demolition, if not already burnt, new buildings are being built and real-estate speculation has begun. Not long ago were years when not a single building permit was issued in the entire city, and on the open spaces that masked the disappearance of what stood before walked lonely souls strangled by the architecture of despair. Soon to appear are the images of adolescent nostalgia, in the form of town houses and strip malls.

The message on the street is clear. The people from the suburb will move into the city, leaving their three-car garage to rot and their manicured lawns to go wild.

And the people who stayed in the city will be pushed out to the new ghettos at the outskirts – as in Europe – between giant but hollow shopping malls. The 'American Dream' is ready to move back into the city.

So here in the four square miles of urban devastation – the lower east side of Detroit – I have begun the International Center for Urban Ecology (iCUE). An interdisciplinary experimental school, the purpose of iCUE is to develop and exercise a new urban paradigm, using Detroit as an ideal site to plan and seed a new economic, political, and social structure. Within the mayor's vision of 'World Class City', the lower east side, the largest ghetto in Detroit, is destined to become the subject of terrible greed and land grab – the area is bounded by the construction of two new major league stadiums near the downtown, the demolition of 2 million square feet J.L. Hudson's Department Store, which would start a New Urbanism, inspired commercial development called Campus Marts and 2-billion-dollar development of Vegas-styled casinos on the waterfront. With only 25 per cent of buildings and houses still standing – half of the remainer are unoccupied or burnt – the neglect of this community will soon end as more fires and bulldozers will appear to clear-cut the area toward a class- and race-based redevelopment. Under the principle of 'demolition means progress', and backed by a black mayor who represents white and suburban interests, the lower east side is about to be 'sold' to the highest bidder.

Thus, the initial work of iCUE has been an 'Architecture of Resistance', which started in the summer of 1999. With the notion that this community is the highest existing example, so far, of a sustainable community – the community had the time to build an urban ecology of its own, because no one cared for it or even knew it existed – the intent of iCUE is to protect the area from detrimental speculations. Unlike countless master plans and megaprojects that have failed time after time, this community, as it is, is a true testament to the idea of a city as an evolution and a ghetto as a utopia. A landscape latent with hard lessons to be learnt, for planners and architects, iCUE has located itself here, in this community, in order to reconstruct this community with the land and its people. Hence, 'Architecture of Resistance' will start by demolishing the burnt houses in this community. Instead of using bulldozers, iCUE will take apart these houses using only hand tools, and with the help and consent of the neighbours. All reusable building materials will be saved so that they can be used to build new structures later on, or to stabilize the vacant houses for the future renovations. The basements of the demolished houses will be kept, for their remains may help to preserve the original urban landscape by influencing the design of future buildings and houses. By using the floor plate of the first floor to shield the basement from the weather, they can be used as a storage facility for the neighbours and salvaged building material. In addition, a series of temporary structures will be designed and built on top of them – artistic, symbolic or functional – so that they can immediately serve the community as their common and public spaces.

Over the years, iCUE hopes to garner public and governmental support to acquire more buildings and properties, so that we can continue to renovate, stabilize and build new structures. Once made into usable spaces, they can be rented or sold to the community members at an affordable price. The process will bring new capital to iCUE, which then can be reinvested so that additional buildings and lots can be bought every year. Every year, iCUE can rebuild more land and buildings, and gradually spread itself across into Detroit.

The accumulative and annular way of reconstructing the community resembles the way nature reincarnates itself every year. With several key members of the community already beginning to rebuild and farm on empty lots, iCUE is simply extending and reorganizing this urban paradigm. In fact, the office of iCUE is located in one of these farms.

Therefore, the strategy of iCUE is simple – to evolve with the land and its people. Over and above that, iCUE brings architecture back to its most fundamental sphere, by setting itself the task of rebuilding a new city straight from the burnt houses and buildings. The ideology behind the practice is that architectural theory is seeded in urban reality and that sweet labour leads to higher grounds in design. Therefore, the master plan of this new city will not be drawn until the community has been completed, and that the ecology of urbanism is parallel to life itself. ❖

The Spectre of Research

| Andreas Ruby |

A change is occurring in the paradigm of contemporary architecture which in many ways can be seen as a generational change. The latent breach between 'young' and 'old' was already perceptible in the mid-1990s but did not come out into the open for the first time until the 1997 Anyhow Conference in Rotterdam. Sanford Kwinter used his opening address as a manifesto to fire a polemical broadside at the current 'Any-Garde' from Eisenman to Tschumi. According to Kwinter, experimental architecture has allegedly been dominated to excess over the last two decades by the ideology of the process of postmodern crypto-transcendentalism, which basically amounts to forcing acceptance of form generation logic as an arbitrary process. In opposition to this theory 'from outside in' (as linguistic, philosophical and other models), younger architects such as Kwinter are searching for the 'formative potential' of architecture 'from inside out', that is,. to develop it out of themselves. This brings to the end an era during which representation, meaning and history were the essential dimensions of an architectonic project and in which the role of the architect was to reflect a given context critically and make sense of a given ideology. Younger architects such as Greg Lynn, MVRDV and FOA no longer have a critical project. They are instead interested in as opportunistic as possible a perspective with regard to the situation of a project.

From Site to Situation

The consequences of this radical pragmatism are apparent on many levels, and especially in the redefinition of 'site'. In the major projects of the 1970s and 1980s (for instance, the Canareggio project of Peter Eisenman and the Parc de la Villette of Bernard Tschumi), the site generally had a passive role. It served as neutral background against which was projected the design concept developed in theory beforehand, often independently of the site. On the contrary, in the above-mentioned opportunistic perspective, the site itself plays the leading role in creation of the project (examples of this are the H2 Pavilion of Greg Lynn in Schwechat, Austria, and the bus station of Ben van Berkel in Arnhem, Netherlands). Here, the site no longer has the passive function assigned to it by the traditional dialectic between form and background, but becomes an active 'background' already enriched with its 'form'. In opposition to the location-specific premises of the 1970s (critical regionalism), the term 'site' no longer designates a historically and culturally specific location whose particular genius loci the architectonic project is supposed to express or enhance, but is instead a 'space of currents' (Manuell Castells) of various natures: sound, temperature, light, odours, material strength. Today, a site is almost better described by the concept of 'situation', encompassing the totality of all the measurable information on a given area. During the site analysis process, using sophisticated software, a data set on this situation is ultimately extracted and visualized in diagrams.

The 3-D diagram as design generator

These diagrams are articulated spatially according to preferences. Instead of dry two-dimensional graphs, the data are arranged in exciting constructs which resemble exotic grottoes or natural rock formations. In the datascapes of MVRDV it is almost possible to see the expression of the romantic notion of the beauties of nature (Kant) in the diagram. In any case, the desire to be able to read the spatial diagram and transpose it directly as an architectonic structure is very recognizable. This means that the design of an architectonic project has basically been redefined, from an intuitive search by a subjective creator for individually fulfilled forms to the systematic generation of forms based on empirical analyses of the material data sets. In the age of post-critical research-based architecture, the architect turns his back once and for all on the idea of the creator as visionary of a utopian configuration to become data manager of an increasingly complex reality.

Empirical Architecture

This radical rationalization of the architectonic design process involves an immense difficulty, that of removing the creative expertise for architectonic projects from the sphere of the creator and transplanting his technical creativity to operating conditions. Research, as the new paradigm for contemporary architecture, is the dream of an objective architecture, whose empirical rigor is ultimately at the mercy of subjective decisions on architecture. It is questionable whether this dream will come true. It appears unlikely that the creator will disappear merely because architecture today uses statistical methods and digital computers. What have surely changed are the conditions of creativity, comparable to the evolution from painting to film in the art of the 1920s. The architect is being transformed from creator of autonomous forms to organizer of form processes. Instead of drawing, he now decides what form-generation parameters should be monitored and what software is best suited to the design. He must therefore also be made responsible for an architecture of datascapes and research with its own arbitrary aspect. The gap between concept and space is not merely smoothed over but requires making creative decisions which are not legitimized by any method. Perhaps even more serious is the question of the lasting impact that will be left by an architecture which is generally conceived from an opportunistic standpoint. Although this strategy may be seen by Rem Koolhaas as a provocative antithesis to vanguard rhetoric, it can solidify into an unpleasantly rigid dogma in the work of his students and followers – usually as the full application of a once-fruitful premise of the moderns, leading to their own failure. If architecture today can be increasingly defined as the optimal satisfaction of the needs of capital, which is what the 'critical accommodation' strategy of Alejandro Zaera-Polo seems to say, the question automatically arises of the added value that architecture can contribute to future society. Since, without added value, contemporary architecture would be worthless. ✦